Major Problems in Latina/o History

MAJOR PROBLEMS IN AMERICAN HISTORY SERIES

GENERAL EDITOR
THOMAS G. PATERSON

Major Problems in Latina/o History

Documents and Essays

EDITED BY

OMAR VALERIO-JIMÉNEZ
University of Iowa

CARMEN TERESA WHALEN
Williams College

CENGAGE
Learning

Australia • Brazil • Mexico • Singapore • United Kingdom • United States

CENGAGE
Learning·

Major Problems in Latina/o History: Documents and Essays
Omar Valerio-Jiménez and
Carmen Teresa Whalen

Product Director: Suzanne Jeans

Content Developer: Larry Goldberg

Content Coordinator: Megan Chrisman

Product Assistant: Kati Coleman

Executive Brand Manager: Melissa Larmon

Market Development Manager: Kyle Zimmerman

Art and Cover Direction, Production Management, and Composition: PreMediaGlobal

Manufacturing Planner: Sandee Milewski

Rights Acquisitions Specialist: Jennifer Meyer Dare

Cover Image: © David Pham

For product information and technology assistance, contact us at **Cengage Learning Customer & Sales Support, 1-800-354-9706.**

For permission to use material from this text or product, submit all requests online at **www.cengage.com/permissions.** Further permissions questions can be e-mailed to **permissionrequest@cengage.com.**

Library of Congress Control Number: 2013942741

ISBN-13: 978-1-111-35377-3

ISBN-10: 1-111-35377-8

Cengage Learning
200 First Stamford Place, 4th Floor
Stamford, CT 06902
USA

Cengage Learning is a leading provider of customized learning solutions with office locations around the globe, including Singapore, the United Kingdom, Australia, Mexico, Brazil, and Japan. Locate your local office at **www.cengage.com/global**.

Cengage Learning products are represented in Canada by Nelson Education, Ltd.

To learn more about Cengage Learning Solutions, visit **www.cengage.com**.

Purchase any of our products at your local college store or at our preferred online store **www.cengagebrain.com**.

Printed in the United States of America
1 2 3 4 5 6 7 17 16 15 14 13

Contents

Chapter 6   Labor Recruitment and Community Formation in the World War I Era   173

Preface

The Latina/o population is among the fastest growing groups in the United States. Yet Latinas and Latinos also have a very long history in the United States—a history sometimes eclipsed by contemporary debates about current immigration and its impact. Geographic areas that are now part of the United States were first settled by Native Americans, and subsequently by Spaniards and Mexicans. The first large-scale Latina/o communities in the United States took shape in 1848, at the end of the war with Mexico, when the boundary between the two nations moved and Mexicans found themselves living within the newly expanded territory of the United States. In 1898, U.S. expansion again fostered the emergence of Latina/o communities in the United States, but this time those communities were Puerto Rican. Cubans also settled in the United States in the nineteenth century, coming as political exiles to fight for Cuba's independence from Spain and as cigar makers working in an industry that crossed national borders. Thus began the growth of Mexican, Puerto Rican, and Cuban communities in the United States. Migration from these countries continued, and U.S. involvement in other Caribbean and Central and South American nations facilitated other migrations and the growth of an increasingly diverse Latina/o population in the United States.

Each national origin group came to the United States with a distinct migration history and created discrete geographic settlement patterns. This population was diverse in their countries of origin—each country had its own national history, culture, and economic composition, as well as racial, religious, and linguistic diversity. The political and economic intervention of the United States in Latin America fueled immigration, but the migrants and their departure dates varied depending on the specific historical context both in the sending country and in the United States. U.S. immigration and refugee policies shaped who arrived and how they were received. Employers, sometimes with the assistance of the state and sometimes in conflict with its policies, recruited low-wage workers from many of these countries in order to meet labor needs and increase profits. Labor recruitment, the availability of jobs and housing, historic settlement patterns, and social networks all shaped where immigrants and migrants settled. The result is an incredibly diverse Latina/o population in the United States— differences in national origin, time of arrival, citizenship status, region of settlement, race, language, religion, gender, and sexuality create an incredible mosaic. Indeed, this diversity has led some to question the utility of the umbrella terms, Hispanic and Latina/o, as well as of fields such as Latina/o history and Latina/o Studies.

Yet despite this diversity, there are parallels in the histories and experiences of Latinas/os. These parallels lead to the common themes covered by the essays and documents in this volume and provide the foundations for comparative history. The following chapters focus on (1) the connections between immigration and U.S. military, political, and/or economic interventions; (2) Latinas/os' recruitment as workers and their struggles to be accepted as equal U.S. citizens; (3) the ongoing transnational connections Latinas/os forge between their countries of origin and their new homes in the United States; and (4) the emergence of pan-Latino alliances and identities. In developing these principal themes, the chapters also explore topics such as racial and ethnic identities among Latinas/os, internal divisions within Latina/o communities based on gender and sexuality, and the role of U.S. popular culture in identity formation. Hence, *Major Problems in Latina/o History* is organized chronologically, introducing each national origin group during the era of their peak migration(s) to the United States, and thematically, emphasizing key concepts critical to the development of comparative historical analysis.

One major theme in this volume is the connection between immigration and U.S. intervention in Latin America and the Caribbean. Direct military interventions, such as the U.S.-Mexican War and the Spanish-Cuban-American War, have certainly fueled migration. But so have other actions, such as U.S. financial and logistical support for military dictatorships throughout the region. In addition, the expansion of U.S. economic investments has often resulted in the concentration of land and the displacement of workers, as well as the limited options of low-wage jobs in U.S. industries that have relocated overseas. Thus, economic displacement has been a significant factor causing emigration. Why would Latina/o immigrants choose to migrate to the United States after it had intervened in their nations of origin? The answer to that question lies in their economic displacement at home and their labor recruitment by U.S. employers, as well as in the social networks created by trade and political ties between the U.S. and Latin America. These networks join with family and community-based social networks, which also facilitate migration, sometimes even after the original conditions have shifted.

The essays and documents in this volume also highlight the labor recruitment of Latina/o immigrants and their subsequent struggles to gain acceptance in the United States. Labor recruiters, including the U.S. government, have had a large influence on the establishment of migratory flows and settlement patterns in the United States. Employers have frequently sought Latinas/os as low-wage laborers, but their goals have often conflicted with those of the communities where workers have arrived. Residents of these communities have routinely not welcomed Latina/o workers, viewing them as foreigners with different cultural and political values, as competitors for scarce jobs, and as disruptive to their communities. Moreover, Latinas/os have been characterized as racial others, who do not fit into the nation's traditional white–black racial binary. Although some workers, such as Puerto Ricans, have arrived as U.S. citizens, many others have not. Those who arrive as undocumented immigrants are particularly vulnerable to the violation of U.S. labor laws and workplace abuses, as the threat of deportation looms large. Meanwhile, the U.S. public and government officials have repeatedly failed to distinguish between citizens, permanent residents, guest workers, and undocumented immigrants. As a result, many Latina/o groups share the experiences of confronting hostile receptions and of struggling to be accepted as community members. What does the ongoing nature of these struggles tell us about the ways in which the United States defines membership and how these notions have shifted over time?

The third theme explored in this volume is the maintenance of transnational connections by Latinas/os living in the United States. These transnational linkages are not new, as they began in the nineteenth century, but they have grown stronger in subsequent years. Connections to countries of origin have been facilitated by the continuous arrival of new immigrants, return migration, increased communications, and popular culture. The growth of Latinas/os' transnational connections highlights the economic and social impact that immigration has on both sending and receiving communities. One important influence has been the practice of sending money (remittances) back to the home countries, which not only helps the immigrants' immediate families but also contributes significant income to their countries of origin. Improvements in transportation have made it easier to maintain such connections, while increased border enforcement has become an obstacle for those immigrants who are undocumented. Transnational links have also facilitated chain migration and the dispersal of U.S. popular culture throughout Latin America and the Caribbean. Conversely, Latina/o communities in the United States have been reinvigorated by the continuous arrival of new immigrants and the corresponding infusion of their culture. These transnational connections, as well as various dimensions of globalization, invite explorations of the meaning of nation and of borders. Why are some border crossings welcomed and promoted, while others remain severely restricted by the still powerful nation-state?

The emergence of pan-Latina/o alliances and identities is the fourth theme of this volume. As previously mentioned, the Latina/o population is incredibly diverse. Yet, despite distinct national origins and migration histories, as well as other differences, Latinas/os have shared parallels in their histories, experiences of racialization, and living spaces. In the nineteenth century, possibilities for inter-Latina/o interactions involved labor alliances and local community organizations in cities with diverse Latina/o communities. As the Latina/o population has dispersed throughout the nation and as immigrants from different regions have arrived, the opportunities for alliances have increased. While workplace experiences and community organizations continue to offer instances of cooperation, popular culture, sports, and politics have expanded the avenues for the creation of pan-Latina/o alliances. Younger generations are growing up in pan-Latina/o communities and sometimes in inter-Latina/o families, as well as in a national context that uses umbrella terms such as Hispanic or Latina/o and where globalization and transnationalism blur boundaries. How will Latinas/os continue to balance identities rooted in their specific national origin with emerging identities of latinidad?

As with other volumes in this series, *Major Problems in Latina/o History* includes primary documents, scholars' interpretations, and suggestions for further readings in each chapter. We have sought to include the widest range of primary sources available, from a variety of government documents to the many diverse forms of personal narrative sources. In each chapter, we have selected some documents that link to the essays and others that cover important topics and perspectives for the time period. Whenever possible, we have included essays that employ a comparative perspective. Yet most of the scholarship still focuses on a single national origin group, as comparative historical treatments are just emerging in the scholarship. Our selection of essays thus seeks to provide coverage of the various national origin groups and to provide a foundation for that comparative perspective. Although historians have authored most of the essays, other selections reflect the interdisciplinary nature of the field of Latina/o Studies and the fact that the scholarship on more recent arrivals is often written by social scientists. There is much less scholarship on those national origin groups with smaller numbers or a more recent history in the United States, and the structure of our volume and selection of essays inevitably reflect the overall state of the scholarship.

Because this volume covers various national origin groups, it is important to explain our use of terms. When we are discussing one particular group, we always use a national origin designator, such as Mexican, Puerto Rican, Cuban, Dominican, Salvadoran, or Guatemalan. This reflects the importance of specific national origins and historical specificity, as well as the way many people continue to self-identify. When we are discussing more than one group or speaking generally, we have chosen to use "Latino" rather than "Hispanic" as an umbrella term. Latino is often the preferred term of self-identification, and it references the regional origins and ancestry of the population. In contrast, government officials instituted "Hispanic" as an umbrella term, and its use often implies connections to Spain rather than to Latin America and the Spanish-speaking Caribbean. Both terms are relatively new constructions because there is no historically appropriate umbrella term that has been used throughout the nation's history. Because Spanish terms are gendered, we use "Latina/o" to indicate that we are referring to both females and males, rather than letting "Latino" stand as a reference to males alone or to both males and females. Occasionally, we write out the term as "Latinas and Latinos" to emphasize our subjects' gender. For the Mexican-origin population, we use "Mexican American" and "Chicana/o" to identify those with U.S. citizenship, "Mexican nationals" for those with Mexican citizenship, and "Mexicans" and "ethnic Mexicans" to refer to the population regardless of citizenship status. Although we use "Puerto Ricans" in our chapter introductions, some of the essays, documents, and studies in the further readings use "Boricuas," which comes from the native term for the island of Puerto Rico and became a popular self-referent during the political and social movements of the late 1960s and 1970s. For other populations, we identify the immigrant population by country of origin (e.g., Cubans, Dominicans), and indicate those with U.S. citizenship and/or long-term residency by adding "American" (e.g., Cuban Americans, Dominican Americans). The use of these terms, however, varies by time period, region, class, immigration experience, political perspective, and educational background. In our use of accents and tildes, we have remained consistent with how they are used or not used in the primary documents and the essays.

Readers seeking additional information on the topics in this volume may consult a variety of resources. At the end of each chapter, we have included a short bibliography of related works under the heading Further Reading. You may also consult several journals including *CENTRO Journal of the Center for Puerto Rican Studies* (http://centropr.hunter.cuny.edu/centro-journal), *Aztlán* (http://www.chicano.ucla.edu/publications/aztlán-journal-chicano-studies-0) for Chicana/o Studies, and *Latino Studies* (http://www.palgrave-journals.com/lst/index.html) for a wide range of works on Latina/o Studies. Scholars of Latina/o history publish in a variety of national and international journals. For the latest scholarship in such journals as well as recent dissertations, readers may use the subject heading "Latino/a" when consulting the "Recent Scholarship" listing created by the Organization of American Historians (http://www.journalofamericanhistory.org/rs/). Readers might also be interested in several professional organizations devoted to the advancement of Latina/o Studies scholarship, including the Puerto Rican Studies Association (http://www.puertoricanstudies.org/), the National Association for Chicana and Chicano Studies (www.naccs.org), and in the Latino Studies section of the Latin American Studies Association (http://lasa.international.pitt.edu/).

This project has been a collaborative one, as we have worked together as co-editors and have reached out to many of our colleagues in the field of Latina/o history and beyond. We want to thank the scholars whose syllabi we studied, as we looked to see not only how Latina/o history is being taught but also how it might best be taught. Many of the scholars whose essays we have included helped us select and provided us with the primary documents that accompany their essays. We realize that our work and this volume are made possible by earlier generations of Chicana/o and Puerto Rican Studies scholars and their pioneering efforts to produce scholarship and institutional homes that are the foundations of Latina/o history and Latina/o Studies. Too many to name individually, we hope you recognize yourselves and our deepest appreciation in these words.

We would also like to thank the editors and staff at Wadsworth/Cengage. For the idea of a volume devoted to Latina/o history, we are grateful to the series editor, Thomas G. Patterson. Sponsoring editor Jeff Greene diligently shepherded this volume through multiple editing stages, and sponsoring editor

Ann West helped us bring the project to completion. For his patience and skills, we thank development editor Larry Goldberg. We would also like to recognize the production, permissions, and support staff at Cengage. We thank the following reviewers for their helpful comments and suggestions: Miroslava Chávez-García, University of California, Santa Barbara; Lilia Fernández, Ohio State University; Nancy Mirabal, San Francisco State University; Natalia Molina, University of California, San Diego; Mark Overmyer-Velazquez, University of Connecticut; and Marc Rodriguez, University of Notre Dame.

We also have some individual thanks to express. Omar Valerio-Jiménez is grateful to his colleagues at the University of Iowa for their support of Latina/o Studies: Carolyn Colvin, Claire Fox, Teresa Mangum, Tlaloc Rivas, Leslie Schwalm, Santiago Vaquera-Vásquez, and Darrel Wanzer. It has been a great experience to meet colleagues who participated in "The Latino Midwest" Symposium at UI, and to participate in the efforts to create a Latina/o Studies working group in the Committee on Institutional Cooperation (CIC). Most importantly, I thank my family for their constant support and encouragement.

Carmen Teresa Whalen thanks her colleagues for making Latina/o studies such a vibrant program and intellectual space at Williams College: María Elena Cepeda, Ondine Chavoya, Jacqueline Hidalgo, Roger Kittleson, Mérida Rúa, Devyn Spence Benson, and Armando Vargas. I thank Williams College alumni and students for demanding and then supporting Latina/o Studies and for creating a wonderful environment for studying Latina/o history together in the classroom and beyond. As always, my deep appreciation goes to Janice, Marcus José, Mateo, and all of my family, as their love and support enrich my work and my life.

OVJ

CTW

CHAPTER 1

Latina/o History
and Latina/o Studies

Latina/o history traces its origins to the late 1960s and 1970s. During this era of social and political movements, the fields of Chicano Studies and Puerto Rican Studies took root, as student activists demanded access to institutions of higher learning and a curriculum that included their histories and experiences. Reflecting the regional dimensions of these communities, Chicano Studies emerged in the Southwest and Puerto Rican Studies in the Northeast. Both developed as interdisciplinary fields of study, as scholars challenged the disciplines that had too often rendered Mexican Americans and Puerto Ricans invisible, inferior, and/or stereotyped, and as scholars sought new research methods and theoretical approaches to tell the histories and experiences of those long overlooked. The historical analysis of Chicanas/os and Puerto Ricans in the United States paralleled the emergence of other "new" histories that sought to uncover and tell of people's everyday lives, moving beyond historical accounts that focused exclusively on leaders, institutions, and major events like wars. Influenced by civil rights struggles and feminist movements in the United States, as well as decolonization movements in developing countries, Latina/o history sought to highlight the struggles of Latina/o workers, activists, and community organizers in the United States. Hence, Latina/o history emerged as a field in dialogue both with the new social histories and with the interdisciplinary fields of Chicano and Puerto Rican Studies.

As the diversity of Latina/o populations in the United States increased and geographic dispersion brought Latina/o populations to shared communities, more encompassing approaches to Latina/o history and Latina/o Studies took shape. Including peoples whose ancestry links them to the many countries of Latin America and the Hispanic Caribbean, Latina/o history is necessarily comparative history, paying attention to the specificity of country of origin and national identities, while seeking overarching theoretical and thematic lenses. It is also often transnational history, looking to the causes of migration and the ongoing connections that people, institutions, and global dynamics create between countries of origin and Latinas/os in the United States. Latina/o history remains part of the broader interdisciplinary field of Latina/o Studies. Indeed, interdisciplinarity is often the only way to begin telling the histories of more recent arrivals to the United States.

ESSAYS

The first essay, by Pedro Cabán, professor of Latin American, Caribbean, and U.S. Latino Studies at the University at Albany, traces the emergence of Chicano Studies and Puerto Rican Studies during the late 1960s and early 1970s. Noting the "insurrectionary and somewhat turbulent origins" of these fields, he explores how they laid the foundations for the field of Latina/o Studies. Cabán considers Latina/o Studies as a vibrant field of study, as well as the challenges that Latina/o Studies has faced as an academic unit in higher education. In the second essay, Vicki Ruiz, professor of history and Chicano/Latino Studies at the University of California–Irvine, reflects on the long history of Latinas/os in the United States and on the ways that including that history reshapes the broad contours of U.S. history. Focusing on three important historical moments, she illuminates how including Latinas/os as "meaningful actors" recasts our understandings of empire and citizenship in U.S. history. In the third essay, Frances Aparicio, professor of Spanish and Portuguese at Northwestern University, turns to a central challenge in the field of Latina/o Studies. The great diversity of peoples embraced by the term Latina/o includes distinct national origins, time and place of arrival in the United States, race, gender, sexuality, class, religion, language, and immigration/ citizenship status. Highlighting the interdisciplinary nature of the field, she argues that this "heterogeneity challenges scholars to find new, interdisciplinary approaches that can address our multiple and shifting realities." Hence, in addition to comparative approaches, Latina/o Studies must also explore interlatino relations and the emergence of new interlatino subjectivities, or Latinidad. In the fourth essay, María Josefina Saldaña-Portillo, professor of Social and Cultural Analysis at New York University, argues for transnational and comparative approaches to Latina/o Studies. Using the aftermath of hurricane Katrina in 2005 and New Orleans as a lens, she demonstrates how these approaches deepen our understandings of the United States and of its relations to countries beyond its borders, as well as to the diversity of peoples within its borders.

From Chicana/o Studies and Puerto Rican Studies to Latina/o Studies

PEDRO CABÁN

Latino Studies has evolved from its insurrectionary and somewhat turbulent origins as Chicano and Puerto Rican Studies into its current incarnation as a multidisciplinary academic field that explores the diversity of localized and transnational experiences of Latin American and Caribbean national origin populations in the United States. In this essay, I draw a distinction between Latino Studies as a field of study and Latino Studies as an academic unit of

Pedro Cabán, "Moving from the Margins to Where? Three Decades of Latino/a Studies," *Latino Studies* 1:1 (March 2003): pp. 5–35. Reproduced with permission of Palgrave Macmillan.

instruction and research in the university. It is evident that as an academic field Latino Studies has matured in terms of the quantity and quality of the scholarship produced, the numbers of programs of instruction, the formation of professional associations, the publication of specialized journals, the growing numbers of doctorates minted each year in Latino and Latina-related subject matter, and other achievements. In the process the field has attained increased academic legitimacy and more universities have targeted hires specifically in Latino Studies.

The development of Latino Studies as academic units has not fared as favorably. As is the case with most race and ethnic studies, Latino Studies has a contested, and in some cases still undefined, status in the academy. The academy's response to Latino Studies has varied widely. As a consequence, Latino/a Studies academic units are configured in a multitude of forms. Hundreds of programs, departments, centers, and institutes have been established in the last three decades. Some academic units enjoy autonomy in hiring and in curriculum design and operate with respectable budgets, while others are merely paper programs with part-time directors. Some are exclusively research-based centers and others provide limited undergraduate instruction....

How Latino Studies is positioned as an academic unit will figure prominently in the development of the field and the nature of its contribution to fulfilling the mission of the university....

Ultimately, I am interested in explaining the gradual shift from a virtually universal hostility and rejection of Chicano and Puerto Rican Studies, the precursors of contemporary Latino Studies, to the current situation in which a growing number of universities are exploring alternative forms of incorporating Latino/a-based knowledge into their academic mission....

[D]espite the inhospitable greeting, Puerto Rican and Chicano Studies endured and helped pave the way for Latino and Latina Studies. What explains the staying power of an academic endeavor that was once perceived to have merely a fleeting and inconsequential impact on US higher education?

The reason simply is that Chicano and Puerto Rican Studies produced scholarship of academic excellence. It has developed academically viable curricula and consistently enrolled large numbers of students in its courses. Student activism has also served to sustain existing programs and remains one of the more powerful forces for the creation of new Latino/a Studies programs. In the 1960s, university and college education was a privilege and inaccessible to the vast majority of students of color, virtually all of whom were from the working class. Working-class and poor students launched the first militant campaigns to restructure the urban public universities in order to include ethnic studies instruction and research. However, the struggle was not only to achieve educational diversity. Given the entrenched racism, Chicano and Puerto Rican leaders realized the indispensability of these programs for retention by improving the self-image, confidence, and academic capabilities of those poor urban youth who were fortunate enough to attend college. The struggle for Chicano and Puerto Rican Studies was steeped in political urgency and would have a major impact on the advancement of their communities.

As the Latino population grew and became increasingly diversified in terms of national origin, social class, and demographic characteristics, the necessity of research and instruction on this population became more pressing and the content more varied. Thirty years ago university administrators could not have envisioned the phenomenal growth of a Latino/a college student population, let alone one that would continue to demand Latino Studies instruction. Yet in the absence of student political activism and protests, academic bureaucrats chose to ignore the growing social and educational importance of providing Latino Studies instruction. In fact, during the 1990s, the refusal of university administrators to consider seriously the reasonable student calls for Latino Studies provoked strikes, building takeovers, and militant activities in a number of Ivy League colleges and prestigious research universities. The intensity and determination of some of these protests by Latina and Latino students, many from a more privileged socioeconomic stratum than the rebels of the 1960s, surprised university officials. This resolve has convinced recalcitrant academic bureaucrats that the demand for Latino-focused instruction is not a transitory political phenomenon....

Nonetheless, the role of Latino Studies in higher education remains a controversial issue for a large number of universities. Advocates for Latino Studies still envision themselves as engaged in a campaign to democratize the academy by broadening the scope of inquiry and instruction. However, now, 30 years after the student sit ins and building takeovers, Latino Studies (and ethnic and race studies in general) has generated new scholarship that reinterprets important episodes and processes of US history and society, produced an array of innovations in curricula, design[ed] ... culturally sensitive pedagogy, developed interdisciplinary research initiatives that generate new ways of knowing, and experimented with novel methods of delivering university generated knowledge to the community. In the process, Latino Studies has posed epistemic challenges to the hegemony of the disciplines....

★ ★ ★

Although a number of studies are available, a detailed, historically grounded comparative analysis of the beginnings and evolution of Chicano, Mexican American, and Puerto Rican Studies needs to be written. In 1968, the first Chicano Studies Department was established in California State College, Los Angeles, as a result of vigorous demands and strikes by the United Mexican American Students. In March 1969, the Chicano Coordinating Council on Higher Education organized a conference at the University of California, Santa Barbara. The participants drafted [El] Plan de Santa Barbara for college level instruction on the Chicano/a experience in the US and outlined the elements of a new academic enterprise that linked the creation of knowledge with community empowerment. The organizers wrote, 'We recognize that without strategic use of education, an education that places value on what we value, we will not realize our destiny.' Higher education was to be employed 'for the development of our community', which necessitated that the 'university work for our people.' The conference also resulted in the unification of regional Chicano student organizations into the national Movimiento Estudiantil Chicano de Atzlán (MEChA), which assumed a leadership role in

promoting Chicano Studies. Soon other programs and departments were established in the California State University system.... By 1984, 19 Chicano Studies
programs had been founded in the University of California and California State
University systems. In 1970, the University of Texas Austin established the Center
for Mexican American Studies. The current Center for Chicano-Boricua Studies
at Wayne State began as the Latino En Marcha Leadership program in 1971.

In April 1969, the Black and Puerto Rican Student Community took over
the walled-in South Campus of the City College of New York and closed the
university until the board of trustees agreed to establish a School of Black and
Puerto Rican Studies. The Puerto Rican Student Union issued a pronounce-
ment, 'Somos Puertorriqueños y Estamos Despertando,' in 1969 that vowed 'to
bring the services of the university to the community which is denied the
knowledge beyond those "ivy walls" that are made to keep the majority of the
people ignorant.' The same year the New York City Board of Education provided priority funding for Black and Puerto Rican Studies in the City University
of New York (CUNY). The establishment of other departments and programs
followed quickly. In 1970, Livingston College of Rutgers University established
the first Puerto Rican Studies Program in New Jersey. By 1973, 17 CUNY units
had established Puerto Rican Studies programs and departments. Programs were
established in a number of SUNY campuses and private institutions. In 1973,
CUNY established the Centro de Estudios Puertorriqueños as a research unit
with a permanent staff of professional research associates. The Centro was the
product of the demands of a politicized social movement that was linked to the
struggles of other racialized communities....

A point of departure for the scholarship in this formative stage in the development of Latino Studies was a critique of the epistemological foundations of the
social sciences and historical inquiry, and a repudiation of canonical claims of
value neutrality in the pursuit of knowledge. The university was implicated as a
crucial component of an overarching structure of racial and class oppression.
Chicano and Puerto Rican Studies disavowed the assimilationist discourse and
eschewed social science positivism as a static and ahistorical mode of analysis ill-
suited to the task of reclaiming a history long denied. To counter the racism of
the university, which expounded an ideology of assimilation but practiced the
politics of exclusion, Chicanos and Puerto Ricans adopted an essentialist posture
and viewed with deep skepticism the process of negotiation and compromise
practiced by these institutions.

Chicano and Puerto Rican Studies emphasized a radical historiography of
colonialism and territorial conquest and displacement, racialization of subject
peoples and their economic exploitation, denial of equal citizenship, and a
quest for symbols and practices of resistance and national affirmation. Given
that Mexican Americans and Puerto Ricans had been systematically excluded
from the historical narrative of the United States, the pioneering scholarship
questioned long-standing preconceptions regarding their contributions to
building this society. Rodolfo Acuña's 1972 path-breaking study recast
long-established depictions of Chicanos as passive subjects who aspired to be
assimilated into the dominant society. He documented a history of the Chicano

resistance to the onslaught of Anglo colonization and displacement, and portrayed Chicano/as as agents in the making of their own history. A new narrative that centrally inserted Chicanos into the history of the Western United States was a vital antidote to the sanitized renditions of Manifest Destiny. According to Alberto Camarillo, the purpose of these early historical works was 'the recovery and reconstruction of an ignored and obscured past'—which challenged a 'history in which people of Mexican origin in the Southwest were cast into the shadows if not altogether omitted from historical consideration.' Almost two decades ago Renato Rosaldo … observed that Chicano Studies 'shared in the broader endeavor of combating ideological, political, and economic forms of oppression confronted by their research subjects.' In addition to the critique of history as practiced in the academy, Chicano and Chicana scholars confronted the racially biased methodology of social science inquiry as practiced in the academy, and were committed to undertake applied research on education, migrant workers, and healthcare delivery.

Frank Bonilla, the founding director of the Centro de Estudios Puertorriqueños, observed that the Puerto Rican Studies research agenda 'meant a rejection of the defeatist visions of Puerto Rican reality promulgated in academic research.' Puerto Rican Studies exists, he argued, because enough Puerto Ricans 'reject any version of education or learning that does not forthrightly affirm that our freedom as a people is a vital concern and an attainable goal.' … Historical rediscovery, national affirmation, and knowledge for political empowerment and community development fueled the incipient intellectual project of creating a new Puerto Rican and Chicano subject who was imbued with agency and capable of using the existing institution.

This formative stage of the field was also characterized by a search for appropriate paradigms that could be deployed to theorize the conditions of Chicanos/as as displaced and Puerto Ricans as colonized people. Chicanos refashioned [the] concept of internal colonialism to explicate the array of institutions and practices that subjugated the Chicano community. By the early 1970s, the Center for Puerto Rican Studies began to theorize the relation between capitalist development, colonialism, and migration to comprehend the 'massive presence of Puerto Ricans in the United States' and their collective condition as a cheap, disposable proletariat in metropolitan labor markets.

Although often informed by Marxist and structural analysis, much of the academic production of this period (late-1960s to mid-1980s) failed to interrogate adequately the practice and mechanism of race, gender, and sexual orientation oppression within the national formation. Neither was the scholarship sufficiently comparative in approach, and it often opted for an analytical perspective that explored the relations between the oppressor and the oppressed as recalcitrant oppositional binaries whose behavior was racially motivated. Political analysis relied on a discursive practice that essentialized both actors, and discouraged more nuanced thinking on strategies of resistance to the assimilationist power of the university. The reliance on historical and political analysis, as opposed to other disciplinary-based perspectives, to generate an understanding of the conditions of Puerto Ricans and Chicanos reflected the dominance of males as the intellectual workers of this early era of Latino Studies. Major theoretical and political challenges to male-centered, nationalistic discourse would be launched in the 1980s and 1990s, initially by feminists, and subsequently by queer scholars who explored the intersections of sexual orientation with other counter hegemonic discourses and practices of identity formation.

The early Puerto Rican and Chicano Studies scholarship shared many of the same normative concerns and analytical perspectives, but they differed in one significant area. Whereas the Chicano historiography and the emerging social science literature primarily explored the Chicano experience in the US, early Puerto Rican Studies was heavily invested in reinterpreting the economic history of Puerto Rico under US colonial domination. Sociologist Clara Rodríguez observes that prior to the 1970s the literature was 'reflective (and in some cases supportive) of Puerto Rico's colonial relationship.' During the late 1960s and early 1970s, the bulk of the literature was critical of US colonialism, 'and attempted to deconstruct the earlier literature and contextualize Puerto Rico and Puerto Ricans.' However, research and theorizing soon focused on the nexus between colonialism, capitalist development, and migration to the United States.

During the 1980s and 1990s, Latino Studies achieved significant academic maturation and professional development. The philanthropic foundations were important in training a cohort of Latino scholars.... Research centers attempted to deliver on early movement goals to undertake policy-relevant research that could be utilized to empower the Latino community. These fellowships and research initiatives served to validate academically the presence of Latinos and Latinas and their scholarship in the academy.

Latinos established national professional associations in order to facilitate the sharing of research, to create intellectual communities and to enhance the academic development of the field.... A number of journals on Latino and Chicano Studies were published....

The rapid expansion of the Cuban and Dominican college age populations in Florida and New York City generated demand for research centers and undergraduate programs that explored the histories of these communities in the United States as well as in their home countries. In 1991, Florida International University established the Cuban Research Institute, which supports, generates, and disseminates research on both Cuba and Cuban Americans. A new scholarship on the Cuban American experience is evolving that is indicative of a sea change in the academic community's self-perception. Second-generation Cuban American scholars are not as inclined as the émigrés of the 1959 revolution to view themselves as an exile community. Their scholarship has focused on issues of identity, exile politics, community development, Cuban Americans in US foreign policy-making, and women as economic agents. By the early 1990s, the large Dominican population of New York City was beginning to exercise its growing commercial and political influence. The Dominican Studies Institute (DSI) was established in 1994 in response to pressure from the Council of Dominican Educators for CUNY to create an institute to address the glaring gap of knowledge on the Dominican community. Current research focuses on the socio-economic characteristics of Dominican communities, the characteristics of the migration experience, transnational community formation, the construction of national identity, and the impact of returning migrants on the Dominican Republic.

During the 1990s, Latino/a Studies underwent considerable redefinition. A new generation of scholars employed the analytical tools and conceptualizations of diverse disciplinary traditions to broaden the scope of historical inquiry and theorizing on the Latino/a experience. The scholarship included postmodernism and more theoretically nuanced applications of historical materialist analysis. The national unity that was perceived as indispensable to advance La Causa gave way to the reality that no national origin group was homogeneous; that all these formations were socially constructed and riddled by class, racial, gendered and sexual orientation divisions. The notion of ethnic identity became profoundly complicated and contested.

Latina feminist scholarship was an early and important intellectual challenge to the essentialist and male-centered orientation of the early Chicano and Puerto Rican Studies research. Chicana feminists shattered the male-imposed notion that nationalism supersedes and subsumes internal differences. They revealed that the monolithic, hegemonic construction of Chicano identity was not only male derivative, but was an exclusionary formulation that imposed a gendered division of intellectual labor. As it questioned the established chronicles of the western experience and colonial practice, Latina feminism offered a gender-based reconsideration of the historical narratives of the Chicano, Mexican American and Puerto Rican experiences....

Citizenship, civil rights, language rights and identity occupied the concerns of sizable contingents of Latino/a scholars. Empirical studies on Latino/a political behavior, immigration and naturalization were also published with increased regularity....

By the early 1990s, Latino and Latina Studies was evolving along at least the following five tracks: (1) the new history that emphasized the areas of urban communities, women, and political and institutional histories, and the frontera or border as an analytical and theoretical construct; (2) literary and cultural studies that made major contributions to the discourse of identity and racial formations, sexual subjectivity, analysis of cultural production, and cross border identities; (3) politics and political economy, with a focus on political participation and electoral behavior, economic justice and labor markets, social movements, immigration, Diaspora studies, and legal citizenship; (4) interdisciplinary scholarship on social constructions of identity, critical race studies, sexual subjectivities, language and cultural citizenship; (5) feminist scholarship that has informed all these analytical and theoretical concerns with new gendered perspectives.

Virginia Sánchez Korrol observed of the new historically oriented scholarship, 'the result was a historical interpretation that conferred agency on US Latinos, bringing them out of the shadows and on to center stage where their reality contrasted and contested the dominant Anglo experience.' ...

During the late 1980s and throughout the 1990s postmodern scholarship generated a critical rethinking of the social construction of identities and made evident the artificiality of cultural, racial uniformity within Latinidad. More recently, a new generation of scholars has embarked on theoretical and empirical explorations of sexual orientation and [its] relationship to identity, transnationalism, and popular culture, the politics of language usage and bilingualism, Latino cultural studies, local electoral politics and mass political behavior, and analyses of the impact of national economic changes on Latino communities.

This intellectual effervescence did not occur in a vacuum. The impact of globalization, Caribbean and Central and South American immigration, the growth of US Latino populations and their heightened electoral importance, the development of information technologies, and growth of the college age Latino student population were among the more notable changes that compelled many universities to rethink the role of Latino Studies. The paradox of growing economic and political interdependence between Latino communities in the United States and their countries of origin heightened policy interest.

★ ★ ★

The rethinking of the role of ethnic studies in higher education is taking place during a period of US global supremacy and unilateralism in world affairs. A triumphalist discourse attributes this supremacy to the superiority of US institutions and way of life. As they acknowledge the vibrant cultural and ethnic diversity of the country, national leaders are reasserting a singular patriotic credo that likens loyalty to the government with patriotism, and which equates dissent with disloyalty. The current re-emergence of American exceptionalism is degrading constitutional liberties and citizenship rights. In the post-9/11 context, difference and diversity are tolerated to the extent that they do not clash with an ideology of political conformity.

The debate on ethnic studies is framed in terms reminiscent of this discourse on difference and conformity....

An earlier phase of US global pre-eminence at the turn of the 19th century was attributed to the country's democratic institutions, efficient capitalist economy, and the superior moral fiber of its people. Ultimately, greatness was attributable to a core set of values that was rooted in a deeply held conviction of racial and sociocultural Anglo-Saxon superiority. National greatness was explicitly associated with male-gendered whiteness....

Historically, US elites have taken comfort in the extraordinary power of civil society and its key institutions to socialize new immigrant populations into the norms of political and economic behavior, and to legitimate the prevailing hierarchy of power. However, when these benign institutions fail to 'make Americans,' the US state has demonstrated time and again its willingness to enforce conformity and compliance.

That is why efforts of new arrivals to preserve their cultural and linguistic distinctiveness, of racialized minorities to rediscover and expose a history that contradicts the central tenets of US exceptionalism, and of activists who daily challenge the practice of race, gender, and sexual orientation oppression pose a threat to the carefully constructed ideology of US greatness, which is still based on a barely disguised discourse of white supremacy. The success with which Latino/as have nurtured a cultural identity and maintained symbolic, as well as real, ties to their countries of origin is an affront to those who believe in the intrinsic superiority of 'American' values. Consequently, Latino/as are often depicted as an undifferentiated mass of foreigners whose first language is Spanish and who nurture the anti-democratic cultural values and anti-Western social practices of their countries of origin. In this context, conservative forces have sought to deprive immigrant Latinos of state-mandated benefits or restrict the citizenship rights of Latinos. These voices proclaim that universities should not provide Latinos the opportunity to study their experience since this only serves to foment balkanization and undermine national unity. For many who fear the growing influence of racialized minorities, Ethnic Studies programs and departments are seen as nurturing values that are antithetical to their notions of E Pluribus Unum.

Yet the history of ethnic and race studies refutes the thesis that careful and critically engaged scholarship on the experience of racialized minorities in this country leads to balkanization, alienation, and social tensions. A monolithic discourse that seeks to eradicate difference, or subsume difference, invariably is more destabilizing than an alternative approach that recognizes and values the reality of difference, but which explores the prospects and opportunities for building unity and strength from this difference.

Recasting Empire and Citizenship in U.S. History

VICKI L. RUIZ

As historians, many of us have had the experience of encountering a memoir, diary, or letter in which the individuals mentioned are far more intriguing than the author of the document. The chatty reminiscences of Señora Doña Jesús Moreno de Soza serve as a case in point. Born in California in 1855, she came of age, married, and cared for her family near Tucson, Arizona. When she was eighty-four, she recounted the following incident that had occurred at a local park some fifty years earlier:

> They used to have a dancing platform. Once it happened that an Apache squaw called Luisa was dancing when Petrita Santa Cruz ... came along, and looking at the Apache squaw said, "That is enough, get out, we want to dance." The Apache squaw replied, "I am a person, too."

Moreno de Soza noted that Luisa later married the Apache son of a prominent Euro-American doctor. Given Luisa's rise in status, Moreno de Soza began to greet her as "comadre" (a term of endearment suggesting kinship). But Luisa kept her distance and purportedly responded to the overtures of friendship with the phrase, "Why don't you call me, Mrs. Handy?"

This tale from the 1880s reveals subtle registers of negotiation and contestation.... The remembered interaction between Moreno de Soza and Luisa Handy lends insight into the ways Mexican Americans, American Indians, and

Vicki L. Ruiz, "Nuestra América: Latino History as United States History," *The Journal of American History.* Vol. 93, No. 3 (Dec 2006), pp. 655–672. Reprinted by permission of Journal of American History.

Euro-Americans could inhabit the same social spaces and thus complicate U.S. western narratives that privilege a binary relationship between Euro-Americans and a designated "other." This unusual vignette also shades our understanding of the Spanish borderlands in showing that interactions between Spanish/Mexican settlers and native peoples could occur outside the specter of bonded labor. Yet, despite a florescence of scholarship on the Spanish borderlands over the past fifteen years, U.S. historians frequently give both the region and the era no more than a passing glance.

One reason for that erasure is simply structural. Having finite time and space to devote to the colonial era, teachers and textbooks place an understandable emphasis on the thirteen British colonies as the background to the American Revolution. But such logic should not preclude discussions of other European settlers, notably the Spanish who arrived in St. Augustine in present-day Florida four decades before the founding of Jamestown, Virginia. Another reason harks back to the Black Legend. With roots in the Reformation and in the competition for New World empires, the Black Legend counterpoised virtuous English families against rapacious Spanish *conquistadores*.... The Black Legend would feed into the currents of Manifest Destiny; however, once the borderlands became territories and states, the diverse histories of pre–United States settlements, if acknowledged at all, became reduced to romanticized images of quaint New Mexican villages or crumbling California missions. Yet disdain and distrust lingered. By 1920 Spanish-speaking people in the Southwest were frequently relegated to either of two categories—the "Spanish" descendants who were living reminders of a bygone era or the larger (and more threatening) group of Mexican immigrants who required guidance and surveillance....

From carving out a community in St. Augustine in 1565 to reflecting on colonialism and liberty during the 1890s to fighting for civil rights through the courts in the 1940s, Spanish-speaking peoples made history within and beyond national borders. Certainly, one essay cannot comprehensively convey the legacies of individuals of Latin American origin. So instead, in a survey of the state of the field, I emphasize three historical moments pivotal to reimagining an American narrative with Latinos as meaningful actors—1848, 1898, and 1948....

★ ★ ★

With the conclusion of the U.S.-Mexican War and the Treaty of Guadalupe Hidalgo, 1848 marked the end of the Spanish and Mexican frontier era, an era that remains shrouded in myth and misconception.... The idea of a prestatehood California controlled by fun-loving swashbuckling rancheros was also enshrined in an earlier historiography of moonlight and mantillas where fiestas and fandangos were the order of the day. However, as the historian Douglas Monroy has pointed out, the ranching elite represented only 3 percent of the Californio population in 1850.

Typically, Californios did not preside over sprawling properties but instead tended small family farms.... Spanish-speaking settlers, according to a more recent account, lived in a society where "the entire family awoke at three o-clock and men and women worked until dusk."

What does contemporary scholarship reveal about the peoples who journeyed north to regions that would become the American Southwest, people establishing communities such as Santa Fe (New Mexico) in 1610, San Antonio (Texas) in 1718, and Los Angeles (California) in 1781? They were a heterogeneous lot representing a range of colonial *castas* that demarcated to the nth degree Spanish, African, and indigenous ancestries. Over one-half of the founding families of Los Angeles, for example, were of African heritage. In addition to mixed-race settlers born in Mexico, Jews from the Iberian Peninsula sought refuge from the Inquisition in the far-flung province of New Mexico. Combing an array of colonial documents, including baptismal records, the historian Omar Santiago Valerio-Jiménez calculated the way economic mobility determined the racial identification of Spanish-speaking villagers in the Rio Grande region of southern Texas and northern Tamaulipas in the eighteenth and early nineteenth centuries. Using the notion of "pigmentocracy," he claimed, "Individual examples abound of poor vecinos … 'whitening' their caste as their wealth increased. Particularly successful individuals not only entered the upper class but also recreated themselves as españoles."

Inventing or reinventing oneself—is that not the hallmark of the mythic American frontier? But before we enshrine the early Spanish-speaking settlers in the pantheon of western lore as rugged individuals who trekked the wilderness in search of opportunity, it is critical to recognize that the Spanish borderlands encompassed caste-based communities with bonded labor at the center of social and economic relations. Indentured servitude was prevalent on the colonial frontier and persisted well into the nineteenth century with Indians and, to a lesser extent, people of African heritage pressed into bondage. In San Antonio, Texas, for instance, in 1735, Anttonía Lusgardia Ernandes, a "free mulatta," sued her former master for custody of their son. She recalled her servitude: "I suffered so much from lack of clothing and mistreatment of my humble person." Moreover, she declared, the patrón, "exercising absolute power, snatched away from me my son—the only man I have and the one whom I hope will eventually support me." Admitting paternity, the man claimed that his former servant had relinquished the child to his wife. The court, however, remanded custody of the child to Ernandes on the condition that she provide her son with "a proper home." …

Borderlands scholars have provided compelling narratives of societies rife with conflict and accommodation, pain and possibilities, effectively destabilizing popular notions of a peaceful pastoral era. With the conclusion of the U.S.-Mexican War and the Treaty of Guadalupe Hidalgo, Spanish-speaking settlers confronted dramatic changes in their lives and in their communities. If one considers Texas in the accounting, Mexico lost one-half of its national domain and between 75,000 to 80,000 of its colonist-citizens, the vast majority residing in New Mexico. Yet, the narratives of these people remain hidden within the American experience, overshadowed by the national implications of conquest.… Historians generally focus on the U.S.-Mexican War as "the fire bell in the night" with the subsequent acquisition (not conquest) of new lands, a feat that would open up the incendiary issue of slavery in the territories.…

But what happened to those Spanish-speaking settlers who remained in the Southwest, ostensibly citizens after a period of one year? Simply put, Mexicans on the U.S. side of the border became second-class citizens, commonly divested of their property, political power, and cultural entitlements....

Concurrently with the economic, political, and cultural upheavals occurring in the Southwest, many Cuban exiles to the east embraced Manifest Destiny. Rodrigo Lazo in his stunning literary history interrogated the publications of Cuban expatriates whose thriving print culture, based in New York and New Orleans from the 1840s through the 1860s, encouraged the United States to set its sights on Cuba. These writers fashioned themselves as emissaries of liberation who believed that Spanish colonialism should be supplanted by American annexation. In *Writing to Cuba,* Lazo teased out the contradictions among Latin American intellectuals who coveted American ideals of freedom while they acknowledged antebellum slavery and U.S. imperial designs. Not a monolithic group ..., they faced off in internal debates, and some founded an abolitionist newspaper, *El Mulato.*

Cirilio Villaverde and Emilia Casanova de Villaverde were exiles whose views would more closely align with those of a younger and more famous compatriot, José Martí. During the Ten Years' War (1868–1878), Casanova de Villaverde, in a letter to the Italian freedom fighter Giuseppe Garibaldi, asserted "that 'the beginning of our revolution means the freedom of our slaves, giving them arms, and incorporating them in our patriotic ranks.'" ... Emilia Casanova de Villaverde turned away from the privileges of the family plantation and advocated abolition. Only recently have historians acknowledged her role as an early leader in the quest for Cuban independence, a rebel in her own right, separate from her husband.

★ ★ ★

While 1848 burned in the consciousness of Mexican Americans during the decades that followed and of Chicano activists a century later, 1898 symbolized a similar transhistoric threshold for Cubans and Puerto Ricans. The Filipino-Cuban-Spanish-American War ... had roots both in the jingoistic stories published by the Hearst press and the protection of U.S. business interests in Cuba (valued at $50 million). But what has remained unacknowledged is the effort of Cubans and Puerto Ricans in the United States who vigorously championed the cause of Antillean independence from Spain.

With New York City as his primary base, José Martí established the Cuban Revolutionary party (Partido Revolucionario Cubano) in 1892, and within a short span over forty branches appeared in New York, New York, New Orleans, Louisiana, and in Florida at Key West and Ybor City (near Tampa). The party also included a chapter dedicated to the freedom of Puerto Rico. On January 29, 1895, Martí was one of four insurgents to sign a declaration of war—the 1895 Cuban War of Independence had begun. Though he fell in battle early in the campaign, Martí's deeds, poetry, and essays would assume a life of their own. Revered as an "apostle" of Cuban liberation, Martí left multiple legacies extending into the twenty-first century....

Within the last decade many scholars in Latin American and American studies have also looked to José Martí for inspiration, interrogating the meanings inscribed in the 1891 essay "Nuestra América" (Our America) in which he laid out a hemispheric vision of independent nation-states in a concerted dialogue with their powerful "neighbor" to the north. Perhaps portending a century of U.S. intervention in Latin America, Martí warned that

> the pressing need of Our America is to show itself as it is, one in spirit
> and intent.... The scorn of our formidable neighbor who does not
> know us is Our America's greatest danger. And since the day of the visit
> is near, it is imperative that our neighbor know us, and soon....

For contemporary academics, Nuestra América not only locates cognition of imperialism among those who would feel its weight but also points to a new paradigm of "the Americas." ... On the one hand, Martí's "Nuestra América" has become emblematic of a truly transnational, hemispheric interdisciplinary discourse, but on the other, Martí as a person should be placed in his own historical moment in the United States. As Nancy Raquel Mirabal has so adroitly and succinctly argued, "Martí represents an intellectual tradition of U.S. based Latin American thought and exile that challenges assumed silences and invisibility."

Martí's contemporaries, both men and women, who had worked tirelessly toward Cuban and Puerto Rican liberation would find their hopes dashed by war's end. Cuba gained its independence in 1902 with the caveat of the Platt Amendment, a clause in the new nation's constitution that authorized U.S. intervention. Puerto Rico, however, remained under U.S. dominion as a "non-incorporated territory." "Are we brothers and our property territory or are we bondsmen of war and our islands a crown colony?"—in 1900 a delegation of Puerto Rican leaders directed that pointed question to the U.S. Congress. Economic dependency on the United States significantly recast the lives of Puerto Ricans and Cubans in the decades ahead. A verse from a poem by the Puerto Rican *independista* Lola Rodríguez de Tió perhaps expressed it best: "Cuba and Puerto Rico/are two wings of one bird."

... [T]he economic restructuring that occurred in Puerto Rico with U.S. capital investment in sugar, large corporate landholdings, and the decline of coffee resulted in the massive dislocation of the island's rural folk. Ignoring the impact of American business interests, federal policy makers tended to interpret rampant unemployment as rooted in overpopulation. As a result, they promulgated plans to disperse families away from the island through job recruitment or contract labor. For example, in 1900 over five thousand Puertorriqueños arrived in Hawaii to harvest sugar cane, filling a labor shortage caused by the Chinese Exclusion Acts, and for two decades more families would follow. In 1917, with the passage of the Jones Act, Puerto Ricans became U.S. citizens; yet for many the free exercise of their rights proved elusive. Unlike cigar rollers in Florida, who exerted some control over their labor, Puerto Rican sugar workers in Hawaii found their movements so restricted that they "could not move from one plantation to another without the planters' consent."

By 1920 Puerto Ricans had migrated as contract workers or free agents to forty-five of the forty-eight states, creating communities in such distant locales as Louisiana and Arizona. However, as the historian Virginia Sánchez Korrol revealed, over 60 percent called New York City home....

Luisa Capetillo, the passionate Puerto Rican labor leader and feminist, certainly found New York a hospitable place during her brief residence from 1919 to 1920. A veteran labor organizer in Puerto Rico and Florida, she used her position as a *lectora* (reader) to cultivate and reinforce the consciousness of cigar rollers on trade union issues, socialism, anarchism, and women's rights. In New York she ran a boardinghouse and adjoining restaurant dishing up revolution and vegetarian fare. In her feminist manifesto, published in 1911, Capetillo stressed a radical version of republican motherhood, emphasizing women's education for their own sake and for the sake of their children.... Envisioning a future of women emancipated in every respect, Capetillo declared, "women are capable of everything and anything."

The Spanish-speaking cigar workers of Ybor City welcomed both José Martí and Luisa Capetillo. Beginning in 1886, Cuban, Spanish, and Puerto Rican cigar rollers and their Italian counterparts in that city had created thriving, militant work cultures in addition to extensive ethnic community networks.... During the 1895 war, Cubans of all colors contributed their wages, savings, and jewelry for the cause of independence. Such solidarity, however, was fleeting....

Afro-Latinos across generations and regions confronted the color line at every turn.... [T]he imprints of those negotiations can be traced across the entire canvas of Latino history from the borderlands to the present.

Patterns of economic dependency, like those unleashed by the Filipino-Cuban-Spanish-American War, could also be located in Mexico and the U.S. Southwest....

In *Culture of Empire*, Gilbert González complicated the standard "push/pull" interpretation of early twentieth-century Mexican immigration that privileges the Mexican Revolution (1910–1920) as providing the crucial push north for over a million people. According to González, large-scale immigration began before 1910 with the uprooting of villagers whose common lands were seized as the regime of Porfirio Díaz attempted to modernize Mexico by opening the country to foreign investment, particularly in agriculture, mining, and transportation. González argued that the emphasis on push/pull bifurcates a more fluid, transnational migration, a migration significantly shaped by U.S. businesses on both sides of the border.

... Instead of Manifest Destiny as territorial conquest that culminated in the U.S.-Mexican War, Manifest Destiny as economic empire building retained (and still possesses) considerable currency.

★ ★ ★

Was World War II a catalyst for civil rights among Latinos in the United States?...

Approximately five hundred thousand Latinos served in World War II, and that figure does not include the tens of thousands who labored in defense plants and other industries vital to the war effort, such as food processing.... I contend that for the individual in the local community, World War II did signal a significant shift in social relations and daily praxis. Men in uniform challenged seating sections in town theaters, demanded table service at "whites only" restaurants, and desegregated public pools. Yet, those protests did not occur in a vacuum but drew strength from two different political traditions forged during the depression, as represented by the League of United Latin American Citizens (LULAC) and El Congreso de Pueblos de Hablan Española (the Spanish-Speaking Peoples' Congress).

Founded by Tejanos in 1929, LULAC within a decade developed into a very influential middle-class Mexican American civil rights organization with local councils scattered across the Southwest. Envisioning themselves as patriotic "white" Americans, LULACers restricted membership to English-speaking U.S. citizens. As the historian David Gutiérrez notes, LULAC, taking a cue from the early National Association for the Advancement of Colored People (NAACP), stressed the leadership of an "educated elite" who would guide their less fortunate neighbors. He continued, "From 1929 through World War II LULAC organized successful voter registration and poll tax-drives ... and aggressively attacked discriminatory laws and practices." One could interpret LULAC's strategy or performance of whiteness as an organizational orchestration of "passing." While Afro-Latinos confronted the color line, güero (fair-skinned) Latinos could at times situate themselves quite differently....

In 1936 Blanca Rosa Rodríguez de León, a Guatemalan immigrant with a young daughter, could have passed given her complexion, education, unaccented English, and elite background. However, this young radical labor organizer chose to forego any potential privileges based on race, class, or color. Deliberately distancing herself from her past, she chose the alias... Luisa Moreno [and] would become one of the most prominent women labor leaders in the United States.... From the Great Depression to the Cold War, Moreno journeyed across the United States mobilizing seamstresses in Spanish Harlem, cigar rollers in Florida, beet workers in Colorado, and cannery women in California. The first Latina to hold a national union office, she served as vice-president of the United Cannery, Agricultural, Packing, and Allied Workers of America (UCAPAWA), in its heyday the seventh-largest affiliate of the Congress of Industrial Organizations (CIO). Moreno also served as the principal architect of El Congreso de Pueblos de Hablan Española....

On April 28–30, 1939, in Los Angeles the first national civil rights assembly for U.S. Latinos convened—El Congreso de Pueblos de Hablan Española. Although the majority of the 1,000 to 1,500 delegates hailed from California and the Southwest, women and men traveled from as far away as Montana, Illinois, New York, and Florida to attend the convention. Over three days, they drafted a comprehensive platform. Bridging differences in generation and ethnic background, they called for an end to segregation in public facilities, housing, education, and employment and endorsed the rights of immigrants to live and work in the United States without fear of deportation. While encouraging immigrants to become citizens, delegates did not advocate assimilation but rather emphasized the importance of preserving Latino cultures, calling upon universities to create departments in Latino studies. Despite the promise of the first convention, a national network of local affiliates never materialized; only a few fragile southern California chapters limped along during the war years.

The stands taken by ... Congreso delegates must be placed in the milieu of the deportations or repatriations of the early 1930s. Between 1931 and 1934, an estimated one-third of the Mexican population in the United States (over five hundred thousand people) were either deported or quasi-voluntarily repatriated to Mexico even though the majority (an estimated 60 percent) were native U.S. citizens. Viewed as foreign usurpers of American jobs and as unworthy burdens on relief rolls, Mexicans were the only immigrants targeted for removal. They were either summarily deported by immigration agencies or persuaded to depart voluntarily by duplicitous social workers who greatly exaggerated the opportunities awaiting them south of the border. Given that recent history, advocating for immigrants was courageous. Speaking before the 1940 conference of the American Committee for the Protection of the Foreign Born, Luisa Moreno contrasted the exploitation of Mexican workers with their indispensability to western agribusiness, "making a barren land fertile for new crops and greater riches." She continued, "These people are not aliens. They have contributed their endurance, sacrifices, youth, and labor to the Southwest."

While many scholars (myself included) have profiled the possibilities for social change in the postwar era, the chill of the Cold War hastened the demise of ten progressive CIO unions and the deportations of suspected immigrant radicals, Luisa Moreno among them. LULAC and El Congreso would imprint different legacies, the former institutional, the latter ideological. LULAC continued to rely on the courts to redress discrimination, while El Congreso's platform resonated decades later in the voices of Chicano activists and political stalwarts, such as Bert Corona, who in bridging generations, would build effective coalitions among trade unions, grass-roots networks, and students in pursuit of immigrant rights.

Two California court cases ... reveal the intersections of Mexican American civil rights campaigns with a larger African American freedom movement. In 1945 Gonzalo Méndez, a naturalized U.S. citizen born in Mexico, and his wife Felícitas, born in Puerto Rico, joined with four other families to sue four Orange County school districts. They challenged the common practice of drawing school boundaries around Mexican neighborhoods to ensure de facto segregation. Mexicans who lived in "white" residential areas were also subject to school segregation. [In 1947, the] renowned California writer Carey McWilliams noted a further precaution taken by school officials, placement by phenotype. "Occasionally the school authorities inspect the children so that the offspring of a Mexican mother whose name may be O'Shaughnessy will not slip into the wrong school." During the trial, superintendents reiterated well-worn stereotypes. Referring to Mexicans as a "race," the Garden Grove superintendent told the court with an air of authority that Mexican children were inferior in "personal hygiene," "scholastic ability," and "economic outlook." The trope of the dirty Mexican appeared prominently throughout the proceedings. The plaintiffs' attorney, David Marcus, questioned the constitutionality of educational segregation and called in expert witnesses—social scientists who challenged these assumptions about Mexican American children and the supposed need for separate schools. When she took the stand, Felícitas poignantly summed up her family's struggles: "We always tell our children they are Americans." Taking almost a year to formulate his decision, Judge Paul McCormick in 1946 "ruled that segregation of Mexican youngsters found no justification in the laws of California and, furthermore, was a clear denial of the 'equal-protection' clause of the Fourteenth Amendment." In 1947 the U.S. Court of Appeals for the Ninth Circuit upheld McCormick's decision.

Méndez v. Westminster assumes national significance through its tangible links to *Brown v. Board of Education*…. "[I]t was the first time that a federal court had concluded that the segregation of Mexican Americans in public schools was a violation of state law" and unconstitutional under the Fourteenth Amendment because of the denial of due process and equal protection of the laws….

The courtship of Andrea Pérez and Sylvester Davis had all the makings of a 1940s Hollywood movie—pretty Rosie the Riveter strikes up a friendship with her dashing co-worker; he leaves to fight for their country; on his return, they fall in love and plan to marry. Credits roll—well, not quite. Pérez was the daughter of Mexican immigrants, and her fiancé Sylvester Davis was African American. Fully aware that California's antimiscegenation code prohibited their union, they hired the civil rights attorney Dan Marshall, a leader in the liberal Los Angeles Catholic Interracial Council. After a Los Angeles County clerk denied the couple a marriage license, Andrea Pérez filed suit.

In 1948 the California Supreme Court ruled in Pérez's favor, becoming the first state supreme court to strike down an antimiscegenation law. As [scholar] Dara Orenstein brilliantly showed, the decision hinged in part on *mestizaje*. She argued that the court found the statute "too vague and uncertain" since it did not take into account people of "mixed ancestry" and since government employees could not consistently determine degrees of whiteness. In addition, Judge Roger Traynor, writing for the majority, ruled that the law violated the equal protection clause of the Fourteenth Amendment. At the time of the decision, Earl Warren was still governor of California; nineteen years later, he would preside as chief justice in *Loving v. Virginia,* the U.S. Supreme Court case that struck down all remaining state antimiscegenation laws….

The year 1948 marked several events of significance to Latino history, including *Pérez v. Sharp* [and] the founding of the American G.I. Forum…. In contrast to the close of the U.S.-Mexican War in 1848 and the Filipino-Cuban-Spanish-American War of 1898, the years after World War II did not represent a drastic transformation in Latino history, but one better compared to slow continuous shifts in plate tectonics. This period represented a claiming of public space as Latinos, through protest, politics, and popular culture, attempted to bridge the fault lines of inequality. The three defining moments discussed in this essay—1848, 1898, and 1948—are suggestive of the ways Latino history recasts and complicates constructions of empire and citizenship.

Over the last fifty years, U.S. Latinos have become even more diverse. According to the 2005 census figures, the Latino population has reached 41.3 million and can be categorized as follows: 64 percent Mexican, 10 percent Puerto Rican, 3 percent Cuban, 3 percent Dominican, 3 percent Salvadoran, and the remaining 17 percent divided among a bevy of other Latin American–origin groups. It is crucial to understand their histories within and beyond the borders of the United States and to contextualize present and projected demographic realities by exploring the pasts that preceded them. A recent National Research Council study predicts that by 2030 one-quarter of all Americans will be of Latin American birth or heritage.

With an utopian bent, José Martí dreamed of a "new America," a trans-hemispheric union between north and south, rooted in democracy, dialogue, and equality. "There can be no racial animosity," he wrote, "because there are no races." He added, "The soul, equal and eternal, emanates from bodies of various shapes and colors." Racism, nativism, and economic imperialism, which shaped Martí's world, remain with us in the twenty-first century. Contrary to popular media depictions of Latinos as people who arrived the day before yesterday, there exists a rich layering of nationalities, generations, and experiences. I seek a fuller recounting of this history, encompassing both transhemispheric and community perspectives. Nuestra América *es* historia americana. Our America *is* American history.

Confronting Diversity and Latinidad in Latina/o Studies

FRANCES R. APARICIO

One evening last year in Chicago, I attended a Latino concert at a local music venue downtown with some friends and colleagues. Around the table we were all Latino, yet each of us embodied very different social, class, cultural, linguistic, gendered, and racial experiences. We were all of Latin American descent; some were born and raised in Chicago, others were more recent immigrants, having arrived to the US five years ago, and others, like me, had been in the United States for most of their lives as adults. Most outsiders would have grouped us all together as Latinas/os, minorities, foreigners, and Spanish-speaking. But a closer look at the complex and contradictory identities and experiences among us all reveals a much more complicated picture about Latino America. This is, indeed, one of the most central challenges that Latina/o studies faces as a field of study....

How can we explore the mutual interactions, transculturations, conflicts, and power struggles among the 38 million Latinas/os in the United States, not to mention the power asymmetries between Latinas/os and dominant society? As a multi- and interdisciplinary site of academic inquiry, Latina/o studies examines the multiple factors that affect the everyday lives of US Latinas/os. Such

Frances R. Aparicio, "(Re)constructing Latinidad: The Challenge of Latina/o Studies." In *A Companion to Latina/o Studies*, ed. Juan Flores and Renato Rosaldo. Copyright © 2007 Blackwell Publishing. Reproduced with permission of John Wiley & Sons Ltd.

heterogeneity challenges scholars to find new, interdisciplinary approaches that can address our multiple and shifting realities.

Since the early 1990s, Latina/o studies has produced cutting-edge knowledge that responds to the historical shifts witnessed by our communities: colonialism and subordination, border crossing and transnationalism, racism and racialization, gendered identities and sexualities, stereotypes and representations, and the constitution of hybrid identities. These areas of inquiry are also located at the intersections between individual selves, collective groups, and the institutions of civil society, the media and the state. If identity is defined by the dialogic struggles between notions of the self and the constructions imposed from the outside (other individuals, institutions, and discourses), then Latina/o identities need to be understood at the interstices of both.

Scholars have debated the usefulness of the term "Latino" as a rubric that incorporates or fails to account for the heterogeneous experiences of US Latinas/os. Because it is an umbrella term that erases our cultural specificities, or that mostly foregrounds the conflicts and segmentations among the various national groups— … the term itself has been the object of suspicion and debate within the field. Yet now it is becoming a site from and around which to discuss the implications of the demographic diversification of the Latina/o population in the United States. Let us go back to the circle of my Latina/o friends in Chicago in order to explore the complexities behind Latina/o identities.

A middle-class immigrant from Venezuela, Sarita came to the US to study English originally in the late 1990s, but decided to stay in Chicago and brought her children over at the beginnings of the Hugo Chávez turmoils. Yet she also stayed because she fell in love with a Chilean man. Sarita and her children are undocumented, but their lives are informed by the middle-class values and aspirations that were part of her life in Venezuelan society. Their preoccupations range from being deported anyday to maintaining their social status through consumerism and social circles. José, a gay, Puerto Rican professor, has been in the United States since he was a graduate student, yet he is still very connected to Puerto Rican Island culture, to Spanish, and to Latin America. His long-term partner is an Anglo man who doesn't speak Spanish. They live in the suburbs and attend the Chicago opera and theater after work when they can. José grew up very poor on the Island, yet he is perceived as an Anglo because of his light skin color and blond hair. His gay identity, however, makes him vulnerable to homophobia and exclusion. Rosario, a Mexican woman in her fifties, a single mother of two young men, has not found full-time employment in years because she does not have a degree, yet she doesn't have enough money to pay for her tuition to complete her bachelor's degree in a continuing education program in the city. She is a citizen, but she cannot afford to pay her gas bills. She has no medical insurance, but she owns a small home in the south side of the city. Her car is always breaking down, and she is constantly struggling to make ends meet. Yet her cultural life is very rich. She has been an active participant of various Latino arts and theater organizations in the city for more than twenty years and she possesses a particular social capital in terms of her knowledge about the community. Dave (for David), half Puerto Rican, half Mexican, was born in Chicago but raised in the suburbs by his Mexican mother, who wanted to escape life in the inner city after her divorce. Despite his suburban identity, he grew up poor, lacking any sort of luxury and having to work since he was a child. Like many native-born Latinas/os, he speaks English and feels uncomfortable speaking Spanish. Many of his acquaintances assume he is privileged and assimilated because of his suburban, Anglophone identity. Yet he is deeply connected to his biological father and his family, who live in a very poor area of the city. His identity integrates the suburbs and the inner city, for he has been a part of these two worlds, cultures, and families. He knows about gang violence, about inner city high schools, and about unemployment through the experiences of his half brothers. He also knows about middle-class lifestyles, an individualist work ethos, and Anglo families and neighbors. And myself, a Puerto Rican blanquita who has lived in the United States for thirty years, been married to two working-class Chicanos, and have felt less and less connected to the Island as the years go by. A single mother of two Puerto Rican/Mexican daughters, and having lived in most regions of the United States, my own experience has connected me to both US Puerto Rican and Chicano/Mexicano cultures. I have in-laws in El Paso, Texas, and sisters in Boston and New York. Chicago is now my home. I call my girls niñas (the Mexican term) instead of nenas (the Puerto Rican term), I spend more time with my Mexican mother in law than with my own mother, but I definitely love to dance salsa and merengue more than cumbias or nortenas. In my case, class, gender, and cultural identities have all been marked by my personal connections to the Mexican American community.

This small group of individuals represents a small slice of the heterogeneous identities and experiences that constitute today what we call Latino. First, the different experiences among economic immigrants, political refugees, exiles, and native-born historical and racial minorities structure Latino lives, yet they do not determine them. Indeed, the contradictions in the lives of Sarita, Rocío, José, David, and myself reveal that individuals' multiple and contradictory identities unfold differently and lead to divergent results in terms of material and social survival. Sarita's undocumented status has made it very difficult for her to purchase a home, while Rocío's citizenship has not significantly improved her living conditions. Yet this past summer Rocío was able to travel to Mexico with a school tour and Sarita and her daughter were not able to go. While David's suburban upbringing may be seen as the most privileged experience in the group, this has not shielded him from poverty nor from witnessing the challenges and social problems of the inner city. In turn, José and I have been in the United States as part of the brain drain that has significantly robbed the Island of the talents and resources of young professionals. Yet gender issues, more than salaries, have kept José and I from returning to the Island.

Despite the fact that Spanish has been repeatedly hailed as the common denominator among Latinas/os, the linguistic diversity within this sector continues to be hybrid, fluid, and politically contingent. That evening, José refused to speak in English to David, asserting the dominance of Spanish at the table. If David has been privileged socially and in educational institutions for his knowledge of English and for not having an accent, contrary to José's heavily accented English despite his many years in the US, that evening David became a linguistic minority, silenced by the dominance of Spanish among the group, an experience of exclusion that he has faced multiple times. This moment of linguistic conflict represented the inverse of language politics in the United States, whereby Spanish is usually subordinated and racialized. In this case, José's Latin American subjectivity and linguistic power exerted dominance over a US-born Latino.

Elements of socioeconomic status and class also become significant in accounting for the Latino experience. While most US Latinas/os are working class or working poor, there is an emerging middle class and professional sector that has become an intermediary between institutions and those with less power and social capital. The case of Rocío is interesting in this regard. While she considers herself an upper-class venezolana, in the United States she has been struggling to maintain that lifestyle while earning much less than what she made in her country. Simultaneous to this shift in her own class experience, she has become an activist and advocate for immigrant and refugee rights. She has used her skills in networking, communications, media, and marketing to speak publicly for the undocumented. This differs from the more common phenomenon of middle-class Latin American immigrants being privileged over US Latinas/os in the workplace, given their levels of education in their home countries and their native skills in Spanish. In Chicago, for instance, the Spanish-language media—television and newspapers—recruit professionals directly from Latin America rather than US Latinas/os because of a perceived deficiency in the use of Spanish among the latter. It is not a coincidence that Rosario, despite her citizenship, has not found a decent, full-time job in the city. While Latin American professionals are displacing US Latinas/os from particular jobs, some, like Sarita, are also using their skills and resources to advocate for the larger community.

The term "Latino" carries with it internal semantic tensions that reflect the multiple sites from which it has emerged. Most scholars and many community members have embraced the term because it has represented a more organic alternative to the government-imposed term "Hispanic," coined and used since the 1970s. Yet this acceptance has not precluded the recognition that the term itself homogenizes the diverse power locations among US Latinas/os. As an umbrella term, it can be used strategically to indicate the oppositional location of Latinas/os versus, or outside of, dominant society. Likewise, it can be used to erase the specificities of the various national groups and historical experiences outlined above. Many second-generation Latinas/os use the term to identify themselves vis-à-vis Anglos, yet they also use their national identity to identify themselves in relation to other Latino groups. It is also increasingly common for hybrid Latinas/os, that is, those who are descendants of two national groups, to use the label Latino in order not to erase either of their identities. Thus, the use of labels is contingent, fluid, and relational, used strategically and structurally depending on the context. I define myself as a Puerto Rican professor among other Latina/o colleagues, but I also define myself as a Latina cultural critic in the larger context of my university colleagues. The term "Latino" then does not necessarily displace the significance of the national identifiers, but is used to signal the multiple and relational selves of colonized subjects.

Many Latina/o scholars have argued against the use of the term "Latino" because the media has deployed it historically to homogenize and lump us all together as one undifferentiated mass. This media discourse has had egregious consequences for the communities involved. For instance, the literary market sells Latin American literature as part of their Latino market. This conflation has less to do with the mutual influences or literary continuities between these two canons than with the economic benefit of attracting additional readers and buyers.... The experience of confronting racial, cultural, and linguistic marginalization and subordination in the United States as a result of the colonized status of our communities is a strong argument that distinguishes US Latino writers from their Latin American counterparts....

★ ★ ★

In Chicago, as in the other major Latino urban centers in the United States, communities from all Latin American countries live, work, dance, and interact throughout the cities that they are also transforming. Chicago is the third largest city in the US and home to the second largest Mexican and Puerto Rican communities nationwide. It is also home to a growing Guatemalan sector that has become the third largest Latino group in this urban area. As of the 2000 Census, Latinas/os constitute 26 percent of Chicago's total population. Of that, Mexicans constitute 70.4 percent, Puerto Ricans 15 percent, Guatemalans 1.8 percent, Ecuadorians 1.2 percent, and Cubans 1.1 percent. The fact that the Guatemalans and Ecuadorians have outnumbered the Cubans suggests that the traditional trinity of the three major historical minorities—Mexican American, Puerto Rican, and Cuban American—is shifting, creating a much more complex mosaic of Latin American national encounters. Indeed, recent Census figures show that Chicago ranks ninth in the metropolitan areas receiving large numbers of South American immigrants. Certainly, Peruvians have long made Chicago their home. In addition, the so-called "new Latinas/os"—Dominicans, Colombians, Ecuadorians, and other South and Central Americans—are all represented in the growing Latino demographics of the city....

This social mosaic leads to new forms of interaction, affinities, and power dynamics between and among Latinas/os from various national groups. It is interesting that media and journalism seem to zero in on the ensuing cultural conflicts and national tensions that have arisen from these new social spaces.

Yet we are also witnessing different forms of affiliations, solidarity, identifications, desire, and intermarriage among Latinas/os. This is not necessarily new, for Chicago and the Midwest witnessed similar interactions between Puerto Ricans and Mexicans, particularly since the 1940s. Yet the growing numbers and the dimensions of this demographic revolution call for a recognition that the term "Latino" is a real thing, an emerging social and cultural experience and experiment, and not just a label or construction imposed from the outside. If in the past decades, paradigms of national identity served to understand and produce a sense of collectivity grounded in particular geo-cultural locations and regions—the Chicanos in the West and Southwest, the Puerto Ricans in New York and the Northeast, the Cuban Americans in Miami—nowadays national identities are still significant, but they are not the exclusive axis of reference from which to understand Latino lives. In fact, national identities are restructured and reorganized as a result of these increasingly hybrid spaces. New interlatino subjectivities are emerging and we need to examine them at various levels....

First, there are myriad examples of mutual transculturations among different Latino nationals. From the impact of Afro-Caribbean music in Mexican culture (Carlos Santana's music), to the linguistic borrowings and influences, let's say, between Cubans and Nicaraguans in Miami, to the ways in which new Latino cuisine fuses Mexican ingredients with Caribbean ones, Latinas/os from various nationalities are creating new cultural objects and practices that are the result of two or more national influences.... Secondly, there are outright cultural conflicts among Latinas/os, most of which stem from the ways in which we racialize each other. These negative constructions of the national Other are usually fueled and informed by stereotypes and racializations that have been historically shared and internalized, but that also point out differences in behavior that may result from gender and racial subordination and from the larger forces of colonization.... There are also instances in which perceived differences of power inform the dis-identification or the gesture toward differentiation from our national others.... For undocumented Latinas/os, Puerto Rican US citizenship is seen as a privilege, while many Puerto Ricans consider it another reminder of their colonial and second-class status within the United States. At the same time, Puerto Ricans are continuously racialized by many other Latinas/os for their Caribbean Spanish, for their darker skin color, and for their high poverty rates. Many Latinas/os also refuse to be confused for a "Mexican," an attitude that reveals their fear of being racialized themselves as much as their internalization of that very same dominant discourse. Many of these disavowals and discourses of subordination, then, are rooted in larger structural forces rather than in individual prejudices.

... [T]he hybrid Latino subjects who are the offspring of Latinas/os of two different national groups ... negotiate their identities in ways that differ from the Anglo-Latino power dyad that has structured most of our understandings about Latinas/os in the United States. These younger Latinas/os may identify with each national culture in more relational ways and in more specific contexts, rather than in the linear ways in which we tend to think about national awareness or cultural reaffirmation. Mérida Rúa's research about the MexiRicans and PortoMex subjects in Chicago suggests that, in fact, hybrid Latinas/os make strategic decisions about national differentiation based on a variety of contextual, family, and social factors. Thus, their identity constructions tend to be more concentric, multiple, and diffused than what we are accustomed to....

Like interlatino racializations, these forms of passing for a national other are likewise informed structurally by the political positions and cultural presence of specific nationalities. For instance, factors such as the power and visibility of each group in relation to the others, or the mainstream acceptance of some identities over others, or the political rights and citizenship accorded to some, have an impact on the ways in which hybrid Latinas/os foreground one identity over another. For David, who is half Puerto Rican and half Mexican, it is easier to identify with the Mexican culture, partly because he was raised by his Mexican mother, but also because, according to him, he has been keenly aware of the fact that Mexico and Mexican history—iconized through its pyramids and the epic grandeur of its Aztec culture—have been much more visible in the US imaginary than its Puerto Rican counterpart. This canonization of particular national groups reveals the uneven ways in which our specific histories have been integrated as part of the US official knowledge. Given his suburban upbringing and his US citizenship by birth, David has not had to take into account the racialization of Mexicans in the context of US labor and immigration policy, nor the privilege of Puerto Rican citizenship.... [These] identities transcend the national/regional segmentation of our fields as well as of the identity paradigms that have traditionally informed our way of thinking. Because our fields of study have developed in such segmented ways and because cultural nationalism and Cuban exceptionalism have informed the boundaries of our research and thinking, this epistemological segmentation has prevented us from exploring these other very significant hybrid Latino sites, moments, and identities.

The history of interlatino relations in Chicago dates back at least to the 1940s when, as Elena Padilla (1947) documented, Puerto Rican newcomers were welcomed, housed, and offered social and economic support by the Mexican community.... While the diversification and increasing internal hybridity of the Latino communities is now coming to the fore as a result of the great migration of the 1980s, the fact is that this hybridity is not altogether new, but rather increasing as a result of these demographic changes. Yet these sites of Latinidad do not necessarily imply a utopian, egalitarian dynamic, nor do they suggest altogether that power differentials are decreasing, but rather, that new power relations emerge from these encounters.

★ ★ ★

What are the implications of this increasing Latinidad for Latina/o studies as a field of study? Rather than reproducing the national and geographical segmentation that has structured the way we organize knowledge in teaching and research, Latina/o studies can become the space in which these diverse experiences, identities, and power dynamics can be accounted for in the construction of a new social imaginary that transcends the old paradigms and nationality based conflicts. By studying and reflecting on interlatino dynamics through interdisciplinary approaches we can produce more nuanced knowledge that moves even beyond comparative studies. The demographic changes also call for the establishment of new programs in areas where Latinas/os are new communities in the making. For instance, the Southeast faces new challenges in terms of incorporating Latino communities in discussions about race, culture, language, and labor that have been historically informed by Anglo–Black relations.... Likewise, approaches to Latinidad will enhance current discussions about internal diversity and power differentials within national groups. The increasing hybridity of younger Latina/o subjects who embody and constitute two national groups, or a Latino and other racial group, will inevitably force us to transform the existing identity paradigms that still inform our thinking. PortoMexes, Cubolivians, Mexistanis (Mexican and Pakistani) are but a few of the possible hybrid identities that populate our urban centers. Will a new Latino melting pot develop as a result of this internal *mestizaje,* or will we continue to use national identities as the dominant criterion for exclusion and inclusion in the community? Redefining Latinidad from this point of view, rather than rejecting it altogether, will yield meaningful knowledge for the future of both Latino and non-Latino sectors in the United States.

Toward Transnational and Comparative Approaches to Latina/o Studies

MARÍA JOSEFINA SALDAÑA-PORTILLO

I begin this essay on Latina/o studies with … two [scholars] … for the tenor of each author's observations. Elliott Young, the historian, … calls for a new border history that gazes ever forward, in search of scholarly paradigms to move us beyond the limitations of nations and national time. Meanwhile Lisa Lowe, the literary critic, calls for a future American studies that turns its gaze resolutely backward, in a reexamination of the United States' imperial past, a reexamination that might help us to better critique the interminable national present. Surely, the aftermath of hurricane Katrina [in 2005] makes the importance of Lowe's call painfully clear, as the United States' past of racial exploitation and segregation vibrantly informs the present. Only by coming to terms with the country's historic dependence on a racialized labor force, subject to extra-economic forms of coercion, can we fully analyze the meaning of the tens of thousands of impoverished blacks waiting at the Superdome, on rooftops and balconies, waiting to be counted as citizens while news images laid bare their disenfranchisement and the Bush Administration's calculated indifference to it. And yet, even as the media focused our attention on the racialized structure of class hierarchy in this country, news anchors fully participated in the *representational* racism undergirding it. For how else to explain unsubstantiated rumors of widespread raping and killing ("looting") throughout the city, which later proved to be completely unfounded, repeated as fact by grim-faced news anchors? This demonization of black masculinity and sexuality is so ritualized in the national news media as to have become banal.

Meanwhile, the very scope of the tragedy made evident the inadequacy of the nation-state as a unit of analysis. The government of the "wealthiest nation on earth" was itself inadequate, incapable of behaving like a truly national government, inept at rescuing its own citizens. Unparalleled military power could not protect US borders from the resolutely global effects of global warming; an administration accustomed to deriding the United Nations was forced to accept relief aid from it. Moreover, even as the predominantly African American and impoverished white victims of Katrina suffered the catastrophic effects of racial and class violence in the local, state, and federal government's failure to evacuate them before or too long after the hurricane, many rejected the internationally used term "refugee" to describe their condition. Rev. Jesse Jackson, NAACP president Bruce Gordon, and members of the Congressional Black Caucus all denounced the term as racist and as discounting blacks as citizens. Three major US papers (*Washington Post, Miami Herald,* and the *Boston Globe*) immediately banned the use of the term.

María Josefina Saldaña-Portillo, "From the Borderlands to the Transnational? Critiquing Empire in the Twenty-First Century," in Juan Flores and Renato Rosaldo, eds., *A Companion to Latina/o Studies* (Blackwell Publishing, 2007), pp. 502–512.

Yet, the very anxiety expressed over the use of the term belies its uncomfortable suitability, drawing our "attention," as Young insists, "to the stories that fit poorly into national narratives." A *transnational* ethnic studies scholarship would analyze this anxiety by elucidating the *lack* of US exceptionalism, as well as its integration into a world system. If the use of the term "refugee" was technically incorrect, substantively it hit the mark. The 1951 Refugee Convention of the United Nations defines a refugee as "a person who, owing to well-founded fear of being persecuted for reasons of race, religion, nationality, membership of a particular social group or political opinion, is outside the country of his [*sic*] nationality." Although the use of the term "refugee" has loosened in the last half century to include victims of natural disasters (and women!), the majority of victims of hurricane Katrina are undeniably US citizens who remain in their own country. Nevertheless, what were these victims fleeing when they finally fled New Orleans, if not the effect of generations of formalized racial and economic disenfranchisement? The abandonment of the predominantly poor and black population in New Orleans by the federal government after hurricane Katrina only made evident an active structure of political violence faced daily by racialized populations in the United States, not just in New Orleans, but in all major US cities. Indeed, this abandonment—the very poverty and racism it exposes—"fits poorly" into the narrative of the universal privilege of US citizenship. In the face of this, one can imagine that, in the hey day of black nationalism and black Marxism, black leaders might have articulated their demands for enfranchisement precisely by emphasizing the similarities between the treatment of African American hurricane victims and African political refugees. Instead, the objections expressed by African Americans toward the word "refugee," as if it were a derogatory term, reveals a national minority finely attuned and attached to a *global* hierarchy of racial differentiation and nationalist privilege.

What hurricane Katrina made evident in August 2005 was that the periphery persists in the heart of the metropole. Unsurprisingly, it was Latina/o pundit Richard Rodríguez, a child of immigrants, who made this astute observation:

> … we discovered that New Orleans, *like any other city,* had been in the third world all along. These faces of terror and want and despair and menace and stoicism are faces from the third world. They are American faces. (Emphasis added)

In Rodríguez's words a transnational Latina/o scholarship should hear the echo of the "internal colonialism" paradigm deployed by minority nationalist movements in the early 1970s with such political alacrity and force to articulate their demands before the state. Indeed, this internal colonialism paradigm provided the theoretical impetus for Chicana/os to create Aztlán as mythical homeland and for Native Americans to reclaim Alcatraz as sacred ground.

A transnational Latina/o scholarship, however, would hear a call toward a post-nationalist analysis as well. For Rodríguez's statement "that New Orleans, like any other city, had been in the third world all along" shakes the United States out of the false comfort of privileged dichotomies, out of its quaint exceptionalism, reinserting it into a continental history of labor flows. New Orleans, like any other global city in the Americas, has always depended on peripheral populations whose racialization facilitates their hyper-exploitation. Indeed, New Orleans, like other global cities so dependent on undocumented immigrants, contained its very own international division of labor. Indeed, the Mexican and Honduran governments had to establish "mobile consulates" in the region, in the hopes of locating tens of thousands of undocumented Mexicans and Hondurans who worked in the oil, agricultural, and service industries in and around New Orleans, but who were too afraid of deportation procedures to seek government aid. According to a *News Standard* article from September 28, 2005, New Orleans was a veritable "Organization of American States":

> Hondurans and other Central American immigrants made up the bulk of the service sector working in casinos and restaurants in the New Orleans area, while Mexicans and other Latin American immigrants also constituted a large agricultural workforce in the surrounding region. The immigrant population in areas affected by Katrina included the 150,000 Hondurans and 40,000 Mexicans along with about 9,600 Salvadorans, 10,000 Brazilians, and immigrants from Perú, Venezuela, Chile, Panama, Trinidad and Tobago, and Costa Rica, according to numbers provided to the press by consulates.

Lowe and Young suggest a transnational American studies, and by extension ethnic studies, must flourish in a temporal paradox, one that seeks to move beyond the nation as the sole unit of analysis, even as it must revisit the past of the United States to continue to understand its trans(post?)national present. To step into this temporal paradox, I begin a deliberation of transnational Latina/o studies with a necessary diversion into hurricane Katrina. The racial logic revealed by hurricane Katrina returns us to an examination of the militant and filial origins of African American and Latina/o studies. (After all, behind every image of a lascivious black man poised to take advantage of an innocent's sexuality at the Superdome lurks the image of a cunning "illegal" Latina/o immigrant poised to take advantage of hurricane relief at the Astrodome.) Over the last thirty years Africana and Latina/o studies have too often evolved into the guardians of *petit* national cultures that serve to round-out the "American" student's liberal education; however, Katrina reminds us that the radical student movements that led to the founding of these departments were deeply *internationalist,* taking their cues from anti-colonial national liberation struggles in Africa, Asia, and Latin America. Through walkouts and sit-ins, student coalitions in the 1970s demanded minority knowledge production within the university; but they also demanded a counter-hegemonic scholarship that would dedicate itself to the analysis of the structural inequalities impacting subaltern peoples beyond American borders. I suggest, then, that a call for a transnational Latina/o studies is but in part a return to these early militant origins of African American and ethnic studies: it is a call to the analysis of a past and present *process* of racial and economic peripheralization of minority populations as it unfolds within—but always exceeds—the boundaries of the United States.

★ ★ ★

Border studies and border theory, which emerged with such scholarly and theoretical force in the 1980s, have been central in precipitating the move toward a
transnational American studies focused on the empire-building origins of the US,
as Young indicates. And yet, border theory and scholarship, precisely because of
the binomial focus of their central trope, too often serve to reinforce a "nation
within a nation" model of Latina/o studies: the focus of such scholarship is
almost exclusively on the historical and cultural "contact zones" which occur
along a border where two national cultures meet. Generally, the focus is the
US–Mexico border, which produces a third space occupied by a hybridized, lim-
inal Chicana/o culture.... Thus, though there have been invaluable titles in the
area of border studies, the question still pertains: what might a truly transnational
Latina/o studies look like? How might it differ from the contemporary
bi-national focus of Puerto Rican, Chicana/o, Cuban, or Dominican scholarship,
and why might we desire such a reformulation of the field?

A transnational Latina/o studies is necessarily comparativist and deeply his-
toricist. However, it is not simply the comparison of Latina/o cultural production by group "X" with the cultural production of Latin American country "Y,"
as necessary and valuable as this kind of scholarship continues to be for our field
more generally conceived. Rather, the call for a transnational Latina/o studies ...
is a call for a totality critique that moves beyond the nation as a unit of analysis
precisely because "Latina/o" identities begin their formation not in the US but
in Latin America, as an effect of US intervention and compulsory neoliberalism.
A transnational Latina/o studies, like transnational American studies, must proceed from an analysis that

- foregrounds United States nation-formation as an expansionist project in the
  Americas, with neocolonial interventions in the nineteenth and twentieth
  centuries that have generated wave after wave of "Latina/o" immigration;

- demonstrates the continued dependence of the US economy on Latin
  American markets, natural resources, *and* undocumented immigrants whose
  racially marked bodies are easily subjected to extra-economic forms of
  exploitation;

- compares the distinct racial legacies of the Anglo-American and Spanish
  colonial governmentality, and analyzes how Latina/o subjectivity is forged
  between these competing racial ideologies;

- analyzes the improvisation of resistive identity and cultural production in the
  wake of this history of racial migration.

When seen from this angle, African Americans and undocumented Mexicans
and Central Americans, equally displaced by hurricane Katrina, are no longer
populations vying for resources. Instead, these are populations sequentially racialized in the service of both an expanding rate of profit and the reproduction of
US nationalism. An expanding rate of profit and nationalist sentiment inevitably
pit racialized laboring populations against each other. Thus, a transnational
Latina/o studies would provide a coherent analysis of the seemingly contradictory positions taken by the Bush Administration in the immediate aftermath of

the storm. On one hand, President Bush, in his September 15 national address, attempted to re-suture the nation's racial divide at the expense of the undocumented (and predominantly *mestizo*) immigrants. He assured an American public— reunited by the iterative gesture—that undocumented immigrants would be ineligible for temporary housing, subsidies, Social Security checks, or even the mail delivery promised to legal residents displaced by Katrina. Furthermore, the Department of Homeland Security (DHS), going against standard procedure following natural disasters, "declined to promise that immigrants would not be placed in deportation proceedings if federal authorities find them through relief efforts." On the other hand, Bush suspended the 1931 Bacon-Davis Act, which would have required federal contractors rebuilding the Gulf region to pay the local prevailing construction wage, and the DHS simultaneously suspended penalties imposed on employers who hire employees without documentation of citizenship, presumably to facilitate the hiring of US citizens who lost their documents in the storm. These apparently opposing policies actually work in concert. Bush reassured his right-wing constituencies *and* segments of the African American community by refusing aid to undocumented immigrants and threatening to deport them, while he shifted reconstruction jobs to those very undocumented immigrants by suspending labor standards. Unsurprisingly, undocumented immigrants were among the first employed in clean up after the disaster struck. The lack of relief services and threats of deportation serve to create docile brown bodies on site and desperate for work....

Hence, slavery, segregation, and continued racial violence against blacks can be placed on a continuum with the "voluntary" immigration generated by US-backed genocidal regimes in Central America during the 1980s; by the IMF's structural adjustment policies imposed on South America during the same period; by the neoliberal reforms that have reformed away the livelihoods of Mexicans in the 1990s. I do not mean to suggest that a transnational Latina/o studies would indiscriminately equate the experience of US slavery and segregation with the experience of political exile and economically driven immigration produced as a violent consequence of US neocolonial and neoliberal policies in Latin America. However, such an approach would require us to place the slavery, genocide, and racial violence experienced inside US national boundaries within the larger context of US colonialism in the Americas, so that slavery and segregation are properly seen as the antecedents of the contemporary extra-economic forms of coercion (threatened deportation, debt peonage, repatriation of the costs of labor reproduction, vigilante violence) employed against undocumented immigrants from Latin America in the US today. Then and now, these extra-economic forms of coercion depend upon a racial economy of visibility and invisibility, or more accurately stated, the (in)visibility of racial labor. Then and now, such forms of subordination have produced cultures of resistance improvised precisely in that paradoxical space of (in)visibility, which at once obliges the brown laborer to disappear into the landscape of restaurant kitchen or agricultural field or hurricane debris, but also summons him or her to loom large as threat to white nationalism and black equality. Between such untenable imperatives, Latina/o immigrants use subaltern knowledge, queered spaces, mutual aid networks, weapons of the weak, rhetorical inversion and perversion, parody and humor, to produce both spectacular and speculative identities that enable them to resist this subordination and, under optimal circumstances, transform what it means to be human in the United States.

A transnational approach to the study of US Latina/o populations corresponds to Lowe's suggested approach to the study of Asian American populations....

Transnational Latina/o studies, like its Asian American counterpart, should provide such a critical consciousness of empire, a critical scholarship that is "tirelessly reckoning with America's past," but also with its present, through an examination of how displaced cultures of racialized immigrants trouble national narratives of democracy and equality. It requires less a fluency in multiple languages than a fluency of multiple Latin American national histories as they intersected with the United States' bloodied quest for hegemony in the region.

★ ★ ★

While Mexico may still predominate as country of origin for new Latina/o immigrants to the United States, the last thirty years of immigration from Central and South America have permanently decentered Chicana/o studies' dominance in the field nationwide. Similarly, the sheer diversity of Latin Americans immigrating to the east coast of the United States (including unprecedented waves of Mexicans) has dethroned Puerto Rican studies from its position of prominence in the region. Demographically, the Latina/o population in this country demands different approaches from us in our teaching, in the organization of our departments and programs, and in our hiring plans. We can no longer think within a cumulative model of Latina/o studies, where Chicana/o or Puerto Rican history and culture form the core of the curriculum, with other Latina/o experiences seen as providing variety to these paradigmatic cases. These changing demographics require us to reconsider the pedagogical reasons for and implications of internationalizing our approach to the study of Latina/o culture, politics, and history....

Mexico and Puerto Rico are indeed the only Latin American entities to have directly experienced US annexation. However, no Latin American country is left untouched by US intervention, and as such, there is no Latina/o immigrant population in the United States which does not [bear] the trace of this imperial legacy. Between 1898 and 1933, US governments landed marines in different Central American and Caribbean countries on a *yearly* basis, including a 20-year occupation of Nicaragua (1912–33), a 19-year occupation of Haiti (1914–34), and an 8-year occupation of the Dominican Republic. With notable exceptions, US administrations rarely deployed troops in the hemisphere after the mid-1930s. Nevertheless, CIA-directed *covert* operations to overthrow progressive Latin American governments or to repress progressive social movements occur on an almost yearly basis during the second half of the century. Such covert operations culminated in CIA-directed and US-financed counter-insurgency movements of the 1980s and 1990s and generated the latest waves of immigrants from the Central American countries. Neoliberal programs, which followed the success of these covert operations, have only exacerbated immigration to the US. Thus, while Chicana/o and Puerto Rican experience with US colonialism is unique in form (direct annexation), it is by no means singular....

I would like to end my plea for a transnational and comparative model of Latina/o studies by underscoring what it is not. While I firmly believe that our field needs to move towards a transnational approach in order to confront the challenges of US empire in the twenty-first century, I do not mean to frame this plea as an "either/or" choice. In other words, a transnational approach would not require that each and every Latina/o scholar change his or her research to a transnational project. Clearly, projects which focus on the experiences of particular Latina/o immigrant communities—their labor histories, their artistic practices, etc.—will always be essential to the field as a whole.... I am suggesting a paradigm shift, one that would permanently decenter the *petit* nationalisms that still dominate our field. However, such a paradigm shift is just that, a decentering rather than a dismissal or a disparagement. What a transnational Latina/o studies would do would be to put comparison and the critique of US empire at the center of our field, because we're not in Kansas anymore. Or more precisely stated, Kansas, like New Orleans, is no longer Kansas. Like the rest of the country, its major cities are an "Organization of American States" in miniature....

FURTHER READING

Frances R. Aparicio, "Jennifer as Selena: Rethinking Latinidad in Media and Popular Culture," *Latino Studies* 1, no. 1 (2003), 90–105.

Arturo Arias, "Central American Americans: Invisibility, Power and Representation in the US Latino World," *Latino Studies* 1, no. 1 (2003), 168–187.

Pedro A. Cabán, "Moving from the Margins to Where? Three Decades of Latino/a Studies," *Latino Studies* 1, no. 1 (2003), 5–35.

David Carrasco, "Cuando Díos y Usted Quiere: Latina/o Studies between Religious Powers and Social Thought," in Juan Flores and Renato Rosaldo, eds., *A Companion to Latina/o Studies* (2007).

Juan Flores, "Latino Studies: New Contexts, New Concepts," *Harvard Educational Review*, 67, no. 2 (1997), 208–221.

David G. Gutiérrez, "Significant to Whom? Mexican Americans and the History of the American West," *Western Historical Quarterly* 24, no. 4 (1993), 519–539.

Gaye Theresa Johnson, "'Sobre Las Olas': A Mexican Genesis in Borderland Jazz and the Legacy for Ethnic Studies," *Comparative American Studies* 6, no. 3 (2008): 225–240.

Nancy Mirabal, "'Ser De Aquí': Beyond the Cuban Exile Model," *Latino Studies* 1, no. 3 (2003), 366–382.

Carlos Muñoz, Jr., "The Development of Chicano Studies, 1968–1981," in E. García, F. A. Lomelí, et al., eds., *Chicano Studies: A Multidisciplinary Approach* (1984).

Centro: Journal of the Center for Puerto Rican Studies. Special Issue: Activism and Change among Puerto Ricans in New York, 1960s and 1970s. Vol. 21, no. 2 (Fall 2009).

Devon G. Peña, "The Scope of Latino/a Environmental Studies," *Latino Studies* 1, no. 1 (2003), 47–78.

Richard T. Rodríguez, "Serial Kinship: Representing La Familia in Early Chicano Publications," *Aztlán: A Journal of Chicano Studies* 27 (Spring 2002), 123–138.

George J. Sánchez, "Y tú, ¿qué?" (Y2K): Latino History in the New Millenium," in Marcelo M. Suárez-Orozco and Mariela M. Páez, eds., *Latinos: Remaking America* (2002), 45–58.

Silvio Torres-Saillant, "Inventing the Race: Latinos and the Ethnoracial Pentagon," *Latino Studies* 1, no. 1 (2003), 123–151.

Silvio Torres-Saillant, "Pitfalls of Latino Chronologies: South and Central Americans," *Latino Studies* 5 (2007), 489–502.

Carmen Teresa Whalen, "Radical Contexts: Puerto Rican Politics in the 1960s and 1970s and the Center for Puerto Rican Studies," *Centro: Journal of the Center for Puerto Rican Studies* 21, no. 2 (2009), 221–255.

CHAPTER 2

U.S. Conquest and Mexican

American Communities

Several Mexican communities in today's U.S. Southwest can trace their origins to the Spanish colonial era. Colonists from New Spain (Mexico) began establishing European settlements in New Mexico in the late sixteenth century. However, New Spain struggled to colonize its Far North due to resistance from American Indians and the region's distance from other Spanish settlements. To overcome these difficulties, officials used missions to convert Indians into Spanish subjects, forts to defend Spanish settlements, and towns to promote civilian populations. Nevertheless, the Far North remained unappealing due to its isolation and the danger of Indian attacks. Worried about its inability to attract colonists and facing advancing French and Euro American settlements, New Spain allowed foreigners to settle in its Far North.

Mexico's successful war for independence from Spain (1810–1821) left the young nation's economy devastated. During the colonial era, the isolated northern settlements lacked regular communications and dependable trade with central New Spain, whose officials frequently neglected to pay and equip soldiers. The devastation caused by the independence war exacerbated Mexico's inability to provide military and financial support to its northernmost settlements. Feeling neglected by their central government, northern residents gradually began establishing economic and social ties with Euro Americans. Mexico's leaders expanded the colonization program by offering land and tax exemptions to foreigners willing to settle in its Far North. Euro Americans, who immigrated into Texas legally and illegally, were the largest group to participate in Mexico's colonization program. They soon outnumbered Mexican Texans (Tejanos) in Texas, where the newcomers spread U.S. culture, manufactured goods, and political influence. To control the flood of Euro Americans into Texas, Mexico curtailed its colonization program.

The U.S. conquest of Mexico's Far North began with Texas' separatist rebellion (1836), launched by Euro Americans and Tejanos. Nine years later, the admission of Texas into the Union, combined with a border dispute, triggered the U.S.-Mexican War (1846–1848).

Although most Tejanos remained neutral during the separatist struggle, Euro Americans accused them of siding with Mexico. The negative portrayals of Mexicans resulting from the Texas rebellion combined with the belief in manifest destiny generated public support for the war. "Manifest destiny" encapsulated Euro Americans' beliefs that the United States was predestined to expand westward and justified to spread its "superior" culture, ideas, and institutions throughout the conquered lands of American Indians and Mexicans who had long resided there.

The Treaty of Guadalupe Hidalgo ended the war and redrew national boundaries, as the United States acquired half of Mexico's territory. The Mexican residents of the annexed territory confronted a vastly different environment under U.S. rule, in which they struggled to defend their property and lost political power. This chapter examines the dramatic changes experienced by Spanish Mexican residents during the first part of the nineteenth century, as well as the U.S. conquest of Mexico and its implications for those made "Mexican American" by the moving of the border.

 # DOCUMENTS

Mexican residents of the distant and isolated northern settlements grew apart from those living in central areas of Mexico. In Document 1, José María Sánchez, a Mexican military official visiting Texas, expresses alarm about U.S. influence on Mexicans, and about Euro Americans' disregard for Mexican laws and customs. Mexicans in San Antonio offer a more optimistic view in Document 2, which argues for more Euro American immigration to augment the city's population, and promote trade. Such trade provided the northern settlements with inexpensive and plentiful U.S. manufactured items. During the U.S.-Mexican War, the U.S. Congress debated how much of Mexico's territory to acquire. In Document 3, Senators John C. Calhoun and John A. Dix share similar views of Mexicans but they disagree about the pending territorial acquisition. The selected passages from the Treaty of Guadalupe Hidalgo in Document 4 describe various promises made to the Mexicans who resided in the annexed territories. The U.S. occupation of Mexico and the terms of the Treaty of Guadalupe Hidalgo generated widespread debate among Mexican citizens and politicians concerning the nation's future relationship with its northern neighbor. Document 5 contains Mexican politician Manuel Crescencio Rejón's arguments against Mexico's acceptance of the treaty. The treaty transformed Mexicans living in the ceded lands into Mexican Americans with U.S. citizenship, and guaranteed them property rights. Throughout the U.S. Southwest, Mexican Americans, like María Rita Valdez in Document 6, struggled to defend their property in courts. The political and social turmoil resulting from the Texas rebellion and the U.S.-Mexican War led Juan Seguín, the former mayor of San Antonio, to describe himself, in Document 7, as a "foreigner" who no longer recognized his native city.

1. Mexican Military Officer Criticizes Mexicans and Anglos in Texas, 1828

BEJAR

Although the soil is very rich, the inhabitants do not cultivate it because of the danger incurred from Indian attacks…. For months, and even years at times, [the] troops have gone without salary or supplies, constantly in active service against the Indians, dependent for their subsistence on buffalo meat, deer, and other game they may be able to secure with great difficulty. The government, nevertheless, has not helped their condition in spite of repeated and frequent remonstrances…. The character of the people is care-free, they are enthusiastic dancers, very fond of luxury, and the worst punishment that can be inflicted upon them is work. Doubtless, there are some individuals, out of the 1,425 that make up the total population, who are free from these failings, but they are very few….

The Americans from the north have taken possession of practically all the eastern part of Texas, in most cases without the permission of the authorities. They immigrate constantly, finding no one to prevent them, and take possession of the *sitio* [location] that best suits them without either asking leave or going through any formality other than that of building their homes. Thus the majority of inhabitants in the Department are North Americans, the Mexican population being reduced to only Bejar, Nacogdoches, and La Bahía del Espíritu Santo, wretched settlements that between them do not number three thousand inhabitants, and the new village of Guadalupe Victoria that has scarcely more than seventy settlers….

NACOGDOCHES

… The population does not exceed seven hundred persons, including the troops of the garrison, and all live in very good houses made of lumber, well built and forming straight streets, which make the place more agreeable. The women do not number one hundred. The civil administration is entrusted to an *Alcalde,* and in his absence, to the first and second *regidores,* but up until now, they have been, unfortunately, extremely ignorant men more worthy of pity than of reproof. From this fact, the North American inhabitants (who are in the majority) have formed an ill opinion of the Mexicans, judging them, in their pride, incapable of understanding laws, arts, etc. They continually try to entangle the authorities in order to carry out the policy most suitable to their perverse designs….

José María Sánchez, "A Trip to Texas in 1828," trans. Carlos E. Castañeda, *Southwestern Historical Quarterly* 29, no. 4 (April 1926), pp. 249–288.

The Mexicans that live here are very humble people, and perhaps their intentions are good, but because of their education and environment they are ignorant not only of the customs of our great cities, but even of the occurrences of our Revolution, excepting a few persons who have heard about them. Accustomed to the continued trade with the North Americans, they have adopted their customs and habits, and one may say truly that they are not Mexicans except by birth, for they even speak Spanish with marked incorrectness....

2. San Antonio's Tejanos Support North American Immigration, 1832

What shall we say of the law of April 6, 1830? It absolutely prohibits immigrants from North America coming into Texas, but there are not enough troops to enforce it; so the result is that desirable immigrants are kept out because they will not violate the law, while the undesirable, having nothing to lose, come in freely. The industrious, honest North American settlers have made great improvements in the past seven or eight years. They have raised cotton and cane and erected gins and sawmills. Their industry has made them comfortable and independent, while the Mexican settlements, depending on the pay of the soldiers among them for money, have lagged far behind. Among the Mexican settlements even the miserable manufacture of blankets, hats and shoes has never been established, and we must buy them either from foreigners or from the interior, 200 or 300 leagues distant. We have had a loom in Béxar for two years, but the inhabitants of Goliad and Nacogdoches know nothing of this ingenious machine, nor even how to make a sombrero.

The advantages of liberal North American immigration are innumerable: (1) The colonists would afford a source of supply for the native inhabitants. (2) They would protect the interior from Indian invasions. (3) They would develop roads and commerce to New Orleans and New Mexico. (4) Moreover, the ideas of government held by North Americans are in general better adapted to those of the Mexicans than are the ideas of European immigrants.

It is unquestionable that the lack of a government which shall feel directly the needs of Texas and understand the means necessary to multiply its population and protect its welfare has been, is, and will continue to be the chief source of our sufferings.

Eugene C. Barker, "Native Latin American Contributions to the Colonization and Independence of Texas," *Southwestern Historical Quarterly* 46, no. 3 (January 1943), pp. 317–335.

3. The Treaty of Guadalupe Hidalgo Establishes Rights for Mexicans in the Annexed Lands, 1848

TRANSCRIPT OF TREATY OF GUADALUPE HIDALGO (1848)

Article I

There shall be firm and universal peace between the United States of America and the Mexican Republic, and between their respective countries, territories, cities, towns, and people, without exception of places or persons....

Article III

Immediately upon the ratification of the present treaty by the Government of the United States, orders shall be transmitted to the commanders of their land and naval forces, requiring the latter ... immediately to desist from blockading any Mexican ports and requiring the former ... to commence, at the earliest moment practicable, withdrawing all troops of the United States ... and such evacuation of the interior of the Republic shall be completed with the least possible delay....

Article VIII

Mexicans now established in territories previously belonging to Mexico, and which remain for the future within the limits of the United States, as defined by the present treaty, shall be free to continue where they now reside, or to remove at any time to the Mexican Republic, retaining the property which they possess in the said territories, or disposing thereof, and removing the proceeds wherever they please, without their being subjected, on this account, to any contribution, tax, or charge whatever.

Those who shall prefer to remain in the said territories may either retain the title and rights of Mexican citizens, or acquire those of citizens of the United States. But they shall be under the obligation to make their election within one year from the date of the exchange of ratifications of this treaty; and those who shall remain in the said territories after the expiration of that year, without having declared their intention to retain the character of Mexicans, shall be considered to have elected to become citizens of the United States.

In the said territories, property of every kind, now belonging to Mexicans not established there, shall be inviolably respected. The present owners, the heirs of these, and all Mexicans who may hereafter acquire said property by contract, shall enjoy with respect to it guarantees equally ample as if the same belonged to citizens of the United States.

Selections from the Treaty of Guadalupe Hidalgo, U.S. Congress, Senate Executive Documents, 30th Congress, 1st Session, 1847, no. 52. (Accessed at www.ourdocuments.gov and at memory.loc.gov: "A Century of Lawmaking for a New Nation: U.S. Congressional Documents and Debates, 1774–1875.")

Article IX

The Mexicans who, in the territories aforesaid, shall not preserve the character of citizens of the Mexican Republic, conformably with what is stipulated in the preceding article, shall be incorporated into the Union of the United States, and be admitted at the proper time (to be judged of by the Congress of the United States) to the enjoyment of all the rights of citizens of the United States, according to the principles of the Constitution; and in the mean time, shall be maintained and protected in the free enjoyment of their liberty and property, and secured in the free exercise of their religion without restriction....

Article XII

In consideration of the extension acquired by the boundaries of the United States, ... the Government of the United States engages to pay to that of the Mexican Republic the sum of fifteen millions of dollars.

4. Congress Debates Incorporating Mexicans, 1848

Mr. CALHOUN said: ... [I]t is without example or precedent, either to hold Mexico as a province, or to incorporate her into our Union. No example of such a line of policy can be found. We have conquered many of the neighboring tribes of Indians, but we never thought of holding them in subjection—never of incorporating them into our Union. They have either been left as an independent people amongst us, or been driven into the forests.

I know further, sir, that we have never dreamt of incorporating into our Union any but the Caucasian race—the free white race. To incorporate Mexico, would be the very first instance of the kind of incorporating an Indian race; for more than half of the Mexicans are Indians, and the other is composed chiefly of mixed tribes. I protest against such a union as that! Ours, sir, is the Government of a white race. The greatest misfortunes of Spanish America are to be traced to the fatal error of placing these colored races on an equality with the white race. That error destroyed the social arrangement which formed the basis of society....
[W]e are the only people on this continent which have made revolutions without being followed by anarchy. And yet it is professed and talked about to erect these Mexicans into a Territorial Government, and place them on an equality with the people of the United States. I protest utterly against such a project.

Sir, it is a remarkable fact, that in the whole history of man, as far as my knowledge extends, there is no instance whatever of any civilized colored races being found equal to the establishment of free popular government, although by far the largest portion of the human family is composed of these races.... Are we to associate with ourselves as equals, companions, and fellow-citizens, the Indians

John C. Calhoun, January, 4, 1848, *The Congressional Globe,* pp. 96–100, and John A. Dix, January 26, 1848, *The Congressional Globe,* pp. 250–257.

and mixed race of Mexico? Sir, I should consider such a thing as fatal to our institutions....

I come now to the proposition of incorporating her into our Union.... You can establish a Territorial Government for every State in Mexico, and there are some twenty of them. You can appoint governors, judges, and magistrates. You can give the people a subordinate government, allowing them to legislate for themselves, whilst you defray the cost.... There is no analogy between this and our Territorial Governments. Our Territories are only an offset of our own people, or foreigners from the same regions from which we came.... It is entirely different with Mexico. You have no need of armies to keep your Territories in subjection. But when you incorporate Mexico, you must have powerful armies to keep them in subjection. You may call it annexation, but it is a forced annexation, which is a contradiction in terms, according to my conception. You will be involved, in one word, in all the evils which I attribute to holding Mexico as a province. In fact, it will be but a Provincial Government, under the name of a Territorial Government. How long will that last? How long will it be before Mexico will be capable of incorporation into our Union? Why, if we judge from the examples, before us, it will be a very long time. Ireland has been held in subjection by England for seven or eight hundred years, and yet still remains hostile, although her people are of kindred race with the conquerors....

But, Mr. President, suppose all these difficulties removed; suppose these people attached to our Union, and desirous of incorporating with us, ought we to bring them in? ... Are they fit for self-government and for governing you? Are you, any of you, willing that your States should be governed by these twenty-odd Mexican States, with a population of about only one million of your blood, and two or three millions of mixed blood, better informed, all the rest pure Indians, a mixed blood equally ignorant and unfit for liberty, impure races, not as good as the Cherokees or Choctaws?

We make a great mistake, sir, when we suppose that all people are capable of self-government. We are anxious to force free government on all; and I see that it has been urged in a very respectable quarter, that it is the mission of this country to spread civil and religious-liberty over all the world, and especially over this continent. It is a great mistake. None but people advanced to a very high state of moral and intellectual improvement are capable, in a civilized state, of maintaining free government; and amongst those who are so purified, very few, indeed, have had the good fortune of forming a constitution capable of endurance....

Mr. DIX said: ... Having thus declared myself in favor of the occupation of Mexico until she shall consent to make peace, I deem it proper to say, in connection with this subject, that I have been uniformly opposed, and that I am still opposed, to all schemes of conquest for the acquisition of territory....

Sir, no one who has paid a moderate degree of attention to the laws and elements of our increase, can doubt that our population is destined to spread itself across the American continent, filling up, with more or less completeness, according to attractions of soil and climate, the space that intervenes between the Atlantic and Pacific oceans....

... Our whole southern line is conterminous, throughout its whole extent, with the territories of Mexico, a large portion of which is nearly unpopulated. The geographical area of Mexico is about 1,700,000 square miles, and her population something more than 7,000,000 souls.... The aboriginal races, which occupy and overrun a portion of California and New Mexico, must there, as everywhere else, give way before the advancing wave of civilization, either to be overwhelmed by it, or to be driven upon perpetually constructing areas, where, from a diminution of their accustomed sources of subsistence, they must ultimately become extinct by force of an invincible law. We see the operation of this law in every portion of this continent. We have no power to control it, if we would. It is the behest of Providence that idleness, and ignorance, and barbarism, shall give place to industry, and knowledge, and civilization. The European and mixed races, which possess Mexico, are not likely, either from moral or physical energy, to become formidable rivals or enemies. The bold and courageous enterprise which overran and conquered Mexico, appears not to have descended to the present possessors of the soil. Either from the influence of climate or the admixture of races—the fusion of castes, to use the technical phrase—the conquerors have, in turn, become the conquered. The ancient Castilian energy is, in a great degree, subdued; and it has given place, with many other noble trails of the Spanish character, to a peculiarity which seems to have marked the race in that country, under whatever combinations it is found—a proneness to civil discord, and a suicidal waste of its own strength.

With such a territory and such a people on our southern border, what is to be the inevitable course of empire? It needs no powers of prophecy to foretell. Sir, I desire to speak plainly: why should we not, when we are discussing the operation of moral and physical laws, which are beyond our control? As our population moves westward on our own territory, portions will cross our southern boundary. Settlements will be formed within the unoccupied and sparsely-peopled territory of Mexico. Uncongenial habits and tastes, differences of political opinion and principle, and numberless other elements of diversity will lead to a separation of these newly-formed societies from the inefficient government of Mexico. They will not endure to be held in subjection to a system, which neither yields them protection nor offers any incentive to their proper development and growth. They will form independent States on the basis of constitutions identical in all their leading features with our own; and they will naturally seek to unite their fortunes to ours. The fate of California is already sealed: it can never be reunited to Mexico. The operation of the great causes, to which I have alluded, must, at no distant day, detach the whole of northern Mexico from the southern portion of that republic. It is for the very reason that she is incapable of defending her possessions against the elements of disorder within and the progress of better influences from without, that I desire to see the inevitable political change which is to be wrought in the condition of her northern departments, brought about without any improper interference on our part. I do not speak of our military movements. I refer to the time when our difficulties with her shall be healed, and when she shall be left to the operation of pacific influences—silent, but more powerful than the arm of force.... Acquisition by force is the vice of arbitrary governments.... For the sake of the national honor, as well as the permanency of our political institutions, I desire not to see it. The extension of free government on this continent can only be arrested, if arrested at all, by substituting war for the arts of peace. Leave it to itself, and nothing can prevent the progress of our population across the continent.

5. Mexican Liberal Manuel Crescencio Rejón Opposes the Treaty of Guadalupe Hidalgo, 1848

... [O]ur national government has entered into those negotiations which are so humiliating to us, thus committing us to grave imputations of perfidy if we should reject the treaty, which we should surely do. This government has demonstrated its misunderstanding of the nature of the institutions by which we live.... The result is that we are unable to disapprove a shameful treaty without rendering our country almost defenseless against the disasters of a war which has been so disadvantageous to us because the government has not prepared the country to resist and to continue the war to a successful end. Ultimately, the very nationhood of the republic will be undermined. Now is our last chance to sustain it. Otherwise, it will disappear within ten or fifteen years with the loss of the rest of the national territory, without there being either the means or the sense of national glory with which to resist.

... The social advantages which would accrue to us by accepting a peace now have been exaggerated, as well as the ease with which we would be able to maintain our remaining territories. It would be necessary, in order to sustain such illusions, to underestimate the spirit of enterprise of the North American people in industrial and commercial pursuits, to misunderstand their history and their tendencies, and also to presuppose in our own spirit less resistance than we have already shown toward the sincere friends of progress. Only through such illusions might one maintain that the treaty would bring a change that would be advantageous to us—as has been claimed.

With the borders of our conquerors brought closer to the heart of our nation, with the whole line of the frontier occupied by them from sea to sea, with their highly developed merchant marine, and with them so versed in the system of colonization by which they attract great numbers of the laboring classes from the old world, what can we, who are so backward in everything, do to arrest them in their rapid conquests, their latest invasions? Thousands of men will come daily to establish themselves under American auspices in the new territories with which we will have obliged them. There they will develop their commerce and stockpile large quantities of merchandise brought from the upper states. They will inundate us with all this, and our own modicum of wealth, already so miserable and depleted, will in the future sink to insignificance and nothingness. We will not accomplish anything by lowering our maritime

Cecil Robinson, ed., *The View from Chapultepec: Mexican Writers on the Mexican-American War* (Tucson: University of Arizona Press, 1989), pp. 95–97.

duties, abolishing our internal customshouses, or suppressing our restrictive laws. The Anglo Americans, now situated so close to our populated provinces, will provide these areas with the marvels of the world, passing them from the frontier zones to our southern states, and having withal the advantage over us of attracting our own merchants as well as our consumers, who will favor these foreigners because of the low prices at which they will be able to buy American goods.

6. Los Angeles Board of Land Commissioners Confirms Mexican Woman's Land Title, 1852

Case No. 371 SD San Antonio (o Rodeo de las Aguas), Maria Rita [V]aldez, Claimant.

Petition to Land Commissioners. Nov. 4, 1852.

"Valdez ... claims ... [name of ranch] containing one square league ... she claims the same under a title from the Mexican government in long ownership firstly by virtue of property in the said tract of land acquired under a temporary title extended to herself and Luciano Valdez in 1831 and constant occupancy under the same in conformity with the Mexican customs until 1838. Secondly by virtue of a grant under the Mexican Government on 1838 by [Governor] Alvarado... since which time the claimant and those under her have been in constant occupancy with this date and without any knowledge of any interfering claimant...." Henry Hancock, Attorney for Plaintiff.

Deposition of Valdez.

"... That she after receiving the [title] from Monterey ... [no date] always kept it stored in a certain trunk of hers which was left with other things in her house at the time of the political disturbances of 1846 at or about the time of the Americans coming to this place.... That on their approach herself and family fled and her house had been pillaged and the said trunk rifled by some unknown part either of Californians Indians or Americans since which time the deponent has not been able to find the said grant [papers]...." Nov. 11, 1852.

7. San Antonio's Former Mayor Juan Seguín Identifies Himself as a "Foreigner in My Native Land," 1858

A native of the city of San Antonio de Béxar, I embraced the cause of Texas at the sound of the first cannon which foretold her liberty, filled an honorable role within the ranks of the conquerors of San Jacinto, and was a member of the legislative body of the Republic. In the very land which in other times bestowed

U.S. District Court, Land Cases, Southern District, Bancroft Library, Berkeley, California Case No. 371, SD San Antonio (o Rodeo de las Aguas), Maria Rita [V]aldez, Claimant, November 4, 1852.

Juan Nepomuceno Seguín, *Personal Memoirs of John N. Seguín, From the Year 1834 to the Retreat of General Woll from the City of San Antonio, 1842* (San Antonio: Ledger Book and Job Office, 1858). Copy from Jesús F. de la Teja, *A Revolution Remembered: The Memoirs and Selected Correspondence of Juan N. Seguín* (Austin: State House Press, 1991), pp. 73–74, 90.

on me such bright and repeated evidences of trust and esteem, I now find myself exposed to the attacks of scribblers and personal enemies who, to serve *political purposes* and engender strife, falsify historical fact with which they are but imperfectly acquainted....

I have been the object of the hatred and passionate attacks of a few troublemakers who, for a time, ruled as masters over the poor and oppressed population of San Antonio. Harpy-like, ready to pounce on everything that attracted the notice of their rapacious avarice, I was an obstacle to the execution of their vile designs. They therefore leagued together to exasperate and ruin me, spread malignant calumnies against me, and made use of odious machinations to sully my honor and tarnish my well earned reputation.

A victim to the wickedness of a few men whose false pretenses were favored because of their origin and recent domination over the country, a foreigner in my native land, could I stoically be expected to endure their outrages and insults? Crushed by sorrow, convinced that only my death would satisfy my enemies, I sought shelter among those against whom I had fought. I separated from my country, parents, family, relatives and friends and, what was more, from the institutions on behalf of which I had drawn my sword with an earnest wish to see Texas free and happy. In that involuntary exile my only ambition was to devote my time, far from the tumult of war, to the support of my family who shared in my sad condition.

Fate, however, had not exhausted its cup of bitterness. Thrown into a prison in a foreign country, I had no alternatives left but to linger in a loathsome confinement or to accept military service.

On one hand, my wife and children, reduced to beggary and separated from me; on the other hand, to turn my arms against my own country. The alternatives were sad, the struggle of feelings violent. At last the father triumphed over the citizen; I seized a sword that pained my hand. (Who among my readers will not understand my situation?) I served Mexico; I served her loyally and faithfully. I was compelled to fight my own countrymen, but I was never guilty of the barbarous and unworthy deeds of which I am accused by my enemies....

★ ★ ★

I will also point out the origin of another enmity which, on several occasions, endangered my life. In those evil days, San Antonio swarmed with adventurers from every quarter of the globe. Many a noble heart grasped the sword in the defense of the liberty of Texas, cheerfully pouring out their blood for our cause, and to them everlasting public gratitude is due. But there were also many bad men, fugitives from their country who found in this land an opportunity for their criminal designs.

San Antonio claimed then, as it claims now, to be the first city of Texas. It was also the receptacle of the scum of society. My political and social situation brought me into continual contact with that class of people. At every hour of the day and night my countrymen ran to me for protection against the assaults or exactions of those adventurers. Sometimes, by persuasion, I prevailed on them to desist; sometimes, also, force had to be resorted to. How could I have done otherwise? Were not the victims my own countrymen, friends, and associates? Could I leave them defenseless, exposed to the assaults of foreigners who, on the pretext that they were

Mexicans, treated them worse than brutes? Sound reason and the dictates of humanity precluded any different conduct on my part.

ESSAYS

Mexican citizens living in Texas and California faced complex choices in the early nineteenth century. By the 1830s, Tejanos had forged social and economic ties with Euro American immigrants, grown dependent on U.S. manufactured goods, and become disenchanted with the policies of their central government. Mexico suspended Euro American immigration into Texas and the centralists gained control of the presidency during the early 1830s. Both developments had far-reaching repercussions in Texas as Raúl Ramos, professor of history at the University of Houston, explains in the first essay. The outbreak of the separatist rebellion in Texas forced Tejanos to make a choice among siding with the rebels, remaining loyal to Mexico, or attempting to stay neutral. An individual's class, social contacts, and political ideology influenced this choice. Ultimately, the outcome of the Texas conflict affected Tejanos' identity, in which ethnicity increasingly played a larger role than nationalism.

American property laws introduced significant changes to landownership practices throughout the U.S. Southwest. As a result, Mexican Americans lost property as they struggled to have their Spanish and Mexican land titles confirmed in U.S. courts. Their loss of land was uneven—it occurred more rapidly in regions with a large Euro American presence, and more slowly in majority Mexican American areas. The reasons for the loss of property included the owners' unfamiliarity with paying property taxes (which did not exist under Mexican law), and their inability to weather economic downturns and natural disasters. In addition, Mexican Americans lost land to pay for legal fees in lengthy property litigation and property confirmation. According to Miroslava Chávez-García, professor of Chicana/o Studies at the University of California, Santa Barbara, these losses were most acute for Mexican American and Native women, as described in the second essay.

Tejanos and the War of Texas Secession in 1836

RAÚL A. RAMOS

In early fall of 1835, the citizens and government officials of Béxar gathered to prepare for the upcoming Independence Day celebration.... A month before the celebration, fifty Bexareños gathered in the political chief's council hall to elect the *junta patriótica,* or patriotic commission, in charge of organizing the event....

... The men elected to serve in the junta included the most prominent civil and military elite in Béxar....

From BEYOND THE ALAMO: FORGING MEXICAN ETHNICITY IN SAN ANTONIO, 1821–1861 by Raúl A. Ramos. Copyright © 2008 by the University of North Carolina Press. Used by permission of the publisher. www.uncpress.unc.edu

After its formation, the junta selected forty-four prominent citizens and officers to participate in six committees to plan, fund, and oversee various aspects of the Diez y Seis de Septiembre celebration....

Along with the civic and religious celebrations, Bexareños planned two dances for the *fiestas patrias*....

After the parade, the crowds gathered around a podium erected at one end of the plaza to hear speeches on civics and elegies to the nation....

Almost immediately, the escalation of violence and demands for Texas secession from Mexico put the meaning and strength of nationalism in the Independence Day parade to the test. Tejano participation on the side of what eventually became a secession movement underscores the limits of ideas like nationalism. When a group cheers an Independence Day parade together one day and fights against each other the next, then nationalism must be more complex than allegiance to a flag. In this case, external events constrained the choices and alliances available to Bexareños, forcing them to take sides on a growing borderland battle between two nations. In the long run, the changes resulting from the war of Texas secession strengthened the importance of ethnicity over nation or region as the central element of Tejano identity.

Tracing Tejano activities before and during the war of Texas secession puts nationalism in relative perspective regarding concerns. Many Bexareños present at the Independence Day celebration participated in a rebellion against the nation in the following months. Ultimately, nationalism operated at different levels within the Tejano community, dividing along lines of social class or family connection. The shared bonds that appeared during the Independence Day celebration can be understood as civic identity as much as nationalism. The range of Tejano responses to events that transpired between 1834 and 1837 demonstrates the variety and complexity of their identity. While they all claimed a Mexican identity, the political, cultural, and social meaning of that identity differed from person to person. The contours of those choices appear in their actions taken during the war of Texas secession, a war now reduced in the popular culture of our time to a single monument known as the Alamo.

After two days of celebration, the cold weather and harsh realities of Béxar's political situation in late 1835 began to set in. On September 21, Commander Ugartechea received reports of Anglo-American immigrant disregard of an order to return a cannon taken from Mexican troops in Gonzales. The cannon incident followed a string of problems with Anglo-American immigrants beginning with the Law of April 6, 1830, and leading to the imprisonment of Stephen F. Austin in Mexico City. These became the first steps in a revolt against the Mexican government led by Anglo-American immigrants, who began to call themselves Texians.... Throughout this period, the largely Mexican town of Béxar became the symbolic and strategic center of that war....

... Within the span of a year, Béxar first would be invaded by Texian forces and later recaptured by the Mexican military. While the battle for Texas secession was largely Anglo-led, it also included significant Tejano participation. Among the Tejanos holding prominent roles in the Texan rebellion were several of the Bexareño elite who had planned the Diez y Seis celebration only months before....

The Texas rebellion and the secession of Texas from Mexico devastated the city of Béxar, leaving it in ruin and without much hope for the future.... For Tejanos, Béxar stood at ground zero of the battle between Anglo-Texans and Mexico....

The variety of ways in which Tejanos participated for and against the secession of Texas along with the economic and social reorganization of the state reveal a shifting priority within Tejano identity: toward an ethnic and regional consciousness and away from the official nationalism displayed on Independence Day. While Tejano support for the Texian secession movement might appear anti-Mexican, the larger social and political context forces other interpretations to explain their participation. Growing disputes between centralist and federalist factions in Mexico provide the background for Tejanos' political identity....

... [T]he secession of Texas also reconfigured ethnic relations even further by affecting national sentiments. The choices Tejanos made during the centralist/federalist conflicts and the war of secession resulted both from a reaction to these external events and within the continuation of their existing social system that gave high value to honor and region. Instead of brokering disputes between Anglo-Americans and the Mexican government, elite Tejanos now officially and unofficially represented Tejanos in San Antonio and south Texas to the new Anglo-Texan power structure. Yet, even that role would constantly shift during the Republic period, as the politics and economics of Texas changed.

★ ★ ★

During 1834, two external issues began to take center stage in the world of Tejano politics. First, pressure and unrest from Anglo-American immigrants continued to increase since the turning point of the Law of April 6, 1830.... Anglo-American demands for exemptions from federal legislation, particularly around slavery, and increased autonomy through Texas statehood put Tejano elites in increasingly more difficult positions relative to the government in Mexico City. Matters took a turn for the worse when Stephen F. Austin traveled to Mexico City to lobby directly and ended up imprisoned for much of 1834. And second, the growing conflict between centralist and federalist political factions on the national level began to reverberate in Béxar. Political leaders on the state level joined other states around the Republic in expressing their discontent with centralist policies emanating from Mexico City. Federalism became the prism that defined Tejano political action beginning in 1834.

After his release from Mexico City, Austin began to suggest his belief that Texas would one day join the United States....

But in his correspondence with Tejanos and leaders in Béxar, Austin portrayed his political cause in terms of federalism versus centralism. He insisted that he and other Anglo-Americans had taken up arms to support the federalist constitution of 1824 and to resist the centralization of political power in Mexico.... As a result of Austin's characterization of Anglo-American dissatisfaction, few Tejanos believed the growing Texian rebellion sought to totally separate Texas from Mexico, or worse, annex Texas to the United States. Instead, most Tejanos viewed the rumblings in their region as part of a larger Mexican movement already underway in Yucatán, San Luis Potosí, and Zacatecas....

During Austin's imprisonment in Mexico City, politics in Mexico and in Coahuila y Texas turned contentious. Tejanos found themselves embroiled in a national political schism between two parties: the federalists, advocating for greater autonomy at the state level, and the centralists, who looked to concentrate power in the presidency. From 1833 to 1835, General Antonio López de Santa Anna presided over a series of national coalition governments that negotiated power between the two factions. On several occasions, Santa Anna managed to use his political savvy combined with his military skills to leave office and return as part of the opposition. In fact, he started his term in 1833 as a federalist but slowly moved toward the centralist faction....

Events in other parts of Texas soon distracted the citizens and military in Béxar, turning their attention back to the Anglo-American colonists. On May 23, 1835, an Anglo-American militia attacked the customs house at Anáhuac, on the Texas coast, expelling the Mexican military from the fort. Anáhuac had been the scene of previous protests in 1832 and a point for tax collection, and the military presence there represented the Mexican state to Anglo-Americans living on the frontier. The actions at Anáhuac amounted to a first strike against the Mexican army by the Texas militia....

Despite the turmoil occurring on the state and national level in the summer of 1835, Bexareños still managed to come together, both civilian and military alike, to celebrate the independence of Mexico from Spain on September 16.... Before the dust settled from the *fiestas patrias,* reports returned from the town of Gonzales that Anglo-American rebels refused to return a cannon to the local military commander.

Once again, Tejano citizens would be thrust into taking sides on an issue. But instead of choosing between federalist and centralist in Mexican politics, they faced the new option of a growing Anglo-American immigrant rebellion. Old tensions and distrust died slowly, though, and many Tejanos still resented the centralist military presence in Béxar....

★ ★ ★

... By November, organized military pressures from Anglo-American rebels put Béxar in the front and center of a national challenge to Santa Anna's presidency. In order to respond more rapidly to problems in Texas, military commander [Martín Perfecto de] Cos went to Béxar to lead the military response to immigrant colonist threats. For Bexareños, problems began to surface even before Cos's arrival.

[Military Commander Domingo de] Ugartechea encountered resistance from elite Tejanos unwilling to lend their homes to Cos during his stay. For separate reasons, both Angel Navarro and Erasmo Seguín refused to open their homes to Cos.... While Seguín and others stopped short of raising arms, they nevertheless opposed the centralist government and refused to accommodate its representatives while they dealt with the Anglo-American-led rebellion....

The reasons Tejanos chose to fight with either the Texas militia or the Mexican military or to flee to the countryside during times of conflict were not always clear or uniform. Even when they articulated their reasons in writing, their personal situations often made it difficult to understand their motivations....

Understanding Tejano choices during 1835 depends greatly on the narrative frame used to explain the Texas war. For Tejanos, the split between centralists and federalists created a civil war in Mexico. The split created a political space where opposition to the government could be voiced while maintaining loyalty and patriotism to the Mexican nation. Another narrative frame recalls years of trade and economic entanglements with Anglo-Americans, which led to cooperation and interdependence between Tejanos and the rebel Texians. Other narratives also explain Tejano choices, including family connections and obligations, *compadrazgo,* and survival. In all these cases, their choices appear less as either/or decisions and more as a complex and changing gray area reflecting political and social realities.

By the fall of 1835, Tejanos confronted difficult choices regarding the future of their homeland. Texians proposed an armed rebellion against the Mexican government. As a result, the Mexican government tapped into nationalist sympathies to maintain the allegiance of Tejano citizens who were in opposition. But a third choice existed. Tejanos could avoid the conflict altogether and leave their cities for ranches and farms in the hinterland. Most Tejanos chose this option, waiting for the political and military dust to settle, as they had done twenty years previously during the 1811 and 1813 insurgency battles. But, unlike the battles for Mexican independence, the results of this war prevented Tejanos from staking out a neutral stance during the clashes and reentering civil life just as they left it....

With the cannon incident at Gonzales, Anglo-Texans committed themselves to armed rebellion. In October 1835, Anglo-Texans attempted to raise an army to wrest Texas from the power of the centralist government.... Next, Texian forces set their sights on Béxar, the capital of the Mexican government in Texas. Preparations were made in November to mount a siege and invasion of the town....

As tensions rose in anticipation of a Texian invasion, Angel Navarro attempted to stem the flight of Tejanos to rebel forces.... After informing the citizens of the fall of La Bahía, he defended the current Mexican government as magnanimous, especially in matters of religion....

... Navarro framed his plea by tapping into the early frontier ethos of the defense against Indian attacks and the border imperative of protecting Mexico against American invasion.... Some ... took up Navarro's call to defend the integrity of the nation.

Even before Cos arrived in Béxar, the military garrison under Ugartechea contained a cavalry company of about ninety locals. These troops remained loyal through the days leading up to the siege on Béxar. Whether because of Navarro's plea or mounting threats to the town or fear of American annexation, additional Bexareños enlisted in the Mexican military....

But Navarro's call to support the Mexican government failed to sway Juan N. Seguín. Seguín had already raised a company of Tejanos to aid in the Anglo efforts to oppose the Mexican army.... The twenty-eight-year-old Seguín rode through the ranches outside of Béxar and into the city itself recruiting his boyhood friends to join him in the war against the centralist government.... By this point, citizens and soldiers in Béxar knew a confrontation would occur....

For the next month, Béxar remained in a state of siege, with the rebel companies camped on several sides of the city and Mexican troops struggling to bring in supplies and reinforcements. Soon after the battle of Concepción, more Texian troops arrived from the north to aid the rebels. Likewise, during this month, the numbers of Tejano participants in the rebellion also increased....

[Edward] Burleson quickly readied the [rebel] attack on Béxar, and the invasion began on December 5. The fighting lasted five days.... The rebel forces slowly gained ground a block at a time until they encircled the Mexican military. Reports from Texian soldiers fighting in the invasion occasionally mention aid they received from Bexareños living in the houses they occupied....

Tired, depleted, and out-positioned, Cos raised the truce flag and negotiated a capitulation of Béxar.... But evicting the Mexican government from Béxar only achieved a temporary victory for the Texian rebels, since the full Mexican military had yet to respond to the secession attempt. From this point forward, the war took on a decidedly different appearance in regard to both the Texan troops and relations between Anglos and Tejanos....

The siege and storming of Béxar occupied most of November 1835, with approximately 1,300 Texas separatist troops encamped at the outskirts of town....

... An analysis of the pension applications for Texas Revolution veterans lists approximately 138 Tejanos who served during the entire rebellion, 97 (or 70 percent) of whom participated at some point in the siege on Béxar....

... While most Tejanos probably avoided conflict and left the city, many joined the Army of Texas, principally under two commanders, Juan N. Seguín and Manuel Leal.... Approximately 56 percent of the soldiers in Seguín's units were born in Béxar. Ethnic Mexican members of other battalions appear to be mostly from outside of Béxar (78 percent), a quarter overall migrating from within Mexico to Texas....

Seguín's decision to support the Anglo-led rebellion stands as perhaps the single most influential factor in encouraging Tejanos to join the Army of Texas. The overwhelming participation of native Bexareños and Tejanos in Seguín's troops indicates the personal connection many of the troops shared when gathering as a force....

The search for reasons Tejanos entered in the service against the Mexican government reveals both personal and ideological motives. Personal ties heavily influenced the decision to fight on one side or the other. The rank and file under Seguín's command had shared the bonds of friendship since childhood. Furthermore, Seguín himself had spent much of his adolescent years with the family of Stephen F. Austin, both in Béxar and in northeast Texas. These connections, between Seguín and his soldiers and between Seguín and Austin, established ties of trust that allowed these Tejanos to put their lives in danger under the direction of Anglo-American leaders. The personal connections forged in Texas elevated the importance of local concerns and region over ties to the nation at this crisis moment.

Tejanos also fought for political causes relating to their regional autonomy. In the weeks leading up to the siege on Béxar, Austin's exhortations to Tejanos often included calls to protect the federalist guarantees of the constitution of

1824.... For many Tejanos joining the Texian forces, the battle for Texas meant the battle to uphold and defend the constitution of 1824....

Whether for friendship or for political ideology, many Tejanos chose to fight against Santa Anna's government and to expel the military from their hometown of Béxar. Unlike Anglo-Texans, Tejanos participating in the rebellion fought from within their own homes and homelands. Being Mexican, Tejanos stood to lose not only their homes but also their livelihoods in the event of defeat. During the rebellion, many Mexican political and military officials voiced vitriolic denunciations of Tejanos siding with Anglos.... Because they joined a rebellion identified with Anglo-Americans rather than simply oppose[d to] the centralist government, Tejanos were labeled by many Mexicans as secessionist collaborators rather than as government critics....

On a more personal level, by fighting in their homeland, these Tejanos also alienated themselves from and fought against neighbors and family. Much of the eventual invasion of Béxar involved house-to-house battles. Places such as the Veramendi home and Zambrano Row became notable sites of crucial confrontations. The Navarro brothers, Angel and José Antonio, supported different sides in the battle. Francisco Esparza chose to fight in the Mexican army, while his brother Gregorio died fighting on the Texian side inside the Alamo.

To others, though, the reasons to choose sides defied generalization.... While Tejanos sought to create a space in between the demands of the Mexican state, as was once possible on the frontier, external events limited their options. While most Tejanos chose to stay out of the conflict, Anglo-Americans and Mexican officials both interpreted inaction as disloyalty....

★ ★ ★

Even though Anglo-Texans and Tejanos fought side-by-side in the siege and capture of Béxar, taking the town itself produced different results for each group. While Tejanos had aided in expelling Mexican officials from Béxar, they now lived under a new regime led by the Texian militia commanders.... In general, Anglo-Texans handled the occupation of Béxar as though they were invading foreign territory, as in a sense they were. Even while Tejanos fought for the Texas army, tensions between Anglo-Americans and Tejanos increased in the period prior to the entrance of Santa Anna's forces into Texas. As the hostilities escalated, Anglo-Texans demanded that Tejanos demonstrate their loyalty to the Texan cause. Moreover, Tejanos who supported the Texian cause in 1836 could no longer claim to fight in the name of the constitution of 1824.

The initial occupation of Béxar made readjusting to life after the siege difficult for Bexareños.... Many Anglo-Texan soldiers were mercenaries from the United States who had no home or family to go to in Texas. Instead, they remained in Béxar at the command of charismatic captains. Unlike the relative racial harmony practiced by long-term Anglo-Texan residents, these recent arrivals into Texas strained relations between Anglo-Americans and Bexareños. They lacked prior contact with Mexicans and brought with them negative stereotypical views. As a result, the months between the fall of Béxar and the arrival of Santa Anna's army in March proved unsettling and even dangerous for the local population of Béxar....

... While Anglo-Texan officers rewarded with governing positions those Bexareños who participated in the rebellion, the Bexareños could act only with the oversight and support of Texian commanders.... In the previous decade, a few Anglo-Americans had made some effort to learn Mexican culture and the Spanish language, and some even developed close friendships and business contacts with Tejanos. Those friendships and enterprises account for much of the eventual Tejano participation in the rebellion. But the recently arrived volunteers from Kentucky and Tennessee lacked such contact with Mexican people and instead developed negative impressions through the experience of war.... The recently arrived Texan volunteers relied on cultural and racial markers to determine who stood on their side of the conflict. Even when Tejanos fought with them, Anglo-Texans raised questions of mistrust or followed leaders who tapped into the suspicion of all Mexicans. Again, this general stance toward Tejanos raises questions about the racial nature of Texas secession. While not all Anglo-Texans shared the same views of Mexican people, the underlying resistance to fully embracing Mexican civil society resulted in some part from views of Mexicans as inferior.

Not all Anglo-Texans shared or fueled these prejudices.... [S]ome Anglo-Texans felt it necessary to include Tejanos in the Texian movement....

Even with sizable Tejano participation in the siege of Béxar, many Anglo-Texans questioned Tejano loyalty. One of the staunchest anti-Tejano voices came from Henry Smith, who eventually served as the first American governor of Texas.... Smith removed the possibility of neutrality or self-preservation from the list of acceptable Tejano actions. Smith summed up his feelings: "Under existing circumstances, I consider one fact plain and evident: that they who are not for us must be against us." Once again, regardless of Tejano motivations, Anglo-Texans defined and limited the meaning and range of Tejano choices....

After the Texas Declaration of Independence, Tejanos could no longer rationalize their participation in the Texan war as upholding the constitution of 1824. This was now a war of secession....

... Most Tejanos ... simply desired to be left alone by any invading army. The statements by Governor Smith, while inflammatory, point out the underlying fact that many Tejanos chose not to fight on either side of the Texan rebellion and abandoned the city for the countryside. Later memorials recounting the battles of this period mention flight as a common reaction to violence in the city.

Since few Tejanos explained for posterity why they left Béxar, their actions need to be understood in the larger context of the rebellion.... On a basic level, flight meant survival.... The choice by many not to join reveals the limits of allegiance to the constitution of 1824 among the general Tejano population. By refusing to raise arms against the Texian army, Bexareños might have anticipated some benefits or at least benevolence from the future Anglo-Texan government. Finally, Bexareños might have believed that Mexico would defeat the Anglo rebellion. In that case, joining the Anglo-Texans would result in severe punishment for treason.

When the Texian leadership met to write the Declaration of Independence, Bexareños returned to their town somewhat reluctantly.... [T]hey came back to a situation that remained uncertain and threatened to turn violent again. Three months after the retreat of Cos's army from Béxar, signs of another battle surfaced with reports in April of the return of the Mexican army led by Santa Anna. Once again, many Bexareños left town to avoid the ravages of war in the countryside....

After the siege and battle for Béxar in late 1835, most of the Tejano troops still in the Army of Texas went to Gonzales to regroup with the remainder of the Texas troops. A force of mostly Anglo-American soldiers remained in Béxar in the Alamo fort, a former mission.... [T]he retaking of Béxar by the Mexican army [is] better known as the battle of the Alamo....

While most histories of Texas depict the second battle for Béxar in terms of a heroic last stand for independent Texas, few situate the conflict in the lives of Béxar's longtime citizens. The battle was less an act of self-defense against the Mexican army than a defense of conquered land by secessionist Texans. A few Tejanos were among the soldiers fighting on the Texan side of the second battle for Béxar, but in a much smaller proportion than in the first battle in December 1835....

Many Bexareños endured this second battle in the same way they did the first siege on Béxar: they simply fled to the countryside.... Family survival played a central role in the decision many Bexareños made regarding allegiances during the war....

Other Tejanos stayed in Béxar either to defend the Anglo-Texan position or to provide services to the Mexican army. In either case, Tejano actions defy clear categorization as supportive of Anglo-Texans or Mexican troops.... Bexareños also participated in the military confrontation on both sides of the second battle, though non-Tejanos made up the bulk of both forces....

The second battle for Béxar concluded with the Mexican army storming the Alamo on March 6, 1836.... The Battle of the Alamo itself appeared to be simply another disruption in the routines and commerce of Bexareños. Events of lasting significance to Tejanos took place soon after, with the defeat of the Mexican army at San Jacinto and the creation of the Republic of Texas. Those events immediately imbued the war of secession and the Alamo itself with new meaning for Tejanos.

At San Jacinto, the Texas army led a surprise attack on Santa Anna's troops, leading to the Mexican surrender. Tejano troops again participated in significant numbers in this battle....

After their action in the battle of San Jacinto, the men of Seguín's company continued to aid the secessionist cause by escorting Mexican troops south....

Santa Anna's capitulation resulted in the secession of Texas from Mexico and the formation of the Republic of Texas. But acceptance of Texas secession by the Mexican government took several more years of skirmishes and another war. Battles continued in the Tejano homeland.... Nevertheless, Anglo-Texans initiated their independent government with an eye toward annexation with the United States. Tejanos who supported the Texan secession movement were rewarded for their loyalty with important government positions. Among these were such Bexareños as Erasmo and Juan Seguín and José Antonio Navarro. Juan Seguín had two companies of mostly Anglo-American soldiers added to his command.

Yet, despite Tejano participation in the siege of Béxar and the battle of San Jacinto, many Anglo-Texan leaders still questioned their loyalty and allegiance.

Broad ethnic stereotypes, such as those found in Henry Smith's comments after the siege of Béxar, continued to spread within the Anglo-Texan military leadership. Smith based his attacks on lack of Tejano involvement in Texan secession. While most Tejanos did avoid fighting, they did so for reasons that Smith did not consider. Sitting out the war was a typical response by residents across the region, Anglo-American and Tejano alike, not a declaration of opposition to Texan secession. As [historian Paul] Lack notes, "For a people of such fabled militancy, the [Anglo-]Texans turned out for army duty in this period of crisis at a low rate of participation." Over the course of the entire war of secession, a maximum of 3,685 out of about 40,000 Anglo-American immigrants fought in any battles, peaking at 60 percent of the Texian forces at any time. Most joined the army during the early months of the conflict. Perhaps Tejanos' lack of participation appeared more striking since a large part of the battles in the conflict occurred in the midst of Tejano homes. Nevertheless, it was Tejano loyalty and allegiance that remained suspect....

... Tejanos and their towns remained the center of tension and conflict between Anglo-led Texas and Mexico for years after the battle of San Jacinto. This tension accelerated Tejano alienation from Texan authority over the years of the Texas Republic and into American annexation in 1845. As a result of these changes, Tejanos began to function in a new social context that defined their identity in primarily ethnic terms, though one where Mexican became the marker of difference.

★ ★ ★

... The turn of events in Béxar from the fall of 1835 to the spring of 1837 indicates a more complex operation of national, local, and ethnic identification than simply Anglo, Texan, or Mexican. Family, friendship, business, violence, and history entered into the decision-making matrix for Tejanos. While the celebration of independence held on September 16, 1835, appeared as a unified expression of national identity, the differing actions taken by Tejanos during the war of secession exposed the contours of nationalism in Béxar during this period. To make room for such a contingent notion of nationalism requires modification of that identity to include various types of economic and social relations.

Rather than an absolute category, nationalism is but one factor of identity within the combination of family, friendship, politics, status, and history. Mexican nationalism not only was different in Béxar than in Mexico City or Guadalajara but also differed from person to person in Béxar itself. The various paths taken by Bexareños during this moment of crisis indicate that these differences had some connection to a shared notion of Mexican nationalism. Some might argue that those who either fled or fought with the Texians held other identities higher than nationalism, which influenced those actions. Yet those same Tejanos continued to refer to themselves as Mexican, just as those who supported the Mexican army did. Mexican identity must be expansive enough to make room for all those choices taken in 1835.

At this point, a deeper shift in the idea of Mexican identity in Texas was underway. These fissures in Mexican identity and reactions to Texan anger suggest "Mexican" shifts from a national identity to an ethnic/cultural identity. These changes provide evidence of an emergent culture developing in relation to the new social order presented to Tejanos.... Bexareños ... still considered themselves Mexican for reasons that went beyond the issues of the moment. They continued to be the frontier people who built colonies in the rugged territory, made treaties with and fought against the indigenous populations, and participated in the protracted effort to attain independence from Spain. Those experiences, based on residual elements of culture extending from the previous decades, defined being Mexican for Tejanos.

Californians' Loss of Land after U.S. Annexation in 1848

MIROSLAVA CHÁVEZ-GARCÍA

... [L]and policies ... dispossessed most Californio-Mexican and native landowners—women and men, the elite, the middle strata, and the poor. Articles 8 and 9 of the Treaty of Guadalupe Hidalgo (1848) [See Document 3] guaranteed the property rights of Mexicans who remained in the newly conquered territories would be "inviolably respected." ...

For the owners of ranchos, the principal culprit was federal legislation that violated the spirit of the treaty by creating an extraordinarily time-consuming, and hence costly, process for confirming land titles. By the 1880s, nearly half of the rancho owners had sold or lost significant portions or all of their holdings. Apart from the insurmountable debts incurred as a result of the court delays, floods and droughts in the late 1850s and early 1860s (which decimated crops and cattle herds), a generally weaker cattle market (created by the introduction of stronger and better grades of stock from the Midwest), and high-interest loans taken to cover these [losses] and to pay for taxes ... led many to bankruptcy.

For owners of property within the limits of [the] pueblo of Los Angeles, the problem was not federal legislation but rather increased land values and the new property taxes. Within the first decade, Spanish-speaking angeleños found themselves overrun by Euro-Americans who acquired much of the most valuable city real estate. During the 1860s and 1870s, most of the original residents of Los Angeles sold, transferred, or in other ways lost their property. They were reduced to living in an ethnically segregated and economically marginalized barrio, where they were joined by recently arriving and equally impoverished immigrants from Mexico. The Native Americans who had been residing in rancherías on the outskirts of town had been forced off their lands and had fled to other parts of the region and state.

On March 3, 1851, the U.S. Congress approved a bill ... "to ascertain and settle private land claims." ... For ranchos, it called for the appointment of three commissioners, who, with the help of a secretary fluent in Spanish and English, were responsible for determining the validity of land titles dating to the Spanish and Mexican eras.... [T]his meant that rancho holders—Californios and natives, individuals and corporations—had to hire lawyers (all of whom, with one

From *Negotiating Conquest* by Miroslava Chavez-Garcia. © 2004 The Arizona Board of Regents. Reprinted by permission of the University of Arizona Press.

exception, were Euro-Americans) to prove the legality of their land titles under Spanish and Mexican law....

... [V]arious complications arose around the grants that had been made in the Spanish and Mexican periods. All claimants had to produce documents or oral testimony concerning the authority under which they had received their land grant, the kind of grant received, and when they received it. Evidence of continuous residence and property improvements had to be supplied, along with proof that the owner had been a Mexican citizen....

The 1851 Land Act also held that all titles, whether rejected or confirmed by the commission, could be appealed within sixty days to the U.S. District Court by either the claimant or the U.S. District Attorney, each of whom would then have the option of appealing that court's ruling to the U.S. Supreme Court....

The process was burdensome, but, in 1852, when Congress ordered that all the commission's rulings be appealed automatically to the district court, the process became punitive. That requirement would create immense delays and hardships for the Californios. Finally, in 1860, Congress eased the situation somewhat and allowed a claimant to order the survey while title confirmation was being sought in the courts, reducing the number of years it took to obtain a patent. However, because the change came so late and the appeal was still required, it took an average of seventeen years for claimants to obtain a patent to their rancho property.

Ironically, although most claims on ranchos were upheld (604 of the more than 800 presented), nearly half (46 percent) of the original owners in the Los Angeles area went bankrupt in the process of defending those claims. That most titles were confirmed reflects not only the leniency of the land commission but also the diligence with which claimants sought out *expedientes* (files of grant papers).... Unsuccessful claimants lost their property.

Native Californians living on rancherías, land that had never been formally granted by the Spanish or Mexican governors, also lost their property. Those lands reverted to the public domain and were opened to settlement and acquisition under preemption or homestead legislation. Preemption laws, enacted by Congress in 1841 and extended to California in 1853, recognized the claims of heads of families, widows, or single individuals to 160 acres of public land, and it allowed them to buy the property at a minimum price of $1.25 an acre.... The enactment of the 1862 Homestead Act by the U.S. Congress attracted more settlers by allowing squatters on the public domain to acquire a patent to 160 acres so long as they could prove five years of residence on the property. Unfortunately, homestead and preemption legislation encouraged squatters to trespass on rancho lands and to take possession of lands on which Native Californians as well as Mexican Californios were residing. Anticipating that the titles acquired in the Spanish and Mexican periods would eventually be denied and that they could then file a preemption or homestead claim to the property, newcomers illegally moved onto ranchos, which provoked conflicts with the owners. Those tensions, in turn, exacerbated racial conflict and further complicated (and, hence, made even more costly) the Mexicans' efforts to confirm their titles.

Confirmation of titles to ranches came slowly for both Spanish-speaking and native peoples, but women, especially married women, encountered additional burdens created by the limitations placed on their rights to manage and control their property. An 1850 California statute gave married women an equal interest in marital or common property, but a husband had the authority to manage his wife's property as if it were his own. Only when the wife had the juridical status of "sole trader," which she acquired by registering an official declaration of her "intent to conduct business in her own name" with the county recorder, could she carry out transactions alone.

The 1850 law also enabled a wife to retain separate property, though her husband (or other legal agent) managed those assets and needed the woman's written and oral permission to sell or transfer her property. Moreover, when it came to separate or community property, a wife could challenge her husband if he grossly mismanaged her share or attempted to dispossess her of it. In such situations, she could ask the First District Court to appoint a trustee, or receiver, to take control of the property. Widowed, divorced, and single adult women, in contrast to their married counterparts, faced fewer difficulties: They could engage in legal transactions on their own, though they (like most other claimants, including Californio men and Native American men and women) often had Euro-American lawyers representing them in the municipal, state, and federal courts.

During the three decades following the American takeover, women and men of different ethnicities brought ninety-four cases before the board of land commissioners to establish title to ranchos in the former Mexican district of Los Angeles. Eighteen (19 percent) involved Californio women, three (3 percent) Native American women, forty-three (46 percent) Californio men, six (6 percent) Native American men, and twenty-four (26 percent) Euro-American men, seventeen of whom had purchased their holdings from original Californio or native grantees in the 1840s and early 1850s. Of the cases petitioned by Californio women, sixteen (89 percent) resulted in title confirmation and two (11 percent) in rejections, but of these, nine (50 percent) sold their ranchos or portions of them during and after the hearings. As for those cases involving Native American women, two of the three claims were successful, and in one of the two successful cases, the owner sold an interest in her rancho while the proceedings were underway. Among the men, twenty-two (92 percent) of the Euro-Americans who filed petitions obtained titles, whereas two (8 percent) did not. During the hearings, eight (33 percent) sold their ranchos. Most of the claims brought by Californios and Native Americans were also successful, though a greater number of cases involving Californio men ended in sales before the termination of the legal process.... Of the forty-three petitions initiated by Californios, thirty-seven (86 percent) led to title confirmation and six (14 percent) to rejections.... Most claims made by neófitos—five of six cases (83 percent)—received titles, and only one (17 percent) was rejected. Only one rancho, claimed by a group of native men, was sold during the proceedings.

The high success rate of all ethnic groups and both genders stemmed largely from the land commission and U.S. District Court's commitment to rule leniently in reaching decisions. The courts ruled favorably even when boundaries remained unclear, title papers had been lost, and grants had been made only days prior to the July 7, 1846, deadline....

The land commissioners accorded both women and men equitable treatment. Vicenta Sepúlveda's 1852 petition for title to the four-sitio Rancho Sierra, for instance, aroused suspicion but was nonetheless approved. (One sitio is equivalent to a square league or about 4,440 acres.) The grant was dated June 15, 1846, less than a month before the July 7 deadline, and she had not taken possession until July 9, 1846. To resolve any doubts held by the commissioners, she called upon others to testify on her behalf, including a close friend and prominent citizen, Antonio Francisco Coronel.... The commissioners ... nonetheless concluded that she and her family had lived on the rancho for nearly twenty years before she took legal possession. That was enough for them to affirm her title in 1855 and then to appeal the case, as now required, to the district court, which upheld their decision the following year. It took more than ten additional years for the surveyor general to complete the survey and the land office to issue a patent.

The land commission and federal courts also treated men, regardless of ethnicity, in a fair and flexible fashion. However, like the women claimants, men endured delays....

Neófitos ... petitioned for grants that were much smaller than those of Californios ... but they were just as successful, even when their claims lacked some of the proof required to establish their claims. In 1852, José Domingo ... initially had difficulty because he lacked evidence that he had inherited the property from his father, Felipe, a former mission native at San Gabriel.... The commissioners expressed skepticism about the claim until Michael White, a former mayordomo at the mission ... verified that José was Felipe's son and verified the family's long residence on the property.... They ruled that under Mexican law, Felipe's widow, Pascuala, "was entitled to one-half of all the [marital] property." Though she had not filed a claim, the commissioners awarded titles to both Domingo and Pascuala in 1853. That decision then went to the district court, which upheld the commission's ruling. Eighteen years later, the surveyor general completed the survey, and the land office approved the patent in 1871.

The commission also closely scrutinized and questioned claims made by Euro-Americans. Though lenient, the commission investigated everyone, regardless of gender or ethnicity....

The federal courts, though flexible and fair in their decisions, nonetheless rejected claims that rested on grossly insufficient or false evidence. Of the twenty-one petitions filed by women (eighteen Californio women and three neófitas), the board initially rejected six (submitted by four Californio women and two neófitas), three of which (from two Californio women and one neófita) were approved on appeal and the other three rejected.

... [M]ost rancho owners secured titles to their land. Sadly, establishing title did not guarantee continued ownership, for more than 46 percent (twenty-eight of sixty Californio-Mexicans and Native American claimants whose titles were found proven) had lost their property by the 1880s. They were dispossessed by financial burdens brought on by the years of delay in getting their titles, high-interest loans, new taxes—which had been unknown in the Mexican era, depressed cattle prices, and droughts and floods that killed livestock and ruined crops in the late 1850s and 1860s.... County property values, though steady in the 1850s, decreased significantly in the 1860s, with the onset of the cattle and crop devastation of that decade. Not until the 1870s, when the region emerged from the natural disasters, did that trend reverse.

Most ranchers, nearing bankruptcy, were forced to sell part or all of their property before they had the titles in hand. Those sales occurred because of indebtedness resulting from the newly instituted land taxes; from crop and cattle losses, especially in the mid-1860s; and from the heavy costs of proving land titles, which required paying attorneys and court fees as well as the costs for the land survey. Appeals and bureaucratic delays in Washington meant that these costs continued for years, sometimes for decades. Some married women lost their lands because of desperate husbands who, when faced with personal financial reverses of their own, overstepped their legal authority and disposed of the wife's property. The available evidence indicates that at least eighteen ranchos claimed by Californio-Mexican men, nine by Californio-Mexican women, and one by a Native American woman were lost during and after confirmation hearings....

María Merced Tapia and her husband, Victor Prudhomme, prominent members of California Mexican society, had to sell their three-sitio Rancho Malibu Simi Sequit because of debts accumulated in appealing their claim to the district court and in maintaining the property. The land commission rejected their petition in 1854 because of their failure to prove that the original landholder, José Bartolomé Tapia, had lawfully obtained the rancho from Spanish governor José Joaquín de Arrillaga in 1804....

While Tapia and Prudhomme were accumulating heavy legal expenses, other rancho holders were incurring crushing debts because of droughts and floods that came in 1857 and again in the early- to mid-1860s. Andrés Duarte, owner of Rancho Azusa, was among those forced to sell properties because of debts acquired as a result of the bad climatic conditions. In 1864, fourteen years before a patent was issued for the rancho, Duarte lost the property because of a debt owed to William Wolfskill, a Euro-American citrus grower and lender. The sheriff foreclosed on the property, selling it at auction for $4,000 to Wolfskill....

Some ranch owners held onto their properties—at least for a while—by subdividing and selling portions of them. For instance, Victoria Reid sold a portion of Rancho Huerta de Cuati in 1858, one year before she received final confirmation of the title, because she needed cash to maintain the property. The sale meant the loss of two-thirds of the original grant, leaving her with only 128 acres.

... These Californios, whose lives had begun in the previous century, witnessed—indeed, they experienced first-hand—the devastating social and economic changes wrought by the American conquest.

In contrast to the struggles of the rancheros, who were coping with the legal system, the economy, and even the climate, landholders inside Los Angeles had fewer difficulties. The process for confirming title to pueblo lands was relatively simple and quick. The 1851 land act vested officials with the authority to affirm private titles to land within the new American towns that had emerged from the former Spanish and Mexican pueblos. Property types included *solares* (building lots) and *suertes* (agricultural lots) granted from *propios* and *ejidos* (municipal and common lands). Acting on behalf of the town were the mayor and members of the Common Council, positions that had replaced Mexican alcaldes and ayuntamientos. They represented all property holders in the municipality.... Since the land act did not stipulate a process for determining the legality of titles in the towns, the state legislature delegated that responsibility to municipal leaders.

In the case of Los Angeles, it did so implicitly in 1850, when it approved the pueblo's incorporation as a city.... Los Angeles's authority over 17,172 acres of pueblo property was made official in 1866.

Town leaders did not wait for such legal niceties to deal with the fundamentally important property issues. In 1849, officials hired Lieutenant E.O.C. Ord to complete the first survey of Los Angeles. Ord's map established the boundaries of preexisting properties held by long-time residents, and it subdivided the remaining vacant land into lots of 2,200 square yards (close in size to a Mexican solar). In early 1850, the town council passed the first of several ordinances allowing for the sale of the newly created city lots. The purpose was threefold: to stimulate the growth of agriculture, the town's major business; to attract new settlers; and to stabilize and increase the city's land values and, hence, the revenue that the city could generate from those properties with the land taxes that the council was soon to enact. With the taxes, the council funded public works projects, such as the paving of streets and the building of sewer and potable-water systems.

... Those best positioned to acquire land under these conditions were the newcomers from the United States, who possessed cash or credit and a willingness to engage in real-estate speculation.

The town council also took steps to facilitate confirmation of Mexican land titles. In 1854, it passed an ordinance that approved the titles of those "persons who themselves or whose ancestors have occupied them without interruption, peaceably, and in good faith for a term of twelve years." Unlike the system for determining rancho titles, this broad declaration led to swift approval and, hence, was a less costly process, even for those who lacked the original title issued by Spanish and Mexican officials or the Mexican ayuntamientos. Petitions for titles or deeds went to the city's "committee on lands," which investigated the claims, usually through an examination of Mexican titles, if extant, or through the testimony of neighbors or former pueblo leaders. The committee then made its recommendations to the mayor, who either confirmed or denied the petitions....

When the town council passed its first ordinance, in 1850, Californio-Mexicans made up 75 percent (1,215 residents) of the city's population of 1,610, whereas Euro-American and other foreign-born residents numbered only 395 or 25 percent. During the next decade, the city's ethnic ratio reversed in response to a stream of migrants from northern California and from the eastern United States, especially New York, Missouri, Illinois, Ohio, Indiana, and Pennsylvania. By 1860 Euro-Americans constituted 53 percent (2,316) of the town's 4,385 residents, whereas Californio-Mexicans were now in the minority with 47 percent (2,069).... In another harbinger of the future, immigrants from Mexico had come close to outnumbering the original Californio residents. By 1880, the number of city residents had doubled, swelling from 5,728 to 11,183, with Euro-Americans making up 81 percent (9,017) and Californio-Mexicans, whose real numbers had remained nearly unchanged in the ten years, were only 19 percent (2,166) of the city's residents.

The city's changing ethnic composition paralleled shifting patterns of property holding. In the 1850s, most landowners were Californio-Mexicans, but by the decade's end, they held less land than Euro-Americans. Soon after Ord completed his survey, Euro-American men, who had cash and credit, began to purchase municipal lots that the city sold at public auction....

In the next few years, ... [m]ost city land went to Euro-American men, enabling them to build at a relatively low cost a new commercial center, located south and west of the plaza and Mexican barrio, the traditional heart of Los Angeles. Thus emerged a new social and economic elite.

Not only were incoming Euro-American and foreign-born men acquiring land at rates that outpaced those of Californio-Mexicans, the value of their properties—land and improvements, such as structures or buildings—would rise substantially during the 1870s, following a city-wide economic depression in the mid-1860s. In the town's early years, property values had risen primarily as a result of the distribution and improvement of the donation lots. That mild real estate boom soon subsided, and by the early to mid-1860s property values had fallen sharply as a result of natural disasters—the same droughts and floods that left many rancheros bankrupt. Property values decreased significantly as a result of torrential rains in 1862 and 1863 and a smallpox epidemic. Euro-American men weathered the city's socioeconomic disasters better than did the Spanish-speaking inhabitants....

... Californio-Mexicans were hit hardest by the depression and smallpox epidemic, suffering losses in property and lives. The storms washed away adobe homes and fences as well as vineyards and gardens, which were important sources of subsistence for the community. The epidemic struck in winter 1863, killing at least 500 people and further wracking the ailing economy....

... [T]he city-wide depression affected primarily the Mexican population of the pueblo. Californio-Mexicans, along with landless native peoples, not only made up the poorest segment of the population but also suffered the greatest loss of life during the winter of 1863, when smallpox took its heaviest toll. Initially, the epidemic severely impacted residents who lived north of the plaza, primarily Spanish speakers, though the disease later spread to other parts of the city. The inability to pay for medical care or vaccines, which arrived only intermittently by ship from San Francisco, worsened their prospects for a recovery.

As the city recovered from the epidemic and the natural disasters, residents and the recent arrivals witnessed marked improvements in the city's economy and society. The creation of new municipal services and formation of businesses, including a gas plant, an ice factory, two banks, and a local railway connecting Los Angeles to the port of San Pedro, signaled the renewal of economic life. The population also continued to expand, as the systematic foreclosure, subdivision, and sale of rancho land in the 1860s brought land-hungry migrants to the region. The newcomers, a significant number of whom settled in local townships, including El Monte, Santa Ana, and Los Nietos (all former ranchos), fueled the demand for municipal services, businesses, and, especially, property....

Real-estate values and the city's infrastructure continued to grow in the 1870s, but few Californio-Mexicans reaped the benefits of that prosperity. In 1874, city property values reached $1,778,956, more than double their 1860 levels. Californio-Mexican men and women combined held only 28 percent of land and improvements, valued at $496,813. In contrast, Euro-Americans held 72 percent, valued at $1.28 million, with almost $1.09 million of that held by men.... The number of Euro-American real-estate owners and the value of their properties continued to increase following the arrival of the Southern Pacific Railroad in 1876, which brought thousands of Euro-Americans to the city, and the real estate boom of the 1880s. By the 1870s, the Californio-Mexicans ... held only a portion of real estate in the city, a miniscule amount in comparison to what they had held previously....

Californio-Mexicans struggled not only to hold onto real estate but also to personal property. The tax records indicate that, in the 1870s, on average, a Californio-Mexican man and woman held less in personal wealth—cash, bank notes, or other movable goods—than he or she did in the 1850s.... Comparing Californio-Mexicans' personal property values to those of Euro-American men reveals the decreasing economic power of Californio-Mexicans vis-à-vis Euro-American men.... [W]hereas Californio-Mexican men and women's personal property values remained nearly the same or declined between 1857 and 1874, Euro-American men holdings increased nearly 400 percent in that same period....

The indisputable point is that the Californio-Mexican residents of Los Angeles were losing their personal wealth and real estate....

Tax liens caused other foreclosures. Nicolasa Carreaga owned two 10 acre lots on Main Street, which she had acquired through the donation system. When she could not pay city and county taxes in 1853, the sheriff seized and sold her property at public auction. Francisco Ballestreros, a mid-strata man who owned a home on a lot and a vineyard, lost everything. The vineyard went first in 1852 to cover monies owed to Louis Lamoreau, John Chapman, and two other unnamed creditors. Two years later, the lot was seized and sold to cover unpaid city taxes....

The sale and loss of land, homes, vineyards, and small gardens resulted in the leveling of social classes among Californio-Mexicans, leading them to cluster in the central area of town, near the plaza. By the 1880s, the locale housed 83 percent of Los Angeles's Spanish-speaking population, which had become the most economically marginalized and ethnically segregated sector of society. Residents of the barrio, including recently arrived immigrants from Mexico and an increasing number of Chinese immigrants, ... lived in dilapidated housing underserved by public facilities. As late as 1879, according to the annual health department report, the area lacked a proper sewage and drainage system. Also crowding into that area of town, increasingly designated a "slum" by outsiders, were unsavory business establishments—brothels, saloons, and gambling halls—and their clientele.

Notwithstanding the declining conditions of their homes and neighbor-hood, Californio-Mexicans found ways to survive impoverishment and adapt to the changing economy. The federal censuses of the 1860s, 1870s, and 1880s, though incomplete, reveal that Californio-Mexican men and women increasingly drifted into manual or domestic jobs in the growing urban and agriculture economy. By the 1870s, nearly 80 percent of the men were in unskilled jobs, toiling as day laborers, laying bricks, repairing city structures, or picking crops. Women also took on unskilled jobs, working as seamstresses, washerwomen, housekeepers, and farm laborers, enabling them, alongside their spouses, brothers, and fathers, to eke out an existence for themselves and their families.

Within a relatively short period after the American conquest, a Euro-American-dominated, Protestant, capitalist society had emerged in Los Angeles, displacing and transforming the world of the original residents. Owners of town property easily confirmed their titles, but the increase in land values in the late 1860s and 1870s, high-interest loans, and taxes strained the resources of the original residents—women as well as men—and led to widespread property loss and impoverishment of both the well-to-do and mid-strata residents. They joined the poor in the barrio, struggling to survive as unskilled laborers.

… For the rancheros, it came as a consequence of time-consuming and costly legal proceedings to confirm their land titles as well as from natural disasters that decimated cattle and crops between 1857 and the mid-1860s.… [M]en and women, regardless of ethnicity, shared the loss. As for the landless Native Americans, their scattering into the rural countryside, which had begun in the 1830s and 1840s, and population decline due to disease and abuse accelerated as the newly impoverished Californio-Mexicans displaced them as laborers in the towns and on the ranchos. Some established themselves in small, isolated communities or they survived by working in the expanding commercial farming industry. Those survivors, like natives elsewhere, remained the most culturally and socially marginalized people in California.

The experiences of Spanish-speaking and native property owners varied little across gender, ethnic, and social-class lines: Californio-Mexican and Native American men and women of all social levels lost their land and became impoverished. By examining and analyzing the experiences of Californio-Mexican and Native American women … we have seen that women also bore the brunt of the conquest. For the single, widowed, separated, or divorced women (whose numbers were on the rise in the post-conquest period), the loss of personal wealth had a direct and severe impact on their families, who depended upon them for support. With the rise of female-headed households … women had to find innovative ways in which to deal with the social, economic, and cultural upheaval of their rapidly changing world. Their solutions, however, were not always welcomed and, in many ways, challenged the values espoused by the Californio-Mexican community.

FURTHER READING

Armando Alonzo, *Tejano Legacy: Rancheros and Settlers in South Texas, 1734–1900* (1998).

Virginia Bouvier, *Women and the Conquest of California* (2001).

Albert Camarillo, *Chicanos in a Changing Society: From Mexican Pueblos to American Barrios in Santa Barbara and Southern California, 1848–1930* (1979).

María Raquél Casas, *Married to a Daughter of the Land: Spanish-Mexican Women and Interethnic Marriage in California, 1820–1880* (2007).

Antonia I. Castañeda, "Gender, Race, and Culture: Spanish-Mexican Women in the Historiography of Frontier California," *Frontiers* 11, no. 1 (1990): 8–20.

Miroslava Chávez-García, *Negotiating Conquest: Gender and Power in California, 1770s to 1880s* (2004).

Brian DeLay, *War of a Thousand Deserts: Indian Raids and the U.S.-Mexican War* (2008).

Roxanne Dunbar-Ortiz, *Roots of Resistance: Land Tenure in New Mexico, 1680–1980* (2007).

Arnoldo De León, *They Called Them Greasers: Anglo Attitudes Towards Mexicans in Texas, 1821–1900* (1983).

Laura E. Gómez, *Manifest Destinies: The Making of the Mexican American Race* (2007).

Deena González, *Refusing the Favor: The Spanish-Mexican Women of Santa Fe, 1820–1880* (1999).

Michael J. González, *This Small City Will Be a Mexican Paradise: Exploring the Origins of Mexican Culture in Los Angeles, 1821–1846* (2005).

Ramón Gutiérrez, *When Jesus Came, the Corn Mothers Went Away: Marriage, Sexuality, and Power in New Mexico, 1500–1846* (1991).

Albert L. Hurtado, *Intimate Frontiers: Sex, Gender, and Culture in Old California* (1999).

Douglas Monroy, *Thrown Among Strangers: The Making of Mexican Culture in Frontier California* (1990).

Raúl Ramos, *Beyond the Alamo: Forging Mexican Ethnicity in San Antonio, 1821–1861* (2009).

Andrés Reséndez, *Changing National Identities at the Frontier: Texas and New Mexico, 1800–1850* (2004).

Bárbara O. Reyes, *Private Women, Public Lives: Gender and the Missions of the Californias* (2009).

David J. Weber, *The Mexican Frontier, 1821–1846: The American Southwest Under Mexico* (1982).

CHAPTER 3

Life in the Borderlands

As newly incorporated U.S. citizens, Mexican Americans faced a myriad of new laws, social changes, and political practices. While the Treaty of Guadalupe Hidalgo guaranteed them full citizenship rights, few exercised those rights in practice. Elites gained easier acceptance as citizens than the poor. Yet, as a group, Mexican Americans lost land, political power, and social standing throughout the second half of the nineteenth century. The extent and pace of their loss, however, varied by region and by individuals' socioeconomic class and gender.

Mexican Americans' ability to hold onto political power depended partly on demographics. They were likely to remain in office in regions where they constituted a majority. Mexican American politicians retained office by forging alliances with Euro Americans, dispensing political patronage, and encouraging bloc voting. The obstacles facing Spanish-speaking communities included U.S. laws, limited English-language fluency, and the denial of the right to vote. Vigilantes physically intimidated Mexican American voters throughout the U.S. Southwest, newspapers discouraged them from exercising the franchise, and Euro American politicians manipulated voters to maintain themselves in office.

As they lost political power, Mexican Americans became more vulnerable to discriminatory laws. Throughout the Southwest, local governments passed legislation that prohibited or limited Mexican cultural practices such as dances, gambling, and bathing in rivers. Influenced by manifest destiny and notions of superiority, Euro American legislators restricted cultural practices considered uncivilized, immoral, and barbaric. Newspapers portrayed Mexican Americans as criminals, and courts incarcerated them in larger numbers. In California, competition over mining claims during the Gold Rush led Euro American vigilantes to attack those who looked "foreign," including Mexican, Chilean, and Chinese miners. Encouraged by nativist sentiments, California's legislature passed the Foreign Miners Act in 1850, which required foreigners to pay a prohibitive tax in order to mine for gold. Throughout the region, Mexican Americans lost their land through legal challenges and vigilante actions.

Responding to their criminalization and rising ethnic tensions, some Mexican Americans launched rebellions. During the 1850s, Californios (Mexican Californians) engaged in banditry after experiencing violent attacks, killings, and evictions from the gold mines. Property disputes in New Mexico led some to organize into secretive groups that carried out raids, cut fences, and destroyed property. In southern Texas, land disputes and Tejanos' increasing incarceration ignited a six-month insurrection led by Juan N. Cortina, a land-grant heir. To offset the decline in their economic and social standing, some Spanish-speaking elites established alliances with Euro Americans. Intermarriage between elite Mexican American women and Euro American men created mutually beneficial social ties. While the newcomers profited from Mexican Americans' extensive familial and friendship networks, the latter sometimes protected their property and maintained political and economic power with the help of Euro American in-laws. This chapter examines how the U.S. government and Euro American settlers exercised their control over newly acquired lands and how Mexican Americans adapted to the U.S. political and legal system.

DOCUMENTS

Although unfamiliar with U.S. laws when they became U.S. citizens, Mexican Americans soon adapted to the legal system. While they had appealed to religious officials to marry and separate in Mexico, they learned that U.S. civil authorities now held jurisdiction over marital concerns. In Document 1, Sarah Garcia Clay, a Mexican Texan woman married to a Euro American man, sues for divorce in a civil court. Marriage and property laws varied throughout the U.S. Southwest, and these differences had significant effects on women's property rights. Unlike the states of California and Texas, the territory of New Mexico incorporated U.S. coverture laws, which subsumed a married woman's rights under her husband, as described in Document 2. Tejanos struggled to obtain justice within the legal system because of widespread bias among judicial officials and jury members. In Document 3, a visiting French priest describes the legal consequences of anti-Mexican views. Western states passed liberal divorce laws that motivated residents of neighboring states to move west and engage in the so-called interstate divorce trade. Along the U.S.-Mexico border, this divorce trade assumed international dimensions as couples who married in Mexico crossed into Texas to divorce, as shown in Document 4. Among the rebellions resulting from the rising ethnic tensions in the postwar period was one that broke out in southern Texas in 1859. Juan N. Cortina issued a proclamation, Document 5, listing the rebels' grievances, including the inability of local governments to uphold the citizenship rights of Tejanos. Intermarriages between elite Mexican American women and Euro American men increased in the postwar period, and were the subject of two elite Californios' frank discussion in Document 6. Among the harshest anti-Mexican views were those directed against poor residents. In Document 7, a Euro American journalist characterizes poor Tejanos as criminals.

1. Sarah Garcia Clay Seeks a Divorce from an Interethnic Marriage in Texas, 1856

Now on this day came the parties by their attorneys, and also came a jury as follows, … good and lawful men who being duly sworn and empanelled proceeded to hear the evidence in the cause and the allegations in the Petition set forth, being proved to wit, that the said James H. Clay had in the month of September AD 1848 married the said Sarah formerly Sarah Garcia[,] and that soon thereafter in the year AD 1849[,] the said James H. Clay had departed from the State of Texas and had since that time wholly neglected to furnish support to the said Sarah his wife[,] and that he had wholly abandoned his said wife and the said witnesses being men well known to the jurors herein, the cause was submitted under the charge of the court to the Jury who rendered the following verdict, to wit, we the Jury find for the plaintiff and that all the facts stated in the petition are true. Robert B. Kingsbury, foreman.

Whereupon it was ordered adjudged and decreed by the court that the said Sarah Clay and James H. Clay be and they are hereby finally and forever divorced from the bonds of matrimony heretofore existing between them and that the defendant pay all costs of court in this cause incurred.

2. New Mexico's Ruling Places Women under Coverture, 1857

This bill was a bill in chancery in the district court of the second judicial district, for the county of Taos, by Mariana Manuela Martinez against her husband, Tomas Lucero. The complainant alleges that on or about the thirtieth day of September, 1828, she intermarried with Tomas Lucero, and that at the time of said marriage and afterwards, a large amount of money, property, chattels, and real estate, the absolute property and inheritance of the said complainant, was delivered to the said Tomas Lucero as her husband, in trust for her use and benefit, and for the use and benefit of both, while they should live together as man and wife. The bill further alleges that they lived together as man and wife for the space of eight years, and that then, from various causes, a separation between them took place; that a few years afterwards, in the year 1847, they were reunited and lived together in the matrimonial relation for the space of eleven months; that at the expiration of that eleven months, they again separated, without issue, and have never since lived together. The complainant further alleges that her said husband has for years past been living in open adultery with another woman, by whom he has two children, and that he has been wasting and dissipating the property and effects of said complainant for the benefit of his said

---

Cameron County District Court Minutes, #1016155, Case #485, *Sarah García Clay v. James H. Clay,* 25 July 1856.

Mariana Manuela Martinez v. Tomas Lucero. Report of Cases Argued and Determined in the Supreme Court of the Territory of New Mexico, Vol. 1 (January 1857), pp. 208–218.

paramour and her two children, and she has good reason to believe that he will continue to waste, dissipate, and so convert the same until the whole amount thereof shall have been consumed. The petitioner therefore prays that the said Tomas Lucero be enjoined from further waste and dissipation of her estate; that he be compelled to answer the allegations of her bill; that he be compelled to account with her for the full amount of her property and estate, as well as the rents and profits thereof, since their last separation, and that such further relief may be granted as the nature of the case may require.

The respondent, Tomas Lucero, in his answer, admits that he intermarried with the complainant as alleged in her bill, and that they lived together for some seven or eight years. He avers that about seven or eight years after their marriage, he discovered that his said wife had proved faithless to him by the commission of adultery with one Mariano Martinez, and that she then, of her own accord, left her house and lived with the said Mariano Martinez in different houses; that in the year 1839, he went to California to escape the infamy and injuries his wife was heaping upon him; that at the time of his departure, she was living with the said Mariano Martinez; that upon his return to New Mexico, in 1842, he found her living in adultery with Mariano Lucero, a priest of the holy Catholic church, and first cousin to him, the respondent; and that she continued to live in adultery with said Mariano Lucero until the year 1846, when, through the solicitations of the respondent and the intercession of one Jose Antonio Martinez, she returned to her house and promised to live a reformed life and continue to live with the respondent. About nine or ten months after, she presented herself before Jose Maria Valdez, an alcalde of the county of Taos, and before him they separated by mutual consent, and the complainant at the time of separation released the respondent from any claim whatever that she might have had against him. And he further avers that immediately after their last separation his said wife returned to the house of the said priest, Mariano Lucero, and contin- ued to live in open adultery with him up to the period of the filing of his answer to the complainant's bill. He also avers that in order to comply with his conjugal duties and his religious obligations, he made many sacrifices to induce her to return to him, and discontinued his effort only when all hope of reformation had gone.

The respondent admits that he had at the time of his answer a woman living in his house to aid and assist him in his household duties, and that the said woman has two children, but avers that he does not know whether he is the father of said children or not. He denies the allegation that he is wasting and dissipating the property of the complainant upon the said woman, and avers that he never took the said woman or any other into his house until he had made several efforts to induce his wife to live with him; and that as late as the year 1854 he requested said complainant to return to her home and perform the duties of a wife towards him, and that she refused so to do. The respondent further avers that he has paid to his said wife the full amount of property which he received as her separate estate....

According to the principles of the civil law, a separation from bed and board, or a dissolution of the conjugal association, must be decreed by a competent tribunal and not by the consent of the parties. It does not appear from the record that any separation had been decreed by a competent tribunal; but the separation which took place between the parties appears to have been voluntary, against the policy of matrimonial law, without legal sanction, and therefore powerless for the purpose of dissolving the conjugal tie. The complainant, in her bill, did not even allege, as a cause of separation from her husband, any one of the causes which would have availed her in a prayer for separation before a competent tribunal....

We are, then, to view the complainant in the character of the lawful wife of the respondent, and it is a principle of the civil law ... that a wife can not, during the conjugal association, recover from her husband her separate dotal property, or resume the administration thereof, without showing waste or dissipation of the same on the part of her husband; for the administration of the dotal property, whether appraised or not, belongs exclusively to the husband during the existence of the marriage....

... The complainant, according to her own allegations, separated from the respondent as his wife without the assignment of any cause which would have justified her in so doing.... She still stood in the eye of the law related to the respondent as his lawful wife, and as such the court could not grant to her the administration of the property, which she claimed without proof of waste and dissipation of the same on the part of the respondent. The bill of the complainant alleges waste and dissipation; but the respondent in his answer denies the charge, and no testimony is introduced to establish the truth of the allegation.

3. A French Catholic Priest Describes Anti–Mexican Views in the Legal System, 1858

The Americans of the Texian frontiers are, for the most part, the very scum of society—bankrupts, escaped criminals, old volunteers, who after the treaty of Guad[a]lupe Hidalgo, came into a country protected by nothing that could be called a judicial authority, to seek adventure and illicit gains....

The magistracy is far from giving adequate guarantees for the security of the public; and in criminal matters it is barefaced as it is revolting. Let the criminal be an American, and though he were the worst ruffian in the town he is let off scot-free, with a mere promise to pay a sum of money, which of course he never pays. Should the crime be of too glaring a nature to escape punishment, the perpetrator, be he robber or murderer, gets off with imprisonment, a mockery in its duration.... This shameless partiality of the American judges is the best justification of Lynch-law. And hence this Draconian code is in full force in all the new States of the Union. As to Germans, Irish, and Mexicans, the civil law is enforced in their cases with all its rigour. Even frequently, where the crime remained to be proved, they would in the first instance be thrown into prison

Emmanuel H. D. Domenech, *Missionary Adventures in Texas and Mexico: A Personal Narrative of Six Years' Sojourn in Those Regions* (London: Longman, Brown, Green, Longmans, and Roberts, 1858), pp. 228–229, 237–240.

in irons, there to await their sentence, or rather their condemnation, in which the sentence most generally is terminated.

Towards the Irish and Mexicans excessive rigour used to be employed, savouring glaringly of bigotry and religious hate.... I saw at Brownsville Mexicans whom the sheriff was flogging to death with his ox-hide lash. They were bound, half-naked, their arms extended across the prison door, and then scourged on the sides and loins with the most brutal violence. To save the expense of their support, pending sentence, they were not sent to prison, but were sent back untried, having their frames lacerated with stripes. Some died from the effects of these barbarities.

I could never comprehend the Mexican's submission, supporting, as he did, at once the cruelty and the contempt of a nation which he sovereignly detested, had I not been so often the witness of his incredible *nonchalance* and imperturbable meekness. In these badly-organised regions, the Mexican might have an easy vengeance on his persecutors, who are quite the minority on the Texian frontiers; but vengeance is not in his heart; he would rather forget an injury than take the trouble of avenging it.

Still there is no lack of courts of justice. Some are stationary and periodical in their sessions; others are itinerant, and courts of appeal. Every village ... has its magistrates for civil and criminal cases. Over them is a more important tribunal, which despatches annually a Judge of Appeal to the principal places of the country of Texas. The man that came to Brownsville was a large handsome Yankee, neither over unpolite nor unreasonable. He even decided equitably enough in the rare moments of his sobriety....

From judges of this stamp, people can hardly expect "*Just Justice*," and hence they dispense it for themselves. When drunkenness is the only defect of a judge, you may hope ... that out of many sentences, some few may be fair, and yours among the number. But when to drunkenness is added ignorance of the law, of the nature of a contract, of the general rules on which property and society itself rest secure; and when to drunkenness and this ignorance too, is further added venality, fear of the strong hand, and party feeling, then it is only a Mexican, a simpleton, or a coward, that would appeal to law for justice. The Americans, and the Europeans who know how things stand in these still savage regions, dispense with magistrates; and the dispensers of justice never interfere in the disputes of such people, knowing well the consequence of their intermeddling.

4. Antonia Diaz Marries in Mexico but Divorces in Texas, 1859

The State of Texas to the Sheriff of Zapata County,

Greetings,

You are hereby commanded, that you summon by publication Felipe Cuellar, [whose] residence is in Mexico, to be and appear before the District Court, to be holden in and for the county of Zapata, at the court-house thereof,

The Ranchero (Brownsville), May 12, 1860.

in the town of Carrizo, on the 11th day of June, 1860, then and there to answer the petition of Antonia Diaz Cuellar filed in said court against the said Felipe Cuellar, and alleging in substance as follows, to wit: That she, the said Antonia Diaz Cuellar, a resident of the said county of Zapata, on the 13th day of August, 1852, was in the town of Guerrero, in the State of Tamaulipas, in the Republic of Mexico, lawfully united in the bonds of matrimony with Felipe Cuellar; that for some years before and continuously up to the time of the celebration of the rites of said matrimony, her husband, Felipe Cuellar, and herself, were residents of the town of Carrizo, in said county of Zapata, in said State of Texas, and ever since said marriage up to about the beginning of February, 1859, her said husband, Felipe Cuellar, and herself, continued to reside at the said town of Carrizo, when her said husband left the said county and State, and up to the present time has temporarily resided out the said State of Texas, to wit: in the said town of Guerrero, in Mexico; while she, the said Antonia Diaz Cuellar has continued up to the present time to reside in said town of Carrizo. The plaintiff further says, that during the residence of herself and her said husband, the said Felipe Cuellar was guilty of excesses, cruel treatment, and outrages toward her of such a character as to render their living together insupportable; and particularly the plaintiff says, that in the month of January, 1856, in the said town of Carrizo, her said husband struck and beat her severely and cruelly; that he has during the whole term of their said marriage, at various times, applied to her opprobrious and disgraceful epithets and language, putting her in bodily fear, and has thus rendered her unhappy and their further living together insupportable.

Came to hand the 22nd day of April, A.D. 1860, and executed by publishing in The Ranchero, a newspaper published in the county of Nueces, being the nearest county where a newspaper is published, (there being no newspaper published in the county of Zapata), for four weeks previous to return day.

Dated this 22nd day of April, A.D. 1860. Pedro Dias, Sheriff, Z.C.S.T.

5. Juan N. Cortina Defends Tejanos' Sacred Right of Self-Preservation, 1859

An event of grave importance, in which it has fallen to my lot to figure as the principal actor since the morning of the 28th instant, doubtless keeps you in suspense with regard to the progress of its consequences. There is no need of fear. Orderly people and honest citizens are inviolable to us in their persons and interests. Our object, as you have seen, has been to chastise the villainy of our enemies, which heretofore has gone unpunished. These have connived with each other, and form, so to speak, a perfidious inquisitorial lodge to persecute and rob us, without any cause, and for no other crime on our part than that of

Juan Nepomuceno Cortinas to the inhabitants of the State of Texas, 30 September 1859, "Difficulties on the Southwestern Frontier," 36th Congress, 1st Session, Vol. VII, No. 52, 1859–1860, Serial No. 1050 (Washington Thomas H. Ford, Printer, 1860), pp. 70–72.

being of Mexican origin, considering us, doubtless, destitute of those gifts which they themselves do not possess.

To defend ourselves, and making use of the sacred right of self-preservation, we have assembled in a popular meeting with a view of discussing a means by which to put an end to our misfortunes.

Our identity of origin, our relationship, and the community of our sufferings, has been, as it appears, the cause of out embracing, directly, the proposed object which led us to enter your beautiful city, clothed with the imposing aspect of our exasperation.

The assembly organized, and headed by your humble servant,... we have careered over the streets of the city in search of our adversaries, inasmuch as justice, being administered by their own hands, the supremacy of the law has failed to accomplish its object....

... Three of them have died—all criminal, wicked men, notorious among the people for their misdeeds. The others, still more unworthy and wretched, dragged themselves through the mire to escape our anger, and now, perhaps, with their usual bravado, pretend to be the cause of an infinity of evils, which might have been avoided but for their cowardice.

They concealed themselves, and we were loth to attack them within the dwellings of others, fearing that their cause might be confounded with that of respectable persons, as at last, to our sorrow, did happen. On the other hand, it behooves us to maintain that it was unjust to give the affair such a terrible aspect, and to represent it as of a character foreboding evil; some having carried their blindness so far as to implore the aid of Mexico, alleging as a reason that their persons and property were exposed to vandalism. Were any outrages committed by us during the time we had possession of the city, when we had it in our power to become the arbiters of its fate? Will our enemies be so blind, base, or unthinking, as to deny the evidence of facts? Will there be *one* to say that he was molested, or that his house was robbed or burned down[?]

The unfortunate Viviano Garcia fell a victim to his generous behavior; and with such a lamentable occurrence before us on our very outset, we abstained from our purpose, horrified at the thought of having to shed innocent blood without even the assurance that the vile men whom we sought would put aside their cowardice to accept our defiance.

These, as we have said, form, with a multitude of lawyers, a secret conclave, with all its ramifications, for the sole purpose of despoiling the Mexicans of their lands and usurp them afterwards. This is clearly proven by the conduct of one Adolph Glavecke, who, invested with the character of deputy sheriff, and in collusion with the said lawyers, has spread terror among the unwary, making them believe that he will hang the Mexicans and burn their ranches, &c., that by this means he might compel them to abandon the country, and thus accomplish their object. This is not a supposition—it is a reality....

[Glavecke] *is the assassin* of the ill-starred Colonel Cross, Captain Woolsey, and Antonia Mireles, murdered by him at the rancho de las Prietas, the theatre of all his assassinations. It is he who instigated some, and aiding others, has been the author of a thousand misdeeds; and to put down the finger of scorn that ever points at him, and do away with the witnesses of his crimes, he has been foremost in persecuting us to death. The others are more or less stamped with ignominy, and we will tolerate them no longer in our midst, because they are obnoxious to tranquillity and to our own welfare.

All truce between them and us in at an end, from the fact alone of our holding upon this soil our interests and property. And how can it be otherwise, when the ills that weigh upon the unfortunate republic of Mexico have obliged us for many heart touching causes to abandon it and our possessions in it, or else become the victims of our principles or of the indigence to which its intestine disturbances had reduced us since the treaty of Guadalupe? [W]hen, ever diligent and industrious, and desirous of enjoying the longed-for boon of liberty within the classic country of its origin, we were induced to naturalize ourselves in it ... and contributed with our conduct to give evidence to the whole world that all the aspirations of the Mexicans are confined to one only, *that of being freemen;* and that having secured this ourselves, those of the old country, notwithstanding their misfortunes, might have nothing to regret save the loss of a section of territory, but with the sweet satisfaction that their old fellow citizens lived therein, enjoying tranquillity, as if Providence had so ordained to set them an example, of the advantages to be derived from public peace and quietude; when, in fine, all has been but the baseless fabric of a dream, and our hopes having been defrauded in the most cruel manner in which disappointment can strike, there can be found no other solution to our problem than to make one effort, and at one blow destroy the obstacles to our prosperity.

... Our oppressors number but six or eight. Hospitality and other noble sentiments shield them at present from our wrath, and such, as you have seen, are inviolable to us.

Innocent persons shall not suffer—no. But, if necessary, we will lead a wandering life, awaiting our opportunity to purge society of men so base that they degrade it with their opprobrium. Our families have returned as strangers to their old country to beg for an asylum. Our lands, if they are to be sacrificed to the avaricious covetousness of our enemies, will be rather so on account of our own vicissitudes.... [O]*ur personal enemies shall not possess our lands until they have fattened it with their own gore.*

We cherish the hope, however, that the government, for the sake of its own dignity, and in obsequiousness to justice, will accede to our demand, by prosecuting those men and bringing them to trial, or leave them to become subject to the consequences of our immutable resolve.

It remains for me to say that, separated as we are, by accident alone, from the other citizens of the city, and not having renounced our rights as North American citizens, we disapprove and energetically protest against the act of having caused a force of the national guards from Mexico to cross unto this side to ingraft themselves in a question so foreign to their country that there is no excusing such weakness on the part of those who implored their aid.

6. María Amparo Ruíz de Burton and Mariano Guadalupe Vallejo Discuss Intermarriage between Mexicans and European Americans, 1867

M. G. Vallejo to M. A. Ruíz de Burton

"… Do you believe that our race is inferior to the Yankee? … I believe that our blood is better and that they (the Yankees) surpass us … in mercantile spirit, industrialists, crazy without any God but money. We [have] taste, pleasures, romanticism, etc. Thus, having these two opposite elements in the mass of the blood of both races, the mixture of them cannot but produce a third, more beautiful, more energetic, stronger, sweeter in character, more temperate, and I believe stronger."

M. A. Ruíz de Burton to M. G. Vallejo

"Yes, it is true that the Yankee and the Mexican race is pretty, and 'prettier still is that of a Belgian and a Mexican,' but more attractive is that between a Protestant and a Catholic.' … Yes, it is true. The mixed races are sometimes very beautiful and good…. Onward, let this process continue, and our nationality will die walked upon by the foot of the Saxon."

7. Texas Newspaper Characterizes Poor Mexicans as Thieves, 1867

To speak within bounds, three-fourths of the inhabitants of this border town are thieves, and live more or less by stealing. In fact, the name of the thieves in this community is legion. Three-fourths of our population consists of Mexican *pelados,* born, bred, and matured thieves. They live in sinks, sewers, and shanties. They infest the alleys day and night. The habits and customs of every family in the place is intimately known to them. They will work by the day or week for almost nothing, in order to find midnight access to some depository of valuables. Not a clothes line can be stretched, not a washing of clothes can occur, that the eyes of a practiced thief does not behold the moments made.

Nine out of ten Mexican *jacal[e]s* are but receptacles for stolen goods, and nine out of ten families live by stealing. These are facts known to our whole community. What work these miscreants do is mainly for the purpose of stealing. We are suffocated and hemmed in by the most adroit thieves the world or Mexico ever produced; so adroit, indeed, that detection appears to be out of the question….

What is the remedy for these ills of which we complain? The first is to close up the alleys and all back door ingress and egress. This is the first most important

Rosaura Sánchez and Beatrice Pita, eds. *Conflicts of Interest: The Letters of María Amparo Ruíz de Burton* (Houston Arte Público Press, 2001), pp. 158–159, 270–271.

Daily Ranchero (Brownsville, Texas), May 29, 1867.

step to be taken. The entire and complete exclusion from our back doors of thieving greaser eyes....

We say abolish the alleys. They are only traversed by thieving *pelados* and are reservoirs for disease, death, and hell ... for no man nor woman, only *pelados,* dare walk the alleys after dark.

ESSAYS

The legal changes from Mexican to U.S. law at midcentury introduced widespread transformations. However, the legal effects varied because the region's states and territories implemented distinct laws. In territorial New Mexico, the national government enacted property legislation while in neighboring Texas, the state legislature had more influence over its property laws. In the first essay, María Montoya, professor of history at New York University, focuses on the owners of the vast Maxwell land grant in New Mexico as a window into the transformation of property law in the territory. The implementation of U.S. law had devastating effects on the property rights that peons and married women had enjoyed under Mexico. Peons lost the informal rights and reciprocal obligations under a *patrón* (landowner) in Mexico because U.S. lawmakers refused to recognize such rights. Married women lost specific property rights under Mexican law that protected their independent holdings. In New Mexico, married women became subject to coverture, which tied their property rights to their husbands.

The U.S. annexation of Mexico's Far North transferred control over marital issues from Mexican religious officials to U.S. civil authorities. This jurisdictional change meant the loss of Mexico's courts of conciliation, where legal officers and the local community exerted pressure over wayward spouses. While couples lost this avenue for reconciliation, they gained several legal opportunities under U.S. law. In the second essay, Omar Valerio-Jiménez, professor of history at the University of Iowa, explains that women facing domestic abuse had more direct ways of stopping the violence by charging their husbands with a crime, and U.S. courts were more likely to punish abusive husbands then were Mexican tribunals. Moreover, U.S. marriage laws gave women more independence because they removed religious marriage restrictions and made absolute divorce possible and relatively easy.

Mexican Married Women, Coverture, and Peonage

MARÍA E. MONTOYA

When Col. Stephen Watts Kearny led the U.S. Army of the West into Santa Fe in 1846 he was not merely conquering a Mexican province for the U.S.

Translating Property: The Maxwell Land Grant and the Conflict Over Land in the America West, 1840–1900, by Marísa E. Montoya, © 2003 by the Regents of the University of California. Published by the University of California Press.

government. Kearny was also leading a moral crusade against what some U.S. political leaders, such as John C. Calhoun, regarded as a despotic and feudalistic system of government and property....

[P]roponents of the U.S.-Mexican War were correct in noticing the enormous differences between the systems of land tenure dominant in Mexico and the United States, at least north of the Mason-Dixon line. The Spanish and, after 1821, Mexican governments had distributed huge land parcels through royal or executive grants to particular individuals or communities favored by the crown, president, or provincial governors.... By contrast, U.S. law distributed lands owned by the federal government through auction to the general public for standardized prices and, later, through uniform systems of possession and patent under the Homestead Act.... Such a collision of property regimes led to enormous uncertainty among people who held their property under the Spanish/Mexican system of royal or executive grant. Former Mexican citizens who were now incorporated into the United States feared that the U.S. government would confiscate their land, throw it into the public domain, and open it to U.S. settlers.

The Treaty of Guadalupe Hidalgo, which ended the U.S.-Mexican War in 1848, provided Mexican landowners with only limited legal protection. The original treaty contained Article 10, which clearly recognized the property rights that former Mexican citizens had enjoyed under Mexican law, guaranteeing that U.S. courts would be obliged to enforce their rights. But the U.S. Congress refused to ratify Article 10 because many congressmen had justified the war as a way to free Mexican *peones* from the domination of the hacienda system and the *patrón*.... Some congressmen argued that by ratifying Article 10 they would be undermining the republican ideals of equality and individualism that had justified the war in the first place. Ironically, while Congress's failure to ratify Article 10 did dispossess large Mexican landowners, particularly the Californios, the failure of Article 10 also hurt small landholders who held land through community grants.

Thus Kearny's occupation of New Mexico threw land titles into confusion, causing leading landowners such as Guadalupe Miranda to sell to people such as Lucien B. Maxwell who were willing to speculate on the validity of these Mexican land grants under U.S. law. The concern over the validity of land titles was the direct result of irreconcilable differences between the two property regimes. It was also the result of U.S. ideological hostility to what Americans saw as Mexican feudalism and the hierarchy of landowners over landless *peones*. Yet there was a deep irony in this American reluctance to recognize Mexican systems of land tenure. In refusing to enforce rights defined by Mexican law, U.S. courts ultimately relegated other members of Mexican society, married women, to the state of "feudalistic dependence" from which U.S. law was supposedly liberating Mexican *peones*. While U.S. lawmakers were quick to point out the inequalities inherent in the hacienda system, they turned a blind eye to analogous sources of hierarchy and subordination in the United States: enslavement of African Americans and unequal treatment of women. More specifically, Anglo-American law, and especially the law of coverture—which allowed husbands to control their wives' property, barring its sale, lease, or bequest without the husband's signature—was just beginning to be reformed in the United States.

Mexican law denied husbands such extensive power over their wives, because the civil law on which Mexican law was based lacked any substantial rule of coverture. Under Mexican law, a married woman could own, sell, lease, and bequeath her property without her husband's signature. By refusing to recognize Mexican practices, U.S. courts stripped Mexican married women of these rights, re-creating them as common-law dependents of the husband, master of the household.

... [T]he uncertainty surrounding land title after the U.S. conquest of New Mexico aided Lucien B. Maxwell in acquiring his vast estate.... He acquired the grant by marrying María de la Luz Beaubien, who was the daughter of the wealthy and prominent Carlos Beaubien, one of the original owners of the Beaubien/Miranda Land Grant. Maxwell obtained the core of his vast estate as the result of a dynastic alliance in the Mexican feudal tradition. He was not unambiguously the "sole owner" of the Maxwell Land Grant because his wife was co-owner of the parcel with the right to control its disposition. In fact, the doctrine of coverture may have aided Maxwell's property acquisition, for it gave Maxwell's sisters-in-law an enormous incentive to sell their holdings to him and thus avoid the legal consequences of the new U.S. property regime.

... The New Mexican system of peonage and *patrón* domination persisted after 1848 in New Mexico despite the efforts of U.S. courts to eradicate it. Lucien Maxwell continued as the *patrón* of his hacienda until he and Luz sold the grant in 1869. As feudal overlord, he owned slaves, dispensed justice among his tenants, and ruled his estate through quasi-familial relationships rather than through contractual formalities, which he disdained. In short U.S. law did not eradicate the feudalism of the *patrón/peón* system during the two decades of Maxwell's tenure. But U.S. law did install the Anglo-American feudal regime of coverture. The conquest of 1848 did not represent a radical break with the hierarchy of the hacienda system, but rather a perfection of it; the law preserved the informal quasi-familial control of *patrón* over *peón* and extended this control to the *patrón*'s wife and other female relatives.

★ ★ ★

After the U.S. victory over Mexico in 1848 and the U.S. occupation of New Mexico, Carlos Beaubien and Guadalupe Miranda became concerned about the status of their property holdings, particularly the extensive grant they had received from Governor Manuel Armijo in 1841. The two grantees, however, dealt with the changes quite differently. Miranda sold his claims and share to Lucien and Luz Maxwell soon after the Americans arrived. Miranda, a Mexican loyalist, saw no future for himself in the new territory of the United States. After Santa Fe's fall to Kearny's troops, Miranda fled over the border with Governor Armijo to Mexico, where he remained. The Beaubien family, however, took over Miranda's shares, remained on the grant, and attempted to perfect their title to the full extent of the grant's boundaries. Carlos Beaubien died before the U.S. government gave the final patent to the land grant, but his family—particularly his son-in-law, Lucien B. Maxwell—carried on the enterprise.

In 1848, while Mexicans hurried to establish their property rights, the enterprising Lucien Bonaparte Maxwell profited from this confusion by speculating that

Mexican property rights and land grants would be recognized by the United states under the Treaty of Guadalupe Hidalgo. Through his marital connections, Maxwell eventually gained control of the entire grant. As a result of his property acquisition, Maxwell was probably the richest man in all of New Mexico Territory during his lifetime, and he ran very profitable mining, ranching, and farming enterprises. These typical western American businesses, however, were not based on his own individual effort or even on that of his family. Instead, they depended on his use of feudalistic practices reminiscent of Mexican haciendas, such as peonage labor and sharecropping-type relationships between himself and his tenants. His persona as a benevolent yet often violent *patrón,* a huge hacienda owner, a wild gambler, and a generous friend has taken on legendary proportions....

The romantic mystique that surrounds Maxwell's life stems in part from his early career as a trapper and trader.... While settling himself into the [Taos] community, he courted and then, in 1844, married the thirteen-year-old María de la Luz Beaubien, one of Carlos Beaubien's six children. Beaubien, himself a French-Canadian turned Mexican trader, was by this time one of the most prominent citizens in colonial New Mexico.... Maxwell had managed to make an excellent marriage, which brought with it social mobility and financial opportunity through his wife's family.

Intermarriage between *ricas,* unmarried women from wealthy families, and outsiders such as Maxwell occurred frequently on the Mexican-American frontier and played a significant role in acculturating foreigners into New Mexican society.... Whether to establish trading alliances or to acquire property, through intermarriage Anglos allied themselves with prominent families, thus uniting the outside Anglo world with the local Hispano culture....

Maxwell['s] ... wealth and power had been derived from the more traditional alliances provided by marriage and family.... [T]he Maxwells acquired the remaining shares of the grant when Carlos Beaubien died in February 1864, leaving his estate to his six children.... As was common practice when a Mexican father passed property to his heirs, Beaubien bequeathed his interest to all of his children, male and female, in equal shares....

Over the next five years, after Beaubien's death and the acquisition of Luz Beaubien Maxwell's inherited share, the Maxwells purchased the other five undivided shares from her siblings....

... Maxwell has come to epitomize the diligent frontiersman who conquered the American West by making a large expanse of land economically profitable. Yet he did not acquire the land through the mythical attributes that have come to be associated with these so-called "pioneers": diligence, industry, and individual effort. Rather, Maxwell acquired his wealth through such Old World tactics as marriage, inheritance, and peonage. He also benefited from the change in government, capitalizing on the uncertainty that his sisters-in-law faced with regard to their own property holdings....

★ ★ ★

Historians of the Maxwell Land Grant and biographers of Lucien B. Maxwell have generally dismissed the presence of María de la Luz Beaubien Maxwell.... Luz ...

had a large family and household, which would have kept her occupied and apart from the affairs of the outside world. Furthermore, Luz spoke no English during her years on the land grant and probably did not read or write....

Nevertheless, historians cannot so easily dismiss the role of Luz Beaubien Maxwell. Historical evidence indicates that Luz was a successful businesswoman both during and after her husband's lifetime. After Lucien and Luz sold the bulk of their propertied estate in 1869, they continued to sell other parcels of property jointly. In some cases, however, only Maxwell's signature appears on deeds. These variations in their transactions suggest that Luz had influence over some aspects of their financial affairs, while Maxwell kept other dealings separate. One might even surmise that the transactions for which Lucien cosigned were for Luz's property, and that he cosigned only because U.S. law required his consent in his wife's business transactions. Furthermore, twenty years after Lucien's death, court documents show that Luz owned her own cattle business.... Luz was not a quiet and passive *doña* of the Maxwell hacienda, but an active and integral part of New Mexico's cattle industry.

Likewise, upon the sale of the whole estate to an English syndicate in 1869, Luz's signature again appears on the documents, indicating that she was the co-owner and coseller of the property....

Luz Maxwell's signing of her name was no trivial act: it signified a vast difference between the restrictive Anglo-American system and the relative autonomy women enjoyed under the Spanish-Mexican legal regime.... Prior to the U.S. conquest of New Mexico, women frequently willed property to their heirs independently, made contracts with persons outside of their family, often without the signature of their husbands, and in general disposed of their property as they chose....

Luz Maxwell's signature, under Mexican civil law, was a crucial detail in legal transactions disposing of the Maxwell estate. Since she had inherited a share of the grant from her father, and since she and her husband had acquired other shares, she shared control over such transactions, at least to the extent that Mexican law governed them. Thus she played an important legal and social role in acquiring property from her family both through inheritance from her father and by purchase from her siblings. By stark contrast, Lucien Maxwell came to New Mexico with very little capital and no real social standing. Had he not married Luz, he would have found it difficult to generate business dealings with the wealthy and influential Beaubien and Miranda families. Absent his marriage to a *rica,* he was an outsider, and a cash-poor one at that....

During the 1840s, two contradictory impulses ran through American society: liberalization of married women's status and anti-Mexican sentiment. Although since 1839 various states had been passing Married Women's Property Acts, which in theory gave more property rights to married women, the law of coverture remained quite powerful.... Though the irony provoked no comment at the time, the Married Women's Property Acts were promoting the kind of legal equality that Mexican law already took for granted. So while the status of American women, at least in theory, appeared to be improving throughout the nineteenth century, the status of Mexican women who now found themselves living under U.S. rule declined.

A female American citizen in the middle of the nineteenth century could expect to have very little control over the property she brought into marriage as dower, through inheritance, or through contract. She, unlike Mexican married women, could not make a will on her own property unless her husband gave his consent in writing to the court.... American women in the nineteenth century retained almost no control over their property and had to rely on their husbands to take proper care of their assets....

★ ★ ★

While the rest of the United States was liberalizing through Married Women's Property Acts, legislation and court cases from New Mexico's early territorial period were instituting coverture as the prescribed law for the newly conquered population. For example, territorial legislation in 1852 explicitly stated that women could engage in property transactions only if their husbands cosigned the contract. Furthermore, one of the earliest territorial cases involving the rights of married women made it quite explicit that coverture was the law. In 1857, Mariana Martínez brought before the Territorial Supreme Court a complaint against her husband, Tomás Lucero. Martínez and Lucero had been legally married for seven years but had separated amicably.... Lucero and Martínez had moved in with other partners.... Martínez sued Lucero because he was using and "wasting" the dowry she had brought to the marriage on maintaining his new family. [See Document 2.]

The territorial court disagreed, however, with Mariana's assessment of her marital situation. According to the law, [they] were still legally husband and wife....

The territorial court punished Mariana Martínez but not her husband, Tomas Lucero, for the act of adultery.... Using phrases such as "derelict in her conjugal obligations" and "sullied by the unrefuted charge of guilt," the Territorial Supreme Court of New Mexico made her responsible for the failed marriage. Furthermore, the court punished her by protecting her estranged husband's right to use her property to maintain his new family. She, on the other hand, was left with none of the money or property that she had brought into the marriage. As a married woman under U.S. common law, Martínez possessed no legal ability to control her property....

... From a legal point of view, then, affluent Mexican women had every reason to be skeptical about their ability to control property as the U.S. legal regime was gradually, but securely, being locked into place after 1848....

These changing legal conditions may have played a significant role in the decision that the Beaubien women made in disposing of their propertied interest; however, their social and economic position, as well as the location of the grant, may also explain their actions. The Maxwell Land Grant ... was far away from Santa Fe and Taos. These geographic barriers made the property difficult to work and also economically risky....

[P]eople also questioned the extent of the grant's boundaries.... The various heirs and claimants to the land grant sold at below-market prices because of pending litigation and questions surrounding the grant's validity and limits....

... During the Maxwells' tenure on the grant, however, the boundaries made little difference as they went about their business of building a home, a family, and a ranching business in the heart of what would later be patented by the U.S. Congress as a 1.7-million-acre estate....

... Another sort of uncertainty, and perhaps the most decisive reason, concerned which legal regime governed the land grant. If U.S. law applied, the Beaubien sisters would not have retained control over the estate at all: their husbands would have had legal control over the land. Their right to use the land in any manner they thought proper would have been worthless if conflict ever arose between the sisters and their respective spouses.... The sisters may have sold as a rational reaction to the likelihood that U.S. law had already stripped them of the rights they were waiving with quitclaim deeds to the Maxwells. While the women could hold cash as their own personal property, they could not hold land. Luz Maxwell, on the other hand, benefited from her sisters' strategic decisions only because she maintained a solid marriage to Lucien. Maxwell, however, suffered the unfortunate circumstance of dying relatively early in life in 1875, leaving Luz a wealthy widow. After Maxwell's death, Luz was free to act as a *femme sole,* or single woman, and run her own cattle business.

★ ★ ★

... The failure to recognize the wide variety of property rights under Mexican law was due in part to U.S. lawmakers' deep disdain for what they understood to be the hierarchical, aristocratic, and feudalistic hacienda system of land tenure in Mexico. Ironically, these were the same congressional leaders who had fewer problems justifying the continued existence of slavery, as well as women's lower political and economic status. Members of Congress had ratified the Treaty of Guadalupe Hidalgo, which legally protected the rights of Mexican citizens, but at the request of President James K. Polk, they had also refused to ratify Article 10, which specifically guaranteed the property rights of Mexican citizens. Polk and Congress ... instead assured the Mexican negotiators that land grants would be protected under U.S. law. Moreover, many congressmen did not want to give unequivocal recognition to the property rights of feudal landlords who held vast estates in Texas, New Mexico, and California. They considered such extensive land parcels inimical to the Jeffersonian ideals of equality and individualism that they imagined to be the foundation of U.S. property law....

The irony, however, was that congressional refusal to recognize Mexican property law relegated Mexican women to precisely the state of feudalistic dependence from which they intended to rescue Mexican *peones* on hacienda estates. This is to say that as a matter of plain legal description, the position of women under U.S. law and *peones* under the rule of the *patrón* were similar. Neither held clear title to property. Neither married women in the United States nor *peones* in New Mexico could use or dispose of the land they inhabited as they chose. This similar legal status, however, does not mean that Mexican married women and *peones* were ever conscious of their common subordination, let alone that they united to resist it....

To better understand the parallel relationships between married women and the *patrón,* and *peones* and the *patrón,* we must look more closely at the *patrón* and *peón* relationship on the New Mexican frontier. The modified hacienda system was part and parcel of the Mexican grant system.... The *patrón* took on the obligation of settling families on the grant, which was usually in a frontier location, as a condition of receiving enhanced acreage. In effect, the Mexican government intended *patrones* ... to be the leaders, overlords, and *alcaldes* of their communities in addition to fulfilling their responsibilities as private property owners.... While the *patrón*'s tenants had no formal legal rights recorded in any deed, they did possess a set of circumstances and informal customs that limited the discretion of the legal owner, and which informally protected their interests. The *patrón* was, in effect, head of an extended family—an informal, closely knit association. While the rhetoric of familial association may seem exaggerated, Maxwell at least respected the duties of the *patrón* insofar as he did not evict his tenants without cause....

When the United States took control of New Mexico, the debt-peonage system that provided the workforce for large ranches and farms like the Maxwell grant concerned the federal government. Congressmen were troubled by a land tenure system that placed so much land in the hands of a few owners and left a whole class of workers to fend for themselves against hacienda owners. The problems associated with *peones* and *patrones* were of particular concern in New Mexico, because the institution persisted long after U.S. occupation. In 1857, the Territorial Supreme Court first took up the issue of peonage in the case of *Mariana Jaramillo v. José de la Cruz Romero*. Mariana, a young girl of thirteen or so, ran away from her *patrón*, José de la Cruz, for reasons not outlined in the case. Romero sued Mariana and her father, claiming that she still owed him $51.75 in cash or services on her debt. The justices ruled that since Mariana was a minor ..., Romero could not force her to repay the debt and hold her in servitude. Although this was a clear-cut case, the Territorial Supreme Court took the opportunity to examine the history of debt peonage in the region and tried to make sense of where this labor relationship might fit into the U.S. legal system....

... The court found few laws that regulated the practice of people selling their labor and personhood to a *patrón*. The court concluded that in the absence of any clear, historically specific legal description, the *peón/patrón* relationship would be best viewed by the U.S. government and territorial officials as a contract in which both parties willingly engaged in the exchange of labor for credit or cash—free labor. For the court, the most important element of the contract was "the consent of the parties [which] was invariably the foundation upon which a servant became bound to service." The court also noted that the relationship went beyond economics since it was based on the "personal interests" of parties who chose to live in close proximity to one another and shared cultural and social ties as well. For example, the *patrón* often acted as a *padrino,* or godfather, to children being baptized or young couples getting married. Moreover, *peones,* servants, and even Indian slaves often lived within the familial household.

Nevertheless, although the court viewed the relationship as socially beneficial and economically lucrative, ... the court felt the relationship was basically uneven and despotic.... [A]nti-Mexican sentiment reverberates throughout the opinion.... The court detested the Mexican legal regime, with its odd labor, social, and property practices. Yet ironically, they did not seem interested in eradicating peonage.

The court's main concern was how to label, codify, and then regulate the practice of debt peonage within the U.S. legal system. This type of servant/

master relationship, while possessing many similarities to southern slavery, still held as one of its basic tenets the right to freely choose one's *patrón*.... One change the New Mexico territorial legislature made in 1852, however, was to take away from the *patrón* the legal right to punish *peones*.... [T]he court eradicated the use of corporal punishment, which had been the *patrón*'s prerogative, and instead mandated imprisonment as the only method of punishment, which was to be determined by the courts, not by the *patrón*. By agreeing to view the *patrón/peón* relationship as a contractual relationship between two "equal" and willing partners, the court deftly avoided the thorny issues that would have arisen if comparisons to slavery were made too closely....

Significantly, these debt-peonage cases more often than not involved the abuse of a woman or girl. On one side of New Mexican society, women like the Beaubien sisters could own property and control economic assets, but many, many more women lived and worked under the control of the upper classes....

While court officials rightly stopped the abuses that came before them, ... the ... cases involving ... young female children reveal the kind of abuses that took place within the debt-peonage system.... Moreover, these ... cases came to the court's attention only because the *patrón* or mistress believed that he or she had unfairly lost service due to him or her and sought legal relief. We have no evidence of *peones* using the courts to punish unfair or abusive *patrones,* which illustrates the skewed power relations between classes in territorial New Mexico, where not everyone stood as equals under the saw. The court, even with such evidence of abuse, did not seek to eradicate the entire labor system but instead contented itself with simply punishing its abuses and regulating its practices.

★ ★ ★

Maxwell inhabited the legal arena in which the U.S. government sanctioned the *patrón/peón* relationship. Indeed, he created a world of intimate and complex labor relations with his settlers who came freely, *peones* who worked the land, and Indian slaves he owned. Through his enterprises ... he attracted and settled hundreds of settlers and *peones* who worked on his land and paid him rent through in-kind payments such as crops and livestock. Maxwell also had Native American servants who were probably slaves captured during the myriad Indian wars that raged on this frontier during the late nineteenth century. Indeed, one of his closest associates, Kit Carson, was known for his role in leading campaigns against Indians and taking captured Indian children into his home. These captured Indians were often used as slaves in New Mexican households and thus were incorporated into this frontier world. In 1860 the Maxwells had three Indian servants living in their household. By 1870 the Maxwell household had fifteen servants, including seven Indians under the age of fifteen....

Maxwell comfortably played the complex role of *patrón*. While these labor relationships seem complicated and multifaceted to historians, for Maxwell his role was relatively similar whether he was dealing with his sisters-in-law, wife, slaves, *peones,* workers, lessees, or business associates. He was the leader of an insular community that depended on him to negotiate with the outside world, which was rapidly moving toward the Maxwell estate: he was the conduit through which most of the cash flowed on the grant....

The relationship between Lucien B. Maxwell and the Hispanos, almost five hundred by some estimates, ... was really a modernized Mexican hacienda system suited to New Mexico's frontier conditions. The *patrón/peón* bond between Maxwell and individual Hispanos and Jicarillas was a personal and informal relationship between dominant and subordinate persons involving nontransferable rights and duties for both. Regardless of the kind of intimacy suggested by friendship or *compadrazgo*, the tie between Maxwell and his *peones* remained mainly a financial one that was an especially lucrative one for Maxwell....

... The workers on Maxwell's hacienda produced surplus commodities for the nascent market economy created by the presence of the U.S. Army, the Indian agency, and the arrival of the Santa Fe Trail trade.

Despite the intrusion of the market into the workings of the estate, Maxwell maintained the informal economic obligations on his estate by personal ties rather than by legal contracts or state enforcement. The grant was much too extensive for Maxwell to manage single-handedly, so he allowed Mexican settlers to hold plots of land on which they built homes and farms. In turn, these settlers paid "rent" to Maxwell in grain, cattle, wool, or sheep, which he then traded to outside markets. Although not as strong as U.S. homesteaders' rights, squatters did have rights to their small parcels. In fact, Maxwell carried out the original intention of the Beaubien and Miranda grant by acting as a Mexican empresario who took a large grant of land and agreed to settle it for the Mexican government. He developed the land, brought settlers onto the estate, and created a stable economy for the migrants. Social and economic relations on the Maxwell grant were inherently unequal in terms of power, but the system was mutually beneficial because the settlers improved the land, and Maxwell protected their homes and farms from Comanche and Kiowa raids on their livestock, as well as from the Anglo settlers moving into New Mexico....

★ ★ ★

The problems that *peones* and married women faced during this early history of the Maxwell Land Grant grew out of the U.S. legal system's inability to accommodate different labor and property regimes. Consequently, Mexican land tenure, which encouraged intimate relations between *patrón* and *peón,* and married women's property rights were not preserved in their original form or with the original set of reciprocal obligations. U.S. lawmakers failed to see the economic and social functions that Mexican land grants and property systems had served and were deeply offended by the notion of haciendas and feudalism existing on U.S. soil. By replacing Mexican with U.S. land law, however, Congress encouraged the creation of a *patrón* system not for Hispano *peones,* but for Mexican married women. Women's legal position in the United States was analogous to the position of the *peón* in the *patrón* system: a theoretically benevolent and familial dependence that meant to protect those deemed incapable of participating in the property regime.

Ironically, the United States law that regulated married women's property was more feudal and paternal than the Mexican law it replaced. While they remained under Mexican law, and later after the Americans moved in—under

New Mexican custom—the Beaubien sisters were quite autonomous and free to deal with the *patrón* as they chose, at least in terms of property relations.... Under U.S. saw, and particularly as a result of coverture laws, however, the Beaubien sisters could not necessarily expect to enjoy the same rights that they had exercised earlier in their lives.

In the end, the power of market capitalism—which demanded of its participants a knowledge of markets, bonds, stocks, and interest—as well as the uncertainty of their legal status as married women under the U.S. regime, proved overwhelming for the Beaubien sisters. For them it was easier to sell their land ... to the Maxwells and move on to other enterprises. All continued to be prominent citizens of New Mexico and to engage in ranching and farming enterprises within the confines of early territorial society....

... The story for Mexican American women is a declensionist tale, a loss of autonomy as individuals capable of contracting and holding property became wards of their husbands, on whom they were legally dependent.

This transformation in property and legal regimes brought drastic changes to both the *peones* and women owners on the grant. Both suffered, but for opposite reasons. The *peones* lost because their informal property rights as squatters or tenants, recognized and enforced by the *patrón,* had no equivalent in U.S. law and consequently could not be recognized: they lost their land and livelihood. The Beaubien/Maxwell women also suffered under the U.S. system, but they lost because the very formal property tights that had been recognized under Mexican civil law were called into question. Now women had to rely on the informal communal property system established for them by U.S. law: coverture. They now had to rely on the good will of their husbands (their *patrones*) to protect their interests. In the end, both *peones* and Mexican women suffered loss of property and livelihood because their old Mexican property rights would not be incorporated into and recognized by the new system of law.

Getting Un-Hitched along the Rio Grande: Mexicans, Anglos, and Divorce

OMAR VALERIO-JIMÉNEZ

In 1834, María Nepomucena Benavides appeared in a Laredo court to accuse José María Cisneros, her husband, of striking and insulting her. Cisneros countered that he had asked Benavides about her lack of attention to their children; unsatisfied and angry at her response, he struck her. Benavides, in turn, accused him of ignoring the family upon his return from outings and dances. She also faulted his negative attitude towards their children and his refusal to help with the housework.... Benavides explained feeling overwhelmed since she was solely responsible for the housework and childcare. The court admonished the feuding

Omar Valerio-Jiménez, "New Avenues for Domestic Dispute and Divorce Lawsuits along the U.S.-Mexico Border, 1834–1893," *Journal of Women's History* 21, no. 1 (Spring 2009), pp. 10–34.

couple about their marital obligations and convinced them to reunite. The agreement, however, was obtained only after the court threatened Cisneros with punishments should marital problems persist. According to the judgment, Cisneros would incur a five-peso fine and eight days in jail if he continued to abuse his wife. The court also warned Benavides to avoid angering her husband with her responses.

This was a typical outcome for nineteenth-century domestic dispute cases in the *villas del norte* (northern towns) near the Rio Grande's mouth at the Gulf of Mexico. Spanish-Mexican residents had been living along the river since the middle of the eighteenth century when they established these seven towns. The churches, government offices, and businesses in the *villas del norte* served a population living not only in the towns but also in a geographically large rural area consisting primarily of livestock ranches. Couples who aired marital grievances before the municipal courts often felt pressured to reunite under threats of punishment. Some women resisted this pressure, but others rejoined unhappy marriages. The resolution of such marital disputes in Mexico depended on the courts, the community, and the Catholic Church. This arrangement changed abruptly in 1848 when the United States annexed Mexico's Far North. Residents of the newly annexed territory could no longer seek the municipal court's assistance in reconciling troubled marriages. But Mexican Americans, who had acquired American citizenship, did gain an easier way to end those marriages....

... Divorce in colonial Latin America was not permitted. Ecclesiastical divorce (i.e., a legal separation that prohibited remarriage) was possible but rare because numerous obstacles dissuaded couples from legally separating, including the Catholic Church's disapproval. For the American West, the opposite was true, because western states passed liberal divorce laws to attract westward-moving migrants....

This [essay] explores changes in domestic dispute and separation lawsuits created by shifting legal jurisdictions in the nineteenth century. It compares the lawsuits of residents of the Lower Rio Grande border region living under Mexican jurisdiction in the first half of the nineteenth century to those living in the same region under American jurisdiction in the second half of the nineteenth century. The jurisdictional change transferred control of marital relations from Mexican religious authorities to American civil officials.... [T]his region underwent dynamic change as different cultures, religions, and civil communities intermixed to create a new society. The transformation of domestic disputes and marriage separations illustrates an increase in women's legal freedom to resolve domestic disagreements, new legal expectations regarding spousal responsibilities, and a decrease in the legal influence of the Catholic Church over marital relations.... American annexation did not lead exclusively to negative changes; it also opened new opportunities for women.... [R]ather than being an era of decline, it was a more complex period with both positive and negative results.

If marital woes interrupted domestic life in Mexico, an aggrieved spouse could appeal to acquaintances or relatives.... [W]ives asked such male allies as relatives, priests, or employers to intervene on their behalf. Antonio Castillo of

Laredo interceded in such a manner by charging his son-in-law, Andrés García, with striking Castillo's daughter in 1834. The court sided with Castillo, reprimanding García for easily resorting to violence, and suggesting that Garcia "correct his wife's faults by scolding or advice rather than [by] blows." When persuasion did not alter their husbands' behavior, some wives left their home to live independently or with relatives. Most who did so suffered from physical abuse or a lack of financial support. However, women were still legally bound to return to their spouses.... Men initiated far fewer domestic dispute lawsuits than did women, and usually after their wives abandoned them. Once women left to escape physical mistreatment, they were unlikely to return. Often they had decided to separate permanently from their husbands—either through an unofficial arrangement or an official legal separation.

When extralegal means failed, wives filed charges in *juicios de conciliación* (trials of conciliation), accusing their husbands of a range of mistreatment, including financial neglect, physical attacks, and adultery. Trials of conciliation were held in each of the *villas del norte,* where a judge (a councilman) presided over the court with the assistance of two arbitrators (elite men). Residents of various class, gender, and racial backgrounds had access to the courts of conciliation. Seeking to preserve marriages, officials attempted to reconcile couples by reaching compromises. A successful conciliation often involved a judge's threat of future punishment should problems persist, a husband's promise to reform, and a reminder for the couple to adhere to their marital obligations. Among twenty-nine domestic dispute cases from 1832 to 1846, the courts secured eighteen reconciliations. The courts of conciliation relied on social pressure from the arbitrators, judge, and community to enforce the compromise agreement. Magistrates could also legally pressure feuding couples. In seventeen of eighteen cases where reconciliation was reached, the judge threatened or fined the couples in order to obtain their agreement.

In seeking marriage reconciliations, the civil courts followed the Catholic doctrine on marriage, which stipulated that "those whom God united under the bond of matrimony cannot and should not be parted." The civil courts' rulings predictably reminded spouses of marital obligations and Catholic responsibilities.... Thus civilian judicial officials cooperated with ecclesiastical authorities in enforcing the Catholic Church's view of marriage as a sacrament that could not be dissolved.

If marital difficulties could not be overcome, a spouse could seek an ecclesiastical divorce, but success was nearly impossible. Mexican law required that couples attend two *juicios de conciliación* before seeking a legal separation. In these civil trials, officials actively sought to preserve marriages, especially when both spouses were culpable for marital discord.... The aggressive attempts of civil authorities to reunite bickering couples ensured that few obtained permission to file for an ecclesiastical divorce....

During the first half of the nineteenth century, the Catholic Church was the only institution authorized to grant marital separations in Mexico. Since the church sought to preserve marriages, ecclesiastical divorces and annulments were very rare. An ecclesiastical divorce permitted the couple to separate legally but neither individual could remarry while their spouse still lived.... Permanent separations were granted only if a spouse (but not both) committed adultery and witnesses corroborated the transgression. Divorce was not permitted in Mexico under civil law until 1917.

The spouse who lost the separation proceedings incurred severe economic and personal penalties. An ecclesiastical divorce was granted in favor of a litigant and against her/his *guilty* spouse. A guilty man not only lost child custody, his wife's dowry, and their community property, but also was required to provide financial support for his family after the legal separation. A guilty woman lost custody of her children older than three years of age and forfeited the right to her husband's financial support. If convicted of adultery, a wife also lost ownership of her dowry and community property. The court required the guilty party to pay for court costs. These punitive consequences made the *threat* of an ecclesiastical divorce an effective tool to pressure husbands to reform.... Due to the severity of ecclesiastical divorce proceedings, a legal separation was typically the last resort for women....

Women benefited more than men did from legal separations because they gained independence and regained legal rights previously held by their husbands.... Once legally separated, women gained the right to litigate independently and to live apart from their husbands, who were required to provide them with financial support. However, enforcing this financial support after a legal separation was difficult.... The legal right to live independently was especially important for women who suffered from domestic abuse. Wives also recovered control of their dowries, their share of community property, and custody of their children. Upper- and middle-class women were more likely to seek legal separations to regain control over their property than poor women, who often chose informal separations. Economic independence proved critical for women whose husbands' lack of support had brought misery upon their family and forced them to work for wages outside the home.

During the lengthy separation proceedings, women lived in a safe-house called a *depósito*. The *depósito* protected the wife from her husband's influence and possible physical assaults while she pursued litigation. It also protected the family's honor as the residents of the *depósito* were entrusted with ensuring the wife's faithfulness; the courts did not make similar arrangements to confirm the husband's fidelity, reflecting [a] double standard of honor and sexual purity....

Husbands maintained a considerable financial advantage during legal separation proceedings because they controlled the couple's property. This economic control allowed elite men to live comfortably, hire attorneys, and to punish their wives by refusing to pay for their *depósito* expenses. The bitter disagreements during separation proceedings were further aggravated by child custody disputes....

The acrimony of legal separation proceedings increased the possibility of violence and the need for the *depósito*. Some wives feared their husbands based on past patterns of violent behavior.... In 1833, a priest testified about the danger faced by María Concepción Flores. While walking past her residence, the priest and a parishioner had come to her aid as Flores ran away from her knife-wielding husband. Subsequently, the priest placed Flores in *depósito* at his own residence while she sought an ecclesiastical divorce to escape a fifteen-year marriage plagued by physical abuse and a lack of financial support; her husband provided no support during her *depósito*. Though they urged most feuding couples to reconcile, local Catholic clergy were supportive of legal separation for marriages involving domestic violence....

Women suffering from domestic violence were the most likely to persevere through the numerous legal obstacles and press for an ecclesiastical divorce. Escaping domestic violence was women's most common reason to seek separations.... After unofficially separating from her abusive husband, one woman sought a legal separation in response to her husband's legal attempts to force her to return home. For the eleven women from the *villas del norte* who refused to reconcile with their husbands, the danger posed by their violent husbands outweighed any social stigma attached to an ecclesiastical divorce. It is unclear from extant documents if these eleven litigants were successful.

Documents from trials of conciliation and divorce petitions provide a window into legal marital expectations.... [W]omen who filed for a legal separation often contrasted their husband's violent behavior and other failings with their own fulfillment of domestic responsibilities. Their arguments, shaped by the law, strategically employed their society's prescribed gender roles, including an acknowledgement of a wife's subordination to her husband. In one petition, a woman described herself as an ideal wife who offered the "caress of a woman who is tender, friendly, and docile." Women argued that they fulfilled their domestic duties by assisting their husbands, raising their children, and preparing the family's food. In return, women expected their husbands to provide for and protect their families. One petitioner accused her husband of abusing the power entrusted to him in marriage. She observed that the canonical teachings that assigned "men as head of the home" did not have the desired legal effect when men "forgot their obligations and abused that superiority." ... Women who filed for separations were not claiming equality with men. Rather, they pursued such lawsuits because women disagreed about the extent of their subordination or believed husbands had abused their "superior position." ...

Rio Grande society underwent a great transformation in the mid-nineteenth century due to jurisdictional changes. The Republic of Texas, independent from 1836 to 1845, claimed but did not control the disputed region between the Nueces and Rio Grande rivers. Instead, Mexico held jurisdiction over the *villas del norte* until the conclusion of the [U.S.-Mexican] War in 1848. Thereafter, residents saw their communities split by the new international border.... [O]nly Laredo and Dolores ... became part of the United States.... Mexicans continued living across a vast rural area encompassing livestock ranches, but now an international boundary divided those with newly acquired American citizenship from their families and friends with Mexican citizenship.

American annexation altered the lives of Mexicans in the ceded territories. As former Mexican citizens became Mexican Americans, they gradually lost economic, political, and social power to newcomers. Anglo-American squatters, lawyers, and speculators obtained property from the old Mexican American landed elite through legal and extralegal means. Mexican Americans also struggled to adjust to an American society that criminalized their cultural activities, racialized them as nonwhite, and limited their civil rights. As Mexican Americans' occupational opportunities shifted from skilled to unskilled labor, women entered the work force in greater numbers while witnessing few gains in literacy and enduring suspicions for moral laxness. Nevertheless, Mexican Americans adapted to the new legal system by filing several types of litigation, including domestic abuse and divorce suits....

The legal avenues to combat domestic abuse in the newly annexed territory decreased after American annexation. Unlike their counterparts across the river, women in southern Texas could not appeal to courts of conciliation to resolve marital problems. This loss worked against women who sought legal means to reform their marriages. Women's first legal option was the mayor's court, where the officials were typically Anglo-American and non-Spanish-speaking. Unlike Mexican courts of conciliation, the mayor's court in Texas was not required to reconcile feuding couples, but rather to punish any violations of the law.... Women could only appeal to the mayor if they wished to charge their husbands with a crime. Some did, while others chose such extralegal means as relying on community pressure to reform their marriages....

Although courts of conciliation were not available after 1848, women in Texas gained the ability to punish their husbands for domestic violence more readily. However, women who pursued criminal charges against their husbands had to accept the possibility that their husbands' punishment might hurt their families' financial standing. In 1866, for example, Mrs. Echarete protested her husband's arrest despite suffering his vicious assault, which provoked a miscarriage and threatened to end her life; she eventually dropped domestic violence charges against him because the family needed his financial support. A mayor could impose a fine, jail time, or hard labor on public works projects for men guilty of domestic abuse.... If officials determined that a domestic abuse case involved felonious assault, they transferred the case to the district court, where men could receive up to ten years in the penitentiary.

While women in Texas lost a legal option to reconcile marriages, they gained the recourse to legally and unequivocally end marriages. Divorce was not an uncomplicated benefit for all women. Some might have preferred the option to legally reconcile their marriages rather than ending them to assume sole responsibility for supporting and raising their children. However, women who believed their marriages were unsalvageable no longer had to endure two trials of conciliation before requesting a divorce. Like marriage, divorce became a civil matter. Border residents witnessed the Catholic Church's loss of power over matrimonial matters in the United States, but its continued control over marriage in Mexico. Since American civil courts were not bound by any church's policies, Texas residents witnessed more religious freedom in matrimonial matters than their counterparts in Mexico. Texas gave the district courts jurisdiction over divorce in 1837, and four years later established precise grounds for granting a divorce. The grounds included adultery, abandonment, and cruel treatment "which made living together insupportable." Violence was not an immediate cause for divorce unless "it was a 'serious' danger and might happen again."

The availability of divorce after 1848 had a tremendous impact; the number of divorce petitions along the border in Texas increased dramatically [from just 12 lawsuits between 1849 and 1863 to 115 between 1879 and 1893].

Marital separation proceedings in Texas were similar to those in Mexico. Men continued to hold the upper hand during divorce proceedings in Texas because husbands controlled the couple's property until the divorce was finalized. The judicial audience (judges, jurors, lawyers, and interpreters) in Texas, as in Mexico, remained elite and male. However, its ethnic composition changed because Anglo-Americans were more prominently represented. Like their counterparts in Mexico, Texas women seeking a divorce typically did so because their husbands had committed adultery, inflicted physical abuse, or failed to provide financial support. Husbands usually filed for divorce after their wives abandoned them. As in Mexico, a spouse lost custody of his/her children if the court determined that he/she was guilty of adultery.

... Unlike in Mexico, where the Catholic Church might grant temporary legal separations, Texas laws granted only permanent divorces. The process was speedier in Texas.... Moreover, the Catholic Church lost all legal influence in civil court proceedings in Texas.... While few couples legally separated in Mexico, most who sought divorce in Texas succeeded. Among 169 divorce petitions in Cameron and Webb counties between 1849 and 1893, 133 (78.7 percent) were successful, three were denied, seventeen were dropped, and six were dismissed. The outcome of the remaining ten lawsuits is unknown.... The percentage of Mexican Americans suing for divorce was significant, but less than their proportion of the population....

Among the acceptable grounds for divorce, adultery was the hardest to prove in court.... The court required a plaintiff who accused her/his spouse of adultery to provide a third party as witness.... Since adultery was hard to prove, spouses of unfaithful parties frequently sued for divorce on other grounds. Adulterous spouses often deserted their marriages, so plaintiffs could charge abandonment, cruel treatment or multiple failings.... Texas laws enforced a double standard in divorce cases charging adultery. A man could obtain a divorce if his wife "shall have been taken in adultery" once. In contrast, in order to obtain a divorce based on adultery, a woman had to prove her husband "*lived in* adultery with another woman."

Texas law gave judges latitude to interpret "cruel treatment" to include both physical and mental abuse reasons for divorce. A woman could charge mental cruelty if her husband wrongly accused her of infidelity in public but failed to prove his accusation. Spouses could also be held liable for mental anguish if they repeatedly insulted, outraged, or provoked their partners.... The option to use "cruel treatment" as grounds for divorce gave women in Texas more choices to leave bad marriages than their counterparts in Mexico....

Abandonment was the easiest charge to prove. Texas law defined abandonment as physical separation with an intention to leave the marriage. An individual had to wait three years after their spouse's desertion before suing for divorce.... [A] wife who left her husband to escape his cruelty could sue for divorce based on abandonment.... Texas officials, unlike Mexican authorities, could not pressure a married woman to live with her husband. However, women in Texas could not obtain financial support while they remained separated from their husbands during the three years required to claim abandonment.... Among nineteen abandonment lawsuits in Cameron and Webb counties, seventeen were successful, one was denied, and the outcome of one is unknown....

Abandonment lawsuits depict marriages plagued by several problems. Wives described partners who were physically abusive and neglected to provide financial support. Husbands complained about wives who refused to accompany them to their present residence.... Several women ... returned to their former homes because they were unhappy with the rustic environment in southern Texas.... Spouses in Mexico also deserted their marriages without official sanction, but abandoned spouses had limited legal recourses. An abandoned wife in Mexico was required to prove that reconciliation was impossible in order to obtain a temporary legal separation. Only then could she reclaim her financial and physical independence. But the couple remained legally married. In contrast, an abandoned spouse in Texas could divorce and sever all links to the wayward partner. Divorce permitted an abandoned wife to reclaim her birth name, exercise full custody of her children, and remarry....

Lax legal and residency requirements made Texas a convenient place to divorce. Like other western states, Texas implemented liberal residency requirements to make it easier for newcomers to vote. But they also made divorce easier. By the mid-1880s, Texas consistently ranked among the top ten divorce-granting states.... The national divorce rate increased five times faster than the nation's population growth rate throughout the latter half of the nineteenth century. The number of Texas divorces was affected by the so-called "interstate divorce trade" as residents of neighboring states moved to Texas specifically to divorce....

Texas women had more freedom while divorce lawsuits were pending than did their counterparts in Mexico, who were placed in *depósito* by the courts. Authorities in Texas allowed women to arrange their own lodging. By the time they filed for divorce, most plaintiffs were living apart from their spouses. Texas law, like Mexican legislation, allowed the husband to retain control of the couple's community property while awaiting the trial's outcome. It also gave women the right to file for alimony while the divorce lawsuit was pending. Among the 169 divorce petitions ..., however, only six plaintiffs secured alimony payments. The majority of men had fled the area, and the courts struggled to enforce alimony—a trend common throughout the United States.... Women's success in securing divorces despite enduring economic hardships in the absence of alimony underscores their determination to abandon abusive marriages.

The high number of Texas divorces can partially be attributed to the relatively mild consequences of divorce under U.S. law. A legal separation was more detrimental to a spouse who lost a lawsuit in Mexico than in Texas. A guilty spouse in Mexico lost control over property and child custody. Texas courts charged the losing party with litigation expenses, but avoided exacting harsh punishments unless a party was guilty of cruel treatment or adultery. Spouses guilty of adultery forfeited their right to any community property and usually lost child custody as well....

The legal advantages of marital separations in Texas, as in Mexico, were greater for women than for men. A married woman retained ownership (but not control) of her separate property and shared ownership in the couple's community property. Her husband controlled her separate property and any community property. Furthermore, a married woman could not establish any business contracts without her husband's permission. However, divorcées regained legal control over their separate property and their share of community property in the majority of cases. They could also litigate and establish contracts freely.... For upper- and middle-class women, regaining control of their property was critical because it prevented their spouses from mismanaging or selling it. While poor women did not have property on which to rely, their legal and economic independence after divorce became critical as they became single heads of households. For example, Rosalía Galves, a fifty-seven-year-old divorcée, lived alone while working as a servant. Divorce also appealed to men because it allowed them to leave unhappy marriages, abandon aging wives, and/or absolve themselves of family responsibilities. However, women filed the majority of lawsuits until 1879, when men began filing for divorce in larger numbers. The increase is partly explained by a change in Texas divorce law that altered child custody determinations, requiring judges to consider the children's interests. As a result, magistrates usually gave custody of younger children to mothers and custody of older boys to fathers....

One of the most important consequences of divorce in Texas was the option to remarry. This option was particularly useful for individuals who had limited financial resources to provide for their children.... [L]egally separated individuals in Mexico could only appeal to friends and family for support or they could establish informal unions, but they could not legally remarry until their spouse died. Both women and men in Texas benefited from the ability to remarry because life on the border during the nineteenth century was harsh and could be considerably easier for a couple than for a single person....

Divorce petitions demonstrate that the legal expectations concerning marital relations in southern Texas had changed from those held in prewar Mexico. Texas court cases continued to describe gendered marital expectations where wives were responsible for childcare and housework while men were responsible for financial support.... In addition to caring for their children, many women worked to supplement their husbands' income. Yet husbands continued to enjoy greater legal rights than wives and marriages were not examples of domestic parity.... Nevertheless, a change did occur in the manner that spouses described their roles within marriage. Absent from divorce petitions is any mention of wives' subordination to their husbands—an essential element in marital dispute cases in Mexico. In legal records, at least, women no longer had to profess subservience in marriage in order to fulfill social expectations. Moreover, women sought divorce for reasons other than cruel treatment, in contrast to the majority of wives in Mexico. The large number of abandonment cases suggests that deserted wives could gain legal redress under Texas law by divorcing, and thus regain financial and legal independence from absent husbands. As in other parts of the American West, women in southern Texas filed for divorce more often than men (eighty-nine women versus eighty men) from 1848 to 1893.... While a legal marital separation was exclusively a female option in the *villas del norte,* it became more complicated after 1848 as men increasingly filed for divorce.

The availability of divorce in the United States provided new avenues for women and men to end troubled marriages, but the application of American laws did not create marital separations nor increase their number. Spouses in Mexico had been separating long before American annexation in 1848. Many had chosen to resolve their marital problems through unsanctioned separations, and a few attempted to obtain an ecclesiastical divorce. After 1848, American laws made divorce available for the first time in southern Texas. Subsequently, the number of legal marital separations in the region increased. Women and men left unsatisfactory marriages, obtained legal custody of their children, and remarried through civil channels. The increasing number of Mexican Americans who filed for divorce demonstrates their adaptation to a new legal system and suggests their departure from the Catholic Church's teachings on marriage. Yet spouses who divorced did not completely abandon their religious beliefs as they negotiated the contradictions between civil society and their Catholic faith. Several divorced individuals continued attending church services, baptisms, and their children's religious wedding ceremonies. Mexican American women's use of American civil courts to obtain divorces also demonstrated a willingness to exercise new rights, which gave them more power within marriage.... Nevertheless, divorce did not solve all problems.... [L]aws continued to favor men and many divorcées struggled economically after escaping bad marriages.

American annexation in 1848 began a period of economic dislocation, land dispossession, and political marginalization for Mexican Americans, but it also created new opportunities. The transfer of jurisdiction from Mexico to the United States opened new avenues for women and men to begin, negotiate, and end their marriages. Although the international border separated two distinct legal systems, it did not sever social relations. Border residents occasionally chose spouses who lived on the other side of the Rio Grande, and sometimes individuals crossed the border to escape unhappy marriages (with or without previously securing a divorce). The porous nature of the border offered some individuals a choice of legal options with radically different possibilities. After 1848, women living in the southern Texas region lost the recourse to appeal to a Mexican court of conciliation to resolve marital disputes. But these women gained the ability to more easily punish their husbands for domestic abuse crimes. They also gained the right to divorce. Domestic dispute and divorce lawsuits suggest that women in Texas enjoyed more independence than their counterparts in Mexico. The right to divorce was the most important change since it restored women's independent juridical rights and provided each spouse with the option to remarry.

FURTHER READING

Arnoldo De León, *Tejano Community, 1836–1900* (1982).

Sarah Deutsch, *No Separate Refuge: Culture, Class, and Gender on an Anglo-Hispanic Frontier in the American Southwest, 1880–1940* (1987).

William Deverell, *Whitewashed Adobe: The Rise of Los Angeles and the Remaking of Its Mexican Past* (2004).

David G. Gutiérrez, "Significant to Whom? Mexican Americans and the History of the American West," *The Western Historical Quarterly* 24, no. 4 (November 1993), 519–539.

Linda Heidenreich, *"This Land Was Mexican Once": Histories of Resistance from Northern California* (2007).

Timothy Matovina, *Tejano Religion and Ethnicity: San Antonio, 1821–1860* (1995).

John Mckiernan-González, *Fevered Measures: Public Health and Race at the Texas-Mexico Border, 1848–1942* (2012).

Eric V. Meeks, *Border Citizens: The Making of Indians, Mexicans, and Anglos in Arizona* (2007).

Pablo Mitchell, *Coyote Nation: Sexuality, Race, and Conquest in Modernizing New Mexico, 1880–1920* (2005).

David Montejano, *Anglos and Mexicans in the Making of Texas, 1836–1986* (1987).

María E. Montoya, *Translating Property: The Maxwell Land Grant and the Conflict over Land in the American West, 1840–1900* (2002).

Anthony Mora, *Border Dilemmas: Racial and National Uncertainties in New Mexico, 1848–1912* (2011).

John Nieto-Phillips, *The Language of Blood: The Making of Spanish-American Identity in New Mexico, 1880s–1930s* (2004).

Louise Pubols, *The Father of All: The De la Guerra Family, Power, and Patriarchy in Mexican California* (2010).

Thomas E. Sheridan, *Los Tucsonenses: The Mexican Community in Tucson, 1854–1941* (1986).

Omar Valerio-Jiménez, *River of Hope: Forging Identity and Nation in the Rio Grande Borderlands* (2013).

CHAPTER 4

1898: U.S. Imperialism, Conquered Territories, and Ambiguous Citizenship

The Spanish-Cuban-American War of 1898 marked the beginning of U.S. expansion overseas. By the end of the nineteenth century, the United States had realized its westward expansion across the continent through the conquest of lands formerly belonging to Native American nations and Mexico. In an 1893 essay, historian Fredrick Jackson Turner worried about this "closing" of the frontier, which had, he asserted, shaped the American character and led to the success of the U.S. economy and politics. The answer, for Turner, was foreign policy and the expansion of U.S. influence abroad. With notions of manifest destiny continuing to shape their thinking and their actions, U.S. policymakers agreed. Although ostensibly seeking markets rather than territory, the United States did acquire territory, and increased its military, political, and economic interventions in other countries.

In Cuba, the first revolt against Spanish colonial rule was waged between 1868 and 1878, the Ten Years' War. Though unsuccessful, the revolution reemerged in 1895. U.S. officials pressured Spain to protect the $50 million dollars of U.S. property in Cuba and to grant sufficient autonomy to squelch the revolution. Instead, as Spain lost control in late 1897, President William McKinley moved a warship into Havana harbor, and on February 15, 1898, an explosion sank the Maine, killing 250 U.S. sailors. The United States declared war in April 1898, hoping to gain more than the protection of U.S. lives and property. Indeed, plans had already been laid to wrest control of the Philippines from the crumbling Spanish empire. There, revolutionaries also fought to end Spanish rule, and the United States saw the opportunity for a naval base from which to maintain an open-door policy in China. Some U.S. policymakers had long desired the annexation of Cuba and now wanted Puerto Rico, as well, though others worried about incorporating multiracial populations into the United States.

96

U.S. intervention transformed Cuba's war for independence into the "Spanish-American War," eclipsing Cubans' struggles and their claims to sovereignty.

Three months after declaring war, the United States emerged as a world power. The consequences for Cuba and Puerto Rico, as well as for the Philippines and Guam, were significant and lasting. Cuba was neither granted its independence nor annexed. Instead, the United States insisted on the Platt Amendment to Cuba's Constitution, protecting U.S. rights to intervene in Cuba and to establish a military base. Puerto Rico was annexed and defined as an unincorporated territory, indicating a lack of intention to grant independence or to move toward statehood. The U.S. political sovereignty over Puerto Rico persists to this day. The new role of the United States as a world power and its willingness to intervene politically, militarily, and economically in the Caribbean and Latin America shaped Latina/o migrations in the short and long term. This chapter explores various perspectives on the Spanish-Cuban-American War and its consequences.

 # DOCUMENTS

The United States interpreted its role in 1898 differently from those affected by U.S. imperialism. In Document 1, José Martí explains Cuba's fight for independence from Spain, critiquing colonialism and asserting the existence of a Cuban nation. As war raged, the United States turned its sights beyond Cuba to other possessions of the Spanish empire. Amos K. Fisk, in Document 2, argues that the United States should take Puerto Rico as a "permanent possession," revealing popular rationalizations and racialized notions of U.S. superiority. In Document 3, Eugenio María de Hostos expresses his concern that the United States will annex Puerto Rico without the consent of the Puerto Rican people, thereby violating its own democratic principles. A week later, U.S. Major General Nelson A. Miles issued a proclamation, Document 4, declaring the U.S. military occupation of Puerto Rico in "the cause of liberty, justice, and humanity." Document 5 is an 1898 editorial cartoon portraying U.S. attitudes toward the inhabitants of its new territorial possessions. Document 6 contains excerpts from the First Organic Act of Puerto Rico, which marked the transition from a military occupation to a civilian government in 1900. The Act defined limited self-government for Puerto Rico, and declared Puerto Ricans "to be citizens of Porto Rico," a designation without clear meaning in the United States or internationally, given the colonial status of Puerto Rico. Although not rendered a U.S. colony, Cuba was also not left to determine its own future, as Document 7, the Platt Amendment of 1901, reveals. Colonial ties increased Puerto Rican migration. Document 8, excerpts of the 1903 report of the commissioner of labor, depicts the recruitment of Puerto Ricans as a source of low-wage labor for Hawai'i's sugar plantations. In Document 9, Isabel Gonzalez, plaintiff in the Supreme Court case *Gonzalez v. Williams*, criticizes the lack of self-government for Puerto Rico in her letter to the *New York Times*.

1. José Martí Explains Cuba's Struggle for Independence from Spain, 1895

The New York Herald has nobly offered the publicity of its newspaper to the Cuban Revolution waged on behalf of the island's independence and the creation of a stable Republic. As representatives-elect of the Revolution, empowered until such time as this revolution chooses leaders befitting its new form, it is our duty to explain as clearly as possible to the people of the United States and the world, the reasons, composition and purposes of the revolution fought in Cuba since the beginning of this century. The revolution has been waged heroically from 1868 to 1878, and today is revitalized through the organized efforts of this nation's sons, both within the island and abroad. Through these efforts we wish to establish an independent nation worthy of the government that releases the wealth of the island of Cuba, thus far stagnated. We wish to live in the peace which can assure man's dignity, freedom to work for its citizens, and free access by the entire world.

Cuba has taken up arms with the joy of sacrifice and the solemn determination of possible death.... [O]ur purpose has been the emancipation from Spain of an intelligent and generous people with a universal spirit but special responsibilities in America. Spain is inferior to Cuba in her abilities to adapt to the modern world with a free government. Spain wants to shut off the island—so exuberant with native strength and the native character to unleash it—from the productivity of great nations by violently oppressing a useful American nation. Cuba is the only market for Spain's industrial production, and these Cuban revenues pay for Spain's debts on the continent. In this manner Spain maintains the unproductive and wealthy class in leisure and power, a class which does not seek in manly effort the rapidly gained and plentiful fortunes which they have been expecting day after day from Spain's conquests in America and which they are obtaining from the colony's venal occupations and iniquitous taxes.

Only superficial thinking, or a certain kind of brutal disdain can, by overlooking Cuba's armed and intellectual struggle for freedom throughout this century, claim that the Cuban Revolution is the insignificant desire of an exclusive class of poor Cubans living abroad, or an uprising of the majority of blacks in Cuba, or the country's sacrifice to a dream of independence unsustainable by those who achieve it....

Cuba wants to be free so that man can there be fulfilled, so the world can go work there, and so Cuba's hidden riches can be sold in American markets where the Spanish master now prohibits her from buying.... A quick review of the national composition of Spain and Cuba would be enough to convince an honest mind of the need and justice of the revolution.... An honest mind is convinced that the two nations' objectives cause them to clash in the modern, hard-working American island's subjection to the backward European fatherland. It is convinced of the loss of modern energy in keeping an agile and good people dependent, during the world's most fraternal and hard-working era. It is convinced that this throne must deny the natural beauty of Cuba, as well as the energetic Cuban character, from working together to resolve her own superficial conflicts and those of other nations, because of the corrupt makeup of her decadent majority....

This is Spain in relation to Cuba....

2. *New York Times* Reveals Desire to Take Puerto Rico as a "Permanent Possession," 1898

There can be no question to perplex any reasonable mind about the wisdom of taking possession of the Island of Puerto Rico and keeping it for all time. There has been the same depressing misrule there as in Cuba.... The comparatively small and compact territory and the military weakness of the population have enabled Spain to crush out any attempt [at revolt] with merciless promptitude. At the same time she has taxed the little colony to help put down insurrection in Cuba as well as to enrich the Spanish officials. There can be no doubt that the people of the Island, very few of whom are Spanish by birth, would rejoice to be relieved of the oppressive and exhausting rule of Spain, although they have been powerless to resist it, and have hardly dared to give vent to a desire to be rid of it.

There is the same reason for driving the corrupt despotism of Spain out of Puerto Rico as for driving it out of Cuba, save for the melancholy difference between a hopeless submission to wrong and a hopeless struggle against it.... It is fortunate for Puerto Rico that Spanish outrages in Cuba have brought about an intervention which will rescue both islands at once. We are under a pledge to leave the fate of Cuba in the keeping of her own people when the Spanish sovereignty over them shall have been destroyed. They have created a claim to this by their own long and costly struggles for independence and by their own part in achieving it, and they have only to justify the claim by proving themselves capable of self-government and worthy of their heritage in order to become a free and prosperous nation.... But we shall free Puerto Rico from Spanish rule practically without any effort on the part of its own people.... We are not pledged to give Puerto Rico independence, and she will have done nothing to entitle her to it at our hands. Besides, it would be much better for her to [c]ome at once under the beneficent sway of the United States than to engage in doubtful experiments at self-government, and there is reason to believe that her people would prefer it. It would be in accordance with the genius of our institutions to accord them self-government in local affairs as

Amos K. Fisk, "Puerto Rico as Permanent Possession," *New York Times*, July 11, 1898, p. 6.

soon and as far as they showed themselves capable of it, and experience would soon teach them how much they had gained by their providential escape from the cruel stepmother country.

The circumstances of the conflict for the enfranchisement of Cuba and Puerto Rico fully entitle us to retain the latter as a permanent possession. Our need of a foothold in the West Indies for naval purposes has long been recognized.... Now we have it within our grasp ..., with Congress and the people in a mood for taking and keeping it, and with every just and proper consideration in favor of our doing so....

The most deliberate choice of a naval station in the West Indies could not have placed it better than the course of events, which has put the Island of Puerto Rico at our disposal.

And it is an island well worth having—the real gem of the Antilles.... In spite of misrule, exhausting taxation, and a backward state of industry, it is a populous island.... This is because the soil is most prolific and the climate exceptionally salubrious; and twice as many people could live there in ease and comfort....

Of the commercial value of Puerto Rico as a possession there is no possibility of doubt. Under a government that discouraged enterprise and prevented improvement, with an almost complete lack of roads and bridges in the interior to make communication and transportation economical, with primitive methods of cultivation and practically no manufactures, and with a stifling system of taxation and official corruption, it has supported a relatively large population and had a foreign trade of $35,000,000 a year. What is it not capable of under an enlightened policy and with a systematic application of enterprise and industry? ...

[T]he labor force [in Puerto Rico] has never been half utilized.... The white population is mainly like the native element of Cuba—creole descendants of European colonists alienated from the Spanish stock. There are many blacks, possibly a third of all the people, and much mixed blood, but the population is not ignorant or indolent or in any way degraded. It is not turbulent or intractable, and there is every reason to believe that under encouraging conditions it would become industrious, thrifty, and prosperous.... [T]he island could be rendered of no small commercial value to us and to its own people.

There is no reason why it should not become a veritable garden of the tropics and an especially charming Winter resort for denizens of the North. Apart from the attractions of climate and scenery, there is a quaint picturesqueness in the old Spanish towns, and many interesting associations with the infancy of America.... There are many relics of the aboriginal races of the Antilles in Puerto Rico.... There are neglected opportunities for the study of American ethnology in the island, as well as political, naval, and commercial advantages to be gained, and infinite attractions of tropic scenery and climate to be visited. Whatever may be said or thought of keeping the Philippines or acquiring the Hawaiians, there can be no question of the wisdom of taking and holding Puerto Rico without any reference to a policy of expansion. We need it as a station in the great

American archipelago misnamed the West Indies, and Providence has decreed that it shall be ours as a recompense for smiting the last withering clutch of Spain from the domain which Columbus brought to light and the fairest part of which has long been our own heritage.

3. Eugenio María de Hostos Fears U.S. Intentions in Puerto Rico, 1898

"It is my intention to ascertain as far as possible the plans of the United States Government relative to the disposition of Puerto Rico when that island becomes by right of capture its possession. It looks now as if my native land is destined to become American territory whether the inhabitants desire it or not, and to this I as well as many of my associates can interpose serious objections. I wish, however, at the beginning to deny any reports to the effect that several Puerto Rican Juntas in foreign countries or in this country have advised their compatriots to offer any resistance to the United States troops in any manner. I fully realize that an expression of that character made on American soil would be treason, and I am quite sure that no sane person would ever utter it.

"Should I succeed in obtaining the desired interview with President McKinley I shall endeavor to impress upon him the fact that if Puerto Rico is to be annexed to the United States it should be with the consent of its population expressed through a regular plebiscite. If the majority of the people desire it we shall all bow to the majority and accept the inevitable.

"But neither I nor any other Puerto Rican patriot and republican would like to see the American people violate their mission as a great democratic nation by forcing our native island to become a dependency of the United States, instead of assisting it to shake off the yoke of its Spanish oppressors and then leave it to build up its own independent government and work out its own destiny.

"We should be only too glad to have the American people act in the capacity of our mentors, our teachers in the art of enjoying and making use of our liberty, which to the masses of the people who have lived for so many years under the ban of Spanish tyranny is a new feeling....

"I am certainly entirely in sympathy with the course pursued in sending an expedition to Puerto Rico....

"Spain must be driven from the Western Hemisphere, and to do this requires men and arms; but there is another provision in this joint resolution which I think should not be left entirely out of sight. I refer to the declaration which says emphatically that this is not a war of conquest, but for the sake of humanity and the independence and liberty of a people entitled to both.

Eugenio María de Hostos as quoted in the *New York Times,* "Senor [sic] E. M. Hostos Talks," *New York Times,* July 22, 1898, p. 2.

"If Cuba is to be free and its people their own masters, are not Puerto Ricans entitled to the same privileges? Have we not suffered long enough under the yoke of an oppressive government and should we not have an opportunity to show our capability of governing ourselves? …

"Let them establish over all their conquered territory not a protectorate, that is too much on the order of a sovereignty, but rather a mentorate, backed by a show of actual interest, … as will insure their own interests and at the same time guarantee the rights of their protegés."

4. Major General Nelson A. Miles Declares U.S. Military Occupation for "Liberty," 1898

In the prosecution of the war against the Kingdom of Spain, the people of the United States in the cause of liberty, justice, and humanity, its military forces have come to occupy the Island of Porto Rico. They come bearing the banner of freedom, inspired by noble purpose to seek the enemies of our country and yours, and to destroy or capture those who are in armed resistance. They bring you the fostering arm of a nation of free people, whose greatest power is in justice and humanity to all those living within its fold. Hence, the first effect of this occupation will be the immediate release from your former political relations, and it is hoped, a cheerful acceptance of the Government of the United States. The chief object of the American military forces will be to overthrow the armed authority of Spain and to give to the people of your beautiful island the largest measure of liberties consistent with this military occupation. We have not come to make war against a people of a country that for centuries has been oppressed, but, on the contrary, to bring you protection, not only to yourselves but to your property, to promote your prosperity, and to bestow upon you the immunities and blessings of the liberal institutions of our government. It is not our purpose to interfere with any existing laws and customs that are wholesome and beneficial to your people, as long as they conform to the rules of military administration, of order and justice. This is not a war of devastation, but one to give all within the control of its military and naval forces the advantages and blessings of enlightened civilization.

Major General Nelson A. Miles, "To the Inhabitants of Porto Rico," July 28, 1898, as quoted in U.S. War Department, Division of Insular Affairs, *Report of the Military Governor of Porto Rico on Civil Affairs* (Washington, DC: Government Printing Office, 1902), pp. 19–20. [Accessed via Open Library.]

5. Editorial Cartoon Portrays Attitudes toward Cuba, Puerto Rico, and the Philippines, 1898

HOLDING HIS END UP

John Bull—It's really most extraordinary what training will do. Why, only the other day I thought that man unable to support himself.

6. U.S. Congress Defines "Citizens of Porto Rico" in the Foraker Act, 1900

Be it enacted by the Senate and House of Representatives of the United States of America in Congress assembled, That the provisions of this Act shall apply to the island of Porto Rico and to the adjacent islands ..., which were ceded to the United States

Fred Morgan, "Holding His End Up," *Philadelphia Inquirer,* August 9, 1898.

U.S. Congress, Fifty-Sixth Congress, Session I, First Organic Act of Puerto Rico (Foraker Act), April 12, 1900; Ch. 191, 31 Stat. pp. 77–86.

by the Government of Spain by treaty entered into on the tenth day of December, eighteen hundred and ninety-eight....

That all inhabitants continuing to reside therein who were Spanish subjects on the eleventh day of April, eighteen hundred and ninety-nine, and then resided in Porto Rico, and their children born subsequent thereto, shall be deemed and held to be citizens of Porto Rico, and as such entitled to the protection of the United States, except such as shall have elected to preserve their allegiance to the Crown of Spain on or before the eleventh day of April, nineteen hundred, in accordance with the provisions of the treaty of peace between the United States and Spain ...; and they, together with such citizens of the United States as may reside in Porto Rico, shall constitute a body politic under the name of The People of Porto Rico, with governmental powers as hereinafter conferred, and with power to sue and be sued as such.

That the laws and ordinances of Porto Rico now in force shall continue in full force and effect, except as altered, amended, or modified hereinafter, or as altered or modified by military orders and decrees in force when this Act shall take effect, and so far as the same are not inconsistent or in conflict with the statutory laws of the United States not locally inapplicable, or the provisions hereof, until altered, amended, or repealed by the legislative authority hereinafter provided for Porto Rico or by Act of Congress of the United States....

That the official title of the chief executive officer shall be "The Governor of Porto Rico." He shall be appointed by the President, by and with the advice and consent of the Senate; he shall hold his office for a term of four years and until his successor is chosen and qualified unless sooner removed by the President; he shall reside in Porto Rico during his official incumbency, and shall maintain his office at the seat of government....

That there shall be appointed by the President, by and with the advice and consent of the Senate, for the period of four years, unless sooner removed by the President, a secretary, an attorney-general, a treasurer, an auditor, a commissioner of the interior, and a commissioner of education, each of whom shall reside in Porto Rico during his official incumbency and have the powers and duties hereinafter provided for them, respectively, and who, together with five other persons of good repute, to be also appointed by the President for a like term of four years, by and with the advice and consent of the Senate, shall constitute an executive council, at least five of whom shall be native inhabitants of Porto Rico....

That all local legislative powers hereby granted shall he vested in a legislative assembly which shall consist of two houses; one the executive council, as hereinbefore constituted, and the other a house of delegates, to consist of thirty-five members elected biennially by the qualified voters....

At such elections all citizens of Porto Rico shall be allowed to vote who have been bona fide residents for one year and who possess the other qualifications of voters under the laws and military orders in force on the first day of March, nineteen hundred, subject to such modifications and additional qualifications and such regulations and restrictions as to registration as may be prescribed by the executive council....

That all laws enacted by the legislative assembly shall be reported to the Congress of the United States, which hereby reserves the power and authority, if deemed advisable, to annul the same....

All pleadings and proceedings in ... court shall be conducted in the English language....

That the qualified voters of Porto Rico shall ..., every two years thereafter, choose a resident commissioner to the United States, who shall be entitled to official recognition as such by all Departments, upon presentation to the Department of State of a certificate of election of the governor of Porto Pico.... *Provided*, That no person shall be eligible to such election who is not a bona fide citizen of Porto Rico, who is not thirty years of age, and who does not read and write the English language.

7. U.S. Shapes Cuba's Constitution with the Platt Amendment, 1903

Whereas the Congress of the United States of America, by an Act approved March 2, 1901, provided as follows:

... That in fulfillment of the declaration contained in the joint resolution approved April twentieth, eighteen hundred and ninety-eight, entitled "For the recognition of the independence of the people of Cuba, demanding that the Government of Spain relinquish its authority and government in the island of Cuba, and withdraw its land and naval forces from Cuba and Cuban waters, and directing the President of the United States to use the land and naval forces of the United States to carry these resolutions into effect," the President is hereby authorized to "leave the government and control of the island of Cuba to its people" so soon as a government shall have been established in said island under a constitution which, either as a part thereof or in an ordinance appended thereto, shall define the future relations of the United States with Cuba, substantially as follows:

"I. That the government of Cuba shall never enter into any treaty or other compact with any foreign power or powers which will impair or tend to impair the independence of Cuba, nor in any manner authorize or permit any foreign power or powers to obtain by colonization or for military or naval purposes or otherwise, lodgement in or control over any portion of said island."

"II. That said government shall not assume or contract any public debt, to pay the interest upon which, and to make reasonable sinking fund provision for the ultimate discharge of which, the ordinary revenues of the island, after defraying the current expenses of government shall be inadequate."

"III. That the government of Cuba consents that the United States may exercise the right to intervene for the preservation of Cuban independence, the maintenance of a government adequate for the protection of life, property, and individual liberty, and for discharging the obligations with respect to Cuba

Treaty Between the United States and the Republic of Cuba Embodying the Provisions Defining Their Future Relations as Contained in the Act of Congress Approved March 2, 1901, signed May 22, 1903; General Records of the United States Government, 1778–2006, RG 11, National Archives.

imposed by the treaty of Paris on the United States, now to be assumed and undertaken by the government of Cuba."

"IV. That all Acts of the United States in Cuba during its military occupancy thereof are ratified and validated, and all lawful rights acquired thereunder shall be maintained and protected."

"V. That the government of Cuba will execute, and as far as necessary extend, the plans already devised or other plans to be mutually agreed upon, for the sanitation of the cities of the island, to the end that a recurrence of epidemic and infectious diseases may be prevented, thereby assuring protection to the people and commerce of Cuba, as well as to the commerce of the southern ports of the United States and the people residing therein."...

"VII. That to enable the United States to maintain the independence of Cuba, and to protect the people thereof, as well as for its own defense, the government of Cuba will sell or lease to the United States lands necessary for coaling or naval stations at certain specified points to be agreed upon with the President of the United States."

"VIII. That by way of further assurance the government of Cuba will embody the foregoing provisions in a permanent treaty with the United States."

8. Puerto Rican Contract Laborers in Hawai'i, 1903

Hardly a locality in the world exists where there is a surplus of unskilled labor that has not been visited and investigated by Hawaiian labor agents. Attempts to recruit field workers have been made in many European countries, in various parts of the United States, in the East Indies, the islands of the Pacific, and in Asia, but nowhere was a people found combining the civic capacity to build up a state with the humility of ambition necessary for a contract laborer.

The present plantation labor of Hawaii, exclusive of skilled labor and superintendence, is composed of a few Europeans and Portuguese from the Azores, Hawaiians, American Negroes, Porto Ricans, Chinese, and Japanese....

The Porto Ricans ... gave the least promise, either as citizens or as laborers, of any immigrants that ever disembarked at Honolulu. The men had been carelessly recruited at a time when the laboring population of Porto Pico was in a condition of acute distress.... They were mostly people from the coffee country of their own island, who had been starved out of the mountains when that region was devastated by the hurricane of 1899. This was followed by a year of idleness, semidependence, and mendicancy in the coast country before they left for Hawaii. They were half starved, anæmic, and, in some cases, diseased. A considerable number of petty criminals, wharf rats, and prostitutes from Ponce and other coast towns accompanied them. They were not so much representatives of the people of Porto Rico as of famine and misery in the abstract when they arrived in Honolulu.... But this was hardly the fault of the Hawaiian planters, who spent nearly $565,000 to get these men, or more than $192 passage

---

Report of the Commissioner of Labor on Hawaii, 1903, Bulletin of the Department of Labor, No. 47, Washington, D.C.

money and recruiting expenses for every adult male arriving, and who were practically interested in their physical well-being....

The hardships of traveling merely prevented any recuperation from the deplorable physical condition in which they had left their homes. When they reached the plantations where they were to be employed, many ... were taken directly to the hospitals, which some of them never left alive. Those who were not actually ill were in no condition to work and had to be fed with specially prepared food for some weeks before they could do a full day's labor in the fields.... They were morally upset by their long travels and changed environment, and many could not acquire the new habits of life necessary to their new condition. So a considerable number became strollers and vagabonds, and, wherever possible, flocked into the towns....

The Porto Ricans arrived in Hawaii in 11 expeditions, beginning in December, 1900, and continuing until October 19, 1901. There were about 450 in each party, the total number of immigrants being about 5,000, of whom 2,930 were men and the remainder women and children....

[T]he planters appear to have fully kept their side of this agreement. In most cases, however, the men have left the plantations originally employing them and wandered from place to place, taking such positions as their fancy or necessity dictated, like other free agricultural laborers....

The Porto Ricans, on their part, have not been uniformly contented with the conditions they have encountered in Hawaii. Complaints of ill usage and injustice were made. It was claimed that they were charged exorbitant prices at the plantation stores, and were obliged to be at work at unreasonably early hours. A careful investigation failed to disclose any extortion in the prices charged by the plantation stores or any discrimination as to hours of labor.... The hours of labor generally observed in Hawaii would naturally seem a hardship to those accustomed to the somewhat easy going Porto Rican methods. Other plantation laborers work rainy days as a matter of course, but over this point considerable trouble with the Porto Ricans in Hawaii occurred.... [T]he industrial regimen of the islands is a strict one. Hawaii is a country where no encouragement is given to idlers. It is probably the most energetic tropical country in the world.

But the condition of the Porto Ricans in Hawaii has another and pleasanter side. The hopelessly ill have died, some of the discontented have left for California, and the criminal element has been largely weeded out of the working population in the country. There remains upon the plantations a considerable body of fairly efficient laborers. Representatives of these were interviewed upon all the islands, and without exception they were satisfied with their present condition. There are 539 Porto Rican children in the schools of Hawaii, enjoying educational facilities that are exceedingly rare in their own country. Some of the better educated men are employed in positions of responsibility, as overseers, storekeepers, office men, and mechanics. Intelligent medical treatment, wholesome diet, and steady labor have improved both their physical condition and their morale. They have lost the dejected, drooping walk that characterized them on their arrival, and step out as freely and vigorously as the jaunty little Japanese. Some of them are saving money....

Of course many of the men are homesick, and probably a very large majority of them would welcome an opportunity to return to Porto Rico....

From the planters' point of view an important result of the Porto Rican immigration was the moral effect that their arrival had upon the Japanese. The latter had begun to fancy that with the enforcement of the Federal Chinese exclusion and contract laws after annexation they were complete masters of the labor situation in Hawaii. They formed temporary combinations for the purpose of striking at critical periods of the planting and grinding season, and in this way had succeeded in forcing up wages.... The regular arrival of monthly expeditions of Porto Rican laboring people throughout an entire year largely disabused them of this sense of monopoly and made them much more reasonable in their relations with their employers.

The ultimate effect of the Porto Rican immigration upon the islands will probably be unimportant. Those who remain will doubtless amalgamate more or less with the Portuguese during their transition into Hawaiian Americans. They and their descendants will in all probability be vastly better off than they had any prospect of being in their own country.... His careless disregard of cleanliness renders the Porto Rican a less pleasant neighbor or employee in many respects than an Oriental. But to an outside observer it would seem that despite all his faults he is more desirable as a permanent settler. He possesses the heredity of the Caucasian, and with the discipline of regular work and the encouragement of the social and political environment he finds in Hawaii, he ought to turn out in the course of time a fairly intelligent and industrious citizen.

9. Plaintiff Isabel Gonzalez Voices Demands for Puerto Rico, 1905

As for the selection of the persons to be nominated for office in Porto Rico, the nominations that the island will accept as fitting and proper must not be made in Washington but in San Juan....

The selection should be made by the insular public opinion. This is the only course that will satisfy the Porto Ricans, and Congress please take notice that there will not be moral peace in the island while the actual conditions exist. We know more about our own affairs than the President does; we are more concerned about our future than the President is; and just as New York and Philadelphia do not allow the Chief Magistrate to appoint any individual to be local ruler, so in Porto Rico we cannot tolerate anything of that kind.

The country wants its own.... We are going to ask that our own [liberties and franchises] be given back to us—those that we exercised when Gen. Miles went to Porto Rico to save us, and proclaimed to the wide winds his "liberating" speech, which turned out later to be nothing but bitter mockery and waste paper.

Isabel Gonzalez, "What Porto Rico Demands," *New York Times,* December 20, 1905, p. 10.

 # ESSAYS

The United States' empire building affected many countries and peoples, often limiting their self-determination and their self-government. In the first essay, John Nieto-Phillips, professor of history and Latino Studies at Indiana University, explores how the United States limited self-government for Mexican Americans in New Mexico and for Puerto Ricans in Puerto Rico. He focuses on the impact of U.S. imperialism and of U.S. racial ideologies in both locations. Developing a comparative historical approach, he argues that Mexican Americans and Puerto Ricans were "linked by parallel struggles for greater political empowerment through self-government." In the second essay, Sam Erman, a sponsored affiliate at the University of Michigan, homes in on a 1904 Supreme Court case to explore how the United States laid the groundwork for an ambiguous and second-class citizenship for Puerto Ricans coming to the continental United States. In *Gonzalez v. Williams*, the Supreme Court ruled that Puerto Rican Isabel Gonzalez was not an alien in terms of U.S. immigration law and hence should be admitted to the country. Yet the Court declined to rule on whether Gonzalez and other Puerto Ricans were citizens of the United States. For Erman, the details surrounding this case and the decision itself provide the basis for an analysis of the ways in which inequalities among U.S. citizens were crafted on the foundations of empire, race, and gender. In the third essay, Gerald Poyo, professor of history at St. Mary's University, explores how political and economic ties between the United States and Cuba shaped Cuban migration and the experiences of Cubans in the United States before and after 1898. Both the political turbulence in Cuba, as it struggled for independence from Spain, and the international cigar industry were key to the movements of capital and people between the two countries.

U.S. Imperialism Limits Self-Government in New Mexico and Puerto Rico

JOHN NIETO-PHILLIPS

Puerto Rican and Mexican American—or, in this case, New Mexican—pasts have been shaped by very distinct forces and circumstances. Yet they remain linked by parallel struggles for greater political empowerment through self-government. Those struggles converged and overlapped most clearly between 1898 and 1917. During this age of confident imperialism, as Congress debated the political status of the nation's continental territories and newly acquired islands, the peoples of Puerto Rico and New Mexico sought to redefine their relationships to the United States' body politic. Central to the respective outcomes was how local and national leaders contested the notions of citizenship and self-government.

John Nieto-Phillips, "Citizenship and Empire: Race, Language, and Self-Government in New Mexico and Puerto Rico, 1898–1917," *Centro: Journal of the Center for Puerto Rican Studies* (Fall 1999), pp. 51–74.

During the latter part of the nineteenth century and beginning of the twentieth, "self-government" connoted several things, depending upon the context in which it was invoked. In the case of New Mexico, taken by the U.S. from Mexico in 1848 along with most of the present-day Southwest, it invariably meant statehood. Admission into the Union, proclaimed the territory's political factions—predominated by merchants, property owners, and a small but growing number of Anglo-American immigrants—would empower local officials elected by the largely Mexican populace by providing it with greater control over natural resources and political offices. At the same time, statehood would substantially limit the ability of the federal government to administer the territory's resources from afar while denying them voting representation in Congress....

In the case of Puerto Rico, however, self-government meant something entirely different. When the United States invaded the island in 1898, Spain had just months before granted it an autonomous government. Some Puerto Rican leaders felt that under U.S. protection the island's interests ... would be best served if it were annexed to the United States. Annexation, they believed, would lead either to an autonomous relationship with the United States similar to that which the island had initiated with Spain or to eventual incorporation into the Union as a state. But during the early years of U.S. occupation, Congress repeatedly ruled out statehood and, instead, imposed on Puerto Rico a restricted civil government headed mostly by U.S. officials. This move emboldened local movements for greater autonomy or independence. With the Foraker Act (1900) [See Document 6] and the Insular Cases (1901–1905) the United States equivocated on its promises of self-government and revealed its true design for Puerto Rico: to maintain the island as a possession. In the years leading up to the 1917 Jones Act, which proclaimed Puerto Ricans U.S. citizens and declared the island an unincorporated U.S. territory, calls in Puerto Rico for greater integration into the metropolis via statehood were matched by calls for greater autonomy and even complete separation or national sovereignty. Thus, unlike the case of New Mexico, self-government in Puerto Rico meant several things, depending on the individual or group who invoked it, including autonomy or independence.

U.S. citizenship, too, connoted many things during this period, and possessed qualifications based on—among other things—an individual's "race," education, and gender. As numerous scholars have pointed out, U.S. citizenship did not apply equally to men and women; rather, there existed a range of intersecting subordinate forms. "Full" citizenship—which involved an array of political rights and obligations to the state—accrued primarily to white men. This fact was so broadly understood among politicians in Washington, New Mexico, and Puerto Rico that, during congressional debates over the political status of the two territories, lawmakers made almost no direct reference to women's suffrage, property rights, or civic obligations. Instead, they focused on race and language as the defining features of U.S. citizenship. Prior to ratification of the Fourteenth Amendment in 1868, which extended citizenship to persons of African descent, U.S. citizenship was limited to "white" persons. Yet even after the amendment's ratification (and well into the twentieth century), a racial qualification remained in effect for persons seeking citizenship. As Ian Haney López points out in his recent monograph, one had to be "white by law" to become a naturalized citizen. It serves to reason, then, that when New Mexico sought statehood, detractors pointed to the mixed (Spanish and Indian) blood of the population, noting that few nuevomexicanos could claim sufficient "white blood" in their veins to qualify as full participants in the nation's (or their own) political affairs. Similar charges were leveled against Puerto Ricans, whose "African blood" some congressmen judged undesirable (though legally permissible) for U.S. citizenship. Arguments against statehood for New Mexicans and citizenship for Puerto Ricans largely hinged on their not being "white enough" for full incorporation into the body politic, a charge that leaders in both lands vehemently denied. Indeed, to the extent they downplayed the degree of non-white blood in themselves and in their constituents, local leaders were complicit in maintaining the racial standard. Language, too, represented a criterion for citizenship. English was widely accepted—even by people of the territories—to be the lingua franca of the United States' body politic. Those who aspired to U.S. citizenship often declared themselves eager to learn English, but not at the expense of their native language and culture....

Born in very different contexts, the quests for self-government in New Mexico and Puerto Rico illustrate how the United States' imperialist actions and racial ideologies went hand in hand, each justifying the other, both rendering subordinate forms of U.S. citizenship.

★ ★ ★

When U.S. troops invaded Santa Fe in August, 1846, they were met with limited resistance.... Many Mexicans opposed the U.S. invasion and, for years to come, defended their land and lifeway against Anglo-American encroachments. Others, however, including some landed families, merchants, and military officers, initially welcomed los americanos.... The people of New Mexico, leaders believed, would soon reap the benefits of increased commerce and more political autonomy and would form their own state and local political institutions, thereby gaining the kind of self-determination long denied them by Spain and Mexico. Their swelling optimism, however, faded when they realized that few congressmen would ever be willing to support the formation of a state comprising more than fifty thousand Mexicans and about ten thousand Native Americans. Rather than grant New Mexico statehood, Congress, after replacing its military regime with a civil one in 1850, proclaimed it an incorporated U.S. territory....

Under the Treaty of Guadalupe Hidalgo, which marked an end to U.S.-Mexican hostilities in 1848, U.S. citizenship was conveyed to Mexicans residing in the vanquished land. [See Document 3, Chapter 2.] ... [F]ew lawmakers in Washington viewed Mexicans as racially white.... [T]he taking of Mexican soil gave rise in Congress to questions about Mexicans' racial character, presumed "fitness" for democracy, and relationship to the nation's body politic....

Thus, "Mexican" evolved into a social category unto itself, at once racial and political in nature. Although, by law, Mexicans were held to be U.S. citizens, they were more often deemed by self-identified "Anglo-Saxons" to be not just different in racial and national origins, but inferior in both regards. This perception ... generally prevailed throughout the country and justified Anglo-American efforts ... to obstruct the political rights of Mexicans who had become U.S. citizens....

New Mexico's political status was swept into the volatile mix of sectional (North-South) politics. Anticipating swift admission into the Union in 1850, a group of Santa Fe politicians drafted a state constitution in which they declared, among other things, that New Mexico would forever remain free of slavery. This prompted southerners in Washington to oppose New Mexico's admission. As part of the Compromise of 1850, which made California a state, New Mexico was proclaimed an incorporated territory of the United States....

[I]n 1876, frustrated at congressional inaction, Santa Fe lawmakers began to demand statehood based on their constitutional rights and on the promise of self-government that the United States had made in the Treaty of Guadalupe Hidalgo. By maintaining New Mexico's territorial status, they argued, Congress had breached that treaty and rendered to New Mexicans an inferior form of citizenship. They had become, effectively, citizen-subjects of the federal government.... Whereas, earlier, the assembly's petitions were met with indifference, the 1876 entreaty drew virulently racist responses from certain lawmakers. Opponents contended that New Mexico possessed neither the "population, industry, intelligence, [nor the] wealth to entitle this Territory to admission in the Union as a sovereign state." It remained too "savage" and "undemocratic" to merit a state government, they said....

Over the next three decades, popular opposition to New Mexico's admission mounted....

Although ... Mexicans were proclaimed U.S. citizens and were, therefore, ostensibly "white by law," they were not perceived or treated as such.... Most white U.S. citizens, however, did not interact with Mexicans in face-to-face situations, but relied on newspapers and magazines for their stereotypes and opinions. Throughout the nineteenth and well into the twentieth century, these journals depicted Mexicans (including nuevomexicanos) as nonwhite and as "grossly illiterate," "morally decadent," indolent, idolatrous, and mixed-blood "greasers." ...

By the twentieth century, ... [s]tatehood proponents—Anglo-Americans and nuevomexicanos alike—made congressional approval of statehood possible by recasting as "Spanish" nuevomexicanos' racial geneology, culture, and history, and as "American" their citizenship and national loyalty.

Though citizenship turned on whiteness, it was also predicated on linguistic homogeneity. Since English was widely accepted and promoted as the exclusive code of the body politic and as a qualification for citizenship, it is not surprising that English-language acquisition became a principal objective of statehood proponents in New Mexico, prompting officials (both nuevomexicanos and Anglo-Americans) to pursue the expansion of the public school system.... Nuevomexicano educators readily agreed with their Anglo-American counterparts that the teaching of English was crucial to the enterprise of molding students into model citizens. But they also held that students should be fully literate in their native Spanish as well as English and consequently advocated instruction in both languages....

Between 1891 and 1903, Congress rejected more than twenty statehood bills for the territory....

By 1906 the growing influx of whites from the East and Midwest—both as tourists and as transplants to the region—served to countervail earlier congressional impressions of New Mexico as a mostly nonwhite territory....

[A] powerful senator from Indiana, Albert J. Beveridge, ... who would be instrumental in the Puerto Rico debates, succeeded in stalling action on a statehood bill until 1910, when, at the urging of President William Howard Taft, Congress passed separate statehood bills for New Mexico and Arizona. Two years later, both officially entered the Union. Beveridge nevertheless managed to insert into the legislation a provision calling for English to be the exclusive language of instruction. That provision, however, was successfully challenged by nuevomexicano delegates to New Mexico's constitutional convention.... Thus, in 1912 New Mexico entered the Union as (and today remains) the only state to possess two official languages—English and Spanish....

Despite New Mexico's admission, many Anglo-Americans remained unconvinced that New Mexico's "Spanish Americans" were sufficiently white or English-speaking to merit a role in self-government and, therefore, continued to deride them as "a race speaking an alien language" and a people not possessing the "best blood on the American continent." Discrimination, territorial displacement, linguistic suppression, Americanization, cultural commodification through ethnic tourism, and political subjugation followed statehood as more and more Anglo-Americans streamed into the state. The admission of Arizona and New Mexico in 1912 may have signaled the official end of Manifest Destiny, or continental expansion.... While Congress closed this chapter in its imperialist record, it was still grappling with the results of its misdeeds elsewhere, particularly in the Caribbean.

★ ★ ★

The U.S. invasion of Puerto Rico in 1898 marked the end of one colonial era for the island and the beginning of another. Because the assault liberated Puerto Rico from Spain's colonial grasp, it was initially welcomed by many. Liberation promised great things, assured General Nelson Appleton Miles. [See Document 4.] ... The United States' ultimate aim, however, was to acquire a strategic naval base from which to carry out future military, economic, and political designs in the Caribbean; for the island, from the outset, was but a pawn in the larger scheme of U.S. military expansion and its quest for new markets. Very soon it became transparent that leaders in Washington were more interested in the island's strategic value than in the well-being of its people, prompting Puerto Rican leaders, like Eugenio María de Hostos [See Document 3] ... and Luis Muñoz Rivera, to insist on more say in the island's internal affairs and its relationship to the United States. Over the next two decades, they called, variously, for national independence, for some form of political autonomy vis-à-vis the United States, or for U.S. citizenship as an initial step toward possible admission as a state. But Washington lawmakers seldom heeded their calls.

Although the geographic and historical contexts, as well as outcomes, differed significantly, congressional debates over Puerto Rico's status sounded much like New Mexico's debates, which both predated and coincided with them. U.S. lawmakers wrestled with similar patronizing questions that revealed their unequivocal belief in white Anglo Saxon supremacy and in the United States' superiority: Did the guarantees of the Constitution extend to peoples of the new possessions? Of what race are the people, and are they entitled to either U.S. citizenship or self-government? …

By 1900 Congress was of two minds about its new possessions. On the one hand, there were those who believed that the United States possessed a special mission—a so-called white man's burden—to liberate, uplift, educate, and civilize nonwhite countries; to teach them presumably Anglo Saxon, Protestant values, such as hard work, thrift, hygiene, and honesty; to apprentice them in the virtues and practice of republican government; and to prepare them for their ultimate destiny: independence. Until the civilizing mission was achieved, argued the imperialists, the holding of colonies was perfectly justified. But this mission was not merely altruistic, for it promised material returns, as Senator Chauncey Mitchell Depew of New York that year pointed out. Depew reminded his colleagues that the United States could maintain possession of other lands, irrespective of the will of their inhabitants.

> Puerto Rico, Hawaii, Guam, Tutuila, and the Philippines are to be held and governed by the United States with an imperative duty on our part to their civilization …, and also for their and our commercial progress and growth. I do not believe we will incorporate the alien races, and civilized, semicivilized, barbarous and savage peoples of these islands into our body politic as States or our Union.…

Despite their rhetoric about eventually liberating the islands, imperialists like Depew saw many advantages in making them permanent fixtures in the United States' domain. To that end, the civilizing mission was a perfect justification for delaying indefinitely the granting of self-government in the form of independence. And since statehood was repeatedly deemed out of the question, perpetual political limbo was the status many imperialists advocated for U.S. possessions.

Anti-imperialists, on the other hand, feared that continued expansion would only yield deleterious consequences for U.S. workers and industry. It would lead to an oversupply of cheap nonwhite labor and products that would reduce the wages of white workers at home; it would open the floodgates to immigration and bring about the "contamination" of white society by what one California anti-immigration league referred to as "the mongrel breeds" of the world; and it would pave the way for the corruption of the body politic by persons believed not capable or worthy of citizenship. Though anti-imperialists shared with imperialists a deep conviction about white (and, more specifically, Anglo-Saxon) supremacy, they disagreed on the means by which supremacy should be institutionalized. Less, not more, U.S. engagement in the nonwhite world was needed, they said, for if the people of the possessions were indeed capable of eventual self-government, as their counterparts argued, then they ought to be set free to establish their own governments without delay, and not a thought should be given to their admission into the United States as citizens or as states. Hence, any mention of a permanent relationship to the metropolis aroused fierce anti-imperialist resistance.

Among U.S. possessions, Puerto Rico was exceptional, claimed the imperialists, because it owned many distinguishing traits that made it an invaluable asset, to be maintained as a permanent possession. [See Document 2.] ...

Discontentment in Puerto Rico was born out of colonial oppression and continued subjugation by foreign powers.... By way of the Autonomist Charter of 1897, Spain had accorded the island ... equal political status with peninsular Spaniards and local self-government. That apparatus, however, was quickly dismantled by U.S. officials following the invasion. Congress then set about defining the future political status of the island and its people. Though Puerto Ricans initially demanded preservation, in some form, of their autonomous government, their demand went largely ignored. They began to ask themselves and Congress when they were to reap the promised benefits of their liberation from Spain and enjoy their own government.... [A]sked a group of nine Puerto Rican leaders in a memorial to Congress, ... "Are we citizens or are we subjects? Are we brothers and our property territory, or are we the bondmen of a war and our island a crown colony?" Claiming to represent "the people of Puerto Rico and their interests," these leaders—among them Tulio Larrínaga, Puerto Rico's delegate to Congress between 1905 and 1911—called for an end to the United States' military government of the island....

Invoking the very racial criteria that had been used to deny New Mexico statehood, these Puerto Rican leaders pointed to the presumed whiteness of most of their countrymen as a fulfilled qualification for U.S. citizenship and territorial status. There was no reason why Puerto Rico should not join Arizona, New Mexico, and Oklahoma in gaining such a status, petitioners argued.... This argument apparently gained the favor of Senator Alfred Allen of Ohio, a proponent of granting territorial status and U.S. citizenship.... In the minds of some congressmen, all Spanish-speaking people, including New Mexicans and Puerto Ricans, were of mixed race but counted among them a sufficient number of "pure blood" whites to merit (and be capable of) self-government.... Puerto Ricans, [other congressmen] argued, had not yet acquired the language, habits, or culture of the metropolis that would allow them to become integral members of its citizenry; moreover, their island was far too valuable a U.S. possession—and the people supposedly still ill prepared—to grant it national independence or autonomy. One proponent of granting citizenship without self-government was Senator Joseph Benson Foraker of Ohio, who retorted simply that Puerto Ricans were not entitled to "rights that the American people do not want them to have." ... Foraker's citizenship proposition failed to make it into the final version of his bill in 1900; rather, islanders were declared to be "citizens of Porto Rico," a title that bore no official political status and that, U.S. officials later claimed, was never meant to imply Puerto Rican sovereignty....

During deliberations over legislation that bore his name, Senator Foraker concluded that very few Puerto Ricans could read or write, that none of them had experience in democratic self-government, and that few could even conceive of U.S.-styled institutions of government. "They are of the Latin race," he pronounced, "and are of quick and excitable temper, but they are at the same time patient, docile, frugal, and most of them industrious." ... This characterization ... made the case to "Americanize" the island all the more compelling and set in motion a campaign to impose the English language on the schoolchildren and "teach" them the values, history, and ways of white U.S. citizens.

Rather than clarify the status of Puerto Rico, early congressional debates merely obfuscated, then postponed the question by naming the island an unincorporated U.S. territory—meaning the island, unlike New Mexico (an incorporated territory), was not predestined to incorporation through statehood at some future date. The Foraker Act of 1900 [See Document 6] established a government composed mostly of U.S. officials and placed little power in the hands of the Puerto Rican electorate and a great deal of power in the hands of the president and Congress. The "citizens of Porto Rico" were to be governed by institutions predominated by mainlanders....

Thus, the Foraker Act transformed Puerto Rico into a U.S. possession that would neither be admitted into the Union nor ultimately liberated as a nation. Aiding that transformation—indeed, legitimizing it—were a number of Supreme Court decisions that arose from the Insular Cases between 1901 and 1905. These decisions, in their essence, confirmed the imperialist notion that the U.S. could possess a territory and govern it without the consent of its people and without any plan as to its eventual liberation or future admission as an incorporated territory or state. The people of Puerto Rico, the Supreme Court determined, were not to be entitled to full protection under the U.S. Constitution and could be taxed without representation.

From 1900 to 1917, Puerto Rican leaders responded to the U.S. takeover and the Foraker Act in various ways. Their divergent positions on Puerto Rico's political status reflected the shifting political alliances that evolved following the invasion.... With ties to the Republican Party in the United States, republicanos believed the island's eventual admission as a state would bring prosperity to the people, or at least to their business-minded constituents. Although these partisans initially criticized the Foraker Act, fearing that under it Puerto Rico would be treated by the United States "as mere chattel," they eventually came to view it as merely a transitional step to territorial status and eventual U.S. citizenship....

Headed by former Autonomist Party leader Luis Muñoz Rivera ... the Unionist Party ... [was] united by a common disdain for the United States' domination of the island, as well as by their shared desire that Puerto Ricans be granted some clear, unequivocal form of "self-government." Thus, the founding platform of the Unionist party in 1904 called for one status or the other: statehood or independence. Either status, claimed Unionists, would bring an end to the federal government's subjugation of the island and would mark the beginning of self-government....

The granting of U.S. citizenship became a central feature of the U.S. Republican platform in 1909. There was in Congress another brief and rancorous discussion of it in which racial and linguistic requirements for citizenship again predominated. Opponents to the proposition, such as Representative Atterson Walden Rucker of Colorado, decried the high rate of illiteracy in either English or Spanish, saying, ... "it is perfectly safe to say that to-day not as many of the native voting population can neither read nor write either their own language or ours; and it can be furthermore fairly said that 60 percent of these native voters are colored people." Rucker stated what many congressmen believed: to be capable of self-government or deserving of U.S. citizenship meant to be racially white, male (i.e., a member of "the voting population"), and able to read and write in the language of the nation-state.

To be granted U.S. citizenship, Puerto Ricans were first expected by lawmakers to be literate in English. Education officials on the island, predominated by white monolingual U.S. teachers, devoted their energies to this end. U.S. citizenship and preparation for some form of self-government, then, was the rationale behind the Americanization campaign that U.S. officials instituted in 1900 and that prevailed well into the 1930s. As happened in New Mexico, most monolingual U.S. officials sought to stamp out any vestiges of the Spanish language in the education system and therefore implemented drastic reforms to expand the school system and simultaneously enforce English-language instruction.... But their efforts proved largely in vain. As was true in New Mexico, difficulties that arose from extreme measures resulted in less effectiveness and the ultimate failure of the monolingual approach....

Though political leaders in Puerto Rico fought over the eventual political status of the island, all parties and interests nevertheless demonstrated to Congress a longing for greater control of the island for the benefit of their respective constituencies....

[I]n 1912 Congress again examined the issue of U.S. citizenship for Puerto Ricans. A proponent of the idea, President Taft's noted secretary of war, Henry Stimson, praised Puerto Ricans for their loyalty to the United States.... But Stimson steered far clear of endorsing eventual statehood for Puerto Rico. Citizenship and statehood, Stimson declared—and Taft agreed—were separate concepts....

Reintroduced in 1914, the Jones Act was abandoned without hearings. Frustrated, Puerto Ricans that year began to press for something other than citizenship, which most Unionists viewed (rightly) as a mere token to appease them. They wanted statehood or independence, but not continued tutelage under the U.S.... Citizenship—be it U.S. or Puerto Rican—meant something far different for many Puerto Ricans than it did for U.S. officials. It meant self-government either by way of statehood, in the first case, or national independence, in the second....

[W]hen the Jones bill was reintroduced in 1916, [s]peaking before the House, Muñoz Rivera, Puerto Rico's resident commissioner ..., argued that U.S. citizenship without statehood amounted to a continuation of federal subjugation of the island. [See Chapter 5, Document 6.] ...

[C]ongressional opponents to citizenship and statehood for Puerto Ricans again resisted admitting as citizens persons whom they deemed were not white....

[In 1917] Congress passed the Jones Act [See Chapter 5, Document 8]. This act not only proclaimed Puerto Ricans to be U.S. citizens, but it also reorganized the government of the island, instituting ... an elected senate, but retaining numerous checks on the power of the assembly. Its passage, however, did not assuage the growing popular sentiment for independence, as many lawmakers had hoped.... Puerto Rico's status remained dubious.... Hence, Puerto Ricans began to conclude that they had been granted precisely what Muñoz Rivera most feared: "a citizenship of an inferior order, a citizenship of a second class."

★ ★ ★

The contexts and political objectives that shaped U.S. citizenship and inspired these two struggles for self-government at the turn of the century—as well as the outcomes—could hardly have been more distinct. New Mexico's vast terrain and relatively sparse population, along with its location, in the heart of the U.S.-Mexico borderland and in the path of the tremendous Anglo-Saxon march to California, made for kinds of race and ethnic relations in New Mexico that were very different from those in Puerto Rico, whose population was much larger and was less impacted by immigration. The stream of Anglo-American migrants and tourists that flowed into New Mexico and fueled their rise to political, economic, and linguistic predominance in the territory played an important role in crafting the illusion of a whitening populace that, in 1912, was still mostly Spanish-speaking and racially diverse. Moreover, the war and treaty that brought New Mexico into the United States' domain set it on a path toward eventual incorporation as a state, something that nuevomexicanos and local Anglo-Americans overwhelmingly welcomed. In stark contrast, the war and treaty that, fifty years later, brought Puerto Rico under U.S. dominion failed to clarify the island's political destiny and gave rise to diverse factions that proffered distinct means for attaining their divergent notions of self-government. The Foraker Act and Insular Cases, along with Congress's repeated denial of either statehood, autonomy, or national self-government for Puerto Rico, galvanized the island's struggle for independence.

In general terms, the histories of New Mexico and Puerto Rico reveal how U.S. lawmakers invoked racial and linguistic qualifications for citizenship and self-government to justify their imperialist ambitions while disregarding the will of the people they presumed to govern. More specifically, they help to explain how Puerto Ricans and nuevomexicanos have arrived at their respective forms of subordination. The achievement of statehood in 1912 did ... further "incorporate" nuevomexicanos (men) into the nation's body politic; it gave them full representation in Congress and greater control over local resources and political offices.... By contrast, the Jones Act of 1917 did not convert Puerto Ricans (men or women) into full U.S. citizens, if citizenship is understood as incorporation into the nation's body politic through statehood and national voting representation. Rather, the law maintained Puerto Ricans in a subordinate status and denied them either independence (and their own citizenship), autonomy, or statehood. Despite these differing outcomes, the popular will that sustained the struggles for self-government, the debates that shaped and responded to them, and the racial ideologies and rhetoric that enveloped them were strikingly similar....

Significantly, what also emerges from these vastly different experiences is how leaders of New Mexico and Puerto Rico viewed themselves and wished to be viewed—as viable members of the United States' white, English-speaking body politic. Leaders of both territories presumed to have met the white racial standard for U.S. citizenship and erroneously believed that they and their constituents would eventually be treated as equals to Anglo-Americans. However, their presumption of whiteness and common desire to govern themselves masked one of the more revealing features of Latinos' diverse experiences in the U.S.

orbit: that, at various junctures in history and in similar ways, Latinos have occupied, sometimes self-consciously but nearly always unwillingly, the legal/social frontiers of both citizenship and whiteness. As neither full-fledged, integral participants in this nation's body politic nor as sovereign citizens of their respective homelands, Puerto Ricans and Mexican Americans were placed in and, in large part, still endure (though in distinct forms) a subordinate political status.

Defining a Limited and Ambiguous Citizenship for Puerto Ricans

SAM ERMAN

Isabel Gonzalez's trajectory from detained "alien" to Supreme Court litigant illuminates links between the legal history of U.S. empire and the legal history of race and immigration in the United States. Her case, *Gonzales v. Williams* (1904), was the first in which the Court confronted the citizenship status of inhabitants of territories acquired by the United States during its deliberate turn toward imperialism in the late nineteenth century. As with many cases, a combination of Gonzalez's actions and circumstances gave rise to the challenge. A single, pregnant mother, Gonzalez headed to New York from Puerto Rico in the summer of 1902. Subject to inspection at Ellis Island as an alien, she failed to gain entry to the mainland under an immigration policy that advocates of racial exclusion had shaped in line with their concerns about the sexual morals and family structures of immigrants. Gonzalez responded by drawing on familial social networks to challenge immigration authorities in federal court. She claimed that she was not an alien but a U.S. citizen. The Court would ultimately give her a narrow victory, holding that Puerto Ricans were not aliens but refraining from deciding whether they were U.S. citizens.

Steaming away from Puerto Rico aboard the S.S. *Philadelphia* in the summer of 1902, Gonzalez departed a homeland both within and beyond the U.S. nation. Puerto Rico was within the United States because on July 25, 1898, the United States invaded the island and then annexed it through the Treaty of Paris, congressionally confirmed on April 11, 1899, that brought an end to the war between the United States and Spain in Cuba, Puerto Rico, and the Philippines. That treaty recognized U.S. authority over these islands and Guam. Puerto Rico lay beyond the United States because a combination of congressional and judicial action had denied the island full-fledged entry into the U.S. federal system. Prior to 1898 the United States had organized new acquisitions from nontribal governments into largely self-governing territories as a prelude to statehood and had generally extended broad constitutional protections and U.S. citizenship to free, nontribal residents.... After 1898 this precedent of relatively uniform treatment disintegrated. In Puerto Rico, for instance, Congress instituted a centrally controlled administration and declined to recognize Puerto Ricans as U.S. citizens....

Closely followed by politicians, scholars, and the public, *Downes* [*v. Bidwell* (1901)] was the most important of the *Insular Cases,* a set of primarily early-twentieth-century decisions creating the constitutional underpinnings of the newly self-conscious U.S. empire. There, Justice Edward White introduced the doctrine of territorial nonincorporation. He reasoned that unlike prior territories, Puerto Rico had not been incorporated by Congress or by treaty into the U.S. Union. It was thus "foreign to the United States in a domestic sense"—that is, foreign for domestic-law purposes—but also part of the United States under international law. White here purported that the exigencies of empire could be reconciled with constitutional and democratic norms because the Constitution did not need to apply uniformly throughout the territories.... [T]he decision permitted establishment of unequal, undemocratic polities in such territories, did not demand that those territories eventually be incorporated, and granted wide latitude to Congress and the executive in structuring those polities....

Though vagueness struck some as a questionable legal principle, nonincorporation nevertheless would become (and remains) accepted constitutional law. *Downes* thus settled the question of the administration of nonincorporated territories.... But, it left the status of the population of those territories undecided. After *Downes,* Puerto Ricans lived in institutional limbo, uncertain whether they held U.S. citizenship or remained alien to their new sovereign. Treasury official F. P. Sargent stepped into this breach, instructing immigration officials to treat Puerto Ricans as aliens. This policy caught Gonzalez in its web, but it also gave her and her allies the chance to press courts to decide whether, as a native of an unincorporated territory, she was an alien or a national, a citizen or a subject.... As the *New York Times* would write, Gonzalez's challenge to her exclusion at Ellis Island presented a "Porto Rican test case" on "the status of the citizens of Porto Rico." When the Supreme Court scheduled the case on an "advanced" basis, it confirmed what Gonzalez, her attorneys, and U.S. officials already understood: the construction and administration of a U.S. empire injected the status of colonized people into debates over U.S. citizenship, which remained unsettled long after *Dred Scott* (1857) and its 1868 reversal by the Fourteenth Amendment.

Responding to her detention, Gonzalez and her family initially focused not on the question of citizenship but on the immediate goals of preserving Gonzalez's honor and bringing her to New York. They thus challenged the implication that she was a single woman without support. Once she lost her administrative appeal, Gonzalez switched tactics, turning to a judicial arm of the state to overturn the administrative decision that she was an alien. In that dispute, the modestly situated Gonzalez tapped into familial social networks to secure assistance....

Rather than specifying the citizenship of the inhabitants of the new U.S. possessions, the Court unanimously issued a ruling as vague, in its own way, as *Downes.* Overruling immigration authorities—Gonzalez, the Court held, was not an alien for purposes of U.S. immigration laws—justices declined to decide whether she was a citizen. Again, the Court in its vagueness facilitated U.S. imperialism.... At the time, the distinction between citizen and subject made little practical difference; because the Court had eviscerated its constitutional content in postbellum cases involving women, immigrants, and people of color,

U.S. citizenship promised Puerto Ricans few new rights.... The status of Puerto Ricans thus implicated hard-to-reconcile strands of Supreme Court jurisprudence involving the great conflicts of citizenship haunting the U.S. polity: gender, race, and empire. By assiduously steering clear of deciding whether Puerto Ricans were U.S. citizens, the Court avoided these issues....

[T]he parties involved [in *Gonzales v. Williams*] all understood the problem of the citizenship status of Puerto Ricans to be inseparable from the many citizenship questions involving "dependent" and "unequal" populations in and around the United States. The U.S. empire-state included states of the federal union, incorporated territories like New Mexico, and colonial possessions like the Philippines. Until 1902 U.S. troops occupied the military protectorate of Cuba. All of these parts of the United States held populations whom the courts and political branches had determined enjoyed sharply unequal access to protections that many associated with citizenship. At the turn of the twentieth century, the U.S. Supreme Court sustained the Chinese exclusion, Jim Crow, and black disfranchisement polic[i]es implemented by the political branches of state and federal governments. Aspects of coverture continued to receive judicial support. Detribalization, conquest, and allotment extended U.S. authority over American Indians and their lands. In the Caribbean, the United States exercised informal but powerful influence. Deciding the citizenship status of Puerto Ricans meant carefully weighing and possibly upsetting this many-layered system of exclusion and domination....

★ ★ ★

A key participant in ... the *Gonzales* case was Frederic R. Coudert Jr. In 1895 Coudert began a career in New York as an international-law attorney and public intellectual.... In 1901 he became front-page news after launching two Insular Cases—*DeLima v. Bidwell* (1901) and *Downes v. Bidwell*—for clients protesting tariffs levied on goods shipped between Puerto Rico and the United States. That January he argued before the U.S. Supreme Court that U.S. annexation of Puerto Rico had made it part of the United States, hence exempt from U.S. tariffs. The Court agreed in part.... Justice White's opinion for three justices in *Downes* ... [argued] that unless "the United States is helpless in the family of nations," it required the power to annex territories without extending inhabitants U.S. citizenship.... [His] proposition—that U.S. citizenship might be too substantive for some inhabitants of U.S. territories to enjoy—had important implications for Puerto Rico, Puerto Ricans, and the U.S. empire-state....

A second key participant was Federico Degetau y González, a prominent Puerto Rican politician familiar with battles over the colonial status of Puerto Rico. Degetau spent the mid and late 1890s in Spain advocating greater autonomy for his island. After 1898 Degetau refocused his advocacy of Puerto Rican self-government and liberty into support for U.S. statehood and citizenship for the island ... In 1899 Puerto Rican politicians reorganized political coalitions ... [into] the Republicanos and the Federales. Degetau cofounded the former party.... The Republicanos nominated Degetau to be resident commissioner.... Degetau and his party won handily, becoming crucial allies to a United States then setting up and legitimizing the civil system laid out in the Foraker Act. Degetau, in his platform, insisted "that the inhabitants of the Island of Porto Rico are citizens of the United States." This position aligned him with the many mainlanders who believed that U.S. annexation had brought Puerto Ricans U.S. citizenship and full constitutional protections and Puerto Rico eventual statehood....

[A] test case would come to Degetau and Coudert the next year from an unexpected source, a young mother named Isabel Gonzalez who was detained by immigration inspectors in New York.... Still living in Puerto Rico, she became pregnant for the second time shortly before her fiancé left to find a factory job in Linoleumville, Staten Island, the neighborhood where Gonzalez's brother worked. When she sought to follow and marry him in mid-1902, she had reason to hope that she would join many Puerto Ricans who, Degetau noted, had "frequently disembarked unmolested in New York." The Treasury Department, however, issued new immigration guidelines that changed Gonzalez's status while her ship was en route. On August 2, 1902 she and other Puerto Ricans had become "subject to the same examinations as are enforced against people from countries over which the United States claims no right of sovereignty." Following the new rules, port officials transferred Gonzalez to Ellis Island.

There, Gonzalez confronted a powerful arm of the U.S. administrative state. Exercising prosecutorial and judicial functions and insulated from most judicial review, hundreds of immigration inspectors determined the residence rights of as many as five thousand immigrants a day. Their line inspections were standardized, high volume, and summary. They sent ambiguous cases before Boards of Special Inquiry that could conduct their nonpublic hearings in mere minutes and deny immigrants rights to an attorney and to see or rebut evidence. Several months earlier William Williams, a Wall Street lawyer, had become the new commissioner of immigration at Ellis Island. Promoting cleanliness, politeness, and strict, efficient enforcement of immigration laws, he doubled his exclusion rate in his first year by aggressively construing the statutory bar on aliens "likely to become a public charge." As a practical guideline, he directed inspectors to treat aliens as suspect if they traveled with less than ten dollars. Like reformers and the welfare laws they would soon institute—both of which conceptualized women and children as dependents (though in fact many worked)—inspectors often attached the label of "public charge" to unmarried mothers and their children. Ellis Island policy dictated that "unmarried pregnant women were always detained for further investigation" and that single women were only released if family members came to claim them.

Although Gonzalez carried eleven dollars in cash and telegrammed ahead to her family to pick her up, officials discovered her pregnancy during her ... line inspection....

The next day Gonzalez's uncle, Domingo Collazo, and her brother, Luis González, joined her at a hearing turning on whether she was "going to persons *able, willing and legally bound* to support" her and not entering for immoral purposes. Here the ostensibly administrative inquiry reflected a movement for racial exclusion that overlapped, in immigration policy, with ideas about moral behavior and proper relations between women dependents and male family members. Inspectors weighed proof of legitimate family relations through presumptions that certain kinds of women were inadequate mothers and certain kinds of men were insufficient fathers and husbands....

For Gonzalez and her family, the hearings touched on traits to which Puerto Ricans and mainlanders attached negative honor, class, and race connotations: lack of membership in an economically self-sufficient man's home; absence of sexual propriety; and classification as pregnant and abandoned. Collazo and Luis González sought to portray Isabel Gonzalez as an upstanding, dependent woman in an honorable man's household. Isabel Gonzalez explained her first child through widowhood. For the second pregnancy, Collazo converted a missing fiancé into a husband whom he had seen "[a]bout two weeks ago" but who "could not come today" because "he is working." Collazo hedged his bets, however, offering to assume the role of patriarch. He earned "$25 a week" as "a printer" and was "willing to take [Isabel Gonzalez] and provide for her." Inspectors, who likely began with racial and class prejudices, were wary. They sent Collazo and Luis González home, opining: "his wife is here and he should come for her." Two days later, still with no help from the father of Isabel Gonzalez's expected child, another attempt was made, this time by Domingo Collazo's wife, Hermina Collazo.... While inspectors solicited Hermina Collazo's claims to moral supervision, they ignored her work and income, questioned her for coming to testify unaccompanied by her husband, and failed to record her name. They also refused to reconsider their demand to see Isabel Gonzalez's husband.

When Isabel Gonzalez's brother, Luis González, testified, he tried a new tack, portraying Isabel Gonzalez as a victim of *rapto,* or seduction, but assuring the inspectors that her family had taken the necessary steps to restore her honor [by arranging for a church wedding].... Although Luis González apparently believed that this would mollify the inspectors' concerns about Isabel Gonzalez's family's capacity to care for her, the inspectors were indignant: "An arrangement then has been made by which a marriage is to take place without the husband's consent?" Luis González affirmed that this was the case. The Board excluded Isabel Gonzalez from entry.

When these attempts failed, Isabel Gonzalez depended upon Domingo Collazo and his access to male political and professional networks. In the 1890s Collazo had been active in a radical wing of the Cuban Revolutionary Party that sought an Antillean social revolution to improve the status of workers and people of color. He had attended meetings with Antillean activists Arturo Schomburg [and others].... On August 18, 1902 he swore out a habeas corpus petition for Isabel Gonzalez.... [T]he U.S. Circuit Court for the Southern District of New York, [s]even weeks later, ... issued its opinion. Narrowing the issue to "whether or not petitioner is an alien," it ruled that she was an alien and upheld her exclusion.

Although unaware of the Gonzalez case, ... several weeks after Gonzalez disembarked at Ellis Island, Resident Commissioner Degetau wrote to the secretary of state in protest of the new rules that made Puerto Ricans subject to immigration laws.... [T]he secretary of the Treasury called Degetau's attention to the Circuit Court opinion, which had recently affirmed the legality of Treasury policy.... Here was the test case for which Degetau and Coudert had been looking.... The case could, Coudert wrote, "settle the status of all the native islanders who were in existence at the time the Spanish possessions were annexed by the United States." ...

Isabel Gonzalez, whose voice is absent from the administrative and trial records, nevertheless seems to have made a concrete decision to join the shift from an argument designed to redeem her individual honor and secure her entry to New York to one intended to secure citizenship for all Puerto Ricans. Indeed, while Gonzalez was out on bond, "the young man, whom she came here to find, turned up," the two wed, and she became "a citizen of this country through marriage," thus acquiring a right to remain stateside. Rather than end her appeal on these grounds, however, she hid her marriage, delaying public redemption to press her claim that all Puerto Ricans were U.S. citizens. Partly as a result of Gonzalez's efforts, the official record came to portray her as did immigration inspectors: dependent, silent, and an object of state policy. There is an irony here. Gonzalez made huge efforts to put claims to dignity and belonging before a federal state that would preserve and disclose many of the documents its officials created and received. Yet because her efforts succeeded, the Supreme Court would read and repeat the "legal story" that immigration inspectors had crafted out of the testimonies witnesses had generated to sway them. Historians have not corrected this depiction of Gonzalez as a passive victim of governmental machinations. Yet her efforts caused people to create documents—later archived—that reveal a different woman: one who pressed and, as we will see, articulated claims to citizenship.

★ ★ ★

The U.S. Supreme Court received the briefs in *Gonzales v. Williams* in late 1903. U.S. solicitor general Henry Hoyt's filing on behalf of the United States focused on the peculiar purposes of U.S. immigration laws. Reviewing bars to entry by Chinese, prostitutes, idiots, insane persons, paupers, certain diseased persons, and anarchists, among others, he highlighted Congress's desire to protect the mainland from harmful immigration. Hoyt then described how Puerto Rico and the Philippines were remote in time, space, and culture and suffered (in his eyes) problems of climate, overcrowding, primitive hygiene, low standards of living and moral conduct, and the extreme and willing indigency that characterized the tropics.... Hoyt concluded, the Supreme Court ought to respect Congress's intent to protect the mainland from these "very evils at which the law was aimed."

... Frederic R. Coudert Jr. opposed the government with his brief on behalf of Isabel Gonzalez. He argued that (1) the Treaty of Paris transferred sovereignty over, and hence the allegiance of, Puerto Rico from Spain to the United States, and (2) under English and U.S. law, such transfers effected transfers of subjection or nationality. If accepted, these two points were sufficient to win Gonzalez entry to the mainland; existing immigration laws only excluded aliens. But, Coudert argued, the Court had to do more. Finding Puerto Ricans to be U.S. subjects or nationals without also holding them to be U.S. citizens would replicate the *Dred Scott* case of 1857, again creating a U.S. status between citizen and alien. He therefore made his third argument, that current U.S. law appropriately deemed all U.S. subjects or nationals also to be U.S. citizens. Moreover, he assured the Court, recognizing Puerto Ricans as U.S. citizens would not hamper U.S. imperial designs. U.S. women and minorities, he explained, possessed a U.S. citizenship similar to the statuses that other empires bestowed upon their subordinated peoples....

Significantly, he did not cast Puerto Ricans as white men who deserved full membership in the U.S. political community....

Turning to case law, Coudert portrayed a U.S. citizenship which generally accompanied U.S. nationality and that, similar to nationality in other empires, was widespread and largely inconsequential. He chose cases in which the Court affirmed that men and women born within U.S. jurisdictions were U.S. citizens whatever their sex, race, and ethnicity. In the same cases, the Court eviscerated those aspects of the Fourteenth Amendment that protected the content of U.S. citizenship....

Appealing to judges' paternal tendencies, Coudert framed the issue in terms of honor and gender.... Allegorically casting Puerto Rico as a woman in need of the protection of the masculine United States not only resonated with the "facts" of the case, it also pointed the way to a solution. Puerto Ricans could be citizens on the model of other dependents, including women. The Court, he suggested, could synthesize U.S. jurisprudence on citizens of color with sister empires' treatments of colonized peoples. Doctrines limiting the claims of U.S. blacks, American Indians, and women, among others, could serve as a model for the legal status of residents of the newly acquired territories: grant citizenship, but withhold rights....

Coudert delineate[d] what he took to be the central confusion in the case: a failure to distinguish tiers of citizenship and subjection.... Thus, the Court had three options: declare Puerto Ricans to be aliens; recognize an intermediate status between alien and citizen; or follow a model even more flexible than those of other great powers and grant Puerto Ricans acknowledgedly rights-poor U.S. citizenship.

Coudert argued that, practically, the Court had to choose between deeming Gonzalez a mere U.S. subject or also a U.S. citizen, neither of which would guarantee her full political or civil rights.... There already was a status in U.S. law that the Court had adapted to the needs of U.S. imperialism: U.S. citizenship. Because the Court had already drained much of the content from U.S. citizenship, the justices needed not deny U.S. citizenship to Puerto Ricans....

★ ★ ★

In his brief to the U.S. Supreme Court, Resident Commissioner Federico Degetau y González took a dramatically different approach than did Coudert. Writing from an official, male, and Puerto Rican perspective, the former Spanish citizen associated his island with markings of male honor like economic self-sufficiency, martial experience, and exercise of political and civil rights.... He did not seek "passive" U.S. citizenship akin to that enjoyed by women and people of color, nor did he seek to gain active citizenship for other colonized and marginalized people. Instead, he claimed—for Puerto Ricans like him—a robust U.S. citizenship associated with white men; civilization; economic, legal, and political opportunities; and military and tax obligations.

A key to this argument was the contention that Puerto Ricans were not "natives" in the colonial sense.... [T]hese natives, he argued, encompassed "the uncivilized tribes of the Philippine Islands," not "Spanish citizens born in Porto Rico." Under Spanish rule, he noted, Puerto Ricans enjoyed such rights as representation in the national legislature, national citizenship accompanied by constitutional protections, "the same honors and prerogatives as the native-born in Castille," and broad autonomy.... He indicated that Puerto Ricans resembled the French and Mexicans who had been incorporated into U.S. citizenship in earlier U.S. cessions when he claimed that Puerto Ricans differed from Filipino "*tribes,*" "*Mongolians,*" and the "*uncivilized native tribes [of] Alaska.*"

The United States, Degetau admonished, was tardy in extending appropriate treatment to his traditionally rights-bearing, self-governing people.... Now the Court could redeem U.S. democratic traditions and leadership....

Focusing on fields dominated by men, Degetau also illustrated how Puerto Ricans needed U.S. citizenship to exercise autonomy and control within business and law.... Although the Foraker Act indicated that Puerto Rico ought to benefit from most U.S. laws, many statutes applied only to U.S. citizens. Degetau's arguments asked the Court to consider him, an accomplished civil servant, rather than Gonzalez, an unmarried mother, as the model for Puerto Rican citizenship. He closed on a personal note: "If I were an alien, I could not have attained the highest honor in my professional career, that of taking, as a member of the bar of this Honorable Court, the oath to maintain the Constitution of the United States, this oath being incompatible with allegiance to any other power."

★ ★ ★

Two months later, Chief Justice Melville Fuller announced the Court's unanimous holding: "[W]e ... cannot concede ... that the word 'alien,' as used in the [immigration] act of 1891, embraces the citizens of Porto Rico." Reviewing U.S. law, he explained that the United States had made "[t]he nationality of the island ... American" and integrated Puerto Rico into the United States. It had in Puerto Rico created a civil government with heads named by the U.S. president; implemented congressional oversight; established a U.S. district court; ... and put most U.S. statutes into force. The opinion was a modest victory for Puerto Ricans. It struck down the Treasury guideline under which Gonzalez had been held but did not address Congress's power to regulate the movement of Puerto Ricans from the island to the mainland.... Justices declined the choice between either reenacting *Dred Scott* by reintroducing "subjects" into U.S. law or acknowledging that U.S. citizenship was largely inconsequential. As in *Downes v. Bidwell,* vagueness proved valuable as the Court sought to accommodate U.S. empire and constitutional democracy.

Although technically the Supreme Court handed Isabel Gonzalez a victory in her case while avoiding the broader question of Puerto Rican citizenship, she did not see it that way. During the hearings and trials her voice was noticeably absent, but when modest media coverage accompanied the decision, she took the opportunity to break the silence. Her first intervention was to correct the false picture of her that she had allowed to stand during the trial. As reporters described her, she "had come here in search of a man who had promised to marry her and had failed to keep his promise." ... On the day of the Court's ruling, one of her lawyers, Orrel Parker, told the *New York Times* of her matrimony and consequent change in status. Her honor, it was thus revealed, had been restored.

Next, and this time in writing, Gonzalez addressed the case more broadly, attacking the decision as an insult. A year after the ruling, still married and thus still a dependent, Gonzalez seized a public voice. She addressed the *New York Times,* writing in published letters [See Document 9], "Gen. Miles went to Porto Rico to save us, and proclaimed to the wide winds his 'liberating' speech." But instead of U.S. citizenship, Puerto Ricans got "the actual [current] incongruous status—neither Americans nor foreigners,' as it was vouchsafed by the United States Supreme Court apropos of my detention at Ellis Island for the crime of being an 'alien.'" The romance between the United States and Puerto Rico in her tale ended in a *rapto*—a breach of promise. Having deceived Puerto Ricans out of one honorable status—Spanish citizenship—the United States was obliged to extend Puerto Ricans a new honorable status—U.S. citizenship. But instead of meeting its obligation to Puerto Rico, the United States made the plight of the victim, Puerto Rico, into Gonzalez's "crime." The island's predicament became the basis of investigations into Gonzalez's honor. In using this romantic metaphor to protest U.S. policies in Puerto Rico, Gonzalez did not seek a passive citizenship like that which Coudert described. Instead, she sought restoration of the "liberties and franchises" that constituted the active, male citizenship advocated by Degetau. Her claim was that having been harmed like a woman, Puerto Rico ought to be recompensed like a man.

Like Coudert, Gonzalez drew lessons from other colonial experiences, and like Degetau she complained that the United States treated civilized Puerto Ricans with less dignity than other empires treated their natives. Thus, the United States was an inferior empire for failing to extend U.S. citizenship and autonomy to Puerto Ricans....

★ ★ ★

Isabel Gonzalez's challenge to immigration officials' attempts to exclude her as an alien likely to become a public charge sparked administrative, legal, and media discussions about the status of Puerto Ricans. These discussions explicitly linked problems of colonial administration to issues of immigration and to U.S. doctrines acquiescing in [the] treatment of U.S. citizens—chiefly women and people of color—as dependent and unequal. Gonzalez and lawyers in the case moved easily among these legal realms, aided by shared languages of race, gender, and morality. Stories about honor tied together claims about the desirability of Puerto Ricans as immigrants, their fitness for self-government, and the suitability of Puerto Rico for traditional territorial status. For Coudert, Puerto Ricans were abandoned women, Puerto Rico a waif. Degetau described a manly island, and Gonzalez depicted Puerto Rico as a victim of seduction. Hoyt, like Williams, saw failed parents, rearing children outside moral, economically self-sufficient homes.

Gonzales v. Williams also capped a constitutional counterrevolution half a century in the making. After decades of judicial ambiguity as to the meaning of U.S. citizenship, Chief Justice Roger Taney, in his 1857 *Dred Scott* opinion, described a U.S. citizenship rich in rights; the Founders, he argued, did not intend free blacks—whom he depicted as long denied many rights by states—to possess this robust U.S. citizenship. Eleven years and a civil war later, the Fourteenth Amendment reversed, recognizing "the privileges or immunities of citizens of the United States" but insisting that "all persons born or naturalized in the United States and subject to the jurisdiction thereof, are citizens of the United States." As Coudert recognized, even though the U.S. Supreme Court had eviscerated the Privileges and Immunities Clause, it had, for thirty years, construed the Fourteenth Amendment to mandate U.S. citizenship for all people subject to U.S. jurisdiction and born in lands under U.S. sovereignty. During those years, U.S. expansion had all but ceased. Justice White gave one reason why: the specter of inhabitants of new territories gaining unspecified rights as new U.S. citizens could operate as a brake on U.S. expansion.

... Opinions varied as to the consequences of the annexations for the U.S. constitutional democracy and its new possessions. Some mainland politicians and commentators held that the U.S. Constitution allowed the United States to have colonies; others promoted partial incorporation into the U.S. polity; a third group contended that U.S. annexation brought inhabitants of new territories a U.S. citizenship that was accompanied by full constitutional protections and eventual U.S. statehood.... Yet when Gonzalez confronted justices with the question of whether inhabitants of newly acquired territories had become U.S. citizens, they ducked.

... In 1905, untethered from litigation and speaking in her own voice, Gonzalez explained that the decision and surrounding events marked Puerto Ricans as inferior to "full-fledged American citizens" and showed General Miles's pledges on behalf of the United States "to be nothing but bitter mockery and waste paper." Later, some island leaders came to oppose U.S. citizenship as promising few rights and foreclosing Puerto Rican independence.

Political and Economic Connections Shape Cuban Communities in the U.S.

GERALD POYO

Contrary to popular perception, the Cuban experience in the United States is not an exclusively post-1959 phenomenon. Cubans have resided in the United States since the 1820s, and well-defined and integrated communities emerged during the 1870s. For the most part, however, scholars dedicated to the study of Cuban Americans have considered this early experience colorful and exotic, but essentially irrelevant to the contemporary scene. In fact, Cubans in the United States have themselves been generally unaware of the longstanding migratory tradition that has linked Cuba to the United States....

"The Cuban Experience in the United States, 1865–1940: Migration, Community, and Identity," by Gerald Poyo, from *Cuban Studies* 21, edited by Louis A. Pérez, Jr., © 1992. Reprinted by permission of the University of Pittsburgh Press.

[T]he Cuban experience in the United States should be understood from its origins in the nineteenth century. The broad historical context of Cuban migrations north during the last 150 years needs to be understood in a holistic fashion despite the sometimes dramatic differences in the various stages of emigration. The popular impression that the Cuban-American experience represents a conservative elite tradition does not stand up to close examination. Contemporary stereotypes should not usurp an entire historical tradition. As with all other immigrant groups to the United States, Cubans are a heterogenous group, and generalizations are not always useful.

★ ★ ★

During the final third of the nineteenth century, socioeconomic changes and political turbulence in Cuba, together with developments in the United States, gave birth to a Clear Havana (100 percent Cuban tobacco) cigar industry in New York, Key West, and Tampa. This created pressures for emigration from Cuba, a situation that continued until the second decade of the twentieth century.

Changes in the international cigar market during the mid-nineteenth century precipitated Cuban migration to the United States. Until the late 1850s, Cuban cigar exports expanded throughout Europe and the United States.... Beginning in the 1850s, however, Cuba began to lose export markets. Protectionist pressures in France and Germany led to tariffs that caused an overall decrease of Cuban cigar exports. To compensate, Cuban manufacturers increased exports to the U.S. market on which they became highly dependent.

Cuban cigar exports to the United States increased through the 1880s, but signs of trouble for the island's manufacturers emerged during the U.S. Civil War when tariffs began to rise. Increasing tariffs on cigars and relatively low duties on tobacco leaf enabled entrepreneurs to recreate a genuinely Cuban industry within the borders of the United States.

Many Cubans who arrived in the United States during the Ten Years' War [1868–1878] took advantage of this favorable economic [situation]. With the outbreak of the insurrection, Cubans emigrated to New York, New Orleans, and Key West....

Besides conditions in international markets, a variety of local social and economic developments in Cuba contributed to dislocations and migration. The Ten Years' War weakened sugar production during the 1870s. Destruction of sugar plantations in Cuba and the growing beet sugar industry in Europe led to a reduction of exports and loss of markets. These troubles were compounded by decreasing sugar prices during the mid-1880s. Cuba fell into depression. Rural workers wandered in search of employment.... Many left the country. Caught in the general economic decline, and affected by the protected and growing cigar industry in Florida and New York, production in Cuban cigar factories declined in the late 1880s. Cuba's general economy plummeted further as a result of the McKinley Tariff in 1890 and the outbreak of the war of independence against Spain in 1895. As a result, during the 1890s emigration from Cuba increased dramatically.

Preferential treatment for Spanish immigrant workers in the Havana factories between the late 1880s and early 1900s created additional pressure forcing Cuban workers to migrate. Spaniards owned and managed many of the factories in Cuba and preferred to hire compatriots as employees....

Many Cuban emigrés returned home [from] the United States after independence [in 1898], but could not find jobs since the managers and foremen in the factories continued to be Spanish. Although Cuban workers demanded equal employment opportunities ..., most Cubans who had been cigarmakers in the United States found little opportunity in Havana. Additional thousands of workers left Cuba during the first decade of the century.

Labor strife in the cigar factories also kept workers on the move. Militant anarchist labor organizations appeared in Cuba in the mid-1880s and, after the turn of the century, Marxist-oriented unions protected workers interests. Unions also formed in Cuban communities in Tampa, Key West, and New York. Solidarity was strong. During strikes in one locality workers in the other centers customarily provided economic and moral support. In fact, strikers usually left their homes en masse for one or another of the cigar centers.... Labor unrest contributed to the highly mobile character of the cigar industry work force.

The penetration of the North American tobacco trust into Cuba during the late 1890s and the early twentieth century was the final factor spurring emigration from the island. The McKinley Tariff had initiated the collapse of cigar exports, a phenomenon aggravated by the independence war. As a result, many large Cuban cigar establishments sold out to North American tobacco interests, which were able to consolidate their position during the U.S. occupation of Cuba. The American Tobacco Company bought up tobacco lands and many cigar and cigarette factories.... After an initially rapid expansion between 1902 and 1905, Cuban cigar exports to the United States began a decline from which they never recovered. The Cuban industry failed to compete with the U.S. factories, which were controlled by the same trust. Slowly, the trust transferred production for the U.S. market to Florida, causing Cuban workers to seek work in the United States in record numbers until the early 1910s.

This accelerated migration did not last long in the new century, however. Technological changes in the North American cigar industry, as well as shifts in fundamental market demand for cigars, reduced migratory pressures. After World War I, mechanization revolutionized the U.S. cigar industry. Machine operators replaced the skilled cigarmakers; the traditionally highly regarded workers from Cuba were no longer needed. Moreover, consumer tastes shifted dramatically: cigarettes increasingly displaced cigars. As demand for cigars declined, so too did production and employment. The longstanding North American cigar labor market closed down, and by the 1930s migrations of workers from Cuba had slowed considerably.

These trends in the United States also affected the Cuban industry. Cigar exports from Cuba declined, plunging the industry into crisis and retrenchment.... [T]he number of cigar and cigarette workers in Cuba declined by more than half between 1899 and 1944. Formerly a world leader in cigar manufacturing, Cuba was reduced to providing leaf to a highly mechanized and productive North American industry with which it could not compete. The vibrant labor markets for handmade cigars that encompassed Havana, Key West, Tampa, New York, and other cities no longer existed. The traditional workers not only lost jobs in the United States, dramatically altering the nature of Cuban communities there, but lost jobs in Cuba as well.

Migrations from Cuba to the United States between 1865 and 1940, then, reflected the socioeconomic dynamic that converted Cuba from a cigar manufacturing center to a net exporter of tobacco leaf. This process culminated in the obsolescence of hand-rolled cigars for mass markets that slowed the migration of cigar workers to the United States after 1910. The decline in migration was a temporary phenomenon, however. The immediate postwar period brought about a resurgence of Cuban migration to the United States.... Cubans traveled to New York and, increasingly, to Miami, as a result of a new set of socioeconomic relationships unconnected to cigar markets, but clearly within the economic framework that tied Cuba to the United States.

* * *

Cuban communities emerged during the nineteenth century as a result of both the rise of the U.S. hand-rolled cigar industry and Cuba's economic and political problems. By the 1870s the first integrated communities, with distinct leaders, institutions, and economic traditions, reflecting the class and racial composition of Cuban cities, had appeared in New York, New Orleans, and Key West. Although Cubans arrived and lived in the United States before the Civil War ..., they were scattered primarily in New Orleans, Mobile, Savannah, Philadelphia, and New York and were, for the most part, white professionals, businessmen, and students, many of whom were exiles who interacted primarily within a political context. In the mid-1870s an estimated 12,000 Cubans lived in the United States; some 4,500 in New York, 3,000 in New Orleans, 2,000 in Key West, and perhaps another 2,500 in other cities such as Jacksonville, Savannah, Washington, Boston, and Galveston.

In New York a broad cross section of Cuba's urban population took hold. Among those living in New York during the 1870s were members of Havana's *criollo* elite, middle-class entrepreneurs and professionals, and a significant multiracial (white, mulatto, black, Chinese) working class employed in the tobacco factories. After the Ten Years' War in 1878, many middle-class Cubans returned home and more workers arrived, strengthening the community's working-class character. During the 1880s, the Cuban population fluctuated between 2,000 and 3,000, but increased with the outbreak of the war of independence in 1895.

Cuba's political problems and the difficulties in the cigar industry also gave rise to a Cuban community in Key West. Exiles and migrant cigarworkers quickly gave the town a national reputation for its anti-Spanish political agitation and high-quality Havana cigars. While the first cigar factories in Key West belonged to non-Cubans, during the 1880s many Cubans entered the trade and soon dominated it. By 1885 almost 100 Key West cigar factories of various sizes employed some 3,000 workers. At the end of the 1880s, Key West produced some 100 million cigars annually. In 1885, some 5,000 Cubans resided on the isle.

... Of employed Cubans fourteen years of age and over in 1880, 79 percent worked in the cigar establishments. Of these, some 18 percent were black and mulatto and 9 percent were women. The remaining 21 percent of working Cubans included unskilled laborers, service workers, artisans, and professionals. The Cuban social structure in Key West included a wide variety of occupations, but it was an overwhelmingly working-class community that relied heavily on the cigar industry.

... The second major Cuban center in Florida appeared in Tampa during 1885 when a powerful labor movement in Key West prompted Martínez Ybor to search for an alternate site for his cigar operations. He and Ignacio Haya, a Spanish manufacturer from New York, obtained tracts of land on the town's outskirts where they constructed their factories in 1886. But it was a fire in Key West during the closing days of March that launched the Tampa cigar industry toward becoming the most important cigar center in the United States. The fire destroyed eighteen cigar factories and forced hundreds of homeless Cubans to migrate again in search of work—to Havana, but mostly to Tampa. During its first decade as a manufacturing center, Tampa grew from less than 1,000 inhabitants to almost 20,000, surpassing Key West's population. Factories moved there from Key West, New York, and Philadelphia. By 1900 Tampa had clearly supplanted Key West as the primary producer of Havana cigars in the United States and was home to a vibrant Cuban community.

While the Cuban communities in New Orleans, New York, Key West, and Tampa developed separate identities, leaders, and institutions, they all operated within the context of the cigar industry labor market. Cuban families usually had economic and social ties in more than one community, and connections with Havana were often strong since political disturbances, strikes, and economic cycles produced considerable movement in both directions across the Straits of Florida. Indeed, for many Cubans, Key West and Tampa were mere extensions of Havana.

At the inception of Cuban enclaves in the United States, emigrés were concerned more with developments in Cuba than with the North American society around them. Their daily routines intersected with Cuba's struggle for independence from Spain. Despite the fact that many Cubans arrived in the United States primarily to seek employment, they were influenced by the nationalist ambience that characterized the communities. Throughout the nineteenth century, opponents to Spanish colonialism assumed leadership in Cuban centers.... [Although] the political activists were in the minority, they usually controlled community organizations and published the newspapers. Accordingly, Cubans who arrived in the communities seeking employment, but without a general political awareness regarding Cuba's colonial situation, often were politicized and enrolled in the independence cause.

Cubans born in the United States were also raised with a similar awareness. Tampa-born writer Jose Yglesias notes in his autobiographical novel that after the Ten Years' War many veterans moved to Florida where they recounted their experiences and exhorted emigrés to support the idea of Cuba Libre.... [See Chapter 5, Document 1].

In Key West, the most important community institution, Instituto San Carlos, served not only as a mutual aid society, educational facility, and social club, but also as a center of nationalist activity. The Instituto provided moral and financial support to dozens of patriotic organizers who passed through Key West during the final thirty years of the century. When Cubans founded Ybor City, similar nationalist organizations appeared....

So intense was the nationalist sentiment among Cubans in the United States that it dissipated only slowly after the termination of the war with Spain in 1898. Cubans who participated in the struggle and remained abroad continued to identify with their homeland after it had become a republic. The important role of the emigré communities in cultivating nationalist thought and promoting the insurrection assumed legendary proportions as the history of the Cuban insurrection was written. Key West and Tampa became known as the "cradles of Cuban independence," and Cubans from those towns, the progenitors of that tradition. Cubans in Florida were justifiably proud of their history, which they associated more with Cuba than the United States.

Instituto San Carlos continued as the primary community institution in Key West, which gained official recognition in Cuba for its contributions to the independence war.... [T]he Cuban legislature appropriated funds to rebuild the institution when a hurricane destroyed it in 1919.... Furthermore, San Carlos' identity became even more closely linked with Cuban nationality when it occupied its new Cuban-owned building that also served as the Cuban consular office. Travel between Key West and Havana was frequent, and through the 1930s, the Cuban community in Key West maintained its deep sense of *cubanidad*. In Tampa, Cuban organizations also maintained a strong nationalist flavor. The Círculo Cubano and Unión Martí-Maceo, two of the most important community organizations in Ybor City, reflected a similar pride and commitment to a Cuban identity.

★ ★ ★

When Cuba finally separated from Spain, emigrés in the United States faced the critical decision of whether or not to return to their homeland. Political exiles generally returned and usually found a place within the new republic. The absence of employment opportunities in Cuba, however, meant that most Cubans employed in the cigar industry had little choice but to remain in the United States. Those who stayed, and their descendants, slowly shed their exile identity. The nationalist intensity that had historically molded community identity and values dissipated as Cubans turned from patriotic endeavors to the challenge of carving out a permanent livelihood in their immigrant communities. Along with others who arrived in subsequent years, Cubans in the United States became immersed in what became a Cuban-American experience.

This process of refocusing from an exile to an immigrant identity is evident in the experiences of Tampa and Key West. Many who lived through the pre-1900 experiences remained committed to their nationalist feelings, but the end of the war also removed the factors that had traditionally sustained nationalist fervor. The separatist press ceased to exist, patriot clubs disbanded, and the romanticism associated with the desire for self-rule declined as the political realities of the Cuban republic caused disillusionment....

A WPA report on San Carlos Institute offers another illustration of what Cubans underwent: "The most significant thing about San Carlos at the present is that its students are taught to be good Cuban-Americans—to become Americanized and yet to maintain their cultural identity as Cubans and Spanish-speaking people. They are taught to be proud of their race, language, and culture." But, the report also noted, "San Carlos cannot compete with the public schools in moulding [sic] the present generation of Cuban children in Key West. For the public schools are intent upon a program of complete Americanization; their only concern with Cuban culture is to obliterate it entirely."

At the same time that increased interaction with U.S. society weaken[e]d the emigré sense of *cubanidad,* socioeconomic realities threatened the viability of the communities and intensified radicalism, which had strong roots in the communities. Cuban centers had evolved in the nineteenth century within an environment of class differences and antagonisms. From the 1870s, when Cubans first entered the Key West cigar factories, until the 1930s when Tampa's hand-rolled cigar industry entered a crisis, a working-class, and often radical, culture associated with the tobacco industry was an inseparable aspect of Cuban identity in the United States. Just as with nationalism, community institutions, newspapers, and activities reflected this cultural and ideological reality. On arriving in Key West during the early 1870s, workers from Havana did not find established labor organizations. They created their own, based on experiences and traditions from home; and once established, they had no need to embrace North American unionism when it finally arrived in Florida after 1880. Workers from Cuba in Florida maintained their own perspectives and looked to their homeland for values and ideas. They embraced anarchism, socialism, and, later, communism, as tools for defending their interests in the evolving industrial communities.

One of the central institutions which promoted this radical identity was the *lectura,* a practice in the cigar factories whereby workers hired individuals to read to them while they labored. As Abelardo Gutiérrez Díaz, a *lector* in Tampa explained, "We continued in Tampa the system that had accompanied the cigar industry from Cuba.... It was a veritable system of education dealing with a variety of subjects, including politics, labor, literature, and international relations." The *lectura* served as one of the important vehicles through which radical thought was disseminated and became associated with the Cuban experience in the United States....

After 1900, with the exodus of the patriot leaders to Cuba, radical activists took the place of the nationalists as Tampa's primary immigrant leaders.... Cubans organized to defend their traditional prerogatives and they acted in solidarity with Spanish and Italian radicals, producing a dynamic immigrant community that was in periodic conflict with their Anglo-American neighbors through the 1930s.

While Cubans turned to radical concepts to defend their communities against the ravaging forces of change, they were eventually overwhelmed by developments that undermined the cigar industry and thus the traditional framework of their community. The seeds that eventually destroyed the hand-rolled cigar industry in Tampa gestated in the 1910s, matured in the 1920s, and flowered during the Depression. Changing tastes and mechanization eliminated jobs, forcing tobacco workers to return to Cuba or to find work in environments where social solidarity was of little importance. Furthermore, the educating and unifying roles of the *lectura* were lost in 1931, when the cigar manufacturers abolished the practice despite a bitter strike over the issue. Finally, the economic crisis in tobacco loosened the traditionally close ties between the Cuban center in Tampa and Havana. United States–based unions with conservative ideologies increasingly displaced the radical labor organizations that had traditionally set the agenda for Cuban workers in Florida. The disruption of traditional employment patterns and, thus, processes of ideological socialization, in addition to the inevitable effects of public school education on longstanding value systems, led to a dissipation of the radical culture that had influenced tobacco workers in Key West, New York, and Tampa for a generation.

The end of the nationalist era in 1900 also brought changes that deeply influenced the centers' racial dynamics. Since their foundation, Cuban communities in the United States reflected the multiracial character of Cuban society, which included whites, mulattos, blacks, and an occasional Chinese. While the various races understood the reality of racial differences and the political and socioeconomic implications of being one race or another, they all recognized that Cuba was, in fact, a multiracial society. This would seem self-evident, except that earlier in the century many white Cubans interpreted *cubanidad* to be a white phenomenon. As far as they were concerned, being Cuban meant participating in a Hispano-Cuban cultural tradition. *Criollo* nationalism was deeply racist, highly exclusive, and did not easily accommodate the island's mixed racial character....

Cuban communities in the United States, and particularly Florida, were in the Vanguard of accepting and promoting a multiracial version of *cubanidad*. The emigré centers' guiding ideologies, in fact, required the building of unified communities. The defeat of the Spanish could never be accomplished without the support of an overwhelming number of the island's inhabitants. This was recognized by Cubans in New York during the mid-1860s, who called on slaves and mulattos to join in the creation of the Cuban nation-state. Two decades later, José Marti called on compatriots of all races to build a nation devoid of harmful distinctions....

Racial attitudes of Cubans in the United States, particularly in Florida, appear to have changed after 1900. The acceptance of a multiracial identity in theory and in practice before 1900 gave way to a dichotomized racial identity, as Cuban whites and blacks adhered to the institutionalized racism of the U.S. South.... After independence and the dissolution of the traditional patriot organizations, new clubs formed and from their inception allowed only white Cubans to join....

The broader significance, of course, was that the Cuban community and its identity became fragmented. The dynamics of race changed as Cubans sought to accom[m]odate to a new social reality....

Emigré strategies, individual and collective, began to reflect conditions in the local communities.

FURTHER READING

Esther Allen, ed., *Jose Martí: Selected Writings* (2002).

Laura Briggs, *Reproducing Empire: Race, Sex, Science, and the U.S. Imperialism in Puerto Rico* (2002).

Pedro A. Cabán, *Constructing a Colonial People: Puerto Rico and the United States, 1898–1932* (1999).

Christina Duffy Burnett and Burke Marshall, eds., *Foreign in a Domestic Sense: Puerto Rico, American Expansion, and the Constitution* (2001).

Aviva Chomsky et al., *The Cuba Reader: History, Culture, Politics* (2003).

Mariola Espinosa, *Epidemic Invasions: Yellow Fever and the Limits of Cuban Independence, 1878–1930* (2009).

Walter LaFeber. *The American Age: United States Foreign Policy at Home and Abroad Since 1750* (1989).

Juan F. Perea, "Fulfilling Manifest Destiny: Conquest, Race, and the Insular Cases," in Christina Duffy Burnett and Burke Marshall, eds., *Foreign in a Domestic Sense: Puerto Rico, American Expansion, and the Constitution* (2001).

Louis A. Pérez, Jr., *Cuba: Between Reform and Revolution* (1995).

Louis A. Pérez, Jr., *The War of 1898: The United States and Cuba in History and Historiography* (1998).

Kelvin A. Santiago-Valles, *"Subject People" and Colonial Discourses: Economic Transformation and Social Disorder in Puerto Rico, 1898–1947* (1994).

Kal Wagenheim and Olga Jiménez de Wagenheim, eds., *The Puerto Ricans: A Documentary History* (1994).

CHAPTER 5

Early Pan-Latino Communities

As the migration of Cubans and Puerto Ricans increased during the late 1800s and early 1900s, vibrant working-class Latino communities emerged in New Orleans, Key West, Tampa, Philadelphia, and New York City. These diverse communities included Latinas and Latinos from many countries, as well as African Americans, European immigrants, Asian immigrants, and whites. Yet the contours of diversity varied markedly based on specific location. As with some Mexican American enclaves in the Southwest, communities were more racially and ethnically mixed than the scholarship has explored. Critical in their own right, the histories of these communities also counter misperceptions. Too often Latinas/os are portrayed as recent arrivals and Cuban migration as a solely post-1959 phenomenon. Similarly, too many think of Latina/o diversity as the result of the Immigration Act of 1965, and hence a relatively recent phenomenon.

Instead, Cuban cigar makers and exiles struggling for Cuba's independence from Spain crafted communities that focused both on their homeland and on the issues confronting them in the United States. In 1880, José Martí (1853–1895) came to New York City, following his arrest and exile to Spain for his participation in the Ten Years' War. In 1892, he established the Cuban Revolutionary Party (PRC), which soon had branches in New York City, Tampa, Philadelphia, and Boston. In New York City, Cubans and Puerto Ricans forged political ties and created several clubs and newspapers to further their shared goals of liberation from Spain. Having followed the circuits of the cigar industry, Cubans and other cigar makers also struggled to retain workers' autonomy, as well as decent working conditions and wages. Workers forged cross-border solidarities. Puerto Rican cigar makers shared these work spaces and labor activism, particularly in Philadelphia and New York City. After 1898, Cubans' and Puerto Ricans' efforts embraced many forms of community building, and Puerto Ricans now faced a long struggle with U.S. colonialism.

In 1917, the U.S. Congress passed the Jones Act, declaring all Puerto Ricans to be U.S. citizens. As with the Treaty of Paris that ended the Spanish-Cuban-American War, Puerto Ricans were not consulted in the declaration of U.S. citizenship. Indeed, many Puerto Ricans worried that given the continued colonial status of Puerto Rico, U.S. citizenship would be that of an "inferior order," a second-class citizenship. Recruited as low-wage workers and traveling on their own to seek increased opportunities, Puerto Rican migration to the United States increased dramatically following World War I. Some communities became perceived as "Puerto Rican," obscuring their earlier pan-Latino makeup. Merchants and other professionals settled in cities such as Bridgeport, Connecticut, and Boston, Massachusetts, creating a more dispersed settlement pattern. This chapter explores the early pan-Latino communities formed by Cuban and Puerto Rican political exiles, cigar makers, and other Latinos, many of whom were working class, with vibrant ties to their homelands and strong stakes in building communities in the United States.

 # DOCUMENTS

In Document 1, Cuban American Jose Yglesias writes autobiographically about his grandfather's encounters in Key West with Cuban revolutionaries, including José Martí. Yglesias reveals differences among Cubans, as well as the gulf separating his Cuban community and the broader community. In Document 2, the founding of an Afro-Cuban Club in Tampa in 1901 is described by the Federal Writers Project, a project funded by the federal government during the Great Depression. In Document 3, a 1910 report, Father Antonio Casulleras highlights the accomplishments of Philadelphia's Spanish Chapel in its first year and the need for additional resources to meet the religious and social needs of the city's "Spanish-American Colony." In 1911, Afro-Puerto Rican Arturo (Arthur) Schomburg began collecting books and other materials of "historical value to the Negro race," as noted in Document 4. These materials constitute an important archive of the African diaspora to this day. In Document 5, excerpts from his 1914 novel, Colombian Alirio Díaz Guerra portrays the hardships and temptations that a young immigrant confronts in New York City, illuminating the diverse Latino population and their shared challenges. In Document 6, Puerto Rican statesman Luis Muñoz Rivera testifies before the U.S. Congress in 1914, arguing that the political status of Puerto Rico and the citizenship status of Puerto Ricans are linked. For Muñoz Rivera, U.S. citizenship should come with statehood or Puerto Rican citizenship should come with independence. Otherwise, he fears a U.S. citizenship of an "inferior order," unacceptable to most Puerto Ricans. In Document 7, excerpts from his memoir, Puerto Rican cigar maker and activist Bernardo Vega describes his 1916 journey to New York City and the diverse community of Harlem. In Document 8, excerpts from the Organic Act of 1917 (the Jones Act), the U.S. Congress declares all Puerto Ricans to be U.S. citizens, while simultaneously retaining sovereignty over Puerto Rico, albeit with increased self-government on internal matters.

1. Cuban-American Jose Yglesias Depicts His Family's History in Florida, 1890

[Grandfather] began showing up evenings at Sociedad de Cuba quite self-consciously, as if being in the presence of the men of the community would give him adult self-control. At first he went only to the canteen, where he sat at the edge of tables where dominoes were played and listened to the conversations there and at the bar. A year earlier the last fighters for Cuban independence were defeated in Cuba, and some of the veterans had found their way to Key West. When they arrived, there had been public meetings to honor them, but already that seemed to Grandfather to have happened long ago, for those events had occurred in the days before he entered the cigar factory as an apprentice. Now the subject entranced him; the notion that there was an island called Cuba ninety miles from their pebbly shore determined to be an independent nation, that he was a Cuban by virtue of his parents and the language he spoke, was a revelation he owed to these men who did not play dominoes but sat on the balcony on the second floor and relived old campaigns and speculated about new ones.

He was a Cuban. This sudden knowledge became one with his experience of working in the factory. It confirmed his adulthood....

Hector Beltran had been General Jose Miguel Gomez's youngest lieutenant, and had been captured by the Spanish army some four years earlier. If he had not been the son of a wealthy Creole family—sugar plantations in Oriente and coffee in the mountains of Las Villas—he would have been executed or held in the dungeons of the military fortress in Havana. His father bargained away the coffee plantations, and the slaves that went with them, and an order arrived from Her Majesty recalling young Beltran to Spain.... [I]t was months before the Court learned that he had left ... for Paris. But here he was now, accepting Grand-father's cigars, more or less stolen from the best coronas made that day, a marvel-ously democratic, handsome young man of twenty-five, at ease everywhere, particularly among Cubans....

[E]veryone there knew that he had come to Key West to organize expeditions to liberate the homeland....

Grandfather's trips to the piers in those days were made to welcome Cuban patriots canvassing the Latin colonies in New York, Philadelphia, Tampa, and Key West to organize help for those again fighting on the island. There had been many attempts to invade it from Key West, and while Grandfather was in New York, Lieutenant Hector Beltran had drowned when one of the fishing boats taking his group to a rendezvous in Pinar del Rio capsized. The Havana manufacturers who had begun the cigar industry in Key West some four decades earlier to escape the radical activities of the nationalists back home were no lon-ger surprised at all this; some had already ten years earlier set up a company town in Tampa to get their businesses away from the ferment in Key West, but there too the fervor for Cuban independence was accompanied by strikes for higher wages, a closed shop, sometimes simply for a better grade outer leaf for the cigars they made. The manufacturers were in the main Spanish and they seemed at a loss to diagnose the fever that swept their workers everywhere....

That southwest corner of Key West was Grandfather's Athens. Jose Martí was its philosopher-king. He formed the Cuban Revolutionary party there, and there and in Tampa delivered some of his most important speeches. When he arrived from New York for one of his stays, Grandfather was in the committee that welcomed him—though well in the background because Grandfather was its youngest member. He was also the youngest member of the strike committee at the factory, and each Saturday set up a small table he brought from home at the factory entrance, opened a folding chair, and checked off in a notebook the names of the workers who paid the ten percent of their salaries pledged to the revolutionary movement. Grandmother was so proud of him that as often as it was possible to do so without shaming him she walked by casually leading the girls and accompanied him to Sociedad de Cuba, where he turned over the week's take.

Before I started grammar school in Tampa, I used to think, listening to Grandfather on our porch, that everyone knew about Jose Martí, but after a week of hearing American teachers speak only English I began to suspect that the years before I entered Ybor City School had been wasted. Martí's name was not mentioned in junior high or in high school either, and one of the things I learned in school was that there were many things you were expected to forget....

"You really shook Jose Martí's hand, Grandpa?" I would ask, though I knew the answer well, just to get him to talk. He was a widower and lived with my mother and sisters and he was also my father now, since mine was not allowed to return from Cuba by the immigration authorities. I was eight, it was three years since we had visited Father in Havana, and I was long ago used to the idea that he could not come home.... Grandfather belonged to me. Especially when we sat by ourselves on our little porch in Tampa. Not Tampa but Ybor City. Tampa was where the Americans lived.

... [F]rom our porch ... [y]ou could see ... the red brick structure of the Clock, the largest cigar factory in Ybor City. For most of my childhood Grandfather worked there and came home early, and when I asked him the question about Martí, he would always pause and study the Clock, I thought, before he replied. Just when I'd decide I should ask the question again, he would nod and say, "He was a simple, great man."

In Key West, Grandfather had twice been on the committee to welcome Martí at the pier and because he was, as I said, the youngest man on it, Martí singled him out for a special embrace. That was the time Grandfather sat on the platform when Martí spoke. It was at the meeting that my aunt Chucha, who had been born in Brooklyn, appeared on the program. She had been selected to greet Martí—she was five and had a strong voice that carried far; a voice that was to be of great use in later years when she was the mother of twelve children— and wore a white dress that Grandmother had designed and sewn for the event.

Chucha recited a verse composed by an older member of the committee, and seventy years later she stood on her porch in West Tampa to say it to me.

> Here on this sister island
> A place has been made for me
> By a little band of men
> Who say—Our flag will fly free!

In her right hand, which she kept behind her during the recitation, she had held a small Cuban flag, also sewn by Grandmother, and when she got to the last line she brought it forward and waved it and then handed it to Martí.

Grandfather never forgot the passage in Martí's speech that day in which he talked about Key West. Inspired, we all liked to think, by Chucha's performance. In Ybor City Grandfather got up from the porch swing to recite it, although he and I were alone....

Social distinctions among the cigarmakers of Ybor City? Yes. At sixteen all that occupied me were the oppressive differences between us in Ybor City and the Americans I first met in high school. Yet I knew, as a fact of life, that Uncle Candido went to the Centro Asturiano, at whose canteen you met Spaniards with better jobs, and Cousin Pancho to the Centro Español where the Spaniards who gathered there were livelier and more democratic; while Abel and Grandfather naturally went to the Cuban Club where no foreman ever entered (and where they were less strict about Cuban blacks) except on gala fiestas to enjoy the superior rumba bands. My dead father was born in Spain and my mother was wholly of Cuban descent, but I claimed neither. I was stubbornly intent on being American, a singular view of myself that no one in or outside that anomalous Southern community shared....

Grandmother ... was never to run a household that did not continually reach out for new members.

Indeed, when they moved to West Tampa in 1896, Grandfather's parents and two sisters were able to come along because Grandmother, without his knowledge, sold an old diamond ring and gave them the money. West Tampa was the newest of the cigarmaking communities. Ten years earlier Ybor City, at the eastern end of Tampa, had been started by the same manufacturers who owned the factories in Havana and Key West and New York; it was their naïve hope that here, where even the rows of frame houses belonged to them, the cigarmakers would somehow be tamed.... Grandfather found a house on Cypress Street that did not belong to the factories. Grandmother set up house and never moved again.

It was there that my mother was born. She was the last of the girls, but Grandmother drew others to her—girls who had come from Cuba and Key West alone, others who were orphaned in their adolescence, and nieces and nephews of Grandfather's....

Every May 20, which is the equivalent in Cuba of the Fourth of July, Mother followed Grandfather into the front yard, where he straightened the flagpole that the rains had loosened in the fall, and together they raised the Cuban flag. Grandfather began this ritual in Key West before Mother was born, the year after Jose Martí was killed, as a way of keeping his spirits up. Later, because the war was at its climax. Finally, as a gesture of defiance in the country that had imposed a humiliating overlordship on Cuba. In time he stopped. Not because his opinions had changed but because he disliked rhetoric and playing the patriot. He would not go to the commemorative celebrations at the Cuban Club either, where the Platt Amendment was denounced—if they were not going to fight, he said, then they should stop talking.

2. Afro-Cuban Club Established in Tampa, 1901

The Cuban negro emigrated from Cuba to the United States to work in the cigar factories the same as the white Cubans. They cooperated with the white Cubans in their patriotic fight against the Spanish oppression. The Cuban negro could work in the cigar factories and at the same time develop their ideals.

The Marti-Maceo Club was organized in 1901 with Jose Y. Ramos as the first president. The club was named for Jose Marti, the apostle of liberty of the Cuban Revolution, and Antonio Maceo, the Cuban mulatto warrior. The club established itself in a house on 8th Avenue between 13th and 14th streets. This house was adapted for the purpose of holding dances and other recreational activities for its members, where they could gather at night and read the newspapers from Cuba and play games.

On the 26th of October 1901, a dance inaugurated the club. The club maintained itself as a social group charging a small monthly membership fee until 1905. At this time the club decided it should have a medical aid department for the protection of its members during illness, similar to the other Latin clubs.

At this time La Union, a welfare society headed by Juan Franco as president and founded in 1904, had a large membership and this fact interfered with the growth of the medical aid department of the Marti-Maceo club. It was finally decided after several meetings of both organizations to merge the two clubs into one which would offer the services of doctors and medicine as well as recreational facilities. This was done in 1905 and the name of the new organization became "La Union Marti-Maceo".

The merger made the club double in membership and by the payment of 50 cents a week dues on the part of the member gave him all recreational and medical privileges.

Because of this increase of membership a series of festivals were given to raise funds for a new clubhouse. With the proceeds from the festivals the club bought a lot and constructed a two story brick clubhouse at the corner of 6th Avenue and 11th Street, containing an auditorium, dance hall and club rooms. A mortgage of $18,000 was borrowed from Mr. Adam Katz, a merchant. The clubhouse was completed in 1908 and is still being used by the club at the present time.

The club is governed by a board of directors of 15 members, who are elected for a period of two years.

"Study of La Union Marti-Maceo: Cuban Club for the Colored Race" (1940). Federal Writers Project Archives, Work Projects Administration, Special Collections University of South Florida.

3. Father Antonio Casulleras Describes Philadelphia's Community, 1910

The purpose for which this small pamphlet is written is to show the progress made by the Spanish-American Chapel since its foundation a year ago under numerous difficulties and handicaps.

The Spanish-American Colony of Philadelphia consists of about 2000 Spanish-speaking people, dispersed all over the city, including Spaniards, South Americans, Central Americans, Mexicans, Cubans, Porto Ricans and Filipinos....

About two years ago the first gathering was held; until then they did not realize that so many of their fellow countrymen were in Philadelphia.

From this nucleus ... a society was formed for all the Spanish-speaking people. Many who had not spoken their native language for years met; they held social gatherings and talked of their old homes. The teachings of former years soon asserted themselves and with the thought of religion came the desire to form a Spanish Congregation....

[T]hey communicated their desires to the Most Reverend P. J. Ryan, Archbishop of this City, who gave his consent to the project and decided that Very Rev. James McGill ... would bring one of his community from Spain to take entire charge of the work.

When we landed in this beautiful and busy country, we understood that a great and difficult task was committed to us, both in the religious and social ways.

Religion is the first thing that needs protection and needs to be cultivated in the minds of the people of different nationality that emigrate to this great Republic, and it is especially needed by our Colony....

All the Latin American countries have the Catholic Religion as the foundation of their lives, and at home no matter how lukewarm some of them may become, they will never entirely fall.

But it is not an easy matter to comprehend the obstacles which are placed in the way of carrying out the necessary acts of religion, when a person arrives in a strange country, where customs and language are entirely different. The younger generation especially, their own masters, away from parental advice, easily forget the teachings of their childhood. They are surrounded by temptations on every side, and, with no guiding hand, fall an easy prey to the seductive influences of baneful associations.

Before the opening of the Chapel, probably 90 per cent. of the Latin Americans did not attend any Church, many children did not receive the Holy Sacrament of Baptism, many parents were not united before the Altar and many of them had allowed relatives and friends to die without receiving the last Sacraments.

During the first year of our labors abundant fruit has been gathered.... Owing to the scattered condition of the Colony the average attendance has not

---

Antonio Casulleras, C.M., "First Annual Report of the Spanish-American Colony" (1910). Philadelphia, Pamphlet Collection, St. Charles Borromeo Archives, Archdiocese of Philadelphia.

been large, but nevertheless it is encouraging. The spark that was almost extinct in the hearts of many is now burning resplendent.

During the first year of our ministry several marriages have been blessed, 10 children have been baptized and the last Rites of the Church have been administered to several seriously ill. Many others made their Easter duty and young folks have been sent to Catholic Parochial Schools.

... [O]ur mission would not be fulfilled were we to limit it to religious work alone.

The greatest difficulty confronting foreigners arriving here is to master the language.... [I]t is our intention to establish a night school where English and other branches will be taught.

Our social programme includes the creation of an association for mutual benefit and protection, an employment bureau for those who believe our mediation may prove beneficial to them. We have already laid the foundation for this work. We have assisted more than 40 needy persons; 32 have been placed in hospitals and gratuitously assisted; 8 persons have received return passages home; we have obtained positions for 25; 10 destitute children have been placed in charitable institutions, and some prisoners visited and attended.

... Were a permanent institution founded for the mutual benefit of all Spanish Americans here it could do incalculable good.

... We need a house for this association and we need the necessary means for the development of our plans. To obtain these is our most fervent prayer to God to move some one charitably inclined to aid us in accomplishing this project.

4. Afro-Puerto Rican Arturo Schomburg Begins Archives on African Diaspora, 1911

Several months ago Arthur Schomburg of New York [C]ity, and J. E. Bruce of Yonkers discussed at the latter's residence, in Yonkers, the feasibility of establishing a society with a limited membership for the purpose of gathering information from books and through correspondence of historical value to the Negro race. Their ideas agreed, and a number of men known to be interested in work of this character were invited to intend a meeting in Yonkers not long ago, at which time the plans of Messrs. Schomburg and Bruce were outlined and cordially approved by those present, and the society was organized. The name Negro Society For Historical Research was adopted and a full complement of officers was elected.... Membership in the society is limited to twenty active members and the entrance fee is $10, with a monthly tax of 25 cents.

The society purposes to gather through its correspondents in the United States and foreign countries books, pamphlets and valuable manuscripts written by Negroes and when opportunity presents to reprint such books or pamphlets now out of print and coming into possession which have any historical value

---

N. Barnett Dodson, "Select Society for Research," *The Pittsburgh Courier*, September 2, 1911, p. 4.

or which will be useful for reference. These it will endeavor to dispose of to members of the race who are interested in knowing what Negroes who wrote books fifty or a hundred years ago had to say and how they said it.

The society is also making a collection of pictures, old wood cuts, photographs of Negroes here and abroad. But this feature of its work will be attended with some difficulty, as there are few pictures of noted Negroes of the early period in this country. It recently came into possession of a splendid steel engraving of Nat Turner, the Virginian Negro who headed and led an insurrection in that state in 1833, which it contemplates reproducing and disposing of for the purpose of adding to its book fund. The books thus far gathered by Messrs. Schomburg and Brace embrace over 150 titles....

5. Colombian Novelist Alirio Díaz Guerra Portrays Immigrants' Struggles in New York City, 1914

... [T]he young scholar had lived in New York City for three years now. During a time when the young ladies inhabiting the boardinghouses were more attractive to Lucas than the books designated to provide a new light to Santa Catalina, it just so happened that—as a complement to his misfortunes and as a result of an inveterate custom through which the great majority of Hispano-American governments display their civilizing instincts—all postal service between the Republic of ★★★ and the outside world came to a screeching halt: surely, not so much because of the civil war which had just broken out and the fact that the government would have to dedicate all rudimentary means of transportation to the war effort, but rather, because it often occurred that, even in times of peace, one never enjoyed truly efficient mail service, which is only provided for fear of a public outrage; therefore, in cases of popular uprisings, the accursed mail does not matter in the slightest....

As soon as the New York newspapers announced that a revolutionary movement had erupted in the Republic of ★★★, events which were not relevant to the Americans nor any other foreigners due to the exponentially small frequency with which they find themselves in Hispano-American countries, the mercantile exchange firm of Jimeno, Marulanda & Co. wrote to Lucas, notifying him that they would not be able to continue to provide him with his monthly pension in the future.

Stunned and confused, the poor young man hurried off to have a word with Señor Jimeno as soon as he read the letter; he explained the desperate situation in which he found himself to Don Arnulfo; he cried; he wailed; he called upon every resource one makes use of when facing life's most difficult trials and tribulations in order to soften Señor Jimeno's hardened heart; but Don Arnulfo proved to be unmoved, and practically pushing and shoving him out the door, he expelled Lucas from his office.

Alirio Díaz Guerra, *Lucas Guevara*; translated into English by Ethriam Cash Brammer (Houston, TX: Arte Público Press, 2003 [originally 1914]), pp. 103–107, 173–175, 181–182.

Lucas's problem remained unresolved as fate threatened to spread open its black jaws and devour him whole. With reddened eyes, swollen cheeks and nervous spasms besieging his entire body, he took to the street. The impetuous, feverish crowd which passed by him on the sidewalk caused him to feel even worse. Lucas found himself in the heart of New York City: that terrifying vortex which consumes everything, where an individual's value or worth is predicated upon the greater or lesser number of coins that he carries in his wallet; where no one knows anyone else; where the pauper is persecuted more strongly than the criminal; where every job, regardless of how insignificant it may be, has thousands of postulants knocking their heads and subjecting themselves to whatever humiliation necessary to acquire it; where the charitable institutions only open to accident victims and the infirm; where, crammed into unsanitary edifices, the disenfranchised perish by the hundreds, succumbing to the cold and hunger in the wintertime and dying of inanition and asphyxiation during the summer. That is how he perceived New York, that immense, heterogeneous and hybrid mass, home to every race of mankind, shelter of every human culture, ocean of every desire, marketplace of every virtue, receptacle of every ambition, a desert where every soul is lost and a feverish bazaar whose heat turns every heart to stone.

This is how Lucas contemplated that gigantic city in his fervent imagination. Jacinto Peñuela had baptized Lucas by throwing him into a lifestyle impossible to sustain when he could no longer count on such abundant financial resources; he had tossed Lucas into a current which was more powerful than the strength of human will; he had led him to discover secrets in a condition and at an age when he should have remained innocent of the ways of the world.... Señor Jimeno, the commodities broker, demonstrated to him, at the most important moments of his life, all of the paltriness of spirits who do nothing more than pursue wealth, those for whom friendship, similarity of blood or race and even shared familial bonds have no value on the marketplace of affection—unless the mesmerizing glitter of gold coins shines on the horizon—and are regarded with utter disdain....

Lucas had no other hope than the very vague notion of finding some job which would be remunerated with what was absolutely necessary in order to prevent the landlady from throwing him out into the street to go without food or shelter. His natural instincts led him to think about his fellow countrymen residing in New York, who he believed could save him from this disaster without too much trouble and without encroaching too much upon their own personal interests. He knew that many of them were living under very comfortable circumstances, that they had business associates, and their own offices in which they ventured to earn a living from the multitude of people whom they were not tied to by any special bond....

After exploding with indignation and outrage, Lucas concluded that it was absolutely absurd on his part to continue with the plan he had initiated, especially when he had heard Peñuela ... on many occasions summarize the moral and material biography of all those fortunate individuals in New York who did not appreciate being approached by, nor did they favor the company of, anyone who could not do them any favors or those who were unable to pay back the favors they did for them.

He thought it would be more prudent and practical to direct himself to those who perform the role of hackney, laboriously earning their daily bread in incessant toil which kept them in bondage from eight in the morning until six in the afternoon, enduring the vain and vulgar impertinence and rudeness of their patrons. Perhaps these hapless souls, who have neither hopes nor happiness, would be able to provide him with more useful and practical recommendations....

And he was not mistaken in his reasoning. If he did not find material support, at least he was given wishes of goodwill instead of frivolous wagon loads of empty promises. But no amount of goodwill or empty promises were going to satisfy his landlady.

So, the original problem, without an apparent solution or even a sign of one anytime in the near future, remained unresolved and became more complicated with each passing hour. Lucas had spent his last dime and was left to the mercy of God and man alike....

★ ★ ★

The boardinghouse where Don Emeterio found lodging was like a holy Mecca for him. Only the Castilian tongue was used inside its walls, and it was spoken in shouts, with excessive rhetoric, just the way he liked it. There were residents of various Hispano-American nationalities: stripling young men, who were cadets at some military academy or students at some Jesuit school; married men, who were faithfully wed to the precepts of holy matrimony, not so much as a result of their virtue, perhaps, as much for aesthetic considerations; honorable matrons, who generally belonged to the society of intolerable mother-in-laws; the chronically ill, who, inspired by the international acclaim of American medicine, resolved to go and place their bodies under the blade of Yankee scalpels, and in many cases once informed about the nature of the malady they were suffering, disguised by the noxious odor of iodoform or carbolic acid, they often met the fate of ending up in the hands of not some famous American physician, but rather in the care of some charlatan or butcher from their own race who is less qualified but certainly more expensive and more inconsiderate than the doctors in their native countries; old spinsters, who were active stewards of world history and who admired or scorned the male tenants in proportion to the greater or lesser amount of flattery and attention they showed; businessmen, who have parted from their native shores for the first time and travel to the United States with the goal of putting a few Yankees up their sleeves; politicians, who aspired to glean more efficient forms of administration and government from American leaders, while they were too often discovered acting as agents of conspiracy or revolution against the heads of state of their own countries; members of the fraternity of the priesthood, usually en route to Rome, who would remove their sacramental vestments and who, instead of passing through the church doors, would embark on missions, like any local boy and with greater avidity than the common man, of the same nature as those selected by Peñuela on that memorable night when Lucas Guevara first lost his virginity ...; venture capitalists, who could not explain why they were not able to locate a buyer for some patent pending, such as sandals made from banana peels, for example, and who were forced to return to their native land, yelling at the tops of their lungs that the Yankees were imbeciles; legendary local artists, who sought to have the tambourine figured among the instruments in an orchestra, and who, because they were unable to achieve their objective, swore by heaven and earth that, as soon as they returned to their countries, they would cause the national presses to resound with their denouncements of the idiocy and anti-artistic sentiments of those who have inherited Washington's glories; military officers, who disembarked from their respective steamships with their swords in their scabbards, wearing combat boots and a pair of gun holsters, and who refused to accept that they should not walk down the streets donning such attire; at least half a dozen young whippersnappers, who heavily contributed to the excitement and din within the boardinghouse with their pranks, shrieks, and mischievous behavior; in a word, there was a kaleidoscope of people of both sexes, representing every shade of skin color and every style and manner of dress....

At mealtime, the dining room turned into pandemonium: the person with the best pair of lungs was considered the most fortunate. The residents discussed politics, religion, and social events; ... and they were always sure to allow the name of some fellow countryman who was not present to trickle into the conversation....

★ ★ ★

Almost on a daily basis, Guevara experienced the delight of coming across other Lucases, and although they may not have shared his same baptismal or Christian names, they were, however, the exact reproductions of that Santa Catalina son when he first made his arrival in New York City; they were Lucases of different nationalities, but their appearances were identical, and, for each one, there was a Señor Jimeno who dedicated himself to leading him by the nose, then sucking him dry; they were Lucases like himself, innocent, helpless, ignorant of the conditions in which they had come to find themselves, victims of circumstance and of an unforgivable lack of judgment, who were shipped out of their native lands like packages, without so much as a distinguishing mark or tag, while the senders remained on the familiar shores of their homelands, satisfied and secure in the knowledge that, simply by virtue of the names that the bundles bear, New York City would open wide its doors to welcome them, and the commodities firms that were responsible for them would send a carriage with a liveried postilion to the pier to greet them and escort them to their hotel....

In a word, wherever he was found to be reproduced, whenever he saw the scenes of his own life represented by other actors, on similar or on the very same stage, it often made Lucas smile when realizing that he did not represent the most advanced form of classic Guevaraism.

6. Luis Muñoz Rivera Criticizes "Inferior" Citizenship for Puerto Ricans, 1914

MR. RIVERA. Mr. Chairman and gentlemen of the committee, I introduced in the House a bill to provide a civil government for Porto Rico, but when I did so it was not my purpose to conflict with the bill of Mr. Jones, which is now under consideration, but only to present in printed form, the true aspirations of my country in regard to matters of home rule....

[T]he Republican and Unionist Parties, in their very recent platforms, declared that they aspire to home rule, with a legislature elected by the people, with a cabinet appointed by the governor with the advice and consent of the insular senate, and with ample legislative authority to pass upon all matters of a local character; and therefore when I demand here a liberal reform which covers these grounds, I can and must speak in the name of all, of almost all my countrymen.

The Unionist Party, the majority party, in its platform, until three months ago, embodied two final aspirations, statehood accompanied by American citizenship, and national independence, with Porto Rican citizenship; either one of these measures to be granted by the Congress of the United States after a period in which my countrymen, under a system of self-government, should have opportunity to demonstrate their preparedness to govern themselves. The Republican Party, the minority party, had in its platform, and continues to maintain there, only one final proposition, statehood combined with American citizenship.

During the last two years there has been discussed in Congress and in the press this question of citizenship; and its own defenders state clearly that American citizenship for Porto Ricans does not suggest the most remote intention on the part of the United States to ever grant statehood to my people, and that it was necessary for them to realize the impossibility of statehood. Among other prominent statesmen Mr. William H. Taft, then President of the United States; Mr. Henry L. Stimson, at that time Secretary of War, in charge of insular affairs ..., made the statement hereinbefore referred to, and not a single voice was heard in Congress or in the press dissenting to this ultimatum, so bitter to the Porto Rican people....

For that reason, when the Committee on Insular Affairs is now studying the question of our citizenship, my 93,000 constituents urge that the resolution be postponed and that Congress leave the question open in order that it may be settled at a later date.... One year ago, when a similar question was under discussion, the House of Delegates of Porto Rico, then in session, unanimously voted to send a cablegram, which read as follows:

"Statement of Hon. Luis M. Rivera, of Porto Rico"; Hearings Before the Committee on Insular Affairs, House of Representatives, 63rd Congress, 2d Session, on H.R. 138118, 1914, pp. 53–67.

The House of Delegates of Porto Rico considers it a very high honor for any human being of this world to be invested with American citizenship, but under present circumstances it prays that Congress take no action upon this matter without direct consultation and in accordance with the will of the Porto Rican people....

Seven months ago the same legislative body sent to the Senate another telegraphic dispatch, as follows:

House acknowledges and is grateful for noble purpose of author of bill granting American citizenship to Porto Rico, but respectfully requests no action be taken thereon without first consulting the will of the people of Porto Rico.... We tender through you to American people our sentiment of cofraternity and our confidence that their great spirit of democracy will respect the inviolable right of our people to decide their destiny.

The sentiments of the Porto Rican people could be condensed into declaring to this committee: "If you wish to make us citizens of an inferior class, our country not being allowed to become a State of the Union, or to become an independent State, because the American citizenship would be incompatible with any other national citizenship; if we can not be one of your States; if we can not constitute a country of our own, then we will have to be perpetually a colony, a dependency of the United States. Is that the kind of citizenship you offer us? Then, that is the citizenship we refuse." ...

In its present form the bill under consideration ... invests the governor with an absolute personal power.... [I]f it becomes a law, there will be in Porto Rico a government of bureaucrats for and by the bureaucrats, and not a government of the people for and by the people.... Porto Rico once more places its confidence and hope in the fairness of the American Congress and in its loyalty to the principles which the American Nation represents in the world as the standard bearer of liberty and justice....

THE CHAIRMAN. Your idea is that the bill should declare the inhabitants of Porto Rice to be citizens of Porto Rico?

MR. RIVERA. Yes; to be citizens of Porto Rico....

THE CHAIRMAN. I understand your position to be that there is one of two courses that would be satisfactory to you, as the representative of your people. One of those things is that they be granted statehood, and the other is that they be granted independence; that you are not willing to accept any other status than one or the other of those things; is that so?

MR. RIVERA. Yes, sir....

MR. TOWNER. Your people believe, Mr. Rivera, that granting citizenship would interfere in some way with the obtaining of their independence?

MR. RIVERA. The people of Porto Rico believe that the granting of citizenship will prejudice the question and will place the Porto Rican people in the almost impossible position of defending their own ideas of national independence....

MR. TOWNER. It seems to me your people ought to understand, also, Mr. Rivera, that it will not affect one particle the question as regards their attainment of statehood, either one way or the other, because in our previous history we have had a great many instances in our Territories where after the people had become citizens the Territories have become States.

MR. RIVERA. But not independent people: never independent nations.

MR. TOWNER. Of course, we have never allowed any part of our territory to get away from us, and the probabilities are that we never will....

THE CHAIRMAN. ... Now, it seems ... that the people of the United States desire that Porto Rico shall remain a permanent possession of the United States, but that it shall be given the most liberal form of territorial government that its people are capable of directing.... To postpone the settlement of this question means, in my judgment, that it will become a very live and most disturbing political issue in Porto Rico; that one part of them will favor Statehood, another independence, and still another a liberal territorial government such as we are seeking to provide in this bill. To postpone longer the settlement of this question is to invite its discussion in Porto Rico when nothing can be gained thereby.... This bill is framed upon the idea that Porto Rico is to remain a permanent possession of the United States. It proposes to settle this question and thus remove it from Porto Rican politics....

MR. RIVERA. ... [T]he final aspiration of my party is nationalism, with or without an American protectorate, and as the Porto Rican people understand it, the granting of citizenship will interfere with their aspirations for independence....

I think the people of Porto Rico will demonstrate that they are able to manage and maintain their own government.

THE CHAIRMAN. I do not think that would change sentiment in the United States, and, I think, speaking for myself, this talk of independence is an idle dream ..., and that it would be much better to have the matter settled now, better for the Porto Rican people themselves....

MR. RIVERA. ... We prefer always national independence, but I am sure that the immense majority of the Porto Ricans would be not only very well satisfied, but that they would be proud to

have statehood promised now and granted a little later in the
future by the United States of America, because we know the
United States to be a great, liberal Nation, and we feel a great
pride to be a part of the United States. But you know that
national independence is a sentiment, a very natural sentiment,
in the hearts of all people....

MR. MILLER. Suppose this matter relative to statehood as drawn remains in
the bill; in other words, the conferring of citizenship upon the
Porto Ricans there....

You think a majority of your people would prefer Porto Rican citizenship
rather than to become citizens of the United States?

MR. RIVERA. Yes.

MR. MILLER. Suppose the bill should provide that only American citizens could
vote and hold office; what effect would that have?

MR. RIVERA. I could not believe that the Congress of the United States would
include that provision in the bill, because this is one despotic and
tyrannical provision which is equivalent to compelling the natives
of Porto Rico to become American citizens, and that is not a
desirable position for the American people to take.

7. Bernardo Vega Describes New York City's Pan-Latino Community, 1916

Early in the morning of August 2, 1916, I took leave of Cayey. I got on the bus
at the Plaza and sat down, squeezed in between passengers and suitcases.... I just
stared at the landscape, sunk in deep sorrow. I was leaving a girlfriend in
town....

I left Cayey that hot summer, heavy of heart, but ready to face a new life.

From an early age I had worked as a cigar-roller in a tobacco factory. I had
just turned thirty, and although it was not the first time I had left my hometown,
never before had I put the shores of Puerto Rico behind me. I had been to the
capital a few times. But now it meant going farther, to a strange and distant
world. I hadn't the slightest idea what fate awaited me.

In those days I was taller than most Puerto Ricans. I was white, a peasant
from the highlands (a jíbaro), and there was that waxen pallor to my face so typical of country folk....

I arrived in San Juan at around ten o'clock in the morning....

I spent the afternoon taking leave of my comrades.... They all were
unhappy about my decision to leave because of the loss it would be for our

Republished with permission of Monthly Review Press, from *Memoirs of Bernardo Vega: A Contribution to
the History of the Puerto Rican Community in New York*, ed. César Andreu Iglesias, trans. Juan Flores (1984);
permission conveyed through Copyright Clearance Center, Inc.

newly organized workers' movement. But they did not try hard to dissuade me. As socialists, we dig our trenches everywhere in the world.

I boarded the boat, the famous *Coamo* which made so many trips from San Juan to New York and back. I took a quick look at my cabin, and went right back up on deck. I did not want to lose a single breath of those final minutes in my country, perhaps the last ones I would ever have....

Sunrise of the first day and the passengers were already acting as though they belonged to one family.... The topic of conversation, of course, was what lay ahead: life in New York. First savings would be for sending for close relatives. Years later the time would come to return home with pots of money....

When the fourth day dawned ... [w]e saw the lights of New York....

First to disembark were the passengers traveling first class—businessmen, well-to-do families, students. In second class, where I was, there were the emigrants, most of us *tabaqueros,* or cigar workers.

★ ★ ★

Ambrosio [Fernández] himself was out of work, which led me to ask myself, "Now, if Ambrosio is out of a job, and he's been here a while and isn't just a cigarworker but a silversmith and watchmaker to boot, then how am I ever going to find anything?" My mind began to cloud over with doubts; frightening shadows fell over my immediate future. I dreaded the thought of finding myself out in the streets of such a big, inhospitable city. I paid the landlady a few weeks' rent in advance. Then, while continuing my conversation with Ambrosio, I took the further precautionary measure of sewing the money for my return to Puerto Rico into the lining of my jacket. I knew I only had a few months to find work before winter descended on us. If I didn't, I figured I'd send New York to the devil and haul anchor....

The next day I went out with Ambrosio to get to know New York....

We walked up Manhattan Avenue to 116th, which is where the León brothers—Antonio, Pepín, and Abelardo—were living. They owned a small cigar factory. They were part of a family from Cayey that had emigrated to New York back in 1904. The members of that family were some of the first Puerto Ricans to settle in the Latin *barrio* of Harlem.... In all, I'd say there were some one hundred and fifty Puerto Ricans living in that part of the city around the turn of the century.

Before our countrymen, there were other Hispanics here. There was a sizable Cuban colony in the last quarter of the nineteenth century.... They must have been people of some means, since they lived in apartments belonging to Sephardic Jews on 110th Street facing Central Park.

... [W]hen I took up residence in New York in 1916 the apartment buildings and stores in what came to be known as El Barrio, "our" barrio, or the Barrio Latino, all belonged to Jews. Seventh, St. Nicholas, and Manhattan avenues, and the streets in between, were all inhabited by Jewish people of means, if not great wealth.... The ghetto of poor Jews extended along Park Avenue between 110th and 117th and on the streets east of Madison. It was in this lower class Jewish neighborhood that some Puerto Rican and Cuban families, up to about fifty of them, were living at that time. Here, too, was where a good many Puerto Rican cigarworkers, bachelors for the most part, occupied the many furnished rooms....

Many of the Jews who lived there in those days were recent immigrants, which made the whole area seem like a Tower of Babel. There were Sephardic Jews who spoke ancient Spanish or Portuguese; there were those from the Near East and from the Mediterranean, who spoke Italian, French, Provençal, Roumanian, Turkish, Arabic, or Greek. Many of them, in fact, could get along in five or even six languages....

I began to recognize that New York City was really a modern Babylon, the meeting point for peoples from all over the world....

At this time Harlem was a socialist stronghold. The Socialist Party had set up a large number of clubs in the neighborhood. Young working people would get together not only for political purposes but for cultural and sports activities and all kinds of parties. There were two major community centers organized by the party.... All kinds of political, economic, social, and philosophical issues were discussed there; every night speakers aired their views, with the active participation of the public....

It was late, almost closing time, when we reached the León brothers' little cigar factory. Antonio, the eldest, harbored vivid memories of his little hometown of Cayey, which he had left so many years ago. His younger brothers, Pepín and Abelardo, had emigrated later but felt the same kind of nostalgia. There we were, pining for our distant homeland, when Ambrosio finally brought up the problem at hand: my pressing need for work. "Work, here?" the elder brother exclaimed. "This dump hardly provides for us!" Thus, my dream of rolling cigars in the León brothers' little factory was shattered. My tribulations in the iron Tower of Babel had begun.

★ ★ ★

In 1916 the Puerto Rican colony in New York amounted to about six thousand people, mostly *tabaqueros* and their families. The broader Spanish-speaking population was estimated at 16,000.

There were no notable color differences between the various pockets of Puerto Ricans. Especially in the section between 99th and 106th, there were quite a few black *paisanos*. Some of them, like Arturo Alfonso Schomburg, ... later moved up to the black North American neighborhood. As a rule, people lived in harmony in the Puerto Rican neighborhoods, and racial differences were of no concern.

That day we visited a good many cigar factories. The men on the job were friendly. Many of them even said they would help us out if we needed it. That's how cigarworkers were, the same in Puerto Rico as in Cuba, the same in Tampa as in New York. They had a strong sense of *compañerismo*— we were all brothers. But they couldn't make a place for us at the worktable of any factory.

8. U.S. Congress Declares U.S. Citizenship for Puerto Ricans, 1917

Be it enacted by the Senate and House of Representatives of the United States of America in Congress assembled, That the provisions of this Act shall apply to the island of Porto Rico and to the adjacent islands belonging to the United States....

SEC.2. That no law shall be enacted in Porto Rico which shall deprive any person of life, liberty, or property without due process of law, or deny to any person therein the equal protection of the laws....

That no law shall be passed abridging the freedom of speech or of the press, or the right of the people peaceably to assemble and petition the Government for redress of grievances.

That no law shall be made respecting an establishment of religion or prohibiting the free exercise thereof, and that the free exercise and enjoyment of religious profession and worship without discrimination or preference shall forever be allowed....

SEC.5. That all citizens of Porto Rico, ... and all natives of Porto Rico who ... are permanently residing in that island, and are not citizens of any foreign country, are hereby declared, and shall be deemed and held to be, citizens of the United States: *Provided,* That any person hereinbefore described may retain his present political status by making a declaration, under oath, of his decision to do so within six months of the taking effect of this Act before the district court in the district in which he resides, the declaration to be in form as follows:

"I,   , being duly sworn, hereby declare my intention not to become a citizen of the United States as provided in the Act of Congress conferring United States citizenship upon citizens of Porto Rico and certain natives permanently residing in said island."

... *And provided further,* That any person who is born in Porto Rico of an alien parent and is permanently residing in that island may, if of full age, within six months of the taking effect of this Act, or if a minor, upon reaching his majority or within one year thereafter, make a sworn declaration of allegiance to the United States before the United States District Court for Porto Rico, setting forth therein all the facts connected with his or her birth and residence in Porto Rico and accompanying due proof thereof, and from and after the making of such declaration shall be considered to be a citizen of the United States....

SEC.12. That the supreme executive power shall be vested in an executive officer, whose official title shall be "The Governor of Porto Rico." He shall be appointed by the President, by and with the advice and consent of the Senate, and hold his office at the pleasure of the President....

Organic Act of 1917 (Jones Act), 64th Congress, 2nd Session, Chap. 145, 39 Stat. pp. 951–968.

SEC.25. That all local legislative powers in Porto Rico ... shall be vested in a legislature which shall consist of two houses, one the senate and the other the house of representatives....

SEC.26. That the Senate of Porto Rico shall consist of nineteen members elected for terms of four years by the qualified electors of Porto Rico....

SEC.27. That the House of Representatives of Porto Rico shall consist of thirty-nine members elected quadrennially by the qualified electors of Porto Rico....

SEC.34. ... All laws enacted by the Legislature of Porto Rico shall be reported to the Congress of the United States ..., which hereby reserves the power and authority to annul the same....

SEC.35. That at the first election held pursuant to this Act the qualified electors shall be those having the qualifications of voters under the present law. Thereafter voters shall be citizens of the United States twenty-one years of age or over.

ESSAYS

Scholarship in Latina/o history and Latina/o Studies is increasingly attentive to the complexities in interethnic and interracial dynamics in the shaping of Latina/o identities and experiences. In the first essay, Nancy Raquel Mirabal, professor of Raza Studies at San Francisco State University, explores how Afro-Cubans negotiated "being black, Cuban, and immigrants in post-Reconstruction Florida." Defined by Florida law as black, Afro-Cubans faced Florida's increasingly segregationist laws and customary practices. Yet Afro-Cubans lived in racially integrated immigrant neighborhoods and worked in racially integrated cigar factories. Mirabal argues that Afro-Cubans negotiated the complexities of race via the racial dynamics among Cubans, the context of segregationist southern Florida, and their interactions with African Americans.

In the second essay, Víctor Vázquez Hernández, professor of history at Miami-Dade College, turns to Philadelphia to describe the pan-Latino community that took shape by the 1890s. Spaniards, Cubans, Mexicans, Puerto Ricans, and other Latinas/os lived together in Spanish-speaking enclaves and worked side by side in the city's cigar making shops. Increasingly, they built community organizations, including a mutual aid society, a Spanish-language Catholic chapel, a Spanish-language Protestant church, and a Spanish-language local of the Cigar Makers International Union, as well as other clubs and groups. The International Institute also built pan-Latino bridges through the community. During the World War II era, Puerto Rican migration increased dramatically and organizational activities surged. Vázquez Hernández argues that pan-Latino diversity had early roots and that those roots were an important precursor to the renewed diversity after the Immigration Reforms Act of 1965.

Afro-Cubans and African-Americans in Ybor City and Tampa

NANCY RAQUEL MIRABAL

On October 26, 1900, twenty-three people attended the first meeting of the Martí-Maceo Society of Free Thinkers of Tampa, at the home of Ruperto and Paulina Pedroso, located on Eighth Avenue in Ybor City. With a copy of the newspaper *El Pueblo Libre* in his hand, Teófilo Domínguez explained to the Afro-Cuban men seated in the small living room why it was necessary that "men of dignity" form an independent institution similar to the one in Cuba known as the Antonio Maceo Free Thinkers of Santa Clara. The object of the club, Domínguez explained to the men, should be to "help finish their intellectual education." ...

There are hardly any references to the fact that only a few months earlier the male Afro-Cuban members of a newly organized racially integrated Cuban club known as El Club Nacional Cubano, October 10 had been expelled. There is no indication from the words recorded that the very reason for the meeting in Ruperto and Paulina Pedroso's small home was to organize a separate Afro-Cuban club. The minutes say little about the changes in Ybor City after the end of the Cuban War for Independence in 1898 and the subsequent military occupation of Cuba by the United States. There is no mention of the sudden shift in the political climate, the [cigar makers'] Weight Strike of 1899 in Tampa, or the reasons behind the dissolution of the local chapter of the Partido Revolucionario Cubano (Cuban Revolutionary Party) only eight months after the end of the war.

The first meeting of what was later to be the club called La Unión Martí-Maceo lasted late into the evening, adjourning at half past midnight. Yet the minutes that Pablo Folas took that evening, filled with suggestive silences and omissions, only hint at what must have kept the members arguing for hours in the Pedrosos' living room....

This understanding ... enables us to move past what is written to investigate not only those parts of the story that remain untold but also why and how the writing and the "not writing" take place. As a result, we can begin to view the withholding of words, the silencing of experiences, and the fragmenting of memories as strategies employed by Afro-Cuban women and men to negotiate being black, Cuban, and immigrants in post-Reconstruction Florida. For the members of the Martí-Maceo Society of Free Thinkers to have formally documented the reasons behind the organization of a separate Afro-Cuban club would have meant publicly acknowledging that their lives were shaped by factors not only outside of the Cuban immigrant community but also within it—that

Nancy Raquel Mirabal, "Telling Silences and Making Community: Afro-Cubans and African-Americans in Ybor City and Tampa, 1899–1915," in *Between Race and Empire: African-Americans and Cubans before the Cuban Revolution*, eds. Lisa Brock and Digna Castañeda Fuertes (Philadelphia: Temple University Press, 1998), pp. 49–69.

along with their racial identity, being Cuban itself was subject to redefinition once they were in Florida.

When Afro-Cubans arrived in Ybor City they were faced with an imposed definition of race that did not take into consideration their immigrant status or ethnic identity. Since Florida's "Black Codes" defined any person with one eighth Negro blood as black, Afro-Cubans who immigrated to Florida during the late nineteenth and early twentieth centuries were assigned to the same legal category as African-Americans. However, as Cubans living and working in an immigrant community, they occupied a fluid, in-between position where they were neither white nor necessarily black.

At the time, the United States lacked immigration policies restricting Cuban entry into Florida; Afro-Cuban women and men were able to move back and forth between Cuba and the United States with relative ease. This mobility, as well as the possibility of finding work and being part of an established immigrant community, facilitated the creation of "in-between" spaces and strengthened them. Such spaces allowed Afro-Cubans to create an identity that preserved and reflected their Cuban cultural heritage while enabling them to resist being defined racially by the state of Florida.

While Afro-Cubans were able to avoid some forms of racial and economic disenfranchisement, they could not altogether escape certain racial laws and policies. By the late nineteenth century, a series of Jim Crow laws had been passed by the Florida legislature that further entrenched the state's already extensive practices of racial segregation. In 1885 the Florida legislature drafted a constitution to replace the 1868 constitution, which had extended certain rights and privileges to African-Americans. The new constitution effectively revoked those rights and sought both to disenfranchise African-Americans and to dissolve the Republican Party. Four years later a series of Jim Crow laws were passed giving legal sanction to racial segregation in Florida. The 1889 laws were so far-reaching that by 1900 racial segregation had become more widespread than it was in 1865.

For Afro-Cubans this meant that even though they lived and worked in racially integrated neighborhoods and cigar factories, they were still expected to use separate schools, theaters, hospitals, and churches and travel in segregated streetcars and trains. It meant not only having to negotiate multiple levels of racial segregation but also of integration. Afro-Cubans had to "know their place" even when what constituted "their place" was continually changing. The fluid and yet persistent nature of racial definitions and customs emphasized the tenuous and changeable nature of such contested spaces, making it clear to Afro-Cuban immigrants that if they were to have a space to work, live, and socialize, those spaces needed to be asserted and cultivated at all times.

★ ★ ★

In 1895, nine years after Vicente Martínez Ybor built the first cigar factory in the Tampa area and established a company town known as Ybor City, close to 130 cigar factories had already been constructed in Tampa. The large number of cigar factories and the steady influx of Cuban workers transformed Ybor City into an economically independent and bustling immigrant community.... Known as the Havana of America, Ybor City, with its immigrant population, Spanish-language newspapers, "hole in the wall cafes," and Cuban social clubs, eased the transition of Cuban immigrants and exiles into the United States.

The majority of Afro-Cubans who immigrated to Ybor City found work in the cigar factories stemming tobacco leaves and rolling cigars....

Although cigar factories were racially integrated, they were by no means free of gender, class, ethnic, and, to an extent, racial distinctions. These differences shaped the type of employment offered to cigar workers and situated them in what has been called an "occupational hierarchy." Although Afro-Cubans earned the same wages as other workers for comparable labor, they consistently occupied the lowest rungs of the occupational hierarchy. For Afro-Cuban men the hierarchy was relatively fluid, allowing them to work not only cleaning the factories and hauling tobacco leaves but also rolling less expensive cigars. Afro-Cuban women, on the other hand, were offered few jobs apart from stemming tobacco leaves. It was an undesirable job....

Afro-Cuban women labored alongside other immigrant women in work areas separated from the men.... Within these spaces women disseminated information, formulated arguments, and ... create[d] a community within the factories, in labor unions, and in the larger Tampa community.... Their networks reached women who worked as seamstresses, midwives, cooks, domestic workers, and boarding-house keepers. During the mid-1890s these networks became particularly important to Cuban women involved in the effort to liberate Cuba from Spain....

While the number of Afro-Cuban immigrants living in Ybor City remained relatively small, they were well represented within the nationalist movement. Afro-Cuban women and men served as delegates to the Tampa chapter of the Partido Revolucionario Cubano, wrote for revolutionary newspapers, contributed donations, and "performed their duties zealously." Some, like Paulina and Ruperto Pedroso, came to symbolize the very struggle for a free Cuba. The Pedrosos donated money, medical care, and almost all of their possessions to the war effort. They even sold their house in Ybor City to help raise needed funds.... Yet despite the efforts of the Afro-Cuban immigrants, they were given little recognition as a community for their work and offered few positions of power within the movement.

Aware of the obstacles presented by racism and class differences in past nationalist efforts, José Martí worked to build a movement that could withstand deep-rooted divisions. Establishing such a movement outside of Cuba necessitated that Martí emphasize the very element missing among Cubans living and working in the United States: Cuba. Central to the movement was the construction of a shared Cuban identity, a *cubanidad* based on the belief that being Cuban and having connections to Cuba superseded differences of race, gender, and class, as well as immigrant and exile status. In his speeches, including one given on the steps of the Club Ignacio Agramonte in Ybor City, Martí urged Cubans to work together and view the revolution as one belonging to all Cubans regardless of color. In essays published in *Nuestra América, La Nación,* and in *Patria,* the publication of the Partido Revolucionario Cubano, Martí consistently stressed the need for a Cuba free not only from Spanish control but from racism, political oppression, and economic exploitation. Although Martí was able to unify Cubans to the point of transforming Tampa into "one of the most important enclaves of revolutionaries in the United States," he was never fully able to neutralize divisions within the community.

Martí's words constitute one of the few historical sources that speak directly to the existence of division and conflicts among Cuban immigrants. His essays, speeches, and actions interrupt and disrupt the silences by challenging the common perception that "racial prejudice among Cubans never existed." ...

★ ★ ★

In April of 1898 the United States intervened in the Cuban War for Independence. Its ensuing military and political occupation of the island drastically altered definitions of exile, immigration, and nationalism. The U.S. actions, along with Martí's untimely death in 1895, signaled an end to the exile nationalist movement, causing revolutionary clubs to close and the Partido Revolucionario Cubano, founded by Cuban exiles, to disband. Cubans who had been in exile were for all intents and purposes free to return to Cuba. Yet the Cuba they would return to was now under the firm political and economic control of the United States. Military occupation of the island until 1902 and the implementation of the Platt Amendment effectively limited Cuban sovereignty and altered the status of Cuba as nation.

Cuban immigrants were now faced with the dilemma of settling in Ybor City or returning to Cuba during a time of economic devastation and political instability. The decision to remain in Ybor City meant having to re-envision a community that was no longer in exile nor able to use the goal of Cuban liberation as its main tool for unification. As a result, questions concerning what it meant to be Cuban outside of Cuba during a time of U.S. occupation and influence figured prominently in the process of remaking community. Some sites where Cuban immigrants grappled with such questions were the cultural clubs and mutual aid societies [See Document 1]. Organized before, during, and after the Cuban War for Independence, these groups not only provided Cuban immigrants with a place to meet, discuss, argue, and socialize but they also offered members badly needed medical insurance, unemployment benefits, and temporary economic relief.

When a group of veterans of the Ten Years War organized the Club Nacional Cubano, close to a year after the U.S. actions in Cuba, it was with the intention of establishing a place to meet. One of the few racially integrated clubs in Ybor City and Tampa, it was, as José Ramón Sanfeliz remembered, "composed of white and black members—a sort of rice with black beans." While the common thread of involvement in the nationalist struggle operated as a powerful tool for unification, it was not enough, in this period, to make and sustain community. Within a few months and with little explanation, the male Afro-Cuban members were expelled and the club disbanded. For Sanfeliz, the decision to separate was not based on racism, since for him "there was no distinction of races"; rather, it was simply something that "happened" in the process of reorganizing a new club called El Círculo Cubano. As Sanfeliz noted, it was only when El Círculo Cubano was formed that the Afro-Cuban members were, as he put it, "left out."

In a study conducted by the Federal Writers' Project on the origins of La Unión Martí-Maceo, the writers describe its formation without ever mentioning the October 10 Club or the ejection of the Afro-Cuban male members [See Document 2].The writers merely note that while the "Cuban whites organized a recreation club to celebrate their festivals, the Cuban coloreds found themselves without a place to do the same." This, the writers state, is what prompted Afro-Cubans to "organize a club of their own."

The most common explanation for the split ... has been Florida's Jim Crow laws.... While it is certainly possible that segregation played a role in the decision to eject the Afro-Cuban male members, it does not explain why Cuban immigrants failed to consider the consequences of racial segregation when they first formed the club in 1899, how segregation was enforced in the immigrant community, or why certain institutions like the cigar factories remained racially integrated before, during, and after the split.

The sources detailing the split rarely considered the thoughts, emotions, and experiences of the Afro-Cuban members who were left out. We know little of the reaction of the Afro-Cuban members or the impact the decision had on the Afro-Cuban community.... The split formalized and, in a sense, reinforced the existence of a "color line" among Cuban immigrants. Although rarely articulated or formally addressed, the color line affected and shaped the actions, decisions, and experiences not only of the Afro-Cuban club members but of the entire Cuban immigrant community. The decision of white male Cuban members to eject the Afro-Cuban male members of the October 10 Club reinscribed the Afro-Cuban members, and by extension the Afro-Cuban immigrant community in Ybor City, as "black."

By the time the Martí-Maceo Society of Free Thinkers officially merged with the mutual-aid society La Unión in 1904 to form La Unión Martí-Maceo, Afro-Cubans were already making these societies a center of activity in their community. Afro-Cuban immigrants would go to La Unión Martí-Maceo to find out about job openings and housing opportunities, to socialize, and of course to discuss political developments in Cuba. In addition to being a place where Afro-Cubans could gather, the club offered any member who paid a weekly dues of twenty-five cents complete medical care and financial compensation for lost income during illness or injury. Although not allowed to become formal members until the 1920s, Afro-Cuban women were pivotal to the club's success. They exercised decision-making powers and remained active in club affairs through the formation of the *comité de damas* (women's committee). Referred to in the records as early as June 16, 1901, the women who made up the *comité de damas* were responsible for organizing social functions, keeping records, raising funds, and, after 1904, dispensing economic and unemployment benefits.... Whether through their relationships with club members or their presence at club functions, Afro-Cuban women used multiple and distinct avenues, such as discussions and informal gatherings, to suggest and make changes.

An important characteristic of the club was its fervent interest in the political, social, and economic developments in Cuba as well as its devotion to Cuban immigrant issues. The club was so strictly organized around Cuba and being Cuban that its charter prohibited members from endorsing any political organization in the United States and called for all funds and properties to be turned over to the Cuban government in the event of the club's dissolution. These provisions not only made it difficult for the club and individual members formally to support issues that were not directly connected to Cuba or to Cuban immigrants, but it also effectively closed them off from the African-American community....

★ ★ ★

In 1900, the same year in which the Martí-Maceo Society of Free Thinkers was formed, close to 4,400 African-Americans lived in Hillsborough County, Florida. African-Americans made up over 20 percent of the population and were concentrated in racially segregated Tampa neighborhoods....

Florida's legally enforced racial segregation, the Black Codes, and the efforts of local officials to restrict voting rights combined to disenfranchise African-Americans politically and economically....

The relationship between African-Americans and Afro-Cubans during this period was strongly shaped by Florida's racial laws. Although a substantial number of Afro-Cuban immigrants lived in a racially integrated community, extensive segregation laws in Tampa left Afro-Cuban immigrants with little choice but to go to ... parts of the African-American community, to receive medical attention, attend schools, and visit the only theater that admitted black patrons. Despite the inevitable interactions that took place between the two communities, Afro-Cubans preferred to distance themselves socially and politically from African-Americans. They were able to do so by carving out spaces where they could both interact with white Cubans and form organizations that catered solely to their own needs.

Ironically, during the late nineteenth and early twentieth centuries, the social and political ties between African-Americans and Cuba, as nation, were intricately involved and raveled. The connections extended beyond Tampa, where African-Americans sent to fight in the Spanish-American War were stationed, to the war itself, where black soldiers were faced—as an African-American chaplain had observed—with the "glorious dilemma" of relieving Cubans of Spanish tyranny, only to push them "into the condition of the American Negro." Race, as [scholar] Amy Kaplan has deftly argued, loomed large in the minds of U.S. government and military officials, who used race both to control African-American troops and to justify the repression and colonization of Cubans. Blackness and its attributed meanings had been constructed to the point where, as Kaplan observes, "the same argument about the need for white officers to discipline black soldiers was made about the need for the United States government to discipline the Cubans by radically circumscribing their status as nation through the conditions of the Platt Amendment." ...

The collective memory of experiences and lives woven through the constructions and uses of "blackness" were not as binding nor as evident as one
would think ten years later in Ybor City. Any longstanding memory or legacy
of connections between African-Americans and Afro-Cubans seemed to have
given way to everyday concerns.... On February 19, 1908, members of La Unión
Martí-Maceo met to discuss and later vote on Señor Gonzales's offer to set up a
school free of charge for "hombres de color de ambas nacionalidades" (men of
color of both nationalities). The proposition was unanimously rejected by the
members, even though one of the founding tenets of the club was a commitment
to the "intellectual education" of the members. Although little discussion appears
in the club records, the secretary did note that *el señor* Acosta had asked that the
members not say anything in public concerning the decision.

Seven years later, on October 17, 1915, Afro-Cuban male members voted
to permit all eligible "Black individuals regardless of nationality" to become
members of La Unión Martí-Maceo. That night close to sixty-two members
showed up to argue, discuss, dissent, and finally accept the membership of
African-American males.... Of the members present, only twenty-six voted in
favor of the decision; four voted against it, and thirty-two abstained. Although
African-American males were now offered membership into the club, they had
to be recommended by a current member and speak Spanish.

These stipulations enabled Afro-Cuban members not only to control the eligibility of African-American membership but also to designate the club as a distinctly Cuban space in the face of rapid and unavoidable change. The vote to
accept African-American male members shows that on some level interactions
and perhaps even solidarity had developed between the two communities.
This, with the declining number of new members and a waning interest in the
club, motivated Afro-Cubans to consider African-American male membership as
a way to keep the club and mutual-aid society alive. Yet, as the stipulations and
abstentions demonstrate, many Afro-Cuban members were still reluctant to open
the club to African-Americans.

The making of an Afro-Cuban community and identity in Ybor City was
shaped by the multiple applications and uses of silences. In addition to being
woven within and throughout public records and sources, official documents
and published texts, silences were also present in the everyday. Operating on a
more intimate and quotidian level, silences were often a necessary tool for forging alliances and sustaining community. As strategy, silences enabled Afro-
Cubans to theorize for themselves their identity and negotiate an "in-between"
space during a period when such complexities were rarely recognized, accepted,
or easily negotiated.

The silences present in the minutes of the meetings of La Unión Martí-
Maceo provide a glimpse into the workings of silences among the Afro-Cuban
community in Ybor City. As symbol, they serve as a reminder that Afro-Cubans
not only understood their "place" within the United States but that they were
intent on restructuring that "place" to accommodate their race, ethnic identity,
language, and culture, despite the strict legal definitions of race as well as
accepted notions of "blackness" in post-Reconstruction Florida.

Philadelphia's Pan-Latino Enclaves and Puerto Rican Migration

VÍCTOR VÁZQUEZ HERNÁNDEZ

In the 2000 census, the Puerto Rican population of Philadelphia was 91,527 out of a total Latino population of 128,928. While the Puerto Rican portion of the Latino population was still large (73 percent), the census found a steady increase in and diversification of the Latino presence in the city. This supposedly "new" phenomenon of a growing Latino community is actually not so new—a diverse Latino population in Philadelphia was evident as early as the 1890s. This chapter explores how these early pan-Latino enclaves made up of Spaniards, Cubans, Mexicans, and other Latin Americans evolved into a Puerto Rican community in the city of Philadelphia in the aftermath of World War II.

Puerto Ricans were present in Philadelphia in the early twentieth century, numbering less than 100 in 1910; they resided among the larger Latino groups in the city. As the immigration restrictions of the 1920s cut off the immigration of Spaniards, labor recruiters focused on attracting Puerto Ricans, who were U.S. citizens. The number of Puerto Ricans in the city progressively increased. By the 1950s, Puerto Ricans were the premier Latino group in the city and represented the bulwark of the organizational structure. Not until the early 1960s, when Philadelphia began to receive larger numbers of Cuban refugees, did the proportionate numbers of Puerto Ricans experience a decline. The influx of Dominicans after 1965 and refugees from Central America and Colombia in the 1970s and early 1980s contributed to a pan-Latino diversification not seen in the city since the 1930s....

Beginning in the early twentieth century, Puerto Ricans and other Latino residents of the city of Philadelphia initiated a community development process, which gestated throughout the 1920s and 1930s, and came to fruition during the 1940s. Before World War I, Puerto Ricans and other Latinos had founded a mutual aid society and a Spanish-language Catholic chapel. In the 1920s and 1930s, the number of organizations serving the needs of Latinos increased as Puerto Ricans, Cubans, and Mexicans founded a Spanish-speaking Protestant church. By the beginning of World War II, Puerto Rican and other Latino-based groups in Philadelphia were operating across enclave boundaries and sponsoring events that served to unite the different nationality and class groups into a Spanish-speaking *colonia*. It was within the population shifts and economic restructuring in Philadelphia in the early twentieth century that Puerto Ricans and other Latinos organized and built the community institutions to sustain them as they incorporated into the city.

★ ★ ★

Víctor Vázquez Hernández, "From Pan-Latino Enclaves to a Community: Puerto Ricans in Philadelphia, 1910–2000," in *The Puerto Rican Diaspora: Historical Perspectives,* eds. Carmen Teresa Whalen and Víctor Vázquez Hernández (Philadelphia: Temple University Press, 2005), pp. 88–105. Reprinted with permission of the publisher.

During the late nineteenth and early twentieth centuries, many Puerto Ricans were attracted to Philadelphia by contacts made through informal networks developed by earlier Spanish-speaking immigrants. These networks served to get the word out to the island about the existence of Spanish-speaking enclaves in the city, as well as the employment opportunities that existed at the time. This was especially true for cigar makers, who were accustomed to traveling throughout the United States and the Caribbean in search of work. The continuous business transactions between the island and Philadelphia, especially in the sphere of sugar and tobacco, helped promote the city as a point of attraction for Puerto Rican migrants. Communication between Puerto Rico, Cuba, New York, Tampa, and Philadelphia among Spanish speakers, as well as the increased migration of Cubans and Spaniards to the city in the early twentieth century, also helped consolidate this group in the city. Finally, the recruitment efforts of companies, such as the Pennsylvania Railroad, attracted Spanish-speaking workers to the region. Many of these migrants eventually settled in Philadelphia.

By the early 1890s, Spanish speakers were well represented among Philadelphia's cigar makers and cigar manufacturers, especially Cubans and Spaniards. Cigar makers were an important group that contributed a significant number of Puerto Rican migrants to Philadelphia during the late nineteenth and early twentieth centuries. Throughout the second half of the nineteenth century, cigar makers migrated to the principal centers of cigar manufacturing in the United States. Among these centers were Tampa, Philadelphia, New Orleans, and New York. Cigar makers, many of whom were political activists, were well known for their keen sense of organization. They founded some of the earliest Spanish-speaking mutual aid societies in the United States. Cigar makers also played a pivotal role in the development of late nineteenth-century labor movements in the United States, Cuba, and Puerto Rico. As early as 1877, cigar makers had established a Spanish-speaking local of the Cigar Makers International Union (CMIU) in Philadelphia.

During the first years of the twentieth century, Puerto Ricans in Philadelphia became increasingly concentrated in three enclaves located in the neighborhoods of Spring Garden, Northern Liberties, and Southwark. They shared these communities with Italians, Poles, Russian Jews, and African Americans, who were overwhelmingly working class. The settlements were located in these three areas because of inexpensive housing and work available nearby. The earliest Spanish-speaking migrant enclaves depended on the availability of work, and the formation of a subsequent community depended on the accessibility to cheap housing, good transportation, and shopping. Considering these demands, the movement of Puerto Ricans into the aforementioned geographic areas and the conversion of them into distinct enclaves increased during the late 1920s and 1930s....

Puerto Ricans settled in areas in which Spaniards, Cubans, and Mexicans were the predominant Latino groups.... This community existed even though not always visible to scholars or contemporaries.

Puerto Rican migration to Philadelphia accelerated during the interwar period. It occurred at a time when the city's population shifted and housing policies implemented during this time made Philadelphia one of the most seg-regated northern cities.... The shift in population in this period, the move of native-born whites to the suburbs and outer rims of the city, and the substitu-tion of the outbound groups by new immigrants, like Puerto Ricans, contrib-uted to the concentration of Spanish-speaking enclaves in the city. Local and federal housing policies further restricted these newer migrants, especially African Americans and Puerto Ricans, to those specific neighborhoods in Philadelphia....

Puerto Ricans who migrated to Philadelphia during the first half of the twentieth century were overwhelmingly working class. In the early twentieth century, workers in Philadelphia invariably lived near their jobs, and most walked to work.... Housing segregation oftentimes meant that African Americans and Puerto Ricans were relegated to lower blue-collar jobs. Initially, semi-skilled workers like cigar makers and others were more representative of these migrants. Progressively, however, in the 1920s, 1930s, and 1940s, more diverse, displaced laborers from the island joined in the migration to Philadelphia. Possessing few industrial skills, many Puerto Ricans joined other "new" immi-grant workers as well as African American migrants from the South in the City of Brotherly Love.

Puerto Rican migrants in Philadelphia experienced a segmented labor market in the interwar period. Increasingly, the better-paying white-collar and professional jobs were occupied by whites, while African American and foreign-born laborers, including Latinos, were stuck in the unskilled sectors.... Philadelphia had become a premier industrial center in the last quarter of the nineteenth century, but by the 1920s, the city had begun to experience the flight of industries to other parts of the country.... Puerto Ricans and other Latinos' occupational patterns in the city reveal that they labored largely in the blue-collar sectors of the city's economy....

While the Southwark enclave developed around the cigar-making shops, the piers, and economic activity along South Street, the Spring Garden enclave also grew and expanded during the period from 1920 to 1940.... For many Spanish speakers, the allure of jobs, especially at the giant Baldwin Locomotive Works plant, was reason enough to live in Spring Garden. But one of the most impor-tant reasons why Spring Garden attracted so many Puerto Ricans in this period had to do with the establishment of La Milagrosa in the heart of this enclave. La Milagrosa, a Catholic mission, moved from Southwark to Spring Garden in 1912.... The chapel's facilities began to expand beyond religious services to include charity work as well. Institutions like La Milagrosa were central to their neighborhoods in attracting settlers as a hub of activity, and as institutional centers.

The arrival of Puerto Ricans in the first decades of the twentieth century enhanced efforts of Latinos in developing the small but significant organizational network of mutual aid and labor groups that connected the Spanish-speaking enclaves in the city....

★ ★ ★

The three enclaves in Southwark, Spring Garden, and Northern Liberties developed organizations and leadership across the city, which helped them consolidate into one interconnected colonia. Although many Spanish-speaking organizations contributed to this unification, four religious and social groups had the greatest impact on the consolidation of Puerto Ricans and other Latinos in Philadelphia between the early twentieth century and the end of World War II. These organizations were La Milagrosa, the Hispanic American Fraternal Association (La Fraternal), the First Spanish Baptist Church, and the International Institute. This evolving colonia also relied on a diverse but increasingly Puerto Rican leadership....

The period from 1910 to 1940 served as the incubator for several pan-Latino organizations around which the enclaves in Southwark, Spring Garden, and Northern Liberties flourished. Two of these institutions began in Southwark, the oldest Spanish-speaking enclave in the city. La Fraternal was founded around 1908 and La Milagrosa began as a Catholic mission in 1909; both were established within one year and two blocks from each other. Together, these two organizations proved pivotal in the evolution of not only the pan-Latino enclave in Southwark, but of the other two enclaves as well.

The Hispanic American Fraternal Society of Philadelphia, La Fraternal, was formed as a mutual aid group. La Fraternal came about as the result of a mass meeting of a pan-Latino group representing the diversity of Spanish speakers, held during that year. It is unclear exactly when and how this meeting was organized, but writing his first report on La Milagrosa in 1910, Father Antonio Casulleras, the priest in charge, noted that the "gathering ... led to the formation of a ... well known society ... for all Spanish-speaking people." [See Document 3.] ... For Puerto Ricans and other Spanish-speaking residents of Southwark, the formation of La Fraternal, essentially a social organization that also sponsored many evening events, plays, discussions, dances, and festivals, marked a turning point in the development of their communal emergence in the city.

The Latino group that met in 1908 realized that they needed spiritual as well as social organizations that could help them achieve greater benefits and success as a community. This group, which included Puerto Ricans, Spaniards, Cubans, Mexicans, and other Central and South Americans, strove for this goal. One of their first successful projects was the creation of La Milagrosa, with the help of the Archdiocese of Philadelphia. The establishment of Spanish-language masses and other religious services helped bring Latinos together from around the city into this unique institution. Initially located in the schoolhouse of Old St. Mary's Catholic Church in Southwark during its first three years of existence, La Milagrosa quickly developed into a full-fledged chapel.

In the 1920s, the increasing numbers of Puerto Ricans and other Latinos in the city also brought greater religious diversity. Spanish-speaking Protestants, though smaller in number than their Catholic brethren, began to organize their own church. Initially interdenominational in nature, Spanish-speaking Protestants founded the First Spanish Baptist Church in 1929. The fruits of this effort added another organization to the Spanish-speaking enclaves in the city, especially for those residents of Spring Garden, where the Spanish Baptist Church was first housed.... The group was made up of Puerto Rican, Cuban, and Mexican families, some of whom had moved to Philadelphia from New York....

The local International Institute was the fourth organizational entity that had a major impact on the consolidation and development of pan-Latino groups in Philadelphia in the 1920s and 1930s. The institute, a part of a national network of groups initially started by local YWCAs in New York City, supported both cultural and ethnic pluralism, while at the same time seeking "a better integration of immigrants and their children in American society." Beginning in the 1920s, the Philadelphia-based chapter of the International Institute took a special interest in the local Spanish-speaking community. The International Institute was located in Spring Garden.... The ample services provided by the institute's social workers to immigrants, especially to Spaniards, Cubans, Mexicans, and Venezuelans, added to the organization's attraction for Spanish speakers in the vicinity. The institute sponsored the formation of social and cultural groups, including Anahuac, a Mexican dance group, and the Club Juventud Hispana, a predominantly Puerto Rican group made up of youth from La Milagrosa. Other groups representing Cuba, Spain, and Venezuela were organized during the 1930s. Once a year, during the month of May, these groups came together to hold a folk festival at the institute.

These four organizations, among others, were representative of pan-Latino and working-class individuals and families living in Philadelphia at this time. The leadership of La Fraternal was most reflective of the diversity of the enclaves. Led by mostly Spaniards or persons of Spanish descent, the leadership group tended to be made up of professionals or small shop owners who lived in one of the pan-Latino enclaves. Yet their events seemed to gather persons of all classes, including cigar makers. By the late 1930s and early 1940s, La Fraternal's leadership had passed into the hands of Cuban *tampeños* and Puerto Ricans, a reflection of the increase of these two groups in the city. "Tampeños" was a popular name given to Latinos, especially Cubans and Puerto Ricans, who originated from Tampa, Florida, and migrated north to Philadelphia and other cities in the 1920s and 1930s....

By the 1930s and certainly by the 1940s, La Milagrosa had developed into a hub of activity for the community. The chapel organized an Association of La Milagrosa, which handled many of the social aspects of the services provided. The association was responsible for organizing English classes, recreational activities, and picnics. The acquisition of the property at 1836 Brandywine Street, around the corner from La Milagrosa, known as the Spanish Catholic Club, helped the chapel expand its range of activities. This location was used primarily for social functions such as dances and graduations. However, the facility was also rented out for weddings and baptism parties. Social functions at the club attracted many Latinos from the other enclaves as well.

By the early 1940s, a Spanish-speaking, interconnected colonia had begun to take shape in Philadelphia. An affirmation of ethnic and religious belief contributed to consolidated links between the different enclaves. Spanish-speaking churches and the International Institute were strongest institutionally and had the greatest long-term impact on the evolving colonia....

★ ★ ★

World War II was a defining period in the evolution of the Puerto Rican community of Philadelphia.... During World War II, the diverse pan-Latino groups would often sponsor events to foster their language and cultural presence even further and to support the war effort. The efforts of Spanish-speaking residents solidified their colonia and poised it for further community development.... The evolution of a Puerto Rican colonia in Philadelphia by the end of World War II, then, was an indication that the diverse Spanish-speaking enclaves had been transformed. An increase in the level of activity during the war, coupled with a major increase in Puerto Rican migration, enhanced the organizational developments of the period. There was also a proliferation of Puerto Ricans who moved from New York City to Philadelphia. Along with the efforts of men like contract labor recruiter Samuel Friedman and the Reverend Enrique Rodríguez, who preached to Puerto Rican farmworkers in their barracks, the Puerto Rican colonia in Philadelphia grew during and immediately after World War II.

In the early 1940s, the First Spanish Baptist Church under the leadership of the Reverend Enrique Rodríguez became an important religious and community center. The church later branched out, moving north into the heart of North Philadelphia.... Reverend Rodríguez frequently preached to Puerto Rican migrant workers on New Jersey farms and to industrial workers at Campbell Soup Company in Camden, New Jersey, in their respective barracks. Many of these workers sought out Reverend Rodríguez once their contracts were expired. They moved Philadelphia to the neighborhood where his church stood. These new members of the Spanish Baptist Church, once established in Philadelphia, oftentimes sent for their respective families, thus contributing to the expansion of the colonia....

The marked expansion in the social activities among Spanish-speaking groups during the war years was evident in the flyers and other promotional materials used for these events. One interesting feature of these materials is that they were produced in English, probably to attract a wider audience beyond the colonia, as well as some second-generation migrants who may have increasingly used English as their primary language. The use of English and American war symbols may have been intended to appease the larger Philadelphia society, much like the immigrant patriotic rallies that were organized in Philadelphia during the First World War. Events sponsored by Spanish-speaking organizations invariably promoted and sold war bonds....

The locations at which events were held during the war included not only those spots within the pan-Latino colonias ..., but also locations outside of the colonia. For example, the Grand Rally Dance was held in 1943 at the Ambassador Hall, 1701 North Broad Street, in a heavily Jewish section of North Philadelphia. This event is illustrative of the period for several reasons. First, it was promoted as a "United War Chest Rally" and was sponsored by the "Spanish Committee." The Spanish Committee was made up of three of the most prominent Latino organizations at the time: La Fraternal, the Mexican association Anahuac, and the Latin American Club—a reflection of the pan-Latino nature of the enclaves. Highlighted in the program of this event was the American flag, and in large bold letters the words "Buy War Bonds." Clearly, events such as the

Grand Rally Dance reflected not only the coming together of members of the different Latino groups—an important accomplishment in its own right—but of greater significance, the establishment of the colonia as a part of the larger Philadelphia community. Undoubtedly, the American war symbols were not lost on those outside the colonia who attended the event or saw the promotional materials.

The connection between the enclaves was also cemented by the numerous reports in *La Prensa,* an important Spanish-language daily published in New York City during the interwar period. This was a reflection of the continuous connection with colonias in New York City. By the early 1950s, this newspaper had established a regular column entitled En Filadelfia, which was written by Philadelphia Puerto Rican community leader Domingo Martínez. Even before then, *La Prensa* had been reporting regularly on social and cultural events among Latinos in Philadelphia. Family ties between New York and Philadelphia were also very important in connecting both cities....

Puerto Rican labor migrants, who came to work in the Philadelphia area during World War II, found the Spanish-speaking social, cultural, and religious ambiance of the city a welcome relief from the doldrums of barracks-style living of the South Jersey farms or the Campbell Soup factory. Labor shortages in the United States had brought thousands of Puerto Ricans to the area during the war, but a lack of social and cultural activities could not keep them on the farm or in the factory. Also, labor conditions, including meager, plain living quarters, unfamiliar food, and a lack of Spanish-speaking personnel, were often cited as reasons for Puerto Ricans leaving their employment and moving to Philadelphia. Some Puerto Ricans returned to the island when their contracts expired, but many more came following the *"ambiente"* in Philadelphia....

Between 1945 and 1970, the Puerto Rican community of Philadelphia blossomed into the third largest concentration in the United States. Many Puerto Ricans also migrated first to other cities, such as New York, and then found their way to Philadelphia. The Puerto Rican population in Philadelphia increased from 854 in 1940 to 7,300 in 1954. As the Puerto Rican community grew during the 1950s and 1960s, so did its organizational efforts. Supported by leaders from La Milagrosa, the First Spanish Baptist Church, and La Fraternal, new groups began to evolve, especially town-based social clubs representing the migrants' hometown back on the island....

Throughout the 1950s, leaders of the Puerto Rican Affairs Committee like Carmen Aponte, who had come to Philadelphia in 1947, Domingo Martínez, and the Reverend Enrique Rodríguez, among others, struggled to get the city to address the many needs of the Puerto Rican community. Their efforts led to the formation of the Council of Spanish Speaking Organizations, El Concilio, in 1962. The Concilio initially brought together many diverse Latino community groups under one pan-Latino organization made up mostly of Puerto Ricans, but inclusive of all Latinos. In 1968, the Concilio became the first full social service agency funded by city and federal funds....

★ ★ ★

The small but significant organizational network that sprang up within the Spanish-speaking enclaves of Philadelphia became, by the end of World War II, a rich cultural mosaic representing Puerto Rican and other Spanish-speaking national groups in the city. Using a combination of mutual aid, labor, social, and cultural organizational formats, Philadelphia Puerto Ricans and other Latinos established the parameters for the appearance of a colonia. It was this colonia, made up significantly of many Latinos and some Puerto Ricans, that served as a welcome mat for the large numbers of Puerto Ricans who arrived in Philadelphia after 1945. The network of religious, social, and cultural groups that evolved between 1910 and 1945 formed the backbone of the Puerto Rican community that existed in the 1950s and 1960s. The roots of the present-day Puerto Rican community in Philadelphia can be traced directly to the community-building efforts of the pioneer groups in the interwar period.

During the 1990s, the Latino community continued to grow, yet the Puerto Rican population, still dominant in terms of numbers, began to cope with an increase in diversity among other Spanish speakers. Prominent among the new groups were Dominicans, Colombians, Venezuelans, Peruvians, and Mexicans. Members of these respective groups reflected this growth in the establishment of a variety of organizations. The Dominican Community Cultural Center, founded to provide social services, was initially set up in the basement of the Incarnation Catholic Church in Olney and later moved to more permanent quarters at the Concilio in Northern Liberties. Meanwhile, the Colombian community experienced unprecedented growth as many left the war-torn country. Along with pioneers who had lived in Philadelphia for decades, Colombian immigrants formed business and social organizations such as the Colombian Coalition and two weekly Spanish-language newspapers, *Al Día* and *El Sol Latino*. During this period there was also a marked increase in the number of Central Americans, especially Guatemalans. Places like La Iglesia de Cristo y San Ambrosio, a Spanish-speaking Episcopal church in Hunting Park, opened its doors to this group with the Proyecto Sin Fronteras, an adult basic education program.

Certain sectors of the Puerto Rican community, especially in North Philadelphia, began to show signs of an increasingly diverse Latino population. Gone were the days of a dominant presence of Puerto Rican grocery store owners. Dominicans purchased those grocery stores, many financed by their Asociación de Bodegueros Dominicanos, a mutual aid society. Mexican farm laborers, who began to replace Puerto Rican laborers in the outlying areas of Philadelphia, surpassed them in the 1990s. Subsequently, as Puerto Ricans did before them, these Mexican laborers discovered better-paying jobs in the restaurants and hotels of the burgeoning Philadelphia hospitality and tourism industry. This fact lured them to the city. Currently, the biggest Mexican enclave is located in South Philadelphia where 6,220 now live. There, the local community has organized Casa Guadalupe, a multiservice, nonprofit entity. Also, through the help of the local consulate, a Mexican cultural center has been formed.

Just as in the early 1900s, organizations such as the Concilio and the Congreso de Latinos Unidos have reached out to Mexican residents in South Philadelphia and to Colombians and Dominicans in the northern sections of the city, providing them with needed social services. In this regard, although Puerto Ricans continue to predominate as a group, the pan-Latino nature of the community has once again provided the backdrop for working across national lines in the interest of all Latinos in the city of Philadelphia.

 # FURTHER READING

Jossianna Arroyo, "Technologies: Transculturations of Race, Gender and Ethnicity in Arturo A. Schomburg's Masonic Writings," *Centro: Journal of the Center for Puerto Rican Studies* 17, no. 1 (2005), 4–25.

Harold Augenbraum and Margarite Fernández Olmos, eds., *The Latino Reader: An American Literary Tradition from 1592 to the Present* (1997).

Lisa Brock and Digna Castañeda, eds., *Between Race and Empire: African-Americans and Cubans before the Cuban Revolution* (1998).

Adrian Burgos, Jr., *Playing America's Game: Baseball, Latinos, and the Color Line* (2007).

Nancy A. Hewitt, *Southern Discomfort: Women's Activism in Tampa, Florida, 1880s–1920s* (2004).

Jesse Hoffnung-Garskof, "The Migrations of Arturo Schomburg: On Being Antillano, Negro, and Puerto Rican in New York 1891–1938," *Journal of American Ethnic History* 21, no. 1 (2001), 3–49.

Amy Kaplan, *The Anarchy of Empire in the Making of U.S. Culture* (2005).

Iris López, "Borinkis and Chop Suey: Puerto Rican Identity in Hawai'i, 1900–2000," in Carmen Teresa Whalen and Víctor Vázquez-Hernández, eds., *The Puerto Rican Diaspora: Historical Perspectives* (2005).

Nancy Raquel Mirabal, "'No Country but the One We Must Fight For': The Emergence of an Antillean Nation and Community in New York City, 1860–1901," in Agustín Laó-Montes and Arlene Dávila, eds. *Mambo Montage: The Latinization of New York* (2001).

Nitza C. Medina, "Rebellion in the Bay: California's First Puerto Ricans," *Centro: Journal of the Center for Puerto Rican Studies* 13, no. 1 (2001), 82–93.

Louis A. Pérez Jr., "Cubans in Tampa: From Exiles to Immigrants, 1892–1901," *The Florida Historical Quarterly* 57, no. 2 (1978): 129–140.

Louis A. Pérez Jr., *On Becoming Cuban: Identity, Nationality and Culture* (1999).

Gerald E. Poyo, *"With All, and for the Good of All": The Emergence of Popular Nationalism in the Cuban Communities of the United States, 1848–1898* (1989).

Fernando Purcell, "Becoming Dark: The Chilean Experience in California, 1848–1870," in José Cobas, Jorge Duany, and Joe R. Feagin, eds., *How the United States Racializes Latinos: White Hegemony and Its Consequences* (2009).

Virginia Sánchez Korrol, "Latinismo among Early Puerto Rican Migrants in New York City: A Sociohistoric Interpretation," in Edna Acosta-Belén and Barbara R. Sjostrom, eds., *The Hispanic Experience in the United States: Contemporary Issues and Perspectives* (1988).

Bernardo Vega, *Memoirs of Bernardo Vega: A Contribution to the History of the Puerto Rican Community in New York*, ed. César Andreu Iglesias, trans. Juan Flores (1984).

Jose Yglesias, *The Truth about Them* (1999, originally 1971).

CHAPTER 6

Labor Recruitment and Community Formation in the World War I Era

The World War I era witnessed the increased migration of Mexicans and Puerto Ricans to fill labor needs in the United States. Economic and political developments in Puerto Rico and Mexico motivated workers to leave, while labor recruitment and employment opportunities brought them to the United States. As the United States grew increasingly suspicious of "foreigners" and "hyphenated Americans," particularly German Americans, and imposed immigration restrictions, employers sought alternative sources of low-wage workers. Asian immigration had already been restricted by the Chinese Exclusion Act of 1882 and the Gentlemen's Agreement of 1908, which limited Japanese immigration. New laws drastically reduced the immigration of southern and eastern Europeans through quotas based on national origins. So employers turned to southern African Americans, Puerto Ricans, and Mexicans. For Puerto Ricans, the 1917 conferral of U.S. citizenship removed all immigration barriers, facilitated labor recruitment and social networks, and resulted in inscription into the U.S. military. Puerto Ricans were recruited to work in war industries and on military bases during the war, and were drafted into the army. Beginning in 1880, U.S. labor contractors traveled to Mexico to find workers for agriculture, mining, construction, heavy manufacturing, and meat-packing industries in the American Southwest and Midwest. This labor recruitment intensified the debate between employers who wanted to hire low-wage workers and restrictionists, who feared the impact of immigrants on what they deemed "American" culture and society.

Puerto Rican and Mexican migration was also propelled by economic and political conditions in their home countries, wrought in part by U.S. economic interventions. After gaining control over Puerto Rico in the Spanish-Cuban-American War, the United States exerted overwhelming political and economic power. U.S. sugar corporations amassed large plantations, displacing much of the rural population, while the number of tobacco and coffee farms declined. The sugar industry failed to provide full employment for the growing landless and unemployed population. Although not a colony of the United States, Mexico experienced the impact of U.S. investors, particularly in the railroad and mining industries. *Dictator Porfirio Díaz sought to "modernize" Mexico with technological improvements, infusions of foreign capital, and the elimination of communal land holdings. Díaz's economic policies increased landlessness and displaced artisans, and his repression of political opponents led to their exile. With the turmoil of the Mexican Revolution (1910–1920), this combination of factors led approximately 1 in 10 Mexicans to flee to the United States.*

While Puerto Ricans settled overwhelmingly in New York City, Mexican settlement continued in traditional areas in the Southwest and expanded into the Midwest, including Chicago. As they built communities in the United States, Puerto Ricans and Mexicans also maintained ties with their home countries. This chapter focuses on the contradictions between the labor demands that spurred early twentieth-century Mexican and Puerto Rican migration and the growing anti-immigrant and racially divisive environment that migrants experienced.

DOCUMENTS

During World War I, Puerto Ricans and Mexicans filled the nation's labor needs in service, agricultural, and industrial jobs. Revealing policymakers' motives in the labor recruitment of Puerto Ricans, in Document 1, Frank McIntyre, the chief of the Bureau of Insular Affairs (the agency that administered Puerto Rico), proposes shipping workers to the Dominican Republic and bringing others to the United States as manual laborers. Overlooking structural problems caused by the U.S. economic dominance and Puerto Ricans' lack of political representation, he offers solutions to Puerto Rico's so-called "over-population," which U.S. policymakers blamed for the island's continued poverty. Document 2, an excerpt from the memoir of Noble Sissle, an African American drum major and composer, reveals a different form of recruitment—of Puerto Rican musicians drafted into the U.S. Army. Puerto Rican soldiers were skilled musicians who, along with African American musicians, served as U.S. cultural ambassadors in Europe. In Document 3, Puerto Rican writer and activist Jesús Colón describes the impact of false promises and exploitative working conditions in New York City. In Document 4, Elías Sepulveda, a Mexican American from Arizona, comments on Mexico and Mexican immigration, and exemplifies contradictory feelings of respect for Mexican immigrants, dislike of Mexico's institutions, and ambivalence about his acculturation. The editors of *La Noticia Mundial*, a Spanish-language newspaper in Chicago, call for unity among Latinos in the United States to fight discrimination, in Document 5. They reveal the diversity of Chicago's Latina/o community and hint at the transnational influence of ideologies from Latin America. Document 6 contains the congressional testimony of Alfred Thom, a railroad association lawyer, on the widespread use of Mexican laborers throughout the U.S. Southwest. He highlights the tensions between depending on Mexicans as low-wage laborers and some people's desires to restrict immigration from Mexico.

1. U.S. Government Proposes Labor Recruitment of Puerto Ricans, 1917

Possibility of temporary use of Porto Rican men as farm laborers and as untrained manual laborers on railroads, etc. in the United States.

The Bureau has had constantly before it for years the question of the over-population of Porto Rico, and has had in mind various projects to relieve this situation.

As a permanent relief, it favors the colonizing of several hundred thousand of the Porto Rican people in Santo Domingo. This has been discussed with Governor Yager, who is strongly in favor of it, and through Governor Yager the public in Porto Rico has, to some extent, been sounded, and there was no strong opposition.

The present emergency, however, brings to mind a condition which, while helpful to the United States, would alleviate the situation in Porto Rico, pending the establishment of a government in Santo Domingo with which it would be possible to make some arrangement for colonizing Porto Ricans in that Republic and protecting them thereafter. That is, to bring to the United States from 50,000 to 100,000 laboring men to be used on farms as agricultural laborers, for which they are best fitted, or as right-of-way laborers on the railroads or similar work requiring manual labor.

Having this latter thought in mind, I have today cabled Governor Yager as follows:

> "Confidential; Pending the working out of some general emigration scheme such as that to Santo Domingo, would it be possible to secure fairly good Porto Rican laborers to be brought to the United States for work on farms or other work requiring manual labor. How many men could be secured without interfering with Porto Rican industries, and would you anticipate great difficulty, transportation being arranged from this end[?]"

If the reply to this is favorable, the matter may be at once taken up with the Department of Agriculture and possibly the Department of Labor, though I think the Bureau would have no difficulty in placing a great many men needed industrially.

2. Puerto Rican Musicians' Experiences in U.S. Army as Depicted by Noble Sissle, 1917

Their Palm Beach suits were not only of many faded colors, but the trousers were too long for short ones and were too short for long ones. The poor little fellows with the East winds whipping around the edges of their sieve-like

Memorandum for the Secretary of War, April 17, 1917, Records of the Bureau of Insular Affairs, Record Group 350, File 1493, National Archives, Washington, DC. In Center for Puerto Rican Studies, *Sources for the Study of Puerto Rican Migration, 1879–1930* (New York: Centro de Estudios Puertorriqueños, Hunter College of the City University of New York, 1982): pp. 104–105.

Noble Sissle, "Happy in Hell: Memoirs of Lieutenant James 'Jim' Europe [October 1942]," Manuscript Division, Arthur A. Schomburg Center for Research in Black Culture, New York City.

clothes, I fear made their first night in New York far from being a comfortable one.... I spent my time in finding blankets for them as their first night was spent with the Regiment in our temporary Armory (the Harlem Casino) on cots, as we left the next morning for Peekskill. Of course, the next morning the Regiment was in a turmoil, how could it be otherwise with a thousand inexperienced men and officers.... [B]ut my mind was not concerned over the multitude, it was the twenty-eight musicians I had to get assembled to "March" at the head of the Regiment; I say "March" because it was blessed little playing they did.

Everyone was running around with an instruction book in his hand trying to find out how to go to camp and as usual in such circumstances everything came up except what was in the book. For instance, in my case, there was nothing in the manual of arms that explained how to tell fifteen Porto Ricans, all of whom spoke only Spanish, what to do in English.... They could not understand me and I could not understand them. I must take that back; there were two words of English that they spoke perfectly and it went for uniforms, beds, food and in fact everything in general about the army and that was those never forgetable two words: "NO GOOD." Everything was "No good," especially the food. It was pitiful, too, with the little fellows so far from home, most of them mere boys and in their teens, but splendid musicians, whom their mothers had entrusted to Jim Europe's care with his promise to see that they were given every care they could get....

... Jim landed Friday, two days before the regiment was to leave for camp, ... and Saturday was spent buying all kinds of instruments, accessories and music.

The Porto Ricans wanted the most expensive instruments, and the saxaphones, the like of which they had never seen before, were immediately pronounced "NO GOOD," yet, they had none of their own. Jim did not want to hurt their feelings, but their childish enthusiasm was very aggravating in the brief space we had to get ready for the next day's departure. But, Jim's patience was never strained. Between the little Spanish he spoke and his signs, he finally got their instruments. He also bought some Band Selections and marches. (The sudden call to camp had caught him without even a piece of music.) ...

Daybreak Sunday still found us trying to get uniforms for the Band and other things "more important" than rehearsing. By the time we got the men all dressed and fed, the order to "move out" came. Band Master Mikell, in the meantime, had selected a few marches and was passing them out among the men. One was "Semper Fidelis," that popular march.... Before we marched out of the Casino the Band just had time to go through that one number. As they were standing still and were all good musicians, they naturally read the piece right off.... The piece sounded great and a cheer went up from the regiment. But the saying, "All that starts well, does not end well," was very vividly impressed on me by the facts that happened during the memorable parade.

Before the sounds of the cheers for the Band had died out, the order came to "Fall In." From then on for the next two years began my "headaches." ...

Jim was yelling, "Sissle, bring the Band!" for no other reason than the Colonel was hollering at him for the Band. Being my first experience in the

Army, I did not know to whom my rank of sergeant gave me the privilege to holler at. I hollered at the Porto Ricans, as they did not know what I was saying anyway....

By this time Colonel Hayward was getting awfully peeved because of his orders not being carried out; above all, he figured the Band that had been brought together by his influence, should at least pay him some attention, he being the Colonel. However, he saw—quite to his disgust—that a mere Colonel meant nothing to temperamental musicians.... The Colonel tried his luck at giving the command "Forward March," and quite to his surprise the regiment responded and stepped off, not all in step, however ... [Jim] gave his men order to get ready to play the piece selected, the "Semper Fidelis"— ... the band rehearsed the piece so wonderfully in the Armory. But, when the band started marching down Seventh Avenue followed by the sweethearts, mothers and other relatives of the soldiers, crying as though we were leaving for France and not on a two weeks regular National Guard tour of Camp duty, the people yelling out windows, ... and this sight was far more important to the astonished Porto Ricans than playing music. They could see notes any time but these sights they had never seen before and contrary to all military rules, they were jabbering away with one another and stumbling along the street, which kept Jim and me running like wild men from one to the other trying to keep them in formation. Imagine the embarrassment when the streets were lined with people all yelling for Jim to have his band play....

... To look back at it now it was a big joke, but then it was a very serious blow, and the first night in camp spent in cold, heatless tents....

Thus commenced the career of Jim Europe's band that was destined to do more than any one individual organization to blaze the trail for the world-wide popularity that American Negro Music is now enjoying. The two weeks in camp under the musical instructions of Band Master Mikell, and his assistant, Sgt. DeBroite, and tutoring in military formation by Sgt. White, the band began to whip into shape....

... [W]e still could not understand each other in spite of the fact that we had been in camp together over two weeks. However, some of their friends who had been in New York quite some time came around and helped me find out their wants and best of all located a Porto Rican restaurant....

During the interim between [Lieutenant Europe's] two [medical] operations my daily visits to see the Lieutenant were ones of consoling him of the fact that the boys of the band were being taken care of and especially the Porto Ricans. He would send suggestions back to Band Master Mikell concerning the plans for getting the band ready for the military campaign which, about that time was certain, as the Lusitania had just been sunk and all eyes were on Washington, waiting the call which finally came.... The unexpected turn in affairs ... had blasted all my hopes of a concert band that was to develop American music. It looked like we were just to be an ordinary Regimental Band, perhaps to be depleted by the cruelties of a heartless warfare....

Finally the time for the regiment to be mustered into the Federal Army was drawing near.... Once more the band led the "Pride of Harlem" down the street and up to camp; however, it was a somewhat different regiment than that that marched away before. What had been termed Col. Hayward's "Tin Soldiers" outfit was starting on the first lap of a march to fame, honor and glory.

With but a very few exceptions, every member of the band, including the Porto Ricans, who made the maiden parade, was again swinging down 7th Avenue, determined to lead that regiment regardless of where duty called it....

... And here we were the first of all the Negro troops to be ordered to France for duty....

... [W]hen the order came for us to join our regiment at the front, active service began to be a reality....

Our curiosity was greatly aroused by the many stories of adventure told by the first contingent of our boys that returned from the front, and whom we had been entertaining, and that natural-born spirit of adventure that lies in every American was fired by these thrilling escapades. We were very anxious to get into the thick of the fray.

It was particularly amusing to hear the Porto Ricans express their determination to get themselves a "Bush German." You would have thought that they were going to go right straight on through to Berlin.

After riding for twenty-four hours, the stern reality of war was definitely impressed upon us as we began to pass hospital trains bringing back the wounded from the front. All of the soldiers whom we had been listening to were those who had been lucky enough to escape the scenes of terrible slaughter and naturally, we could only visualize the enemy as being the ones in hospitals....

3. Puerto Rican Writer and Activist Jesús Colón Confronts Working Conditions in New York City, 1919

This happened early in 1919. We were both out of work, my brother and I. He got up earlier to look for a job. When I woke up, he was already gone. So I dressed, went out and bought a copy of the *New York World* and turned its pages until I got to the "Help Wanted Unskilled" section of the paper. After much reading and re-reading the same columns, my attention was held by a small advertisement. It read: "Easy job. Good wages. No experience necessary." This was followed by a number and street on the west side of lower Manhattan. It sounded like the job I was looking for. Easy job. Good wages. Those four words revolved in my brain as I was travelling toward the address indicated in the advertisement. Easy job. Good wages. Easy job. Good wages. Easy ...

The place consisted of a small front office and a large loft on the floor of which I noticed a series of large galvanized tubs half filled with water out of which I noticed protruding the necks of many bottles of various sizes and shapes. Around these tubs there were a number of workers, male and female, sitting on

Jesús Colón, "Easy Job, Good Wages," in *A Puerto Rican in New York and Other Sketches* (New York: International Publishers, 2nd ed. 1982 [1961]), pp. 25–27.

small wooden benches. All had their hands in the water of the tub, the left hand holding a bottle and with the thumb nail of the right hand scratching the labels.

The foreman found a vacant stool for me around one of the tubs of water. I asked why a penknife or a small safety razor could not be used instead of the thumb nail to take off the old labels from the bottles. I was expertly informed that knives or razors would scratch the glass thus depreciating the value of the bottles when they were to be sold.

I sat down and started to use my thumb nail on one bottle. The water had somewhat softened the transparent mucilage used to attach the label to the bottle. But the softening did not work out uniformly somehow. There were always pieces of label that for some obscure reason remained affixed to the bottles. It was on those pieces of labels tenaciously fastened to the bottles that my right hand thumb nail had to work overtime. As the minutes passed I noticed that the coldness of the water started to pass from my hand to my body giving me intermittent body shivers that I tried to conceal with the greatest of effort from those sitting beside me. My hands became deadly clean and tiny little wrinkles started to show especially at the tip of my fingers. Sometimes I stopped a few seconds from scratching the bottles, to open and close my fists in rapid movements in order to bring blood to my hands. But almost as soon as I placed them in the water they became deathly pale again.

But these were minor details compared with what was happening to the thumb of my right hand. From a delicate, boyish thumb, it was growing by the minute into a full blown tomato colored finger. It was the only part of my right hand remaining blood red. I started to look at the workers' thumbs. I noticed that these particular fingers on their right hands were unusually developed with a thick layer of corn-like surface at the top of their right thumb. The nails on their thumbs looked coarser and smaller than on the other fingers—thumb and nail having become one and the same thing—a primitive unnatural human instrument especially developed to detach hard pieces of labels from wet bottles immersed in galvanized tubs.

After a couple of hours I had a feeling that my thumb nail was going to leave my finger and jump into the cold water in the tub. A numb pain imperceptibly began to be felt coming from my right thumb. Then I began to feel such pain as if coming from a finger bigger than all of my body.

After three hours of this I decided to quit fast. I told the foreman so, showing him my swollen finger. He figured I had earned 69 cents at 23 cents an hour.

Early in the evening I met my brother in our furnished room. We started to exchange experiences of our job hunting for the day. "You know what?" my brother started, "early in the morning I went to work where they take labels off old bottles—with your right hand thumb nail … Somewhere on the West Side of Lower Manhattan. I only stayed a couple of hours. 'Easy job … Good wages' … they said. The person who wrote that ad must have had a great sense of humor." And we both had a hearty laugh that evening when I told my brother that I also went to work at that same place later in the day.

Now when I see ads reading, "Easy job. Good wages," I just smile an ancient, tired, knowing smile.

4. Arizonian Elías Sepulveda Argues for Immigration Quotas, 1926–1927

He is a native of Nogales, Arizona, [and a] *mestizo*.... His parents were Mexicans from "the interior," from Mazatlan, Sinaloa, but he is an American citizen for:

"Destiny wished for me to be born in Nogales, Arizona, and that I should be educated in an American school, and now I am an American citizen. I am twenty-three years old and in that time only once have I gone to the interior of Mexico. I went with my parents to visit some relatives and visited Hermosillo, Guaymas and Mazatlan. To tell the truth I didn't like it because it all seemed to be very poor and old fashioned.... I know ... that everything is modern and like the United States in the Capital of Mexico but you see here one finds modern things everywhere, it doesn't matter how little a town it is. My parents kept me in school until I finished high school and [then] I began to work, starting as an apprentice in a bakery in Nogales until I learned the trade at which I am now working and with which I earn enough for myself, my wife, and my little girl and also to help my parents some.... I don't believe I could make a living as a baker in Mexico for they would not pay me there what I earn here.... According to what I saw in Hermosillo they knead by hand there, ... while here the kneading is all done by machinery, the ovens are of gas and of iron and altogether the work is much easier.... I don't know how to make Mexican bread. I only know how to make American bread. I can read Spanish and write it a little because my parents taught me how.... I am ashamed when I meet a well educated Mexican from the Capital because I can't talk to him, for I speak Spanish very brokenly. I am an American citizen and pay my taxes but I don't fail to recognize on that account my Mexican blood. One can't deny one's race. If there was a war between Mexico and the United States I wouldn't go to shoot my own brothers.... We are all Mexicans anyway because the *gueros* always treat all of us alike.... I believe that it would be a good thing to put a quota on the Mexican immigrants for it would be a good thing for them and for those who are already living here.... Perhaps there might be more work for them in Mexico if it was at peace and then they wouldn't have to come to humiliate themselves before these *gueros*. In addition the Mexicans who are already here wouldn't have so much competition from those who keep coming and they could earn better wages and the Americans wouldn't humiliate us so much because they believe that we are like those who come from Mexico who let them do whatever they want. I remember that after the European War when work was scarce here and there was a great crisis that they would take work from all the Mexicans who had it in order to give it to the Americans. They had to deport the Mexicans who came here from Mexico and they took them in trucks to the border. That was very pathetic. Some of them were even begging. I was working in the bakery of an American and an American baker came and in front of me asked him why he had a 'Mexican' working when the Americans had greater need of that work. I answered that I was a 'Mexican' but that I had more

Manuél Gamio, *The Life Story of the Mexican Immigrant: Autobiographical Documents* (New York: Dover Publications, 1971), pp. 267–271. Reprinted with permission of the publisher.

right than he to the work. First because I was an American citizen born in the United States and secondly because I was from Arizona and I told him that I could even teach him the Constitution of the United States. When he heard me speak English he left.... When I am among Mexicans I feel better than when I am among the Americans. I belong to the Alianza-Hispano-Americana....

"As my parents taught me to be a Catholic when I was little I am Catholic, but it has been three years since I have been in a church and I was there then only to get married. My wife is a Mexican, from Hermosillo, Sonora. I believe that Catholicism such as the priests teach it is nothing but exploitation and that is why Mexico is so backward, for the priests don't let the people progress....

"Another thing which I don't like about Mexico is that they are always in revolution; they don't get tired of fighting. That is why nothing good can be done there. If there was peace Mexico perhaps might be greater and richer."

5. Chicago Newspaper Calls for Pan-Latino Unity, 1928

In Chicago, there are a good number of societies, organizations, and clubs that have the support of the Spanish-speaking residents of the city, but it pains us to admit that few of them tend to unify the Hispanic Americans. Being in a foreign country, and above else in a country that considers itself an enemy of ours, Hispanic Americans should not consider themselves citizens of different nations, but rather of one single country called Hispanic America....

Let's remember that U.S. citizens almost never distinguish between us, and always identify us as simply "Spanish." For them (because of their lack of knowledge of geography), it is the same whether one is Mexican or Spanish, Chilean or Nicaraguan, Argentinian or Salvadoran. To them we are all "Spanish." Let us then redeem our race. Let us make sure that the "Spanish" (which we will translate as Hispanic Americans) are recognized in the group of important communities in Chicago....

Wouldn't it be better for these groups, now completely disunited, to join in forming one strong and powerful group, which would reveal much about our Indian-Spanish race in this city? ...

6. Alfred P. Thom Characterizes Southwestern Industries as Dependent on Mexican Labor, 1928

Mr. Thom. ... [T]here is now a supply of common labor which to a considerable extent we have drawn from other countries. If that supply is cut off, the statesmanship of this country must find a substitute, because we can not exist as a people unless we can cultivate our farms; unless we can maintain our transportation

---

"La Union es la Fuerza [In Unity There Is Strength]," *La Noticia Mundial* (Chicago), January 28, 1928. Translation: Omar Valerio-Jiménez.

Testimony of Alfred P. Thom, General Counsel, Association of Railroad Executives and National Railroad Association, in House Committee on Immigration, *Immigration from Countries of the Western Hemisphere: Hearings*, 70th Congress, 1st Session, 1928, pp. 386, 389–391.

facilities; unless we can have the common labor essential to these important enterprises.

It happens, Mr. Chairman, that in a vast territory in America common labor has been supplied to a very large extent from Mexico....

Now, as to the railroads ... [in the Southwest and Midwest] we find that of the section laborers about 67 per cent are Mexicans. Of the extra gang laborers about 90 per cent are Mexicans....

I am told that it is also in evidence before you that from 68 per cent to 75 per cent of the labor engaged in agricultural pursuits in the State of California are Mexicans, and I presume the same would apply throughout the other territory to which I have referred.... From that territory, more than 500,000 carloads of agricultural products move annually....

So that what is produced in that section is largely the product of Mexican labor....

... The question arises as to what is going to be the economic effect upon that vast territory and its vast agricultural industry, if the supply of common labor is made inadequate. What could be more destructive of the prosperity of a people; of their contentment; of their general welfare; than to have their entire labor situation disrupted? ...

THE CHAIRMAN.   If we can not limit [Mexican labor] immediately, is it advisable to devise a plan to slow it down and regulate it?

MR. THOM.   That is a very difficult and delicate task, Mr. Chairman. Of course, you have got a sociological question as well as an economic question. You have got to be wise enough to settle them both without any abrupt and hurtful effect....

Let us go a step further. A great deal of this section of the country has a climate and living conditions where you can not get any other class of labor to go—any class but the Mexicans. White men will not undergo the hardships incident to the life. On the other hand, negroes can not be obtained.

But let us glance for a moment at what will be the situation in the event you do cut off this supply of labor. As I have indicated, you are involving two of the fundamental enterprises of our civilization, namely, the farming industry and the transportation industry. You have gone so far in your legislation as to emphasize the importance of both of these.

 ## ESSAYS

During the World War I era, Puerto Ricans and Mexicans were recruited to the United States, but continued to experience stereotypes and discrimination. Like labor recruitment, community building was shaped by ongoing interactions across borders, as these three essays reveal. The first essay, by Ruth Glasser, lecturer in urban and community studies at the University of Connecticut–Waterbury, examines the recruitment of Puerto Rican musicians into the U.S. armed forces' African American military bands. Although this social and musical interchange among African Americans and Puerto Ricans was unprecedented, the cross-border and interracial dynamics that shaped music were not. Puerto Rican musicians found opportunities within African American ensembles in the military and later in civilian life, but they also faced strict racial restrictions unknown to them in Puerto Rico.

As Mexican immigration increased dramatically and settlement became more dispersed, contradictions emerged both within U.S. society and within Mexican American communities. In the second essay, David Gutiérrez, professor of history at the University of California, San Diego, analyzes U.S. employers' dependence on Mexican immigrant labor and the nativist views of immigration opponents. Racial assumptions shaped arguments on each conflicting side. While reinforcing existing Mexican American communities, Mexican immigrants' arrival also stoked tensions as both groups vied for job opportunities, housing, and acceptance. The third essay, by Gabriela Arredondo, professor of Latin American and Latino Studies at the University of California, Santa Cruz, explores the identity of Mexicans in Chicago. Although racial discrimination divided Mexicans by accentuating schisms based on class and complexion, it also served to unite them. Mexican ideologies of *indigenismo* and *mestizaje,* as well as pan-Latino anti-imperialism, shaped their sense of Mexicanidad (Mexican identity). All three essays shed light on diversity within Puerto Rican and Mexican communities, and on their interactions with the larger racial and ethnic communities of which they were a part.

Afro–Puerto Rican Musicians in the U.S. Army and in New York City

RUTH GLASSER

"Jazz Won the War!" declared the genre's most ardent fans at the end of 1918.... [T]he Allied victory of World War I owed a great deal to the efforts of nearly four hundred thousand African-American soldiers, among whose ranks were numerous bands and singing groups that had charmed their way through France. Christened with regiment nicknames, the "Hellfighters" of the 369th, the 350th Field Artillery Band, the "Buffaloes" of the 367th, and the "Black Devils" of the 370th put ragtime, vaudeville tunes, spirituals, and southern melodies on France's musical map. Their musical conquests both symbolized the importance of American blacks in the Great War and presaged significant cultural innovations for the United States and Europe....

... Within the ranks of these black soldiers was still another subculture, Puerto Rican brass and reed players who contributed their considerable talents ... to this

My Music Is My Flag: Puerto Rican Musicians and Their New York Communities, 1917–1940, by Ruth Glasser, © 1996 by the Regents of the University of California. Published by the University of California Press.

musical and military effort. These men, recruited directly from Puerto Rico, were among the pioneers who introduced jazz to France. They were also among the first Puerto Rican musicians to sojourn in the mainland United States, exchanging musical ideas with their erstwhile companions and bringing new sounds back to the island.

Within the context of World War I began a process of migration and a cultural exchange between two groups, African-Americans and Puerto Ricans, that would last for many years.... Puerto Ricans and other Latinos played trumpets and tubas and composed and arranged for some of the best-known black and white jazz orchestras in the United States. In turn, they brought jazz orchestrations and harmonies back to Latino ensembles. In many respects World War I was the kickoff point for a creative intermingling that was often invisible to outsiders.

★ ★ ★

That Puerto Ricans formed part of African-American military bands was the result of ... two significant historical events: Congress's passage of the Jones Act, which made Puerto Ricans citizens of the United States, in March 1917; and, just one month later, Congress's declaration of war with Germany and the U.S. entry into World War I. In the flurry of registration that followed, over 236,000 Puerto Rican men were declared eligible for the draft. Nearly 18,000 of these were mustered into the U.S. armed forces. Some 4,000 soldiers were sent to guard the Panama Canal, and the rest trained in Puerto Rico.

[For the] thousands of Puerto Rican men who donned the uniform of the United States Army for the first time ... with that uniform came a new and potent identity, that of the black man in the United States. Even men who trained for the war on their own island were put into racially segregated camps. Although this was standard policy within the U.S. military, it was a new configuration for the Puerto Rican soldiers in training. Puerto Rican society was not devoid of color consciousness or prejudice, but racial categories were different than in the United States. Not only did Puerto Rico have a greater degree of racial mixing than its northern colonizer but its racial classification scheme comprised fluid and diverse categories.... Puerto Ricans defined themselves and each other on a continuum from white to black, with facial features, hair texture, and even wealth or occupation helping to determine how a person was classified. For these new soldiers in the American army, the "white" and "Negro" camps in which they were placed represented an alien social experience.

No Puerto Rican soldier, however, had an experience as acutely bittersweet as that of those members of the African-American regimental bands who played and fought overseas. In artistic terms, to be a Negro meant to be in the vanguard of popular music; however, in social terms, it counted for innumerable abuses in the lives of these soldiers. Within just a few months these new recruits felt the sting of racism in northern and southern training camps, as well as the adulation and apparent colorblindness of the French. They were abruptly thrust into the cultures of Harlem and southern-born African-Americans. A white world that

saw all people of color as essentially alike expected these Puerto Ricans to identify themselves with this new ethnic group both socially and musically.

As musicians and soldiers, moreover, Puerto Ricans were asked to be emissaries of that adopted culture, ... as overseas representatives of the United States.
Part of regiments whose members the outside world labeled American Negroes,
these men had to absorb new musical forms and make them their own. Within
this linked renegotiation of their ethnic and musical identities, Puerto Rican military musicians ... learned firsthand the extramusical implications of this apparently innocent entertainment. As best they could, they interpreted their position
in the midst of some of the social, political, and economic difficulties plaguing
African-Americans....

★ ★ ★

The musicians brought to the mainland from San Juan were actually among only
a handful of Puerto Ricans who fought the war in France.... Although relatively
few in number, these Puerto Ricans formed a particularly prominent part of the
United States Army's most famous musical ensemble, the 369th Infantry "Hellfighters" Band, led by Lieutenant James Reese Europe. Europe himself recruited
some eighteen musicians from San Juan's bands and orchestras....

Victoria Hernández still remembers the "americano de color" who arrived in
Puerto Rico looking for army musicians. It was May of 1917. Her brother
Rafael had left Aguadilla and toured the island with a Japanese circus, and then,
like many of his peers, he had gone to San Juan in search of more musical
opportunities. Now he was playing violin in the Orquesta Sinfónica of San Juan
and trombone in Manuel Tizol's municipal band....

... With centuries of connections to the colonial military, public bands like
Tizol's were decidedly martial in instruments and orchestration. The musicians
within both the band and the orchestra were adept at reading sheet music, and
most could play several instruments. Europe grabbed Rafael Hernández, his
brother Jesús, and sixteen more musicians and took the next boat back to
New York....

[T]his recruitment brought about a significant encounter between two
groups whose histories had telling differences as well as striking intersections and
similarities....

The life history of the man who scouted for Puerto Rican instrumentalists
itself testifies to the heights a talented and ambitious black musician, composer,
and conductor could reach in the United States, as well as the restrictions a
socially constructed racial identity placed upon him.... Born in Mobile, Alabama,
in 1881, James Reese Europe was a highly trained musician who spent years in
New York City as a writer and orchestra leader with black musical shows. But
the opportunities for African-Americans in a white-dominated entertainment
industry were often transient and dependent on prevailing racial attitudes....
A talented organizer and advocate for African-American musicians, Europe
founded the Clef Club in 1910. Much more than a gathering place for
musicians, the club functioned as a union and booking agency for New York
City's African-American artists, who were all but ignored by the American

Federation of Musicians.... Europe directed the Clef Club's enormous orchestra of more than one hundred musicians.... Their appearance in Carnegie Hall in 1912 marked the first time a black orchestra had ever appeared on that stage and the first time anyone had made the hallowed auditorium resonate with popular tunes....

... No doubt it was this pioneering ability, as well as his organizational and musical skills, that led Colonel William Hayward to ask Europe to form an army band.

When Jim Europe enlisted in the Fifteenth Infantry of the New York National Guard in 1917, he was stepping into a recently formed Negro regiment that already had a troubled history. It was only because of pressure from local black leaders and the efforts of Colonel William Hayward that skeptical government and army officials had grudgingly conceded that "the great colored population of New York" could yield soldier-worthy material.... Colonel Hayward, the regiment's white commander, begged Europe to organize "the best damn brass band in the United States Army," undoubtedly to give the beleaguered regiment some prestige.... Europe hoped that this increased visibility for black performers would raise their status within the United States and lead to funding for his personal dream, a black symphony orchestra.... Europe informed Hayward that he needed to go farther afield than the continental United States in order to recruit superior musicians.... Europe was on his way to Puerto Rico, while his drum major, Noble Sissle, a vocalist, composer, and arranger in civilian life, auditioned musicians back in New York....

[Europe] knew that island blacks and *mulatos* had access to the type of training many of their counterparts could not get in the United States. Jim Europe's Puerto Rican "finds" included a variety of clarinetists, valve trombonists, saxophonists, and tuba, French horn, bassoon, and *bombardino* players in their teens and twenties. Whether they were first-generation musicians ... like Rafael Hernández and his brother Jesús, or the scions of illustrious musical families, all could read music and play in a wide variety of social and musical contexts....

... On both sides of the ocean, music was one of the few careers open to people of color. In both places distinct musical cultures often developed within the context of black or *mulato* people's working-class trades. Whereas in Comerío or Cayey *tabaqueros* sang, played, and composed together as they worked, in black barbershops in New Orleans or New York proprietors, employees, and patrons experimented with new types of vocal harmony.

In Puerto Rico, however, where perceptions of race were partially based on the amount of money and education a person possessed, working-class people of color could utilize music for social mobility and added prestige. Additionally, there was a degree of solidarity among working-class Puerto Ricans, regardless of color, that was not to be found in the United States. In Puerto Rico music as a career choice was most commonly the province of black and *mulato* members of the working class. But whatever the complexion of the musician, once he had chosen this career, he experienced a rough equality in training, genres played, and performance opportunities....

... For African-American musicians a more pointed racism was overlaid upon the basic instability of the profession.... Unlike in Puerto Rico, there was no racial stigma attached to music making in the United States. Indeed, for a succession of ethnic groups, ... music provided an honorable form of recreation, cultural preservation, and, occasionally, social and economic mobility.... [E]nterprising whites had thoroughly organized and commercialized virtually all aspects of musical training, performance, and distribution by the late nineteenth century.

Within such an atmosphere, those African-Americans who were fortunate enough to get training often did so almost inadvertently, through army, orphanage, and other publicly supported bands. Needless to say, these bands were segregated, and African-American musicians usually had less access to decent instruments and funding than their white counterparts. In the realm of popular music, African-American musicians played in black theaters within segregated circuits, generally controlled by whites. With the lines between classical and popular music more strictly drawn in the United States than in Puerto Rico, even the most qualified African-American musician would more likely be found in a minstrel show than in a symphony orchestra....

... White ideas about black musical abilities had a life of their own within the North American context. African-Americans were supposed to be natural and spontaneous musicians....

The Puerto Rican performers in Jim Europe's band were recruited precisely because of their outstanding musicianship, but the image white America had of black artistry worked against their training. It must have been extremely difficult for the "Porto Ricans," taught to read and display their craft openly in island orchestras and small groups, to come to a country where the very qualities they were recruited for had to be concealed, to get used to being "Negroes" with an instinct for music rather than a painstakingly labored skill and a generations-old guildsman's pride. These *boricuas* had to learn to adapt to the stereotypes of blacks as natural musicians. This translated into working without sheet music. Classically trained, they were sometimes unfavorably judged by audiences and colleagues alike as technicians without improvisational abilities.

In addition to these concerns, the Puerto Rican musicians had to adjust to daily life within the black regiment.... Noble Sissle's memoirs of the regiment's experience in the war make mention of the Puerto Rican musicians, although not as individuals. He portrays the "Porto Ricans" as a collective and childlike unit, pathetic, demanding, although ultimately loyal. This portrait is ironic, given the not dissimilar white depictions of blacks in contemporary minstrel shows and popular literature. Nevertheless, Sissle gives us some insight into the process of adjustment faced by these musicians who came to New York [See Document 2]....

While the adjustments between the Puerto Ricans and the black American musicians were significant, looming ahead were the far greater challenges of performing and fighting a war as members of a racially segregated division. Even after the difficulties of forming the regiment were resolved, Colonel Hayward struggled to equip it and to keep it going.... The residents of Harlem watched with disbelief as the men trained with broom handles, for the Army was reluctant to issue them real weapons. The regiment was even denied permission to participate in a march with the rest of the New York National Guard before leaving the state....

After many difficulties in getting a place to practice, the Fifteenth was finally assigned to a camp in Spartanburg, South Carolina.... While the regiment's white officers exhorted members to keep their head even under strong provocation, they employed the bands of the regiment in an active public-relations effort.

Simultaneously, the Puerto Ricans had to learn the importance of the distinctions the Spartanburg whites made between northern and southern blacks and to actively participate in peacemaking through music. Jim Europe's outfit took part in semiweekly open-air concerts and was subsequently invited to play at a dance at a white country club. Nevertheless, after a series of tense confrontations with hostile townspeople, the black soldiers were hastily removed from the camp with orders to go to the front.... On New Year's Day of 1918, the Fifteenth became the first black regiment to arrive in France. Its troops had had a scant three weeks' training for their war efforts....

... While the musicians certainly had some celebrity status within their regiment and later throughout France, their nonmusical work was decidedly unglamorous. Rafael Hernández and several of his *compatriotas* spent much of their time as part of the Ambulance Corps.... In a rare comment on his war experience Rafael Hernández remarked in 1962 that he was relieved when he got his sergeant's stripes because it enabled him to get away from doing cleaning and other menial tasks. As musicians he and the other band members were warmly received by the French, but as soldiers they were exposed to racial epithets, poor camp conditions and equipment, and restrictive army rules that were not applied to white soldiers.

On the musical level as well the Puerto Rican recruits must have learned a great deal, for carefully selected, eclectic programs were the hallmark of the regimental band's experience in the United States, on the ship, and throughout France. While their work in the Cine Tres Banderas and at dances in the San Juan area had undoubtedly given most of the Puerto Rican recruits some familiarity with North American popular music, here they were exposed to a greater variety of U.S. regional, primarily African-American forms....

This intertwined musical and social reeducation for the Puerto Rican musicians continued in France as well. In between bouts of manual labor and months of trench warfare, Jim Europe's outfit toured France playing open-air and formal concerts, operas and vaudeville. As the band traveled, its members were told by their commanders "that they were upon a mission of great importance; that they were not merely musicians and soldiers of the American Army but that they were representatives of the American nation." ...

The band clearly worked hard to please its diverse audiences. Jim Europe challenged the ensemble by accepting requests from civilians, working from sheets of favorite folk songs or handwritten compositions timidly proffered to him. From all reports, the group gave remarkable concerts featuring a wide variety of music....

... Both African-American and Puerto Rican music were based largely on the interactions between the members of a forced African diaspora and a European colonizer. Ongoing infusions of African, Latin American, Caribbean, and European migrants added to the musical melange, as did internal migrations within each country. The resemblance between the musical development of New Orleans, the birthplace of much of the most innovative African-American music, and that of the islands of the French and Spanish Caribbean was particularly striking.

Musically speaking, therefore, James Reese Europe and Rafael Hernández perhaps had more in common than at first met the eye. As composers and performers, they had worked within somewhat analogous musical forms. Hernández, who had begun to write songs when he was fourteen, had already composed several *danzones,* a Cuban form with more than a passing similarity to ragtime. Both were syncopated descendants of various strains of rather marchlike nineteenth-century European dance music....

... The *danzón* and ragtime had influenced each other as a result of close commercial ties between the ports of Havana and New Orleans.... Europe was himself involved in the spread throughout the United States of the *tango,* already popular in Puerto Rico.... While the people of Harlem went "tango mad" in 1914, Puerto Ricans were beginning to hear fox-trots as accompaniments to silent films and to dance to them in *casinos.*

In many ways, then, the World War I interaction between African-American and Puerto Rican musicians made sense.... In New York, such collaborations were reinforced by demographic and social factors that often grouped North American blacks and Puerto Ricans together. The parallel oppressions and musical developments of the past combined with close quarters in the present to promote ongoing musical exchanges.

★ ★ ★

After the armistice in November 1918, the members of the 369th U.S. Infantry went home heroes both for their bravery in prolonged combat and for their music.... The entire 369th was awarded the croix de guerre. On February 17, 1919, the regiment finally had its triumphal parade up Fifth Avenue in New York City. Warmly greeted by a spectrum of the city's population, they were even more fervently cheered when they reached Harlem.

James Europe's 369th U.S. Infantry Band went on a postwar tour of the United States and began recording for the Pathé label. The Hernández brothers, Rafael Duchesne, and the other Puerto Rican band members were almost certainly involved in Europe's recording of early ragtime, jazz, and blues classics.... In May 1919 James Reese Europe was fatally stabbed in a quarrel with his drummer, and the band abruptly dissolved....

... The public's enthusiastic reception of the regimental bands and the many African-American veterans with impeccable war records had led numerous black leaders to believe that racial barriers were being erased through both patriotism and good music. But the war's end heightened white racial anxieties that had been exacerbated by significant demographic changes.

During the war, xenophobic fears of "hyphenated Americans" had led government leaders to accept, albeit reluctantly, the recruitment of black and Puerto Rican troops. In the context of the anti-German hysteria these people of color were thought to be more loyal than many white immigrants and their scions. In turn, thousands of African-Americans and Puerto Ricans welcomed the opportunity to prove their loyalty to the United States. By showing that they were good Americans, many blacks hoped to achieve basic social and economic rights within the United States. Similarly, leaders in Puerto Rico felt that this demonstration of loyalty would win them more economic and political autonomy for their island.

But during and after the war, as Congress sharply curtailed migration from Europe and Asia, a tremendous exodus of African-Americans from the South began to change the racial contours of northern cities. In New York, this situation was compounded by the in-migration of thousands of Puerto Ricans whose economic situation on the island was deteriorating rather than improving. Once again, there were parallels between the Puerto Rican and the African-American experience: members of both groups left behind the constant struggles of farming under increasingly difficult conditions or the disappearing crafts that had sustained them in urban areas to look for factory jobs in the North.... Puerto Ricans and African-Americans were both swept up in the tensions surrounding this adjustment between blacks and whites in the urban North. In the period during and immediately after the war there were race riots, and a revived Ku Klux Klan spread throughout many states. In New York City the two groups faced increasing segregation in housing and discrimination in jobs and unions. Within both their daily lives and their artistic careers, Puerto Rican musicians within a rigidly biracial North American society were caught up in "Negro" problems. Thus, their musical development in New York City must be understood within the context of opportunities for black artists....

... The postwar period demonstrates the ever-shifting fortunes of black musicians in New York City, dependent on a fickle, white-dominated music industry and audience that placed them in and out of fashion. The fate of black performers often depended both on the achievements of individual African-American personalities and on a variable American racial climate rather than on a systematic and progressive acceptance by white America. Moreover, the perennial stereotypes plaguing black musicians before and during the war continued to haunt them afterwards.

While the goodwill spread by the Hellfighters and other wartime bands did not eradicate existing or growing social tensions, it did create some new opportunities for black musicians. On the heels of their success during World War I, black bands became almost fixtures on Broadway during the 1920s.... The efforts of black musicians before and during the war combined with a surge of Prohibition era entertainment activity to produce a new black theater. While this entertainment was generally backed and produced by whites, who received most of the financial benefits, it gave black performers an opportunity to do significant work both in Harlem cabarets and on Broadway....

Not surprisingly, some of the Puerto Rican musicians who had triumphantly marched with Jim Europe's band down Fifth Avenue in 1919 became a part of these new musical ventures, as did other recently arrived *boricuas*.... [A] number of musicians who became well-known jazz players, particularly on brass and woodwind instruments, came from Cuba and Puerto Rico, as well as Panama, Mexico, and other parts of Latin America....

... With the advent of Prohibition, white and black entrepreneurs and organized-crime figures developed Harlem into a paradise of forbidden nocturnal pleasures for whites.... [T]he black bandleaders hired for these nightspots incorporated Puerto Rican and other Latino musicians into their groups.... Noble Sissle['s] ... orchestra became a veritable incubator of such musicians.... In turn, such musicians formed a network that helped other Latinos to get jobs....

... In the postwar period Puerto Ricans were still a nearly invisible minority among New York's ethnic populations. While an estimated 35,000 Puerto Ricans lived in New York by the war's end, the African-American population there had reached about 150,000. Black American musical groups received the support of both their own sizable communities and the white audiences with whom they were currently popular.... There were few Latino ensembles in New York City during the 1920s, and Puerto Ricans of color were barred from participation in white orchestras. Thus Puerto Rican and Latino participation in African-American ensembles was conditioned in part by their prior experiences and in part by the range of options they saw around them....

When Jim Europe's band broke up, ... ex-sergeant Rafael Hernández took off for Cuba, where he spent five years as the director of a cinema orchestra in Havana. Returning to New York in 1925, he formed his own ensemble of Puerto Rican musicians, which had a triumphant debut in the prestigious Palace theater. Hernández spent several months touring the United States with the band of Charles Luckeyth "Lucky" Roberts, one of the finest black stride pianists of his time, and soon after formed his own *trío*. Hernández, and undoubtedly other Puerto Ricans as well, sandwiched musical jobs with African-American groups between performances in Latino musical ensembles.

Puerto Rican experiences in African-American orchestras were also conditioned by the needs and desires of black musicians, who were constantly battling pernicious stereotypes. Jim Europe's polished society bands before World War I and Sissle and Blake's Broadway performances afterwards sought to bring dignity to African-American music and theater....

Dignity was important to these musicians, who had spent years performing in impeccable dress before New York's elite, top U.S. military brass, and respectful European audiences. But the stereotype of African-Americans as instinctive musicians continued to plague them and to determine their performance strategies.... The band of *Shuffle Along* and the bands of ensuing productions had to commit entire scores to memory....

Puerto Rican musicians had to adapt to both white racist expectations and African-American strategies to subvert stereotypes. Just as the white world believed that blacks were natural musicians, it tended to categorize all their music as "hot" or "jazz." ... New York–based musicians ... were careful orchestrators and arrangers who resented being categorized as "hot" jazz musicians. Their enthusiasm for Puerto Rican musicians probably represented their desire to combat prevalent stereotypes by producing a smooth, refined sound. In an atmosphere where training often counted more than improvisational ability, Puerto Ricans and other Latinos from a municipal band background were prized figures.... Duke Ellington describes ... a group he saw in Washington, D. C., in 1920: "... I met Juan Tizol, the trombonist.... This group impressed us very much, because all the musicians doubled on different instruments, something that was extraordinary in those days."

Ellington was so impressed that several years later he invited Tizol, the nephew of San Juan's municipal bandleader, to join his orchestra in New York, starting a musical association that would last many years....

Other indignities and problems were chronic for black musical groups and, in turn, for their Puerto Rican members.... Underpayment, lack of union protection, and tremendous difficulties in making sleeping and eating arrangements when on tour (usually in segregated theaters) were standard in the lives of black musicians of the period. While black shows were popular on Broadway during the 1920s, they operated on shoestring budgets, which all but evaporated during the Depression era. Only a small number of black performers made it to the big-time vaudeville theaters, and they were taboo in most of the elegant downtown hotels and nightspots. And the Harlem nightclubs where they could perform were often barred to black patrons....

★ ★ ★

The Puerto Rican musicians who participated in African-American bands ... had to play the same music and face the same humiliations and dangers as American blacks. When they returned home, however, their identities might undergo a change.

Puerto Rican musicians generally lived among their nonmusical *compatriotas* in working-class neighborhoods. While the demographic accident that had brought Puerto Ricans and African-Americans to New York City at the same time resulted in a proximity that meant opportunities for cultural and occupational mingling for those who were musicians, it created competition for most members of both groups, who fought for jobs and housing in an era of increasing occupational and residential restrictions for people of color. Within New York, newly arrived as well as established African-Americans and Puerto Ricans and other "West Indians" jostled each other for the few jobs that would accept them and apartments in the few neighborhoods not off-limits to them.

The day-to-day tensions between African-Americans and Puerto Ricans were undoubtedly exacerbated by the struggles of nonwhite *boricuas* to come to terms with the monolithic "Negro" identity imposed upon them from the outside by a racist North American society. In case they forgot, the signs on many New York City apartment buildings that read "No Dogs, No Negroes, and No Spanish" reminded Puerto Ricans and other Latinos that many whites put them in the same inferior category as they did black Americans....

... [T]he geographically and culturally divided nature of ... society forced the issue of ethnic loyalty and identification in racial terms.... For Puerto Ricans, who spanned both American race categories, it meant complex intra-ethnic divisions and confusing choices.

Puerto Rican artists' struggle to earn a living in New York almost inevitably involved some measure of crossover to the North American mainstream popular music scene. But that scene presented very different choices to musicians of darker and lighter complexions. The bluntly bipolar racial situation, manifested so strongly in music as well as in daily life, did a great deal to bifurcate the career paths of Puerto Rican musicians. Unlike the relatively isolated North American black and white musicians, a spectrum of Puerto Ricans might know each other intimately through Puerto Rican and New York community ties, shared professional experience on the island or mainland, or *compadrazgo* (godparenthood) or even family connections....

... [W]hite or light-skinned Latinos with talent and ambition found success, if they were lucky, in ways that were not open to even the finest Afro-Latin musicians....

★ ★ ★

With the onset of the Depression and the scarcity of jobs, white swing bands crowded most black ensembles out of the musical scene.... [T]he racism affecting the development of the North American popular bands in which Puerto Ricans played also had its effects on the Latin music scene.... The difficulties experienced by most African-American bands undoubtedly led to severe unemployment and underemployment for the Latino members. It is likely that the circumstances pushed many Puerto Rican and Latino musicians who had dreamed for years of creating Latin orchestras to strike out on their own.

But when Puerto Rican and other Latinos decided for commercial or personal reasons to "go back" to Latin music, the choices for darker- and lighter-skinned musicians were again geographically and racially separated. The downtown Latin "relief" bands, which alternated with featured orchestras in elegant hotels and clubs, were usually made up of whites only. While the rules may have been made by the ballrooms and hotels, the bandleaders rarely challenged them....

... Hernández may have been restricted to uptown live-performance sites in New York, but he became internationally famous partly as a result of racism. Seeking countries where he could be a respected orchestra leader, composer, and radio personality, Hernández and his compositions traveled to Cuba, Mexico, and finally back to Puerto Rico. Conversely, the light-complexioned Latin relief bands that were fixtures in downtown ballrooms during the 1930s had a high social status in a society that equated white skin and plush surroundings with success. At the same time, their very categorization as relief bands was a ruse that allowed club owners to pay them less than union wages for work under grueling conditions.... [Mario] Bauzá was making much more money in the African-American ensembles than his ostensibly higher-status compatriots were making in the relief bands. He also claims that the musicianship in his groups was far superior. According to Bauzá, light-skinned Latin relief bandleaders' pandering to the racism of white club owners not only hurt them musically but socially and economically divided the Latino artistic community....

... Among Latino musicians in New York there was no ... alternative to racist or inadequate performers' institutions such as the American Federation of Musicians' local.

In the meantime, musicians such as Bauzá and legions of other dark-skinned Latinos were channeling their apparent liability toward the formation of an exciting uptown Latin music scene. This scene was largely made up of veterans of the African-American popular orchestras. To a certain extent these artists were going back to their musical roots, thus belying the stereotyped picture of ethnics on a slow and steady road toward assimilation into "American" culture. At the same time, they were following a particular musical path shaped by their racial circumstances. Moreover, the whole concept of going back was tempered by the inevitable influence of their years in one particular kind of North American ensemble. These musicians returned to El Barrio to play Latin music before Hispanic audiences; the music itself was greatly influenced by African-American jazz....

"Mexican Immigrants and the Development of the American Southwest"

DAVID G. GUTIÉRREZ

... Geographically isolated and mired in the lowest levels of the [Southwest's] economy, by the 1890s the United States' Mexican American population had become, in one scholar's apt phrase, "the forgotten people."

... [A]s the century drew to a close, the resident ethnic Mexican population began to grow at a significantly higher rate.

... Displaced from the land by the draconian land policies instituted by Mexican dictator Porfirio Díaz and drawn to the United States by the rapidly diversifying and expanding southwestern economy, the number of Mexican immigrants entering the United States climbed steadily after 1890. When the Mexican people revolted against Díaz's regime in 1910, the stream of Mexicans into the United States increased even more. By the 1920s their rate of entry for a short time rivaled the great European migrations of the late nineteenth century.... [A]t least one million, and possibly as many as a million and a half Mexican immigrants entered the United States between 1890 and 1929.

... Accustomed as they had become to seeing Mexicans as an inherently inferior and internally undifferentiated racial minority, most Americans failed to recognize the significance of large-scale Mexican immigration for the simple reason that they recognized no distinctions between Americans of Mexican descent and more recent immigrants from Mexico. This was true largely because the vast

Walls and Mirrors: Mexican Americans, Mexican Immigrants, and the Politics of Ethnicity, by David G. Gutiérrez, © 1995 by the Regents of the University of California. Published by the University of California Press.

majority of Americans never came into direct contact with the resident Mexican population....

The effects of large-scale immigration were readily apparent, however, to Americans of Mexican descent. Although the increasing flow of immigrants into the Southwest was welcomed by some Mexican Americans because the immigrants helped to rejuvenate Mexican culture, customs, and use of Spanish in their communities, immigration of this magnitude also tended to exacerbate the many social, economic, and political problems Mexican Americans faced in American society....

★ ★ ★

The rapid expansion of the Southwest's ethnic Mexican population was the result of a number of interrelated economic and political developments that unfolded in both the United States and Mexico during the last quarter of the nineteenth century.... In the last decades of the century, ... important infrastructural and technological advances in the region—particularly the extension of vast railway networks, the introduction of the refrigerated boxcar, and the construction of an intricate network of privately and publicly financed irrigation projects—laid the foundations for one of the most explosive periods of economic growth in American history.

The construction and expansion of the great western railroads ... tied the region both to the national economy of the United States and to the newly constructed Mexican rail system, thus enabling western entrepreneurs to transport and market their goods in unprecedented quantities.... The expansion of irrigated agriculture in the arid Southwest was even more impressive. In 1890 the combined total of irrigated land in California, Nevada, Utah, and Arizona amounted to a mere 1,575,000 acres.... By 1909 nearly 14 million acres were under irrigation in the Southwest.

In California the combined effects of these developments—particularly the expansion of the railroads and the rapid growth of highly specialized irrigated agriculture—were dramatic. The extension of the Southern Pacific into Los Angeles (and the heart of the state's citrus growing region) in 1876 and the link with the Santa Fe in 1887 allowed southern California growers to increase production and reach distant markets. As irrigation systems slowly snaked into new areas throughout the state, millions of additional acres of rich agricultural land were brought into intensive production.... By 1930 California alone accounted for one-third of the United States' fresh fruit, one-fourth of its vegetables, eight-tenths of its wine, and nearly the entire American output of almonds, artichokes, figs, nectarines, olives, dates, and lemons.

To accomplish this massive increase in agricultural production, California growers expanded the scale of their enterprises and in the process laid the foundations for the development of American corporate agriculture, or agribusiness. Employing economies of scale by expanding the acreage under cultivation, by the turn of the century California growers had already established a pattern of encompassing prime agricultural land into huge corporate farms....

... With the extension of the railroads into southern and western Texas during the first two decades of the century, vast new areas were opened to mining, livestock raising, and agriculture—especially the cultivation of citrus fruits, vegetables, and cotton, perennially Texas's top cash crop.... Texas accounted for between 35 and 42 percent of the total United States' cotton crop and an amazing 20 to 30 percent of the world crop.

The concomitant growth of Texas's rail network and irrigation systems spurred growth in other areas of agriculture [and] made possible the integration of the Texas economy into national markets and provided an unprecedented boom to the local economy as well.

★ ★ ★

The rapid expansion and growing scale of the agricultural, mining, transportation, and construction sectors of the southwestern economy would not have been possible without a massive infusion of labor....

Frustrated by ... early attempts to stabilize the regional labor supply [of Asian workers] in the rail, mining, construction, and agricultural industries, American employers began to look to Mexico as a source of cheap labor.... When the Chinese Exclusion Act and the Gentlemen's Agreement significantly reduced the available labor supply, employers began to hire Mexican immigrants to fill the steadily increasing demand for low-skilled, low-wage jobs in the southwestern economy.

Fortunately for American entrepreneurs, their increasing demand for labor coincided with the serious deterioration of the position of workers in Mexico during the Porfiriato. Forced off the land and into a growing migratory labor stream by the movement toward export-crop farming under Díaz's regime, thousands of Mexican workers had begun to wander within Mexico well before they thought of making the journey north to the United States. But facing the painful realities of declining wages combined with rapidly rising food prices, growing numbers of landless Mexican workers began to look to the United States for work....

... This movement was aided and abetted by American labor agents, who traveled into the interior of Mexico seeking agricultural and railroad construction and maintenance workers....

... By 1920 the Mexican-born population residing in the United States had more than doubled, to at least 478,000 individuals.

Mexican immigrants filled a wide variety of occupations, ranging from agricultural labor, mine work, and railroad construction and maintenance, to common day labor on innumerable construction sites throughout the Southwest. By 1910 Mexican immigrant workers had become the backbone of the work force in many industries and could be found in smaller numbers working as auto and steel workers in the Great Lakes region and as fishermen and cannery workers in Alaska. By the 1920s Mexican immigrant and Mexican American workers dominated the unskilled and semiskilled sectors of the regional labor market....

★ ★ ★

Given the long history of racial antipathy toward Mexicans in the Southwest, it may seem surprising that Mexican immigrants were allowed to become such a vital component of the region's economy.... The need for cheap labor, however, provided a powerful inducement to southwestern capitalists to change their thinking about Mexicans. Faced with the persistence of anti-Mexican sentiment among the American public, employers had to devise ways to justify the recruitment and employment of large numbers of Mexican workers.

Most employers invoked many of the same negative racial and cultural stereotypes Americans had developed over the years about Mexicans to explain their use of them as low-paid labor. Thus in the years after 1910 southwestern economic interests exploited Americans' traditional perceptions of Mexicans as an inherently backward, slow, docile, indolent, and tractable people. By the mid-1910s southwestern employers argued that these characteristics constituted the very virtues that made Mexicans an ideal (and cheap) labor force.

The basic tenets of the elaborate rationale American employers first developed about the use of Mexican labor would be heard again and again over the course of the next sixty years. Spokesmen for the Southwest's commercial farmers, mine operators, railroad corporations, and large construction firms reiterated their old complaints about the region's chronic labor shortage. Second, they argued with no small justification that the kind of work required by these industries was not work that white Americans would tolerate. The hours were too long, wages too low, and working conditions too harsh to attract white American workers in sufficient numbers to fill the ever-growing demands for labor in the Southwest [See Document 6]. And last, American advocates of the use of Mexican labor blandly asserted that Mexicans were a race that was both culturally and physiologically suited to perform the arduous manual labor required in these industries....

As increasing numbers of Mexican immigrants entered the labor market after World War I, however, southwestern industrial and agricultural spokesmen recognized the need to allay other Americans' fears about what many perceived as an invasion of foreign workers. In an era in which American nativists clamored for ever more stringent restrictions on the immigration of non-Nordic peoples to the United States, advocates of the use of Mexican labor had to tread a very fine line in developing and advancing their arguments. Consequently, in a pattern that characterized the region's debate over Mexican immigration for the next six decades, employers and their allies tried to dampen criticisms of the use of Mexican labor. To this end they developed a public relations strategy that painstakingly explained the reasons why Mexican immigrant workers did not represent a threat to American workers or to the cultural (and racial) homogeneity of American society....

... [P]erhaps the most important part of the southwestern employers' argument [was] that Mexicans were a temporary foreign work force and therefore represented no lasting social or economic threat to American citizens. Arguing in all seriousness that Mexicans had an ingrained homing instinct like that of migratory birds, western lobbyists repeatedly assured congressional committees that Mexican workers came to the United States seeking only to earn a stake before they ultimately returned to Mexico....

Over time, southwestern extractive, agricultural, and transportation corporations ... honed their arguments.... By the mid-1920s the litany espoused by southwestern economic concerns about the benefits of temporary Mexican labor was presented to the American public as a set of scientific facts....

... The region's corporate lobbyists, though they admitted that their industries might have become overreliant on temporary foreign labor, insisted that Mexican immigrants had become indispensable to the economic well-being of the Southwest. During hearings over proposed restrictions on Mexican immigration in the late 1920s, Alfred P. Thom, a representative of the American Railroad Association, ... concluded, "We are not employing men on account of their dispositions. We are employing them to have them exercise their strong backs at hard work. We are not employing them because they are of a high type of intellectuality [for] if we employed men because of their mental attainments, we could not employ either Mexicans or these colored people. We employ these men because we have the world's work to do and we must do it well." [See Document 6.]

★ ★ ★

At the same time that ... southwestern industrial and agricultural lobbyists ... were advancing their case for the suitability of Mexican immigrant labor, forces were building within the regional society that would severely undermine their efforts. The most serious of these was the resurgence of anti-Mexican sentiment that was prevalent during and after World War I. Although some Americans had expressed vocal opposition to Mexican immigration even before the war, in the late 1910s and early 1920s the immigration debate assumed new levels of vituperation.

Much of the increase in anti-Mexican sentiment stemmed from the generally high levels of xenophobia and nativism that had increasingly characterized American society since the last years of the nineteenth century. Alarmed at the rapid increase in immigration from southern and eastern Europe and convinced that the so-called new immigrants were racially and culturally inferior to white Americans of Anglo-Saxon heritage, American protectionists had begun to agitate for restrictive federal immigration legislation as early as the mid-1880s.... Congress responded to these pressures by slowly revising U.S. immigration law in an effort to stem the flow of undesirable immigrants.... Laws passed in 1917 and 1921 and the omnibus Johnson-Reid Immigration Act of 1924 not only imposed strict literacy requirements but also established a stringent national-origins quota system, which placed severe limitations on immigration from southern and eastern Europe, the Far East, Africa, and most countries of the Middle East.

Mexican immigrants initially were not subject to most of these restrictions. Bowing to the intense pressure exerted by southwestern agriculture, transportation, and construction lobbyists, Congress either exempted Mexican immigrants from the restrictive provisions of the new laws or relaxed them through various administrative procedures. As a partial consequence of these practices, Mexican immigration continued to increase steadily in the years after World War I....

... Although Mexican immigrants were not yet considered quite the menace that immigrants from southern and eastern Europe represented, as early as 1910 some influential Americans had already voiced concern about their poor health and hygiene, "cultural backwardness," and general "unassimilability." Over time, however, restrictionist sentiment against Mexicans became more pronounced.... From the point of view of a growing number of Americans, the rapid growth of the Mexican population represented just as serious a threat to the racial, cultural, and social integrity of the United States as did the entry of any of the other undesirable peoples. Indeed, by the mid-1920s many Americans were beginning to conclude that Mexicans were inferior even to the lowliest European immigrants.... According to the restrictionists Mexican immigration, if allowed to continue unabated, would surely "change the complexion of [the Southwest] ... and bring about a hyphenized, politically unstabilized, Latinized majority throughout the [region]." In the opinion of the vocal East Texas Congressman John C. Box, Mexican immigration was bound to create in the Southwest a race problem which would exceed that of the South....

Acting on this basic assumption, immigration restrictionists like Box mounted a concerted campaign designed to counter the arguments earlier advanced by the proponents of Mexican labor. Although the restrictionists shared many of the ethnocentric or racist assumptions held by their opponents, spokesmen for this position turned these assumptions on their heads, arguing that the characteristics southwestern employers had long touted as reasons for the use of Mexican labor were precisely why Mexican immigrants should be *barred* from the United States. The restrictionists' fundamental premise was that Mexicans constituted an inherently "un-assimilable" group.... In Box's view the only way to protect "American racial stock from further degradation or change through mongrelization" was to bar all future immigration from Mexico. Other restrictionists were even more rabid in their assessment of Mexicans, as an editorial in a local Los Angeles magazine made clear in January 1928. In the view of its author, Mexicans were "diseased of body, subnormal intellectually, and moral morons of the most hopeless type." ...

American immigration restrictionists hoped to bolster this line of argument by asserting that lenient U.S. immigration policies would inevitably result in the creation of a serious new race problem in the United States. Undoubtedly influenced by the racial strife that had erupted in Texas, Chicago, East St. Louis, and other areas at the end of World War I, restrictionists argued that similar outbreaks might occur if Mexican immigration continued unabated.... Thus for restrictionists the question, as [Vanderbilt University economist Roy L.] Garis put it, was "whether we shall preserve the Southwest as a future home for millions of the white race or permit [it] ... to be used ... as a dumping ground for the human hordes of poverty stricken peon Indians of Mexico." "We must decide now before it is too late," he argued, "whether we wish the complete Mexicanization of this section of our country with all which it implies—enormous decreases in the value of all property; the economic organization based upon peon labor, exploitation, and oppression; the complete nullification of the benefits derived from the restriction of European and the exclusion of Oriental immigration; a lowering of our standards of morals and of our political and social ideals; the creation of a race problem that will dwarf the negro problem of the South; and the practical destruction, at least for centuries, of all that is worthwhile in our white civilization."

Restrictionists augmented such flagrantly racist arguments by insisting that Mexicans were depriving American citizens of jobs. As important sectors of the American economy slipped into recession in the mid-1920s, immigration restrictionists intensified their accusations against the Mexican peons they saw competing with American citizens. As a member of the Texas State Chamber of Commerce put it, Mexican workers "living constantly on the ragged edge of starvation" were driving hard-working Americans out of jobs....

★ ★ ★

Although the debate that raged among Americans over the so-called Mexican Problem reflected many of the demographic, economic, and social changes that had altered the face of southwestern society in the 1910s and early 1920s, the rhetoric employed by both sides of the immigration debate made it abundantly clear that many Americans continued to view Mexicans as faceless abstractions rather than as a group of human beings. For the proponents of the use of foreign labor, Mexicans represented little more than a huge, tractable labor pool to be exploited at the whim of American industry. To immigration restrictionists Mexicans constituted a foreign menace both to the cultural and racial homogeneity of American society and to the institutional foundations on which the nation had been built. Thus, whether one argued that Mexicans should be allowed to work in the United States or not, Americans continued to subscribe to stereotypical images of Mexicans as members of an inferior, debased race....

... [I]mmigration from Mexico had also created a deeply complex and troubling set of issues for the Southwest's growing ethnic Mexican population. The arrival of so many Mexican immigrant workers in a political environment that was already hostile toward Mexicans stimulated deeply ambivalent responses in the Mexican American communities of the Southwest.... Mexican immigrants rejuvenated and enriched the social and cultural life of those communities. Pouring into the region and settling in, or next to, existing Mexican American barrios and colonias in Texas, Arizona, and California (and to a lesser degree, New Mexico, Colorado, and some areas of the industrial Midwest), Mexican men, women, and children dramatically expanded the Mexican cultural community of the United States. By bringing the Spanish language, Mexican customs and folkways, or merely the latest news from the hinterlands of Mexico, Mexican immigrants helped to reinforce the distinctive Mexican atmosphere of existing Mexican American enclaves. Indeed, by the mid-1920s the influx of new immigrants was so large that the immigrant population soon vastly outnumbered the native-born population in many areas and thus changed the character of Mexican American neighborhoods that had stood for more than a century.

... [I]n California and Texas, the ultimate destinations for the majority of recent immigrants from Mexico[,] ... the growth of the Mexican immigrant population were similar, with that of Texas growing from 71,062 in 1900 to 262,672 in 1930 and that of California from 8,086 to 191,346 in the same period.

Not all Mexican Americans regarded this process of Mexicanization as a positive development.... Although all of the recent immigrants shared a common language and cultural heritage with their Mexican American neighbors (and many shared even more intimate friendship and kinship ties), contact and interaction between natives and immigrants of Mexican descent in the United States were also marked by conflict and mutual distrust....

... Some of the friction apparent between U.S.-born Mexican Americans and Mexican immigrants in the twentieth century could be traced to a tradition of misunderstanding and suspicion that had divided the residents of Mexico's northern frontier provinces from the Mexicanos *del otro lado* (Mexicans "from the other side" of the border) since early in the nineteenth century.... [A]t that time the independent Norteños often chafed at the arrogance and cultural chauvinism displayed by Mexican government and military officials. In the view of many nineteenth-century Californios, Nuevomexicanos, and Tejanos, working-class Mexicans "from the other side" were even worse. From their point of view, common Mexicanos from Mexico were little more than uncultured, vulgar peasants....

The migration of hundreds of thousands of Mexican immigrants into the Southwest after the turn of the century created an even more complex and volatile set of issues for the growing ethnic Mexican population of the border region. Thrown together in a sociopolitical context in which Mexican Americans occupied an inferior social status and Mexican immigrants were, by definition, aliens, both groups found themselves viewed as outsiders in American society. Consequently, as immigration rates increased Mexican Americans and Mexican immigrants confronted each other in an ambiguous and often contradictory social milieu where potentially crucial distinctions between native and foreigner, citizen and alien, and American and Mexican, were called into question.

These confusing issues played themselves out in countless ways in the everyday interactions between U.S.-born Mexican Americans and recent Mexican immigrants.... Despite the cultural affinities Mexican Americans may have felt toward immigrants from Mexico, as their numbers grew, many Mexican Americans began to worry that the recent arrivals were depressing wages, competing with them for scarce jobs and housing, and undercutting their efforts to achieve better working conditions....

Mexicans and Mexican Americans ... were well aware of the many regional differences that had long characterized Mexican society, both within the Mexican Republic and in the extended Hispanic-Mexican Southwest. Although Mexican Americans often resembled recent immigrants physically, spoke the same language, and shared many customs, subtle, mutually recognized distinctions in language usage and vernacular, folkways, and social mores often served as internal boundaries demarcating various subgroupings of Mexicans from one another....

[P]erhaps most important ... [a]lready subject to the stigma of being Mexican in American society, many Mexican Americans feared that the mass immigration of impoverished, uneducated Mexican peasants would reinforce and inflame the negative stereotypes Americans already held about Mexicans....

... In one of the most detailed analyses of evolving Mexican American–Mexican immigrant relationships during this period, a research team led by the distinguished Mexican sociologist Manuel Gamio illuminated some of the most important sources of the ambivalence in relationships between the two groups....

... Summarizing his findings, he observed, "The attitude of the Mexicans who are American citizens toward the immigrant is a curious one. Sometimes they speak slighteningly of the immigrants (possibly because the immigrants are their competitors in wages and jobs), and say that the immigrants should stay in Mexico.... Furthermore, they are displeased, possibly because of racial pride, at the miserable condition in which most Mexicans arrive." On the other hand, Gamio noted that the Mexican immigrant "considers the American of Mexican origin as a man without a country. He reminds him frequently of the inferior position to which he is relegated by the white American." [See Document 4.]

Yet Gamio also noted the strong ties that bound Mexican Americans to Mexican immigrants and thus complicated the range of their interactions even further. He observed,

> ... both are called Mexicans by white Americans; they live together in the same districts; they belong to the same social stratum; they talk the same language; they wear the same clothes and possess the same needs and ideals; and most significant of all, they frequently intermarry....

Many Mexican immigrants expressed their own ambivalence, if not outright resentment, about their experiences with Mexican Americans in the United States.... Considering themselves part of what they called *Mexico de afuera*—Mexico outside Mexico—they believed themselves the only true Mexicans and often dismissed the Mexican Americans, whom they called *pochos* (faded or bleached ones), as a mongrel people without a country or a true culture....

Voicing a criticism of Mexican Americans that many Mexicans continue to make to the present day, [one] immigrant charged that Mexican Americans had "lost their culture." As he put it, "Mexicans who are born and educated here are people without a country." Another young man interviewed by Gamio's survey team was more temperate in his criticism yet communicated essentially the same message. "I don't have anything against the Pochos," he said, "but the truth of the matter is that although they are Mexicans, for they are of our own blood because their parents were Mexicans, they pretend that they are Americans. They only want to talk in English and they speak Spanish very poorly. That is why I don't like them." ...

★ ★ ★

[S]ustained large-scale immigration from Mexico helped to rejuvenate a strong Mexican cultural presence in the United States. With hundreds of thousands of immigrants settling in or near existing Mexican American communities after the turn of the century, the culture, language, and customs most Americans believed had disappeared in the United States experienced a new flowering in Mexico's former northern territories.

Although these developments were welcomed by Mexican Americans who continued to feel strong cultural attachments to the Mexican people and to Mexico, the rapid growth of the United States' ethnic Mexican population raised some troubling issues for both Mexican Americans and Mexican immigrants.... Forced to compete against the recent arrivals for scarce jobs, housing, and access to social services in a social and political context in which Mexicans were already stigmatized, many Mexican Americans argued that large-scale immigration represented a clear danger to ethnic Mexicans already living in the United States.

At another level, potential ethnic solidarity between U.S.-born Mexican Americans and recent immigrants was undermined by the subtle internal differences that had always characterized Mexican society and culture. Sensitive to regional variations in customs, language usage, and social mores, Mexican Americans and Mexican immigrants often found as many reasons to distrust and dislike one another as they found reasons for amity. In the increasingly pressurized social context of the Southwest, these mutually recognized distinctions would often be much more significant than they would have been in a less politically charged atmosphere.

The various cleavages that divided Mexican immigrants from Americans of Mexican descent were reflections of much deeper social changes occurring in the Southwest.... By maintaining elements of Hispanic-Mexican culture and identifying themselves as Mexicanos, as Hispanoamericanos, or as members of the more metaphysical La Raza, Mexican Americans had asserted an oppositional set of defining characteristics that helped demarcate their community from the Norteamericanos. Thus, although the bifurcation between "us" and "them" ... reflected the racially stratified character of southwestern society, by providing Mexican Americans with a basis of solidarity and action these ethnic boundaries served as an effective defense mechanism against discrimination....

... Prior to 1910 it had been fairly easy for Mexican Americans to define themselves vis-à-vis Anglo Americans by adhering to a formula that simply distinguished "us" from "them," but the presence of a large population of Mexicans "from the other side" greatly complicated the boundary-marking process. Although many Mexican Americans may have continued to consider themselves culturally Mexican when comparing themselves to Anglo Americans, the unprecedented influx of Mexicans from Mexico raised some confusing questions about what now defined a Mexican in the United States. As increasing numbers of Mexican immigrants entered their communities, Mexican Americans were compelled to reconsider the criteria by which they defined themselves....

... As more Americans became aware and alarmed over the rapid growth of the resident ethnic Mexican population and as the American economy rapidly slid toward a deep depression at the end of the [1920s], Mexican Americans and Mexican residents of the United States would be forced to consider, and to make initial decisions about, those issues of ethnic and national identity that Mexican immigration brought to the surface of regional politics.

Becoming Mexican in Chicago through Transnational Practices

GABRIELA ARREDONDO

In Chicago, Mexicanidad emerged as a fragile but proud identity that wove together elements of postrevolutionary Mexican nationalism and nostalgic conservative histories of "Mexico Lindo" (Beautiful Mexico) with the acknowledgment of growing anti-Mexican biases. It took the negative racialized connotations that "being Mexican" increasingly carried in Chicago and turned them on their head by celebrating Mexicanness. Played out in Chicago against a Latin American backdrop, Mexicanidad provided Mexicans with expressions of national allegiance....

Unlike their European neighbors, Mexican communities in Chicago were continually reinforced by new migrations from Mexico and the U.S. Southwest, at least throughout the 1920s. Moreover, the geographic proximity of Mexico and the particularities of preexisting histories between Mexico and the United States—indeed, the very connectedness of land and histories—meant that Mexicans in Chicago lived in dynamic, ongoing ways with Mexico. Multiple migration routes flowed into and out of Chicago: up and down the railroad lines, through states in northern and western Mexico and the central United States, and snaking along transportation routes throughout the Midwest. Taken together, these ongoing movements of people (and thus of news, ideas, cultural and social practices, etc.) and the distinctiveness of U.S.–Mexico relations enforced a raw awareness of Mexico in Chicago's Mexicans. Building on the ideals of the revolution and the nationalist projects in Mexico, Mexicans in Chicago found themselves creating a Mexicanidad that was fundamentally transnational and imbued with the mandate to redress anti-Mexican sentiments. Because of the particularities of Chicago, Mexicans also understood themselves within a broader Latin American context....

★ ★ ★

... At the popular level, nationalists culled Mexico's histories for useful events, myths, and memories that collectively could be used to create and appeal to popular visions of "Mexican tradition." ... Much of this was captured in various flavors of *indigenismo*....

... In the early nineteenth-century struggles for liberation from Spain, prominent ideologues ... effectively "proclaimed what was essentially a fiction, the myth of a Mexican nation, which was the lineal heir of the Aztecs." ...

Indigenismo of the early twentieth-century postrevolutionary period moved beyond valorization of a neo-Aztec past to include a celebration of the *indio* specifically.... Working toward agrarian reform programs, many *indigenistas* of the revolutionary era looked to the *indio* as the model member of a reconstructed Mexican state. That is, the *indio* represented a gendered-male communalism that supported moves toward land reform and that challenged those Porfirian holdovers. As an ideology, *indigenismo* appeared to be progressive, yet *indios* themselves faced only two real options: remain frozen in time as representatives of an imagined pre-Columbian Mexican past, or incorporate into the Mexican state only if they could be transformed into homogenous *mestizos*.... Those who participated in and cooperated with representatives of the postrevolutionary nation-state were deemed "more Mexican" than those who resisted....

The notion of the new *mestizo* arose concurrently....

Unspoken yet very much a part of these ideologies were racial divisions. Being a much more explicitly classed society than that of the United States, social status in Mexico closely correlated to racial categorization. Markers of race included physiological indicators of *indio*-ness, including body type, physical strength, skin color, hair texture, amount of body hair, and facial features, but they also included other cultural features like dress, practices, and language....

Race in Mexico, ... as in the United States, was a malleable and unfixed phenomenon, and *indigenistas* ... came to realize that *mestisaje* better captured the realities of the Mexican nation-state. "Racially," prominent nationalist Moisés Sáenz wrote, "the mestizo is the real American, and his number is on the increase.... It is inaccurate, therefore, to refer to Mexico as a nation of Indians; it is, rather, a nation of mestizos." ...

... Mexican nationalist ideologies of unity, whether of *indigenismo* or *mestisaje,* harmonized with an understanding of American identity that echoed the continental Pan-Americanist rhetoric of Latin American and Caribbean intellectuals and activists.... Simón Bolívar had written of unifying the former colonies of Spain into a continental republic.... Uruguayan José Enrique Rodó [called] on Latin America to resist the rise of U.S. imperialism by embracing common beliefs and cultural values.... Hispanofilia, grounded in a critique of U.S. imperialism, also provided the political and ideological mortar for other Latin American and Caribbean revolutionaries and thinkers like Cuba's José Martí. One of Latin America's most famous political philosopher-activists and considered the father of Cuban independence, Martí devoted his life to fighting for Cuban freedom from Spain and to keeping the tentacles of U.S. imperialism from creeping into Latin America. In his most famous essay, "Nuestra America" (Our America), first published in newspapers in Mexico City and New York in 1891, Martí expounded his views on the need for the peoples of the Americas to unify to prevent imperialist incursions....

... [M]any Latin Americans at the turn of the century ... were outraged at the stark imperialism of the United States after the "liberation" wars of 1898. This was closely followed by U.S. support of a revolution in Panama in 1903, during which the United States gained control of territory upon which they built the Panama Canal. Shortly thereafter, in December 1904, Theodore Roosevelt proclaimed his corollary to the Monroe Doctrine that explicitly allowed the United States to exert "international police power" to quell unrest in the Western Hemisphere....

... In Mexico, the dictator Porfirio Díaz and his U.S.–friendly policies came to stand for ... authoritarian modernity. U.S. foreign policy through the 1910s and early 1920s confirmed Mexican fears of U.S. authoritarian and expansionist designs in Mexico. President Woodrow Wilson's direct meddling in Mexican affairs culminated in the U.S. naval occupation of the Mexican port city of Veracruz in April 1914. Only two years later, in another unauthorized incursion into Mexican sovereignty, General Pershing led six thousand U.S. army troops through northern Mexico in search of Pancho Villa. Added to long memories of the U.S. invasion of Mexico City in the mid-nineteenth century and its conquest of nearly half of Mexico's landmass in 1848 and 1853, these events fueled fears of U.S. imperialist designs on Mexico.

Mexican postrevolutionary nationalists, most notably José Vasconcelos, Manuel Gamio, and Moisés Sáenz, in the 1920s and 1930s took up these anti-imperialist, Hispanocentric sentiments in their attempts to create a new, unified nation-state of Mexico....

The principal postrevolutionary solution for integrating all Mexicans into a national collective was the educational system....

An attorney, social philosopher, and later minister of education under President Obregón, José Vasconcelos advocated his vision of *la raza cósmica* as a way of incorporating the vast diversity of Mexico's peoples into the new nation-state of Mexico. Through a public-education system, Vasconcelos believed that the country could incorporate the *indio* into the *mestizo* mainstream, thus creating *la raza cósmica*. As minister of education (with Moisés Sáenz as the undersecretary), he oversaw the establishment of several thousand rural schools and an estimated two thousand libraries through which teachers sent into the countryside could work on the national mission: teaching the rural populations how to be Mexicans per his vision. This involved basic reading, writing, and arithmetic skills, along with Mexican history.... All of "the fundamental tools [were given] in Spanish," since Vasconcelos believed that knowledge of the Spanish language was crucial to the incorporation of the *indio*.

... [H]owever, ... rhetorical nods to *indio* incorporation did not match the socio-economic and political realities of most *indios*....

José Vasconcelos visited Chicago several times during the 1920s, and by 1929 a Clúb Pro-Vasconcelos had been formed to support his bid for the presidency of Mexico. When he visited in June 1928, he took time to speak to Chicago's Mexican *colonias*....

[Vasconcelos'] agenda became clear: to keep Chicago's Mexicans within the purview of the Mexican state, to ensure that Mexico did not permanently lose these obviously productive and resourceful citizens. Undoubtedly he was aware of the anthropologist Manuel Gamio's research tracing the remittances Mexicans sent back to Mexico, and he must have calculated the financial implications of these wages for the Mexican economy....

★ ★ ★

Perhaps the Latin Americanist orientation of Chicago's Mexicans was also encouraged by the presence of Cubans, Puerto Ricans, Guatemalans, Nicaraguans, Colombians, and Brazilians within Chicago's Mexican *colonias*.... Mexicans predominated in the Latin American population, but Central and South Americans formed a notable percentage....

... [Latin American immigrants of various nationalities] lived interspersed throughout areas of Mexican settlement.... Although Mexicans predominated in the Latino population, they were not the dominant group in any single neighborhood....

... [T]he presence of significant numbers of other Latin Americans potentially complicated moves toward a hemispheric Americanism, or Latin Americanism. Moreover, this diversity simply added to the already heterogeneous Mexican population. Mexicans and other Latin Americans recognized the desirability of and the need for unity between them. [See Document 5.]

... Mexican calls for unity in Chicago operated on two levels: they were reminiscent of Mexican nationalist rhetoric seeking to unify the nation-state; however, they were also truly concerned with unifying the Mexican population in Chicago, not simply out of nationalist leanings but also to fight against rising anti-Mexican prejudices and discrimination. In this sense, Mexicans in Chicago wielded the tools of Mexican nationalism to combat local conditions.

★ ★ ★

As being Mexican carried with it an increasing liability, Mexicans sought ways to redress the inequities. However, the overwhelming majority did not seek U.S. citizenship, for they did not see citizenship as a means toward that redemption. Señor Alonzo summarized the issue: "If you carry naturalization papers in your pocket ... you may hold your head up and say to yourself, 'Now I am as good as anybody.' But that won't prevent an American from kicking you and saying, 'Get out of here, you damned Mexican!'" Clearly, naturalization papers were not sufficient to protect one from being branded "Mexican" and suffering the discriminatory consequences of that label....

Mexicans in Chicago found that they were treated as "Mexicans" regardless of their legal status. Thus, their primary task was to "make the colony understand our great need of remedying our collective status." Those remedies came in the form of appeals to pull together....

By the mid-1930s formalized groups sprouted, organized specifically to unify the Mexican *colonia* to combat anti-Mexican prejudice....

Racial prejudice against Mexicans in Chicago worked in two contradictory ways. It separated people from each other depending on the extent to which one carried various markers of "Mexican" identity, such as skin color, proficiency with English, dress, economic status, work habits, or cultural practices, all of which fed into creating one's "reputation." ...

Racial prejudice also worked to unify Mexicans as they found themselves tagged "Mexican." In a perverse way, the effect of being branded pejoratively ... provided Mexicans with a unifying weapon that they could brandish against those people and institutions that discriminated against them. The net effect of this brand of prejudice was to homogenize Mexicans in the eyes of these same institutions and people.... Manuel Bravo's experience ... points ... to the anonymity that racial prejudice effectively created for Mexicans in the eyes of their employers.

Bravo described a practice common among Mexican workers in the area by which one would fill out job applications and take physical exams posing as someone else. In Manuel's case, it allowed him to pass a physical exam to work in the steel mills that he would have failed otherwise because of a bad eye.... And in other cases, according to Bravo, men were able to gain jobs that they otherwise would not have gotten because of their limited English....

These innovative solutions to the conditions under which they labored also diluted the strength of labor's appeal to the Mexican worker. Not only did they know this kind of flexibility was not yet available through unions, but Mexicans also knew there was racial prejudice against them....

... [I]f conditions became intolerable, they could choose the common option of simply leaving....

[T]he few Mexicans who joined labor unions explained that they did so not primarily to better their wages and working conditions but rather to combat the prejudice and discrimination they faced in the workplace. Their fights for improved wages and working conditions thus became symptoms of much larger issues and not their primary motivation. Angelo Soto ... was one such Mexican who joined the steel workers union in South Chicago because he never moved up in the work he did. He knew this was a form of discrimination against him as a Mexican, and he "saw the Union as a way of combating" this prejudice....

★ ★ ★

Mexicanidad functioned as an ethnic and racial identity, a collectively imagined and experienced way of "being Mexican in Chicago." As in other areas in the U.S. Southwest, immigrant identification with *lo mexicano* "helped bridge *patria chica* [small fatherland] allegiances to the home village and class divisions." In Chicago, however, against a Latin American and Euro-ethnic backdrop, pride in being "Mexican" at once acknowledged racialized negativity and at the same time celebrated "being Mexican" through a nostalgic tradition that empowered and unified.

Valorizing heroes of a past that was imagined to be collective included annual celebrations of Mexican independence from Spain in 1810. At such a celebration in 1924—marking the 114th anniversary—sponsored by the Mexican Fraternal Society of Chicago, festivities began before an altar to the *patria* displaying "pictures of the Father [Hidalgo]" and the "Heroes of Independence." ... The fiesta was also attended by non-Mexicans, which served an ulterior motive: to demonstrate Mexican unity and thereby blunt criticism of the social disorganization of the Mexican communities....

... [C]ommemorations of major historical events and actors helped to build and solidify a commonly agreed-upon heritage among Chicago's Mexicans. Such a collectively imagined history necessarily included major Catholic figures like Father Hidalgo.... Appeals to an imagined Aztec past ... included the naming of popular local sports clubs, including Clúb Anáhuac (after the Aztec name for the Valley of Mexico where Mexico City is located) and Clúb Atlético Cuauhtémoc (after the last ruler of the Aztec empire [1520–21]).... In the 1930s, ... Chicago's Mexicans celebrated Cinco de Mayo, publishing celebratory histories of the Battle of Puebla while groups from a variety of mutual-aid societies organized parades and dances. Spurred on by Mexican consuls, Mexicans organized feasts to honor Benito Juárez....

In 1935, representatives from several Mexican groups and social societies, along with many individual Mexicans and the Mexican consul, Eugenio Prequeira, worked together to form the Comité Pro-Mexico (the Pro-Mexico Committee), a confederation that apparently existed for several years....

As it matured, the Comité Pro-Mexico fought against ... generalized derogatory stereotyping of Mexicans in Chicago and served "to unify the *colonia Mexicana* in Chicago and to remind it of its civic duties." These reminders of their civic duties along with consular concern with *Mexico de afuera* spoke vividly of the degree to which successive Mexican governments worked not to lose their nationals. The tremendous irony, of course, is that most of these people would not have been noticed much by government structures at any level, beyond perhaps the local, had they stayed in Mexico. Once outside of Mexico in the United States, however, Mexican citizens represented a vibrant, productive, and therefore valuable citizenry that the Mexican nation-state targeted with resources and support. Thus Mexican consuls, as the official representatives of the Mexican national state, concerned themselves with reinforcing these people's Mexicanness in a variety of ways.

★ ★ ★

Like the postrevolutionary nationalists in Mexico, the Mexican consulate in Chicago relied on unity as its principal organizational theme, and they labored during the 1920s and 1930s to unify Mexicans throughout Chicagoland....

As seen through its participation in the fiestas, the Pro-Mexico Committee, and other examples, the consulate centered its high-profile activities around social and cultural events in Chicago. The consul and his local allies, especially businessmen and the editors of a few of the newspapers, used political events and knowledge of political conditions in Mexico to maintain ties with Mexico and among Mexicans. Accordingly, Spanish-language newspapers announced, and at times sponsored, *fiestas patrias*, parades, and theatrical productions about political conditions in Mexico.

Beyond their concerns with social and cultural events to promote Mexico and positive images of "Mexicanness," the Mexican consulate in Chicago did take an active part in mediating conditions for Mexican nationals....

... Primarily, the consul was charged with three duties: facilitating business and commerce between the United States and Mexico, providing protection to Mexicans living and working in the area, and defending the good name of the Republic of Mexico. In practice, these duties often conflicted. The interests of Mexican workers ... often collided with those of business and commerce. Nevertheless, a few of Chicago's consuls worked doggedly to resolve wage disputes between Mexican workers and American employers. In spite of this, many

Mexicans tended to view their consul with suspicion. In part, their distrust grew from the simple fact that the consul represented an authoritative government that they had known always to be corrupt and in which they held little direct representation. In addition, the frequency with which Mexico changed presidents, especially during the 1920s, meant that alliances with the consulate were usually short, and therefore people did not work as vigorously to build or maintain those ties. Moreover, the instability of the Mexican nation-state only confirmed the trepidation with which many Mexicans approached their government. After all, connections to one consul or government could be costly politically during sudden shifts in which opponents gained power.

The mobility of Mexican migrants into and out of Chicago and throughout the United States and Mexico added to their detachment from the consulate in Chicago. A consul's active involvement with the U.S. and Mexican governments to expedite and promote the repatriation campaigns of the 1920s and 1930s did not make him any more popular with Chicago's Mexicans. Yet many saw no contradiction in going to the consul when they were in trouble or needed his help. This was especially true when Mexicans came to him to perform what they believed to be his official duties. These ranged from cultural events like sponsoring (and funding) *fiestas patrias* to intervening with negligent employers on behalf of Mexican workers....

Just as Mexicans held expectations of their consulate, so too did the consulate and its allies expect Mexicans to comport themselves as true patriots.... As true Mexicans, they were expected to have strong clubs and societies ..., to have "irreproachable conduct, public and private," and to develop "business[es] which increase the wealth and the prestige of our country." It was no accident that this enumeration of the duties of the true patriot mirrored the official mission of the Mexican consulate.

★ ★ ★

Of course, other views on the "true Mexico" existed in Chicago. Ignacio Elizalde, for instance, "a quick, nervous, bald-headed white Mexican ... friendly and talkative," bemoaned that North Americans "did not appreciate the true Mexico." Betraying clear class and race biases, he explained that this was because "North American[s] saw only the crude Mexicans, los rudos, los Indios." ... Neither was he the "typical Mexican" as racialized in Chicago, given his light skin and education.... Again, being Mexican carried with it certain markers in physiognomy and comportment—white skin, fair complexion, and education somehow didn't signal "Mexican" to a non-Mexican, and by implication, "Mexican" really meant dark complexion with little or no education.

In attempting to depict the "real Mexican," another Mexican expressed views that echoed those of Elizalde. "'... In Mexico a lot of the people that are here were either servants or mountain Indians. There are many *peones* from the haciendas here too. There they were uncultured and savage. Here they dress like civilized people and eat well but do not pick up any education or manners.'" Clearly, the fear among these men was that in Chicago they would be lumped together with these "lesser" peoples into one derogatory category called

"Mexican." They were concerned that non-Mexicans would not understand or even notice what to them were vast differences in their qualities as national representatives of Mexico. As one man said, "'I am not ashamed of being a Mexican. But I am not proud of the Mexicans in Chicago. They are mostly Indians of the lower uneducated classes of peones.'" These views offer a direct window into the complexity of perspectives that existed among Chicago's Mexicans and also neatly capture the difficulties facing those who might aim for solidarity across these differences....

Even though Mexicans spoke this way of each other, they increasingly presented a more unified front when attacked from outside the *colonias,* particularly by racial prejudice.

Evidence suggests that Chicago's Mexicans were interested in celebrating their Mexican identities even in the face of rising discrimination against them. By the late 1920s, they used the term "de-Mexicanization" to refer to negative changes they saw among their populations in Chicago. Nostalgic conservative nationalist sentiments became especially transparent when dealing with children, the future generations of Mexicans in Chicago. Children who had little or no experience of Mexico itself were told stories and given descriptions of a romantic place frozen in time, frozen the moment their parents left.... Chicago's Mexicans created formal and informal institutional structures to keep their children's Mexican heritage by teaching them the Spanish language, Mexican history, and Mexican cultural and social practices....

Elements of a collectively imagined history could also be frozen in time as familiar cultural markers. In this sense, memory became another tool through which Mexicanidad was constructed in Chicago, for Mexicans drew from their memories of Mexico and their knowledge of history, beliefs, and practices in Mexico to hold the line against, de-Mexicanization....

Remembered places and longed-for locations also were frozen in the names of restaurants, barbershops, and billiard halls. El Chapultepec was a South Chicago restaurant and pool hall whose name evoked the beautiful central park in Mexico City where the Aztec emperor had his home. There was also a poolroom/barbershop near Hull-House with this name and a restaurant in Packingtown named El Chapultepec. Bello Jalisco (Beautiful Jalisco) was a restaurant on the Near West Side, and there was a similarly named restaurant in Packingtown....

★ ★ ★

The appropriation of historical elements in such simple ways helped to bolster the belief in a common heritage and to offer some measure of pride in this frozen, nostalgic history. Indeed, elements of pre-Columbian history and of nineteenth-century national heroes blended to provide Mexicans in Chicago with a shared sense of heritage. Even as they sought ways to take pride in "being Mexican," they continually faced anti-Mexican prejudice and discrimination....

Pride in their Mexicanidad provided comfort and an empowering belief in themselves as Mexicans, which helped to counter growing prejudices many faced by virtue of being Mexican. To those Mexican nationals living in Chicago who refused to change flags and who did not see changing citizenship as effecting any real change, Mexicanidad provided a means of coherence. It was their growing sense of national identity that emboldened many and provided the seeds for collective action, whether through fiestas, sports clubs, or parades. And its Latin Americanist bent allowed some Mexicans to actively claim their American identity by virtue of continental, or hemispheric, citizenship, not U.S. citizenship.

For, as is clearly the case with Mexicans in Chicago, lack of U.S. citizenship—and lack of desire to become U.S. citizens—did not indicate a fundamental indifference to their lives in Chicago, as social workers and others had thought. They struggled to lay claim to their American identity and to maintain their Mexican citizenship even while seeking lives outside the Mexican nation-state. The active involvement of the Mexican state (in the form of ... presidential tours, or consular work) and the prevalence of Mexican revolutionary/nationalist rhetoric all fed into Mexican determinations not to change flags. Indeed, in an ironic testament to the powers of nationalist sentiments, Chicago's Mexicans became Mexicans not while in Mexico but rather once outside of the bounds of the nation-state of Mexico.

Mexican attempts to maintain their continental citizenship while constructing their Mexicanidad, however, were stunted by the weight of insular Eurocentric forces of Americanization and by deep economic hardship. As economic conditions worsened for everyone in Chicago during the early 1930s, Mexicans experienced ever-more profound discrimination. They found themselves passed over for work in favor of European Americans, singled out as "Mexicans" and not "Americans" by relief workers, even formally segregated racially as "Mexicans" on the federal census of 1930.... Ultimately, Mexican visions of themselves as hemispheric Americans dimmed under the burdens of state and federal infrastructure that increasingly solidified the "barrier of prejudices" against which they struggled.

The economic depression and its attendant social and political consequences erected a more effective barrier to any transnational or continental vision than the creation of the Border Patrol had nearly a decade earlier, as it stymied the flow of people, culture, and ideas.

FURTHER READING

Gabriela F. Arredondo, *Mexican Chicago: Race, Identity, and Nation, 1916–39* (Chicago: University of Illinois Press, 2008).

Centro de Estudios Puertorriqueños, *Labor Migration under Capitalism: The Puerto Rican Experience* (New York: Monthly Review Press, 1979).

Jesús Colón, *A Puerto Rican in New York and Other Sketches* (New York: International Publishers, 1982; originally published 1961).

Linda C. Delgado, "Jesús Colón and the Making of a New York City Community, 1917 to 1974," in Carmen Teresa Whalen and Víctor Vázquez-Hernández, eds., *The*

Puerto Rican Diaspora: Historical Perspectives (Philadelphia: Temple University Press, 2005).

William Deverell, *Whitewashed Adobe: The Rise of Los Angeles and the Remaking of Its Mexican Past* (Berkeley: University of California Press, 2004).

Ruth Glasser, *My Music Is My Flag: Puerto Rican Musicians and Their New York Communities, 1917–1940* (Berkeley: University of California Press, 1995).

David G. Gutiérrez, *Walls and Mirrors: Mexican Americans, Mexican Immigrants, and the Politics of Ethnicity* (Berkeley: University of California Press, 1995).

Edwin Maldonado, "Contract Labor and the Origins of Puerto Rican Communities in the United States," *International Migration Review* 13, no.1 (1979), 103–121.

Félix V. Matos Rodríguez and Pedro Juan Hernández, *Pioneros: Puerto Ricans in New York City 1896–1948* (Charleston, NC: Arcadia, 2001).

Natalia Molina, *Fit to Be Citizens? Public Health and Race in Los Angeles, 1879–1939* (Berkeley: University of California Press, 2006).

Douglas Monroy, *Rebirth: Mexican Los Angeles from the Great Migration to the Great Depression* (Berkeley: University of California Press, 1999).

Victoria Nuñez, "Remembering Pura Belpré's Early Career at the 135th Street New York Public Library: Interracial Cooperation and Puerto Rican Settlement during the Harlem Renaissance," *Centro: Journal of the Center for Puerto Rican Studies* 21, no. 1 (2009), 52–77.

Virginia Sánchez Korrol, *From Colonia to Community: The History of Puerto Ricans in New York City* (Berkeley: University of California Press, 1994, originally published 1983).

Lorrin Thomas, *Puerto Rican Citizen: History and Political Identity in Twentieth-Century New York City* (Chicago: University of Chicago Press, 2010).

Carmen Teresa Whalen, "Colonialism, Citizenship, and the Making of the Puerto Rican Diaspora: An Introduction," in Carmen Teresa Whalen and Víctor Vázquez-Hernández, eds., *The Puerto Rican Diaspora: Historical Perspectives* (Philadelphia: Temple University Press, 2005).

CHAPTER 7

The Great Depression
and Dubious Citizenship

As the U.S. stock market crashed and the U.S. economy collapsed, the era of the Great Depression brought new levels of economic hardship to Mexican Americans and Puerto Ricans. They were no longer recruited as sources of low-wage labor. Instead, Mexicans and Puerto Ricans were often the first fired as jobs became scarce. Limited household resources became even more strained. Using existing connections to their home countries, some Mexican and Puerto Rican migrants returned with hopes of finding work and sustaining their households, despite the economic crisis, which wracked Mexico and Puerto Rico's economies as well.

This era witnessed a rise in nativist sentiment. U.S. society questioned the citizenship of Mexican Americans and Puerto Ricans, who were seen as taking jobs and benefits from white Americans. Throughout the American Southwest and Midwest, local governments, federal agents, and charity officials sought to persuade Mexican immigrants to return to Mexico in a repatriation campaign that sometimes forced Mexican American children to accompany their parents to a country they had never visited. Without formal deportation proceedings, at least 400,000 people were repatriated to Mexico, a number that included thousands of U.S. citizens of Mexican descent. Although they were not forcibly repatriated, Puerto Ricans continued to confront a second-class citizenship and a racial hierarchy that defined them, as well as Mexican Americans, as inferior.

The decade of the 1930s was also marked by increased political and social activism among Mexican Americans and Puerto Ricans. Determined to claim full citizenship rights, activists used various strategies from the assimilationist approach of the League of United Latin American Citizens to union organizing to participation in vibrant left-wing organizations. While some sought inclusion in the U.S. mainstream, others strove for the radical transformation of U.S. society. This chapter focuses on the experiences of Mexican immigrants, Mexican Americans, and Puerto Ricans as they confronted continued second-class status, as well as the xenophobia sparked by a severe economic downturn.

DOCUMENTS

As the ravages of the economic crisis impacted individuals and families, some Mexican immigrants sought assistance from the Mexican government to return to their homeland. In Document 1, Mexican immigrants write to the Mexican consulate, depicting their hardships in Rockdale, Illinois, and requesting assistance to return to Mexico. Document 2 reveals that in November 1930, the U.S. consul wrote to the U.S. secretary of state, reporting that large numbers of Mexicans, including many who had lived in the United States for several years, were returning to Mexico through Laredo, Texas. Adding to Mexicans' hardships, private employers were not the only ones to fire or to refuse to hire Mexican immigrants. Document 3 is an excerpt from the California Alien Labor Act of 1931, which prohibits contractors from hiring "aliens" for any public works projects. Document 4 is an excerpt from Puerto Rican activist Bernardo Vega's memoirs. He describes the range of political activities in New York City, including transnational working-class solidarity, and provides his interpretation of the Harlem riot in 1935. Despite hardships, some political gains were made such as the election of Oscar García-Rivera, which is revealed in Document 5. In 1937, he became the first Puerto Rican elected to the New York State Assembly. Document 6 is an excerpt from writer Piri Thomas' now classic autobiography, *Down These Mean Streets*, in which he depicts the continuing impact of the Great Depression on his Cuban/Puerto Rican family in Harlem in 1941.

1. Mexican Immigrants in Rockdale, Illinois, Ask the Mexican Consul for Voluntary Repatriation, 1930

… This letter is addressed to you with the exclusive purpose of communicating the present situation that prevails among us Mexicans in this town of Rockdale, Ill.

Among us are a number of families and single men without work or hope of obtaining work in this town. As far as industries, there is a wire factory and a brick factory. The wire factory has not employed a single Mexican in years but for those who for the past 10 years already worked there. The brick factory was our only option, and on the 29th of this month it laid off all Mexicans in order to hire North Americans and Europeans instead. This leaves you as our only hope against the travails of hunger and cold, to intercede on our behalf before the Prime Magistrate of our country.

Most honorable Consul, we wish that for humanity's sake you will do whatever possible in order to repatriate us with our families before we die of hunger and cold or be forced to crime and dishonor over a morsel of bread for

Francisco Balderrama and Raymond Rodríguez, *Decade of Betrayal: Mexican Repatriation in the 1930s* (Albuquerque: University of New Mexico Press, 2006), p. 115.

our wives and children. The government denies us aid and when we ask for it they answer that Mexicans are exempt from aid. The only way we have managed without work is because those with jobs have, for a long time, helped those without.

We hope His Excellency will act on our behalf, offer us repatriation and collaborate towards the enrichment of our beloved nation.

2. U.S. Consul Richard F. Boyce Reports on Mexicans Returning to Mexico through Nuevo Laredo, 1930

... I have the honor to report that thousands of Mexican residents of the United States have been returning to Mexico during the past two months through Laredo, Texas. In crossing the international bridge each day one can always see a line of cars with licenses from nearly half the states of the United States filled with household effects of Mexicans returning and waiting to make the necessary registrations with the Mexican authorities. Most of the cars are dilapidated in appearance and show the effects of the long journey from northern sections of the country. Those travelling in cars however are less than half of the total who are returning. Many of them are returning to [t]ake up land at the Don Martin irrigation project, attracted by the advertisements of the Mexican National Irrigation Commission. But about 805 are returning because of lack of work in the United States. A Mexican coming from a large Mexican settlement of about a thousand in Colorado stated that almost all were planning to return to Mexico because of lack of work.

No figures are given for those who were legally in the United States and those who were illegal residents. The Mexican immigration authorities do not record either the length of residence in the United States or whether legal admission was made. The American authorities do not "check out" those aliens unless they have proof of legal entry, an identification card from the Mexican consul in the United States and voluntarily call at the American immigration office....

While no figures, or even estimates, are obtainable of these Mexicans who have lived over five years in the United States it is believed quite a number have lived in the United States more than five years. Some claim eight, ten, fifteen, even thirty years American residence.

Number of Mexicans returning to Mexico from the United States through Laredo, Texas:

October, 1930 4,255

November 1–24, 1930 3,995

Francisco Balderrama and Raymond Rodríguez, *Decade of Betrayal: Mexican Repatriation in the 1930s* (Albuquerque: University of New Mexico Press, 2006), pp. 153–155.

... Estimated American residence of Mexican repatriates:

Texas	20%	Colorado	5%
Illinois	15%	Oklahoma	3%
Michigan	15%	Massachusetts	2%
Indiana	10%	New York	2%
Missouri	10%	Wisconsin	2%
Ohio	8%	Pennsylvania	2%
Minnesota	5%	Alabama	1%

3. California Alien Labor Act Prohibits Hiring Foreigners, 1931

... SECTION 1. No person, firm, partnership, association or corporation, or agent thereof, doing any work as a contractor or subcontractor upon any public work being done for or under the authority of the state, ... or for or under the authority of any county, city and county, city, town, township, district, or any other political subdivision thereof, ... shall knowingly employ or cause or allow to be employed thereon any alien, except in cases of extraordinary emergency caused by fire, flood, or danger to life or property, or except to work upon public military or naval defenses or works in time of war.... Such contractor and each subcontractor shall also keep, or cause to be kept, an accurate record showing the names and citizenship of all workers employed by him....

SEC. 3. Work done for irrigation, utility, reclamation, improvement and other districts, ... as well as street, sewer and other improvement work done under the direction and supervision or by the authority of any officer or public body of the state, ... whether or not done under public supervision or direction, or paid for wholly or in part out of public funds, shall be held to be "public work" within the meaning of this act.

The term "alien" as used herein means any person who is not a born or fully naturalized citizen of the United States....

4. Puerto Rican Activist Bernardo Vega Recalls the Harlem Riot, 1935

... On March 21, 1935, Harlem was hit by a major riot. It was sparked off by the arrest of León Rivera, a young boy accused of stealing from the Kress store on 125th Street off Lenox Avenue. Several women who witnessed the event

Statutes of California, (Sacramento: California State Printing Office, 1931), pp. 913–914.

Republished with permission of Monthly Review Press, from *Memoirs of Bernardo Vega: A Contribution to the History of the Puerto Rican Community in New York*, ed. César Andreu Iglesias, trans. Juan Flores (1984), pp. 180–181; permission conveyed through Copyright Clearance Center, Inc.

thought Rivera was a black American, although he was of course Puerto Rican, and rushed out into the street to protest the abusive manner in which the private guards (whites, of course) made the arrest. Hundreds of people gathered around the women, anger flared, and rocks started sailing through the store's windows. Violence spread throughout the neighborhood and lasted for several hours. When order was finally restored, Harlem looked like a city in ruins and was in a state of siege.

The roughing-up of the young boy by the guards and the women's outburst was like pulling a cork, and all of the pain and suffering of the black people rose to the surface. There were thousands of businesses in the area, all of them run by whites. In none of them—from the largest to the smallest—was there a single Afro-American person working. Discrimination was rampant, and was all the more abusive and humiliating because Harlem had the greatest concentration of blacks in New York City. The refusal to hire Negroes, even in businesses largely patronized by them, and at a time when the most severe unemployment was among black people—who, on top of all that, also had to pay higher rents than whites—made racial discrimination all the more disgusting.

Fortunately, Fiorello La Guardia was mayor of New York at the time. As soon as he heard about the riot, he went up to Harlem himself, restrained the police—who thought they could solve the problem with billy clubs—and stated publicly that black people were victims of a grave injustice. He called a meeting right there on the spot, spoke in conciliatory tones, and pledged the resources of the city government to alleviate the most pressing problems afflicting the Negro population—immediate assistance, jobs, and so forth. His quick action prevented a repetition of the violence.

That riot of March 21 seemed to strike panic into the managers of companies operating in Harlem. From then on, nearly all the stores began to hire blacks for menial work. The recently established "relief agencies" recruited blacks to conduct some of their investigations, and employment became available at the Board of Education and in the Police Department. These were some of Fiorello La Guardia's achievements during his first term in City Hall.

If anything taught the Puerto Ricans—including white Puerto Ricans—what life is like in the United States, it was the awareness of discrimination. As we have come to see, racial prejudice takes on many different faces. One form it took, around that time, was exemplified by the New York City Chamber of Commerce. Claiming that it needed to determine the "intelligence quotient" of Puerto Rican children, it sponsored a series of experimental tests. After administering the exam to 240 students, the Chamber announced in the papers that Puerto Rican children were "deficient" and lacked "intellectual development."

That "experiment" provoked a protest from groups representing the Puerto Rican community.... But the Chamber of Commerce showed little or no interest, and turned to other matters....

By that time the Puerto Rican community had spread out considerably. In addition to El Barrio in Harlem, thickly populated neighborhoods had sprung up in the Bronx, Washington Heights, and on parts of Long Island. The owners and managers of apartment buildings actively resisted this Puerto Rican expansion. In many cases, especially up in Washington Heights, they refused to rent to families who had come from Puerto Rico, which is what gave rise to the Comité de Defensa de Derechos de los Hispanos....

5. Puerto Rican Oscar Garcia-Rivera Elected to New York State Assembly, 1937

One of the first things that Oscar Garcia-Rivera, newly elected American Labor candidate for the state assembly in the 17th Assembly District, plans to do as a member of that body is to introduce an emergency rent law to help ameliorate the present crisis in the Harlem housing situation.

"I have lived in Harlem almost all of my life," he told an Amsterdam News reporter at his law offices at 1360 Fifth avenue Tuesday, "that is, since I came from Puerto Rico, and the only thing that made me move away from the community was the high rents."

The young assemblyman explained that he had lived at 35 West 110th street for several years and that when the rent for his six-room apartment was hiked from $60 per month to $90, he was forced to move because he could not aford the higher rate. He is now living at 1263 Fifth avenue, right next door to Mayor LaGuardia....

"To what party do I belong?" he repeated the question. "I was a Republican, but I am now too progressive to be a member of that party. I was endorsed by the Republicans, the American Labor Party and the Fusionists in the last election. I suppose I would be called a Progresive Republican."

Also intensely interested in the federal Child Labor Amendment, Mr. Rivera intends to seek its ratification by the state assembly.

"My political career has been brief," he said. "More than anything else up to this time, I have been engaged in civic work in the community."

As president of the Civic Committee of Harlem, Mr. Rivera recently contacted all of the leading persons in the 17th Assembly District to see what could be done to call the attention of the authorities to the fact that they should devote more time to better the economic, moral and social conditions of Harlem....

Expressing the hope he might wedge the way for the Spanish-speaking people of lower Harlem and residents of other Harlem districts to recognize that their political, social and economic problems are one and the same, the assemblyman declared that "the dividing line between the Spanish-speaking people and the colored American is due to Tammany Hall propaganda, for Tammany Hall benefits by keeping us politically apart."

"Newly Named Assemblyman Tells of Plan: Will Work to Better Conditions for Harlemites," *The New York Amsterdam News*, Nov 13, 1937, p. 24.

6. Piri Thomas, a Writer of Cuban and Puerto Rican Descent, Depicts the Great Depression in Harlem, 1941

Poppa didn't talk to me the next day. Soon he didn't talk much to anyone. He lost his night job—I forget why, and probably it was worth forgetting—and went back on home relief. It was 1941, and the Great Hunger called Depression was still down on Harlem.

But there was still the good old WPA. If a man was poor enough, he could dig a ditch for the government. Now Poppa was poor enough again.

The weather turned cold one more time, and so did our apartment. In the summer the cooped-up apartments in Harlem seem to catch all the heat and improve on it. It's the same in the winter. The cold, plastered walls embrace that cold from outside and make it a part of the apartment, till you don't know whether it's better to freeze out in the snow or by the stove, where four jets, wide open, spout futile, blue-yellow flames. It's hard on the rats, too.

Snow was falling. "My *Cristo*," Momma said, "*qué frío*. Doesn't that landlord have any *corazón*? Why don't he give more heat?" I wondered how Pops was making out working a pick and shovel in that falling snow....

We drank hot cocoa and talked about summertime. Momma talked about Puerto Rico and how great it was, and how she'd like to go back one day, and how it was warm all the time there and no matter how poor you were over there, you could always live on green bananas, *bacalao,* and rice and beans. "*Dios mío*," she said, "I don't think I'll ever see my island again."...

Moms copped that wet-eyed look and began to dream-talk about her *isla verde,* Moses' land of milk and honey.

"When I was a little girl," she said, "I remember the getting up in the morning and getting the water from the river and getting the wood for the fire and the quiet of the greenlands and the golden color of the morning sky, the grass wet from the *lluvia* ... *Ai, Dios,* the *coquís* and the *pajaritos* making all the *música*....

"... I remember the hard work and the very little bit we had, but it was a good little bit. It counted very much. Sometimes when you have too much, the good gets lost within and you have to look very hard. But when you have a little, then the good does not have to be looked for so hard."...

"... [Y]ou have people everywhere who, because they have more, don't remember those who have very little. But in Puerto Rico those around you share *la pobreza* with you and they love you, because only poor people can understand poor people. I like *los Estados Unidos*, but it's sometimes a cold place to live—not because of the winter and the landlord not giving heat but because of the snow in the hearts of the people." ...

The door opened and put an end to the kitchen yak. It was Poppa coming home from work. He came into the kitchen and brought all the cold with him. Poor Poppa, he looked so lost in the clothes he had on. A jacket and coat, sweaters on top of sweaters, two pairs of long johns, two pairs of pants, two pairs of socks, and a woolen cap. And under all that he was cold. His eyes were cold; his ears were red with pain. He took off his gloves and his fingers were stiff with cold.

"*Cómo está?*" said Momma. "I will make you coffee."

Poppa said nothing. His eyes were running hot frozen tears. He worked his fingers and rubbed his ears, and the pain made him make faces....

"It was not always like this," my father said to the cold walls. "It's all the fault of the damn depression."

"Don't say 'damn,'" Momma said.

"Lola, I say 'damn' because that's what it is—*damn.*"

And Momma kept quiet. She knew it was "damn."

My father kept talking to the walls. Some of the words came out loud, others stayed inside. I caught the inside ones—the damn WPA, the damn depression, the damn home relief, the damn poorness, the damn cold, the damn crummy apartments, the damn look on his damn kids, living so damn damned and his not being able to do a damn thing about it.

And Momma looked at Poppa and at us and thought about her Puerto Rico and maybe being there where you didn't have to wear a lot of extra clothes and feel so full of damns, and how when she was a little girl all the green was wet from the *lluvias.*

And Poppa looking at Momma and us, thinking how did he get trapped and why did he love us so much that he dug in damn snow to give us a piece of chance? ...

And Miriam, James, José, Paulie, and me just looking and thinking about snowballs and Puerto Rico and summertime in the street and whether we were gonna live like this forever and not know enough to be sorry for ourselves.

The kitchen all of a sudden felt warmer to me, like being all together made it like we wanted it to be....

... When Poppa finished, he came into the living room and stood there looking at us. We smiled at him, and he stood there looking at us.

All of a sudden he yelled, "How many wanna play 'Major Bowes' Amateur Hour'?"

"Hoo-ray! Yeah, we wanna play," said José.

"Okay, first I'll make some taffy outta molasses, and the one who wins first prize gets first choice at the biggest piece, okay?"

"Yeah, hoo-ray, *chevere.*"

Gee, Pops, you're great, I thought, *you're the swellest, the bestest Pops in the whole world, even though you don't understand us too good.*

When the candy was all ready, everybody went into the living room. Poppa came in with a broom and put an empty can over the stick. It became a microphone, just like on the radio.

"Pops, can I be Major Bowes?" I asked.

"Sure, Piri'" and the floor was mine.

"Ladies and gentlemen," I announced, "tonight we present 'Major Bowes' Amateur Hour,' and for our first number—"...

Everyone took a turn, and we all agreed that two-year-old Paulie's "gurgle, gurgle" was the best song, and Paulie got first choice at the candy. Everybody got candy and eats and thought how good it was to be together, and Moms thought that it was wonderful to have such a good time even if she wasn't in Puerto Rico where the grass was wet with *lluvia*....

The next day the Japanese bombed Pearl Harbor.

"My God," said Poppa. "We're at war."

"*Dios mío*," said Momma....

I wondered if the war was gonna make things worse than they were for us. But it didn't. A few weeks later Poppa got a job in an airplane factory. "How about that?" he said happily. "Things are looking up for us."

Things *were* looking up for us, but it had taken a damn war to do it. A lousy rumble had to get called so we could start to live better. I thought, *How do you figure this crap out?*

I couldn't figure it out, and after a while I stopped thinking about it. Life in the streets didn't change much. The bitter cold was followed by the sticky heat; I played stickball, marbles, and Johnny-on-the-Pony, copped girls' drawers and blew pot. War or peace—what difference did it really make?

 # ESSAYS

Despite racial complexities since it origins, the United States continued to cling to a racial binary that defined people as either white or black, providing privileges to those defined as white. This racial binary did not make room for racial mixing nor for racially heterogeneous groups, rendering the place of Mexican Americans and Puerto Ricans unclear. Indeed, as Natalia Molina, professor of history at the University of California, San Diego, notes in the first essay, only people who were defined as white or black were eligible for citizenship and hence for immigration to the United States. Mexicans, she writes, "were placed into a third, flexible racial category ... of 'non-white.'" While some government officials and nativist groups sought to define Mexicans as "non-white" and hence ineligible for citizenship and immigration, some Mexican Americans sought to claim their rights by demanding official recognition as "white."

In the second essay, Lorrin Thomas, professor of history at Rutgers University, Camden, revisits the Harlem riot of 1935 to explore how the racial binary worked to render Puerto Ricans invisible in the New York City politics of the time and in U.S. history. Although portrayed as an African American event, Puerto Ricans were present in the origins of the incident and in the responses to it. Turning to the pages of New York City's Spanish-language newspapers, Thomas explores how Puerto Ricans negotiated the racial binary and asserted their own sense of themselves. Puerto Ricans drew on notions of race that were salient in Puerto Rico, as well as on their sense of how best to claim rights within the U.S. context. With attention to the different systems of racial classification in Mexico, Puerto Rico, and the United States, these essays highlight the socially and historically constructed nature of race, as well as how racial ideologies cross borders. They also illustrate that racial categories in the United States have changed over time, varied by regions, and have been widely contested.

Mexicans' Tenuous Citizenship

NATALIA MOLINA

... According to the Naturalization Act of 1790 and its revision in 1870, only those who were deemed white or black could become citizens.... The Supreme Court had ruled that neither Japanese persons nor Asian Indians were white in *Ozawa v. United States* (1922) and *United States v. Bhagat Singh Thind* (1923). Moreover, since Section 13 of the 1924 Immigration Act restricted immigration to persons eligible for citizenship, an immigrant needed to be from a group considered white not just to naturalize but even to immigrate to the United States.

... [W]hite supremacists saw an opportunity to nullify Mexicans' eligibility for U.S. citizenship by insisting these landmark citizenship decisions made previous racial designations of Mexicans null and void. The ultimate aim of the proponents was, of course, to shore up the definitional walls of what they saw as the essential distinction between "white" and "non-white" population groups, thereby putting even sharper teeth into the severe racial restrictions on both the naturalization and potential immigration of racially proscribed peoples. In the process, Mexicans were placed into a third, flexible racial category (after those of "black" and "white") of "non-white."

This article provides a revealing look into various efforts by state and private actors to render Mexican immigrants ineligible for U.S. citizenship by having them officially categorized as "non-white." ... While legislation and court rulings may have constituted the legal framework in which race and racial hierarchy were defined, those definitions were always subject to an inherently informal and ad hoc process of human interpretation and intervention that extended the complex process of racialization and racial definition beyond what was formally inscribed in the law....

★ ★ ★

The contest over Mexicans' status was fought not just in naturalization cases, but in immigration policy as well. Until the 1910s Mexicans had crossed the U.S.-Mexican border with relative freedom. The passage of the Literacy Act in 1917 increased immigration requirements for the first time for those who entered from Mexico. The act's imposition of a head tax also proved a financial burden for some Mexican immigrants, and many looked for places to cross the border outside of the supervision of a border checkpoint to avoid paying it. Moreover, stereotypes of Mexicans as carriers of disease who threatened both the health of

Molina, Natalia, "'In a Race All Their Own': The Quest to Make Mexicans Ineligible for U.S. Citizenship," in *Pacific Historical Review*, vol. 79, no. 2 May 2010. © 2010 by the Regents of the University of California. Published by the University of California Press.

the nation and its charity system (and also as a fertile population ready to over-take the nation) resulted in humiliating medical inspections at border-crossing stations, a practice that made entering the United States still more punishing. With the creation of the border patrol in 1924, Mexicans experienced even more difficulty crossing the border.... Border patrol agents played a key role in defining Mexicans as outsiders through their harassment and denigration of Mexicans at checkpoints—even when their papers were in order—or in random stops as they crossed the bridge from Juárez, Mexico, to El Paso, Texas, the larg-est point of entry.

... Throughout the 1920s, the strong lobbying power of large-scale employ-ers, as well as diplomatic and trade interests, kept Mexicans from being included in the quota system. Nevertheless, opponents continued to launch attempts to legislate restrictions on Mexican immigration.

One of the most important immigration restrictionists in Congress was Representative John C. Box of Texas. Box was tireless in his efforts to rally anti-Mexican sentiment and to pass severely restrictive immigration legislation.... Box's arguments may have persuaded many of his fellow Americans, but his attempts in 1926 and 1928 to shepherd legislation that would drastically limit Mexican immi-gration failed. The need to preserve diplomatic and trade relations with Mexico, as well as the State Department's commitment to protecting American-owned oil properties there, proved more powerful than the strong anti-Mexican sentiment of Box, some of his fellow legislators, and assorted citizen groups....

Although restrictionist legislation repeatedly failed to pass, in 1928 the State Department engineered a significant reduction in Mexican immigration by instructing its consular offices in Mexico to curtail the number of visas issued. This change in policy was aimed at appeasing restrictionists and imped-ing future legislation to limit Mexican immigration.... With the consuls scru-pulously following the new visa policy, legal immigration from Mexico decreased drastically....

By 1930 the flow of Mexican immigrants had decreased dramatically. In 1929, the year following the change in visa policy, Congress approved another deterrent, Public Law 1018, which made crossing into the United States without a visa a misdemeanor with a penalty of up to one year in prison. Moreover, the law provided that anyone who was deported, then re-entered, and was caught would be charged with a felony and would face up to two years in prison. Lastly, Congress increased funding to the border patrol, adding to both its real and symbolic power. This combination of decreased visas, increased penalties, and tighter patrolling was highly effective in reducing Mexican immigration. Nevertheless, ... well into the 1930s restrictionists continued campaigning for a quota to be established for immigrants from Mexico and for an end to their eligibility for citizenship.

★ ★ ★

Much as the question of immigration remained unresolved during the 1930s, so too did the question of eligibility for citizenship. Business interests consistently undercut the possibility of a monolithic, race-based approach to the question of

Mexican immigration. Advocates for immigration may have agreed with opponents that Mexicans were of "inferior stock" and "not quite white," but this shared perception made them no less zealous in ensuring that the immigration door remained wedged open enough to allow a steady flow of low-wage labor to continue.

Two major turning points for Mexicans and Mexican Americans living in the United States occurred during the 1930s. The first was the Depression. The collapse of the U.S. economy triggered a dramatic change in the treatment of Mexicans and Mexican Americans. Their marginal acceptance, which had stemmed from their being a source of cheap labor, disappeared as rapidly as the jobs Mexican laborers had been hired to fill. As jobs disappeared, so did the justification for allowing an open immigration policy with Mexico. Opponents of unrestricted immigration began insisting that Mexicans return home and followed up those demands with political pressure at the local, state, and national levels. These attitudes culminated in repatriation programs that sent large numbers of Mexicans—including American citizens of Mexican descent—to Mexico....

The second major turning point was the rise of second-generation Mexican Americans as a politicized group. Depression-era deportation programs made it clear to the second generation and Mexicans residing in the United States that they could no longer move easily back and forth between countries, nor could they anticipate as much help from the Mexican government in protecting their legal rights while they were living in the United States. They increasingly turned to U.S. institutions, joining unions, demanding their rights as U.S. citizens, and using organizations like the Congress of Spanish Speaking Peoples to channel their voices and give them greater political weight....

Mexican Americans fought on many fronts to continue being classified as white for they knew that whiteness afforded them rights. Historians David Gutiérrez and Neil Foley have written about the large-scale organizing Mexican Americans engaged in through organizations such as the League of United Latin American Citizens (LULAC) in both Texas and California. Unlike most other Mexican organizations in the United States, whose main concern was immigrant mutual aid, LULAC's mission was political. The organization aimed to help naturalized Mexicans and Mexican Americans claim their rights as U.S. citizens. Formed in 1929 by Mexicans who had been born or come of age in the United States (including some who had served in the U.S. armed forces during World War I), LULAC pursued an agenda of assimilation, excluding from membership Mexicans who were not U.S. citizens.

When faced with the possibility of losing the few citizenship rights they had, Mexicans fought back. Historian Mario García has told the history of the attempt by the El Paso city registrar and the city health officer to change Mexicans' racial classification from "white" to "colored" in El Paso in 1936. At the time, El Paso had a high infant mortality rate among whites, which would reflect badly on any city, but especially one like El Paso that was working to establish itself as a health resort. Since they believed that Mexicans contributed disproportionately to this high infant mortality rate, they concluded that reclassifying Mexicans as non-white would improve the health statistics. With the help of LULAC, Mexicans and Mexican Americans in the city mounted a campaign against the reclassification and won. Because El Paso city officials had justified the reclassification by citing the precedent set by the U.S. Census to place Mexicans in a racial category of their own, Mexican activists continued their fight and took it to Washington, D.C., where they compelled the U.S. Census Bureau to classify Mexicans as white once again.

Another history-making moment occurred in 1931 in Lemon Grove, located in San Diego County. During the Depression, school officials segregated Mexicans and Mexican Americans into a separate school. Enlisting legal counsel and the help of the Mexican consul, the Mexican community organized and took their fight to the Superior Court of California in San Diego where they won the first school desegregation case.

In addition to legal activism, Mexicans fought discrimination through social and cultural means. Historian Gabriela Arredondo has argued that the Mexican community in Chicago had a more ambivalent attitude toward remaining in the United States permanently; thus, Mexicans there tended to turn less to civic participation, preferring instead to unify among themselves to combat discrimination through everyday acts, such as joining sports teams and enjoying local festivals and parades....

As the definition of whiteness continued to be contested in the 1930s, ... nativist groups finally got what they wanted: a test case. In 1935 Judge John Knight of the U.S. District Court in Buffalo, New York, denied three Mexicans' petitions for naturalization because they had a "strain of Indian blood." Knight's reasoning resonated with what was commonly known as the "one-drop rule," which defined anyone with even one drop of "black blood" as black.... In Knight's view, Mexicans were "outside the category" of aliens eligible for citizenship because they were neither white nor black....

One of the three denied petitions ruled on by Knight was that of Timoteo Andrade. Andrade had been living in the United States for twenty years when he filed a petition to become a naturalized citizen. He originally came from Lagos, in the Mexican state of Jalisco, a town connected to the United States through rail lines, thus facilitating immigration north. Andrade had lived in El Paso, Texas, for a time but had settled in Buffalo, New York, where he worked as a waiter. He had married Sara de la Cruz, also a Mexican citizen, in El Paso. Together, they had three children, ... all born in the United States. He did not need a translator in his naturalization interviews, which demonstrated his fluency in English.... [M]any aspects of his life pointed to ways in which he had become integrated into American life....

Timoteo Andrade's self-description in his declaration of intention to naturalize and the statements by his witnesses speak to the myriad ways in which we understand race as framed by nation, language, heritage, phenotype, history, culture, and desire. He described his physical features as the questions on the form required. He had black hair and brown eyes. His complexion was dark, but his "color" was white. Under race he listed "Spanish," and under nationality he listed "Mexican." When a naturalization examiner asked his witness, Thomas Harding, "What race of people did you consider him to be of?" Harding replied, "Spanish." When the examiner asked the other witness, Bernard Malvern, "Do you know what race he is?" Malvern replied, "I always thought he was Mexican." All of these descriptions spoke to various ways of gauging race.

The racial descriptions above allowed a certain degree of fluidity in terms of racial eligibility for citizenship. What Timoteo Andrade said in his naturalization interview, however, did not.... [H]e told the immigration inspector that he had "Indian blood." When asked how much, he replied, "Maybe I have seventy-five percent; maybe fifty." Because one had to be considered white or black to naturalize, such an answer clearly raised questions about his fitness for citizenship. Knight denied the petition based largely on this testimony.

Timoteo Andrade appealed the denial. With the help of an attorney, Andrade submitted further testimony that showed he was "in error" when he stated that he might have "fifty percent Indian blood" when perhaps he was more like "2 percent" Indian blood. In a follow-up interview, Andrade was frank about why he answered in such a manner. "In Mexico, even if we have full Spanish blood, we say that we have Indian blood, because in Mexico we are all Mexicans," he explained. "We are proud that we are Mexicans and we don't like to be told that we have Spanish or French blood," he clarified.

Timoteo Andrade's definitions of race were clearly shaped by nation-building projects in Mexico. After the Mexican Revolution, under President Álvaro Obregón (who served from 1920 to 1924), Minister of Public Education José Vasconcelos implemented a cultural education program aimed at refashioning Mexican identity. This program encouraged Mexicans to adopt a positive national identity centered on Mexico's mestizo past. The mestizo was a product of Indian and Spanish blood, which together produced a stronger race, *la raza cosmica,* according to Vasconcelos.... In seeking a new life, or at least a new job, in the United States, some Mexican immigrants, like Timoteo Andrade, clearly carried with them the concept of *raza cosmica....*

His mother, Maria Bera Andrade, was also brought in to give testimony on his behalf. Many of the questions directed to her asked about the family lineage—where relatives hailed from and what they looked like, "white" or "Indian." ... The questions could have come from any stock eugenics textbook of the time that linked race and physiognomy. Maria Andrade traced the family lineage to Spain and told of fair-haired relatives, but, like her son, she could not decouple race and nation and also spoke of being of the Mexican race....

With new testimony to consider, the case was once again brought before Knight. Knight reiterated what he had stated in his original ruling: "[M]en are not white if the strain of the colored blood in them is half or a quarter, or not improbably, even less, *the governing test always being that of common understanding.*" That said, Knight reversed his original ruling and granted Timoteo Andrade citizenship.

... [T]he political landscape played a key role in shaping Knight's decision. The Mexican embassy had protested Knight's original ruling, directing the consulate in New York City to formally appeal the decision. In response, the

State Department's Latin American affairs specialist, Sumner Welles, assured the Mexican ambassador in Washington that Knight's ruling would not stand and that Mexicans would be allowed to continue immigrating to the United States and naturalizing.

★ ★ ★

The fight to make, or keep, Mexicans white continued on various fronts outside the courtroom. The same year the Andrade decision was issued, the U.S. Census Bureau announced that it would reverse its decision to classify Mexicans as a race of their own. For the first and only time, the United States placed Mexicans in a racial category of their own in 1930. Upon reversing its policy, the Census Bureau announced that "persons of Mexican birth or ancestry who were not definitely Indian or of other nonwhite race were returned as white."

In line with the Census Bureau's racial classifications, the Immigration and Naturalization Service (INS) issued Circular No. 111 in May 1937, instructing officers that Mexicans were to be listed as white and not as a separate race in all INS proceedings....

Despite this restatement of policy, discrepancies in classifying Mexicans continued. Some INS officers and clerks listed Mexicans' race as white in cases of naturalization but not in cases of immigration registration. This led the INS to issue yet another directive. Circular No. 140, issued in July 1937, stated that, "Whenever the term 'race' is used in the case of any person of Mexican descent, handled in the Central Office or in the field, the classification should be 'white.' This applies to all forms, cards, circulars, and other papers." The INS seemed to be trying to cast a net so wide and far-reaching as to preclude any need for further statements regarding the racial status of Mexicans.

These renewed efforts to categorize Mexicans as white prompted criticism from within the INS....

Some immigration and naturalization personnel ... simply ignored the various departmental circulars, preferring to continue the practice of classifying Mexicans as a separate race, but without drawing attention to themselves. This more passive resistance sparked protest from external sources, including another formal complaint to the INS from the Mexican embassy. Embassy officials also followed up when, despite assurances that immigration officers would comply with the regulations, they continued listing Mexicans as a separate race....

LULAC also became involved in the fight to ensure that Mexicans be formally designated as white. During the 1930s LULAC officials wrote to and personally visited immigration officials to protest the continued listing of Mexicans as a separate race even though that practice violated INS policy. Not surprisingly, given their goal of assimilation, LULAC spokespersons shared the racial paradigm favored by many immigration officers: They readily concurred that some Mexicans were of the "Indian or Red Race" but argued that the "majority belong[ed] to the Caucasian or White Race." Thus, the LULAC officials continued, Mexicans "resented being classified as other than White." ...

During the 1930s the INS and other government offices also fielded complaints from Mexicans living in the United States who had endured discriminatory treatment not only in immigration procedures at the border and naturalization processes in the states where they had settled, but in nearly all aspects of their daily lives. The experiences these letter-writers reported reveal that the same ideologies that compelled border personnel to list Mexicans as a separate race when they first entered the country followed these individuals throughout their lives in the United States. Aurora Davalos, a Mexican woman from San Antonio, Texas, wrote to First Lady Eleanor Roosevelt in 1941, describing the difficulties she and her family faced. She had witnessed her brother being denied access to public places, and yet he was still considering enlisting in the Army, now that the United States stood at the brink of war. Davalos questioned what it meant to fight for a country in order to preserve its rights when you yourself were denied those same rights. Davalos explained that she knew that individuals discriminated, and she had come to terms with this fact by dismissing them as "ignorant, narrow minded people." But when she learned that the government classified Mexicans "in a race all their own," she realized that such discrimination was at both the individual and institutional level. Davalos was referring to government forms that asked an applicant to list his or her race as "White," "Yellow," "Black," or "Mexican."

In the end, none of the Mexican naturalization cases made it to the Supreme Court, and in 1940 the issue became moot. The 1940 Nationality Act extended citizenship "only to white persons, persons of African nativity or descent, and descendants of races indigenous to the Western Hemisphere."

★ ★ ★

... At the same time that Italians, Irish, and other European ethnics "became Caucasian," there was a renewed effort to categorize Mexicans in a race of their own. Thus, while the category "white" was malleable enough to include some groups, such as European ethnics, it was more rigid for others, such as Mexicans and Asians, in terms of immigration, and African Americans under Jim Crow segregation. Such shifts serve as a reminder that, although citizenship may have been clearly defined in black and white terms, black and white and "Indian" could be unstable categories.

Puerto Ricans Negotiate the U.S. Racial Binary in New York City

LORRIN THOMAS

ONE AFTERNOON IN MARCH, 1935, sixteen-year-old Lino Rivera got caught stealing a penknife at a Kress five-and-dime store on 125th Street and Seventh Avenue, a few blocks from his home on Manhattan Avenue and

Lorrin Thomas, "Resisting the Racial Binary? Puerto Ricans' Encounters with Race in Depression-Era New York City," *Centro: Journal of the Center for Puerto Rican Studies* v. 21, n. 1 (Spring 2009): pp. 5–35.

122nd Street. When the store's manager confronted Rivera and detained him, the boy resisted and allegedly bit the man on the hand. Someone called the police, and a crowd gathered outside and in the front of the store. After the manager decided to let the boy go instead of arresting him, a police officer escorted Rivera through the basement to the back exit on 124th Street. When Rivera disappeared with the officer into the basement of the store, a rumor spread through the crowd that he was being beaten; and when an ambulance drove up to the back entrance of the store and drove away empty ... some in the crowd said that the boy had in fact been beaten to death.... The crowd consisted of shoppers in the neighborhood's busy commercial district as well as residents of central Harlem, who were almost entirely African American, and it dispersed for a time after police arrested the woman accused of inciting the disturbance. Several hours later, a group of protesters began an impromptu public meeting about the rumored violence against a black child, and as the police were trying to remove a speaker from his soap box stand and clear the sidewalk, someone threw a rock into the front window of the Kress store. Thus began a full-scale riot in which several thousand Harlemites participated, an event that before long would symbolize the acute suffering and resentment of the country's most storied African-American community.

The Harlem riot of 1935 is amply cited in the history of African Americans' civil rights struggles in the twentieth century, but rarely have historians and other chroniclers written about or even mentioned the fact that the "Negro" or "black" boy whose arrest set off the famous riot was, in fact, Puerto Rican. The Jamaican-born writer Claude McKay's 1940 book *Harlem, Negro Metropolis* included one of the few English-language accounts of the riot that described Rivera as Puerto Rican; the Puerto Rican writer and activist Bernardo Vega noted in his memoir, written in the 1940s, that observers "thought Rivera was a black American, although he was of course Puerto Rican" [See Document 4]. But these accounts were exceptional....

... Racial categories had hardened anew in New York City by 1930, the year that the United States Census dropped its "mulatto" category ..., leaving only "white" and "Negro" thereafter.... The critiques and complaints of many Puerto Ricans in this period betrayed a fear that a proscribed racial identity, forged by the limitations of the binary racial regime, would lead to a circumscribed political identity within the nation, a fear that as a group they would fail to attain the promises of American citizenship. Acutely aware of racist power dynamics within their own island society, Puerto Rican migrants across the political spectrum talked about the pitfalls of "second-class citizenship," of being relegated to the inferior status of the Negro—"citizens without rights"— and excluded from many of the benefits and protections that white citizens expected, demanded, and got....

... The neglected fact of Lino Rivera's national identity in the story of the Harlem riots—a fact deemed unimportant by the vast majority of chroniclers, including historians, even up to the present—represents only one of countless silences that mark the "hidden history" of Puerto Ricans in New York City, where their racial ambiguity added another layer of invisibility to a group already marginalized for its colonial identity in the nation....

★ ★ ★

To a large extent, it was American lawmakers' perception of the "mongrel" Puerto Rican people, members of a mixed and "alien race," that had inspired many in the United States Congress to fight against offering them citizenship after the United States took control of the island in 1898.... The pragmatists in Congress (many of them openly racist) ... argued that ... America would have greater control over the island if the constitution "followed the flag," and they won out in 1917, conferring United States citizenship on a mixed race people already controlled by American law.... With citizenship suddenly in hand, thousands more Puerto Ricans also followed the economic boom inspired by World War I, alighting in New York City alongside the largest urban population of African Americans, many of whom had fled the stagnating South for the industrial North. Side by side, these two groups of largely impoverished migrants took up residence in the city that was experiencing, more than any other place, the social and political impact of restrictionist immigration policies that had radically reduced the number of European immigrants entering the United States by 1925....

Puerto Ricans fit uneasily in this unstable social terrain. Rejected by the increasingly white-seeming ethnics as not white; suspicious, themselves, of the Negro racial identity reflexively imposed on them by white society; and seen by African Americans as "Spanish"—or, at least, distinctly foreign—more than black, Puerto Ricans began to perceive the degree to which the intense and distinctive racisms of the United States would shape their experience as Americans.... New York during the depression years witnessed key changes in race relations, not only because of the exploding populations of African Americans and Puerto Ricans. The economic pressures of the depression also intensified social hierarchies.... In the 1920s, the community of thirty thousand or so Puerto Rican migrants was dominated numerically by a skilled working class and culturally by a small Hispanicized professional elite, some of whom coped with their concerns about North American racism by "passing" for Spanish. During the Depression, though, as their foreignness and their inscrutable racial origins hindered them in their competition with other New Yorkers for jobs and a growing array of welfare funds, and as their increasing numbers inspired intensifying prejudice on the part of whites, racial identity became a subject of intensely concerned debate within the Puerto Rican community....

Puerto Ricans had been taking the measure of that divide, with increasing anxiety, since the early thirties. So when the Harlem riot exploded right alongside the largest Puerto Rican barrio in the city, it begged a kind of reckoning.... [D]id it even matter that the riot's spark was a conflict involving a Puerto Rican boy? It did indeed matter. It mattered first as evidence of the contemporary invisibility of Puerto Ricans and other non-native "colored" people in New York.... The other reason that Lino Rivera's role in the riot matters is [that] returning him to his place in the narrative helps fill in the silences that make the story of the Harlem riot not simply more accurate, but more accurately complicated. This richer version of the story of the riot has resonances that help us to interpret both a larger urban past that is more racially complex than many histories admit, and a present whose racial heterogeneity is hardly new....

... Harlem resident Claude McKay ... remembered the Harlem riot as "a spontaneous community protest against social and legal injustice." "Harlem broke loose," he wrote in 1940.... In the end, seventy-five people were arrested, hundreds of windows were broken, and sixty-three people, including several policemen, were injured. One black boy, shot in the back by a police officer, died several days later. City investigators, reporting a year later, described the immediate sentiments that sparked the riot as linked to much deeper grievances:

> The rumor of the death of the boy ... awakened the deep-seated sense of wrongs and denials and even memories of injustices in the South....

...[T]he Kress Store incident had struck a nerve with black Harlemites who saw an opportunity to publicize the suffering of their community....

The *Amsterdam News,* New York's largest African-American daily, also failed to identify Rivera as Puerto Rican, referring to him instead as a "young Negro boy." ...

... African Americans, and white observers too, seem to have viewed the riot's participants through their own binary racial lens. Many may well have known that Rivera was Puerto Rican, but the only social fact that really mattered was that he was colored, and if he was colored, he may as well be called "Negro." To whatever extent Puerto Ricans took part in the riot, they remained a more or less invisible presence in all of its coverage by the citywide dailies....

New York's Spanish language daily *La Prensa*—headed in the 1920s and '30s by a Spaniard, José Comprubí, and frequently criticized by working class Puerto Ricans as a mouthpiece of the elite—more carefully noted the distinction between the rigid North American social category "Negro" and the more descriptive Spanish term "*negro*," which referred to phenotype but did not necessarily represent a rigid social category. *La Prensa* reporters implied that the "disturbances" were attributable only to "*gente de color, americana,*" and reported that most of the protesting and looting activity actually took place in central Harlem, several blocks west of the East Harlem barrio where most Spanish-speakers lived and shopped. Such elision between description and category in Spanish was characteristic of the way Puerto Ricans (and many other Latin Americans) talked about race.... This non-binary racial vision was illustrated in the "complexion" label of identification cards made available to Puerto Rican migrants in New York between 1930 and 1950, via a program established by the Puerto Rican Department of Labor. About 30,000 migrants applied for ID cards, mainly in order to prove their American citizenship to prospective employers. The Puerto Rican ID office clerks who assigned their complexion labels used terms like "dark," "light," "ruddy," "olive," "*regular*," "brown," "light brown," and "dark brown." Although they were loose translations at best, these complexion descriptions resembled the island's varied racial terminology in that they interpreted the phenotypic dimensions of racial identity with fluidity.

If the African American press and city officials in New York agreed that the causes of the Harlem riot were rooted in the problems of Negroes, not Puerto Ricans, many middle-class Puerto Rican and Hispanic residents were happy to support that perspective. *La Prensa* reported on the rioting in central Harlem in distancing tones, calling the incident "race riots" among the "colored elements of that neighborhood." Here the editors were using the term "colored" in a North American sense, meaning Negro....

La Prensa profiled Rivera as a well-mannered, well-behaved boy from a home "characterized by an admirable cleanliness despite its modesty," who demonstrated loyalty both to his mother (he left high school to help support his family) and to his native country (he remained fluent in Spanish). One report declared that Rivera "involuntarily" caused the "racial clash" and "deplore[d] what happened." ... The main point of the interview emerged when the reporter asked Rivera whether he would have tried to pacify the crowd if it had been possible. "Of course!" Rivera replied, reinforcing the idea that Puerto Ricans had no investment in the "racial hatred" that "exploded" in Central Harlem....

★ ★ ★

The threat of being marked by an "unwanted notoriety" was something that Puerto Ricans in New York, the migrant elite in particular, had been worrying over since the beginning of the decade.... Their first call to alarm came late in 1930, when the *New York American* printed an article on "Newcomers in the Slums of East Harlem." The article referred to migrants as "wretched" and "the lowest grade of labor"—"lower than the colored worker." María Más Pozo, a Nationalist activist and frequent contributor to *La Prensa*'s letters column, attacked the *New York American* article with venom. "It is time to think long and hard about the situation of my compatriots in this country," she said. She continued,

> The Puerto Rican must not be seen as worse than the native blacks of this country. *We do not want a North American citizenship that humiliates us, depriving us of our dignity, after having been stripped, in the name of humanity, of our blessed land.* We want to be pure Puerto Ricans, only proud of single race; that which mixed her white blood with the passionate blood of the indian.

Although she elsewhere criticized the "imposition" of an unequal and debased form of US citizenship on Puerto Ricans—a common Nationalist complaint—Más Pozo insisted here that that United States citizenship should function to protect Puerto Ricans against the ascription of a low social status, one that made them "worse than the native blacks" on the mainland.... [F]or all Más Pozo criticized North Americans for their racial hypocrisy, her concern was not with racial injustice; she complained only about the specific injustice of Puerto Ricans' being paid "worse than Chinese and blacks" in America. A number of similar letters followed....

Only a single reader criticized both the *New York American* article and the commentators who failed to challenge the hierarchy in which Puerto Ricans fell beneath Negroes and Chinese immigrants. Introduced by *La Prensa*'s editors as "a Puerto Rican of the black race," Gabriel Rivera also protested "*los insultos de los yanquis*," but questioned other readers' outrage over being categorized with black Americans:

> I don't see the motivation to feel so profoundly injured because they see us as black Americans; since ... I wouldn't want to be seen as a white Texan or Georgian, either; because ... I am filled with contempt and disgust by the white man for his savage and heretical instinct, which the lynchings in the Southern states have shown us so recently.

Rivera's reference to "the lynchings in the Southern states" would not have surprised *La Prensa*'s readers in 1931, since the rise in racial violence in the South during the twenties was covered regularly in *La Prensa*. More surprising, given the dominance of the slippery discourse of *mestizaje* in Puerto Rico—a discourse with a blind spot regarding the African component of the mestizo—was the way Rivera took Más Pozo to task for her definition of Puerto Rican peoplehood: "What would my countrywoman do with black-blooded *Boricuas* ..., whose blood is mixed as much as white blood is mixed with indian?" Más Pozo defended herself aggressively. "Many times in *La Prensa* and other New York periodicals, I have taken up the defense of the colored man with every ounce of my being." Indeed, in previous letters to *La Prensa*, she had fashioned herself as a champion of the underdog and a proponent of racial enlightenment.

... The several letter writers who followed Más Pozo's lead in decrying Puerto Ricans' social debasement argued for maximizing distance between the Puerto Rican and the American Negro.

Several years after the initial reaction to the *New York American* article, and a year before the explosion of rioting in Harlem in 1935, another sensationalist piece on Puerto Rico appeared in the American popular media. The controversy this time centered on the photographs of dark-skinned peasants for an article on Puerto Rico in the nationally circulating *Literary Digest,* just the kind of snapshot of her country that María Más Pozo was afraid of.... Dr. Augusto Arce Álvarez wrote to *La Prensa* from what was then the middle-class enclave of Washington Heights to lament that "the publication of such photographs in this country... has led the majority of Americans to believe that our island is populated entirely by Negroes." Álvarez called on Puerto Ricans to lean on their status as citizens— though exactly how, he did not say—to counter the putative racial insult: "We must defend our rights before the people, without fear; we must seek the protection of the citizenship given us by the Congress of the United States in 1917."

This time the debate about the dilemmas of Puerto Ricans' racial identity in the United States played out differently. In 1931, all but one of the participants in the debate over the *New York American* article rejected comparisons of the Puerto Rican to black Americans, and refused to acknowledge African roots in Puerto Rican history. Now, however, Dr. Álvarez's passionate expression of this latest "injury" against Puerto Rico "provoked immediate attention within the colonia," according to *La Prensa*'s editors, attention that pointedly criticized Álvarez for his racist views. "I was not born black," wrote one critic, who signed his name M. Callejo, "but if I were I would be proud to be part of a race ...

whose struggle … is that of the oppressed masses.…" … Callejo went on to deconstruct Álvarez's invocation of citizenship as a source of "protection" for Puerto Ricans. "I ask you: 'Is this the way to defend the rights of the people, insulting the majority of your people and bragging about the citizenship which the Congress of the Morgans and the Rockefellers used to send to their death their unlucky soldiers?'" Callejo was referring here to a an interpretation of the 1917 Jones Act, popular among Nationalists and anti-imperialists, which asserted that the Congress granted citizenship to Puerto Ricans when it did—after 17 years of debate—in order to enable the armed forces to draft Puerto Ricans to fight for the United States in World War I. More of a challenge to the status quo was Callejo's claim that "the majority" of Puerto Ricans were black, or at least would identify with Negroes in the United States. Other readers also objected to the racism in Álvarez's letter, but couched their criticism in more genteel terms.… "We are what we are," said another reader. "They can spoil our language, impose their education on us, but they cannot take away our color." In all of these 1934 letters, "our color"—to whatever extent North Americans viewed it as "black"—figured as a distinct source of pride for Puerto Ricans.

… The more progressive letter writers in 1934 … tended to give less credence to the rigid divisions required by racial ideology in the United States: "We are what we are … they cannot take away our color." This assertion could have been interpreted readily in terms of the distinctly *non*-African "gran familia puertorriqueña," what María Mas Pozo referred to as "pure Puerto Ricans, only proud of a single race." But in the context of the series of letters criticizing Álvarez for his anti-black racism, it actually represented a challenge to that discourse—as well as a challenge to the North American racial binary.

In a similar vein of racial justice, one *La Prensa* reader wrote to the editor after the 1935 riots with a passionate critique of the conditions created in Harlem by the "*explotadores capitalistas.*" Libertad Narváez … expressed deep sympathy with the plight and the grievances of the rioters:

> Thousands of black workers, most of them unemployed … took to the streets of Harlem with the sounds of protest against the miserly aid distributed by the "Relief" Administration, and the discriminatory … treatment by officials of this agency of which they are victims; against the high rents and unhealthy conditions of Harlem apartments; against the unconscionable … conduct of the rich business owners who refuse to give employment to those of [the colored] race, despite the fact that they represent almost the entirety of the shoppers.…

Like virtually all of the other commentary on the riot, however, Narváez's letter was silent on both the place and plight of Puerto Rican migrants in Harlem. Not only did it fail to mention the large numbers of Puerto Ricans who would be identified—and might identify themselves—as "Negro workers." It also ignored the fact that Puerto Ricans had been expressing for years the same grievances as African Americans concerning housing, relief, and discrimination. This writer's silence on these parallels reminds us of the pains taken not just by the elite but also by working class, leftist Puerto Ricans to distinguish their countrymen from the black Americans whose plight they so often decried.... The price of accepting the ascription imposed by the racial binary in America—blackness as Negro, not just *negro*—was potentially too steep even for Puerto Rican radicals.

* * *

Mayor Fiorello LaGuardia, who had a solid reputation as a racial progressive, formed a committee to investigate not only the immediate causes of the riot, but the conditions in Harlem that constituted the underlying motivations for protest. Over the course of a year, the Mayor's Committee on Conditions in Harlem (whose members included ten men and one woman, six of them black, five white) investigated Harlemites' experiences with relief, housing, education and recreation, health and hospitals, and crime and the police. After 21 public and four closed hearings, including testimony of 160 witnesses, and months of research, the Committee submitted its report to the Mayor's office in March 1936. It concluded that the Harlem riot was a protest against the "intolerable conditions" wrought by five years of economic depression in an already poor community, "which made [Harlem residents] feel more keenly than ever the injustices of discrimination in employment, the aggressions of the police, and the racial segregation...." ... [T]he Committee turned out to consist only of African Americans and white Americans, despite the fact that Puerto Ricans comprised the plurality of residents on about one quarter of Harlem's residential blocks and was the second-largest national or "ethnic" group in the neighborhood....

In the months following the Harlem riots, Puerto Ricans became the primary victims of a new "anti-Hispanic campaign" in Washington Heights, where middle class Puerto Ricans had begun to settle earlier in the thirties. The Jewish and Irish landlords in the neighborhood had begun raising rents sharply in an alleged effort to "drive out" their Puerto Rican tenants. Spanish-speaking observers saw the landlords' coordinated action as a reaction to two threats: first, that more and more of their Hispanic tenants were recent arrivals of the "lower classes," and second, that these "brown-skinned or darker" new tenants would bring with them the kinds of problems that might turn Washington Heights into "a second Harlem." These observers saw a specifically racial prejudice against dark-skinned Puerto Ricans. "The situation in Washington Heights is not simply a situation of nationality, it is purely and unjustly a question of race," asserted one letter to *La Prensa*. Even the lighter-skinned among them should not feel immune to this kind of discrimination, he warned, since no clear line existed, here, between light and dark complexions; the only line was between *white* and dark. "If it could happen to them, it could happen to you," he warned. That is, any Puerto Rican, no matter his or her complexion, could be discriminated against as a person occupying the non-white side of the binary—the black side....

... The colonia celebrated a ... victory when migrant Oscar García Rivera was elected on a Republican ticket to the New York state assembly in 1937. It was the first time a Puerto Rican held an elective office on the mainland, and the Puerto Rican community saw this achievement as an open door to greater recognition by the major parties [See Document 5]. However, it was soon clear that García Rivera's office could not reverse the political invisibility that the growing Puerto Rican population had been fighting throughout the decade. Nor could it protect them from an identity as colonial citizens in the metropole, a real liability in mainstream politics that proved to be at least as powerful as their ambiguous racial identity. In 1937, when Nationalist agitation reached a new peak of violent conflict in Puerto Rico, Roosevelt appointees on the island—who had sought to rescue Puerto Rico with island-based New Deal programs— suddenly jumped ship, leaving the island's fiscal fate to a hostile American Congress. Puerto Rican nationalists in New York decried the false promises of liberal politicians, formulating an angry challenge to the integrity of American liberalism at the very moment of its ascendance....

... Migrants took a renewed interest in connecting the problems of colonialism with the problems of Puerto Ricans' racial identity in the United States. Pilar Pacheco, a Nationalist activist, wrote a biting letter to *La Prensa* reminding her compatriots that

> Each Puerto Rican is a free and sovereign citizen of the United States ... free and sovereign to chase after his bread, ... which he is denied.... The Puerto Rican in the United States has the privilege of scrubbing plates in restaurants; of rising at five in the morning on harsh winter days to line up at the factory, at the cafeteria, at the docks with the hope of being chosen among the hundreds of foreigners who comprise the working masses of this people.... We are absolutely free to hear how they call us "niggers," to see how they ignore our rights as American citizens....

Puerto Ricans may have marked their difference from black Americans, but now it seemed clear that they would be unable to escape the injustices that confirmed their minority status and excluded them from the category of "free and sovereign citizens of the United States." ...

The more salient conflict for Puerto Ricans had to do with their persistent political invisibility not only as dark-skinned foreigners, but also as colonial citizens. In the realm of island politics, independentista migrants in the 1940s watched the disappearance of what they had seen as their wartime opportunity to hold politicians to account on the question of Puerto Rico's status.... At the local level, Puerto Ricans' energetic activism had brought them no closer to securing the concrete privileges they hoped their American citizenship would give them, including access to decent housing, fair employment, and recognition as legitimate actors in local and national politics. Still fighting off a "Negro" identity, but failing to achieve an identity approaching "white," Puerto Ricans faced an invisibility that circumscribed their political power throughout the thirties, and then was compounded by the explosion of colonial tensions after 1937....

[With] the Harlem riot of 1935[,] ... the imposition of rigid and simplified racial categories robs the narrative not only of a certain amount of its depth, but also of some of its major historical and political meanings.... [M]any Puerto Ricans—even working class radicals and self-proclaimed racial egalitarians— realized the immobility of binary racial discourse and focused their efforts in the

1930s on affirming their place on the powerful side of the binary. This was a strategic denial of a black identity by many migrants, an effort to play by the rules of a powerful racist ideology to fend off disadvantage.... Ultimately, ... New York Puerto Ricans failed in their efforts to sidestep the pitfalls of their ascribed racial identity.... Puerto Ricans ... in the thirties found that they were rarely regarded as white, and would not enjoy the privileges of whiteness unless they managed to "pass." These little-known details provide texture and depth to a very obvious point about the power of a rigid racist ideology to render disadvantage to those on the wrong side. They also illustrate a point only slightly less obvious, about the power of the racial binary to silence those historical actors who don't fit into its categories.... Their reconstructed stories teach us not simply about "agency" or "resistance," but about the creative work of seeking recognition as social actors beyond the racial binary in American society.

 # FURTHER READING

Katherine Benton-Cohen, *Borderline Americans: Racial Division and Labor War in the Arizona Borderlands.* (2009).

Julia K. Blackwelder, *Women of the Depression: Caste and Culture in San Antonio, 1929–1939* (1984).

Lawrence R. Chenault. *The Puerto Rican Migrant in New York City* (1938).

Linda C. Delgado, "Jesús Colón and the Making of a New York City Community, 1917 to 1974," in Carmen Teresa Whalen and Víctor Vázquez-Hernández, eds., *The Puerto Rican Diaspora: Historical Perspectives* (2005).

Juan Flores, ed., *Puerto Rican Arrival in New York: Narratives of the Migration, 1920–1950* (2005; originally published 1997).

Camille Guerin-Gonzales, *Mexican Workers and American Dreams: Immigration, Repatriation, and California Farm Labor, 1900–1939* (1994).

Abraham Hoffman, *Unwanted Mexicans in the Great Depression: Repatriation Pressures, 1929–1939* (1974).

Félix V. Matos Rodríguez, and Pedro Juan Hernández. *Pioneros: Puerto Ricans in New York City 1896–1948* (2001).

Vicki Ruiz, "'Star Struck': Acculturation, Adolescence, and the Mexican American Woman, 1920–1940," in Elliott West and Paula Petrick, eds., *Small Worlds: Children and Adolescents in America, 1850–1950* (1992).

George J. Sánchez, *Becoming Mexican American: Ethnicity, Culture and Identity in Chicano Los Angeles, 1900–1945* (1993).

Lisa Sánchez González. *The Stories I Read to the Children: The Life and Writing of Pura Belpré, the Legendary Storyteller, Children's Author and NY Public Librarian* (2013)

Piri Thomas, *Down These Mean Streets* (1997; originally published 1967).

Zaragosa Vargas, *Proletarians of the North: A History of Mexican Industrial Workers in Detroit and the Midwest, 1917–1933* (1993).

Bernardo Vega, *Memoirs of Bernardo Vega: A Contribution to the History of the Puerto Rican Community in New York*, ed. César Andreu Iglesias, trans. Juan Flores (1984).

CHAPTER 8

Race, Gender, and Continuing
Migration in the World War II Era

With long-established U.S. communities, Mexican and Puerto Rican migration increased dramatically during World War II and after. As men and women joined the armed forces and the home front shifted to a wartime economy, labor shortages appeared in some of the least desirable, lowest paid jobs. The U.S. government turned to its most "domestic" sources of labor—African Americans from the southern states, Puerto Ricans, and Mexican Americans, as well as Mexicans. Begun as wartime emergency measures, contract labor programs that brought Mexicans and Puerto Ricans to work in the continental United States continued into the postwar era. Begun in 1942 during the war, the Emergency Farm Labor, or Bracero Program, recruited Mexicans to work in agriculture and on the railroads. The agricultural program continued until 1964 and constituted part of the U.S. recruitment and subsequent deportation of Mexican workers. In 1954, the U.S. government launched the offensively titled "Operation Wetback," which deported an estimated one million ethnic Mexicans (Mexican immigrants and Mexican Americans). Puerto Ricans were also recruited during the war, but on a much smaller scale. Policymakers sought temporary workers and feared that Puerto Ricans, because of their U.S. citizenship, might be less pliable workers and might choose to remain in the continental United States when their contracts expired. In the aftermath of World War II, however, Puerto Rican women were recruited as domestics and Puerto Rican men as seasonal farm workers. This increased labor recruitment sparked informal networks and fostered more dispersed settlement, with the emergence of new Puerto Rican communities in the Midwest and the Mid-Atlantic states.

Although recruited again as low-wage laborers, ethnic Mexicans and Puerto Ricans were still not fully welcomed. The United States fought against Nazism and fascism overseas, but neglected to ensure that Latinos and Latinas enjoyed democratic rights domestically. Even as Puerto Ricans and Mexican Americans joined the armed services, their citizenship and patriotism were questioned. Racial tensions ran high during the war, as evidenced by the U.S. government's internment of Japanese residents and Japanese American citizens. In 1943, white U.S. servicemen in Los Angeles physically attacked Mexican American youth in what came to be known as the "zoot suit riots." This chapter examines the renewed recruitment and migration of ethnic Mexicans and Puerto Ricans, as well as the continued challenges they confronted as a result of biased perspectives and exploitative working conditions.

DOCUMENTS

In Document 1, the *California Eagle,* an African American newspaper, describes "the zoot suit riots" in 1943, as white soldiers and sailors attacked African Americans and Mexican Americans, revealing solidarities between these two groups, and condemning the roles of the Los Angeles press, the city council, and the police in fanning the servicemen's violent actions. In Document 2, the *Los Angeles Times* reports on the Citizen's Committee's insistence that all participants in the violent episodes be held accountable—servicemen, civilian youth, and police officers—challenging interpretations that blamed Mexican American youth. A 1943 *New York Times* article, in Document 3, calls attention to the labor shortages generated by the war, especially in seasonal agriculture. Contract labor programs designed to meet those labor shortages continued for both Puerto Ricans and Mexicans long after World War II ended. As Puerto Rican women arrived as domestic workers in Chicago in 1946, Elena Padilla, a Puerto Rican graduate student in anthropology at the University of Chicago, writes to activist Jesus Colón in New York City, seeking his assistance, in Document 4. Puerto Rico's policymakers' motives for promoting the contract labor program for women as domestics is revealed in Document 5, a memo from Donald J. O'Connor, chief economist in the Office of Puerto Rico, to Manuel Pérez, Puerto Rico's commission of labor. At the same time that Puerto Ricans were recruited as a source of low-wage labor, a 1947 *Life* magazine article revealed concerns about their in-migration and about Puerto Ricans' citizenship, which made them eligible to vote and for social services. Although most men were recruited as seasonal agricultural workers, a few were recruited for manufacturing jobs. In Document 7, in an excerpt from an oral history interview, José "Cheo" Córtez describes his journey to Lorain, Ohio, in 1948. As the Bracero Program continued, issues remained with the program's implementation. In Document 8, scholar and activist Ernesto Galarza reports on the limited enforcement of contract provisions and the impact on Mexican workers in 1956.

1. *California Eagle* Blames Servicemen for Attacking Mexican American and African American Zoot Suiters, 1943

With sporadic disturbances still tearing loose throughout Southeast Los Angeles, a heroic six-days of zoot suit inflammation by daily papers found Los Angeles facing this morning one of the biggest headaches in its history.

"Rioting Skirts Negro Community," *California Eagle*, June 10, 1943.

Central avenue at 12th street has been the center of several outbreaks between Mexican groups, police officers, and bands of roving service men, both soldiers and sailors.

Negroes have been attacked throughout the downtown area by service men. No mass rioting by Negroes, however, has been reported.

Metropolitan newspapers continued disruptive egging-on of the so-called "zoot suit" crisis today in the face of statements from civic leaders, the Mexican consul, and the State Department condemning their activities.

The City Council solemnly blew its top yesterday afternoon as it unanimously passed an ordinance barring the wearing of long coats and peg-drape pants!

While the City Fathers indulged in this claptrap, reports rolled into California EAGLE offices of beatings and riot provocations against Negroes as well as Mexicans throughout the city.

At two o'clock Sunday night, service men pounced upon John Zion, 1143 East 24th street, grandson of a Baptist minister, beat him, kicked him, and cursed him....

Two officers witnessed Zion's beating, he said.

A 16-year old Negro boy, Joseph Nelson was dragged from a "U" car at Fifth and Main streets. He was beaten and his pants cut. He attends McKinley Junior High school.

At the Orpheum theater and other downtown spots, service men charged into the auditorium, removing citizens whose clothing they disapproved.

Many were beaten and trampled.

All Los Angeles is out of bounds for Army and Navy men today. This belated action was a smashing blow to riot-inciters at the Hearst Examiner and Herald, Harry Chandler's Times, and the butterfly liberal, Manchester Boddy's Daily News.

Each of these papers has encouraged mob spirit of the soldiers, viciously attacking the Mexican people and tending minute by minute to bring the Negro community into their range of attack.

That the police force has attempted to use Negro cops to brutalize Mexican youth was authoritatively reported today. This is a try at splitting the unity of Mexican and Negro minorities.

It was reported that police have asked local Negro Elks to bar mixed dancing between Negroes and Mexicans at the Elks Hall.

One police officer in Vernon has been seriously injured in a reprisal raid by a Mexican gang in which he was run-over by a car assertedly driven by Mexican youth.

Since last Thursday, rioting has spread over the Los Angeles area. It was cut down sharply Wednesday when the Army and Navy ruled Los Angeles out at bounds to service men.

In Watts, Mexicans are said to have stoned passing P. E. red-cars. Several sailors have been cut.

During Tuesday night's rioting, severest of all, serviceman indiscriminately ran down Mexican and Negro youth who were garbed in clothes the metropolitan press has taught them to despise....

Indications are also noted that the riot has spread to Watts, Long Beach and San Diego....

Striking are the facts: (1)—There has been no serious outbreak by the Negro people; (2)—All sections of the Negro community urgently demand full police protection of the Mexican minority; (3)—The pretense that zoot suits denote criminality is roundly condemned.

2. *Los Angeles Times* Reports on Governor Warren's Citizens' Committee Investigating the Zoot Suit Riots, 1943

Punishment of all persons responsible for "crimes of violence" in last week's zoot suit riots, whether servicemen or civilians, was recommended yesterday by a special citizens' committee of investigators as the juvenile warfare died out....

... [T]he committee summed up as follows:

"Immediate curative action, which was called for by the Governor in creating this committee demands that crimes of violence be brought to justice, and the guilty must be punished regardless of what clothes they wear—whether they be zoot suits, police, Army or Navy uniforms."

"The streets of Los Angeles must be made safe for servicemen as well as civilians, regardless of national origins. The community as well as its visitors must learn that no group has the right to take the law into its own hands."

The report then went on to say that all facts of the riot situation should be accurately interpreted, and that "it is a mistake in fact and an aggravating practice to link the phrase 'zoot suit' with the report of a crime."

Because a number of suspects arrested in the recent disorders are persons of Mexican descent, the report took occasion to remark that "the increase of delinquency in the case of youths of Mexican families has been less than in the case of other national or racial groups and less than the average increase for the community."

The committee also announced the investigation disclosed there are approximately 35 neighborhood gangs in Los Angeles, many of whose members have criminal records.

But some of these gangs, it was stated, do not wear zoot suits, while some do.

"Some are Mexican, some Negro, and some are so-called Anglo-American—that is, they include all types of classifications of youth," the report declared....

... Governor Warren's committee made the following main recommendations:

1—Arrests for criminal or gang activity should be made without undue emphasis on members of minority groups....

3—Law enforcement agencies should provide special training for officers dealing with minority groups....

5—A juvenile forestry camp should be established by the county probation department to care for delinquent youth under the age of 16.

"Punishment of All Urged to Break Up Zoot Suit War," *Los Angeles Times*, June 13, 1943. Copyright © 1982. Los Angeles Times. Reprinted with Permission.

6—Lawyers' associations should continue to enlist panels of attorneys to protect the rights of youth arrested for participation in gang activity.

7—Military and shore police should be increased.

8—Additional recreational and group work facilities should be provided in all neighborhoods in a quantity sufficient to meet the needs of the community.

9—Churches of Los Angeles County should increase their program for youth.

10—Discrimination against any race in the provision or use of public facilities should be abolished....

While the committee was in session, the Federal government stepped into the local zoot suit picture by obtaining an injunction against a downtown store restraining the sale of zooters' "uniform"—the finger-length and down-to-the-knees coats and ankle-tight pants that cost about $75 each....

In effect, the suit, first of its kind in the nation, served notice that zoot suits are "out" for the duration—if the government's position is upheld by the courts after a trial....

3. *New York Times* Reports on Expected Postwar Labor Shortage in Agriculture, 1943

Although some observers expect unemployment in California to reach the million mark by the year end, concern already is being expressed in some quarters over the prospect of seasonal farm labor shortages during 1946....

The difference between April farm employment and that at the peak in late September and early October runs about 150,000. By fall the farm laborers in California normally exceed 300,000, of whom about two-thirds are of the migratory type, moving from area to area as crops mature.

The War Department has announced that after June 15 no more prisoners of war will be available for farm work, and there is opposition, especially among local councils of the Congress of Industrial Organizations, to the importation of Mexican nationals this year.

The CIO takes the stand that, with an estimated 500,000 Californians unemployed now, there should be sufficient domestic labor to handle all farm crops if wages are satisfactory....

The Federal Government's attitude is to bring in Mexican and West Indian workers provided their labor is needed and does not displace domestic workers, and provided the State services certify the need.

Last year 119,000 were imported and the tentative goal set for 1946 is 70,000. The California quota has not been established, but Mr. Crocheron, whose State Farm Labor Office distributes the workers where they are needed, estimates that the number will not exceed 22,000, or fewer than half those employed last year.

About 17,000 Mexican nationals who signed contracts in 1945 are still in California, most of them picking oranges in the south. Their contracts expire on May 1 and some may be re-signed.

A survey by the State Chamber of Commerce arrives at the conclusion that seasonal farm labor shortages "are anticipated" and Ray B. Wiser, president of the State Farm Bureau Federation, concurs in this.

"It looks as if, as a general rule, we should have a better labor situation but there will be a shortage of skilled workers, such as pruners and tractor drivers, and of stoop labor, required in such crops as asparagus, sugar beets and cotton," he said.

Relatively few of the Japanese evacuees who have returned to the West Coast are going into the farm labor market, although many are settling in rural areas. Some of the Filipinos who quit farms to work in war plants are returning to the soil, but their numbers are fewer than before.

Many war veterans are interested in acquiring land but not in joining migratory farm labor....

4. Elena Padilla Criticizes Conditions for Puerto Rican Domestic Workers in Chicago, 1946

You would say that I am irresponsible for having offered a visit in June and then not show[ing] up and not even send[ing] you a card informing you why I did not feel obliged to change my plans. As you already know, I suffer from rheumatic fever and the weather in Chicago forces me to stay in be[d] for long periods of time ... (as what happened during June, July, and August).... When I got up, I had to start working to pay debts and subsist.

A fact that I have found scandalous has obliged me to break my silence: the importance of the Puerto Rican workers to Chicago. A few days ago, I read in the job section column of the Chicago Daily Tribune that a so-called Fred Fletcher (employment agent) offered the services of <u>WHITE</u> Puerto Ricans for domestic work for $70 per month (men) and $60 for women. In addition, they will be given housing and food. The Puerto Rican workers sign a one year contract for those services. Muna and I were investigating the matter and we found that in Chicago there is no minimum salary for domestic workers nor is there a union for them. The import of these workers ha[s] the sanction of the Department of Labor in Puerto Rico, according to a note I read that appeared in the New York press from what Ricardo Alegria informed me, a federal employee told him that the federal department of labor had supported the measure. According to what has been informed to me, Angel Perez is very proud of the plan that provides a way of life to Puerto Rican workers at the expense of decreasing the salaries of other domestic workers, while contributing to the racial discrimination of Puerto Rican workers.

Letter from Elena Padilla to Jesús Colón, 3 October 1946 (Box 3, Folder 5, Jesús Colón Papers, Center for Puerto Rican Studies, New York City).

I want to make you aware of this because it seems that there are plans to continue this new slavery. I want to ask you to help me do something. I want to write an article for [the] Puerto Rico press about this matter because it seems like one of the greatest betrayals that the ex-socialist government of Puerto Rico is sponsoring. I think that it is not worth it to try to convince the officials responsible of this matter because everything seems to indicate they knew very well the situation of the domestic workers prior to taking that action.

My most affectionate greetings to your family. And one of these days I will surprise you with a visit ... meaning, after I have done something to abolish the import of Puerto Ricans so that they might die and contribute to the shortage and hunger of other workers.

5. Policymaker Promotes Puerto Rican Women's Migration as Population Control, 1947

If there is a special session, some consideration should again be given to introduction of a bill to assist in the procurement of mainland jobs.... The Insular need of jobs is great. The mainland is incredibly prosperous. Join these two propositions, and it becomes wisdom to take timely advantage of opportunities....

It is, I think, particularly important to provide for the assistance of young unmarried women. They have, as the public might easily understand, fewer opportunities to save enough for a trip to the mainland, and to work their way than do boys. Furthermore, opportunities for their services in the domestic trades and in the lighter factory jobs are more clearly evident than are opportunities for young men (although plenty exist for them). It is also obvious that girls, with their typically strong family loyalties, will send for their kin or send money to their kin at home. What need not be made clear, except in executive sessions of the legislative committees, is the demographic effect of female emigration.

Narrowing the eligibility group to employable women, childless and under 25 years of age, upon proof of lack of adequate funds, would greatly lessen the risk of financing travel of those who would and could come "on their own"....

Can the Insular Government afford to expend a large sum for mainland jobs? More appropriately: Can it afford not to? For one hundred dollars in the form of a loan, or as Gov. Piñero prefers, a scholarship, one young woman and five unborn children can be transported to the States. If each of these children were born on the Island and stayed for four years of schooling, the Insular cost of their education would be over one thousand dollars. For this brood "average" relief costs for twenty years would be at least two hundred and fifty dollars. Probably twice this sum for public health would be required for the one woman and her offspring. Moreover, from the mainland she will, if happily employed, send the amount of her loan, and more, back to her kin for family

---

Donald J. O'Connor, chief economist of the Office of Puerto Rico, to Teodoro Moscoso, Puerto Rico Industrial Development Corporation, 6 June 1947 (National Archives, Record Group 126).

emergencies and for family travel. Polish girls, German girls and Irish girls did. Puerto Rican girls will.

Re-settlement is frightfully expensive.... Job procurement is, in good times, cheap. It can be started quickly.

Hordes of Europeans see opportunities here, but immigration laws bar their coming. For Puerto Rico there are no bars except a language difficulty (not *per se* a barrier), inertia and lack of passage money.

A net of 15,000 young girls sent annually to the States for the next fifteen years would reduce by half what the population will otherwise be. It would provide jobs for girls ready for jobs. It would provide advance-guards which would make easy the entrance of late-comers. It would provide better schooling for those who remained on the Island. It would lessen the necessary outlay for jobs on the Island. It would assure Congressional response to Puerto Rican opinion, just as Polish, Irish and Jewish immigrants and second generation voters have assured Congressional sensitiveness to the needs of these people's relatives abroad. It would, as no other policy would, by bringing up the standard of life on the Island, provide Puerto Rico with a reasonably free choice respecting political status, a choice which its economic condition makes too narrow for satisfaction today.

Much of this reasoning is prompted by my knowledge from the very old Irish and Scotch-Irish who in my boyhood told me much about what emigration had meant to them, to their children and to their own parents. If Ireland could depopulate itself by emigration, Puerto Rico can. If the South can ease its pressures of underemployment by internal migration, so can Puerto Rico....

6. *Life* Magazine Reveals Concerns with Puerto Ricans' Migration and Their U.S. Citizenship, 1947

As he stands at the airport in his Sunday suit and takes his first bewildered look at America, the Puerto Rican ... is the envy of his countrymen. He has just arrived in the promised land, where he will join thousands of others who have taken the northbound journey ahead of him. He is part of a mass migration which since the end of the war has added a possible 50,000 Puerto Ricans to the population of New York's swarming East Side. This month the migration is at a flood tide of almost 1,000 a week.

Puerto Ricans are leaving their Caribbean island for a single compelling reason. If they stay there, they face unemployment, disease and semi-starvation. Generations of ruthless exploitation of the land for the sake of one crop, sugar, have reduced Puerto Rican economy to beggary. This has been foreseen for a long time. Four years ago a Senate investigating committee returned from the island with the verdict that its problems were almost "unsolvable." But almost nothing has been done to aid Puerto Ricans, who are as much American citizens as the residents of Hawaii or Alaska.

Many of the Puerto Ricans now pouring into New York City are illiterate. Many speak no English. All of them are desperately poor. Almost without exception these newcomers squeeze into East Harlem, complicating an already critical housing and relief situation. Puerto Rican and New York authorities are belatedly—and so far ineffectually—looking for a solution. One man who is not worrying is East Harlem's pro-Communist Representative Vito Marcantonio. To the Puerto Ricans he is a fountainhead of advice and help. Day and night they crowd into Marcantonio's "clubhouse" on 116th Street for assistance in their financial, family or civil troubles. They ask his aid in dealing with the welfare workers who issue relief checks. They seek his help in arranging passage for relatives, left behind in Puerto Rico, who would also like to come to New York. After a year of receiving this patronage in the 18th District, however, they may, if they wish, return Vito Marcantonio's favors. They can vote.

Most Puerto Ricans come to the U.S. in the stifling, cramped cabins of ex-Army C-47s....

When they reach New York, proudly wearing their best clothes, most Puerto Ricans are penniless and already homesick. But in Spanish Harlem, where 200,000 of their people are now established, they can find stores where their own language is spoken and an atmosphere that reeks of home. Because they have no money, many Puerto Ricans soon turn to welfare offices, where as American citizens they are entitled to such support as the city's home-relief funds can afford....

7. José "Cheo" Córtez Recalls Leaving the Sugar Cane Fields of Puerto Rico for the Steel Mills of Lorain, Ohio, 1948

I lived in Barceloneta, Puerto Rico, one of the smallest towns in Puerto Rico. I used to work in the sugar cane fields for three months each year, and for nine months: nothing. I did nothing. I earned 75 cents a day. I remember that after the *zafra* there was no work for nine months. If when we were working things were bad, they were worse during those times. We would only eat one meal a day. During the war, things were bad. We would not drink coffee with sugar because, although there was sugar, we did not have the money to buy it. Everything was rationed; even the rice was rationed. There were times when one had a little money and would go to the store and could not buy anything. We would only eat corn meal and fish. We had no equipment. We had no shoes. We had no clothes. We had nothing.... My *compadre* told me that Friedman was bringing people to Ohio. I applied and got the money and went to the office at Fernandez Juncos Avenue. I bought a ticket to migrate. We owed $25 upon arrival in Lorain. We had to agree to pay Friedman from our first paycheck. I arrived in November 1948, Thanksgiving Day....

We left from Isla Grande Airport in San Juan. The airplane seemed in good condition with regard to the engine and equipment but inside it was in critical

José "Cheo" Córtez, Interview by Eugene Rivera, June 1984.

condition. It was very dirty. We were up to our knees in garbage. It was used to transport Jersey cows. There was a fence in the middle, they placed cows on one side and bulls on the other....

When we arrived in Miami, they told us that we would be leaving shortly. The airplane had engine problems. At eight o'clock, they took us to a waiting room where we spent three days. We asked for help because we had no money and they gave ninety-some dollars for the group.... The only thing we ate during those three days was coffee and donuts because that is all we knew in English. They kept testing the airplane on the runway. Finally, they put us on another one....

When I arrived [at the National Tube Company] there were 435 Puerto Ricans. I lived in barrack D, D-15. The only barracks with Americans was barrack A, the others were full of Puerto Ricans. We had no place to go so we would buy food from La Italiana [Grocery Store] and cook it in the barracks.... Since Friedman only brought hard workers here, the majority of the time we worked.

8. Scholar Ernesto Galarza Reports on the Bracero Program, 1956

Asked about working conditions, another bracero said: "Three days ago our crew stopped work right in the field. There were fifty men in the group. It was explained by one of the men who could express himself that it was not our desire to make a strike but we wanted to have eight hours work or to have our board without charge if we worked only one or two hours. The foreman said that assuredly there would be plenty of work and we went back to the cutting. The next day the bracero who had spoken for us was not in the camp. The foreman said he had been taken to the Association but he did not know the motive. In the field the boss said there are plenty more where we came from if we are disgusted. I have read my contract, but it is not worth the pain to insist on the clauses. Here the contract has no value." ...

"I am sleeping in a building that used to be a market," said one National. "We have to cover the holes in the windows and walls with paper. The camp gave me only one blanket. Yesterday I asked the camp boss for another blanket because of the cold. He said, 'No, you are supposed to have only one.' He said, 'There are two hundred men in this camp and everybody would want an extra blanket.' I said, 'There are no stoves in our camp and I have to sleep in my work clothes.' Then he said, 'Lots of people in this town don't have stoves in their houses.'" ...

Mexican Nationals are guaranteed the payment of wages "not less than the prevailing wage rate paid to domestic workers for similar work at the time the work is performed and in the manner paid within the area of employment." This

Ernesto Galarza, *Strangers in Our Fields* (Washington, DC: Joint United States–Mexico Trade Union Committee, 1956. pp. 18, 22, 30, 62–63, 66.).

is both a statement of a legal right and presumably a description of the economic facts underlying it. The enjoyment of that right is, however, as uncertain as the economic assumption on which it is based.

As one bracero put the problem: "We would like for the Government to tell us truly what the local workers get for picking tomatoes. Some of the locals tell us they get 15 cents a box and 90 cents an hour. We get 12 cents a box and 70 cents an hour. But it is hard to find out the truth of this if the government doesn't tell you." ...

Field compliance agents usually operate out of the offices of the state employment agency. In 1955 there were two of these agents in Arizona, 13 in California. They were responsible for compliance with the contracts of nearly 100,000 Nationals. In addition they had to supervise the extension, renewal or termination of all contracts. Compliance officers do not usually roam the camps looking for violations of the Agreement or the contracts. They are instructed to arrange beforehand with the employer for any inspection visits or grievance investigations. Their role is not that of an advocate or representative of the worker.

So far as the bracero is concerned, the keystone of the compliance structure is the Mexican Consul....

"It is a delicate problem to call the Mexican Consul," another said. "Somebody has to take the responsibility. We could write him a letter but the problem is that he might show the letter to the company. We do not know his address. Some say he is in Sacramento and some say he is in Los Angeles." ...

"I can read the contract and I know that several of the clauses are not observed," one of these men said to me. "We talk about the clauses among ourselves in the camp. But nobody would make a complaint for fear of being sent back to Mexico. When you are sent back, you are sent back in a hurry. They give you the notice in the morning, or maybe at noon, or when you get back from work. You tie up your bundle and they put you in the truck to go back to the Association."...

 # ESSAYS

The World War II era was marked by people on the move and by racial tensions. In the first essay, Luis Alvarez, professor of history at the University of California, San Diego, hones in on a dramatic example of the racial tensions of the era, the Los Angeles "zoot suit riots" of 1943, exploring the underlying causes and the broader implications. For Alvarez, the riots revealed both broad societal wartime tensions and the very specific local interactions of white servicemen and youth of color on Los Angeles' streets. Although labor migration has often been portrayed in the scholarship as a male phenomenon, in the second essay, Carmen Teresa Whalen, professor of history and Latina/o Studies at Williams College, explores the ways in which Puerto Rican women were labor migrants in the post-World War II era. Defining labor migration to include women's paid employment and their work in sustaining their households,

Whalen argues that this approach challenges the narratives constructed by policy-makers and social service providers in Puerto Rico and in Philadelphia—narratives that disregarded women's paid employment and disrespected their work within the household. In the third essay, Lilia Fernández, professor of history at the Ohio State University, provides a rare comparative assessment of Mexican and Puerto Rican labor migrations to Chicago, focusing on contract labor programs. She asserts that although there were important differences in the experiences of the two groups based on their citizenship status, shared experiences were also shaped by their recruitment as low-wage, racialized workers.

Youth and the Zoot Suit Riots in Los Angeles

LUIS ALVAREZ

... [H]undreds, if not thousands, of young Mexican American men were violently attacked by white servicemen on the streets of LA during the first week of June 1943. Although most of the violence was carried out by white navy, army, and marine personnel, supported by white civilians, the weeklong series of skirmishes came to be known as the Zoot Suit Riots. Countless youth who wore the drape pants and fingertip-length coats were stripped of their clothes, beaten in front of gathering crowds of onlookers, and subsequently arrested for disturbing the peace, vagrancy, and a number of other offenses.

Most previous accounts of the riots have highlighted Mexican American males as victims of the violence, have noted that the riots served as a flash point for the political mobilization of the Mexican American middle class in Los Angeles, and have focused mainly on the role of the mainstream city press in fanning the flames of the attacks.... Although Mexican American males suffered most of the violence, virtually all zoot suiters, regardless of their ethnicity, and many nonwhite youth, regardless of whether they wore zoot suits or not, were subject to attack....

... [T]he violence carried out by white servicemen and city residents stemmed in large part from the intensification of wartime xenophobia, concerns over domestic security, and attempts to blackball anyone perceived as not contributing to the war effort. This nationalist rhetoric served as the ideological base for the riots, but also functioned as retaliation against the nonnormative race, gender, and sexual behavior of nonwhite youth.... Nonwhite youth in Los Angeles, zoot suiters in particular, were singled out for their sexual, masculine, and sometimes racially mixed behavior, which challenged wartime social mores. If zoot culture enabled the youth involved to explore the possibilities of wartime identity, the Zoot Suit Riots were a resounding statement of disapproval of such activity by white servicemen, urban authorities, and the general public.

The Los Angeles Zoot Suit Riots raised critical questions about what and who was considered a legitimate part or member of U.S. society during World

The Power of the Zoot: Youth Culture and Resistance during World War II, by Luis Alvarez, © 2008 by the Regents of the University of California. Published by the University of California Press.

War II. In what was a very public ground zero during the first week of June 1943, local authorities, the military, the media, and the public fought over nothing less than who was included in and excluded from the wartime polity. The riots underscored the denial of nonwhite youth from full and equal belonging in the United States in that their experiences and cultural identities did not always easily fit within the dominant ethos of wartime patriotism or even within the efforts of nonwhite communities to accommodate to the war effort.... [T]he line between [zoot suiters and servicemen] was increasingly blurred. Large numbers of nonwhite youth—including many zoot suiters themselves—entered the service. Joining the army or navy not only provided a way for them to prove they were as American as anyone else but also threatened the equation white servicemen and other Americans maintained between their white racial identity and masculinity on one hand and patriotism on the other. In their angry response to zoot culture, white servicemen and civilians could draw more exclusive boundaries around U.S. identity. The Zoot Suit Riots illustrate that nonwhite youth and their cultural practices were at the center of debates over national identity.

★ ★ ★

The tension between zoot suiters and servicemen in the Los Angeles area began well before the Zoot Suit Riots. As early as the mid-1930s, when zoot style was just catching on as popular fashion among nonwhites, fist fights and verbal confrontations on city streets between African American and Mexican American civilian youth and white servicemen were not uncommon....

... [T]he increasing U.S. involvement in the war and Southern California's role as a civilian and military center on the Pacific Coast contributed to the escalating conflict between servicemen and zoot suiters. Following the bombing of Pearl Harbor, rumors multiplied throughout 1942 and into early 1943 of Japanese attacks targeting the city. Many Angelinos used such threats to rally for home-front unity.... One result of the increasing war hysteria was open hostility against those considered subversive of the war effort. Just north of LA, the district attorney of Ventura County made clear who was included in such accusations when he claimed that "zoot suits are an open indication of subversive character." The zoot thus emerged as a symbol of anti-Americanness on the home front.

The confrontation between servicemen and zoot suiters was also fueled by their routine contact around the city. The two groups often encountered one another in such popular areas as downtown and Hollywood and even in East Los Angeles, where sailors and soldiers often sought the companionship of young Mexican American women.... [M]uch of the city's military infrastructure, including barracks where enlisted men resided, was located near Mexican American or African American sections of town.... With upwards of 50,000 servicemen on leave pouring into Los Angeles nearly every weekend, the Mexican and black neighborhoods that skirted the downtown area served as a meeting ground for civilian youth and servicemen.

During the early war years the military police recorded hundreds of complaints against zoot suiters by servicemen that reveal the contested nature of race and manhood in wartime LA. During the Zoot Suit Riots the commandant's office of the Eleventh Naval District in Southern California compiled complaints from the months and weeks prior to the riots that highlight at least four major themes: the protection of white women, sexuality, military service, and masculinity.

Among the complaints were a number of charges by white sailors that zoot suiters insulted them and their white female companions....

[A] sailor reported that his wife, who worked at Lockheed, was about to board a streetcar on the corner of Whittier and Euclid when a group of zoot suiters insulted her and tried to entice her to join them....

The reports filed by sailors accusing zoot suiters of accosting, propositioning, and harassing white women reveal important clues about the interconnectedness of race and gender identities during wartime in Los Angeles. For many servicemen, their whiteness and masculinity were inseparable.... Being white and masculine stemmed in large part from protecting the presumed virtuosity of their white mothers, wives, girlfriends, and sisters from the vulgar, hypersexual, and violent threats posed by nonwhite youth. Such white male bravado was intertwined with their patriotism and defined in contrast to the nonwhite, unmanly, and unpatriotic behavior of young African American and Mexican American zoot suiters and the hyperfemininity, sexual purity, and helplessness of white women....

Insults to their patriotism and decision to serve in the military was another theme in the allegations sailors made against zoot suiters....

... [B]ecause insults to military duty was a flash point in the sailor complaints, it is likely that some zoot suiters were voicing an antiwar politics, lashing out at authority figures, or loosely criticizing a home-front society that expected them to serve in the armed forces yet did not afford them first-class citizenship.

Another common theme in the charges made by sailors against zoot suiters was that the latter did not fight fair.... Not only did servicemen consider the zoot suiters' allegedly violent behavior, especially their reported penchant for sucker punches and ganging up, as unmanly, but also their views mirrored the stereotype in wartime Los Angeles of the Japanese and other "enemies" of the United States as being fond of sneak attacks....

... For the white sailors, their whiteness, manhood, and sexuality depended on their ability to protect white women from nonwhite men, their military service and patriotism, and their willingness to fight like men. Juxtaposed with the alleged cowardly, vulgar, and weak zoot suiter, their masculinity and whiteness was the epitome of the wartime hero....

The early months of 1943 also saw an increase in violence carried out by the LAPD, which contributed to racial tension in the city.... During the weeks leading up to the riots, a number of high-profile cases of police aggression occurred involving Mexican Americans and African Americans. In early March, for example, a thirteen-year-old African American boy named Ronald Hudson was shot and killed by police officers when he was caught riding in a stolen car.... Reports showed that the bullet that killed Hudson was fired through his eye, despite police claims that they fired at the car as it was being driven away from them.... In early May, the LAPD was involved in the shooting of a young Mexican American male....

The incident that perhaps most foreshadowed the Zoot Suit Riots occurred in Venice in May, just a week before the rioting began. The Lick Pier and nearby beachfront ... was a favorite hangout for both sailors and zoot suiters.... [A] group of Mexican American zoot suiters were dancing at the nearby Aragon Ballroom when a rumor spread that a white sailor had been stabbed.... [D]espite the efforts of local LAPD officers to quell the unrest, an unruly mob of sailors, white high school students, and other civilians gathered outside the Aragon and attacked the Mexican American youth as they left the dance hall. A group of some five hundred sailors and civilians chased zoot suiters down the board-walk.... The rioters proceeded to beat the Mexican American youth they encountered, and according to one eyewitness.... "They didn't care whether the Mexican kids wore zoot suits or not ... they just wanted Mexicans." Other reports of the incident established that the zoot suiters did not submit weakly to the onslaught but fought back, even attacking police officers.... Even though white servicemen and civilians had been the instigators, police later blamed the Mexican American youth involved....

The trial of eleven of the Mexican American boys arrested during the Venice riot sparked more controversy when the presiding judge in the case, Arthur Guerin, lectured the boys, urging them to join the army as an outlet for their aggression and to serve their country patriotically. Alfred Barela, one of those so admonished by Guerin, ... responded to the judge's charges in a letter.... Barela eloquently articulated his struggle with wartime society, questioning why the police who unfairly arrested him did not earn the judge's wrath:

> Why don't you bawl those cops out? How come he [the police officer] said there were twenty-five hundred people in that mob and only a few Mexican kids, but all the arrests were of the Mexican kids and none of the others arrested? ... You should see the way the cops searched us for knives and guns as though we were gangsters. They didn't let us call our folks and my ma was plenty worried about what happened to me. You say we've got rights like everybody else. Then how can they do this to us?

There is little doubt that zoot suiters' account of the violence and tension sweeping Los Angeles differed from those of servicemen, police, and the general public.... [I]n the weeks leading up to the Zoot Suit Riots, servicemen in the Los Angeles area were reportedly involved in at least eighteen incidents of unlawful violence that did not involve zoot suiters, including events that led to the deaths of seven Angelino civilians in which servicemen were the prime suspects....

By late May 1943, racial tensions in Southern California had reached an all-time high. Signs multiplied that Los Angeles, in particular, was a racial tinderbox....

★ ★ ★

Fears of mass violence in Los Angeles were realized on the night of Thursday, June 3. Eleven white sailors walking along Main Street in East Los Angeles were, they later claimed, jumped and beaten by a gang of at least thirty-five zoot suiters, in this predominantly Mexican American neighborhood.... The group of white servicemen suffered only a few minor injuries. LAPD officers responding to the call, many of them off duty at the time, dubbed themselves the Vengeance Squad and arrived at the scene to arrest Mexican American zoot suiters. The next day, more than two hundred sailors hired a caravan of at least twenty taxicabs and set out for East Los Angeles. When sailors in the lead car spotted a young Mexican American in a zoot suit, a signal was sent to the rest of the procession, and the boy was beaten within minutes. Violence against Mexican Americans and African Americans, many wearing zoot suits and others not, continued for the next four days and nights, leading *Time* magazine to declare a few weeks later, "California's zoot-suit war was a shameful example of what happens to wartime emotions without wartime discipline."

... Ironically, the same night the violence began, a group of at least thirty-five Mexican American boys from the Alpine neighborhood met with police at the Central Police Station on First Street to discuss strategies to reduce juvenile delinquency and keep Mexican American youth off the streets. During the meeting a report was received from a Mexican American sailor that a group of white sailors was roaming the neighborhood hunting for zoot suiters and seeking revenge for alleged attacks on servicemen. The meeting was prolonged in hopes of preventing an incident, but when the boys left the meeting to go home, many of them were attacked and beaten by the sailors....

In one of the few written testimonies of a zoot suiter, Rudy Sanchez, a young Mexican American who attended the anti-gang meeting with LAPD officers, ... related in a letter ... :

> ... The girls, boys, lad[ies], men and manager of the theatre informed us that forty or fifty sailors broke in the show and beat up "zoot suiters," grown up men and even boys as young as twelve and thirteen years old.... [W]hen the sailors of the United States of America beat up twelve and thirteen year old kids of the same country just because [they are] Mexicans, you can imagine how brave they must be. Some of the sailors victims twelve and thirteen year old kids were taken to hospitals for injuries they suffered at the hands of the pitiless sailors.

... The violence soon escalated when white soldiers and marines joined sailors to cordon off sections of city blocks, raid places of business, and form posses in an attempt to purge LA's streets of zoot suiters....

For four days, zoot suiters were beaten, stripped of their clothes, and left humiliated in front of gathering crowds of onlookers. Although much of the initial violence occurred in the northern part of downtown between the city's center and the naval training base, ... virtually any other neighborhood where Mexican Americans lived were targets for the rioting servicemen....

... Servicemen made the rounds of the city's dance halls and public meeting places in search of zooters. Soldiers used army jeeps to transport themselves from one scene of rioting to another, while sailors used naval oars to block off streets in hopes of containing zoot suiters. Streetcars were stopped and motormen forced to open the doors as rioters searched for victims. Rioters targeted theaters, where they forced theater managers to turn on the lights, took youth in zoot suits from the audience, and beat them on the streets outside.... In several cases, young men were taken from beside their wives, girlfriends, and even children....

By June 5, the second night of the riots, Carey McWilliams reported, squads of sailors joined by soldiers and marines paraded through downtown, four abreast, arms linked, stopping anyone whose clothes they did not like and ordering him to change by the following night or else suffer a fate similar to those beaten the night before. In his own eyewitness account, Al Waxman, editor of the *Eastside Journal* and long a sympathizer with the plight of Mexican Americans in Los Angeles, wrote:

> At Twelfth and Central I came upon a scene that will long live in my memory. Police were swinging clubs and servicemen were fighting with civilians. Wholesale arrests were being made by the officers.
>
> Four boys came out of a pool hall. They were wearing the zoot-suits that have become the symbol of a fighting flag. Police ordered them into arrest cars. One refused. He asked: "Why am I being arrested?" The police officer answered with three swift blows of the night-stick across the boy's head and he went down. As he sprawled, he was kicked in the face. Police had difficulty loading his body into the vehicle because he was one legged and wore a wooden limb....
>
> At the next corner a Mexican mother cried out, "Don't take my boy, he did nothing. He's only fifteen years old. Don't take him." She was struck across the jaw with a night-stick and almost dropped the two and a half year old baby that was clinging in her arms....

Mexican Americans in zoot suits were the prime targets of violence by white servicemen, civilians, and police, but others were also attacked, including African Americans, Filipinos, and even some white youth.... Milford Brewer, a twenty-one-year-old African American, and several of his friends were ... targets. After celebrating his induction into the army at a farewell beach party, Brewer and several companions, including three women, at least one of whom was white, were stopped by police while on their way to the bus depot to check the schedule for departures to Des Moines, Iowa, where Brewer was to report for duty. The group was ordered out of their car, searched, and told to "wait there." Within moments, a group of white soldiers arrived and stripped the boys of their trousers. The *Amsterdam News* reported that the violence was "prompted by the presence of a young white woman" with Brewer.

The *California Eagle* reported that black Angelinos were subject to violence whether they wore zoots or not [See Document 1]....

... Reports also indicate that several white zoot suiters came under assault from servicemen. The young white men who lived in black or Mexican areas, had Mexican American or African American friends, and were culturally part of such groups were also attacked....

That sailors and soldiers included black and white zoot suiters in their attacks, as well as non–zoot suiters, is of no small significance.... Their tirades against black and white youth ... suggest that they associated more than a single race or ethnic identity with the zoot's subversive qualities.... Attacks on white zoot suiters further suggest that the rioting servicemen did not see race in monolithic black, brown, and white terms, but rather in varying degrees of each. The white zoot suiters attacked were not quite white enough, or perhaps too black or too brown, to be spared. The servicemen may have seen them as race traitors or foreign to U.S. whiteness, as many of them hailed from Eastern European immigrant communities, some of which shared residential districts with Mexican American and African American Angelinos.

... While the gendered and sexual nature of the riots was evident in the myriad male-to-male interactions that occurred, the role of young women is also worth noting. Young Mexican American women, in particular, actively participated in the riots. Although they were not targeted to the degree that their male counterparts were, young women did endure physical harassment....

A number of observers blamed the violence on competition for young women between male zooters and sailors. Pachucas, it was rumored, appealed to servicemen and thus were jealously guarded by many Mexican American boys, much as white servicemen thought zoot suiters threatened white women. In this scenario, Mexican American women were viewed less as active participants in zoot suit culture and wartime society than as sexual property....

Rumors of another enemy attack on U.S. territory after Pearl Harbor, particularly in Los Angeles and along the Pacific Coast, also fueled the backlash against zoot suiters because they were considered subversive to the war effort. The animosity against zoot suiters grew from rumors spread by the press and general public that zoot suiters were active members in a network of fifth-column *sinarchistas* working on behalf of Hitler's master plan to disrupt the unity of the U.S. home front. Although no evidence supports such claims, the rumors nonetheless indicate that zoot suiters and nonwhite youth in general were labeled enemies of the U.S. state. While the notion that zoot suiters were fascist agents helps explain the servicemen's violence against them, the theory also serves as an apology for their unruly, undisciplined, racist, and violent behavior.

The wartime hysteria in Los Angeles makes more sense as an impetus toward the riots when it is considered in relation to other causes, including the structural conditions in the city. Several local officials cited the economic position occupied by nonwhite youth as a prime factor in their discontent and alleged hatred of servicemen.... [T]he *California Eagle* asserted that although African American and Mexican American youth might be criticized for their role in the violence, it should be recognized that "slums manufacture delinquency" and that poor housing conditions and lack of recreational facilities resulted in problems regardless of race, ethnicity, or the kind of clothes one wore. A report by a civilian group charged with investigating the riots noted ... two other "irritants" for African Americans in Los Angeles: an increasing recognition that the armed forces relegated blacks to low-level positions and refused to protect them from civilian violence, and that city officials were pushing to stop black migration into the city, an apparent violation of constitutional rights....

The economic and social causes of the riots were exacerbated by the role of the mainstream Los Angeles press. Many of the city's progressive political activists ... argued that the press, especially the Hearst-owned *Examiner,* had helped conjure up an imaginary threat of zoot suit youth disrupting home-front stability....

Ultimately, the Zoot Suit Riots were the result of a myriad of political, economic, and social factors that underscored the racial, gender, and sexual conflicts between zoot suiters and servicemen and consistently marked zoot suiters as a threat to the safety of the general public.... The riots were also a direct response by white servicemen, local authorities, the mainstream press, and the general public to the challenges posed by zoot suiters' unorthodox social mores. The multiracial nature of zoot culture, its valuation of different masculine identities, and the propensity of some zoot suiters to value leisure over much-needed wartime labor all helped provoke the violence. Moreover, because so many young nonwhites, including many zoot suiters, did join the military, white servicemen rioters may have felt they were defending the armed forces as a kind of last bastion of whiteness, masculinity, and patriotism. In the end, the conflict between zoot suiters and servicemen was largely about drawing the boundaries of the national polity during wartime. On the one hand, zoot suiters made a case, whether conscious or not, that national belonging and cultural citizenship should be broader, more flexible, and more inclusive. White servicemen, on the other hand, proposed narrower, more rigid, and more exclusive criteria for considering who was an equal member of wartime society....

Although white servicemen initiated and carried out most of the violence, zoot suiters did not submit meekly to the beatings, but actively defended themselves and retaliated with physical and verbal assaults of their own....

In striking back, zoot suiters were responding to the violence against them, but they may also have been taking a jab at the hypocrisy of being attacked because of their race and culture at a time when the U.S. war effort sought to defeat fascism overseas....

... In a letter to Mexican American activist and attorney Eduardo Quevedo, for example, Rudy Sanchez, writing on behalf of the "so called" zooters, wrote, "If these sailors are setting example for the rest of the armed forces we will lose the war. They are dividing us here at home and they call us the hoodlums. We want to help win the war too, and many of us fight in the war. Whose side is the Navy on anyway, Uncle Sam or Hitler?" ...

Young nonwhite women also resented their treatment throughout the riots. A group of eighteen young Mexican American women, for example, submitted a letter to the editor that condemned mainstream Los Angeles newspapers for negative characterizations of pachuca style during the riots, but the letter was rejected by the big-city dailies. Al Waxman's *Eastside Journal* eventually published it on June 16, when the group argued publicly for their own virtuosity and patriotism: "The girls in this meeting room consist of young girls who graduated from high school as honor students, of girls who are now working in defense plants because we want to help win the war, and of girls who have brothers, cousins, relatives, and sweethearts in all branches of the American armed forces. We have not been able to have our side of the story told."

As agents of violence themselves, zoot suiters marked the riots as a struggle over the edges of U.S. identity.... Whether fighting back with violence of their own or sticking up for themselves in the press, both men and women zoot suiters found ways to voice their own displeasure with their treatment. Zoot suiters made known that as much as the riots may have resulted from macro political and social patterns in wartime LA, they were also very much tied to the micro politics of nonwhite youth's struggle for dignity....

★ ★ ★

Although young Mexican American civilian males and white servicemen undoubtedly made up the majority of actors in the riots, young women, African Americans, and civilian whites also actively participated. Broadening the narrative framework of the riots to acknowledge their involvement does more than make the story more inclusive. It also shifts our understanding of the riots' causes and meanings. While many previous accounts have rightly suggested that wartime xenophobia was an important impetus to the riots, those who were involved in the riots were not simply pawns in the geopolitics of World War II. Servicemen, zoot suiters, other civilians, and local authorities each had their own conceptions of Los Angeles and U.S. identity that fueled their behavior. As much as the riots were part and parcel of a more general wave of xenophobia sweeping the nation, as evidenced in the Japanese American internment, they also stemmed from the particular conflict between zoot suiters and servicemen over the nature of race, masculinity, and sex during the war and the ways that entry of nonwhites into the armed forces challenged many military men's interrelated racial, gender, and national identities....

Puerto Rican Women and Migration

CARMEN TERESA WHALEN

Sitting in the Norris Square Senior Citizens' Center in North Philadelphia, Doña Epifanía reminisced about growing up in Coamo, Puerto Rico, and about migrating to Philadelphia. Born in 1919, she was raised with eleven siblings on a farm of eighty-nine *cuerdas*. She recalled, "We lived from the crops and the animals...." She and her mother also took in home sewing. In 1954, as a single parent in search of a "better life," she decided to migrate to the Philadelphia area when a man she knew told her "that there were beans to cook." She cooked for fourteen Puerto Rican agricultural laborers for two years. When she moved to Philadelphia, she stayed with a friend who took her to the garment factory where she worked. Doña Epifania was hired that day and stayed with the company for seventeen years, until the company moved to Florida. Doña Epifanía then retired.

Doña Epifanía considered herself a "worker." ... [Her] definition of "work" included a broad range of reproductive and productive labor. Like Doña Epifania, other migrant women used a broad definition of "work" to validate their many and diverse tasks.... The narratives of Puerto Rican women migrants to Philadelphia suggest the need for a revised definition of labor migration. Puerto Rican women, I argue, were labor migrants in the post–World War II era; they were displaced from Puerto Rico's rural economies, they were recruited as a source of cheap labor, and they migrated in search of work. To consider Puerto Rican women as labor migrants requires attention to sexual divisions of labor in sending and receiving societies and a definition of "labor" that encompasses subsistence labor within the household, paid employment within or beyond the household, informal economic activities, and community work whether paid or unpaid.

... Competing narratives emerged as policy makers in Puerto Rico and in the continental United States constructed their own gendered narratives. Puerto Rican women were at the nexus of policy makers' plans for the island's economic development, which entailed industrialization and the reduction of the population. While policy makers focused on women's reproductive roles, they also portrayed them as a source of cheap labor. In the continental United States, policy makers and social service agencies interpreted the experiences of Puerto Rican women through the emerging culture of poverty paradigm. This was a national discourse that retained the focus on women's reproduction and "overpopulation" while rendering Puerto Rican women's work—their subsistence labor, paid employment, and community work—invisible. This essay examines the ways in which an emphasis on women's reproductive and/or productive roles and definitions of "work" shaped these competing narratives of Puerto Rican women.

★ ★ ★

Puerto Rican women described their migrations from Puerto Rico to Philadelphia in economic terms, emphasizing the impact of changing economic conditions in their local communities and the threats to their rural household economies. In Philadelphia they struggled to recreate their household economies.... Domestic responsibilities were theirs, and, at the same time, paid employment within or outside the household was a very real and constant possibility as well as an economic necessity. Contributing to their households encompassed their reproductive and productive tasks, and, at least in retrospect, they validated the work they did in raising their children. These women balanced "productive" and "reproductive" labor in ways that challenge the scholarly distinction between them and that foster a redefinition of labor migration.

Doña Carmen emphasized the economic motivations in explaining her and her husband's decision to leave San Lorenzo for Philadelphia in 1947.

> ... There were schools, there was a life, you see, in town, but there wasn't enough [work] for everyone to have a better life. So, what we did was plan for the family, like us, we planned to go to the United States.

Her husband, Don Quintín, drove the town's ambulance. She had worked in a library, in a school, and in Humacao's district court. Then, as she recalled, "I started working for myself." She ran a small thrift shop and sold produce, and cooked at home, catering to the town's wealthier residents and providing lunches for the women who worked at the nearby tobacco factory. She enjoyed this work, but rationing during the war had hurt her business. In 1946, Don Quintín came to the Philadelphia area with a labor contract for seasonal farm work. Doña Carmen followed within the year, selling all of their possessions and bringing their four children with her.

Yet Doña Carmen and other Puerto Rican women did not just follow their husbands. Many came with the intention of finding paid employment in Philadelphia. Doña Carmen went looking for work the day after she arrived.... [S]he did find a job—packing shoes at the J. Edward Shoe Company, where she worked for seven years. Married women like Doña Carmen, female heads of household like Doña Epifanía, and single women migrated to Philadelphia in search of jobs. In the postwar era, the city's economy provided jobs for Puerto Rican women in the secondary sector, especially in the garment and food processing industries. By 1950, 33 percent of Puerto Rican women were in the labor force, compared to 34 percent of women citywide.

... In 1954, [Doña Margarita] left Santurce and joined her husband, Don Marcelino, in Philadelphia. They already had four children when her husband came to the States with a labor contract for seasonal agricultural work.... He left the farm, found an apartment in Philadelphia, and sent for Doña Margarita and the children....

Doña Margarita considered her domestic duties "work." She remarked of her life in Santurce, "But at home I had more than enough work because there was the house, the obligations of the house, getting those that were already going to school ready, washing, going to the public spigot to get on line.... Nothing by machine, nothing, nothing of convenience or anything, all of this was by hand." ... In Philadelphia, everyday tasks became easier, while financial hardships created new challenges....

Doña Margarita found paid employment in Santurce and Philadelphia. In Santurce, she contributed to the family's income with paid work within the household. She explained, "I didn't work outside but, yes, there were people who told me 'iron these clothes for me.' ... So they brought me the clothes and at home, I earned a few dollars, too." In Philadelphia, she and her husband worked on farms for several summers. She recalled, "... during the summer we took [our children] to the farms to pick fruits, blueberries.... We took them during the summer, to not leave them alone." ...

... [S]he contributed to her household through informal economic activities. She helped her comadre ..., who ran a day care and a guest house out of her home. Her oldest children were in school and she took her younger children with her.... Hence, while her children were younger, Doña Margarita contributed to the household economy by caring for her children and her household, and by working with her comadre and bringing home food and some money....

In addition to paid employment and domestic responsibilities, Puerto Rican women in Philadelphia included "community work" in their definitions of work and minimized the distinctions between paid and unpaid community work. After several years at the shoe factory, Doña Carmen began a long career in human services. Rather than emphasizing the change in jobs, she stressed the continuity in helping the community.... In the early 1970s, she became the director of the Norris Square Senior Citizens' Center, where she worked for more than twenty years.... In 1992, she reminisced, "I've been a fighter since the first days—for my Puerto Rico.... I'm still fighting."...

Puerto Rican women's narratives reveal the complexities of women's work and provide the basis for a redefinition of labor migration. Women described the impact of economic changes and their search for *mejor ambiente,* or "a better life." Recreating their household economies in Philadelphia meant some combination of caring for their children in a very different environment, finding paid employment, participating in informal economic activities, and fostering the well-being of the Puerto Rican community. They viewed paid employment as part of their responsibilities in contributing to the maintenance of their households; and although most found it challenging to balance household and paid work, they did not express this as a conflict in roles. Instead, paid employment was a possibility, and the nature and rhythm of paid employment were shaped by their other responsibilities to their households.... For many, the balancing of reproductive and productive work resulted in the *double day.* Women remained responsible for domestic duties even as they secured paid employment.... [T]hese women emphasized the continuities in contributing to their households, even as migration changed the contexts of those contributions. Here, their narratives challenge persisting notions that work is something that migrating women discover in the host society. In their narratives, Puerto Rican women used a definition of work that extended beyond paid employment outside the home to include work within the household, paid and unpaid, and community work, paid and unpaid.

★ ★ ★

In Puerto Rico, policy makers' narratives of Puerto Rican women encompassed reproductive and productive roles, but only in limited ways. Instead of identifying the decline of rural household economies, policy makers attributed Puerto Rico's economic woes to "overpopulation" and focused on women in their efforts to reduce the population. Policy makers did not, however, acknowledge women's other reproductive and productive contributions to their households. As policy makers pursued industrialization by invitation, they marketed women as a source of cheap labor. Yet they circumscribed their definition of their work to traditional areas of women's work and to women as supplementary wage earners. These limited notions of women's reproductive and productive roles and the resultant contradictions emerged most clearly in policy makers' program to send women to the continental United States as contracted domestics.

... A 1944 study circulated by the Puerto Rico Planning Board suggested a consensus on overpopulation and emphasized the role of "mothers." According to the study's authors, "that the basic problem of Puerto Rico is the maladjust-ment between resources and population is clearly the conclusion of most serious students." They predicted that "the pressure of population on resources, which is already great, will become intolerably greater." By way of solutions, the authors called for "a conscious policy of emigration and birth control." Sensitive to legal restrictions, the authors ... called for "a continued expansion of the present work" in contraceptive education.... In regard to sterilization, they hinted only that "more could have been performed if facilities had permitted." More sterili-zations were subsequently performed. By 1965, one-third of Puerto Rican women between the ages of 20 and 49 had been sterilized, "a rate significantly higher than that of any other country."

As policy makers promoted industrialization, Puerto Rican women emerged as a source of cheap labor. In addition to a complete tax holiday for U.S. cor-porations in Puerto Rico, the other major attraction of Puerto Rico was low wages for workers, especially women. The minimum wage provision of the Fair Labor Standards Act was not applied in Puerto Rico. Instead, minimum wages in Puerto Rico were determined on an industry-by-industry basis by spe-cial committees appointed by the secretary of labor.... In U.S. congressional hearings in 1949, Teodoro Moscoso, the president of the Puerto Rico Industrial Development Company, argued against applying the minimum wage and for "the beauty of this flexible arrangement." Moscoso insisted that low wages, which were approximately 60 percent of those in the United States, and tax incentives did not constitute an unfair recruitment of U.S. companies. In addi-tion, he asserted Puerto Ricans' willingness to work in the least desirable jobs....

Policy makers encouraged labor-intensive, export-oriented industries, like the garment and textile industries, to come to Puerto Rico.... [A] 1949 pam-phlet entitled "Puerto Rico's Potential as a Site for Textile, Apparel and Other Industries" asserted Puerto Rico's benefits, including an abundance of workers, ... and ... "orderly and tranquil" labor relations.... Emphasizing the availability of women workers, it noted ... [that] [l]abor laws had "recently been liberalized to permit night work for women in textile industries." Perhaps most important, wages in the needlework industry were only 26 percent of those in the United States. The pamphlet concluded, "In virtually all lines and stages of tex-tile and apparel manufacturing the current wage structure of Puerto Rico offers the possibility of substantial advantages to the entrepreneur."

These industries relied on the cheap labor of Puerto Rican women in their homes and in the new factories. By the 1949 congressional hearings, employees of the new U.S. plants numbered 3,793 in shops and 3,440 home workers.... [T]he Economic Development Administration or Fomento became the agency responsible for promoting industrialization. By 1952, the apparel and food pro-cessing industries provided the majority of new manufacturing jobs. By 1963, Fomento plants employed 70,000 workers, and 60 percent of the new jobs were filled by women....

Despite policies that increased women's employment, policy makers contin-ued to define women as supplemental earners and to reinforce existing sexual divisions of labor....

Policy makers' contract labor program for domestics highlighted their concerns with overpopulation and the gender-based nature of their contract labor programs. Policy makers were willing to consider women as workers only in areas traditionally defined as "women's work." In 1947, policy makers turned to contract labor as a solution to "overpopulation," and again they focused on women. Their first postwar program was a contract labor program for young, unmarried women to work as domestics in the continental United States.... This was state-sponsored migration, as the government of Puerto Rico assumed responsibility for recruiting, screening, and training workers and for the labor contract. Labor contracts were signed by the employer and the employee, and were approved by the commissioner of labor of Puerto Rico. The New York State Employment Service arranged the placements for Puerto Rican domestics.

Policy makers' focus on young women revealed their goal of reducing the population. They were optimistic about the demographic effects, but hesitant to proclaim them publicly. [See Document 5] ...

Planners foresaw additional benefits to the emigration of women, based on traditional gender roles. Women would spark informal networks, send money home, foster dispersion, and reduce the social tensions associated with settlement....

Planners emphasized the compatibility of the program with women's roles, merging women's productive and reproductive roles.... Domestic training kept women's limited options open, so that "They need not look forward to a lifetime of domestic service. The capable ones who display initiative will find opportunities in the field of hotel and other institutional housekeeping.... And there is always the possibility of marriage on the continent." ... The possibility that domestics would marry in the States increased the potentials for depopulation, for dispersion, and for an "invisible" and problem-free migration.

Although it contracted women as laborers, the program for domestics was based on traditional notions of gender roles and sexual divisions of labor. As a result, labor contracts stipulated working conditions and appropriate behavior for the domestics.... Hours were specified as a maximum of ten hours per day and forty-eight hours per week, with additional hours on call not to exceed three nights per week nor four hours per night. Yet the contract allowed work in excess of these hours provided that it was compensated at double the hourly wage.... The employees, in turn, agreed to do the work to the employers' specifications, "to maintain a neat and appropriate personal appearance," and "to maintain the decorum of the household, especially with respect to her own guests and her deportment in public."

Despite ambitious goals, the program was short-lived.... The numbers of placements were not high enough for Puerto Rico's policy makers, [who] ... instituted another gender-based contract labor program for men to work as seasonal agricultural laborers on farms in the States.

As Puerto Rican women arrived in the continental United States, policy makers and social service workers constructed a "culture of poverty" narrative to interpret their experiences. The culture of poverty was a national discourse, with important local and gendered dimensions, that attributed Puerto Ricans' perceived problems to their culture. [Writing in 1965, a]nthropologist Oscar Lewis considered "poverty and its associated traits as a culture … with its own structure and rationale, as a way of life which is passed down from generation to generation along family lines." Lewis severed the culture of poverty from the conditions of poverty so that it came to be seen as self-perpetuating and equated with the "national culture" of Puerto Rico. Migrating Puerto Ricans carried this culture of poverty with them; "many of the problems of Puerto Ricans in New York have their origin in the slums of Puerto Rico." For Lewis, the culture of poverty was characterized by little integration with the larger society, little organization in the ethnic community, families that verbally emphasized unity but rarely achieved it, and individuals with a high tolerance for pathologies. The culture of poverty's emphasis on culture, family, and generations implied that women, traditionally held responsible for these domains, were to blame for the "problems" affecting their families and their communities. [This narrative] deemed the Puerto Rican family "defective" in comparison to both European peasant families and perceived U.S. norms.…

Within this narrative, women were portrayed as failures in their reproductive roles. They were "submissive wives" who had too many children, and inadequate mothers. In 1950, C. Wright Mills, Clarence Senior, and Rose Kohn Goldsen summarized the role of the Puerto Rican woman: "The woman is supposed to be submissive, and her submissiveness is guaranteed by a network of manners and politenesses which confines her major sphere of activities to the home, circumscribes her social contacts, and places her under constant surveillance." They contrasted this to their perception of the U.S. norm: "Compared with the continental American family types, however, the despotic father-husband relationship is the dominant island pattern." …

Like their counterparts in Puerto Rico, U.S. policy makers continued to focus on reproduction and attributed Puerto Ricans' "problems" to the fact that they had too many children. U.S. policy makers, however, linked the "population problem" to the other assumed "problem" of Puerto Ricans—lack of a work ethic and welfare dependency. Here, women's roles as workers were ignored, as a basic tenet of the culture of poverty was the lack of a work ethic and the desire for welfare dependency. [Nathan] Glazer and [Patrick] Moynihan defined the "population problem" as a cultural tendency to have too many children, a tendency that migrated with Puerto Ricans to New York City.… Linking overpopulation and dependency, they concluded, "The special misfortune that consigns so many Puerto Ricans to the relief rolls is their large number of children." This became a "circle of dependency," and from this perspective, "The culture of public welfare … is as relevant for the future of Puerto Ricans in the city as the culture of Puerto Rico." …

In Philadelphia, policy makers and social service workers drew on the national discourse and shared many of its assumptions. The local discourse mirrored the national discourse in its focus on "problems," the cultural roots of those problems, the lack of a work ethic, and the lack of community organizations. The clearest articulation of Puerto Ricans' lack of a work ethic and its cultural determinants appeared in a 1958 survey by the Friends' Neighborhood

Guild. As was often the case, these views were expressed by those most involved with and most interested in assisting Puerto Ricans. The study asserted:

> The Puerto Ricans just do not want to work in many cases.... The excuses they invent as to why they didn't need that particular job all cover up the underlying fact that they are very lazy and would prefer to think of ways to collect relief money for not doing anything than look for jobs.... It all has to do with the greatest factor of all we must cope with in dealing with the Puerto Rican, the Latin mentality and the Latin tradition which is against work and which sees fit to have the women of the lower class bring in the pay while the man sits home.

... The root of the problem was cultural, located in "the Latin mentality and the Latin tradition" and not in factors such as the economic structure of Philadelphia or employment opportunities.... At the same time, the survey expressed concern with Puerto Ricans' dependency; "let it [the Guild] be known as a place that one does not just come to when one needs a handout.... The Guild should tell those with whom it deals that they can do it all themselves and that they should want to, furthermore. Otherwise, we are just breeding a generation of outstretched hands."

Puerto Rican women were again portrayed as "submissive wives" and deficient mothers.... [T]he Guild's survey expressed frustration in recruiting Puerto Rican children for summer camp, "I ran into the Latin traditions again as a stopping block ... no mother is willing to take the responsibility of saying that her child can go to camp for fear that something might happen to him and then she could expect the firing squad from her husband. The father is still the boss." Here, the "submissive wife" and the Puerto Rican mother failed to "take responsibility" for her own children.

In Philadelphia, ... [s]ocial service workers suggested that Puerto Rican women worked precisely because they were "submissive wives" and because of their husbands' other "culture of poverty" traits. Yet they also portrayed women's employment as a threat to men's masculinity and to the Puerto Rican family.... The Guild's survey emphasized the "cultural" roots of women's employment:

> [T]here is a tendency because of old Latin traditions to let the wife work among the lower classes while the husband watches television, which he rarely understands, but he likes the noise and pictures! ... In one house I actually found three very healthy men in their mid-twenties sitting around while the wife of one and her cousin worked in a factory.

Social service workers assumed that women's employment was something new and one of the "benefits" for women in the States. Stressing the impact of migration, the Commission on Human Relations noted, "the Puerto Rican woman finds ... it easy to get a job, the pay is far better than on the island and the new wage-earning ability raises her status in the family to the point where she is equal, and sometimes superior, to the male." This employment and women's new ideas about "freedom" caused concern and the Commission cautioned that "they may affect the husband's role as undisputed head of the family...."

When Petra Pagán de Colón, as director of Puerto Rico's Migration Division, attended a meeting of a social service agency in Philadelphia, she challenged social service workers' stereotypes and highlighted the differing narratives in Puerto Rico and the States. In their meeting notes, the Nationalities Services Committee commented with some surprise, "Mainlanders have often misconceptions about family constellation in Puerto Rico. It was brought out that women are not completely subordinate to their husbands, but in meetings it was observed that they make as much of a contribution as do their husbands." There was another revelation, "It was also found that those workers who had the closest contacts with the Puerto Rican migrants, ... discovered that Puerto Ricans had a long tradition of hard, diligent labor."

Social service workers were also concerned by their perceptions that Puerto Ricans lacked community, a defining characteristic of the culture of poverty. The Guild's survey reflected this view, as well as the assumption that community leaders had to be men: "The crux of the problem lies [in] ... a complete lack of any social responsibility." Again, the perceived problem, a lack of community, was portrayed as having cultural roots, "the Latin mentality." The Guild used a narrow definition of community, equating community with organizations.... The survey conceded, however, "There may not be any community unity among the Puerto Ricans, but there is definitely a warmth within the neighborhood itself and those who like it, really like it." The survey concluded by revealing both the limitations of their narrow definition of community and the invisibility of women's community work: "in the process of becoming Americanized, suggestions are always welcome and the way is made easier just by wanting to help. There are groups doing just that at the moment. One is a group of Puerto Rican women who ... work their heads off just going around within the community instructing the Puerto Rican women on the ways of making life easier for themselves in the United States."

In the national discourse, Puerto Rican women's work—their paid employment, their unpaid subsistence labor within their households, and their community work—was rendered invisible by the culture of poverty concept. Instead of being seen as economically displaced and migrating in search of work, Puerto Ricans won the dubious distinction of being among the first to be cast as migrating in search of welfare benefits.... From this perspective, Puerto Ricans could not be labor migrants because they lacked a work ethic and desired welfare dependency. The obstacles that confronted Puerto Ricans stemmed not from a new urban environment, a tight job market, or discrimination, but rather from their own cultural deficiencies. Puerto Ricans were "lazy" and dependent and lacked "any sense of social responsibility." In Philadelphia, the portrayal of Puerto Rican women as "submissive wives" coexisted in a contradictory fashion with an awareness of their roles as workers....

★ ★ ★

... Puerto Rican women wove their reproductive and productive roles into a single narrative of contributing to and maintaining their households in Puerto Rico and in Philadelphia. It was, they reminisced, a lot of work and at times a difficult balance. Yet, at least in retrospect, these women did not experience it as a conflict in roles. Migration changed the context within which they did this work, but it was not a novelty to balance the reality or possibilities of paid employment with the other responsibilities of home. Their narratives challenge the still resilient portrayal of immigrant women discovering "work" in the host society. In their broad definitions of contributing to their households and of work, these women's narratives break down scholarly binaries that do not adequately reflect lived experience and foster a redefinition of labor migration.

In treating oral histories as just one of several competing narratives, this essay suggests the importance of examining the "subjectivity" of policy makers and of supposedly "objective" sources, such as government and social service agency documents. In both Puerto Rico and the States, policy makers constructed narratives of Puerto Rican women. These state narratives were no less "subjective" than oral history memories. In Puerto Rico, the state's narrative of Puerto Rican women was consistent with prevailing assumptions and with policy goals aimed at reducing Puerto Rico's population and attracting U.S. industries to Puerto Rico. In the States, where racialist constructions merged with gender constructions, Puerto Rican women were viewed through the lens of the culture of poverty paradigm. Narratives continued to emphasize women's responsibility for "overpopulation," but now ignored Puerto Rican women's work in all of its dimensions, avoiding their contributions to their households and their communities and their roles as cheap labor for U.S. industries. Policy makers' "subjectivity," their embedded assumptions, shaped policy initiatives and the provision of social services. Migration provides a window to two different, yet connected, contexts, and these competing narratives of Puerto Rican women suggest the complexity of gender constructions in the postwar era.

A Comparative Approach to Mexican and Puerto Rican Labor Migration

LILIA FERNÁNDEZ

In the Spring of 1945 in the city of Chicago, a local Mexican American organization, the Mexican Civic Committee, alerted the Council of Social Agencies' Committee on Minority Groups about the presence of several hundred Mexican migrant contract workers (*braceros*) in the city. Most of the men worked on local rail lines while others had labored in agriculture or on railroads elsewhere in the region and then made their way to the Windy City. By late 1946, the Committee on Minority Groups established a Subcommittee on Social Services to Mexican Migratory Workers to address the population's needs.... Many braceros had poor working and living conditions, insufficient clothing for midwestern winters, inadequate food, and substandard wages. Some men "skipped" their contracts and arrived in Chicago without money, a place to sleep, or a way to get back home.

The subcommittee discussed ways that local social agencies could provide services to these migrants and help those who wanted to return to Mexico.

... [A]nother group of Chicago residents also turned their attention to a different sort of "braceros" who were experiencing comparable conditions—Puerto Rican migrant women and men who had been placed locally as domestic servants and foundry workers, respectively. A group of students at the University of Chicago and other sympathizers began investigating workers' complaints of employer abuses, unfair wage deductions, and overall bad work experiences. Puerto Ricans were not a part of the formal bracero agreements that the United States had established with Mexico, but like Mexicans, they, too, had begun traveling to Chicago and elsewhere as contracted laborers.... [T]his recruitment program took place between the Puerto Rico Department of Labor, American employers, and the United States Employment Service (USES).

Beginning with World War II and throughout the 1940s and 1950s, both Mexicans and Puerto Ricans became subjects of state-sponsored mass labor importation programs in the United States. Mexicans earned "legal" entry into the country as foreign nationals through the Emergency Farm Labor or Bracero Program (1942–1964), a temporary recruitment program initially designed to assuage severe labor shortages during World War II. Puerto Ricans became labor migrants under the auspices of the Puerto Rico Department of Labor Migration Division, as part of the island's modernization and population control effort known as Operation Bootstrap/Manos a la Obra. Broadly speaking, their migration had the two-pronged goals of alleviating the island's widespread unemployment and controlling its putative "overpopulation." ... [T]he similarities and parallels between these simultaneous population movements have gone largely unnoticed.... This may be due to the tendency of some ethnic histories to focus on ethnic/national groups individually, to the exclusion of others. Or this elision might be attributed to geography—the singular attention to the Southwest when studying Mexicans/Mexican Americans and the emphasis on the East Coast for Puerto Rican histories. While the majority of Mexican braceros labored in agricultural fields or on railroads in the Southwest, and most Puerto Rican labor migrants worked on the East Coast, both groups converged in the fields, on the railroads, and in the factories of the Midwest. This confluence in postwar Chicago provides a fruitful site ... for producing a comparative and relational history of Mexicans and Puerto Ricans that reveals the similarities and distinctions of their labor migrations.

... Mexicans and Puerto Ricans both served as viable labor pools to fill American economic needs in the mid-twentieth century.... Mexican migrants (whether bracero or not) entered the country as citizens of a sovereign nation, and therefore were identified legally as "aliens" and popularly as "immigrants." Puerto Ricans came as residents of an American colonial possession and, therefore, as citizens as a result of ... the Jones Act of 1917. They were thus identified as domestic "migrants." ... This distinction kept noncitizen Mexicans (including braceros) in a vulnerable and chronically "deportable" status, while generally affording Puerto Ricans greater and more immediate recourse to governmental protections and greater ease in permanently relocating to the mainland.... While much has been made of this citizenship difference between Mexicans and Puerto

Ricans, and noncitizen status certainly had real material consequences for some migrants, I suggest that their simultaneous recruitment as low-wage workers reinforced their racialization as an exploitable laboring class and provided much more common ground for the eventual affinities and alliances that emerged between the two groups.

... Puerto Rican and Mexican workers ... came to do similar forms of work (e.g., agricultural and low-wage industrial labor) in the mainland United States for specified periods of time and under similar though not always identically exploitative conditions. Two important factors made their experiences much more alike, however, than their distinct citizenship status would suggest. First, although Puerto Ricans enjoyed legal membership in the nation-state, theirs was an unequal citizenship. From its origins, Puerto Rican legal status was fraught with limits, conditions, and qualifications. Their colonial racialization vis-à-vis white Americans and their subsequent incorporation as subordinate citizens (much like African Americans and Native Americans) mutually reinforced one another and thus constructed most of the population as exploitable, low-wage labor both on the island and the mainland. Rather than securing the full privileges and rights of white American citizens, then, Puerto Rican workers were locked into a low-wage labor market, one which they came to occupy alongside ethnic Mexicans upon migrating to the mainland....

A second condition complicates this citizen/noncitizen divide: not all Mexicans in the United States were noncitizens. Puerto Ricans and Mexican braceros on the mainland encountered U.S.-born Mexican Americans ... and naturalized Mexican immigrants. Citizenship, thus, was not necessarily the most salient feature that distinguished these two groups.... Mexicans and Puerto Ricans ... also related to one another as workers in the same factories, neighbors in the same communities, worshippers in Spanish-language churches, patrons of the same ethnic businesses, and ultimately, even relatives in blended families.... Their mutual class position, racial subordination, and cultural affinities rather than state-assigned legal status, I suggest, proved more meaningful in shaping bi-ethnic ... solidarities and alliances....

★ ★ ★

A comparative analysis of Mexicans and Puerto Ricans as raced-classed-gendered transnational migrating subjects in the mainland United States must begin with an examination of their historical economic relationship to and racialization by the U.S. nation-state....

... [T]hese distinct migrations have been the result of American empire. Both Mexicans and Puerto Ricans have functioned as colonial labor in their respective places of origin—Mexicans as miners and petroleum workers for American and European corporations in Mexico, ... and Puerto Ricans as agricultural workers on U.S.-owned sugar, coffee, and tobacco plantations on the island. But their migrations to the U.S. mainland have also been a result of the economic, social, and political dislocations that such imperialism and colonialism have produced. Indeed, most studies of Puerto Ricans underscore the migration phenomenon as part and parcel of the island's colonial relationship to the

United States... Chicano historians and other scholars have advanced this argument in relation to Mexican migrants as well....

The migration of both populations to the mainland United States during the mid-twentieth century carried with it the racial legacies of conquest and colonization at the same time that it perpetuated and reinforced that racialization. Puerto Ricans ... confounded the nation's black-white binary at a moment when European immigrants were consolidating their "whiteness" and black migrants to the urban industrial north had been firmly cast in their "blackness." Puerto Ricans' racial heterogeneity and ambiguity marked them as some "other" nonwhite group despite their American citizenship. Mexican and Mexican American labor migrants reinforced the historical socioeconomic status of ethnic Mexicans in the Southwest as low-wage stoop labor.... [U]ltimately their non-citizen/alien, and perceived un–American status marked them firmly outside the national body. They too represented another type of nonwhite "other." ...

★ ★ ★

World War II propagated tremendous domestic migration within the mainland United States. Internal movement of southern African American, southern white, and Mexican American workers as well as urbanization policies regarding Native Americans all brought increasingly diverse populations of workers to urban areas. Yet the upgrading of many Americans, especially women, to more lucrative industrial jobs and the urbanization of the U.S. population during these years resulted in a dramatic decline in farmers and farm labor. This reality collided with American imperatives for cheaper labor and increased food and industrial production during the war....

... Pressured by powerful agribusiness, manufacturing, and railroad companies during World War II, the U.S. government established agreements for temporary transnational migration from Jamaica, Mexico, the Bahamas, British Honduras, and its own colonial possession, Puerto Rico. The largest labor migration to fill this need issued from Mexico. U.S. imperialism, modernization and industrialization campaigns, agricultural displacement, environmental catastrophe, and government policies made Mexico and Puerto Rico ripe candidates for exporting workers. Both Mexican and Puerto Rican governments pursued labor migration as an economic policy.... Moreover, the labor migration programs of both Mexico and Puerto Rico had differing aims: the Bracero Program was to bring Mexican workers strictly on a short-term basis and return them home at the end of their contracts. Migration from the colonial territory of Puerto Rico, in contrast, was more ambiguous, understood variably to be temporary, permanent, or semipermanent relocation to remove so many unemployed off the island....

The U.S. government established the Emergency Farm Labor Program in April 1942 as a result of pressure from agricultural lobbyists who sought to import foreign workers to tend their crops and fields [See Document 3]. The initial program, popularly known as the Bracero Program, allowed employers to contract Mexican laborers for six months at a time. Contracts purportedly included free transportation from recruitment centers to the workplace, free sanitary housing, water, and nutritious meals provided at cost. Workers were to be paid the local prevailing wage, although local wage boards, composed largely of farmers themselves, and not workers, established these at the beginning of each season. Braceros initially labored in the Southwest, but many began working crops and orchards in midwestern states like Michigan, Ohio, Minnesota, Illinois, and Wisconsin as early as 1944. The negotiation of labor contracts for Mexican workers also extended to the railroad industry. Like agribusiness, the railroads cited severe labor shortages, although evidence suggests that the problem was not so much a dearth of domestic workers as it was the low wages that the railroads wanted to pay for unskilled work.... The Railroad Bracero Program brought over 100,000 Mexican men to work on U.S. railroads in only two and a half years (from 1943 to 1945). Perhaps because of pressure from railway unions, the program did not last as long as the agricultural component....

The Mexican government tried, to a certain extent, to protect its workers from discrimination and prejudice, objecting on various occasions to unfair treatment, including wage differentials, and other worker complaints. It completely excluded Texas from the program in the early years, citing its notorious racism against Mexicans....

The Puerto Rican government was eager to participate in the war effort and send its residents to work on the mainland as well. As early as 1942, insular government officials urged the War Manpower Commission (WMC) to hire Puerto Ricans (U.S. citizens) for jobs that were being filled by imported foreign workers—Mexicans, Jamaicans, Bahamians, and Barbadians.... The program carefully selected more than one thousand skilled workers who could speak English, pay their own travel costs, and met other criteria. After six months, the WMC began recruiting unskilled laborers for placement in railroad, food processing, and mining industries.... Not long after it had begun, however, the program was considered a failure. Migrants protested work and living conditions and many skipped out on their work assignments.... Apparently, neither employers nor the federal government had much control over their mobility, as many chose to vote with their feet and leave unsatisfactory jobs. As a result, many employers chose instead to continue hiring foreign workers who could purportedly be managed more carefully and deported or threatened with deportation as necessary.

The War Manpower Commission discontinued the formal recruitment program and instead allowed private employers individually to seek workers on the island on their own....

... The Puerto Rican government ... began small-scale migration experiments and in 1947 established a Migration Division within its Department of Labor....

★ ★ ★

Mexican and Puerto Rican migrants first began encountering one another in significant numbers in the Midwest in the late 1940s.... Between May 1943 and September 1945, over fifteen thousand braceros came to work in Chicago. Because the city served as a central hub for many of the nation's railroads, braceros came through or worked in the area on a number of lines.... Many braceros who eventually settled permanently in Chicago started on the railroad circuit....

Others who had worked as braceros elsewhere or simply came to the U.S. on their own traveled to Chicago on word of abundant, lucrative job opportunities in the 1950s and 1960s.

When braceros arrived in Chicago, they found a small, established Mexican American community that had lived in the city for more than two decades. Mexican American leaders initially became advocates for braceros....

Shortly after Mexican braceros began arriving in Chicago, the first Puerto Rican contract laborers reached the city as well. In the fall of 1946, the Castle, Barton and Associates employment agency contracted nearly 600 women and men as domestic, foundry, and steel workers. Puerto Rican women began arriving in the city in stages beginning in September of that year. In total, an estimated 398 women came to work as live-in domestics. With the cooperation of Puerto Rico's Department of Labor, the employment agency handled the arrangements and placements of the workers and outlined the contract terms....

Along with the domestics, nearly two hundred Puerto Rican men also arrived that September for industrial employment. The Chicago Hardware Foundry Company in North Chicago, thirty miles from the city, reportedly faced a labor shortage and struggled to find general laborers. Nearly one hundred men came on contracts.... The company agreed to provide migrants housing and meals for a fee. An article in the *Chicago Tribune* spoke highly of the workers, remarking that "many of the men [spoke] English well" and many of them "were former GIs." ...

By December of that year, however, complaints about working conditions and pay deductions from both the household and foundry workers drew attention locally and in Puerto Rico. A small group of Puerto Rican students and sympathizers at the University of Chicago took an interest in the workers and publicly exposed their labor conditions and the contract violations. [See Document 4] ...

... Despite this initial scandal, Puerto Rican migration to Chicago and elsewhere in the Midwest grew dramatically over the next decade.

★ ★ ★

Mexicans and Puerto Ricans occupied a similar racial and socioeconomic position as labor migrants. Many of them worked side by side in the agricultural fields of the Upper Midwest doing similar forms of work and often encountering Tejano or other Mexican American agricultural migrants. They worked often under difficult conditions, suffered abuses, felt the pains of homesickness and culture shock, and experienced Midwest ... winters for the very first time.... [T]hey were continually reracialized as nonwhite laborers and felt the prejudice and discrimination that accompanied that process in the mid-twentieth-century United States.

As early as March 1945, the Mexican consul general in Chicago complained to the president of Mexico "that the laborers were not being treated fairly in the region." Braceros experienced many hardships while on contract—from uninhabitable converted chicken coops or shacks for housing to contaminated water, verbal and physical abuse, and discrimination from employers and local residents. In 1951 President Truman's Commission on Migrant Labor issued a report identifying severe problems with the Bracero Program, including employer abuses, lax enforcement of regulations, and deplorable living and working conditions. The Commission's report ultimately recommended restricting the program. [See Document 8] ...

Much like the government of Mexico and its bracero contracts, the Puerto Rican government could not or did not effectively protect its workers against abuses, low wages, and poor working conditions. Many of the jobs available to contracted labor migrants—particularly those in agriculture and domestic work—were among the most exploited and least protected employment in the United States. Workers had little protection by way of federal or state laws.... The fact that the Migration Division found itself intervening in so many cases of wage disputes and labor complaints ... suggests that many workers faced unbearable conditions, complained about unfair deductions, and encountered unjust treatment.

Mexicans and Puerto Ricans essentially competed with one another for the chance to earn wages on the U.S. mainland. On the one hand, Puerto Ricans had a preferred status as citizens, especially given nativist arguments against the use of foreign labor. On the other hand, some employers favored Mexicans, especially illegal immigrants, for their tractability, deportability, and willingness to work for lower wages. U.S. officials actually used the availability of "domestic" imported migrants to pressure the Mexican government to renew bracero agreements.... If Mexicans would not agree to the exploitative employment terms, the United States would find other workers who would.

The distinction between the juridico-political status of Mexicans and that of Puerto Ricans did not go unnoticed by Puerto Rican officials, either.... Over the years the insular government carried out aggressive marketing campaigns to advertise its workers to American employers.... Puerto Rican officials planned and carried out their labor migration campaign fully aware of the competition posed by "foreign" (read Mexican) workers....

★ ★ ★

The greatest distinction between Mexicans and Puerto Ricans as labor migrants, however, was the threat of deportation by the Immigration and Naturalization Service (INS). Puerto Ricans enjoyed greater ease in migrating to the mainland: they could travel freely with or without labor contracts and did not have to register with authorities to seek permission for their travel. Mexicans, in contrast, either needed to have a bracero permit or other visa to cross the border legally, or attempted to travel undetected by immigration officials or the Border Patrol.... [T]he Bracero Program actually increased illegal immigration during its operation. Many growers welcomed, even preferred, undocumented workers.... For workers, the difference between having a bracero contract and working "illegally" could be negligible, as neither option provided many safeguards or protections. Those who abandoned contract work ultimately increased the circulation of illegal aliens in the United States, revealing the severe limitations of the program....

From 1942 through 1964, the state recruited and, indeed, condoned illegal immigration at the same time that it disciplined those workers through arbitrary roundup and deportation procedures.... Many employers, especially those in

Texas and along border regions, openly hired and recruited undocumented workers while INS and Border Patrol officials simply looked the other way or relaxed enforcement practices. Even more astonishing, the INS regularly "dried out," or legalized, thousands of illegal immigrants already working on U.S. farms. Between 1947 and 1949, for example, the United States imported only 74,600 braceros but reclassified 142,200 Mexican illegal aliens already in the United States as legal contract laborers. This practice benefited farmers, who avoided losing their work force to deportations by instead complying with a perfunctory administrative exercise.... In 1954, in the midst of economic recession, the INS initiated the Operation Wetback campaign, which reached Chicago that fall and expelled approximately one million ethnic Mexicans (some of them citizens or legal immigrants) nationwide. Mexican immigrants were thus at the whim of the state's immigration apparatus, one whose policies fluctuated based on the needs of American markets.

In contrast, Puerto Ricans did not endure compulsory deportation after their work terms expired. Though in some cases wages were withheld until their return to the island and the Migration Division strove to regulate their movement, they were "Americans" according to the law and could move freely throughout the mainland. Still, since Americans could not always distinguish between Puerto Ricans and Mexicans or were simply unclear on the vicissitudes of immigration law, the former could sometimes be mistaken for the latter and asked to produce documentation of their legal status....

Despite their seemingly favored status as citizens, then, Puerto Ricans bumped up against the limits of citizenship as racialized subjects. As racially foreign, recent arrivals, they were deemed inauthentic, unequal members of mainland society. Their legal citizenship was frequently challenged and brought into question.... The claims to citizenship of Puerto Ricans were sharply circumscribed by their racial difference, colonial status, perceived inferiority, and the very poverty that such unequal citizenship perpetuated....

★ ★ ★

But if Mexican and Puerto Rican migrants were subject to different types of regulation based on distinct politico-juridical status, ultimately, their historical twin labor flows, which brought them to urban and rural communities in the Midwest in the postwar years, also brought them in contact with one another. In postwar Chicago—in the workplace, the schools, the neighborhood streets, in the city writ large—ethnic Mexicans and Puerto Ricans ... were two Spanish-speaking populations navigating the same urban terrain.

 # FURTHER READING

Luis Alvarez, *The Power of the Zoot: Youth Culture and Resistance during World War II* (2009).

Rina Benmayor, Ana Juarbe, Celia Alvarez, and Blanca Vázquez, "Stories to Live By: Continuity and Change in Three Generations of Puerto Rican Women," *Oral History Review* 16 (1988), 1–46.

Elizabeth R. Escobedo, *From Coveralls to Zoot Suits: The Lives of Mexican American Women on the World War II Home Front* (2013).

Erasmo Gamboa, *Mexican Labor and World War II: Braceros in the Pacific Northwest, 1942–1947* (1990).

Ruth Glasser, *Aquí me quedo: Puerto Ricans in Connecticut/Puertorriqueños en Connecticut* (1997).

Thomas A. Guglielmo, "Fighting for Caucasian Rights: Mexicans, Mexican Americans, and the Transnational Struggle for Civil Rights in World War II Texas," *Journal of American History* 92, no. 4 (2006), 1212–1237.

Félix V. Matos Rodríguez and Linda C. Delgado, eds., *Puerto Rican Women's History: New Perspectives* (1998).

Eduardo Pagan, *Murder at the Sleepy Lagoon: Zoot Suits, Race, and Riot in Wartime L.A.* (2003).

Gina M. Pérez, *The Near Northwest Side Story: Migration Displacement and Puerto Rican Families*, (2004).

Catherine S. Ramírez, *The Woman in the Zoot Suit: Gender, Nationalism, and the Cultural Politics of Memory* (2009).

Mérida M. Rúa, *A Grounded Identidad: Making New Lives in Chicago's Puerto Rican Neighborhoods* (2012).

Vicki L. Ruiz and John R. Chávez, eds., *Memories and Migrations: Mapping Boricua and Chicana Histories* (2008).

Carmen Teresa Whalen, *From Puerto Rico to Philadelphia: Puerto Rican Workers and Postwar Economies* (2002).

CHAPTER 9

Building Communities in the World War II and Postwar Era

During the post–World War II era, Puerto Ricans and ethnic Mexicans continued their community building efforts and sought to claim recognition and full rights in U.S. society. Latina/o activism surged as veterans felt entitled to demand full democratic and citizenship rights at home after fighting for freedom abroad. Returning GIs joined civil rights activists to press for educational, legal, and voting reforms that would remove the barriers that made Latinas and Latinos second-class citizens. Latinas addressed the issues confronting their children, communities, and neighborhoods in public, vocal, and organized ways. Youth continued to assert their own identities and increasingly their own definitions of citizenship and belonging, forming their own groups during this era.

Yet the patriotism of the war era and the domestic cold war that emerged in the immediate aftermath of World War II changed the context of Latina/o activism. Rampant anticommunism squelched the radical activism of 1930s, as government officials sought to weed out "communists" and "communist sympathizers," and as some politicians fanned the flames of fear, hurling accusations of disloyalty and guilt by association. Hearings and trials were held. Teachers, government employees, and others lost their jobs. Labor unions and community organizations purged members considered too "leftist." Some Latina/o groups were conservative, while others succumbed to the pressures of the times to conform politically.

Still, by invoking patriotism and American ideals of democracy and equality, Latinos and Latinas highlighted the contradictions of fighting for democracy overseas when democracy had not been fully achieved at home in the United States. Several community organizations gradually became radicalized as their initial efforts at liberal reform met with official intransigence and racist opposition. This chapter focuses on postwar Puerto Rican and Mexican American community activism, which laid the foundations for the social movements of the 1960s and 1970s.

DOCUMENTS

For Cubans, Puerto Ricans, and Mexican Americans, the years after World War II bridged long-established communities with increased migration during the 1950s. In Document 1, Afro-Cuban Melba Alvarado shares her reflections with historian Nancy Raquel Mirabal in a 1995 interview. Alvarado describes New York City's pan-Latino communities and relations between white Cubans and Afro-Cubans, hinting at shifts wrought by the Cuban Revolution and increased migration. In Document 2, Puerto Rican historian Virginia Sánchez Korrol writes autobiographically about growing up in the South Bronx. She depicts the strengths of the Puerto Rican community prior to World War II, the impact of the massive postwar migration, and how both motivated her to become an early chronicler of the community's history. Documents 3 and 4 highlight the contradictions that Mexican American veterans experienced. Document 3, a 1949 *New York Times* article, reveals the refusal of a Texas funeral parlor to provide services for a Mexican American veteran and the intervention of then-Senator Lyndon Johnson to secure his burial with full military honors in Arlington National Cemetery. The photograph in Document 4 depicts an American GI Forum float in a Veterans Day parade in Dodge City, Kansas. Demonstrating veterans' pride, the American GI Forum promoted education and equal educational opportunity, as part of the broader activism to assure full citizenship. Document 5, a 1951 *Los Angeles Times* article, reveals the domestic cold war context and language that set the stage for public debates and activism. Here, opponents equate public housing with "socialism." Document 6 is an excerpt from Puerto Rican scholar Andrés Torres' memoir. Depicting a scene on a New York City subway in 1960, he reveals both the challenges his deaf family confronted and the pride with which they challenged bias individually as incidents arose and collectively through a community group. In Document 7, Puerto Rican activist Antonia Pantoja describes the founding of ASPIRA in 1961 as her most important contribution. ASPIRA promotes education and equal educational opportunity, like the American GI Forum, indicating the importance that postwar groups placed on educational issues and activism.

1. Afro-Cuban Melba Alvarado Describes Relations between White Cubans and Afro-Cubans, 1940s to 1961

Since I came, I lived in Manhattan in 113th and Fifth Avenue until the early [19]40s, and then, we moved to the Bronx because we bought a house on Prospect Avenue....

Excerpts from interview with Melba Alvarado by Nancy Raquel Mirabal, July 30–31, 1995, New York City.

... [B]ehind this house where the club [Inter-American Cuban Club] is, this avenue was all trees full of jasmines, it was a very nice environment. All the houses, there were a lot of houses that they call "town houses" where a lot of Hebrew and the like lived. They had some very pretty houses and after the war they started to change. Some of the houses were being torn down, and then there were the projects and other type of housing and a lot of Saxons moved from the neighborhood and it started to transform into a Hispanic neighborhood....

When I came to the Bronx, there were already Hispanics, ... particularly more Cubans ... but ... not as many like now. There were still a lot of other nationalities but now it's almost completely Hispanic, the ones that have come are Hispanics and American people of color....

There were a lot of Puerto Ricans. That's what there was. Over "downtown," there were a lot of Spaniards.... I often went to 102nd and Madison where the Spanish club, Repertorio Casa Galicia, started, this was further down. Over here towards the Bronx, there has always been more of a Puerto Rican environment....

Yes, that was the neighborhood where a lot of Hispanics lived.... [T]here were a lot of Cubans in the Lenox Avenue neighborhood.... [T]here was La Milagrosa Church, 114th and Seventh. That was the Hispanics' church, and they gave the mass of each of the Hispanic countries' patron saints.... And there were a lot of Cubans, ... and a lot of Cubans of color too....

The white Cuban lived in the upper part of Manhattan....

I don't know what to tell you about the separation [of white Cubans and Cubans of color], it's that I had some very sad experiences those years, for example in the beginning of the 60s. When I came to this country, there was a woman named Julia Martínez, who was of color, who started to organize the mass of charity with other Cubans. And at the time, when I came to this country, they gave the mass in La Milagrosa, in 114th Street and Seventh Avenue. Back then I remember that it was an enormous hierarchy because a person of color who was a great musician, Alberto Socarras, played the flute and then the mass did not start until the Cuban consul, Quezada, arrived with his feathered hat and then mass started.... Everyone went to the masses. But they were organized by a woman of color and a group that she had, and I also helped her. And then it turned out that with time and the like, well it turned out that this woman moved to Cuba and a woman who worked in the church said to me, "Melba you have to become in charge of the masses." I was always in charge of the masses. And at that time, well, then the Cubans started to come migrating, and the propaganda started that the real life of charity was on 156th [Street] in La Esperanza church. And the whites began masses on 156th [Street] in La Esperanza church and then the blacks over there on 114th and Seventh Avenue. And it became divided. The priests became very upset because it had already become divided and it stopped being the masses that they were before....

This thing came about around [nineteen]-sixty or sixty-one, in the time of the revolution, when the migration started to come.

2. Puerto Rican Historian Virginia Sánchez Korrol Recalls Her "Intellectual Journey," 1940s to 1971

The sixth-floor, walkup apartment in the South Bronx represented the center of my universe. On that warm, spring-like day the world was close to war, but this factor had a minimum effect on the sweetness of life at that very moment. Following the customary morning routine, a breakfast of buttered bread and warm milk laced with coffee, I sat beside my mother on the red, crushed velvet sofa set opposite tall twin windows that overlooked the neighboring tenement rooftops. The scarlet cushion fabric rubbed against the backs of my legs, making me itch and I gently shuffled my calves from side to side. "¿Qué dice, Mami? ¿Qué dice?" I repeated with four-year-old persistence.... A slight hesitation, then concentrating on the page before her, [my mother] slowly related the comic strip antics of Archie and Veronica, and then Dagwood and Blondie. Gradually, index finger pointing the way, she reached my favorite—Little Lulu. She read in measured, heavily accented English, pronouncing each syllable as surely her third grade teacher in Mayagüez, Puerto Rico, had taught her to do.

If mother and I fully comprehended the funnies' alien words, harsh-sounding linguistic obstacles that conveyed a popular pastime in American culture, I cannot remember for sure. But what was clearly evident was that the cultural lessons I was determined to unlock in that foreign tongue held not an inkling of my own people's proud heritage. It would distance me for a long time from developing an appreciation for the connections between ancestral women on distant shores and those who, like me, would reach maturity in diaspora.

With time and a zealous Catholic school education, I became proficient in the English language. The written word flooded into my home via magazines, newspapers, and the treasured comic books my father salvaged while cleaning out the trains that came into Pennsylvania Station. Before my tenth birthday, small sister in tow, I would barge into the local public library hauling off every book within the limits of my restricted children's card. And while I reveled in this newly discovered world of words and wisdom, heroic adventures, time travel, distressed damsels, and foreign lands, not one book ever told me about me.

It was precisely because experiences like mine were common among the children of the pioneer migrant generation of Puerto Ricans who came to live in New York City during the twenties and thirties that heritage and education were of prime concern in pre–World War II communities....

... At the age of seven I was enrolled in the local parochial school.... Private schooling was made possible through my mother's sacrifices; her careful squirreling away of nickels and dimes made me feel guilty when I did not perform well. Beyond the protection of the home and familiar barrio streets, my initial encounters with ethnic diversity and multiculturalism happened in this school and opened new horizons. Before I realized it, I was "being raised" Irish Catholic!

... It happened almost automatically when you attended St. Anselm's Roman Catholic School in the South Bronx, at the dawning of the great population shifts from Puerto Rico to New York City.... St. Anselm's ... boasted a predominantly Irish American student population, a smaller concentration of Italian Americans, and an even less significant smattering of Puerto Ricans. Nurturing Irish antecedents and catering to a more established immigrant community, the school cultivated close ties to the old country and culture through its many activities....

... [T]he children the nuns taught ensured cultural and spiritual bonds between Ireland and America for decades to come.... I admired the tenacity of a people who so fiercely resisted acculturation. Engaged in the national business of Americanization, replete with civic duties, English-language dominance, democratic values, and worthy founding fathers, these teachers still *remembered* how to infuse pride in the "Old World" heritage. And so at some level I must have internalized the notion that you didn't have to give up one identity in order to assume another—that both strands could coexist without conflict. That understanding, however, would not manifest itself until I was much older.

Contradictions abounded for me and other Puerto Rican youngsters caught in an assimilationist one-way street. For the teachers and administrators, many of whom had not encountered a cohort of non-English-speaking youngsters in the classroom since the great immigrations of the early twentieth century, Puerto Rican children were virtually invisible; their rich multicultural and multiracial history, language, life-cycle commemorations, ritual kinships, and affirming institutions were inconsequential. Hundreds of Puerto Rican children became casualties of an Americanizing cultural onslaught that, coupled with intense wartime patriotism, absorbed them into a national ideal that promoted equality yet maintained a colonial stranglehold on Puerto Rico and sanctioned ethno-racial divisions on its own shores. Throughout those formative years I firmly embraced the American dream even as a nagging inner voice vacillated between my public and private beings.... For most of my generation who experienced this painful dilemma, survival would rest on selective adaptation; the ability to pick and choose cultural elements from both cultures, blending "American" and Puerto Rican ways of being into something unique called U.S. Puerto Rican, *Boricua,* or *Nuyorican.* But it was, nevertheless, a rough job for a kid....

In spite of the dedication of a few Puerto Rican professionals, by the time I entered high school in the mid-fifties, stereotypical attitudes and distortions about Puerto Ricans had increased. Almost from the first discernable Puerto Rican presence in the United States, articles reeked with negative portrayals of our communities.... Throughout the forties and fifties, the media referred to the group as the "Puerto Rican problem." ...

[N]egative and controversial writings titillated a reading public eager to believe the worst about the group. For young Puerto Ricans grappling with identity and self-worth, one of the most damaging was Oscar Lewis's *La Vida.* I borrowed a copy from the library and felt its portrayal of Puerto Ricans, especially women, was insulting. Touted as an objective anthropological study, it overgeneralized both the island and diasporic realities from the experiences of one poor extended family engaged in prostitution.... Despite claims of impartial scholarship, Lewis studied a small sample and used a San Juan ghetto, the city's unofficial red-light district, as a representative site....

Without doubt, such pervasive negativity affected the schooling of young Puerto Ricans....

... Absence from the curriculum, historical invisibility, negative stereotypes, and low teacher expectations meant that if I wanted to continue my education, to strive for that elusive American dream, I had to fight for it every step of the way.... I confronted the senior guidance counselors on the day before graduation.... Preferring to comment on my "poor choice" of lipstick color, the counselors condescendingly informed me about the existence of a free city university system with a campus right there in ... Brooklyn.... Left to research college admissions on my own, ... I nonetheless became the first in the family to attend.... By the time I earned the baccalaureate degree, a mere 1 percent of the graduating classes of the entire CUNY system were Puerto Rican.

My first impression of Brooklyn College, nestled in what seemed to me a bucolic oasis that defied its urban location, was everything I could hope for.... Nonetheless, obstacles appeared at every turn. My bosses in the factory where I worked as a bookkeeper would have preferred that I dedicate all my time to their business, and "What are you going to college for? You'll only get married anyway" became a constant refrain. Few of my neighborhood friends were in school, so there was no one who could understand what I was doing. In time, I became socially and intellectually distant from family and friends as I struggled to open unknown paths for myself....

... I soon discovered the hallowed halls were neither immune from the ethno-racial prejudice of the period nor eager to question social science dogma. In retrospect, I found it difficult to reconcile a nurturing home, the hub of an extended family, and community with social science rhetoric that frequently reinforced a notion of Puerto Rican downward mobility. The pervasive invisibility of anything Latino silently echoed its very absence throughout my education. I was drawn to piecing together evidence to counteract negative Puerto Rican images in the literature....

[In 1971] I sought admission to graduate studies in the History Department at the State University of New York at Stony Brook with a well-defined agenda in mind: to tell the story of the New York Puerto Rican community from my parents' pioneering generation to the present, to set straight the historical record, and to ensure that Puerto Ricans would forever find themselves in the national narrative.... And so began my intellectual journey into the study of Puerto Ricans, Latin Americans, and U.S. Latinos....

3. Mexican–American GI Denied Burial in Texas, 1949

WASHINGTON, Jan. 12—A soldier's funeral and burial were arranged today by the Government of the United States for Felix Longoria, late private, Infantry, Army of the United States, who died in action on Luzon in the Philippines.

He will receive full military honors, in Arlington National Cemetery, where lie some of the more illustrious dead....

Private Longoria's widow, Beatrice, and such of his friends as live in his little town of Three Rivers, Tex., had reported some difficulty in having funeral services there for him.

Dr. Hector P. Garcia informed Senator Lyndon D. Johnson of Texas, in fact, that the manager of the one undertaking parlor in Three Rivers had refused the use of his facilities with the explanation: "Other white people object to the use of the funeral home by people of Mexican origin."

Dr. Garcia is president of a veterans' organization known as the American GI Forum.

"In our estimation," he telegraphed to Senator Johnson, "this action in Three Rivers is in direct contradiction of those same principles for which this American soldier made the supreme sacrifice in giving his life for his country and for the same people who now deny him the last funeral rites deserving of any American hero regardless of his origin."

Mr. Johnson telephoned to old friends in South Texas and, he said, found that the case in its substance had been correctly reported. As a member of the Senate Armed Services Committee he got in touch with the high military authorities and made arrangements for a different sort of burial.

He sent then to Dr. Garcia a telegram of his own, which said in part:

"I deeply regret to learn that the prejudice of some individuals extends even beyond this life.

"I have no authority over civilian funeral homes, nor does the Federal Government."

"However, I have today made arrangements to have Felix Longoria reburied with full military honors in Arlington National Cemetery here at Washington where the honored dead of our nation's wars rest. Or, if his family prefers to have his body interred nearer his home, he can be reburied at Fort Sam Houston National Military Cemetery at San Antonio (Tex.). There will be no cost."

Mr. Johnson then asked Private Longoria's widow to indicate her preference "before his body is unloaded from an Army transport at San Francisco on Jan. 13."

Mrs. Beatrice Longoria, in a telegram to the Senator, then closed these exchanges.

"Humbly grateful," she said, "for your kindness in my hour of humiliation and suffering. Gladly accept your offer for reburial of my husband at Arlington National Cemetery. Please arrange for direct shipment to Washington. Forever grateful for your kindness." ...

Private Longoria was born on April 19, 1919. He began active military service on the anniversary of an old armistice, Nov. 11, 1944. He fell less than a year later—on June 16, 1945, in the last months of action in the Philippines. This is all that could be learned from the War Department records available here.

"I am sorry," Mr. Johnson said, "about the funeral home at Three Rivers. But there is, after all, a fine national funeral home, though of a rather different sort, out at Arlington."

4. Photo of American GI Forum Float at a Veterans Day Parade in Dodge City, Kansas, 1950s

An American GI Forum float at a Veterans Day parade in Dodge City, Kansas. The AGIF motto, "Education is our freedom and freedom should be everybody's business," indicates the emphasis the Forum has always placed on learning as a means to social betterment. From the group's early days, local chapters organized back-to-school drives, attendance campaigns, and scholarship programs, while the national worked through legal channels for equal educational opportunity.

SOURCE: *Dr. Hector P. García Papers; Special Collections and Archives*, Bell Library, Texas A&M University–Corpus Christi.

Reprinted in Henry A. J. Ramos, *The American G.I. Forum: In Pursuit of the Dream, 1948–1983* (Houston: Arte Piblico Press, 1998), p. 33.

5. Opponents of Public Housing Decry "Socialism" in Los Angeles, 1951

The label of Socialism was applied repeatedly to proposed Federal Housing projects for Los Angeles yesterday as scores of persons appeared before the City Council to appeal from decisions of the City Planning Commission approving sites for the government-subsidized building programs.

Nine sites involving 10,000 units to cost $100,000,000 were in the proceedings. The Council chambers were packed as the hearings went into their second day and the city legislative body held one of its first all-day sessions in recent years, hoping to reach an end of the protests.

Particularly vigorous in presenting their case were residents and businessmen from the Rose Hill area where 2000 units, some of them to be incorporated in 13-story buildings, are scheduled to be erected in what is now a single-family residence zone.

"There are many ways that we can handle the housing job and do better through private enterprise—ways far superior to this proposed socialized concentration camp," said one speaker for the Rose Hill delegation. The Rose Hill group even embellished their presentation with a series of stereoptican slides, showing homes which would be demolished if the housing site were approved.

The presentation brought from Councilman Ed Davenport, admitted proponent of the housing projects, the statement that "this is the most forceful and convincing presentation I have listened to in my six years of sitting of the City Council."

Byron Jones, director of the Montecito Hills Improvement Association, was particularly eloquent upon the charge of Socialism.

He said in part:

"The real issue that should govern our decision is the issue between private enterprise and Socialism ... in summation, the questions are, 'Shall we light the match that spreads the conflagration which will destroy private homes and private enterprise in our city? Shall you gentlemen be *the guards at the gate who* tear it down to permit the entry of a Trojan horse which will destroy our American ideal of American privately owned homes?'" ...

H. J. F. Hanemann, a civil engineer, ... labeled the Rose Hill project as "contrary to the city's master plan of zoning and a movement which would perpetuate Socialism in Los Angeles."...

6. Puerto Rican Scholar, Andrés Torres, Reflects on Being "A Hearing Son," 1960

"STEP LIVELY, STEP LIVELY." The conductor's command came sharply over the loudspeaker as they jumped aboard. Life had taught them to regard

---

Andrés Torres, *Signing in Puerto Rican: A Hearing Son and His Deaf Family* (Washington, DC: Gallaudet University Press, 2009), pp. 1–5.

punctuality as a vital habit. Too often they had been overlooked or left behind, so they were already poised at the doors as the subway slowed to a halt. My parents were going downtown to the Friday meeting of the Puerto Rican Society for the Catholic Deaf. Together with their friends Isaura and Oliverio, they were riding the A train to the meeting hall, located in the central office of the New York City Archdiocese, near St. Patrick's Cathedral. I was with them as usual. The year was 1960.

Pop worked as a stock clerk in the garment center where his weekdays were spent packing men's shirts into cardboard boxes. His hands were callused from the daily handling of those boxes, and the years of lifting and lugging molded his body into an athletic frame. He arrived home gritty and tired, but on those Friday evenings of the Deaf Society, of which Pop was president, he was a transformed man. In his grey suit and blue tie, his face sweetly scented with his favorite lotion, he could have passed for someone well beyond his true station in life. As president of an organization, he might as well dress up for the role....

The five of us worked our way through the busy car and in the far corner Mom and Isaura, dressed up and perfumed, found seats. They fit snugly in a double seat, while I grabbed an empty spot some distance from them.... Fortunately, I had already convinced my parents that a twelve-year-old boy didn't need to be making a fashion statement for these meetings. With my blue striped polo shirt, unadorned cotton slacks and Converse sneakers, I was good to go. Pop and Oliverio stood nearby, holding onto a silver pole where there were already two men. As the train pulled out of the station Pop and Oliverio faced each other.

"Do you think there'll be many people tonight?" Oliverio wondered, in signs.

"Maybe twenty-five to thirty. It will be a good crowd," Pop responded with his hands.

Signing on a subway that alternates between a stop-and-go crawl and a bouncing sprint is not the easiest thing to do. Elbows and knees were in constant motion, as the men braced themselves against the gleaming silver pole. Each would've been grateful for the use of a third arm.

"We have a lot of business to discuss: the credit union and planning for the dinner, and Monsignor Lynch wants to talk to us. Then we will have the movie. I hope we do not waste time on silly arguments." Pop liked to run the meetings efficiently and leave time for socializing.

They kept the signs to themselves, trying to conceal the conversation like poker players sheltering their hands. Pop didn't like to verbalize loudly or put his gestures on display, as did other deaf people I knew. Nevertheless, the other two men at the pole were startled; they weren't sure what to do. I had seen this before and I knew what they were thinking: Is it wrong to look? Or do you just pretend they're not there?

These two just stayed where they were, fidgeting and looking away. Pop had been through this often and he didn't care. He wasn't going to be a zombie on the subway. On he went, signing with Oliverio, discreetly, but without shame. Next to me Mom and Isaura were gossiping too, *chismeando* with their hands. As soon as we'd jumped aboard they'd gone straight for the corner seats, to avoid the view of other passengers. They conversed with their hands down on their laps, making only the subtlest of facial movements. I was accustomed to this scene: watching my parents sign in the subway, and watching the hearing people watch them.

Pop and Oliverio continued, as did Mom and Isaura, oblivious to the attention gathering about them. By now the other passengers, not just the two men at the silver pole, noticed the deaf people talking. Then, toward the center of the car, a group of young kids had noticed:

"Hey, look over there," one of them said. "Look over there at the deaf and dumb people!"

Then came the bulging eyes and giggles.

"Oh yeah, look." Another chimed in, pointing at my parents.

A third one let out, "Hey I can do that, can't you?"

They threw their hands about, competing for the loudest laughs. Any exaggerated movement would do: fingers in acrobatic maneuvers, clownish faces, grunting noises. Standing and sitting, they were bunched together and making like they were trading signs. They pretended it was an inside joke, but they must've known my parents could see what was going on.

… The train raced downtown as the show continued. And in the audience I saw a variety of reactions: embarrassment, pity, and fear. I perceived varieties of anger as well. There was anger directed at the troublemakers. And there was another anger reserved for my parents, for starting the whole mess in the first place.

Up to now, I was a bystander, seated apart from them.

"Ahtay!" (I was known as "Andy" in the hearing world, but "Ahtay," with the accent on "tay" is how it sounded in the Deaf world.) Pop waved at me to get my attention. He said for me to get the time from someone.

Of course, Pop knew the time. What he wanted was not the time but for everyone else to know that I was with him. I asked an elderly lady sitting across the aisle. I always preferred approaching older people. I signed the time to Pop; he told me to thank the elderly lady; she told me to tell Pop he's welcome; Pop nodded his head at her, with the trademark grin that barely curled the corners of his mouth. He raised his hand in thanks and the lady smiled at me.

Then the passengers turned to me, interpreting the scene…. And now the confusion deepened, the faces changed again, and I guessed at what they were thinking: "Hey, I don't get this. Don't deaf people have deaf children?" …

I remember what went through my mind in these situations: "Sometimes hearing people, they get so stupid. Like the kids on this train, making fun of my parents with their phony sign language."

Once, earlier, on another subway ride when people were staring at my parents, I felt so bad for them that I got up and screamed, "Hey, what's the matter with you? You never saw deaf people before? They're just regular people, you know!"

… You should've seen them when they realized I could hear and talk *and* sign. How quickly their faces changed. But I knew when it was all over, and they were home, they'd laugh themselves silly. To think they were fooled like that! So yelling or making a scene every time wasn't worth the trouble. I learned that from Pop. He might give a dirty look, but that was about it. But that Friday night, when I was an eighth grader and the kids were mimicking my parents and their friends, something else happened....

As the train screeched into 59th Street, where we would switch to the D line, we were ready to get off. Finally. On the way out, Mom poked at my shoulder: "Ahtay."

She pointed to the kids so they could see her then she angrily signed to me what she wanted them to know. Then she crouched her short, chubby body in their direction, flashed a menacing look that left no doubt what she thought of them, and threw them the middle finger of her right hand.

The kids recoiled, giggled nervously, then stopped laughing.

Mom poked again at my shoulder, ordering me to translate.

I relayed her words. "She says God will punish you for making fun of us; she says your children will be born deaf."

7. Puerto Rican Activist, Antonia Pantoja, on the Founding of ASPIRA, 1961

If you asked me, "What was the most important and impacting work that you have ever done?" I would reply, "The founding of ASPIRA." ASPIRA occupies a very special place in my heart....

This time period actually spans over seven years, ending in 1961....

The original idea that I presented to Dr. [Frank] Horne was called "New Leaders in New York." It was to organize youths into clubs that would become the vehicles to encourage them to find their identity, learn leadership skills by working on problems that their communities suffered, complete high school, and enter college to pursue a career that would allow them to give back to their community. The idea had germinated in my mind as a result of various experiences that I had when I arrived in New York. The idea began to haunt my thoughts after having heard discussions from Puerto Rican high school students who attended the youth conferences that PRACA [Puerto Rican Association for Community Affairs] was holding. These conferences were organized and held by the youths themselves, who were the leaders and speakers telling us how powerless and insignificant they were made to feel by their classmates and teachers. The students discussed their fear of speaking in their classes, their shame because of their native language, their fear of the gangs from other ethnic groups, and their fear of the police. I was deeply concerned about what I was hearing.

The implementation of my ideas would not come easily. I had to pursue many different persons and approaches before I could succeed....

My idea was to ... provide a way for their "hanging out together" (the clubs), following a behavior that was natural to their age group. In the clubs, they would learn about their culture and the country of their parents, and also learn how to survive in the school and the neighborhood. The club would provide opportunities to develop feelings of self-worth and appreciation for their

Excerpt, pages 90–109 is reprinted with permission from the publisher of "Memoir of a Visionary: Antonia Pantoja" by Antonia Pantoja (© 2002 Arte Público Press-University of Houston).

culture as they learned leadership skills to work in their communities. The clubs would substitute for the gangs that were already becoming popular protective groups for Italian, Polish, and black youths....

We needed to design ways to attack the root causes of these myriad fires and begin to develop in the community other people who would join the battle at different points in the problems. The approach I prepared suggested two roads: the immediate help brought by youth clubs that could engage in giving attention to selected problems; and the longer road that would develop educated leaders committed to the resolution of the problems at policy levels, in the political and economic spheres of the total society....

After months of work, our group had prepared a philosophy, a mission, objectives, and a work plan. Everyone agreed that this new leadership program should not become a service agency; instead, in form and methods, it should be a movement. However, we all were wise enough to understand that it had to render some service if it was to be successful in raising funds.

The very important act of naming the project engaged the group in discussions that clearly indicated a philosophical position and a profound understanding that to work with youth we had to impart values, optimism, and the decision to succeed. We wanted an upbeat name, one word to express belief in one's self. The word *aspira* was finally selected. It was chosen because to aspire is upbeat. We all wished the meaning would be "I will aspire and I will attain." The Spanish command form ASPIRA, of the verb *aspirar*, was perfect.

We made fast progress in organizing ASPIRA....

In the autumn of 1961, we received letters from the five foundations accepting our proposals and assigning funds. The Forum board called a meeting.... [T]hey all concluded that I should resign my position with the city of New York to come and direct ASPIRA....

The club programs grew to be very impressive in membership size, number, and impact. The ASPIRA Club Federation became a very powerful organization with very successful programs.... The important fact about the model of the work in clubs was that it was invented by the youth....

The reader will understand why ASPIRA became the most important work of my life. In terms of numbers, ASPIRA of New York alone, from 1963, to 1999, can easily be shown to have touched the lives of approximately 36,000 young people from Puerto Rican and other Latino groups....

... Today, there are seven ASPIRAs: in Connecticut, New York, Pennsylvania, Illinois, Florida, and Puerto Rico. They are served by a national office in Washington, D.C.

 # ESSAYS

Puerto Rican and Mexican American community activism in the postwar era was shaped both by the patriotism invigorated by being a country at war and by the cold war, which took root in the immediate aftermath of World War II. In the first essay, Lorrin Thomas, professor of history at Rutgers University,

Camden, examines how Puerto Ricans and their advocates invoked citizenship rights to defend their interests in postwar New York City. Within the cold war context, a liberal discourse emphasized the individual. Thus, Puerto Rican students confronting ethnic attacks in high school, educational reformers, and Puerto Rican community activists all focused on individuals and citizenship rights. Increasingly, Puerto Rican youth asserted their own sense of the meaning of citizenship and began to shift the discourse to one that also included the rights of groups to be recognized as belonging in American society. Challenging the pervasive negative portrayals of Puerto Ricans, these community activists laid the groundwork for the increasingly radical activism of the late 1960s and 1970s.

In the second essay, Ronald W. López II, professor of Chicano and Latino Studies at Sonoma State University, analyzes the efforts of Chavez Ravine's predominantly Mexican American residents to remain in their homes as the city of Los Angeles invoked eminent domain to remove them from their homes and their community to build public housing in its place. López reveals that women were the most vocal activists in resisting the government's plans. Testifying in city hearings and writing letters of protest, women used a language of "patriotic post-war motherhood," emphasizing their citizenship and their sacrifices to U.S. war efforts as the wives and mothers of veterans. From their perspective, they represented American values of patriotism and home owner-ship, while the government and commercial interests were behaving in ways "un-American."

Puerto Rican Youth Activism in Postwar New York City

LORRIN THOMAS

In 1951, a group of Puerto Rican students from Benjamin Franklin High School (BFHS) in East Harlem wrote a plaintive letter to *El Diario* asking the editors to publicize a series of attacks they were suffering at school. The students reported that members of Italian gangs at Franklin were targeting Puerto Rican boys, stealing their lunch money, and beating them up to the point that several, they said, had left the school in fear. "We believe that we have the right to study without being harassed by anyone," the students wrote, "since we are American citizens and our parents pay taxes just like [the Italians] do." A couple of months later, *El Diario* reported again on gang attacks against Puerto Ricans at Franklin, … and remarking on the principal's handling of the conflicts internally. Leonard Covello, who had steered Franklin through a number of previous anti–Puerto Rican incidents as principal of the progressive and multiethnic high school since he founded it in 1934, made no public statements about the harassment. He did, however, speak on the issue to the school's Club Borinquén, which he had helped organize in the late thirties following the first wave of ethnic conflict

Lorrin Thomas, "'Juan Q. Citizen,' Aspirantes, and Young Lords: Youth Activism in a New World Order," in *Puerto Rican Citizen: History and Political Identity in Twentieth-Century New York City* (Chicago: University of Chicago Press, 2010), pp. 200–244.

between Puerto Rican and Italian youth in East Harlem. In their discussion of the injustice of these attacks, both the students and Covello framed the problem as one of the denial of individual rights in a liberal framework. That is, their status as citizens should protect the students from discrimination at the very least, giving them the freedom to study and thereby, they implied, the opportunity to become even better citizens.

For the Puerto Rican students, this was a new kind of assertion, expressive of the second generation's efforts both to gain a foothold in the city's social landscape and to demand their individual rights as aspiring members of the mainstream. In terms of relations with the Italian community, on the other hand, their lament was old news: members of both communities testified to the Italians' anti–Puerto Rican sentiment dating back to their first contact in the twenties....

[W]ith the postwar migration from Puerto Rico still escalating, Italian Americans all over East Harlem expressed resentment about the changes in their community, as did New Yorkers throughout the city who feared the "dangerous influx." Puerto Rican youth continued to bear a heavy burden of the anti–Puerto Rican fury on the streets. Throughout the 1950s, Puerto Ricans under the age of twenty-five comprised New York's most rapidly expanding demographic group, so they were ready targets of the public's anxiety about a postwar world in flux. Widespread fears about young Puerto Ricans and their fitness as American citizens had developed alongside the national obsession with youth, especially those with dark skin, that dominated the media in the decade following the "zoot suit" riots in 1943.... While Covello and some of his progressive colleagues had been working to counter the vilification of poor youth since the thirties, their efforts on behalf of the growing Puerto Rican population touched only a small fraction of the city's migrants. A larger number of Puerto Rican children and families were drawn into New York's education and social service institutions via the more dominant liberal agendas that would, by the mid-fifties, describe the ideal new migrant as "Juan Q. Citizen." Adult migrants were barraged with messages from the Migration Division and other social service agencies about voting and learning English, as well as about comportment in the workplace and proper standards of dress and housekeeping, and younger Puerto Ricans were targeted by liberal educators who hoped to provide the most promising students with the tools to embark on middle-class lives. The Puerto Rican students at Franklin who publicized their experience of discrimination in 1951 would have heard dozens of versions, sometimes indistinguishable from one another, of these progressive and liberal messages directed at youth.

Shortly after the gang harassment incidents at Benjamin Franklin, in a conformist cold war milieu that intensified nationwide fears about juvenile delinquency, a growing number of Puerto Rican youth leaders began to take the reins from their white liberal allies, defining themselves as the future leaders of their community. They worked to create a new image of Puerto Rican youth, plotting a path of selective assimilation—and navigating around obstacles like *West Side Story*'s gang stereotypes or the publicity surrounding the Capeman murders—to be recognized as equal members of postwar American society.

Theirs was not a direct challenge to the assimilationist ideal of turning the Puerto Rican migrant into "Juan Q. Citizen," although it was an assertion of their power to articulate the ideals of American citizenship for themselves.

Gradually, over the course of the fifties, this first generation of young Puerto Rican leaders began to emphasize demands for recognition as a group alongside more standard claims for individual rights. And, by the early sixties, many of the young mainstream leaders began to challenge the political and institutional assumptions of the social liberals who supported them, for the first time making colonialism part of the mainstream conversation about Puerto Rican advancement in New York....

★ ★ ★

While the postwar emphasis on rehabilitating delinquents and training citizens to fight the cold war dominated the city's education agenda, Covello and Benjamin Franklin faculty quietly if less optimistically persisted in their intercultural programming and bolstered support of Puerto Rican students, whose numbers increased every year between 1947 and 1955. By the time the first big wave of postwar migrants began settling in East Harlem in 1946, Covello and other BFHS staff had modified most aspects of the school programming to include issues concerning Puerto Rican children and their families. Club Borinquén continued to sponsor regular dances and cultural events, and by 1948, it had established the annual "Latin American Festival," which quickly attracted high-profile artists, writers, and performers from El Barrio, who donated their time "for the aid of the poor Puerto Rican student." ... His progressive advocacy notwithstanding, Covello never rejected traditional postwar educational ideals. He noted proudly, for instance, that "we are interested in preparing these [Puerto Rican] boys for active participation and useful citizenship in the U.S."

Their agenda was not limited to Franklin. Partly due to Covello's advocacy on the issue, by 1951 there were ten bilingual teachers in the handful of schools with the highest Puerto Rican concentration.... As early as 1936, following the controversy over Puerto Rican children's IQ scores, Covello also argued that the standard IQ testing practices in the United States were not valid for "foreign-born" children, including Puerto Rican migrants. In 1947, Covello was still demanding that current tests of academic achievement and mental ability for Puerto Rican students should be reevaluated, and "appropriate instruments of measurement should be developed for [them]." ...

During these first years of New York's anti–Puerto Rican backlash, Leonard Covello was second only to Vito Marcantonio in terms of actively fostering the "mutual respect" that so many white liberals talked about. Covello addressed other New York City school principals on what he saw as their obligation to the city's Puerto Rican families: "The post war world requires of citizens and teachers more than mere understanding of their neighbors—immediate or distant. It demands, in addition, an understanding, mutual respect, and a mutual sharing of our cultures. [We have] an opportunity for gaining such an understanding of our fellow Americans—the *Puerto Ricans.*" During the summer of 1947, Covello traveled to Puerto Rico to deliver a series of lectures at the

University of Puerto Rico.... Covello visited twenty or so towns in a quest to "get to know" the island from which so many of his students had emigrated, hand-delivering scores of letters written by Benjamin Franklin students to their friends and family. [T]he *New York Herald Tribune* praised the principal who "walked the walk" of progressive educators. As far away as Pittsburgh, the *Courier* ... tout[ed] the school's "fine program for Puerto Ricans," which offered a "new approach" to educating "foreign youth."

It was no surprise that the nuances of Covello's work, his progressive and pluralist approach to "education for citizenship" that challenged the orthodoxies of traditional assimilationism, were absent from the discussion of what he was actually attempting to do in East Harlem. Although his vision of Puerto Ricans as "just like other immigrants" was in many respects similar to the liberal social service ideal of training the migrant to become "Juan Q. Citizen," Covello's advocacy on behalf of Puerto Rican youth—as in the case of the aggrieved students in 1951, among countless others—helped foster their leadership skills independent of the social service establishment. Ultimately, this generation of young leaders would contribute substantially to the challenging of the old liberal orthodoxies via new discourses of group rights in the 1960s.

★ ★ ★

In 1952, the Mayor's Advisory Committee on Puerto Rican Affairs established a scholarship fund for Puerto Rican students, explaining its primary goal as "to promote maximum integration of our citizens of Puerto Rican background into the general New York citizenry in the shortest possible time." Their publicity materials did not actually use the "Juan Q. Citizen" phrase that the Migration Division included in at least one of its pamphlets in that era, but the idea was the same: assimilation facilitated by a shared national citizenship.... Emphasizing that the scholarship was about more than just educational achievement, a 1953 press release explained the committee's vision of the "next steps" of the scholarship fund: housing; "integration," focusing especially on English-language proficiency; "mutual understanding" and civility; employment; and building a Puerto Rican leadership base in New York.

Around the same time, the Riverside Neighborhood Assembly, a liberal organization on the Upper West Side, established a more experimental leadership program, involving exchanges of promising youth between Manhattan and Puerto Rico. Upon their return, the "Goodwill Ambassadors" would write a weekly newsletter on issues in the Puerto Rican community and speak to New York–area youth groups about their experiences on the island.... The Board of Education's experimental "Higher Horizons" program was part of the same constellation of initiatives geared toward supporting minority children, and it received praise from Puerto Rican educational activists. Unlike other programs that focused on training participants in practices of "good citizenship," which proliferated in the first decade after the war, Higher Horizons provided for educational enrichment broadly conceived: more guidance counselors, remedial reading and math teachers, and specialty teachers in its target schools, as well as trips to the opera, the theater, and science laboratories.

The advocacy of liberals like Covello and the members of MACPRA was only a small part of the story of efforts to change educational outcomes for—and the public image of—Puerto Rican youth in the fifties. Early in the decade, young migrants themselves, including a small but growing cohort of college students, sought to strengthen their community and take control of the negative discourses about Puerto Ricans in New York by creating youth-based leadership initiatives and youth-run community organizing campaigns. Certainly the public's focus on juvenile delinquency helped galvanize Puerto Rican youth to promote their own agenda of "civic pride" for Puerto Ricans by the mid-fifties. But the force of youth activism had more to do with demographic change in the Puerto Rican community. Second and third generations were now attending high schools and colleges, and growing numbers of Puerto Rican youth were inspired to build networks and create alliances with existing community organizations to promote their own agendas for change....

Among the new generation of young Puerto Rican leaders in the 1950s, Antonia Pantoja would become the best known, although, as a migrant herself who arrived in New York in her twenties, her background was different from that of many of the second-generation members of her cohort. Soon after her arrival in the city near the end of World War II, Pantoja fell in with a multi-ethnic group of artists and radicals, lived downtown, and briefly attended the radical Jefferson School for a course on the "Marxist Interpretation of the History of Puerto Rico," a set of formative experiences more cosmopolitan than those of many of her contemporaries who spent their youth in New York's *barrios*. What Pantoja did share with the other young leaders of her generation, many of them students and activists at a number of New York's high schools and colleges, was a sense of anger at the discrimination and exclusion experienced by the people of her community and a determination to challenge the anti–Puerto Rican status quo.

Pantoja had been a youth worker at a community center, a job that was a point of entry for many young activists by the early sixties. She then became one of the leaders of the first formally organized, youth-led Puerto Rican organization in New York, the Hispanic Young Adult Association (HYAA), while she was an undergraduate at Hunter College in the early 1950s. HYAA's goal was to create a forum to bring together the energies of an emerging cohort of activist Puerto Rican youth. One of its central objectives was to influence the images of Puerto Ricans circulating in New York, images that HYAA felt were being "managed" somewhat ineffectively by liberals in the Migration Division and in the city's educational and social service establishment. A growing and increasingly divisive debate emerged within HYAA's leadership between, on the one hand, a moderate, liberal, and nonpolitical response to elevating the community through its youth, and, on the other hand, a more politicized faction that sought to call attention to the ways in which existing institutions and city officials were failing to meet the needs of the Puerto Rican community, and young Puerto Ricans in particular....

This split was partly responsible for the emergence, out of HYAA, of the Puerto Rican Association for Community Affairs (PRACA), in 1956. Pantoja recalled that the motivation for the change in the organization's name came from a desire to make the organization explicitly a Puerto Rican one, a group that would proudly assert its Puerto Rican identity rather than retaining the more vaguely assimilationist label "Hispanic." Though not officially organized to serve youth, PRACA was led by young Puerto Rican professionals and activists. Shortly after the creation of PRACA, Pantoja, who had gotten a master's degree in social work from New York University, was offered a staff position on the new Commission on Intergroup Relations. Her mentor there, Dr. Frank Horne, encouraged her in the creation of the Puerto Rican Forum, a larger and more powerful organization than PRACA. Pantoja modeled the Forum after a similar group that Horne had founded for young African Americans in the South and designed it to support both general institution building in the Puerto Rican community and the fostering of young leaders who would initiate Puerto Rican–run programs. Many of the participants in these groups described them as modeled after "uplift" and "community defense" groups like the NAACP.

Although this movement of youth activists was well under way before the Capeman murders in 1959, the incident, and the renewed flood of anti–Puerto Rican vitriol that followed, inspired a new flurry of organizing by young leaders focusing primarily on educational issues. A group calling itself the Hispanic Association Pro–Higher Education (HAPHE), founded in 1959, sponsored the first in a series of annual conferences for Puerto Rican youth that met throughout the sixties. The second Puerto Rican Youth Conference, in 1960, articulated a goal that still echoed with the Puerto Rican community's trauma following the Capeman incident: "to set a positive image to counter 'pathology and fear' to show the Puerto Rican as ambitious, with a desire and increasing ability to climb upwards, as have all past newcomers to the city." ...

In 1961, members of the Puerto Rican Forum's board of directors created a youth organization that Pantoja had envisioned, she recalled, since the mid-fifties, "an instrument to develop leaders from among our youth." They named the organization Aspira [See Document 7].... Though often accused—especially by Puerto Rican activists in the late sixties and early seventies—of promoting a conservative or assimilationist agenda, Aspira served as an early model of cultural pride and community autonomy that would become central to Puerto Rican community organizing in the sixties. Its programs, emphasizing educational skills and achievement and access to higher education, were indeed more moderate than radical, but its firm commitment to a Puerto Rican–run leadership structure ... and to the teaching of Puerto Rican history and culture marked Aspira as a challenger of the status quo within New York's social service networks.

Pantoja would later describe Aspira's relationship to the Puerto Rican social service sector, dominated by the Migration Division, as an uneasy one. She acknowledged that the Office of the Commonwealth "believed that their mission was to help the community solve its problems" but said that it "was equally concerned with maintaining a position of control over New York Puerto Ricans and keeping the leadership in the hands of the government of Puerto Rico." Moreover, she remembered its approach to community as one limited by racism:

"The leadership of the [Migration Division] office espoused integration and assimilation, but I knew that only those of us who were white-skinned had any hope of this kind of acceptance." ...

... [M]any Aspirante leaders, along with other Puerto Ricans, [pursued] bilingual education.... (And in 1974, Aspira filed a lawsuit against the New York City Board of Education, charging that teaching non-English-speaking children in a language they did not understand violated their constitutional rights.) Gradually, Aspirantes' critical stance about Puerto Ricans' educational experience led to more aggressive positions on the teaching of Puerto Rican history and culture.... In spite of its identity by the late sixties as a moderate and even "assimilationist" organization, Aspira's young members considered it their mission to challenge this prevailing orthodoxy concerning Puerto Rico and its people. It was not just about demanding individual rights for young Puerto Ricans to achieve "respect" in American society. More important, and increasingly, their struggle was about insisting on group justice—an argument for recognition that Jesús Colón, ahead of his time, was making already in the mid-fifties: "The community is struggling to express itself more forcefully, to unite itself, to gain recognition and the rights it is entitled to, in the city at large."

★ ★ ★

When the Board of Education named its new middle school enrichment program "Higher Horizons" in 1956, the presumption was that the many Puerto Rican students it served could look forward to greater opportunity and material gains in the near future. Although for some young Puerto Ricans—those who benefited from new bilingual teachers, social service support for their families, and the strong start of grassroots youth organizations like HYAA—the late fifties and early sixties did look brighter, most Puerto Rican children lived in households in which poverty and insecurity still outweighed opportunity....

Puerto Rican New Yorkers did not need the State Department of Labor or the Bureau of the Census to tell them how things were going on the ground. It was clear that their compatriots were losing the slight income gains they had made in the fifties, and losing the tenuous security and faint hopes for advancement they had nourished just a few years before. The early signs of these socioeconomic losses were alarming but not surprising, and they helped confirm the sense of mission that was already driving activists. Housing was still a persistent problem at the top of the agenda of many Puerto Rican community leaders in this decade, but it was education that became the real focal point. By 1960, with the implications of the *Brown* decision reverberating throughout northern cities, the politics of school integration mobilized parents and activists alike in New York. That year, residents of African American and Puerto Rican communities in Brooklyn, the Bronx, and Manhattan began pushing the Board of Education to site new schools in mixed-race areas or on the borders of more segregated neighborhoods, to encourage racial integration....

A more pressing issue than integration in the early sixties was the lack of any Puerto Rican, or even Hispanic, presence on the Board of Education. Puerto Rican children comprised almost 16 percent of the city's public school population in 1961, and they were the majority or near majority in over a dozen schools in both Manhattan and the Bronx, and in a handful of schools in Brooklyn. Lamenting that "there is no group so completely voiceless" in the city, the Puerto Rican Bar Association petitioned the mayor to appoint a school board member to ensure that the Puerto Rican community would "see [their] role changed from that of a voiceless subject of sociological thesis [*sic*] and studies, to that of equal citizens with a share in the policy making of a system so vital to themselves." ...

By the mid-sixties, activists working on education issues were also asking why so many black and Puerto Rican students were being pushed into vocational training schools instead of academic high schools.... [B]y 1965 African Americans and Puerto Ricans were suggesting that the failures of vocational education and a declining economy exposed the weaknesses, and perhaps the empty rhetoric, of President Lyndon Johnson's new War on Poverty. At an antipoverty conference early in 1965, Michael Harrington, whose 1962 book *The Other America* had painted a shocking portrait of poverty amid prosperity in the United States, joined Aspira's Antonia Pantoja in arguing that the War on Poverty needed to focus on youth.... Both criticized the tendency to steer poor teenagers toward vocational high schools ... ; indeed, one 1963 study cited by the *New York Amsterdam News* reported that over 80 percent of Puerto Rican students who graduated from New York public high schools in 1963 received their diplomas from vocational programs....

Its critics notwithstanding, by 1965 money flowing through Johnson's War on Poverty initiatives supported a proliferation of new grassroots organizations in New York's poor neighborhoods. In 1964, ... the Puerto Rican Forum applied to the Office of Economic Opportunity to fund a comprehensive, citywide agency that would promote, integrate, and supervise a system of projects designed to assist the Puerto Ricans in New York. The Puerto Rican Community Development Project (PRCDP) won a half-million-dollar grant from the city to distribute among twenty-five hometown clubs and other civic groups participating in a coordinated self-help initiative....

To the extent that Puerto Rican activists and community leaders saw their work as insurance against the explosion of poor urbanites' resentments—as in the 1964 riots, which happened in mostly African American neighborhoods—they did not succeed. In the summer of 1967, ... El Barrio exploded. This was its first full-scale riot, and the spark was the fatal shooting by police of a twenty-five-year-old Puerto Rican man who had allegedly stabbed another man. Journalist Peter Kihss, who had covered issues in Puerto Rican neighborhoods for the *New York Times* throughout the sixties, opened his description of the events with the question that many outside the community were asking: "Why did New York City's Puerto Ricans erupt into violence when they had endured ghetto conditions for so many years and had struggled to rise above them without such disorders before?"

The following day, Mayor Lindsay assembled a group of forty Puerto Rican leaders. As Kihss's question suggested, there was no singular cause to which the community leaders could attribute the riot.... [A] young community worker,...

Arnold Segarra addressed the conference, emphasizing the need for "more meaningful dialogue" between East Harlem youth and both police and antipoverty workers.... Meeting attendees decided on the spot to assign Segarra, already an employee of the city's Human Resources Administration, to form a youth council. Kihss interviewed another young man, Aníbal Solivan, a former vice president of MEND (the Massive Economic Neighborhood Development program) involved in several Community Action Program–funded organizations, who more pointedly than Segarra criticized the participants in the Gracie Mansion conference for being removed from El Barrio's problems on the ground: "That's the established power structure of the community. None of those cats was there during the weekend. They're not in the streets when they're needed. They don't relate."

Two months after the riots, Puerto Rican writer Piri Thomas, whose notorious memoir *Down These Mean Streets* appeared in May that year, testified before the National Advisory Commission on Civil Disorders. Thomas posed a series of questions that sounded merely rhetorical only because his real interlocutors, his *barrio* neighbors, were not present:

> Did you ever stand on street corners and look the other way, at the world of *muchos ricos* [sic] and think, I ain't got a damn? Did you ever count the garbage that flowed down dirty streets, or dig in the back yards who in their glory were a garbage dump's dream? Did you ever stand on rooftops and watch night time cover the bad below? Did you ever put your hand around your throat and feel your pulse beat say, "I do belong and there's not gonna be nobody can tell me, I'm wrong?"

In trying to explain why East Harlem had exploded, Thomas had little interest in the local politics of the riot, in the resentments over who controlled antipoverty funds and at what distance from the streets. His interpretation had more to do with what he might have called the existential pain of the rioters, a larger framework for understanding the "why now" question: for how many years can a group of people be told, in a thousand ways, "you're wrong" before they explode? In this sense, Thomas's reading of the riot and the beating pulse of El Barrio was not just about class and the impossibility of Puerto Ricans' belonging to "the world of *muchos ricos.*" It was also about Puerto Rican New Yorkers' ambivalence and anger about the various forms of exclusion they experienced in the United States—the consistent rejection of their claims for recognition as people who "belonged" and whose status as citizens promised some measure of sovereignty, over both their community and their island nation....

Echoing Piri Thomas's suggestion in his postriot testimony [Puerto Rican writer and activist] Andreu Iglesias insisted that poverty itself was only part of the struggle for Puerto Ricans. The lack of sovereignty, the lack of freedom to address their island's problems independently of the United States, was the real key to the riddle. More significant than the material failures they had accumulated during the sixties was Puerto Ricans' intensifying sense of disempowerment ... that created motivations for widespread radicalization in the New York *barrios*.... Young radicals would thus hammer another nail into

Juan Q. Citizen's coffin and ... demand recognition of the "free and sovereign" Puerto Rican in his stead.

★ ★ ★

... [T]housands of activists ... were determined to make a connection between the liberal antipoverty agenda in the United States and a new nationalist vision for Puerto Rico by the late 1960s. The sixties' Puerto Rican nationalist movement still identified itself with Pedro Albizu Campos's Nationalist Party of the 1930s, but now it was also defined by the increasing militancy of young radicals who were animated by the Cuban revolution, by decolonization struggles across Africa and southeast Asia, and by their opposition to the United States' war in Vietnam. In defining the field of struggle in this way, young Puerto Rican *independentistas* connected themselves to a complex network of radicals in the United States and to a worldwide network of radicalism beyond.... [B]y the mid-1960s ... Puerto Rican, Chicano, and African American activists ... sought to hold their liberal democratic society accountable for its violent exclusions and oppressions of so-called minority peoples....

The politicized "inner colonized" of New York's *barrios,* whose families had come from an actual colony, now seized on every opportunity to link their local experience of oppression to the larger problem of colonialism....

In 1951, aggrieved students had appealed simply to their status as American citizens, and their parents' credentials as taxpayers, to defend their rights to an education free from violence and discrimination. Two decades later, Puerto Rican youth (some of them graduates of Benjamin Franklin) ... helped shift the discourse from a language of individual liberal rights to a language of global recognition on the basis of justice.

Defending Chavez Ravine in Postwar Los Angeles

RONALD W. LÓPEZ II

On 8 May 1959, the City of Los Angeles evicted the Aréchiga family from their Chavez Ravine home of 36 years. Once the family had been removed, a bulldozer reduced the home to a pile of rubble. Eminent domain proceedings had begun 8 years earlier, when the city planned to seize the land for a major public housing project. Long before the final evictions, however, the housing project had been canceled, and the Los Angeles City Council was in the process of transferring the land to the Los Angeles Dodgers, for the future site of Dodger Stadium. The 10-year debate over the use of the land leading up to the dramatic final evictions came to be known to the people of Los Angeles as the *Battle of Chavez Ravine.*

This article examines the vocal, organized resistance of the people of Chavez Ravine to the destruction of their community, and the displacement of the

Ronald W. López II, "Community Resistance and Conditional Patriotism in Cold War Los Angeles: The Battle for Chavez Ravine," *Latino Studies* 7:4 (December 2009): pp. 457–479. Reproduced with permission of Palgrave Macmillan.

residents for the construction of a public housing project that was never built. Largely women, they spoke out during public hearings, wrote letters, and made statements to the media in a gendered discourse of resistance to displacement. In a language of patriotic post-war motherhood, the women made direct references to husbands and sons in military service to underpin the moral legitimacy of their statements. And yet, they made it clear that their patriotism was conditional. They had worked hard, purchased property and sent their men to war despite the discrimination that they faced at home. If the Government could take their homes, the symbol of American belonging, it threatened the foundation upon which their patriotism was based, and suggested that the United States had failed to live up to its promise. The people of Chavez Ravine, moreover, challenged projects that were supported by the entire left, liberal, and labor community, projects that promised to help poor communities, including Mexican Americans, nationwide. In doing so, they opposed positions taken by Mexican American leaders, and allied themselves, if only briefly, with local conservatives....

★ ★ ★

In late 1949, the residents of Palo Verde, Bishop Canyon, and La Loma – collectively known as Chavez Ravine – learned of a planned public housing project that required the entire community to be displaced and relocated. Located in the hills immediately northeast of downtown Los Angeles, Chavez Ravine was home to over 1100 families, many who had lived there for several generations. Developed as a Mexican suburb early in the century, Chavez Ravine had become a healthy, multigenerational Mexican barrio by the end of World War II. Since at least that time, the residents had been working to improve their community. They had petitioned the city council to put in streetlights, pave streets and provide bus service to the area. Through their own efforts, they had been successful in decreasing juvenile delinquency and crime, and in increasing attendance at the local schools. After all these efforts, they were shocked to learn that their community had been declared "a blighted area," and that they would have to move so that their homes and community could be destroyed, and public housing put up in its place.

The residents had good reason to defend their community. While Chavez Ravine had its share of social problems, it had the highest proportion of property owners and the highest social indicators of any Mexican American community in the Los Angeles area. Furthermore, a shortage of affordable housing, residential segregation, and the exclusion of Mexican Americans from new housing developments made the prospect of being displaced and finding new homes especially onerous. A public housing project in Chavez Ravine would thus turn a sizeable group of homeowners into renters. Those who moved out did not receive adequate compensation for their homes and land, and found that segregation and high prices excluded them from many areas.

By opposing the public housing project, the people of Chavez Ravine were rejecting a program supported by the entire Mexican American and liberal establishment, including Councilman Edward Roybal, the first Mexican American elected to the City Council since the nineteenth century. Although he was one of the strongest and longstanding supporters of public housing, including the units planned for Chavez Ravine, Roybal steadfastly defended the residents' rights to fair treatment and a fair price for their homes. The City Center District Improvement Association (CCDIA), a Chavez Ravine community organization, publicly rejected assistance from the leftist Asociación Nacional México-Americana, or ANMA, refusing aid from any organization that did not adhere to "American Principles." Instead, the community allied itself with the conservative real estate lobby, which argued that public housing was "socialist," and that adequate low cost housing could be attained by the enforcement of existing laws and building codes. That the residents allied themselves with the real estate interests is not surprising, since their traditional allies were unanimous in supporting public housing. And yet, they were reluctant to denounce public housing altogether, refusing to adopt the real estate lobby's mantra that public housing was "socialist."

Most importantly, the majority of those who spoke out and wrote letters were women – Mexican, Mexican American, white and Asian American – who lived in Chavez Ravine. They spoke and wrote in the language of conservative post-war patriotism, but it was a tentative, conditional patriotism. Their sons, brothers and husbands fought in World War II, and in Korea. Speaking in the gendered discourse of mothers and wives of veterans, they emphasized their contributions to the "war effort" of World War II as citizens who had earned the right to enjoy their homes in peace. Settlers of Chavez Ravine, they were pioneers who built their homes with their own hands, and raised their children to be patriotic citizens, just like earlier generations of Americans. They had worked to improve their community, and they rejected a project that proposed to benefit others at their expense. In doing so, Chavez Ravine residents challenged, head on, the City Council and the dozens of high profile civic leaders and "experts" that supported the public housing projects, denouncing what they saw as an unjustified plan. They walked a fine line, both defining themselves as exemplars of American patriotism and suggesting that if the City forcibly displaced them, they might be radicalized in the process.

Los Angeles, with a city administration dominated by liberal social planners, was one of the first cities to take advantage of the passage of the 1949 Housing Act, applying for $110,000,000 in Federal Funds to construct 10,000 units of low-rent public housing at 11 sites around the city.... In August 1949, the City Council unanimously approved the plan.

Two competing visions of Los Angeles' urban redevelopment had emerged in the post-war era: the conservative vision, favoring the free play of the market, and the liberal vision that included desegregation and an aggressive public housing program. Supporters of the liberal program included organizations such as the Citizens Housing Council, organized labor, veterans, religious organizations, the National Association for the Advancement of Colored People (NAACP), the Community Service Organization (CSO), and Mexican American civic leaders such as Councilman Edward Roybal and, publisher Ignacio López. Advocates for public housing ... argued that the infusion of federal money would provide jobs for workers, contracts for local businesses, housing for the needy, and would stimulate the local economy. They argued that slums and "blighted" conditions caused overcrowding and fostered delinquency and rat infestations that spread disease and endangered public health. A coordinated program of urban redevelopment, coupled with a racially integrated public housing program would address these ills.

... [I]ts most outspoken advocate was CHA Information Director Frank Wilkinson, who epitomized the social engineers who believed that razing the slums and building low-cost public housing would improve the living standards of the poor and reduce poverty, crime, delinquency, disease, and residential segregation citywide.

Conservative interests, such as the real estate lobby that included the *Los Angeles Times,* and smaller groups like the Small Property Owners Association (SPOA) wanted slum clearance and urban redevelopment too, but argued that the need for housing was being met by private developers, and that public housing was socialism, or at least "creeping socialism." They pressured the City Council on public housing, and almost immediately after approving the program, council members shifted, one by one, from unanimous support for public housing, to a slight majority against it. Two weeks after the passage of Proposition 10, which made future housing programs subject to the approval of voters, the City Council approved the selection of 11 sites for public housing projects, this time by a majority. Chavez Ravine was one of the approved sites.

The public housing project planned for Chavez Ravine would have included almost one-third of the units planned for the city. To be called "Elysian Park Heights," the project proposed ... [t]he mostly single family dwellings would be replaced with 163 two-story buildings and twenty four 13-story apartment towers.... For their sacrifice, the displaced residents were promised, in writing, first choice of the new housing, without respect to race.

★ ★ ★

Despite these promises, the people of Chavez Ravine were shocked and angered; they had worked hard, built a thriving community, and many of them owned their own homes. Thus, building public housing there would destroy what was arguably the most successful barrio in the city, and would turn a sizable group of homeowners into renters. Along with the homeowners of a number of other areas, they refused to cooperate with the city's plans, and spoke out vigorously against the choice of their district at public hearings held before the Planning Commission and the City Council. Their resistance, although unsuccessful, was passionate and organized, and the rhetoric they employed and the alliances they forged ran counter to conventional expectations of Mexican American political behavior for that era.

Frank Wilkinson, accompanied by Ignacio "Nacho" López, walked door-to-door convincing Chavez Ravine residents to move. The CHA guaranteed them first priority on new housing, rent scaled to income, and no racial discrimination. On the other hand, some residents reported being threatened with forcible eviction, and were intimidated into selling their homes for a low price. Through guarantees of future rental housing, and through intimidation, a large number of residents reluctantly agreed to sell and left their homes....

The people of Chavez Ravine had been well organized as a community since at least the end of the war, long before the proposed project had been announced. In particular, the CCDIA represented a number of Chavez Ravine residents....

... In the case of CCDIA, their militancy reflects the fact that they viewed themselves not as foreigners but as citizens entitled to all the rights of citizens, including the right to own homes and preserve their community....

At the same time, their protest was couched in the conservative language of post-war patriotism.... They emphasized that their homes were not blighted. Many pointed out that their sons, brothers, and husbands had fought in World War II. Was this what they had fought and died for? ...

★ ★ ★

The women of Chavez Ravine spoke out forcefully against the destruction of their community for the construction of Elysian Park Heights during two sets of public hearings held in ... 1951.... [W]ith the CCDIA clearly occupying leadership, ... men occupied the nominal leadership of the organization in the role of President and lead counsel, [while] women clearly occupied the vanguard of the discursive attack on the housing project.... [T]he arguments presented by the men directly responded to statements made by proponents of the projects, while the women articulated their objections in terms of their role as patriotic mothers and wives of veterans, and spoke from a position of moral authority that the men on both sides of the issue could not....

... Traditionally, Mexican American women were expected not to engage in political or other public activities without the knowledge, assent, and even guidance of family members, ideally fathers or husbands. When women did become active, however, their "activism originated in family concerns and community networks, then generated broader political concerns and networks." Thus, activities that are extensions of women's domestic roles, such as those involving the home, the Church, or the schools, were increasingly seen as acceptable or even appropriate areas for women's activism.... The outspoken testimony by Chavez Ravine women at public hearings in defense of their community was thus consistent with their "family and community relationships," and obligations.

The first set of ... hearings' official purpose was to determine if the project sites should be approved, but in truth, the contract between the City of Los Angeles and the Federal Housing Authority had been made.... The first day of hearings ... was an emotional affair attended by at least 500 persons. Opponents packed the hearing chambers and harangued the council, making it clear that they had no faith in the intentions of the CHA, shouting "Don't believe them. They're trying to take your land. They've never cared about you before. Why should they now?" ... On the one hand was an impressive pantheon of civic leaders speaking on behalf of the proposed project: the CHA, representatives of the Catholic Church, and labor unions. On the other hand, speaking against the project were representatives from Chavez Ravine and their lawyer, Mr G.G. Bauman....

... Stanley Furman, Development Counsel for the CHA, ... asserted that temporarily housed veterans would have first preference at the new housing, making no mention of the people of Chavez Ravine....

... [T]he community, represented by the CCDIA, declared their desire to keep their homes and preserve their community.... The CCDIA, said Baum[a]n, had for several years been trying to improve conditions in the area, but to no avail....

... That public housing would be a tax burden on the community became the most salient and compelling argument to the public, as the debate evolved from one specific site location to a national debate in which public housing was equated with socialism. Another issue, one that was dropped as time went on, was the immigrant and non-citizen status of many of the residents of Chavez Ravine. Baum[a]n refuted earlier assertions that all current residents would be "given priority" for moving into Elysian Park Heights, noting that some of the people of Chavez Ravine were "of Mexican-Spanish descent, some Italians," and that "Federal Law does not permit them [to live in public housing] unless they are citizens." Homeowners were also ineligible for public housing.

Responding to pictures of run down conditions, Manuel Cerda displayed photos of well-maintained properties, stating, "If you call this a slum, I don't know what would be a good house." Cerda emphasized ..., "We have plenty of facilities in there. We have gas, water, lights." He also pointed to the city's failure to maintain the area, noting that, "The streets are very poor – but that is due to the City Engineer and Council. They have not done anything for us."

Mabel Hom, local Girl Scout troupe leader and an Asian American, ... [declared], "I am an American Citizen," [and] spoke at length.... She denounced veteran support of public housing ...[:]

> I should think you know how it feels to go over to protect a piece
> of what you call your home .... We did not know the Veterans were
> against our purpose of keeping our homes and ... I think it is very
> undemocratic of people to place the preference of ... Veterans over our
> 1100 families in Chavez Ravine. We have just as much right to a home
> as they have.

Furthermore, Ms Hom noted, the property owners of Chavez Ravine were "forced" to live there, because "discrimination forced us to buy into this area" when it was considered unsuitable for development. "But now these Capitolists (*sic*) find we have a lovely place, located close to every facility there is, and you want it." ... [R]ather than calling public housing "creeping socialism," Ms Hom suggested that the evicted residents might themselves become un-American ... [:]

> If this plan goes through, I assure you there will be 1100 families that
> will not be as American, with attitudes that they should possess. I am
> sure if you label us 'Reds' from now on it will be the fault of the
> Housing Authority group which has no right to push people around, as
> they have been pushing 1100 families in Chavez Ravine.

The pro-American tone of her statement, her defense of private property rights and her attack on both big government and big capital make her statement especially interesting.... Ms Hom's perspective illustrates the intensity of the anti-public housing feeling that was felt by many, especially those who were threatened with losing their homes, that public housing was a conspiracy of powerful interests arrayed against them....

The final statement recorded in opposition was given by Agnes Cerda, the Secretary of the CCDIA, and the wife of Manuel Cerda. Speaking as a "taxpayer and American Citizen," and speaking on behalf of "the Mexican people," ... [s]he likened the early generations of Mexican American homeowners of Chavez Ravine to other generations of American pioneers.... She also denounced the CHA as un-American for taking their homes ...[:]

> I represent all of ... the Mexican people ... they came out here to the land of liberty and justice for all. They started one by one to build to the best of their ability.... Now, when they have them built, with the sweat of their brow.... The Housing Authority comes in now and tries to take their homes away from them. It is not justice and not American policy.

Mrs Cerda, emphasizing the Mexican people of the community, equated their experience with the American ideals of liberty and justice. Although she denounced the proposed public housing project in Chavez Ravine, Mrs Cerda, like Ms Hom, chose not to suggest that public housing was "socialistic," emphasizing "I don't say housing projects are not right. They might be all right for the people that want to live in them, but we, as property owners, we want to keep our homes." ... [L]ike Ms Hom, Mrs Cerda also warned the Commission about the disenchantment and anxiety that dispossession and dislocation would cause.... Identifying herself as the mother of a combat veteran and an American citizen, she appealed to public sympathy for veterans and their families ...[:]

> Take our homes away from us and you are taking away our incentive to be good American Citizens, [that] ... we are trying to raise our children to be. I know, I had a boy in the Second World War. Thank God he was lucky to come back. I have another one ... is he going to fight over there and have to come and fight over here for a home he hasn't got? Would you put your mother out of your home to give it to the Housing Authority? You would not.

... The women positioned themselves at the center of America's patriotic and pioneering spirit, building their own homes by "the sweat of their brow," and articulating their patriotism by raising their children to be good American citizens, even soldiers in wartime. But it was these idealized American values and trust in government that were now endangered by the very actions of the City Council and the CHA, representatives of both big business and big government. The expression of conditional patriotism was ... clearly well-thought out, but it may also have been true.

Despite the thoughtful and strategic arguments of the residents, the policy-oriented arguments in favor of public housing prevailed. On 17 May, the City Planning Commission approved eight sites for public housing, including Elysian

Park Heights.... The residents did not give up, but appealed the Planning Commission's approval ... argu[ing] that the projects were not properly located and that the CHA did not have legal standing to seize their properties. The City Council agreed to hear the appeals....

On 21 June, the City Council began what turned out to be a week of raucous public hearings. Hundreds of people packed the Council chambers....

Manuel Cerda, leader of the CCDIA, was the first speaker on behalf of Chavez Ravine property owners. Arguing that the will of the community was against the project, he asserted that, "The people of my district don't want to be renters. They want to be honest taxpayers. We don't want anybody else to have to pay our taxes." Finally, he said, "We don't want to be socialized." ... Angie Villa stated that she had lived in Chavez Ravine for 39 years, that she and her father wanted to keep their home, and that public housing had poor living conditions....

Speaking in defense of the projects, CHA chief Holtzendorff argued ... that the real estate lobby was behind opposition to the projects. Others argued that the housing projects would provide better living and a healthy environment for youth, that private development had failed to provide adequate and affordable housing, that it was a community responsibility to provide low-rent housing, that the human rights of the many must prevail over the property rights of the few, and that the benefit to the community as a whole offset the damage to a few individuals. Trinidad Rodrígues of the Railroad Workers union argued that the project would help the Mexican community, since the location was close to downtown where many Mexicans worked.

... Only a few homes were to be lost for the Rose Hills development, while the Chavez Ravine homeowners were to be forced out completely. The Rose Hills site representatives argued, in classic "not-in-my-backyard" fashion, that public housing would lower their property values, and that there were better ways to address the housing problem, in the words of one speaker, than "this proposed socialized concentration camp" [See Document 5]....

There were explicit examples of racial bias as well. Some letters to the City Council denounced the racial integration the public housing program proposed. For example, H. G. Tuthill, a Rose Hills property owner ..., said that he was one of those parents who,

> ... want their children to be free from the influence of a mass of negro, Mexican and a lot of others who have little regard for the better aspirations of American Citizenship ... we ... know it is hard enough to keep children out of trouble without moving them right into a nest of melting pot hudleums (*sic*) who care very little about what their children do or say.... How would you like to have your own little girls (if you had any) be left to play with a bunch of rough negro, and others no better, would you like it?

Tuthill's racial invective was wrapped in the language of citizenship, much like the statements of Ms Hom, Mrs Villa and Mrs Cerda, but to different effect. While they shared an opposition to public housing developments in their communities, Rose Hills residents vociferously embraced the argument that public housing was creeping socialism, and that integration threatened the racial integrity of their white daughters. The people of Chavez Ravine, on the other hand, were defending their already integrated community from complete destruction on the basis of their exemplary upholding of American ideals, such as their military service in World War II....

That same day, the Council approved resolutions denying the appeals of Manuel Cerda and the other residents of Chavez Ravine, and granted the final approval to the CHA to proceed with public housing in Chavez Ravine and the other sites. The *Los Angeles Times* ... echoed Bauman's demand that the Council place the issue on the ballot.... [A] referendum on public housing was placed on the June 1952 ballot.

★ ★ ★

After the approval of the Elysian Park Heights housing project, and with eminent domain looming, many Chavez Ravine residents gave up and sold their land to the CHA. Some held out, hoping for a reprieve, some stubbornly refused to leave, and some wrote, letters to the City Council, protesting their impending evictions. These women continued to express themselves in a discourse of conditionally patriotic mothers, such as Faustina Tele Ibarra, who wrote,

> I do not see the necessity of my paying rent or to be burdened with a debt in buying a home when I already own one, and ask, why it is that we mothers of veterans do not have a right to own property and live in peace without being molested?

At 66 years old and in poor health, Maria Longoria Esparza, caring for her 11 orphaned grandchildren, was no longer able to work. She wrote that she would not be able to buy a new home for the price offered for her house, which was paid in full....

Mrs Esparza's concerns were echoed by a neighbor, ... who reiterated that many people would not be able to obtain new housing for what was offered....

By August of 1951, two-thirds of the Chavez Ravine residents had packed up, sold their homes and land, and moved on. Those that remained refused to sell. Women such as Agnes Cerda, Angie Villa and Arana Aréchiga, who were leaders in the struggle to preserve Chavez Ravine from redevelopment, expressed resentment at their treatment by the City, and their determination to continue the fight to retain their homes.

The concerns of the women mirrored those expressed months before at the public hearings.... Agnes Cerda, one of the guiding forces of the holdouts, ... [argued] that "We built our homes here, not the government.... Taking away our homes takes our incentive to be good American citizens." Avrana Aréchiga concurred, adding that "I know nothing of slums. I only know this has been my home and it was my father's home and I do not want to sell and move. I am too old to find a new home. Here is where I live. Here, in Chavez Ravine."

Their desire to stay was reinforced by the negative experiences of those who had moved out before, only to suffer discrimination and hostility in their new neighborhoods. Mrs de León reported that "There are families that have moved into the City and they have come back to us and they have had tears in their eyes. And they say they are not accepted outside." ... By this time, less than a third of the original property owners remained.

Earlier in the year, the property owners had met with Los Angeles City Councilman Edward Roybal. A progressive Mexican American leader and a consistent supporter of public housing, he understood, from experience, the challenges faced by the residents of Chavez Ravine.... [H]e advised the property owners that they would only be fairly paid for their property if they remained united, collectively refused to sell their properties to the CHA, and demanded a higher price from the CHA....

The residents of Chavez Ravine were supposedly offered "market prices" for their land.... Although the CHA was to provide relocation assistance in finding new living quarters, ... Roybal ... said that the people were not paid fairly.... "Under the right of eminent domain they went in there and took their property." The CHA "told them your house is worth 'so much,' and that's all there was to it."

Many resisters, such as the Aréchigas, ... stayed on, fighting the evictions in the courts. During the Condemnation proceedings the Aréchigas were offered $10,500 for three lots and two houses. Unsatisfied, the Aréchiga family hired a private appraiser, who appraised their properties at $17,000.... [I]n court, the Aréchigas lost and the courts set the price at $10,050. When the Aréchigas refused to accept the money, the payment was placed in an account in their name and the sale declared consummated by the judge. Eviction proceedings began.... In all, the Aréchiga family resisted the City Council, police officers and the courts for 10 years.

★ ★ ★

On 3 June 1952, Los Angeles voters rejected the public housing program in a citywide referendum, but the vote was merely symbolic; the courts had ruled that the measure would have no effect, and that public housing in Los Angeles would continue. The property owners of Chavez Ravine had been unable to prevent the mass condemnation of their properties, and they had been unable to obtain satisfactory prices for their homes. Those who refused to accept the prices offered, like the Aréchigas, found that the CHA brought the matter to superior court, where their lands were condemned, prices set low and "sales" forced on unwilling landowners....

Within a week of taking office [in 1953], the new Mayor [Norris Poulson] suggested a compromise to end the controversy. CHA Director Holtzendorff would agree to renegotiate the contract between the Federal Housing Authority and the City of Los Angeles that would cancel the controversial Chavez Ravine and Rose Hills projects, and Poulson would leave the remaining public housing intact, and ask his allies in Congress and Los Angeles to end their attacks.... [T]he Chavez Ravine and Rose Hills projects [were] canceled....

... [T]he City Attorney's office continued to condemn Chavez Ravine properties until the very minute they received word that public housing there was officially canceled. The Rose Hills properties were left untouched. The people of Chavez Ravine had their land seized under eminent domain for a purpose that no longer existed. Dispossessed of their land and forced to move, they were largely forgotten.... Los Angeles was able to buy the land in Chavez Ravine for a minimal sum, and a few years later succeeded in attracting the Brooklyn Dodgers to the city by offering them 315 acres of Chavez Ravine.

There were still some of the old residents living there, however, who had to be forcibly evicted, including the Aréchigas, who were evicted in May 1959. The home was bulldozed moments after the eviction, and the family conducted a "sit-down strike," camping out for a week on the site. Aurora Vargas, a daughter of the Aréchigas and a war widow, hung her husband's dress uniform up in front of the wreckage of the house with a handwritten sign that declared; "My husband died in World War II to Protect Our Home." The dramatic eviction and its aftermath quickly overshadowed the earlier struggle of the people to preserve their homes 8 years earlier. Although there were other evictions, it was the Aréchiga eviction, filmed by television reporters and covered in detail by the newspapers, that seared the fate of Chavez Ravine into the minds of Los Angeles residents.

★ ★ ★

The residents of Chavez Ravine fought to preserve their community against destruction by the intrusion of a public housing project during the years 1950–1952.... The people who spoke on behalf of Chavez Ravine used a variety of arguments, but were consistent in their expressed belief in American political principles and ideals, and their commitment to the democratic process. Largely women, they spoke in a highly gendered language, making unambiguous references to husbands and sons in military service to underpin their moral legitimacy.... The residents rejected a sacred cow of liberal ideology of the era – that public housing was a greater good destined to help Mexican Americans, and other poor communities. Their protest challenged contemporary expectations of Chicano political behavior of the era: they were not simply poor, hapless slum-dwelling Mexicans, but politically astute Mexican Americans determined to defend their community. In the end, although their opposition to the redevelopment of Chavez Ravine was unsuccessful, ... the struggle to preserve Chavez Ravine became part of the popular memory of Los Angeles' Mexican American community. The residents of Chavez Ravine spoke out in defense of their homes, and their politically complex position impacted Los Angeles city politics. They rejected the liberal establishment's social engineering because, despite their desire to be fully included in the American body politic, it would be they, and not the liberal social planners, who would pay the price.

 # FURTHER READING

Eric Avila, *Popular Culture in the Age of White Flight: Fear and Fantasy in Suburban Los Angeles* (2004).

Lilia Fernandez, *Brown in the Windy City: Mexicans and Puerto Ricans in Postwar Chicago* (2012).

Mario García, *Mexican Americans: Leadership, Ideology, and Identity, 1930–1960* (1989).

Matt García, *A World of Its Own: Race, Labor, and Citrus in the Making of Greater Los Angeles, 1900–1970* (2001).

Gabriel Haslip-Viera, Angelo Falcón, and Félix V. Matos Rodríguez, eds., *Boricuas in Gotham: Puerto Ricans in the Making of Modern New York City* (2004).

Olga Jiménez de Wagenheim, "From Aguada to Dover: Puerto Ricans Rebuild Their World in Morris County, New Jersey, 1948 to 2000," in Carmen Teresa Whalen and Víctor Vázquez-Hernández, eds., *The Puerto Rican Diaspora: Historical Perspectives* (2005).

Anthony Macias, *Mexican American Mojo: Popular Music, Dance, and Urban Culture in Los Angeles* (2008).

Nancy Raquel Mirabal, "Melba Alvarado, El Club Cubano Inter-Americano, and the Creation of Afro-Cubanidades in New York City," in Miriam Jiménez Román and Juan Flores, eds., *The Afro-Latin@ Reader: History and Culture in the United States* (2010).

Felix M. Padilla, *Puerto Rican Chicago* (1987).

Antonia Pantoja, *Memoir of a Visionary: Antonia Pantoja* (2002).

Eugenio "Gene" Rivera, "La Colonia de Lorain, Ohio," in Carmen Teresa Whalen and Víctor Vázquez-Hernández, eds., *The Puerto Rican Diaspora: Historical Perspectives* (2005).

Mérida M. Rúa, *Latino Urban Ethnography and the Work of Elena Padilla* (2010).

Vicki L. Ruiz, *Cannery Women, Cannery Lives: Mexican Women, Unionization, and the California Food Processing Industry* (1987).

Andres Torres, *Signing in Puerto Rican: A Hearing Son and His Deaf Family* (2009).

Dan Wakefield, *Island in the City: The World of Spanish Harlem* (1959).

CHAPTER 10

The Cold War and Cuban Migration

When the Cuban Revolution ended in 1959, the U.S. response was shaped by the Cold War and U.S. anticommunism. After World War II, U.S. policymakers viewed the world as polarized between the United States, as a capitalist and democratic society, and the then Soviet Union, as a communist and authoritarian society. U.S. foreign policy was based on the fear that other countries might fall like dominoes into the throes of Soviet control and communism. Initially, U.S. policymakers accepted that the Cuban dictator they had supported for many years, Fulgencio Batista, had fallen to Fidel Castro and the 26th of July Movement. Yet relations between the United States and Cuba soured quickly—U.S. opposition to Cuba's government solidified, and Castro's policies shifted to the left.

Fleeing dramatic political and economic change, Cuban immigrants coming after the revolution differed significantly from earlier arrivals. Working-class cigar makers, who had struggled for Cuba's independence from Spain and were often socialists, were now met by Cubans predominantly from the elite and professional classes, who were vehemently anti-Castro and who struggled to overthrow the Cuban government from exile. The first two waves of post-1959 migrants set the context for subsequent arrivals, as well as for perceptions of a homogenous Cuban community. The U.S. government defined Cubans as refugees fleeing communism and set out to assist them. The 1961 Cuban Refugee Program provided unprecedented federal aid in the form of direct assistance to meet immediate needs, small business loans, and professional retraining. The 1966 Cuban Adjustment Act enabled Cubans to remain in the United States and become citizens. Cubans established an economic enclave in Miami, a cluster of Cuban-owned businesses that employed other Cubans and provided an economic foundation for the community. Efforts to resettle Cubans beyond south Florida were less successful, as Miami and the surrounding areas remained the largest communities. Still, communities in northern New Jersey and New York City also grew, and other Cubans settled throughout the United States.

In 1980, Cuban migration and U.S. perceptions shifted. Asylum seekers overran the Peruvian embassy in Havana, and the Cuban government then opened the port of Mariel, encouraging Cuban Americans to come by boat to pick up their relatives. Unlike previous waves, the United States exercised no control over this third wave, which was large, rapid, and chaotic. More representative of Cuba's population than previous waves, migrants included more working-class people, Afro-Cubans, and men. The U.S. press charged that Castro was forcing the exodus of criminals and the mentally ill, as well as homosexuals. Most were immediately released to sponsors without media attention, but some were held in camps awaiting sponsors. No longer defined as refugees, third-wave arrivals were labeled "entrants." Migration has continued through legal accords between the two countries, via third countries, and by rafts, constituting the fourth wave. This chapter explores shifts in Cuban migration and in U.S. policies and perceptions, as well as their implications for Cuban Americans.

 DOCUMENTS

Although the U.S. government was quick to define Cubans as refugees fleeing communism, it was not as quick to provide financial resources, hoping that private organizations and charities would meet Cubans' needs. In 1961, however, President John F. Kennedy initiated massive federal assistance, as he described in Document 1, a Department of State bulletin. Despite unprecedented federal aid, not all Cubans arrived with ease. In Document 2, scholar María de los Angeles Torres describes her journey to the United States in 1961 at the age of six, as part of Operation Pedro Pan, a semiclandestine program that brought unaccompanied children from Cuba to the United States. Document 3, the foreword to a 1967 government study, provides a brief overview of "Cuba's Children in Exile" and the federal government's role in assisting them. During the third wave of Cuban immigration, U.S. perceptions shifted dramatically, as captured in Document 4, a 1980 newspaper article from the *National Catholic Reporter*. Whereas previous waves had been depicted as golden exiles, "bad press" depicted the third wave as "criminals, homosexuals, and mental defectives." The article suggests that shifting perceptions were also based on the depressed economy, the labeling of these arrivals as "entrants" rather than refugees, and perhaps on the higher proportion of Afro-Cubans. In Document 5, writer Reinaldo Arenas narrates autobiographically his experiences as a Cuban gay man leaving Cuba for the United States in 1980. Cuban American journalist Mirta Ojito explores the relationships between Afro-Cubans and white Cubans in Document 6, a 2000 *New York Times* article. She chronicles the changing friendship of two men who arrived as *balseros* or rafters in 1994, to find a more racially divided society in Miami than the one they had left in Cuba.

1. U.S. Government Provides Assistance for Cuban Refugees, 1961

I have conferred with Secretary [of Health, Education, and Welfare] Abraham Ribicoff concerning the Secretary's on-the-spot investigation made at my direction on the problems of Cuban refugees in southern Florida.

"President Outlines Measures for Aiding Cuban Refugees," *Department of State Bulletin* 44 (February 27, 1961), pp. 309–310.

Secretary Ribicoff paid tribute to the refugees as a proud and resourceful people, whose courage and fortitude in the face of tragic disruption of their lives is magnificent.

At the same time he reported that many of the refugees are now in serious need. They are living in extremely crowded quarters. Their resources have been exhausted or greatly depleted. Health and educational facilities are badly overtaxed.

Secretary Ribicoff praised the exceptional efforts of voluntary welfare agencies, and State and local officials, to cope with the problems which have been created by the influx of refugees from oppression in their homeland. But he emphasized that the increasing number of refugees, and the personal circumstances of many of them, had become more onerous than private and local agencies could any longer bear alone.

The Secretary said that immigration authorities estimated there are already 66,000 Cubans in this country, with at least 32,000 in the Miami area. To meet their minimal needs the personal resources of many of the refugees have been exhausted and the available resources of voluntary and local authorities badly overstrained.

As a result of the conference this afternoon I have directed Secretary Ribicoff to take the following actions on behalf of the United States Government:

1. Provide all possible assistance to voluntary relief agencies in providing daily necessities for many of the refugees, for resettling as many of them as possible, and for securing jobs for them.

2. Obtain the assistance of both private and governmental agencies to provide useful employment opportunities for displaced Cubans, consistent with the overall employment situation prevailing in Florida.

3. Provide supplemental funds for the resettlement of refugees in other areas, including transportation and adjustment costs to the new communities and for their eventual return to Miami for repatriation to their homeland as soon as that is again possible.

4. Furnish financial assistance to meet basic maintenance requirements of needy Cuban refugee families in the Miami area as required in communities of resettlement, administered through Federal, State, and local channels and based on standards used in the community involved.

5. Provide for essential health services through the financial assistance program supplemented by child health, public health services, and other arrangements as needed.

6. Furnish Federal assistance for local public school operating costs related to the unforeseen impact of Cuban refugee children on local teaching facilities.

7. Initiate needed measures to augment training and educational opportunities for Cuban refugees, including physicians, teachers, and those with other professional backgrounds.

8. Provide financial aid for the care and protection of unaccompanied children—the most defenseless and troubled group among the refugee population.

9. Undertake a surplus food distribution program to be administered by the county welfare department, with surplus foods distributed by public and voluntary agencies to needy refugees.

I hope that these measures will be understood as an immediate expression of the firm desire of the people of the United States to be of tangible assistance to the refugees until such time as better circumstances enable them to return to their permanent homes in health, in confidence, and with unimpaired pride.

I am particularly interested in Secretary Ribicoff's proposal to make effective use of the faculty of the University of Habana, three-fourths of which are reported to be in south Florida at the present time. I have asked Secretary Ribicoff to examine how this community of scholars could be most effectively used to keep alive the cultural and liberal traditions for which this faculty has been justly noted. It represents a great inter-American asset, for their own people, for this country, and for the entire hemisphere. I have asked the Secretary to report by March 1st on how these great intellectual abilities can be most effectively employed.

I also want to commend Secretary Ribicoff for the constructive, humanitarian, and immediate program proposed to assist the Cuban refugees. He said that he hoped that it would be considered first and foremost an essential humanitarian act by this country. But he also wanted it to indicate the resolve of this Nation to help those in need who stand with the United States for personal freedom and against Communist penetration of the Western Hemisphere.

I have consulted with Budget Director David E. Bell on means for financing these interim measures, which are expected to cost about $4 million through the remainder of this fiscal year.

2. Scholar María de los Angeles Torres Recalls Her Experiences with Operation Pedro Pan, 1961

My mother's relatives lived in Yaguajay, a little town nestled between the sea and the foot of the Escambray Mountains in the Las Villas province of Cuba. Two or three times a year, my family took the five-hour drive from our home in Havana to visit them. In the summer of 1961, our trip had a secret purpose. We were coming to say good-bye. We were delivering some of our possessions: a fan, jewelry, photographs. We also brought our longhaired cat, Johnny, for safekeeping until our return. I sat next to Johnny's cage in the backseat; I can still recall the smell of his sweaty coat.

My parents, like thousands of Cubans, had supported the revolution at first; they hid rebels in our home, a risk that could have cost them their lives. In January 1959, the day the *rebeldes* marched into Havana, my father rushed home to pick me up so that we could greet them. When we reached the Avenida de los Presidentes, a wide avenue dotted with statues of Cuba's past presidents, he hoisted me onto his shoulders so that I could see over the crowd. People were

"The Lost Apple: Operation Pedro Pan, Cuban Children in the US, and the Promise of a Better Future" by María de los Angeles Torres. Reprinted by permission of Beacon Press, Boston.

jubilant—dancing, chanting, and reaching out to touch the bearded rebels in their olive green uniforms. One stopped in front of us and reached up to hug me; I was mesmerized by the red glass beads of the rosary that hung from his neck and the silver cross almost buried in his hairy chest. We honked our car horn all the way home. My father told me it was a day I must never forget.

But during the next two years, everything changed. Fidel Castro, once a popular hero in our family, became a ruler we feared. We stopped collecting trading cards featuring heroes of the revolution. I no longer rode my toy military jeep on the back patio, waving the red and black flag of the 26 of July Movement. I had just turned six. Time was moving fast. Turmoil was increasingly becoming a part of our daily lives. Sirens were heard at all hours. Our familiar routines of playing in the park and going to the beach on Sundays were constantly disrupted by threats of bomb raids. Just months earlier, the government had shut down the schools, including mine, Nuestra Señora de Lourdes. There was constant confusion in the air. For reasons I only understood later, my parents decided to go into exile.

The quickest way for the family to depart was to send me to the United States with a visa waiver; I would then claim my parents and sisters, who would join me in a few months. I was to travel with my best friend, Xavier Arruza, also six years old. His older brothers were already in Miami. It was Xavier's father who had obtained the visa waiver for me. I was going to Miami, I was told, to stay with Nenita and Pucho Greer, my parents' friends. We started to pack my things. I felt a strange surge of excitement (I had never been on an airplane before) mixed with apprehension (I had never been separated from my parents). Secrecy shrouded my trip: no one was to know that I was leaving the country. My parents had not even told my younger sister, Alicia.

On July 30, just before dawn, my parents woke me and dressed me in the aqua blue and white checkered dress my grandmother had made for me, on which they pinned a piece of paper bearing my name and the name and phone number of our friends in Miami. They quietly loaded the car: a suitcase, a gray and red vinyl handbag, and my favorite doll. The sky was turning a pale orange pink as we drove to the airport.

Years would pass before I learned how many other children had left the island in the same fashion, to be reunited with their parents at an uncertain date. Some, in fact, never saw their parents again; others experienced long separations. Still others faced terrible hardship in foster homes or institutions. At the time, though, I knew only about my cousins, who arrived in the United States shortly after I did. On Sundays, we visited two of my cousins at a makeshift camp in south Dade County. Church officials in Havana had told their parents that their daughters would receive a *beca* (scholarship) to go to a good school in the United States. Instead they were sleeping in a large room filled with small cots squeezed so tightly together that they had to slide onto them from the pillow end. Later two cousins were shipped to a foster home in Albuquerque, New Mexico, and others to an orphanage in St. Louis, Missouri.

By mid-1961, most middle-class Cuban families knew of the semi-clandestine visa waiver program that had spurred this child migration. But no one spoke about it openly; everyone was sworn to secrecy, both on the island and in the United States. It wasn't until March 8, 1962, that the *Miami Herald* wrote about a secret effort called Operation Exodus that was bringing Cuban youth to the United States to save them from Fidel Castro's brainwashing. The *Herald* reported 8,000 had already arrived in South Florida. In the next seven months, another 6,000 unaccompanied children would enter the United States. In total, between the years 1960 and 1962, more than 14,000 children entered the United States through the program that came to be known as Operation Peter Pan or, in its Spanish translation, *Operación Pedro Pan*....

Despite the headlines about the unprecedented exodus of Cuban children, larger events overshadowed it, and Operation Pedro Pan soon faded from public attention. By October 1962, the world would be at the brink of nuclear war. The United States detected the Soviet Union's nuclear missiles on the island and demanded that they be removed. In turn, the Soviet Union demanded that the United States make a pledge of nonintervention in Cuba. As a result of the standoff, both Cuba and the United States banned travel to and from the island. The plight of these children—many whose parents had not been able to come to the United States—would be forgotten in the unfolding world drama.

3. U.S. Government Assists "Cuba's Children in Exile," 1967

In November 1960, a Cuban mother brought her two children to Key West. She feared that they would be sent to Russia because she and her husband were actively opposed to the Castro regime. She asked the judge of the juvenile court to find homes for them. The judge assumed jurisdiction and placed her children in foster care. The mother returned to Cuba to be with her husband and to continue her work in the counterrevolutionary movement.

This incident marked the beginning of a rapid influx of Cuban children, many of whom would be unaccompanied by their parents and with no relatives here to care for them. The children came from all classes of Cuban society, although the majority were from well-to-do, middle-class families. Most of them were in their teens, and nearly two-thirds were boys.

Voluntary agencies did what they could to provide care and shelter for these children, but it soon became apparent that they could not carry on without the help of the Federal Government.

In January 1961, President John F. Kennedy asked the Secretary of Health, Education, and Welfare, Abraham Ribicoff, to plan and administer a Federal program to deal with the needs of Cuban refugees while in the United States and to expedite their return to their homeland when conditions made it possible.

The Cuban Refugee Program—the most comprehensive program ever devised in this country to meet the needs of incoming refugees—was the first

U.S. Department of Health, Education, and Welfare, Social and Rehabilitation Service, Children's Bureau, "Cuba's Children in Exile" (Washington, DC: U.S. Government Printing Office, 1967).

to entail the distribution of Federal financial assistance for maintenance outside of a refugee center. Provisions for the unaccompanied children were made part of the overall plan.

The Children's Bureau, through delegation, was made responsible for child welfare services, including the care and protection of these unaccompanied Cuban children. The Florida State Department of Public Welfare acted as agent for the U.S. Department of Health, Education, and Welfare, in turn, contracted with HIAS [Hebrew Immigrant Aid Society] and the Miami voluntary Bureau of the Diocese of Miami, the Children's Service Bureau, and the Jewish Family and Children's Service—for arranging the placement of the children.

By April 30, 1967, the Federal Government had been responsible for the foster care of over 8,300 children.

Practical problems that would have discouraged those less convinced of the importance of what they were doing beset the agencies and organizations at every turn. But they persisted—and difficulties were finally overcome.

4. From Golden Exiles to "Bad Press" for Cubans, 1980

BAD PRESS, a depressed economy and a legal technicality have conspired to make the resettlement of 115,000 Cuban refugees more difficult than resettlement of Indochinese refugees in recent years.

"Press coverage of the Cubans has been a disaster for us," said Joseph Battaglia, western regional director of the U.S. Catholic Conference's (USCC) Migration and Refugee Services. "Portraying the 115,000 Cuban emigrants as criminals, homosexuals, and mental defectives is a gross distortion that has hurt the effort to recruit sponsors for their resettlement," said Battaglia.

From several angles the Indochinese resettlement, now totaling 300,000 since 1975, has gone more smoothly than the Cuban. In 1975, the economy was beginning to bounce back from a recession, making jobs easier to find and the new arrivals less of a threat to Americans....

"The Cubans have had little contact with North Americans," said Father John Lightle.... "Particularly the black Cubans—about 30 per cent of the whole—are going to find it hard to adjust here since they're used to going where they want, living and working where they want, and marrying who they want." More than 80 per cent of Cubans have been settled.... Most of the 50,000 were family members, and the USCC now faces the task of settling some 5,500 unsponsored Cubans, 80 percent of them single men.

Father Morton Park of Catholic Charities in Portland, Ore., explained that sponsors of single Cubans must see that the refugees find jobs and set up independent living, all without the support of a family or access to most governmental assistance programs.

Federal money to aid the Cuban resettlement has been scarce because, technically, they are not refugees. Initially classed by the Immigration and

Mark Neilsen, "Bad Press Creating Difficulties in Resettling Cuban Refugees," *National Catholic Reporter* 16 (August 15, 1980), pp. 22–23.

Naturalization Services as "applicants for political asylum" and eligible only for food stamps, the Cubans became officially "entrants" June 20, making them eligible for the same government programs for which citizens are eligible.

Were the Cubans classified "refugees" as the Indochinese have been, they would be eligible for a wide range of federally funded programs including health care and job training. In most states, such services are not generally offered to males under age 65.

To provide for the Cubans, legislation pending in Congress would appropriate $100 million for benefits similar to those covered under refugee status. Although the Carter administration is not fighting such an appropriation, it has denied the Cubans refugee status because in the words of one spokesman, "they came here unscreened, uninvited and contrary to the wishes of the government."...

Without public support and federal money, the Cuban refugee resettlement will proceed, but the going will be slow, say officials around the country. "Right now, people feel overwhelmed by the presence of large numbers of Cubans at a time when the economy is bad," said Mary Gatton of Catholic Charities in Louisville. "If new programs don't open up to help us soon," said Gatton, "we'll reach our saturation point."

5. Writer Reinaldo Arenas on Being Cuban and Gay, 1980

It was paradoxical that those great writers who had left Cuba in search of freedom were now unable to publish their work here.

Such was the case with Carlos Montenegro, a first-rate novelist and storyteller, also living on welfare in a small room in a poor neighborhood of Miami; this is the price to be paid for keeping one's integrity. The sad fact is that Cuban exiles were not very interested in literature; a writer was looked upon a strange, abnormal creature.

In Miami I met wealthy people, bankers and business owners, and I proposed to create a publishing house for the best of Cuban writers, most of them living in exile already. The reply of all those men, all multimillionaires, was categorical: Literature is not lucrative. Almost nobody is interested in a book by Labrador Ruiz; Lydia Cabrera can sell in Miami, but not to any great extent; in short, it would not work out as a business.

"We might be interested in publishing one of your books because you just left Cuba and you are news," they told me. "But those other authors, nobody is going to buy their books."

Montenegro died the following year in a public hospital, completely forgotten. Labrador is struggling to survive in a small room in Miami. As for Lydia, she is completely blind but still writing. Her small editions hardly circulate beyond Miami.

I once went to the presentation of one of her books. I saw an old lady sitting at a small table under a mango tree, signing books: it was Lydia Cabrera. She had left behind all of her past, her huge country estate in Havana, her extensive library, and was now trying to make ends meet in a small Miami apartment. When I saw this blind old lady signing her books under a mango tree, I understood that she represented a greatness and a spirit of rebellion that perhaps no longer existed in any of our writers, either in Cuba or in exile. One of the greatest women in our history, she was completely forsaken and forgotten, or else surrounded by people who had never read a single one of her books and were now just looking for a quick news story, taking advantage of the splendor that old lady still radiated. It was a paradox and at the same time a good example of the tragic fate Cuban writers have suffered throughout our history; on our Island we have been condemned to silence, to ostracism, censorship, and prison; in exile, despised and forsaken by our fellow exiles.... Lydia always urged me not to stay in Miami; she said I had to leave at once, for New York, Paris, Spain. She never found a niche in that flat, envious, mercenary environment, but being eighty years old she had nowhere else to go. Lydia Cabrera belonged to a more refined tradition, one richer in depth and world culture, far removed from those poetesses of boring bad taste and corny inanities, for whom nothing mattered but their current participation in social events, and for whom anyone who managed to publish a book in a foreign country and attain some renown was almost a traitor.

I realized immediately that Miami was not for me. The first thing my uncle told me when I arrived was: "Buy yourself a jacket and a tie, have your hair cut short, and walk properly, tall, firm. Also, have some business cards printed giving your name and saying that you are a writer." Of course, he was trying to tell me that I had to become more of a macho man. The typical Cuban machismo has attained alarming proportions in Miami. I did not want to stay too long in that place, which was like a caricature of Cuba, the worst of Cuba: the eternal gossip, the chicanery, the envy. I also hated the flatness of the scenery, which could not compare with the beauty of an island; it was like the ghost of our Island, a barren and pestiferous peninsula, trying to become, for a million exiles, the dream of a tropical island: aerial, bathed by the ocean waters and the tropical breeze. In Miami the obsession with making things work and being practical, with making lots of money, sometimes out of the fear of starving, has replaced a sense of life and, above all, of pleasure, adventure, and irreverence.

During the few months I lived in Miami, I had no moment of peace. I was surrounded by gossip and difficulties, and by an endless succession of cocktail parties, soirées, and invitations. It was like being on display, a strange creature that had to be invited before it lost its luster or until a new personality arrived to displace it. I had no peace to do anything, much less to write. Moreover, the city—not really a city but rather a number of detached houses peopled by cowboys for whom the horse had been replaced by the car—terrified me. I was used to a city with sidewalks and streets, a deteriorated city but one where a person could walk and appreciate its mystery, even enjoy it at times. Now I was in a plastic world, lacking all mystery, where loneliness was often much more invasive. It did not take long for me to become homesick for Cuba, for Old Havana, but my enraged memory was stronger than any nostalgia.

I knew I could not live in Miami. Now, needless to say, after ten years, I have realized that an exile has no place anywhere, because there is no place, because the place where we started to dream, where we discovered the natural world around us, read our first book, loved for the first time, is always the world of our dreams. In exile one is nothing but a ghost, the shadow of someone who never achieves full reality. I ceased to exist when I went into exile; I started to run away from myself.

In Miami, Lázaro had another crisis of total madness; it was getting worse. Everybody lived in a state of constant paranoia, locked up; even my aunt, whom I had not seen for twenty years, seemed more moonstruck. When I arrived in Miami I think I made some statements that people did not like very much. I said: "If Cuba is Hell, Miami is Purgatory."

In August of 1980 I accepted an invitation to speak at Columbia University, in New York. Without a second thought, I prepared my lecture in less than two hours, and took the plane. I was fleeing from a place that only increased my anxieties and wasn't suited to my way of being; I was also, forever, running away from myself.

The exile is a person who, having lost a loved one, keeps searching for the face he loves in every new face and, forever deceiving himself, thinks he has found it. I thought I had found that face in New York, when I arrived here in 1980. The city took me into its fold. I felt as if I had arrived in a glorified Havana, with great sidewalks, fabulous theaters, a transportation system that worked marvelously, streets that were really lively, and all kinds of people who spoke many different languages; I did not feel like a stranger in New York. That very first night, I started walking around the city; it seemed to me that in another incarnation, in another life, I had lived in this city. That evening, a group of more than thirty friends, including Roberto Valero, Nancy Pérez Crespo, and even Samuel Toca, whom I had forgiven, took cars and drove along Fifth Avenue, which, on the first of September, was beginning to be invaded by the mists of autumn....

6. Journalist Mirta Ojito Explores the Relationships Between Afro-Cubans and White Cubans, 2000

Havana, sometime before 1994: As dusk descends on the quaint seaside village of Guanabo, two young men kick a soccer ball back and forth and back and forth across the sand. The tall one, Joel Ruiz, is black. The short, wiry one, Achmed Valdés, is white.

They are the best of friends.

Miami, January 2000: Mr. Valdés is playing soccer, as he does every Saturday, with a group of light-skinned Latinos in a park near his apartment. Mr. Ruiz surprises him with a visit, and Mr. Valdés, flushed and sweating, runs to greet him. They shake hands warmly.

But when Mr. Valdés darts back to the game, Mr. Ruiz stands off to the side, arms crossed, looking on as his childhood friend plays the game that was once their shared joy. Mr. Ruiz no longer plays soccer. He prefers basketball with black Latinos and African-Americans from his neighborhood.

The two men live only four miles apart, not even 15 minutes by car. Yet they are separated by a far greater distance, one they say they never envisioned back in Cuba.

In ways that are obvious to the black man but far less so to the white one, they have grown apart in the United States because of race. For the first time, they inhabit a place where the color of their skin defines the outlines of their lives—where they live, the friends they make, how they speak, what they wear, even what they eat.

"It's like I am here and he is over there," Mr. Ruiz said. "And we can't cross over to the other's world."

It is not that, growing up in Cuba's mix of black and white, they were unaware of their difference in color. Fidel Castro may have decreed an end to racism in Cuba, but that does not mean racism has simply gone away. Still, color was not what defined them. Nationality, they had been taught, meant far more than race. They felt, above all, Cuban.

Here in America, Mr. Ruiz still feels Cuban. But above all he feels black. His world is a black world, and to live there is to be constantly conscious of race. He works in a black-owned bar, dates black women, goes to an African-American barber. White barbers, he says, "don't understand black hair." He generally avoids white neighborhoods, and when his world and the white world intersect, he feels always watched, and he is always watchful.

Mr. Valdés, who is 29, a year younger than his childhood friend, is simply, comfortably Cuban, an upwardly mobile citizen of the Miami mainstream. He lives in an all-white neighborhood, hangs out with white Cuban friends and goes to black neighborhoods only when his job, as a deliveryman for Restonic mattresses, forces him to. When he thinks about race, which is not very often, it is in terms learned from other white Cubans: American blacks, he now believes, are to be avoided because they are delinquent and dangerous and resentful of whites. The only blacks he trusts, he says, are those he knows from Cuba.

Since leaving Havana on separate rafts in 1994, the two friends have seen each other just a handful of times in Miami—at a funeral, a baby shower, a birthday party and that soccer game, a meeting arranged for a newspaper photographer. They have visited each other's homes only once.

They say they remain as good friends as ever, yet they both know there is little that binds them anymore but their memories. Had they not become best friends in another country, in another time, they would not be friends at all today.

★ ★ ★

They met on a bus, No. 262, the one that took Joel from his home in the racially mixed neighborhood of Peñas Altas to middle school, 35 minutes away. Achmed got on in Guanabo, and they sat together talking, as boys do, about everything and nothing.

Both grew up in orderly homes, with hard-working parents who supported the Castro government. Their fathers worked for the state oil company. Their mothers—Joel's was a nurse, Achmed's an administrator in stores for tourists—knew each other and sometimes met for coffee.

The boys' friendship was cemented through school and sport....

But as they grew older, each became restless with the limitations of life in Cuba....

[Achmed] found work at sea, trapping lobsters and selling them for $4 each. In a country where most people earn less than $10 a month, it was a living, though not a life. When the government allowed thousands of Cubans to leave in small boats and rafts in 1994, he was ready.

His friend Joel was ready, too, though it had taken him far longer to make up his mind. Indeed, given Cuba's racial history, it is hardly surprising that black Cubans have generally been far less eager than whites to flee to America. After all, in pre-revolutionary Cuba, blacks and whites had lived largely segregated, separated by huge disparities in economic and social standing. But two months after he seized power in 1959, Fidel Castro ordered whites to look upon blacks as equals and began leveling the economic and educational playing fields.

When Joel was very small, his family lived crammed into one room of an old carved-up mansion. Soon, the government gave them a three-bedroom apartment in a development that Joel's father had helped build. Before the revolution, Joel's mother had made a living cleaning white people's homes. It was Fidel, she told him over and over, who had given her the chance to become a nurse. And so Joel came to believe that it was no big deal, being black in Cuba.

As for America, he had seen the images on government television: guards beating black prisoners, the police loosing dogs or training hoses on civil-rights marchers.

But as Cuba's economy fell apart in the 1990's, he began to see things differently. He left military school for a cooking program, hoping for a well-paying job at a tourist hotel. Once he graduated, the only job available was washing windows. Look around, co-workers told him, look who's getting the good jobs. The answer was whites.

He noticed, too, when he watched the American channels at Achmed's house, that some blacks seemed to live well in America. He saw black lawyers, politicians, wealthy athletes....

On Aug. 21, 1994, he climbed onto a raft and made for Florida. Like his friend before him, he was intercepted by the United States Coast Guard and sent to the American base at Guantánamo. The next year, they were freed—first Mr. Valdés, then Mr. Ruiz—and headed straight to Miami.

★ ★ ★

In Miami, Joel Ruiz discovered a world that neither American television nor Communist propaganda had prepared him for. Dogs did not growl at him and police officers did not hose him. But he felt the stares of security guards when he entered a store in a white neighborhood and the subtle recoiling of white women when he walked by.

Miami is deeply segregated, and when Mr. Ruiz arrived, he settled into one of the black urban sections, Liberty City. He had family there. His uncle Jorge Aranguren had arrived in 1980....

In Cuba, he says, he had been taught to see skin color—in his case, the color of chocolate milk—as not much more important than, say, the color of his eyes. But this was not Cuba. This was Miami, and in Miami, as the roughly 7 percent of the area's Cubans who are black quickly learn, skin color easily trumps nationality.

Pretty much anywhere else in America, Mr. Valdés would fit nicely into the niche reserved for Hispanic immigrants. If the question of race came up, he would be called a light-skinned Hispanic. Here in Miami, such distinctions do not apply. Here he is not a member of any minority group. He is Cuban and he is white.

This, after all, is a city run by Cubans, white Cubans. Not only are the mayors of Miami and Dade County Cuban, so are 7 of 13 county commissioners and 3 of 5 city commissioners. Spanish is the dominant language heard in the streets.

Mr. Valdés's transition to this world has been seamless, so much so that he does not really think of himself as an immigrant at all. His self-image is of someone well along on a sure, quick path to the middle class....

Ninety miles and four and a half years later, Mr. Valdés has ended up back in Cuba—albeit a new and improved Cuba.

"The only thing I miss from Cuba is being able to see the ocean from my windows," he says. "Everything else I need and want is right here. This is exactly the country that I always imagined."...

 # ESSAYS

Cubans migrated to the United States in distinct waves, punctuated by Cold War events and by changes in U.S. and Cuban policies. In each wave, both the U.S. and Cuban governments sought to achieve geopolitical advantage, while people tried to make the best decisions for themselves and their families. In the first essay, María Cristina García, professor of history at Cornell University, delineates the major waves of post-1959 Cuban migration, highlighting shifts in the migrants' demographics and in the U.S. reception. She argues that many of those who left in the immediate aftermath of the revolution were connected to the Batista regime and hence faced possible retribution, but that subsequent emigrants were disillusioned with the direction that the revolution was taking.

The significant socioeconomic class, race, gender, sexuality, age, and political differences that emerged in each wave created challenges within the Cuban

American community, and resulted in a more diverse community than is often perceived. Delving deeply into the third wave, the 1980 Mariel boatlift, Susana Peña, professor of ethnic studies at Bowling Green State University, explores the experiences of Cuban gay men. In Cuba, the state repressed public displays of what it considered effeminate male behavior and hence "obvious homosexuals." Peña argues that ironically, the Cuba government deemed these men as "undesirables" and approved their departure from the country, which often coincided with gay men's hopes to find a more hospitable home. In the United States, the policy to welcome Cubans as refugees clashed with policies prohibiting the immigration of homosexuals. These policy tensions coexisted with the shifting U.S. perceptions of Cuban migrants more broadly.

Cuban Migration and U.S. Policies

MARÍA CRISTINA GARCÍA

THE MAJORITY of the 1.3 million Cuban Americans presently in the United States arrived after 1959, when revolutionaries led by Fidel Castro assumed control of the Cuban government. Over the next forty years, more than one-tenth of Cuba's present-day population migrated to the United States, and thousands more migrated to other countries in the Caribbean, Latin America, and Europe.... Cuban immigration to the United States is not merely a late-twentieth-century phenomenon. It is a pattern that was established several centuries earlier, the product of commercial ties and geographic proximity. Distinct Cuban communities in the United States were first noticed in the nineteenth century....

By the 1950s, Pan American airlines scheduled as many as twenty-eight daily flights between Miami and Havana. Cubans were vast importers of U.S. consumer goods and cultural forms, from New York fashions to Hollywood movie features. Vacationing in Miami Beach or New York City was as popular for middle-class Cubans ... as vacationing in Havana was for middle-class Americans. The large American presence and financial investments on the island and the close commercial ties between both countries shaped the evolution of Cuban politics. It also influenced language, customs, and traditions. However, this familiarity with American culture and institutions did not guarantee that life for the exiles and immigrants would evolve smoothly in the United States, nor did it exempt them from discrimination, racial violence, and abuse in the workplace. Black and mulatto Cuban workers were particularly harassed, especially those who were involved in labor organizing....

From Exiles, Immigrants, and Transnationals: Cuban Communities, by María Cristina García in David G. Gutiérrez, ed., *Columbia History of Latinos in the United States since 1960.* Copyright © 2004 Columbia University Press. Reprinted with permission of the publisher.

Cubans on opposite sides of the Florida straits maintained contact with each other in multiple ways, and those who lived in the United States strove to maintain a strong sense of *cubanidad*. They kept Cuban traditions alive through cultural pageants and celebrations; they published Spanish-language newspapers with news of the homeland; they wrote novels, plays, and poetry and composed music that spoke of their ties to both Cuba and the United States.... Remittances traveled easily across the border.... Cubans on the island and on the mainland were able to travel back and forth relatively freely, exchanging ideas, importing and exporting one another's goods, investing in one another's future. Like their nineteenth-century forebears, the Cubans on the mainland played an active role in the politics of their homeland, raising money for political causes and candidates.

Ironically, the revolutionary movement that produced the most expansive economic and political reform on the island also scared away the greatest number of people by its radicalism. Some of those who chose—or were forced—to leave Cuba after Castro took power were supporters of the U.S.-backed dictator, Fulgencio Batista.... As in many colonial and authoritarian societies with a history of corruption, the population had long hoped that an idealistic politician would come along and initiate the necessary reforms to create a truly egalitarian society. During the 1950s, many cautiously hoped that Fidel Castro and his July 26th Movement would provide that leadership and restore José Martí's vision for Cuba: a vision that had been thwarted by U.S. military and political intervention in 1898. Thus, when Castro proved successful in ousting Batista from power, many Cubans were euphoric, but that enthusiasm slowly waned in the years that followed. It is unclear if Castro was a communist when he took power in 1959, or if he was compelled to become so because of aggressive U.S. diplomatic and economic policies. Whatever the case, many Cubans became disillusioned with the marxist orientation their nationalist revolution ultimately took. They believed that under Castro, Cuba remained a colony, only this time of the Soviet Union. Cubans who now came to the United States perceived themselves as "exiles" rather than immigrants: people who had been displaced by a government that became increasingly hostile to their basic beliefs about democratic government, commercial enterprise, and equal opportunity....

Cuba's historic ties to the United States made it logical that most exiles would turn to their former American patrons for help, and until the mid-1970s, daily flights between Havana and Miami allowed Castro to export dissent. Arriving during the midst of the Cold War, the Cubans became powerful symbols for Americans of the clash between democracy and authoritarianism, between free enterprise and communism. Popular U.S. magazines like *Time, Life, Newsweek,* and *Fortune* celebrated the refugees' courage, love of freedom, and entrepreneurial spirit. Laws were bent or broken to facilitate the Cubans' entrance into this country and their accommodation and naturalization. No other immigrant group in the second half of the twentieth century received as expansive a welcome as the Cubans.

★ ★ ★

Cuban migration to the United States in the Castro years occurred in distinct "waves." The first occurred from 1 January 1959 to 22 October 1962 and brought approximately 248,070 Cubans to the United States. The first people to leave were those who were in some way connected to the old regime: political leaders, high government officials, and military officers of Fulgencio Batista's government. Associated with the corruption and abuses of the Batista years, these individuals were eager to leave Cuba since they faced retribution from a resentful population....

However, not all who left during this first wave were affiliated with the Batista government. Thousands became alienated by the social upheaval that followed Castro's rise to power. Cuban society underwent radical transformation in the 1960s. Agrarian and urban reform laws changed the character of ownership and production and placed most properties under the control of the state. The nationalization of U.S. properties on the island—a considerable investment ranging from [sugar]mills and factories to railroads and public utilities—angered the Eisenhower administration and led to a severing of diplomatic relations between the two countries and, eventually, an economic embargo. Fidel Castro correctly assumed that the United States would try to overthrow his government, and he proceeded to create a police state obsessed with weeding out any counterrevolutionary activity, real or imagined.... Shortages in basic food staples and consumer goods, brought on by the restructuring of the Cuban economy and later by the trade embargoes imposed by the United States and several other nations also affected Cubans across society....

Cubans of the elite classes were the first to leave, followed by member[s] of the professional middle class....

Most Cubans who traveled to the U.S. did so under the assumption that they would soon return to their homeland. Because of the United States' long history of involvement in Cuban affairs, most exiles believed that it was merely a matter of time before the United States intervened to replace Castro....

South Florida became the principal place of settlement.... Flights between Havana and Miami were the most readily available. Since the first arrivals came primarily from the middle class, Miami was also a place with which they were familiar because they had either vacationed or conducted business there. There was also a fairly large Cuban community in south Florida by 1959—some 30,000—many of whom had migrated a generation or two earlier as exiles from other political regimes.... Florida's climate and topography were also important considerations; and, as an added incentive, the plane ride from Havana to Miami was a short one (fifty-five minutes) and inexpensive (approximately twenty-five dollars).... Cubans ultimately settled wherever they found jobs, even if it meant relocating way up north in cities such as Chicago, St. Louis, or New York....

Acquiring permission to leave Cuba, as well as to travel to the United States, was a long, complicated affair. In order to leave their country legally, Cubans had to acquire an exit permit ..., which allowed the government to screen travelers before they left. While the government wanted to rid the country of dissenters, they also wished to prevent a "brain-drain"; those with skills considered vital to the revolutionary society (particularly in the sciences) and who did not pose a security threat were prohibited from leaving. Those suspected of "crimes against the revolution" were also detained for appropriate punishment. Cubans who could not secure exit permits, or who feared for their safety, took refuge in foreign embassies or sailed clandestinely to the Florida Keys, often on homemade rafts. Those unable to get a seat on a plane to the United States also had the option of traveling to a third country—if they were fortunate enough to acquire the appropriate visas—and either stay in those countries or apply for immigrant visas at the U.S. embassy there....

The U.S. bureaucracy was somewhat easier to navigate. Visas to travel to the United States could be acquired at the U.S. Embassy in Havana or at the American consulate at Santiago, and officials there regularly granted over a thousand "tourist" visas each week to allow Cubans to come to the United States. Once in the U.S., the Cubans were granted "indefinite voluntary departure" or "parole" status. After the United States severed relations with Cuba in January 1961, U.S. officials inaugurated a procedure of "visa waivers," which could be obtained through the Swiss embassy in Havana....

By the end of 1960, almost forty thousand Cubans had arrived in the United States, and their numbers increased by one thousand to fifteen hundred per week. Residents of south Florida panicked, since they knew that their city could not accommodate such sudden population growth. Most jobs were in the low-paying service sector, and Cubans had to compete with a large pool of unemployed workers, mostly African American, as well as northerners that traveled south each winter in search of jobs in the resort economy. The public school system, one of the poorest in the country, was ill-equipped to deal with the hundreds of children who arrived in their classrooms each month.

... [T]he early arrivals from Cuba experienced radical downward mobility. Approximately 36 percent of Cubans of the first wave were professionals (e.g. doctors, lawyers, engineers, and educators) but were unable to practice their professions because they lacked English fluency or did not meet other state licensing requirements. They worked at whatever jobs they could get, in construction, maintenance, and service occupations....

The Eisenhower administration left the task of accommodating the Cubans to local communities and charitable organizations. Like the exiles, the Eisenhower administration believed that it was only a matter of time before the Cubans returned to their homeland.... As early as March 1960, Eisenhower authorized the CIA to begin preparing an invasion of Cuba that would overthrow the Castro government and replace it with a coalition of leaders chosen directly by the United States. However, after many complaints from south Florida residents, who wanted the Cubans moved out of the area, the president finally released one million dollars ... to assist in resettlement efforts.... [I]n invoking the Mutual Security Act, Eisenhower officially recognized that Cuba was a communist state, and thus the Cuban exiles were refugees. The administration also established a "Cuban Refugee Emergency Center" in downtown Miami to coordinate the relief efforts of all the voluntary relief agencies and oversee a resettlement program. However, most of the financial burden of the Cubans' accommodation continued to rest with the volunteer agencies.

It was not until the Kennedy administration that the federal government assumed a more assertive role in refugee relief efforts. Kennedy established a "Cuban Refugee Program" (CRP) under the umbrella of the Department of Health, Education, and Welfare (HEW). [See Document 1]. The CRP provided funding for resettlement, monthly relief checks, health services, job training, adult educational opportunities, and surplus food distribution.... The government also provided partial funding to the Dade County Public School System to help it accommodate the more than 3,500 Cuban refugee children who attended public schools by January 1961.

One major problem the Kennedy administration had to deal with was the over 14,000 children who arrived unaccompanied during this first wave. Many parents unable to leave Cuba sent their children ahead, hoping to be reunited with them at a later date. These parents feared the political indoctrination in the schools and the military draft, and so they took part in what is now known as Operation Peter Pan, an underground network that emerged on the island to send children to the United States. [See Document 1]. Over half of the children who arrived unaccompanied in Miami were between the ages of 13 and 17, and over two-thirds were boys.... [T]he Kennedy administration assumed financial responsibility for the children, providing foster families and institutions with funding for their care. [See Document 3.]

... Working with community groups, the administration funded programs to assist Cuban professionals to prepare for their state licensing boards or to retrain for other types of employment. Programs were established at local universities to assist doctors, lawyers, teachers, and other professionals in their efforts to become certified for practice in the United States.

A number of federally funded vocational training programs targeted the working class.... Women received intensive English-language instruction and training in any of a number of skills: hand-sewing, sewing-machine work, office machine operation, clerical work, nursing, domestic service, and even silk-screen art work. Women were later resettled to cities where jobs were available for them....

Cuban migration to the United States continued even in the wake of the Bay of Pigs invasion of 1961, when the United States unsuccessfully carried out CIA plans to overthrow the Castro government. Migration continued until October 1962, when the Cuban Missile Crisis finally severed all air traffic between the two countries. In just three short years the city of Miami had undergone dramatic change as it accommodated over two hundred thousand "temporary visitors." While the government had resettled a few thousand Cubans out of south Florida, the majority preferred to remain in the area, even if it meant forfeiting any government assistance. They preferred to stay as close to the homeland as possible and within the more familiar and nurturing exile enclave.

Even though air traffic between the two countries ceased after the missile crisis, approximately 56,000 Cubans arrived in the United States from 22 October 1962 to 28 September 1965. The majority came via third countries, particularly Spain or Mexico, arriving with immigrant visas acquired at the U.S. embassies in those countries.... [M]any Cubans also sailed clandestinely from Cuba, arriving on small boats, rafts, and even inner tubes. By 1963, approximately 4,000 men, women, and children successfully crossed the Florida Straits in such craft and either arrived at Key West or were rescued by the U.S. Coast Guard. How many drowned, or were forced to return by Cuban authorities, is unknown.

★ ★ ★

… [O]n 28 September 1965, Fidel Castro announced that Cubans with relatives in the United States who wished to leave the island would be permitted to do so. He designated the small fishing port of Camarioca as a possible gathering place and port of departure and he pledged "complete guarantees and facilities" to exiles returning to Cuba by their own means to get their families out.

Within days of Castro's announcement, hundreds of Cuban exiles sailed to Cuba, mostly on rented craft, to pick up their relatives. The Johnson administration was caught completely by surprise. While the administration agreed to assist all those who wanted to leave communist Cuba, the last thing it wanted was an uncontrolled migration. Johnson announced that the United States would accept more Cuban refugees, but the migration had to be monitored…. The crisis coincided with the passage of the 1965 Immigration Act that abolished the national [origins] quota system in favor of a seven-category preference system that stressed family reunification. Thus, under the terms of the new law, migration preference was given to those Cubans who already had immediate family in the United States. In a "memorandum of understanding" between the two countries, the U.S. agreed to send chartered planes to Varadero twice each day, transporting between 3,000 and 4,000 Cubans each month…. The flights continued until April, when the Castro government once again prevented emigration to the United States. By this date, 3,048 flights had carried 297,318 refugees to the United States.

This "second wave" of Cuban refugees was distinct from the first in several ways. First, both the United States and Cuba were able to exert more control over this migration. The United States limited immigration to the immediate families of those Cubans already in the country …, and the Cuban government protected its own interests by more thoroughly screening the emigrant pool and prohibiting the emigration of those with skills or military service vital to the regime. Secondly, the refugees differed from the earlier arrivals in socioeconomic status: the "second wave" was much more representative of Cuba's working class. During the first wave, 31 percent of the Cubans who arrived in the United States were professionals or managers. By 1970, only 12 percent were professionals or managers, and 57 percent were blue-collar, service, or agricultural workers. Women were also overrepresented in this migration, as were the elderly: a consequence of the emigration restrictions placed on certain types of skilled labor and men of military age….

Cubans of every social class and profession were represented in the population, as were its various ethnic and religious groups. For example, the majority of Cuba's Chinese and Jewish populations settled in the United States.

… [H]owever, blacks remained underrepresented. The 1953 Cuban census revealed that 27 percent of Cuba's population was black or of mixed race, and yet in 1970, less than 3 percent of the Cubans in the United States were black.

This underrepresentation was attributed to three factors. Since racial equality was one of the goals of the revolution, black Cubans were generally optimistic about the future. As the poorest and most discriminated segment of Cuban society, they also stood to gain the most from the revolution's social and economic policies.... Secondly, blacks feared emigrating to the United States due to its history of Jim Crow segregation, lynching, race riots, and other types of race-related violence. During the 1960s, the photographs and news stories coming out of the United States showed a society in violent confrontation over civil rights.... Third, since U.S. immigration policy gave preference to those with relatives already in the United States, this policy tended to benefit whites—the first to leave—rather than blacks. Consequently, it was not until the Mariel boatlift of 1980 that a larger number of black Cubans emigrated to the United States (by the 1990 census, however, only sixteen percent of the Cuban exile population identified themselves as black, Chinese, or of another race). The small number that did choose to emigrate during the 1960s and 1970s were more likely to settle outside of Florida to escape the heightened racial tension in the South and the discrimination from their own white compatriots.

By 1974, the Cuban Refugee Program had resettled 299,326 of the 461,373 Cubans who had registered with them.... [T]he areas to receive the largest percentages were New York (27.1), New Jersey (19.8), California (13.2), Puerto Rico (8.5), Illinois (7.5), and Louisiana (2.8). By the mid-1970s, the Cuban Refugee Program had spent over $957 million in resettlement, relief, and other services, and a gradual phaseout of the program began.

The end of the "freedom flights" did not stall Cuban migration.... Several thousand more Cubans immigrated to the United States over the next few years, mostly via third countries. Clandestine emigration continued.... By September 1977, the total number of Cubans to arrive in the United States (since 1 January 1959) through legal and illegal channels reached 665,043.

★ ★ ★

In 1980, the Castro government once again allowed Cubans to emigrate to the United States. Echoing his actions fifteen years earlier, Castro announced in April that all who desired to leave Cuba were permitted to do so, and once again he invited Cuban exiles to sail to Cuba—this time to the port of Mariel—to pick up their relatives. One more time, thousands of exiles sailed across the Florida straits.... 124,776 Cubans arrived in the United States from April to October 1980, constituting the third official wave of post-Castro Cuban migration. However, unlike the previous two waves, the U.S. government played no role in sponsoring the migration....

During the late 1970s, there was a general thawing in tensions between Cuba and the United States. In 1977, for the first time in almost twenty years, both countries established limited diplomatic representation through the creation of "interests sections" in Washington and Havana. A number of cultural exchanges followed this rapprochement, and hundreds of Americans and Cubans traveled to one another's countries.... In a gesture of goodwill, the Castro government released over four thousand long-term political prisoners in the late

1970s and allowed them to emigrate with their families. In 1978, also for the first time, a few hundred Cuban exiles were allowed to return to their homeland to visit; the following year, over 100,000 exiles were allowed to return to their homeland to visit their families and friends....

For the first time in almost twenty years, Cubans on the island were able to have steady contact with Americans, and especially with their former compatriots, the people their government had long—and angrily—called "*los gusanos*" (the worms)....

These developments also coincided with one of Cuba's periods of economic austerity. Indeed, Castro's decision to allow Cuban exiles to visit their homeland was a move calculated to increase needed revenues.... The number of people who successfully fled the country on homemade rafts increased, as did the number of people apprehended by the Cuban Coast Guard. Beginning in May 1979, Cubans also began smuggling themselves into Latin American embassies to request political asylum. By March 1980, close to thirty Cubans had crashed their vehicles through embassy gates and had taken refuge within the compounds....

The tension climaxed on March 28, when a group of six Cubans stole a city bus and crashed through the gates of the Peruvian embassy. The Cuban guards stationed at the three entrances to the compound shot at the bus, and one of the guards was caught in the crossfire and killed. When the Peruvian ambassador refused to turn these gate-crashers over for criminal prosecution, the Castro government took action. On April 4, Castro pulled all Cuban guards from around the embassy compound, and sent in steamrollers to tear down the embassy gates. In a radio broadcast later that afternoon, Castro stated that his government would no longer risk the lives of its soldiers to protect "criminals."

As news of the event spread through the city of Havana, people left their homes and jobs to go to the embassy to observe. Realizing that they could freely walk into the embassy, many quietly entered the compound and requested asylum. Within 48 hours, approximately 10,800 men, women, and children were standing inside the Peruvian embassy. On April 6, Cuban police finally put up barricades all around the perimeter of the embassy—and for several blocks around—and prohibited more people from entering. For days the fate of the 10,800 was uncertain. The Peruvian government announced that it was unable to accept all the Cubans as asylees and requested international assistance. While they waited to know their fate, conditions in the camp steadily worsened....

The 10,800 remained in the compound for two weeks until an emigration plan was negotiated. Peru agreed to take one thousand asylees, and Costa Rica, Spain, Ecuador, Argentina, Canada, France, and West Germany pledged to accept a total of 2,500. The U.S. accepted a total of 6,200 refugees.

The airlift began on April 16....

Castro abruptly suspended the flights to Costa Rica four days after they began. A few days later, Castro substituted a new plan to rid the island not only of the remaining asylees at the Peruvian embassy, but of thousands of other dissidents.... [T]he government announced that all Cubans who wished to leave the island were permitted to do so, and urged them to call their relatives in the United States to come pick them up. He declared the port of Mariel, located some twenty miles west of Havana, as the port of departure and instructed officials to quickly set up camps around the port to process the thousands of Cubans expected to leave....

By the end of the week, an estimated five hundred boats had arrived in Mariel, and hundreds of others followed over the next few weeks.... The U.S. Coast Guard, the INS, and other federal authorities tried to discourage the boats from sailing out to Cuba, warning them that their actions violated U.S. immigration laws. However, as in Camarioca, these warnings had little effect....

When their relatives finally arrived at the port, Cuban officials informed the ship captains that they had to transport additional passengers—whomever the Cuban government told them to take....

[A] large and complex bureaucracy developed in south Florida to register and assist the new immigrants....

Finding sponsors became an especially difficult task during this third wave, however, since close to half of the Cubans had no friends or family in the United States. The government eventually had to build "tent cities." ... The federal government also opened up three additional camps to house the Cubans.... 62,541 Cubans, or almost half of the Mariel immigrants, waited for sponsorship in one of these camps; some stayed a few days, others remained for over a year....

Over the weeks, it became clear that the Castro government was using the boatlift to rid the country of its "undesirables." Cuban police removed people from hospitals, jails, and other institutions....

Unfortunately, the U.S. press focused an exaggerated amount of attention on the hard-core felons. While the latter constituted less than 2 percent of the total number of entrants, they commanded almost all of the media attention. Few journalists ever mentioned the fact that the overwhelming majority of Mariel Cubans had no criminal history and were hard-working citizens yearning for a better life. [See Document 4]....

The Cuban government finally closed the port of Mariel to further emigration on September 25, and the last boat arrived in Key West four days later. By this date, over 124,000 Cubans had made it to the United States.

Demographically, the Cubans of Mariel were different from the Cubans who arrived during the 1960's. The Mariel population was younger by about ten years (averaging thirty years of age), contained a higher percentage of blacks and people of mixed race (roughly twenty percent), and reflected a wider geographic distribution. Almost seventy percent were male....

The Mariel migration was most distinctive, however, in how it was perceived by the federal government and the larger U.S. society. Unlike the Cubans who immigrated from 1959 to 1973, the Cubans of Mariel were not considered legitimate refugees. The majority cited political reasons for their emigration, and administration officials commonly referred to them as "refugees." But the Justice department determined that under the terms of the 1980 U.S. Refugee Act (which came into effect a month before the boatlift), the Cubans did not qualify for refugee status nor for the special assistance that that status entitled them to receive. This marked the first time since the Cold War began that the govern-ment denied refugee status to individuals leaving a communist state. Instead, the government categorized the Cubans with the rather ambiguous term "entrant: status pending." … It was not until 1984 that the Cubans of Mariel were able to regularize their status.…

The older, more established Cuban exiles initially felt a moral responsibility to assist their compatriots.… Many worried that the new immigrants, raised under an authoritarian socialist system, would never adapt to their new society. Like most Americans, they were scandalized by the news that Castro had released criminals into the boatlift population. Angered that their reputation as "golden immigrants" was now tarnished, the exiles took great care to distinguish them-selves from the new immigrants. They coined a special term for the Cubans—*los marielitos*—that quickly became a pejorative in the community.…

Ethnic relations in south Florida deteriorated in the wake of the boatlift. During the summer of 1980, African Americans in nearby Liberty City rioted. While the riot was a response to a specific act of police brutality, it expressed the larger frustration in this community. For decades African Americans com-plained of having to compete with "foreigners" for jobs and political power, and the 1980s riot was the latest in a series of civil actions where citizens vented their rage against a system they felt had shut them out. In November 1980, in another demonstration of anti-Cuban sentiment, voters repealed the Bilingual-Bicultural Ordinance (originally passed in 1973) and made it unlawful to use county funds "for the purpose of utilizing any language other than English, or promoting any culture other than that of the United States." … To combat the negative images that now dominated the media, Miami Cubans founded the organization "Facts About Cuban Exiles" (FACE) in 1982.…

… Ten years after the boatlift, the term *marielito* had ceased to be pejorative.

★ ★ ★

In 1984, the Reagan administration and the Castro government signed a new immigration accord in which the United States agreed to accept up to 20,000 Cuban immigrants per year. In return, the Cuban government agreed to take back 2,746 criminal and mentally ill detainees of the Mariel boatlift. However, in May 1985 the Castro government suspended the accords in response to the Reagan administration's installation of *Radio Martí,* a radio network founded with the specific purpose of beaming news, music, and sports to the island, twenty-four hours a day, from an undisclosed location in the Florida Keys. By the time of the suspension, only 201 Mariel detainees had been returned to Cuba. It was not until 1987 that both governments once again reinstated the terms of the migration accords. But over the next decade both countries moved slowly on their ends of the agreement.…

The number of Cubans who emigrated clandestinely on rafts and small boats increased dramatically during the 1990s as a result of the worsening economic con-ditions in Cuba. After the dismantling of the Soviet Union, Cuba could no longer rely on its former patron.… The lack of external funding, together with a series of agricultural crises, caused even greater shortages in basic consumer goods.…

The *balsero* crisis peaked during the summer of 1994.... Unlike other undocumented immigrants, Cubans caught entering the United States illegally were allowed to stay under the terms of the 1966 Cuban Adjustment Act. Fearing another Mariel, the Clinton administration suspended this thirty-year policy: he announced that Cubans detained at sea would not be admitted to the United States and, instead, would be sent to the Guantánamo naval base until the Cuban government accepted them or the *balseros* received admittance to a third country.... The Clinton administration also tried to pressure the Castro government to restrict illegal emigration. U.S. officials announced that the sending of remittances to relatives on the island was prohibited, and charter air traffic from Miami to Cuba, available since 1979 to allow Cuban exiles the opportunity to visit their relatives in Cuba, was now indefinitely postponed. Despite these reversals in policy, the *balseros* kept coming. During the last two weeks of August 1994, the U.S. Coast Guard picked up an average of 1,500 *balseros* each day.

Finally, the U.S. was forced to go back to the negotiating table.... Under the terms of the 1994 agreement, the United States committed itself to accept a *minimum* of 20,000 per year, and the Castro government agreed to intercept any *balseros* and to accept the Cubans detained at Guantánamo without reprisals. However, the majority of the Cubans at Guantánamo refused to return to Cuba, and few were able to find admittance into a third country.... [P]roviding for the tens of thousands of camp residents cost U.S. taxpayers an estimated one million dollars a day. Finally, in 1995, the Clinton administration agreed to begin processing the camp residents for admittance into the United States.

The 1994 accords has not stopped illegal boat traffic to the United States or to other countries....

U.S. policy regarding the Cubans remains highly inconsistent, as was seen in the case of Elián González. This six-year-old boy was rescued at sea by the U.S. Coast Guard on Thanksgiving Day 1999, one of two survivors of an illegal expedition that claimed the lives of eleven defectors, including Elián's mother. Under the new policy, the young boy should have been deported back to Cuba and to the father and grandparents who wanted him back. In this particular case, the United States allowed the boy to stay to live with his relatives (a great-uncle and his family) in Miami, prompting a political tug-of-war between Cuba and the United States—and the families in each country—over who had legitimate rights to care for the boy. Elián's relatives in Florida, as well as many in the Cuban exile community, claimed that he was entitled to a life in the United States given the fact that his mother had lost her life trying to reach this country. His father in Cuba, on the other hand, demanded his return based on his rights as the now custodial parent, and traveled to Washington, D.C., to make his appeal. Polls showed that most Americans supported his claim. Editorials and op-ed pieces in the U.S. press criticized the United States for its inconsistent immigration policies and for bowing to pressure from the conservative and vocal elements in the Cuban exile community.

Finally, in April 2000, the INS stormed the house in Little Havana in a predawn raid, seized the six-year-old at gun point, and transported him to Washington, D.C., to await the legal resolution of his case with his father, Juan Manuel. In June, the Supreme Court denied the Miami relatives' claims to keep Elián in the United States, and the boy returned with his father to a hero's welcome in Cuba.

Cases such as this one proved yet again how politicized the immigration and asylum process has become....

Gay Cubans Challenge U.S. Immigration Policies

SUSANA PEÑA

ON THE DAY ARMANDO WENT to the police station to ask for permission to leave Cuba, he wore the gayest outfit he could find. Having been dissuaded from a career in teaching because he was too "obvious," Armando had experienced firsthand the ways in which a visible gay man's life might be limited in Cuba. Although spared the more intense forms of repression faced by others of his generation, Armando had decided to find out if the tumultuous events in Cuba during the summer of 1980—events that would come to be known as the Mariel boatlift—would really lead to the promised authorization to leave the country.

During our interview almost twenty years later, Armando explained how he had purposefully picked out a flowery shirt and a little chain that fit snugly around his neck ... for his interview with the Cuban police officials who would decide whether he should receive an exit permit. In 1980 Cuba these fashion choices were seen as gender transgressive, so Armando hoped they would confirm to the police officers that he was a counterrevolutionary homosexual and, therefore, that he would be permitted, if not encouraged, to leave the country. Before this day he had thought his homosexuality was "obvious," but for this important interview with Cuban officials he did not rely on the everyday visibility of his homosexuality: he made sure to perform the *loca,* the gender-transgressive effeminate homosexual man. Armando successfully passed the test. He was identified as socially undesirable, homosexual *escoria* (scum) by the Cuban state—negative labels that facilitated his exit from the country. At age twenty-six Armando crossed the Florida Straits on a ship named the *Spirit of Ecstasy.*

Armando's own ecstasy, however, soon gave way to confusion and instability. He described a chaotic scene in Florida. Mariel entrants were required to have a sponsor (either a family member or a volunteer) in order to be released from state custody. Although Armando had an uncle who was willing to sponsor him, a miscommunication kept him from making contact with that uncle when he arrived in Florida. Consequently, like many Mariel entrants, he was taken to Fort Chaffee, Arkansas, one of several resettlement camps around the country. Although he spent two months there, he recounts that it felt more like two centuries. He does not remember whether he was asked by camp officials about his sexuality. On 4 July 1980, after successfully being connected with his uncle, Armando left Fort Chaffee.

First published as the article "'Obvious Gays' and the State Gaze: Cuban Gay Visibility and U.S. Immigration Policy during the 1980 Mariel Boatlift," by Susana Peña, from *Journal of the History of Sexuality* Volume 16 Issue 3, pp. 482–514. Copyright © 2007 by University of Texas Press. All rights reserved.

Armando's convincing performance of the ostentatious homosexual facilitated his exit from Cuba, but it was unclear how that same kind of performance might affect his entry into the United States. The clarity with which he recalls his exit interview with Cuban police contrasts sharply with his recollection of how (and if) sexuality was considered in his processing by U.S. authorities. This contrast could be simply explained by the U.S. Immigration and Naturalization Service's (INS) lack of interest in immigrant sexuality, yet the historical record suggests that the INS was concerned rather than apathetic about such matters. Instead, as this article demonstrates, the U.S. government—from national, state, and local politicians to INS officials and local law enforcement—demonstrated a strong yet inconsistently focused interest in the sexuality of Mariel immigrants.

... I examine the state's "gaze" in relation to male homosexuals on both sides of the Florida Straits. I use the term *gaze* both to describe the methods used by the state to identify sexual populations as well as to highlight the ways in which these identification systems intersected with the interests and desires of the Cuban and U.S. states. The Cuban state's gaze relied on an assumption of gay identifiability. In practical terms, Cuban officials' interest in homosexuality necessitated a mechanism by which they could identify this population. As Armando's case makes clear, this mechanism involved openly evaluating visible markers of homosexuality. In contrast, his vague account of his U.S. experience suggests that in the United States, the state's long-standing interest in sexuality conflicted with the special treatment previously accorded Cuban "refugees" under cold war immigration policies. This tension required that U.S. authorities develop a selective gaze that sometimes saw and other times refused to see homosexual Mariel Cubans....

I put the state gaze in national context, analyzing how the state defined homosexuals, the identification procedures it used, and its vested interests in identifying homosexuals....

During the cold war relations between the United States and Cuba were tense. Because of this political acrimony, Cubans as a group had been accorded preferential treatment for their symbolic value as people fleeing communism. However, in the same era homosexuals were formally and categorically excluded by U.S. immigration policy. Even as Armando and other gay–identified Mariel Cubans were traveling by boat to the United States, the country of their destination was recodifying a long-standing immigration policy that explicitly excluded homosexuals. Because of its massive scale, the Mariel migration also posed procedural challenges to any systematic identification of immigrant characteristics. Finally, given the national media attention focused on the boatlift, the identification of homosexuals posed a public relations dilemma for the U.S. government. These complications are clearly seen when focusing on the ways in which homosexual Cuban men entering the United States were seen and not seen by the U.S. state gaze. During the boatlift conflicting immigration policies and procedures clashed as men who were both Cuban and visibly gay entered the country under the glare of the media spotlight.

★ ★ ★

The series of events now referred to as the Mariel boatlift began on 28 March 1980 when a Cuban bus driver took a busload of passengers into the Peruvian embassy in Havana to seek asylum....

... This led to a massive flotilla, and by October 1980 124,776 Cubans had arrived in the United States.

Tense relations between Cuba and the United States had been building since Fidel Castro's 1959 revolution. The nationalization of U.S.-owned property by Cuba, the establishment of an embargo against Cuba by the United States in 1960, the failed Bay of Pigs invasion in 1961, and the Cuban missile crisis of 1962 all contributed to these escalating tensions. Migrants from Cuba to the United States became important symbolic figures manipulated by both sides to prove the superiority of their respective political systems. Early into the Mariel boatlift, the U.S. government and media were able to further a discourse of Cubans desperate to leave an oppressive country and a failed economic system. In order to challenge this discourse, Castro discredited those who wanted to leave and characterized them as undesirables, antisocials, lumpen proletariat, and *escoria* (scum) and added that the United States was "performing a tremendous sanitary service" by accepting them.... In the United States the media picked up on this characterization. News reports repeatedly affirmed that Castro had emptied his prisons by sending criminals to the United States and that the migrants included members of "undesirable" groups such as mental patients, prostitutes, and homosexuals. Both the U.S. media and South Florida's Cuban American community began commenting on demographic and cultural differences between the Mariel immigrants and previous waves of Cuban immigrants. The perceived racial and class difference of the *Marielitos* ... added to their stigmatization and contrasted sharply with the historically preferential treatment of light-skinned immigrants to the United States, a special treatment accorded to previous generations of anticommunist Cuban "refugees." Racialization, class stigma, and sexual deviance were thus embedded in coverage of the Mariel migration, reinforcing the notion that these migrants were no loss to Cuba and posed a potential problem for the United States.

The Cuban government developed a selective process to facilitate the exit of people whom the revolution had already identified as undesirable. By prioritizing "undesirables," Cuban officials hoped to eliminate what they defined as problem populations from the country and reinforce the official story that disparaged all those who wanted to leave. When Cuban Americans arrived in Cuba with empty boats, hopeful that they would be reunited with family members, they were required to transport not only their relatives but also other people the Cuban government had approved for departure, among them, homosexuals, criminals, and the mentally ill.

After the 1959 Cuban revolution, the homophobia and heterosexism that already existed in Cuba became more systematized and institutionalized. Gender and sexuality explicitly entered political discourse even as vaguely worded laws increasingly targeted gender-transgressive men believed to be homosexual. Male homosexuals, in particular, were targeted under these laws, and male homosexuality became a visible and publicly discussed vice, whereas lesbianism remained unnamed and invisible. Between 1959 and 1980 male homosexuals suffered a range of consequences from limited career options to detention in street sweeps to incarceration in labor camps. The state had especially targeted gender-transgressive, "ostentatious," or obvious homosexuals.... Such visible markers not only facilitated enforcement of homosexual repression; more broadly, visibility and gender transgressions themselves constituted a central part of the problem identified by the revolution. Even in the severest period of enforcement ..., private homosexual expression was never the main target.... The gravest crime was not same-sex sexual acts per se but, rather, transgressing gender norms in ways associated with male homosexuality—in other words, appearing visibly or "obviously" gay.

During Mariel this state identification of homosexuality facilitated exit from the country, a situation many aspiring migrants viewed as beneficial. Some Cuban homosexuals were even given the unenviable choice of either serving jail time or leaving the country; it was hoped this ultimatum would encourage their departure. Others, like Armando, were able to request permission to leave.... In a speech delivered in May 1980, Castro denied that anyone was being forced to leave the country but added, "We have the right to authorize the exit of the antisocial elements, and that is what we're doing."

Accounts of gay men who went through this process confirm that declaring their homosexuality facilitated their exit from the country and reveal the ways in which authorities evaluated homosexuality.... [I]n *Before Night Falls* author Reinaldo Arenas described his processing at a local police station: "At the police station they asked me if I was a homosexual and I said yes; then they asked me if I was active or passive and I took the precaution of saying I was passive.... The Cuban government did not look upon those who took the active male role as real homosexuals. There were also some women psychologists there. They made me walk in front of them to see if I was queer."...With his *loca* strut for the psychologists and his previous arrest for having caused a "public scandal," Arenas was certified as visibly homosexual and, therefore, allowed to leave the country. [See Document 5]....

When Armando picked out his flowery shirt ... and Arenas strutted for the psychologists, they were deliberately performing the category of flamboyant, effeminate homosexual for state officials. The category of homosexual was reinforced, constructed, and redefined in these interactions. All of these accounts confirm that the officially recognized (and stigmatized) homosexual was a gender-transgressive male whose public behavior was ostentatious and who took the passive sexual role. As men who understood themselves to be homosexual performed this *loca* character, they reflected the official caricature of the homosexual back toward the state that had heightened its stigmatization. Certainly, some degree of condescension is at work here, for the men exaggerated a stereotype that they knew did not encompass who they were or who homosexuals were more broadly. However, even consciously constructed performances entailed real material and political consequences. If the men were convincing, authorities expedited their exit from the country. If they were not convincing, they might be refused an exit permit but marked as wanting to leave—a quite uncomfortable position given the acts of repudiation directed at *escoria* who preferred to emigrate. Their detailed accounts also suggest an ironic display of liberation: these men exaggerated effeminate or ostentatious mannerisms precisely in front of the government officials from whom they would most likely have hidden under normal circumstances.

At this moment in Cuban history, the state's policy toward homosexuals, while still oppressive, was quite unambiguous. Homosexuals continued to be stigmatized and defined as alien to the Cuban national project....

The interests of the Cuban state and homosexuals wishing to leave Cuba thus coincided in unexpected ways. From the Cuban state's perspective, the opportunity physically to remove homosexuals from the island could both enhance the virile image of the revolutionary nation and prevent possible future resistance from this stigmatized group. The migration of a large number of homosexuals, a minority group also stigmatized in the United States, also helped cast the mass exodus favorably for the revolution. According to the official Cuban discourse, the mass exodus did not prove the failure of the revolution. Instead, the hopeful emigrants were all undesirables, the lumpen dregs of society who did not want to work and were consumed by the vices of capitalism (including homosexuality, crime, and prostitution). By drawing attention to groups also widely stigmatized in the United States, the Cuban state simultaneously further discredited the emigrants, supported its revolutionary image, and generated challenges for future migrants.

Ironically, the interests of the Cuban state aligned with the immediate needs of Cuban homosexuals who wanted to depart.... [T]hose factors that may have motivated emigration are not so easy to disentangle. Some Cuban homosexuals might have wanted to leave the island because of repression they faced due to their homosexuality. Others might have been more motivated by economic concerns. Regardless of their motivation, Mariel provided a brief opening for those who wished to emigrate. In contrast to previous Cuban state policies toward homosexuals, the identification of homosexuals during Mariel, in effect, provided a desired outcome (at least for those homosexuals who *wanted* to leave) as opposed to a repressive consequence.

★ ★ ★

Whereas in Cuba the state actively sought to identify homosexuals in order to expel them and homosexuals, in turn, actively identified themselves to the state in order to facilitate their expulsion, in the United States the interests of the state and homosexuals did not line up so neatly, since the purpose and process of identification were inconsistent and often contradictory. Homosexual Cuban immigrants, ostentatious ones at that, presented three major complications for this receiving nation. First, homosexual Cubans embodied many of the existing contradictions and ambiguities of U.S. immigration policies governing homosexuals and Cubans as separate categories. Second, the identification of Cuban homosexuals was complicated by the fact that Mariel Cubans were processed in different ways by a number of federal, state, local, and voluntary agencies (VOLAGs) in a range of locations throughout the United States. These bureaucratic and jurisdictional differences inevitably led to disparate identification procedures. Third, the flood of national media attention that enveloped Mariel further complicated such procedures. The U.S. government was no less interested than Cuba in the public relations impact of the boatlift. For an international audience, it could confirm the failure of Cuban communism and the supremacy of U.S. capitalism: why else would so many desperate Cubans want to come to the United States? At home, the reinforcement of U.S. superiority might also quiet growing uneasiness about a weak national economy. Given the economic downturn in the previous decade and the upcoming presidential election in 1980, the domestic perception of the Mariel immigrants was especially important. Would voters perceive them as valued immigrants who would contribute to the U.S. economy (as they had perceived the "golden exiles" from Cuba who had preceded Mariel), or would they perceive them as undesirable immigrants who threatened national well-being?

Homosexual Mariel Cubans encountered ambiguous and contradictory U.S. immigration policy. On the one hand, since the rise of the cold war, the United States had warmly received Cuban immigrants and exploited their desire to leave Cuba as tangible proof of the failure of communism. On the other hand, the United States had a long-standing—if selectively enforced—ban against homosexual entrants. These two policies clashed on the bodies of gay Cubans.

It was unclear whether Cuban immigrants entering during the Mariel boatlift would be granted the same level of preferential treatment given to previous Cuban immigrants. In fact, few Mariel Cubans were defined as either political refugees or seekers of asylum. Instead, they were issued "paroles," and a new category was created for them: "Cuban-Haitian entrant (status pending)." This ambiguous status allowed them physical but not legal entrance into the country.... Also, unlike previous Cuban immigrants who had been processed by the Cuban Refugee Program, this new wave became "the first sizeable group of Cuban immigrants to experience the Immigration and Naturalization Service's personnel and operations." Therefore, most Mariel Cubans encountered more difficult immigration procedures and policy hurdles than had the post-1959 Cuban immigrants who preceded them.

Homosexual Mariel immigrants faced an additional hurdle because, precisely as they were entering the United States, the INS was in the process of redefining its homosexual exclusion policy. As Eithne Luibhéid explains, homosexuals had been formally excluded from entering the United States since the early 1950s. Beginning in 1952, people identified as homosexual had been issued Class A medical exclusions because they were classified as having a "psychopathic personality." Between 1965 and 1979 homosexuals were reclassified as "sexual deviates" and still subject to Class A medical exclusions. However, in 1979—six years after the American Psychological Association's 1973 decision to drop homosexuality as a mental illness from the *Diagnostic and Statistical Manual of Mental Disorders*—the surgeon general ordered the Public Health Service to stop issuing automatic Class A medical exclusions to homosexuals. This order denied the INS a bureaucratic identification mechanism to facilitate the automatic exclusion of homosexuals.

The INS had yet to react formally to this new directive from the surgeon general when, between April and late September 1980, a sizeable population of gay men and women—Armando among them—entered the United States from Cuba. It was not until September 1980, with the boatlift almost over, that the INS responded with a new policy on homosexual exclusion that effectively bypassed the surgeon general's order. Given the timing of the decision, we can deduce that the INS felt the need to clarify its policy in order to deal with the sudden mass influx of immigrants and increasing media curiosity about homosexuals among the Cuban migrants. On 8 September 1980 Acting INS Commissioner David Crosland sent an agency memo announcing that new procedures would no longer require medical certification from the Public Health Service. According to the new policy, "aliens" were not to be asked about their sexual preference during "primary inspection." However, if "an alien makes an unsolicited, unambiguous oral or written admission of homosexuality" or if "a third party who presents himself or herself for inspection voluntarily states, without prompting or prior questioning, that an alien who arrived in the United States at the same time and is then being processed for admission is a homosexual," then a private, professionally administered "secondary inspection" of the alien would follow. During this secondary inspection, Crosland's memo directed, the alien "shall be asked *only* whether he or she is homosexual. If the answer is 'no,' the alien shall not be detained for further examination as to homosexuality. If the answer is 'yes,' the alien shall be asked to sign a statement to that effect ... [and] he or she shall be referred to an immigration judge for an exclusion proceeding."

This new policy was perceived as a partial victory by gay rights activists who had been struggling against the INS's broadly construed gay and lesbian exclusion policies....

During the initial stages of the boatlift itself, the INS homosexual exclusion policy was in flux. However, even after clarification, the U.S. state confronted conflicting imperatives. On the one hand, identifying homosexuals would allow their exclusion—a desired outcome from the department's point of view, as its new policy made clear. At the same time, the possibility of excluding a large number of Cuban immigrants because of their sexuality posed a practical problem: What would the U.S. government do with a large group of "excludable" homosexuals who could not be returned to their home country?

★ ★ ★

In addition to this policy dilemma, various practical issues on the ground made the Mariel boatlift a logistical nightmare for the agencies charged with processing immigrants. During their first days on U.S. soil, Mariel Cubans underwent bureaucratic processing by federal agencies, local officials, and VOLAGs. Most Mariel Cubans went through a basic process during which authorities consistently identified personal characteristics they considered to be of interest to the state. For example, officials tested the immigrants for venereal disease and tuberculosis and interviewed them about their criminal history. In these first days of processing, the state gaze was refracted through a range of federal agencies, including those concerned with immigration status (INS), law enforcement and security, and public health as well as several VOLAGs charged with resettlement.

While this initial processing was fairly consistent across the Mariel entrant population, subsequent processing varied dramatically, and the route a Mariel entrant followed to immigration sponsorship had a substantial impact on the subsequent intensity of the state's fractured gaze. Mariel Cubans who were reunited with family sponsors by the VOLAGs within their first seventy-two hours in the United States were held in custody for only a few days and never left South Florida. In contrast, others were held in state custody for months in distant states.

After this initial common processing, Mariel Cubans followed one of three routes: (1) direct resettlement in South Florida for those with available sponsors; (2) review at a federal correctional institution (FCI) for those suspected of having a criminal background; or (3) confinement at a resettlement camp for those without available sponsors. Both homosexuals and nonhomosexuals followed all three routes. However, the focus and intensity of the U.S. state gaze in relation to homosexuality varied considerably, depending on the route.

The most desirable route for entrants was to locate a family or unrelated volunteer sponsor quickly while they were still in the South Florida area. About half of the Mariel entrants were placed directly with sponsors. Those with family members willing to sponsor them and those who were attractive, nonthreatening candidates for volunteer sponsors were placed more quickly. Less attractive candidates (single men, black men, and "obvious homosexuals") were more likely to be sent to resettlement camps outside of South Florida.

Given that about half of entering Mariel Cubans were resettled directly out of South Florida, it is likely that many Cuban gays and lesbians were resettled in this way....

Mariel Cubans who were suspected of having a criminal background, including those who admitted to homosexuality-related arrests in Cuba, were sent to FCIs for further review. Because U.S. authorities were invested in identifying "criminals" among the Mariel entrant population and because certain expressions of homosexuality were criminalized in Cuba, this portion of the homosexual Mariel population did fall directly under the state's gaze....

Given that admission of homosexuality to state officials had very recently facilitated exit from Cuba for many Mariel Cubans, many of whom believed the United States less repressive of homosexuals than Cuba, it is likely that many homosexual Mariel Cubans did not hide their previous homosexuality-related incarceration from INS officials. A review of information about Mariel Cubans released from the FCI in Talladega, Alabama, suggests that homosexuals comprised a significant portion of [this] population....

Although information about the homosexuality of Cubans detained in FCIs was collected, this information was not necessarily made public and did not capture the media's attention (rapists and murderers were much more alarming "criminals" reported in the news). Homosexual Mariel Cubans who were sent to resettlement camps, on the other hand, did attract media attention. Mariel Cubans who had a difficult time finding sponsors were sent to more distant processing camps scattered throughout the country, including Fort Chaffee, Arkansas, Fort Indiantown Gap, Pennsylvania, Fort McCoy, Wisconsin, and Fort Walton Beach, Florida. As negative media portrayals of the Mariel immigrants increased and massive numbers of Cubans continued to arrive, volunteer sponsors were harder to come by, and Mariel Cubans were held in state custody for longer periods of time.

The CHTF [Cuban-Haitian Task Force] was aware of media interest in this population.... The task force's final report reflected on the impact of this media attention: "During the summer months, there was media coverage of the presence of homosexuals among the Cuban entrants. The self-segregation of these homosexuals in the resettlement centers gave them a high visibility which facilitated the media coverage." According to the CHTF, "widespread publicity" increased the difficulty of finding sponsors for the homosexual Mariel Cubans. Federal officials also felt that the visibility of homosexuals contributed to the overall negative perception of the migration.... To challenge this negative impression, the federal government denied any systematic knowledge or identification of homosexual immigrants in the camps. However, because "obvious" homosexuality and gender transgression were obstacles to traditional resettlement, homosexuality had to be taken into account in order to facilitate the processing of homosexual Cubans. Therefore, authorities had to see homosexuals in order to move them out of the media spotlight even as they claimed not to see the homosexuals in order to deny their existence to the media.

The resettlement camp population formed the primary focus of media debates about homosexual Mariel Cubans.... As time went on, the camp populations were increasingly comprised of difficult-to-place Cubans or "special cases." One category of special cases was male homosexuals and, more specifically, gender-transgressive male homosexuals....

Official denials aside, camp officials were clearly aware of the homosexual population.... In a State Department memo in response to direct questions about the homosexual population, Senior Civilian Coordinator Donald Whitteaker described the presence of "two different types of homosexuals at Fort Chaffee, admitted and closet [sic]." According to Whitteaker, the homosexuals were "consenting adults and segregated by their design. Lifestyle is casual and open." This descriptive response signals the government's careful attention to the homosexual population....

Until 7 July 1980, however, the national mainstream media avoided the topic of gay men among the Mariel entrants, did not identify this visible gay presence as a major story, and cited the "unavailability of reliable data" as the reason for this omission. The theme of unreliable data would emerge again and again as state officials attempted to silence the gay Mariel story.

★ ★ ★

The Mariel boatlift offered some homosexual men who had suffered the consequences of visibility in Castro's Cuba an opportunity strategically to flaunt their homosexuality as a way to escape state oppression. Many believed they were coming to a country tolerant of such display. Ironically, many were headed for a nation that had just embarked upon a national Christian backlash against gay liberation, and they had entered it through the city of Miami, where some say that backlash began. This backlash and the potential for assault notwithstanding, inside and outside the camps many embraced the notion that they would no longer have to hide. Gender transgression was one culturally resonant way in which a subpopulation of men who had sex with men and identified as homosexual expressed that identity.

Viewed in this way, the gender transgression of the gay *Marielitos* enacted both political resistance and community formation. However, this visible behavior posed an obstacle to traditional resettlement.... [A] representative of the United States Catholic Conference explained ... : "We have a number of individuals at Chaffee whose lifestyles is [sic] obviously something that we must be very honest [about] with our sponsors.... And if we pick up some facets of their personality which are possibly going to be a surprise to the sponsor, if José, as it turns out, is in fact wearing a dress, it's obviously very important that we discuss this issue with the sponsor." As [this] comment suggests, many religious VOLAGs traditionally involved with resettling refugees were not necessarily well suited to finding sponsors for a dress-wearing José....

As the "deviance" of the Mariel Cuban population increasingly became the subject of sensationalist media stories, the state developed an interest in dispersing the spectacle of visible, gender-transgressive homosexuals concentrated in state custody. In order to move the *locas* out of the media spotlight and facilitate their sponsorship, the U.S. state needed precisely to pinpoint gender-transgressive homosexuals in the resettlement camps—ironically, in order to obscure this population from the media's gaze. However, if the state formally recognized their homosexuality, these migrants could be subject to exclusion hearings based on INS homosexual exclusion policies. In order to navigate these contradictions, the authorities needed to process gender-transgressive homosexuals without officially identifying them as homosexuals at all.

The CHTF responded to a 7 July 1980 *Washington Post* report by Warren Brown that twenty thousand Cuban homosexuals remained in the resettlement camps by taking a series of conflicting official positions. In effect, the CHTF claimed that (1) they did not identify homosexuals in the Mariel population; (2) they did not know how many homosexuals there were; (3) they did not involuntarily segregate homosexuals in resettlement camps; and (4) they did not work with gay organizations to resettle gay immigrants from Mariel....

A close examination of the state's publicly avowed positions on gay Mariel Cubans and internal records of federal agencies reveals what are perhaps expected contradictions. While the task force claimed that they did not identify, count, or segregate homosexuals and that they were not working with gay organizations, federal authorities did (if inconsistently) identify, count, and segregate homosexuals, and they did end up working with gay agencies to resettle the Mariel Cubans and partially funding their efforts....

... [I]t was still unclear whether homosexual Cubans identified by the state in either informal or formal ways were going to be allowed to stabilize their status (shifting from parolees to permanent residents) or whether they were going to be "excluded" as a group. As homosexual exclusion policy stood (after its 1980 clarification), anyone who made two back-to-back "unsolicited and unambiguous" declarations of homosexuality could be excluded. Because of this, gay and lesbian organizations working with the Cuban entrants began to demand clarification from the INS about how this policy would be applied and to counsel gay men to be careful what they said to local and federal immigration authorities.

Partly in response to this pressure from gay and lesbian organizations, the INS clarified its position on gay Mariel Cubans five years later. In 1985 the INS explained that gay or lesbian refugees who entered as part of Mariel and were identified as gay or lesbian would "not be excluded from the U.S. based on that information alone."...

★ ★ ★

When Armando presented himself to Cuban police officials, he wanted to be sure that the Cuban state's gaze would read him as an "obvious," flamboyant, effeminate homosexual. To be identified as *escoria* during that brief moment signified a way out of the country and, in his young eyes, a ticket to a land of freedom and opportunity. In Cuba the state's gaze was relatively consistent during this brief moment. Cuban authorities had a vested interest in identifying an already stigmatized group, "obvious" homosexuals, in order to facilitate their exit or expulsion from the country. The state saw gender-transgressive, ostentatious, passive men as homosexual.... To say that the Cuban state gaze was consistent is not to say that it was necessarily precise. In the case of Mariel, people who had not previously identified as homosexual claimed homosexuality in order to leave the country. Others who did understand themselves as homosexual were not allowed to leave the country because they were not identified by police as homosexual (or homosexual enough) or because other factors restricted their departure, as they nearly did in the case of Arenas.

The U.S. state gaze was neither consistent nor precise. Facing competing imperatives (to welcome victims of communism and to exclude homosexuals), the U.S. state carefully crafted policy clarifications that welcomed Mariel Cubans (although not with the same enthusiasm as previous cohorts) while it maintained a homosexual exclusion policy.... Thus, the state had an interest in not seeing or identifying homosexual entrants since, given the tenor of the relationship between Cuba and the United States, returning Cubans to Cuba was an unlikely scenario. Detaining Mariel homosexuals indefinitely, as the United States tried to do with Mariel entrants identified as criminals, proved an expensive and unattractive option. Despite these disincentives, even authorities who pretended not to see the homosexuals were actively engaged in the politics of homosexual visibility precisely because administrative needs required the identification of those who disrupted camp life or posed a challenge to traditional resettlement.

In addition to inconsistent U.S. policies, the state's identification of homosexual entrants was imprecise. Not all men who thought of themselves as homosexuals were visibly identifiable as gay, nor did they all verbally declare their homosexuality to state officials. When the state recognized the need to identify homosexuals in order to facilitate their resettlement, it acknowledged mostly only gender-transgressive, "obvious" gays. As various federal officials attempted to count this population, the imprecision of the gaze was further revealed.... While the controversial Brown article cited a figure of 20,000 homosexuals, the federal government produced estimates ranging from 200 to 6,800. We simply do not know with certainty how many gay men arrived as part of the Mariel boatlift....

Although inconsistent and imprecise, the federal government did at some levels identify individual homosexual entrants and estimate the size of the homosexual subpopulation. Nevertheless, it is important to note that the power of state identification practices does not lie in their precision.... The processing of immigrants with regard to sexuality provided *Marielitos* with their first socialization into U.S. sexual categories and identities. Whereas in Cuba the distinction between active and passive homosexuality was key (passive homosexuals were the "real" homosexuals and the corrupting force), it is unlikely that U.S. authorities deployed this distinction. However, ... their figures were based not on homosexual identity or same-sex behavior per se but on gender-transgressive expressions. Ironically, then, although the Cuban and U.S. state gazes were differently grounded, in the end both targeted a similar population—gender-transgressive, "obviously" gay men.

Despite their inconsistencies and imprecision, the fractured gazes of both Cuba and the United States entailed real material consequences for those identified as deviant. For the Mariel *locas,* U.S. identification as homosexual did not necessarily lead to exclusion, but it opened up this possibility…. Although the worst-case scenario did not materialize in this case (i.e., the exclusion of all Cuban homosexuals who entered as part of Mariel), the state's refracted gaze still wielded power in its flickering recognition of "negative" characteristics.

 # FURTHER READING

Reinaldo Arenas, *Before Night Falls* (1993).

Ruth Behar, ed., *Bridges to Cuba/Puentes a Cuba* (1995).

Román de la Campa, *Cuba on My Mind: Journeys to a Severed Nation* (2000).

María de los Angeles Torres, *The Lost Apple: Operation Pedro Pan, Cuban Children in the U.S., and the Promise of a Better Future* (2003).

María Cristina García, "The Cuban Population in the United States: An Introduction," in Andrea O'Reilly Herrera, ed., *Cuba: Idea of a Nation Displaced* (2007).

María Cristina García, *Havana USA: Cuban Exiles and Cuban Americans in South Florida, 1959–1994* (1996).

Guillermo J. Grenier, Lisandro Pérez, and Nancy Foner, *The Legacy of Exile: Cubans in the United States* (2002).

Guillermo J. Grenier and Alex Stepick, eds., *Miami Now! Immigration, Ethnicity, and Social Change* (1992).

Felix Masud-Piloto, *From Welcomed Exiles to Illegal Immigrants: Cuban Migration to the U.S., 1959–1995* (1996).

Mirta Ojito, *Finding Mañana: A Memoir of a Cuban Exodus* (2005).

Andrea O'Reilly Herrera, ed., *Cuba: Idea of a Nation Displaced* (2007).

Andrea O'Reilly Herrera, ed., *ReMembering Cuba: Legacy of a Diaspora* (2001).

Silvia Pedraza, "Cuba's Exiles: Portrait of a Refugee Migration," *International Migration Review* 19, no. 1 (Spring 1985), 4–34.

Silvia Pedraza, *Political and Economic Migrants in America: Cubans and Mexicans* (1985)

Silvia Pedraza, *Political Disaffection in Cuba's Revolution and Exodus* (2007).

Gustavo Pérez Firmat, *Life on the Hyphen: The Cuban-American Way* (1994).

Alejandro Portes and Robert L. Bach, *Latin Journey: Cuban and Mexican Immigrants in the United States* (1985).

Alejandro Portes and Alex Stepick, *City on Edge: The Transformation of Miami* (1993).

Gerald E. Poyo, *Cuban Catholics in the United States 1960–1980: Exile and Integration* (2007).

Emily H. Skop, "Race and Place in the Adaptation of Mariel Exiles," *International Migration Review* 35, no. 2 (2001), 449–471.

Victor Andres Triay, *Fleeing Castro: Operation Pedro Pan and the Cuban Children's Program* (1998).

CHAPTER 11

Social Movements and
Self-Proclaimed Identities

The late 1960s and 1970s were an era of social and political movements throughout the United States and internationally. Globally, decolonization struggles sought independence for Third World countries, and sparked social movements in many countries. The United States witnessed the proliferation of movements: civil rights and Black Power; Chicana/o, Puerto Rican, Native American, and Asian American; anti-Vietnam War and student; as well as Women's and Gay Liberation movements. No longer seeking incremental reforms by working within existing political structures, these movements sought "radical," fundamental social change and deployed various protest strategies to achieve them.

Becoming political activists, Latina/o youth participated in many movements and created their own. They built on the legacies of African American civil rights struggles and the social fervent of the era, long-term activism within their respective communities, and historical movements within their countries of origin. Given distinct migration histories and geographic settlement patterns, the movements were separate—the Chicana/o movement, the Puerto Rican movement, and Cuban American activism. Each was based on an assertion of racial and ethnic pride, and a challenge to prevailing stereotypes. Each also had local and transnational dimensions, as well as an internal diversity of perspectives.

The Chicana/o and Puerto Rican movements confronted racism and economic exploitation, seen as the legacies of conquest. Chicana/o youth and activists focused on the conquest of 1848 and the betrayals of the Treaty of Guadalupe Hidalgo. The reclaiming of Aztlán emerged as a powerful concept for claiming the land lost in the conquest, as well as for the assertion of a "homeland." Much of the Chicano movement embraced cultural nationalism, based on "la raza," as a foundation for unity. Puerto Rican activists drew connections among the conquest of 1898, Puerto Rico's continuing colonial status, and conditions in the United States. Much of the Puerto Rican movement embraced international socialism, based on working-class solidarity across racial/ethnic lines. Chicana/o and Puerto Rican activism confronted urban issues, such as gentrification and displacement, police brutality, and economic exploitation. They also supported farm worker activists.

Educational disparities, bias and mistreatment, and inattention to or misrepresentation of their histories fostered educational activism that led to the creation of Chicana/o Studies and Puerto Rican Studies programs in colleges and universities. Women confronted gender inequalities within both movements. Chicanas challenged cultural nationalism's assertion of traditional gender roles, and Puerto Rican women sought to remedy the discrepancy between egalitarian rhetoric and unequal treatment.

Cuban American youths' activism focused on the right to return to Cuba, their "homeland." They wanted to explore the nature of the Cuban revolution and to choose their relationship with Cuba. They also sought to reconnect with their own identities as they defined them. Political and generational tensions ruptured Cuban American communities and helped shift U.S. and Cuban foreign policy. This chapter examines the struggles of Puerto Rican, Chicana/o, and Cuban American activists who began organizing around community issues, as well as becoming involved in national and international political change.

DOCUMENTS

Document 1 is an excerpt of Rodolfo "Corky" Gonzales' 1967 poem, "I Am Joaquín," which became an anthem of the Chicano movement. The poem evokes a personal rendering of Chicano history and the foundations for unity based on shared history and identity. First emerging as a youth gang in Chicago, the Young Lords became political and a foundation for the Puerto Rican movement in 1968. In Document 2, Chicago Young Lord José "Cha Cha" Jiménez reflects on these origins and their activism in a 2012 interview. Document 3 is "El Plan Espiritual de Aztlán," which emerged from the First Chicano National Conference in 1969. The Plan articulated "nationalism" and "brotherhood" as the basis for unity and specified key goals for the Chicano movement. Young Lords branches emerged in New York City, Philadelphia, and elsewhere in the Puerto Rican diaspora. In Document 4, the Young Lords articulate their 13 Point Program and Platform. This 1970 version replaced an earlier one that called for "revolutionary machismo," as women within the movement argued that machismo could not be revolutionary. Document 5 is a 1972 *Mademoiselle* article by Jennie V. Chávez revealing the challenges Chicanas confronted within the Chicana/o movement and the resultant "revolution within a revolution." In Document 6, Puerto Rican activist Esperanza Martell narrates autobiographically the founding of the Latin Women's Collective in 1975, emphasizing the importance of working-class women's perspectives. For Cuban American youth, just initiating contact with their home country was a challenge. Document 7 is the Declaration of the Antonio Maceo Brigade, which was published in *Areito* in 1978. The Brigade enabled Cuban Americans to visit Cuba, and here they outline both their reasons and the criteria for participants. In Document 8, Cuban American writer Achy Obejas depicts in her autobiographical fiction the intense generational and political conflicts that erupted not only within Cuban communities, but also within families.

1. "'I Am Joaquín' Voices Chicano Movement's Goals," 1967

I am Joaquín,
lost in a world of confusion,
caught up in the whirl of a
        gringo society,
confused by the rules,
scorned by attitudes,
suppressed by manipulation,
and destroyed by modern society.
My fathers
   have lost the economic battle
and won
   the struggle of cultural survival....

I owned the land as far as the eye
could see under the crown of Spain,
and I toiled on my earth
and gave my Indian sweat and blood
     for the Spanish master
who ruled with tyranny over man and
beast and all that he could trample.
               But...
     THE GROUND WAS MINE.
I was both tyrant and slave....

I am the mountain Indian,
       superior over all.
The thundering hoof beats are my horses.
The chattering machine guns
   are death to all of me:
     Yaqui
       Tarahumara
         Chamula
           Zapotec
             Mestizo
               Español....

I rode the mountains of San Joaquín.
I rode east and north
   as far as the Rocky Mountains,
      and

Rodolfo "Corky" Gonzales, in *The Latino Reader: An American Literary Tradition from 1592 to the Present*, eds. Harold Augenbraum and Margarite Fernández Olmos (Boston: Houghton Mifflin Company, 1997): pp. 265–279. Reprinted with permission of the author.

all men feared the guns of
                    Joaquín Murrieta.
I killed those men who dared
   to steal my mine,
       who raped and killed

                        my love
                        my wife....

My blood runs pure on the ice-caked
hills of the Alaskan isles,
on the corpse-strewn beach of Normandy,
the foreign land of Korea
                    and now
                    Vietnam....

My knees are caked with mud.
My hands calloused from the hoe.
I have made the Anglo rich,
                    yet
   equality is but a word—
       the Treaty of Hidalgo has been broken
   and is but another treacherous promise.
My land is lost
           and stolen,
My culture has been raped....

And in all the fertile farmlands,
                        the barren plains,
the mountain villages,
smoke-smeared cities,
           we start to MOVE.
   La Raza!
Mejicano!
   Español!
     Latino!
       Hispano!
         Chicano!
or whatever I call myself,
           I look the same
           I feel the same....

I am the masses of my people and
I refuse to be absorbed.
           I am Joaquín.
The odds are great

but my spirit is strong,
>   my faith unbreakable,
>   my blood is pure.
I am Aztec prince and Christian Christ.
>   I SHALL ENDURE!
>   I WILL ENDURE!   [1967]

2. José "Cha Cha" Jiménez Explains How a Chicago Gang Became a Part of the Puerto Rican Movement in 1968

… Lincoln Park as a whole seemed mixed but it was internally divided along racial lines.…

There was a lot of prejudice in the city, especially against Latinos and African Americans. But in terms of growing up, it was like any other community. People were close and friendly. Actually, there were a lot of … Latino social clubs … that became gangs later as there was more poverty and less supervision. Now the Young Lords, we were a gang from the beginning. We wanted to fight, we wanted territory, and we wanted a name. So, we were different. We were also a younger group. Around 1962 they opened an upper elementary school center and that's where we met and we officially got the name, the Young Lords.

… [W]e had gotten into fights with other groups previously.… [A]ll of us were getting chased by other white gangs. Coming from school you would get chased. That was the normal thing.… You know, we were just coming into a Lincoln Park heavily populated by whites. Not that we wanted to be there, it was more that we were pushed into it.…

Once the Puerto Ricans that arrived into Lincoln Park got to know each other, the younger ones started forming their own little groups. Those groups were more for protection. As other Latinos moved into the neighborhood we now wanted to chase those who originally harassed us.…

I was in and out of jail for different things.… I was the head of the group at the time, and they wanted to get rid of the head. They gave my mother a choice, since I was still a juvenile, between staying in jail and going to Puerto Rico. I was put in handcuffs and sent to Puerto Rico. That was good for me because I learned a little about my culture. I started to speak Spanish more, and when I came back I changed my name from "Cha-Cha" to "El Cagüeño" [that is, a native of Caguas].… I returned to Chicago within a year, maybe '64. When I came back, I rejoined the group.…

Then there was a drug epidemic in the neighborhood. You could feel a quick change in the area.… I started using heroin at that time and I got caught with a bag and given sixty days [in the summer of 1968].… While I was there, a black Muslim worked as a librarian.…

"The Young Lords, Puerto Rican Liberation, and the Black Freedom Struggle: Interview with José 'Cha Cha' Jiménez," *OAH Magazine of History* 26, no. 1 (January 2012), pp. 61–64.

From him, I started reading *Seven Story Mountain* which is about a monk [Thomas Merton]. I also started reading about Malcolm X, Martin Luther King, and hearing about the Black Panthers.... Those things got me interested and thinking that I could do the same thing, something similar to what blacks were doing but within the Puerto Rican community.

[When I got out of prison], ... I saw people that I knew being kicked out by the sheriff when they could not pay rent—their clothes splattered all over the sidewalk. I wasn't the only one thinking of this as a problem, the neighbors were also talking about the Latino community being oppressed. Groups such as the Progressive Puerto Rican Youth began to address some of those neighborhood concerns.

Then [in early September 1968] I met this lady, Pat Devine, a white woman who was fighting against urban renewal ... not in defense of Puerto Ricans but for the whole neighborhood in a class basis. She asked me if I could get some people to go to a [local council] meeting [of the Department of Urban Renewal] and I said, "of course, I can get a bunch of people." I was on the corner drinking and bragging about all the people I could get for her and then I started talking to members of the Young Lords gang, but they opposed to go.... I even got in a couple of fights because people started calling me "communist" and things like that.

Finally, the day of the meeting we were able to get around sixty people to come.... Inside the urban renewal office we saw a big display of the remodeling plans. I started telling the group "look, that is your house and they are going to knock it down"—real simple urban renewal analysis.... The people that were meeting that night were mainly white.... Offended by the sight, the guys and I called for the meeting to be over. I told them that if they did not get black or Latino representatives from the community they could not meet there anymore....

The following day I got picked up and sent to the station. The cops were asking me questions about me working with communists to which I laughed. They could not understand that we were not communists we were simply pissed off. About an hour or two later, a lawyer came. He told me there were people outside the station. I did not believe him but when he got me out I saw Pat Devine and a bunch of Young Lords there. That day gave me the motivation to keep working for the community.

... [W]e designed a button that said "Tengo Puerto Rico en mi corazón" [I have Puerto Rico in my heart]. Our main focus was the neighborhood but also self-determination for Puerto Rico. We brought the colonial issue to Chicago on a massive scale. We did not know words like "diaspora" or anything like that but we always knew that we were connected to Puerto Rico....

That was a big part of our beginnings, our roots as a group centered on demanding self-determination for Puerto Rico. We used the term "self-determination" because we tried to find a concept that anybody could understand.... We fought for the right to control our own lives.

For us, it was simple. It was not anything theoretical. It was just like what we saw at Lincoln Park. Other people came to take over the neighborhood and the U.S. did the same thing in Puerto Rico. The whole issue of housing displacement, then, served as a way to explain the issue of U.S. colonialism in Puerto Rico and vice versa.

We went to Denver, Colorado and through Corky González [the founder and central leader of the militant Chicano group Crusade for Justice] we met people from the Brown Berets, a lot of Chicano gangs from Los Angeles, and members from the Council of Aztlán. I also traveled to California for one of Corky's speaking tours. There, I learned more about the Black Panthers.

In Chicago, after the Young Lords made news following a takeover of a police community workshop meeting, we met Fred Hampton and the Chicago Panthers. The Panthers were organizing at the same time that we were, but they mainly worked underground. They were smart; we did it the dumb way. They prepared themselves first before they came out. We went straight from being a gang right into being a politicized group without much preparation....

After we were better known, we started to have Latino students working for us. Before that, we were mainly street people....

... [I]n McCormick Theological Seminary, where Pat Devine and her group, The Concerned Citizens of Lincoln Park, with several other organizations, us included, fought to get the Seminary to invest in low-income housing as a way to slow down urban displacement. After the Seminar's refusal to invest in low-income housing, we decided to occupy their offices [on May 15, 1969].... We were there for almost a week until the people of the Seminary agreed to meet our demands—$50,000 to be invested for low-income housing, $25,000 for two health clinics, to invest in a community legal aid office.... In the end, the city council rejected our plan for low-income housing....

After we met Fred [Hampton], we decided that we had no choice but to come together. The police in Chicago was well connected so we needed to come together and protect ourselves. Besides, we were fighting for the same thing. A group of hillbillies called the Young Patriots also joined. At that time in Chicago, the Appalachian community was suffering from the same displacement issues that we Puerto Ricans faced. Having different people together allowed us to re-educate ourselves. We learned that we were not alone in the world, that there [are] many people fighting for change and we were part of a larger struggle for change.

★ ★ ★

[In the fall of 1969], three weeks before [Fred] Hampton and [Mark] Clark were killed, our reverend Bruce Johnson [pastor of the People's Church, formerly the Armitage Avenue United Methodist Church] and his wife were stabbed to death in their home. It was definitely something planned ahead of time. There was a lot of repression going on against other groups, not just blacks. Still, at that time we did not know what repression meant. We walked down the street and if a cop stopped us and beat us with a nightstick it did not represent anything outside our way of life. For us to get beat up and charged with assault and battery against the police, when we were the ones bleeding from our head injuries, was part of our everyday experiences. So, we did not call it or accuse it of repression....

By constantly arresting people they took away from our funds as well. I remember getting a $30,000 dollars bond for disorderly conduct. I was arrested close to eighteen times in six weeks. They were not targeting me, but the group. They targeted leaders.... They knew that together we were a strong group and they were afraid of the Rainbow Coalition that we had....

I was a pall-bearer at Hampton's funeral.... Not just me but a lot of people got afraid and it had a big effect on the movement in Chicago.

Many abandoned us. Infiltrators started to become more of a problem as well. That was when people started turning on each other. Police also created animosity between groups.... There were splits everywhere, splits between the student groups, the Black Panther Party, and a split between the Young Lords Party and the Young Lords in Chicago.

Theoretically speaking we were for the same goals, but while in Chicago we were more street-talking, in New York the discourse came from their schooling, from their university education. They were very well educated in terms of Marxist theory and literature. For us it was not as important how much Marxist literature we knew, it was how much the people knew about what was going on in their surroundings. The emphasis was on the level of consciousness the people were at, not the level of consciousness I was at. And I think, both groups, the Young Lords in Chicago and the Lords in New York got away from that. We both divorced ourselves from the people.

3. First Chicano National Conference Reclaims Aztlán, 1969

In the spirit of a new people that is conscious not only of its proud historical heritage but also of the brutal "gringo" invasion of our territories, *we*, the Chicano inhabitants and civilizers of the northern land of Aztlán from whence came our forefathers, reclaiming the land of their birth and consecrating the determination of our people of the sun, *declare* that the call of our blood is our power, our responsibility, and our inevitable destiny.

We are free and sovereign to determine those tasks which are justly called for by our house, our land, the sweat of our brows, and by our hearts. Aztlán belongs to those who plant the seeds, water the fields, and gather the crops and not to the foreign Europeans. We do not recognize capricious frontiers on the bronze continents.

Brotherhood unites us, and love for our brothers makes us a people whose time has come and who struggles against the foreigner "gabacho" who exploits our riches and destroys our culture. With our heart in our hands and our hands in the soil, we declare the independence of our mestizo nation. We are a bronze people with a bronze culture. Before the world, before all of North America, before all our brothers in the bronze continent, we are a nation, we are a union of free pueblos, we are *Aztlán*.

"El Plan Espirtual de Aztlán (1969)," in Rudolfo A. Anaya and Francisco Lomelí, eds., *Aztlán: Essays on the Chicano Homeland* (Albuquerque, NM: Academia/El Norte Publications, 1989), pp. 1–5.

PROGRAM

El Plan Espiritual de Aztlán sets the theme that the Chicanos (La Raza de Bronze) must use their nationalism as the key or common denominator for mass mobilization and organization. Once we are committed to the idea and philosophy of El Plan de Aztlán, we can only conclude that social, economic, cultural and political independence is the only road to total liberation from oppression, exploitation, and racism. Our struggle then must be for the control of our barrios, campos, pueblos, lands, our economy, our culture, and our political life. El Plan commits all levels of Chicano society—the barrio, the campo, the ranchero, the writer, the teacher, the worker, the professional—to La Causa.

Nationalism

Nationalism as the key to organization transcends all religious, political, class, and economic factions or boundaries. Nationalism is the common denominator that all members of La Raza can agree upon.

Organizational Goals

1. UNITY in the thinking of our people concerning the barrios, the pueblo, the campo, the land, the poor, the middle class, the professional—all committed to the liberation of La Raza.

2. ECONOMY: economic control of our lives and our communities can only come about by driving the exploiter out of our communities, our pueblos, and our lands and by controlling and developing our own talents, sweat, and resources....

3. EDUCATION must be relative to our people, i.e., history, culture, bilingual education, contributions, etc. Community control of our schools, our teachers, our administrators, our counselors, and our programs.

4. INSTITUTIONS shall serve our people by providing the service necessary for a full life and their welfare on the basis of restitution, not handouts or beggar's crumbs....

5. SELF-DEFENSE of the community must rely on the combined strength of the people. The front line defense will come from the barrios, the campos, the pueblos, and the ranchitos....

6. CULTURAL values of our people strengthen our identity and the moral backbone of the movement.... We must insure that our writers, poets, musicians, and artists produce literature and art that is appealing to our people and relates to our revolutionary culture. Our cultural values of life, family, and home will serve as a powerful weapon to defeat the gringo dollar value system and encourage the process of love and brotherhood.

7. POLITICAL LIBERATION can only come through independent action on our part, since the two-party system is the same animal with two heads that feed from the same trough. Where we are a majority, we will control; where we are a minority, we will represent a pressure group; nationally, we will represent one party: La Familia de la Raza! ...

El Plan de Aztlán is the plan of liberation!

4. The Young Lords Define Their Platform, 1970

1. WE WANT SELF-DETERMINATION FOR PUERTO RICANS, LIBERATION ON THE ISLAND AND INSIDE THE UNITED STATES.

For 500 years, first spain and then united states have colonized our country. Billions of dollars in profits leave our country for the united states every year. In every way we are slaves of the gringo. We want liberation and the Power in the hands of the People, not Puerto Rican exploiters. QUE VIVA PUERTO RICO LIBRE!

2. WE WANT SELF-DETERMINATION FOR ALL LATINOS.

Our Latin Brothers and Sisters, inside and outside the united states, are oppressed by amerikkkan business. The Chicano people built the Southwest, and we support their right to control their lives and their land. The people of Santo Domingo continue to fight against gringo domination and its puppet generals. The armed liberation struggles in Latin America are part of the war of Latinos against imperialism. QUE VIVA LA RAZA!

3. WE WANT LIBERATION OF ALL THIRD WORLD PEOPLE.

Just as Latins first slaved under spain and the yanquis, Black people, Indians, and Asians slaved to build the wealth of this country.... Third World people have led the fight for freedom. All the colored and oppressed peoples of the world are one nation under oppression. NO PUERTO RICAN IS FREE UNTIL ALL PEOPLE ARE FREE!

4. WE ARE REVOLUTIONARY NATIONALISTS AND OPPOSE RACISM.

The Latin, Black, Indian and Asian people inside the u.s. are colonies fighting for liberation. We know that washington, wall streets and city hall will try to make our nationalism into racism; but Puerto Ricans are of all colors and we resist racism. Millions of poor white people are rising up to demand freedom and we support them.... POWER TO ALL OPPRESSED PEOPLE!

5. WE WANT EQUALITY FOR WOMEN. DOWN WITH MACHISMO AND MALE CHAUVANISM.

Under capitalism, women have been oppressed by both society and our men. The doctrine of machismo has been used by men to take out their frustrations on wives, sisters, mothers, and children. Men must fight along with sisters in the struggle for economic and social equality and must recognize that sisters make up over half of the revolutionary army: sisters and brothers are equals fighting for our people. FORWARD, SISTERS, IN THE STRUGGLE!

6. WE WANT COMMUNITY CONTROL OF OUR INSTITUTIONS AND LAND.

We want control of our communities by our people and programs to guarantee that all institutions serve the needs of our people. People's control of

"Young Lords Party: 13 Point Program and Platform," in Young Lords Party and Michael Abramson, eds., *Palante: The Young Lords Party* (New York: McGraw-Hill, 1970), p. 150.

police, health services, churches, schools, housing, transportation and welfare are needed. We want an end to attacks on our land by urban renewal, highway destruction, universities and corporations. LAND BELONGS TO ALL THE PEOPLE!

7. WE WANT A TRUE EDUCATION OF OUR AFRO-INDIO CULTURE AND SPANISH LANGUAGE.

We must learn our long history of fighting against cultural, as well as economic genocide by the spaniards and now the yanquis. Revolutionary culture, culture of our people, is the only true teaching. JIBARO SI, YANQUI NO!

8. WE OPPOSE CAPITALISTS AND ALLIANCES WITH TRAITORS.

Puerto Rican rulers, or puppets of the oppressor, do not help our people. They are paid by the system to lead our people down blind alleys.... VENCEREMOS!

9. WE OPPOSE THE AMERIKKKAN MILITARY.

We demand immediate withdrawal of u.s. military forces and bases from Puerto Rico, Vietnam and all oppressed communities inside and outside the u.s. No Puerto Rican should serve in the u.s. army against his Brothers and Sisters.... U.S. OUT OF VIETNAM, FREE PUERTO RICO NOW!

10. WE WANT FREEDOM FOR ALL POLITICAL PRISONERS AND PRISONERS OF WAR.

No Puerto Rican should be in jail or prison, first because we are a nation, and amerikkka has no claims on us; second, because we have not been tried by our own people (peers).... FREE ALL POLITICAL PRISONERS AND PRISONERS OF WAR!

11. WE ARE INTERNATIONALISTS.

Our people are brainwashed by television, radio, newspapers, schools, and books to oppose people in other countries fighting for their freedom.... We will defend our sisters and brothers around the world who fight for justice and are against the rich rulers of this country. QUE VIVA CHE GUEVARA!

12. WE BELIEVE ARMED SELF-DEFENSE AND ARMED STRUGGLE ARE THE ONLY MEANS TO LIBERATION.

We are oppose to violence – the violence of hungry children, illiterate adults, diseased old people, and the violence of poverty and profit. We have asked, petitioned, gone to courts, demonstrated peacefully, and voted for politicians full of empty promises.... When a government oppresses our people, we have the right to abolish it and create a new one. ARM OURSELVES TO DEFEND OURSELVES!

13. WE WANT A SOCIALIST SOCIETY.

We want liberation, clothing, free food, education, health care, transportation, full employment and peace. We want a society where the needs of the people come first, and where we give solidarity and aid to the people of the world, not oppression and racism. HASTA LA VICTORIA SIEMPRE!

5. Chicanas Assert a "Revolution Within a Revolution," 1972

As the Women's Liberation movement is becoming stronger, there is another women's movement that is effecting change in the American Revolution of the '70s—the Mexican-American women, las Chicanas, *las mujeres*.

In contrast to some of the white women of the Liberation movement, who appear to encourage an isolationist method of acquiring equality, Mexican-American women want unity with their men....

As Chicanas, discriminated against not only by the white dominant society, but also by our own men who have been adhering to the misinterpreted tradition of *machismo*, we cannot isolate ourselves from them for a simple (or complex) reason. We must rely on each other to fight the injustices of the society which is oppressing our entire ethnic group.

On May 28–30, 1971, the first national Mujeres Por La Raza Conference was held in Houston, Texas.... Five hundred Latin women from states as far away as Washington, New York, Michigan and, of course, California attended.

Just six months prior to this conference I was being called a white woman for organizing a Las Chicanas group on the University of New Mexico campus. I was not only ostracized by men but by women. Some felt I would be dividing the existing Chicano group on campus (the United Mexican-American Students, UMAS), some were simply afraid of displeasing the men, some felt that I was wrong and my ideas "white" and still others felt that their contribution to La Causa or El Movimiento was in giving the men moral support from the kitchen....

Now, however, because a few women were willing to stand strong against some of the *macho* men who ridiculed them, called them white and avoided them socially, the organization has become one of the strongest and best-known in the state. Prior to the Houston conference, Las Chicanas was being used as the work club by the other male-run Chicano organizations in the city of Albuquerque. Every time they needed maids or cooks, they'd dial-a-Chicana. Every time there was a cultural event they would call the Chicana Glee Club to sing a few songs. For three months Las Chicanas was looked upon as a joke by most of the UMAS men and some of the other Chicano organizations....

It has taken what I consider a long time for them to realize and to speak out about the double oppression of the Mexican-American woman. But I think that after the Houston Conference they have more confidence (certainly I regained it) in speaking up for our recognition....

... [T]he Chicana is becoming as well-educated and as aware of oppression, if not more so, as the Mexican-American male. The women are now ready to activate themselves. They can no longer remain quiet and a new revolution within a revolution has begun....

6. Puerto Rican Activist Esperanza Martell, Starts The Latin Women's Collective, 1975

The experience of being uprooted from my homeland has had the most profound impact on who I am today; and it is the basis for the deep, justified rage I feel. I am a person without a country. I do not fit there or here, but I carry a deep love for my birthplace, Puerto Rico—the place that could have been my home.

My mother, María de los Angeles Gaetan Martell, has also had a great impact upon me. She passed on to me her love of Puerto Rico through her stories of growing up in Bayamón. In our home, although quietly, Albizu Campos and the Nationalists were seen as patriots and were talked about with love and pride. My mother also passed on her courage, hope, and love for our people. Her adventuresome nature had her riding motorcycles in the forties, and when the economic conditions in Puerto Rico became bleak she left for New York without knowing any English. She was not going to let her two children go hungry; she joined the thousands of Puerto Ricans who were part of the mass migration to the United States in the late forties and early fifties.

I grew up in Manhattan on West 81st Street.... When people came from Puerto Rico, [our home] was the place to go. They knew they could get support.... My mother took care of children and was the neighborhood nurse. She had a room where she would detox addicts cold turkey with herbs and love. She was part of a strong community of women, and I was right in the middle of it. I was the community translator at the welfare center, schools, and hospitals. My mother worked as a hotel maid for twenty-five years. There she learned how to make the union work for her and taught me about the importance of being a union member....

I have survived all the ills of growing up Puerto Rican and part of the working class of New York City. I have experienced physical abuse, rape, alcoholism, and a racist educational system—a system, that when it first learned my name told me to change it. When I spoke Spanish, I was sent to the principal's office, and when I said, "I want to be a nurse," I was given cooking and drawing classes. This is just a small part of my story of living in the belly of the beast and going beyond survival.

I really believed in the American dream, a real patriot. I would even cry when I heard the national anthem, but the atrocities of the Vietnam War, the South, and the killing of President Kennedy turned me around. How could my country be doing these things? I began to look for answers; I became a civil rights and antiwar activist very early on.... My first real political act of defiance against authority was deciding not to salute the American flag at graduation from Julia Richmond High School in June of 1963. A group of my fellow students and I were protesting the hosings, killings, bombings, and general terrorizing of Blacks in the South.... That same summer I was in Washington, D.C., when Martin Luther King Jr. gave his "I have a Dream" speech. I, along with thousands of others, was wading in the Lincoln Memorial pool, standing up against racism and economic injustice.

Esperanza Martell, "'In the Belly of the Beast': Beyond Survival," in Andrés Torres and José Velázquez, eds., *The Puerto Rican Movement: Voices from the Diaspora* (Philadelphia: Temple University Press, 1998), pp. 173–191.

... Once at City College I got involved in organizing evening students during the student strikes of 1968 and 1969. I was on my own now and worked full time, always finding ways to be politically active and to dance. I was a serious *salsera*. I was at the Pentagon demonstration in 1968 putting flowers into the solders' bayonets and running from their tear gas. I was also at Woodstock working in the first-aid tent....

For a while I was even going to the Movimiento Pro Independencia (MPI) meetings.... I was determined to learn and understand what was going on in Puerto Rico and with Puerto Ricans in the United States. I needed to know my history.... As an artist I was also involved in the Puerto Rican cultural movement made up of poets, musicians, and other artists.... I was learning from different people and groups, experimenting with and experiencing the movement on all its levels.

... [I]n August of 1970 I got the opportunity to go to Cuba....

In 1969 I joined the Venceremos Brigade, an anti-imperialist organization that since 1968 had been taking mostly young white people to Cuba to help build the revolution and to see for themselves how socialism was working. More than five hundred youths from every nationality and from all over the country went to challenge the U.S.-government travel ban to Cuba that violated our constitutional rights. Along with Cubans and other international work brigades we planted citrus trees....

Before I left for Cuba, I had been active in supporting El Comité, a community group based on the West Side of Manhattan that was started by a softball team made up of ex-gang members, factory workers, and Vietnam vets.... El Comité was family; we were all from the neighborhood and had strong ties. As part of the squatters' movement in the West Side of Manhattan, El Comité had taken over a storefront on 88th Street and Columbus Avenue. The squatters' movement was the organized response of the poor, working-class, multi-national community to the city's Urban Renewal Program or, as we called it, Herman Badillo's "Urban Removal Program." In Vietnam the government was bombing villages, and in New York it was destroying good, low-income housing to build high-risers for the rich. For us it was one and the same. We organized with "Operation Move-In" in the fight to take back our community.

... By the time I got back from Cuba El Comité was a full-fledged revolutionary organization.... We were witnessing a worldwide revolution; there were liberation struggles in Asia, Africa, Latin America, and right here in the United States with the Black Panther Party and the Young Lords Party. All these organizations were anticapitalist and socialist in nature.... Here in the United States we equated socialism with ending racism and poverty in our communities.... We were working-class youth who ... were living our lives as political activists, working to transform everything around us with revolutionary theory and practice....

It was not until January of 1971 that I became a full-fledged member of El Comité and part of their steering committee, with Federíco Lora, an ex-U.S. Marine from the Dominican Republic, and Americo Badillo, an ex-Jesuit from Puerto Rico. I was in charge of outreach and community organizing and worked as assistant editor of *Unidad Latina*. I was twenty-four, full of energy and revolutionary fervor, and felt I could do anything.... El Comité had made a commitment to develop women's leadership. As a member of El Comité

I helped train many people in community organizing and raised political consciousness all over the city....

In 1975 I was invited to attend the Second Women's Conference in support of Vietnam in Toronto, Canada. I had attended the first conference in 1971 and was part of the national organizing committee, a multi-national group.... [T]he Latinas who attended from New York ... put together a presentation that was to become the political framework for the creation of the Latin Women's Collective. Around the same time I had been discussing with Federíco Lora the need to begin a Puerto Rican women's organization to train sisters in leadership skills for El Comité–MINP and for the movement in general. It all came together in the summer of 1975.... We had worked together in different movements and were coming together for the first time to organize women from a working-class perspective. This was very important to us because as women of color we wanted to separate ourselves from the white feminist movement, which we felt was racist and ignored our needs....

We wanted to create an organization that was reflective of our needs and those of the community—for women by women with working-class politics. Our slogan was "*Liberación De La Mujer Através De La Lucha Obrera*," ("Women's liberation through the working-class struggle"). We believed that working-class women historically had been the backbone of most political and community organizations, but they never took or got the credit for their hard work. To be leaders we had to develop writing, speaking, and analytical skills and the courage to take up the struggle against sexism within us and our community. We took the challenge, and the Latin Women's Collective was born. We combined the personal and the political, applying critical thinking to all aspects of our lives.... We measured our success by the women from the collective who became active leaders in our community.

The organization grew in members, and at our peak close to sixty women attended our monthly meetings. We got incorporated, opened a storefront in East Harlem on 115th Street, institutionalized March 8 as International Working Women's Day, published a newsletter, *La Semilla*, worked with women from the community, and developed a real support network for our members.

7. Cuban Youth Promote Dialogue with Cuba, 1978

The Antonio Maceo Brigade offers a travel opportunity to Cuba to every young Cuban who:

1. **Has left Cuba through a family decision.**
2. **Has not participated in counterrevolutionary activities and does not maintain a violent attitude against the Revolution.**
3. **Self-defines against the blockade and in favor of the normalization of relations between the United States and Cuba.**

As residents of the United States and Puerto Rico, we maintain that it is our right to go to Cuba to visit, not only because that is how President Carter has

"Declaration de la Brigada Anotonio Maceo," *Areito* 4, nos. 3–4 (Spring 1978), trans. by Taisha Rodriguez.

recognized it when he annulled the travelling prohibition towards Cuba in March of 1977, but because as Cubans it is essential for us to resume contact with the reality that today forms an integral part of our nationality and the historical and cultural trajectory of our people. Moreover, we feel that we lack information about contemporary Cuban society. We come from the communities that have maintained the most hostile and closed attitudes regarding the Revolution and therefore it is twice as important to get to know Cuba through a direct experience to at least balance the vision that has been transmitted to us.

However, travelling to Cuba to visit is neither an act of unconditional support to the Cuban Revolution nor a public declaration in favor of socialism. Many go to Cuba out of legitimate interests to get to know not only the achievements of the Revolution, but also their errors and problems. The first group of the Antonio Maceo Brigade reflects a range of political positions that also includes the socialist. Its composition is, partly a result of the events surrounding the Vietnam War and the fight for civil rights during the 1960s, events that led many young Cubans to reconsider the vision of the Cuban Revolution propelled by exile. The circumstances today are not the same and therefore, the political positions of those youths that wanted to go to Cuba will not be the same. The future members of the Antonio Maceo Brigade will necessarily constitute a wider group and more heterogeneous than the first.

It is indisputable that the majority of the exiled do not sympathize with the Cuban Revolution. However, we argue that the majority do agree with a distension process between Cuba and the United States because the majority thinks that it will open doors towards family reunification and the possibility of going to Cuba for vacations. However, the fear, instilled by a minority that does not represent the interests of Cubans in the United States and Puerto Rico, prevents that position from being publicly and freely expressed in a massive form. Despite the environment of fear, various groups in the past years have publically expressed their positions, dissimilar with the current dominant views within our communities. These include publications such as Areito, academic institutions such as the Institute of Cuban Studies, and religious groups such as Pro Justice and Liberty Christians, and the "Good Shepherd" Church in Hialeah.

The Antonio Maceo Brigade unites with these groups to defend the every Cuban's rights to get to know the new Cuba and define their own relation with their homeland.

8. Writer Achy Obejas Describes Generational Conflicts in the Cuban Community, 1994

I'm wearing a green sweater. It's made of some synthetic material, and it's mine. I've been wearing it for two days straight and have no plans to take it off right now.

Achy Obejas, "We Came All the Way from Cuba So You Could Dress Like This?" in *We Came All the Way from Cuba So You Could Dress Like This?* (San Francisco: Cleis Press, 1994), pp. 113–131. Reprinted with permission.

I'm ten years old. I just got off the boat—or rather, the ship. The actual boat didn't make it: We got picked up halfway from Havana to Miami by a gigantic oil freighter to which they then tied our boat. That's how our boat got smashed to smithereens....

As I speak, my parents are being interrogated by an official from the office of Immigration and Naturalization Services. It's all a formality because this is 1963, and no Cuban claiming political asylum actually gets turned away. We're evidence that the revolution has failed the middle class and that communism is bad. My parents—my father's an accountant and my mother's a social worker—are living, breathing examples of the suffering Cubans have endured under the tyranny of Fidel Castro.

The immigration officer, a fat Hungarian lady with sparkly hazel eyes and a perpetual smile, asks my parents why they came over, and my father, whose face is bright red from spending two days floating in a little boat on the Atlantic Ocean while secretly terrified, points to me—I'm sitting on a couch across the room, more bored than exhausted—and says, We came for her, so she could have a future.

The immigration officer speaks a halting Spanish, and with it she tells my parents about fleeing the Communists in Hungary. She says they took everything from her family.... There's an official presidential portrait of John F. Kennedy behind her, which will need to be replaced in a week or so.

I fold my arms in front of my chest and across the green sweater. Tonight the U.S. government will put us up in a noisy transient hotel. We'll be allowed to stay there at taxpayer expense for a couple of days until my godfather—who lives with his mistress somewhere in Miami—comes to get us....

★ ★ ★

My parents escaped from Cuba because they did not want me to grow up in a communist state. They are anti-communists, especially my father.

It's because of this that when Martin Luther King, Jr., dies in 1968 and North American cities go up in flames, my father will gloat. King was a Communist, he will say; he studied in Moscow, everybody knows that.

I'll roll my eyes and say nothing. My mother will ask him to please finish his *café con leche* and wipe the milk moustache from the top of his lip.

Later, the morning after Bobby Kennedy's brains are shot all over a California hotel kitchen, my father will greet the news of his death by walking into our kitchen wearing a "Nixon's the One" button.

There's no stopping him now, my father will say; ... I know he's the one who's going to save us, he's the one who came up with the Bay of Pigs—which would have worked, all the experts agree, if he'd been elected instead of Kennedy, that coward.

My mother will vote for Richard Nixon in 1968, but in spite of his loud support my father will sit out the election, convinced there's no need to become a citizen of the United States (the usual prerequisite for voting) because Nixon will get us back to Cuba in no time, where my father's dormant citizenship will spring to life....

★ ★ ★

In 1971, I'll come home for Thanksgiving from Indiana University where I have a scholarship to study optometry. It'll be the first time in months I'll be without an antiwar demonstration to go to, a consciousness-raising group to attend, or a Gay Liberation meeting to lead.

Alaba'o, I almost didn't recognize you, my mother will say, pulling on the fringes of my suede jacket, promising to mend the holes in my floor-sweeping bell-bottom jeans. My green sweater will be somewhere in the closet of my bedroom in their house.

We left Cuba so you could dress like this? my father will ask over my mother's shoulder.

And for the first and only time in my life, I'll say, Look, you didn't come for me, you came for you; you came because all your rich clients were leaving, and you were going to wind up a cashier in your father's hardware store if you didn't leave, okay?

My father, who works in a bank now, will gasp—*¿Qué qué?*—and step back a bit. And my mother will say, Please, don't talk to your father like that.

And I'll say, It's a free country, I can do anything I want, remember? Christ, he only left because Fidel beat him in that stupid swimming race when they were little.

And then my father will reach over my mother's thin shoulders, grab me by the red bandanna around my neck, and throw me to the floor, where he'll kick me over and over until all I remember is my mother's voice pleading, Please stop, please, please, please stop....

★ ★ ★

There are things that can't be told.

Things like when we couldn't find an apartment, everyone's saying it was because landlords in Miami didn't rent to families with kids, but knowing, always, that it was more than that.

Things like my doing very poorly on an IQ test because I didn't speak English, and getting tossed into a special education track, where it took until high school before somebody realized I didn't belong there.

Things like a North American hairdresser's telling my mother she didn't do her kind of hair.

Like my father, finally realizing he wasn't going to go back to Cuba anytime soon, trying to hang himself with the light cord in the bathroom while my mother cleaned rooms at a nearby luxury hotel, but falling instead and breaking his arm.

Like accepting welfare checks, because there really was no other way.

Like knowing that giving money to exile groups often meant helping somebody buy a private yacht for Caribbean vacations, not for invading Cuba, but also knowing that refusing to donate only invited questions about our own patriotism.

And knowing that Nixon really wasn't the one, and wasn't doing anything, and wouldn't have done anything, even if he'd finished his second term, no matter what a good job the Cuban burglars might have done at the Watergate Hotel....

★ ★ ★

... In college one day, I'll tell my mother on the phone that I want to go back to Cuba to see, to consider all these questions, and she'll pause, then say, What for? There's nothing there for you, we'll tell you whatever you need to know, don't you trust us?

Over my dead body, my father will say, listening in on the other line.

Years later, when I fly to Washington, D.C., and take a cab straight to the Cuban Interests Section to apply for a visa, a golden-skinned man with the dulled eyes of a bureaucrat will tell me that because I came to the U.S. too young to make the decision to leave for myself—that it was in fact my parents who made it for me—the Cuban government does not recognize my U.S. citizenship.

You need to renew your Cuban passport, he will say. Perhaps your parents have it, or a copy of your birth certificate, or maybe you have a relative or friend who could go through the records in Cuba for you.

I'll remember the passport among my mother's priceless papers, handwritten in blue ink, even the official parts. But when I ask my parents for it, my mother will say nothing, and my father will say, It's not here anymore, but in a bank box, where you'll never see it. Do you think I would let you betray us like that? ...

★ ★ ★

When my father dies of a heart attack in 1990 ... I will come home to Florida from Chicago, where I'll be working as a photographer for the *Tribune*....

When my father dies, I will feel sadness and a wish that certain things had been said, but I will not want more time with him. I will worry about my mother, just like all the relatives who predict she will die of heartbreak within months (she has diabetes and her vision is failing). But she will instead outlive both him and me.

I'll get to Miami Beach, where they've lived ... since their retirement, and find cousins and aunts helping my mother go through insurance papers and bank records, my father's will, his photographs and mementos: his university degree, a faded list of things to take back to Cuba (including Christmas lights), a jaundiced clipping from *Diario de las Américas* about our arrival which quotes my father as saying that Havana harbor is mined, and a photo of my mother and me, wide-eyed and thin, sitting on the couch in the processing center....

★ ★ ★

There will be a storm during my father's burial, which means it will end quickly....

Three days later, after taking my mother to the movies and the mall, church and the local Social Security office, I'll be standing at the front gate with my bags, yelling at the cab driver that I'm coming, when my mother will ask me to wait a minute and run back into the house, emerging minutes later with a box for me that won't fit in any of my bags.

A few things, she'll say, a few things that belong to you that I've been meaning to give you for years and now, well, they're yours.

I'll shake the box, which will emit only a muffled sound, and thank her for whatever it is, hug her and kiss her and tell her I'll call her as soon as I get home. She'll put her chicken bone arms around my neck, kiss the skin there all the way to my shoulders, and get choked up, which will break my heart....

When I get home to Uptown I'll forget all about my mother's box until one day many months later when my memory's fuzzy enough to let me be curious. I'll break it open to find grade school report cards, family pictures of the three of us in Cuba, a love letter to her from my father (in which he talks about wanting to kiss the tender mole by her mouth), Xeroxes of my birth certificate, copies of our requests for political asylum, and my faded blue-ink Cuban passport (expiration date: June 1965), all wrapped up in my old green sweater.

ESSAYS

Latina/o youths' activism was shaped by conditions in their local communities and by the transnational histories and ongoing relations between their countries of origin and the United States. In the first essay, Carmen Teresa Whalen, professor of history and Latina/o Studies at Williams College, explores the origins of Puerto Rican youths' activism in Philadelphia and of a branch of the Young Lords Party. Youth sought to understand the racism and poverty that wracked their communities and began to understand those conditions as connected to the colonial status of Puerto Rico. She argues that the Young Lords' bridging of "homeland and barrio politics" was a key component of their ideology and their actions, and shaped the responses to them. Focusing on women, Maylei Blackwell, professor of Chicana/o Studies and Women's Studies at UCLA, examines the origins of Chicanas' activism in the second essay. In 1968, Chicanas founded Las Chicanas de Aztlán at California State University, Long Beach. For role models, these women looked to the strong, activist women of their families and communities, an experience that clashed with the ideology of the Chicano movement. Confronting the challenges of attending an overwhelmingly white college and the contradictions within the Chicano movement, Chicanas started their own groups, and forged a philosophy of *hermanidad*. While Cuban American youth also became activists, as María de los Angeles Torres, professor of Latin American and Latino Studies at the University of Illinois, Chicago, reveals in the third essay, the challenges they confronted differed in important ways. When these youth turned their attention to the "homeland," they encountered a U.S. foreign policy that prohibited most forms of interaction with Cuba and a Cuban émigré community that was dominated by vehemently anti-Castro perspectives and actions. Nonetheless, activists initiated visits to Cuba and then participated in forging a "dialogue" between Cuban Americans and the Cuban government.

Puerto Rican Activists Bridge Homeland and Local Politics

CARMEN TERESA WHALEN

In the early 1970s, Puerto Rican youth defined a politics that bridged the home-land politics of Puerto Rico with the reality of their lives in *El Barrio*. These youth, born or raised in Philadelphia, confronted the poverty and discrimination that affected their working-class neighborhoods. In looking to Puerto Rico, they asserted an identity that was proudly Puerto Rican and that both connected these youth to their island ancestry and allied them with the struggles of people of color in the United States. They linked the colonization of Puerto Rico to the poverty of Puerto Ricans in the United States and defined the issues as imperialism, capi-talism, and racism. They defined the solutions as independence for Puerto Rico and socialism. This coupling of homeland and barrio politics were important in several regards. First, it strengthened their sense of Puerto Rican identity and their political analysis of the larger forces affecting their lives. Second, it created strategic challenges. Although activists saw the two as intricately connected, they found it difficult to balance homeland and local concerns. Third, this bridging shaped the Young Lords' allies and adversaries. The Young Lords were supported by several clergy, who focused on their community work while dismissing their political ideology. The city administration and the police, however, perceived the Young Lords as "radicals" and responded harshly. Finally, the Lords' ideology and confrontational style challenged the established Puerto Rican leadership and forged a realignment of Puerto Rican politics in the city.

Although their tenure as an organization was short-lived, the Young Lords had a lasting impact on Puerto Rican politics in Philadelphia, and their bridging of homeland and barrio politics is key to understanding that impact....

★ ★ ★

In recalling the factors that sparked their political activism, Juan Ramos, Wilfredo Rojas, and Rafaela Colón emphasized their emerging sense of Puerto Rican iden-tity and the poverty and racial discrimination that affected themselves, their families, and the entire Puerto Rican community. They perceived the economic conditions and discrimination as unfair.... They also pointed to a sense of collective responsi-bility that was rooted in their families and their religion. Their politics began as personal experiences and broadened as they began to question the institutions that affected their daily lives and as they became aware of other social movements both within and beyond the city's limits. Their organizing efforts broadened as well. Ramos and Rojas organized high school clubs, then the Young Revolutionaries for Independence, and finally the Philadelphia branch of the Young Lords.

These future activists were struck by the fact that their parents worked hard and remained poor. Rojas recalls, "I became very political ... because I saw that something was not right.... My father cut sugarcane, came from ... Puerto Rico.

Carmen Teresa Whalen, "Bridging Homeland and Barrio Politics: The Young Lords in Philadelphia," in Andrés Torres and José Velázquez, eds., *The Puerto Rican Movement: Voices from the Diaspora* (Philadelphia: Temple University Press, 1998), pp. 107–123.

Here he went through years of discrimination." The contrasts were stark and the place of Puerto Rican men in the community was clear: "The Embassador Hotel was the best, classiest Jewish restaurant in the city, right across the street from my house, and all the cooks were Puerto Ricans, in the back." Ramos' father worked at the hotel for years. Colón's father migrated as a seasonal agricultural laborer, and her mother cooked and washed for the farmworkers. When her family moved to the city, her father worked in a factory, and her mother stayed home to care for their nine children. Colón says, "I think [about] being in the middle and having to use hand-me-downs ... the little ones got the milk, and I was one of the older ones so I didn't get any milk, because we were poor—dirt poor." She explains the impact: "One of the things that I always looked at, since I was little, [was that] we were poor.... I knew I wanted it to be different ... I knew something was wrong with the picture because my father worked, we were church-going, God-loving people."

The three Puerto Rican youths' interactions with the larger society reinforced their sense that "something was wrong with the picture." Rojas felt that his neighborhood was deteriorating: "I saw my neighborhood go from being a Ukrainian, German, Irish, stable neighborhood to being a ghetto. Those things begin to weigh on you. Why is it that when we get here it becomes a ghetto, and all the other Europeans move away?" At school, Rojas and Ramos confronted racism when they were in seventh grade. Rojas explains, "A nun would call us spics [and say] 'you're ruining the neighborhood,' she would smack us around.... and we would have to take this from this nun." They led a student "walk-out" to the principal's office. For Rojas, confronting this racism was an affirmation of his Catholicism.... By the age of fourteen, Colón had to work: "Every weekend I was either baby sitting ... for rich people's kids or cleaning some lady's house.... I was exploited." In spite, or perhaps because, of this experience, Colón says she knew that she wanted to work and go to school. Describing her mother as "a wonderful human being," Colón says: "I knew that I loved my mom, and I knew that I wasn't going to be like that ... the fact that, OK, [my father] worked and busted his chops. So did she at home, and she had no support.... she was dependent, and she was sheltered, you know, and she was tired." For Colón, unequal gender relations were another dimension of what was "wrong with the picture" and another dimension that sparked and informed her political activism.

The three youths' sense of injustice was combined with a sense of responsibility that was fostered by their families, the community, and by Casa del Carmen, a Catholic social service agency. Ramos recalls, "We were part of that system over at Casa del Carmen, we participated in sports, we cleaned up, so we were into giving a little something back. We saw it in our parents." ... Ramos concluded, "I think that we had an upbringing and an education that propelled us to take a leadership role.... [O]ur people were people that were already giving something back to the community." For Rojas, who had wanted to be a priest, "being involved in the Young Lords was an extension of us wanting to do things" for the community.

Aspira, a community organization dedicated to the education of Puerto Rican youth, fostered these activists' sense of identity and provided role models and organizing experience. Yet, … Colón recalls, "Aspira was very conservative then … but you had progressive counselors who allowed students to meet and discuss things…. They had this young person … [who] would teach us about capitalism, about Puerto Rico, about the culture, the relation with the Americans, etc." … Rojas and Ramos organized their high school Aspira clubs….

Ramos and Rojas, nonetheless, disagreed with Aspira's approach…. For Rojas, "Aspira was too conservative…. They didn't want to send [the youth] to college to come back and give something to the community but [wanted to] send them to college so they can make something and … get out of the ghetto…. That's not what I wanted to further my education for." … Rojas's club split, "I was young, vibrant, felt invincible, felt indestructible, and I really wanted to change the world…. Some of the people came with me, and we decided to form the Young Revolutionaries for Independence."

Their awareness of other social movements sharpened Rojas's and Colón's perceptions of the issues confronting Puerto Ricans in Philadelphia. Rojas traveled the country with the Office of Equal Opportunity evaluating youth programs. He says, "I was very inspired by what the African Americans were doing and the fact that they were forging ahead." While in California, his interests broadened: "I read about Ché Guevara…. I started to identify with Ché as a Puerto Rican, and what that did was instilled in me a willingness to fight for Puerto Ricans." … Colón worked with the United Farm Workers and the grape boycott in Washington state through the American Friends Service Committee. She explains, "I saw these people struggling…. It was because I was poor, and the same problems that were existing there, existed in my home." …

For Colón, the trip fostered her political awareness and her independence, and the two were very connected…. When she returned home, she recalls, "I then realized the racism that I had gone through in high school." She attended a peace demonstration. "All of a sudden," she recounts, "we saw the American flag coming down and the Puerto Rican flag went up." She met the Young Revolutionaries for Independence and decided to participate.

Founded by Rojas and Ramos, the Young Revolutionaries for Independence paved the way for the emergence of the Young Lords in Philadelphia. They fashioned themselves after Cuban revolutionaries. Rojas recalls, "… One day we decided to go up—we wanted to meet the Young Lords." In New York the Young Lords explained their organization and their platform. The Young Revolutionaries … switched from red to purple berets, communicated with the New York Lords via letters and telephone calls, and "decided that we wanted to affiliate with New York." Ramos became the captain of defense, Rojas became the lieutenant of education, and Colón became an active supporter. In August of 1970, the Young Lords' *Palante* newsletter announced the new branch….

The Philadelphia Young Lords emerged as the response of Puerto Rican youth to their experiences in the city. They adopted the Young Lords' national platform because it addressed their concerns for the independence of Puerto Rico and the issues affecting their communities. Anticipating the accusation that the Philadelphia Lords were "just trying to copy the Lords in New York," Ramos wrote in *Palante* in 1970, "[t]hese people must realize that the oppression of Puerto Ricans in Philly is the same as the oppression in New York. The conditions in both of these colonies are the same.... The struggle is the same." While they confronted similar issues, the branch retained its own distinctive stamp. Rojas characterizes the differences: "If we can put labels on the different chapters, you would say that Chicago were like street Lords because they came out of being a gang. New York were like college students who brought in some street people.... And in Philadelphia you had a bunch of Catholics—Catholics who got together, brought in some junkies along the way, and dragged in a few students." ...

★ ★ ★

The Young Lords bridged homeland politics—independence for Puerto Rico—with the issues affecting their working-class community. Their ideology linked the colonization of Puerto Rico with the oppression of Puerto Ricans in the continental United States, and their platform proclaimed, "We Want Self-Determination for Puerto Ricans, Liberation on the Island and Inside the United States." Making these connections strengthened their sense of Puerto Rican identity and their political analysis of the larger forces affecting their lives....

For the Young Lords, poverty became a crucial link connecting the homeland and the barrio. Rojas concedes, "We were trying to make the connection ... a lot of people couldn't understand why we wanted Puerto Rico free when we didn't live in Puerto Rico, we lived in the United States." Ramos explains their response: "We were saying that independence was something that was good for the people, basically because ... the status quo did not help the poor—did not help the poor in Puerto Rico, didn't help the poor in our community in Philadelphia." Similarly, Colón says, "We did talk about the independence of Puerto Rico, as being a colonized people, and so they saw the connection of being colonized in the United States—poor education, poor housing...." Ramos describes their efforts: "... we had to do something about the poor in our community because we couldn't do anything about the poverty in Puerto Rico with the exception of saying that independence was an alternative for the poor and that we believed in it.... So we had to help the poor, and in doing so we put out our message of being in support of Puerto Rican independence." Because they "wanted to help our people," they focused on improving conditions in the barrios and relied on political education to promote independence.

This approach defined what it meant to be a Young Lord.... The Young Lords ran two free breakfast programs, one at the Lighthouse for more than one hundred children and the other at St. Edward's Parochial School for more than eighty children. They had a continuous clothing drive. They arranged testing for tuberculosis and volunteered at Casa del Carmen's health clinic.... They approached gangs through political education. Rojas recounts, "Our whole thing was political—we're brothers, we're Puerto Ricans, we're blacks—we shouldn't fight each other. The enemy is the system. We have to beat the system. These young guys weren't trying to hear that. They were about turf."

For the Young Lords, social services became a vehicle for criticizing the "system" and for political education. Their platform called for "a Socialist Society ... where the needs of the people come first" and for "control of our communities by our people and programs to guarantee that all institutions serve the needs of our people." Juan González, a Young Lord in New York City and political activist later in Philadelphia, describes the difference from preexisting social service agencies: "While those agencies sought assistance from the government for Puerto Ricans, the Young Lords *demanded* that assistance as a right." In doing so, they "broke with the more mainstream, less confrontational approach of earlier agencies." The Young Lords, according to one reporter, served breakfast with "a lesson about why the kids' parents can't afford the food boys and girls need in order to do well in school." The reporter continued, "The Lords believe this is the patent difference between their breakfast program and a bread line. The latter is a handout, the former is a vehicle for instilling political consciousness."

The Young Lords provided services and demanded that existing agencies meet the needs of the community....

By focusing on their community programs and dismissing their "radical" ideology, some clergy supported the Young Lords. Father Thomas P. Craven, director of Casa del Carmen, explained, "It is difficult to organize the whole community behind issues, and the Lords are trying to change that.... I think, recognizing their problematic ideology, that the Young Lords have a right to exist.... What I see in them are noble intentions." Similarly, Rev. Gerald Kelleher said, "I think they're great kids. I don't, of course, buy all their politics. But from a priest's point of view, [it's] a lot easier to work with people who have ideals. What I like about them is that they're doing something; they're concerned." For Father Craven, there was also a personal dimension: "Just because young people whom I've known for a long time—and whose families I know—have been radicalized by a different ideology, I see no reason to stop being their friend or to break off communications with them." Casa del Carmen provided office space, while the Lords ran a clothing drive, provided interpreters for the health clinic, and joined in a procession against drugs. Rojas acknowledged, "We were very Catholic. So the thing was that there are these Catholic kids that grew up in the neighborhood, that were always tied to the Casa del Carmen, that are now asking us to take them in and get them an office for them to promote the breakfast program. Because we weren't really talking about revolution, we were talking about a free breakfast program."

Despite their "religious fervor" and ties to particular clergy, the Lords were critical of religious institutions. Ramos criticized churches as "the biggest money-making organizations in the world," yet he explained the ongoing relationship: "I believe in what Christ built the church on, serving the people.... Individual priests have gone back to basic beliefs of serving people. That's why we haven't attacked the church." The Lords' mottos included "If Christ were alive today, he'd be a Young Lord" and "Every Christian who is not a revolutionary lives in mortal sin." Rojas recalls, "A lot of us studied the theology of liberation. We all went to church. It was a weird contradiction in that some of our other chapters were atheists, and we were very Catholic.... We really believed that Catholicism was about changing peoples' lives and fighting for the downtrodden." Yet, on November 5, 1970, the Lords took over the Kingsway Lutheran Church. Ramos reported in *Palante*, "It is becoming apparent that the church, like all other institutions in our community, is not there to serve the people and that the only way they can be made to serve the people is if the people start doing it themselves." They provided a legal information center, an interpreting program, and drug rehabilitation. Rojas reminisced, "What was interesting about this church takeover was that we had the consent of the priest." Like other clergy, Rev. Roger Zeppernick explained, "The Lords are involved in human liberation, and I see more Christian upbringing in them than I do Marxist-Leninist orientation."

The Young Lords were also supported by their families. Colón believed, "So there were some ... older people, that were supportive, who came around and understood[,] ... like my parents. They were supportive of me, you know, because I was a good kid.... They just figured 'she's very patriotic.'" ... The support, for Rojas, rested on family ties and the issues: "Our parents would support us because we were their kids, so whenever an event happened they would come to meetings, they would come to protests. They would be there because they were supporting their kids, and a lot of the things we were saying was true—we were talking about an end to discrimination."

While their community activities generated support from some, the Young Lords' politics triggered the wrath of the city administration and the police. Although police brutality affected the entire Puerto Rican community, the Young Lords' politics heightened the conflict....

For the Young Lords, ... confrontation with the police was not an isolated incident. The national branch concluded, "[T]hey have undergone practically the heaviest attacks of any branch; there have been numerous beatings, false arrests, and several firebombs which have wrecked their offices." Ramos reminisces, "We were scorned by the police. We were talking about community control of the police. We were objecting and protesting the gang warfare going on and the flow of drugs into the community. I mean we were addressing these issues when we were eighteen years old and as a consequence, we had our office bombed." When their office at Casa del Carmen was bombed, Rojas says, "A lot of us had to get out of a little window. And when we came out the police were laughing at us." Rojas was also arrested: "They arrested me, took me to the station, beat the shit out of me and never booked me—they let me go. So I was one of the people that testified at the hearing that I was falsely arrested." ... These memories led Ramos to conclude, "We, at a very early age, had to face a lot of reprisal, a lot of repression ... in retrospect, we were way too young to take on all those responsibilities, but we had no choice."

In addition to spawning allies and adversaries, their dual focus on homeland and barrio politics also created strategic challenges. In 1971, the Young Lords opened branches in Puerto Rico "to unite our people on the island and the mainland with a common goal: liberation." This decision increased repression against the Young Lords, created tensions with independence movements in Puerto Rico, and fostered divisions within the Young Lords. Ramos ... went to Puerto Rico in 1972. He says, "That's where the infiltration really became very, very concentrated and the split of the Young Lords eventually came.... It was the politics of Puerto Rico versus the politics of the big cities.... I took the side that said that we needed not to be in Puerto Rico. *La experiencia de nosotros*—our experience—was strictly a mainland experience, with Puerto Rican hearts and culture and history, *pero* outside of that, the way people moved and did things in Puerto Rico was different." Ramos believed that it was infiltration "that above all destroyed the Young Lords." ...

Although the linking of homeland and barrio politics was strategically difficult and contributed to the splintering of the Young Lords, this bridging had a lasting impact on Puerto Rican politics in Philadelphia. The Young Lords redefined Puerto Rican identity and Puerto Rican leadership.... For Colón, the impact was personal and political: "The Young Lords awakened and discovered that pride to what my culture was. I don't think I would ever have had that going to a Catholic school that was all White and living with parents that were not very sophisticated and who were just surviving." She also credited the Lords, as having "impacted even the leadership now to have that vision that you have to know who you are and where you came from to know where you are going." In June of 1971, the *Evening Bulletin* captured the shift: "A new wave of ethnic pride has been sweeping the Puerto Rican community here recently." Businessman Domingo Martinez was quoted[,] ... "Before, people who made it didn't want to be called Puerto Rican, now they are proud of it. One of the things we won't sell at any price is our culture." And it was a short step from "ethnic pride" to demanding "respect." Rojas remarks, "A lot of folks thought that ... we were crazy for challenging the system, but it wasn't a question of being crazy. It was a question of gaining respect." For one reporter, it was the presence of the Young Lords that "indicates in no uncertain terms that Puerto Ricans do not intend to be victimized for long."

The Young Lords' ideology, while based on ethnic pride, was not narrowly Nationalist and instead opened the doors to discussions of gender and the possibility of political coalitions. Unlike other Nationalist movements of the era, including those in Puerto Rico, the Young Lords did not base their definition of Puerto Rican culture on a reassertion of traditional gender roles for women. They changed their platform from a demand that "*machismo* must be revolutionary" to "We want equality for women. Down with *machismo* and male chauvinism." There were limitations; according to Colón, "I think there was a lot of sexism within the Lords.... I couldn't really be in the leadership or a full-fledged member of the Lords ... because I lived at home. I wasn't going to sleep with every brother, you know, call it 'sister love.'" Clearly, the platform was only a beginning. In addition, the Lords' demand for "Power to all oppressed people!" was inclusive. Their platform called for "self-determination for all Latinos" and for the "liberation of all Third World people," including "Black people, Indians, and Asians." In defining themselves as "revolutionary nationalists" who "oppose racism," the Lords asserted, "Millions of poor white people are rising up to demand freedom and we support them." In Philadelphia, they worked closely with the Black Panthers, especially on breakfast programs and against police brutality. They supported Mexican farm workers and the grape boycott and joined others in opposing the war in Vietnam.

★ ★ ★

The Young Lords' bridging of homeland and barrio politics challenged the established Puerto Rican leadership and fostered a realignment of Puerto Rican politics in the city. They redefined Puerto Rican identity and Puerto Rican leadership, questioned the social service approach of Puerto Rican agencies, and planted the seeds for progressive coalitions. The Young Lords' confrontation with the police and the city administration drove a wedge into the long-standing affiliation of Puerto Rican leaders and Frank Rizzo, who was the city's police commissioner and later was mayor from 1972 to 1980. This wedge became a fissure and Puerto Rican politics shifted. Although the Young Lords Party dissolved, former Lords remained active in city politics, forming a Philadelphia chapter of the Puerto Rican Socialist Party and then the Puerto Rican Alliance. The concern with homeland politics that the Young Lords! inserted into Puerto Rican politics remained, as former Lords and subsequent political organizations continued to grapple with the balancing of homeland and barrio issues....

This shift in Puerto Rican leadership in Philadelphia was the result of Puerto Rican activism from the early 1970s to the 1980s. Despite the changing organizations, many of the activists, the issues, and the confrontational style of politics continued. Writing in the late 1980s, González observes, "[W]e have two of the most committed and politically progressive elected officials of any Puerto Rican *colonia* in the nation.... This is no accident. It is a direct result of the struggles of the past fifteen years." Similarly, Colón concludes, "The Young Lords were critical to any progressive movement in Philadelphia." Concerns with homeland and barrio issues were not mutually exclusive—attention to homeland issues did not prevent activism on issues affecting Puerto Ricans' daily lives in the United States.... Instead, the focus on homeland and barrio issues reflected and contributed to the emergence of transnational communities and an emphasis on biculturalism in the U.S. This dual focus mirrored the ongoing colonial ties between Puerto Rico and the United States. This was a second generation that came of age during an era of political activism and ethnic revitalization. This was a community shaped, not only by its "minority" status, but also as activist and journalist Pablo "Yoruba" Guzmán noted by "our overwhelming preponderance in the working class." These factors had a lasting impact on Puerto Rican politics.

The Chicana Movement on College Campuses in Southern California

MAYLEI BLACKWELL

IN GREATER LOS ANGELES, the Chicano movement of the 1960s and 1970s were heady days filled with personal, communal, political, and social change. The transformations were stunning for those who ... began to learn about the farmworkers' struggle, the ins and outs of political organizing, the right to quality education, and the historical legacy of their people in the Southwest, or Aztlán. While there was a romantic quality to being involved in a community of

Maylei Blackwell, "Chicana Insurgencies: Stories of Transformation, Youth Rebellion, and Chicana Campus Organizing," in Maylei Blackwell, *¡Chicana Power! Contested Histories of Feminism in the Chicano Movement* (Austin: University of Texas Press, 2011), pp. 43–90.

resistance, many young people joined the Chicano student movement in order to confront the new forms of race, gender, and class discrimination they experienced in educational institutions as they collectively entered universities for the first time.... [T]he experiences of this generation and ... the alienation they felt as they entered university pushed them toward social justice activism and educational advocacy. Many became active in the larger Chicano student movement as a survival strategy, finding a political home on campus with deep links to the communities from which they came. Yet it was the contradictions Chicana activists found in the particular ways that "home" was constituted that compelled them to address ... gender and sexual power that were not originally part of the Chicano movement agenda....

Racial hostility, sexual politics, and a lack of reproductive health care and guidance were just some of the issues with which these Chicanas grappled as they tried to find their own voice ... on campuses and in the Chicano movement.

... [I]n 1968 at California State University, Long Beach ... las Chicanas de Aztlán ... [a] group of Chicana student activists, began to name how the racial and economic oppression and educational inequality had gendered and sexual dimensions that influenced their lives as Chicanas but were not addressed by the Chicano student movement. The group ... [ran] consciousness-raising and solidarity-building sessions for Chicanas on campus as well as for incoming female freshmen. This led them to create a philosophy of sisterhood, Hermanidad, and to publish a Chicana feminist newspaper, *Hijas de Cuauhtémoc*, a name they became known by after the newspaper's first issue. In addition to addressing the structural an cultural roots of oppression, the group's efforts to bring gender equality and liberatory ethics to relationships, sexuality, power, women's status, labor and leadership, familial bonds, and organizational structures resulted in enduring historical changes for ... Chicanas....

★ ★ ★

The oral histories of the Hijas de Cuauhtémoc reveal that while several members came from "traditional" (conventionally gendered) backgrounds, many others drew their sense of political agency and gender identity from other community-based "traditions" of female strength and resistance. As descendants of female labor organizers, political party activists, railroad workers, and women who managed family households on scarce resources, most Chicana activists I interviewed stated that it was their mothers, *abuelas* (grandmothers), or *tías* (aunts) who served as their role models. This suggests that Chicana feminism emerged not only from the gendered contradictions of the movement, as scholars have suggested, but also from how gendered movement discourses, based on an idealized nationalist recovery of cultural "tradition," did not resonate with many Chicanas' lived experiences. The construction of gender for women in the movement was based on what Alma García has called the "Ideal Chicana," ... that "glorified Chicanas as strong, long-suffering women who had endured and kept Chicano culture and family intact." The Ideal Chicana prescribed the gender norms of many movement organizational practices. Not only was family used as both a metaphor and a mobilizing strategy, but ideologies of political familialism, which often left patriarchal structures unquestioned, played a role in naturalizing male supremacy and reinforcing women's marginalization....

Chicanas' activism was born out of the everyday strength of women at the center of familial and community life whose sensibilities drew from a structure of feeling or commonsense beliefs about more egalitarian gendered roles based on a long legacy of working-class women's labor participation, activism, and, in some cases, radicalism....

... Some [activists] stated that they shared a sense of injustice around "traditional" gender roles as girls.... Anna NietoGomez challenged patriarchal norms as a girl because ... she was exposed to traditions of both patriarchy and women's independence. Born in 1946 in San Bernardino, California, NietoGomez is a third-generation Chicana on her mother's side, while her father's side of the family has roots in New Mexico that can be traced to the 1600s....

... Even as a girl she had developed ideas about women's position in the family.... "... [M]y grandma did not eat at the same table as my grandpa. He ate by *himself* like a patrón, and for whatever reason, I don't know where I got it, I thought that it was wrong. She would cook[,] ... but my grandma would not eat at that table until everyone was finished—like a servant, like she wasn't family—neither my father nor my other grandfather treated their wives this way...."

NietoGomez explains that there was a diversity of experiences among the women in her own family, illuminating a basic idea that ... the experiences and backgrounds of Chicanas are not monolithic.... NietoGomez took her cues about gendered expectations from her mother and her father. Her mother had graduated from high school and began working for the Santa Fe Railroad in 1944, at the age of eighteen.

NietoGomez's father taught her the importance of independence because he felt that women should be taught how to manage on their own—a perspective he developed while watching his mother fight for survival as a single mom. She also credits her father for teaching her how to cook and sew and for teaching her mother how to build a house and fix the car....

... Sylvia Castillo, born in 1952, resided with her family in Pico Rivera (a working-class neighborhood of Southeast Los Angeles) until her father took a job in the aerospace industry and the family moved to Lakewood, becoming among the first to integrate that largely all-white neighborhood.... Castillo was a politically conscious high school student who came to political organizing through her family's union involvement.... "My mother had climbed the rungs of the Democratic Party and was doing organizing work for the UAW [United Auto Workers]. At sixteen I had exposure to the Chicano movement because in 1966 my mother had started working with César Chávez through the UAW."...

... Leticia Hernández was not politically involved before she went to college, as her family enforced conservative gender roles and political views. Hernández, born in 1952, grew up with her first-generation mother and grandmother and her second-generation father in the East Los Angeles housing project Pico Gardens. After attending Catholic grade school, Hernández transferred to the public school system.... "I was the first to graduate from high school in my family. My last year in high school ... we had a lot of riots [student walk outs of East Los Angeles] and I was always too afraid to join because my dad would kill me if I had gotten caught.... My father insisted that I be home by three o'clock.... So I was very sheltered. My parents were also very conservative; they talked about César Chávez as being a Communist." ...

★ ★ ★

The members of the Hijas de Cuauhtémoc ... began college between 1967 and 1970. They all describe intense isolation and alienation stemming from the fact that there were few Chicanas/os or Latinas/os on campus, let alone other people of color....

NietoGomez recalls that there were only three Chicanas among the students who started the United Mexican American Students (UMAS) organization in 1967 at what was then Long Beach State College.... NietoGomez and Corinne Sánchez were among the first Hijas de Cuauhtémoc members to enter college. Their work in movement politics focused heavily on Chicano recruitment, and they served as counselors, Educational Opportunity Program (EOP) advisers, and peer mentors to prevent dropouts....

In the mid- to late 1960s, as Mexican American youth went to college in unprecedented numbers, they found campus environments that were a radical departure from what anyone in their families or communities had experienced. The transition to college was not just a watershed personal development for this generation; it was an important historical development that changed what it meant to be a Mexican American woman living in the United States....

Although their achievement represented the hopes and dreams of the generations before them and the aspirations of their families, some young women did not receive full support from their families because educational attainment also entailed breaking out of conventional gender roles....

... [T]he transition from the barrio to campus was so radical that many Chicanas either dropped out within the first year or never managed to finish their degrees due to their activism, which put collective survival before individual academic success....

★ ★ ★

NietoGomez described the deep alienation she felt as one of the first Chicanas to step onto a college campus in the late 1960s. She described feeling lost in lecture classes of 250 people and how professors would literally ignore her when she raised her hand or walk away from her while she was talking to them. Chicanos and Chicanas were made to feel invisible—literally, ethnically, and culturally unintelligible....

Finding others like her on campus helped her survive, and the movement provided a haven, "... I went to my first UMAS meeting.... I remember walking in and there were about twelve or fifteen Chicanos—mostly guys, some girls.... I was just so happy to see them, and then we started talking and we were all going through the same experiences.... They also didn't know anybody; nobody would talk to them; they didn't know what they were doing there; they felt so isolated, so alone, and so we decided that we would meet and do things together." ...

By the late sixties the UMAS chapter at Cal State Long Beach included women, and several were among the core activists.... The mostly all-male leadership felt that "women had less political knowledge than themselves and that women need to raise their consciousness. The veteran Chicanas were in charge of this education." These political education groups provided a forum for movement women to meet among themselves, sharing ideas and discussing issues. These meetings eventually became the political vehicle for the first informal support group, las Chicanas de Aztlán.... Formed in 1968 in Long Beach, the group became strong advocates for Chicanas....

As early UMAS members, Corinne Sánchez and Anna NietoGomez, along with several other student activists, were involved in organizing the first Dia de la Raza recruitment day.... As a result, the number of Chicanos on campus tripled the next year....

... [T]hey were disheartened to find that only one-third of new college recruits were women, and over half of those women dropped out before their junior year.... [The] political origins ... [of the Hijas de Cuauhtémoc emerged] out of an effort to solve this problem. "Las Mujeres ... discovered two important facts.... First, Chicanas did not fail because of academic deficiencies.... Second, nebulous support from faculty, peer group, and counselors, as well as from the family, provided little psychological reinforcement for the Chicana to stay in college."

The group found that Chicanas suffered guilt at not contributing to the household income of their families and social pressures to get married. A silent factor that contributed to dropout rates was unplanned pregnancy and lack of access to birth control. In the complex context of the sexual revolution many Chicanas were faced with the contradiction between new freedoms and expectations and continued gender inequality and the sexual double standard.

... [M]any Chicanos relied heavily on programs such as EOP. Yet the lack of support was insidious for young women because the precise places where they could look for support and guidance were undermined by the ways they were often sexualized or endured sexual harassment.... [A]s Leticia Hernández describes, ... "The EOP counselors were peer counselors, but the guys picked up on the girls; it was a big joke in retrospect. At the time, they thought that they were trying to help, but they were really trying to get them in bed...." NietoGomez reflected on her role as a counselor.... "The pill was not yet widely available, so for women the number one reason for dropping out was pregnancy either by the guys on the campus or by their old boyfriends in the community who didn't want them to go on to college.... I think being the EOP counselor is what raised my consciousness.... I often felt it was a curse for a Chicana to be cute and beautiful because it left her very vulnerable because being cute and beautiful does not necessarily mean you have control over your life or especially your body at that time. There was no birth control, there were no legal abortions.... I realized for the women the number one problem was they didn't have control of their bodies. That was the reason for dropping out...."

★ ★ ★

More elaborate than other framing documents of the Chicano movement, *El Plan de Santa Barbara* was written in 1969 and united former Chicano student and youth groups under the name el Movimiento Estudiantil Chicano de Aztlán (MEChA). Written in the new spirit of nationalism embodied in *El Plan*

Espiritual de Aztlán [See Document 2], *El Plan de Santa Barbara* laid out a blueprint for education. Although activist women like Anna NietoGomez participated in creating this collective document, its version of Chicanismo was articulated through culturally mediated concepts of masculinity such as brotherhood, familialism, and *carnalismo* (brotherhood)....

According to female student activists in Southern California, women's marginalization in the Chicano student movement in the late 1960s occurred on at least three levels. First, women often were not seen as the real political subjects of the movement but as auxiliary members. As a result, they were relegated to supporting roles, reinforcing the gendered division of labor. During meetings their ideas were often dismissed on the basis of their gender, marginalizing them in the political and decision-making process. Second, women were discouraged from taking leadership roles and were sometimes outright undermined when they were elected to them. Third, women felt that the sexual politics of the movement were counterproductive to their full participation and treated them as sexual objects instead of encouraging the recognition of their full humanity and creating organizational structures in which they could be fully realized as part of their people's struggle for liberation....

... [W]omen were relegated to secretarial and other support roles, [which] signified to women that although they often provided the backbone of the organizational labor, their ideas, voices, and leadership were not recognized. Chicana student activists increasingly felt their political vision and voice were devalued in political organizing meetings, and some became aware of the informal power structure of movement heavies that women had little access to outside of being someone's girlfriend. Politicized speech had its own language in the movement. At the time this language was largely reserved for men, except for the few occasions when women adopted these codes and the vernacular of el movimiento....

... While the movement embraced carnalismo as a way to create solidarity, it also led to the creation of a social movement culture based on masculinized codes, behaviors, and modes of organizing, thereby creating and reinforcing political philosophies and practices that had gendered implications for how the movement organized and who it validated as organizers and leaders....

Increasingly, many female organizers in the Chicano Movement felt that the gendered division of political work was a reflection not only of male privilege but also of the ways in which Chicanas were disregarded as real political actors and relegated to the kitchens and mimeographing rooms of the movement. Chicanas were in charge of developing, typing up, and mimeographing position papers; doing all the fund-raising, cooking, and organizing events; doing the office work, the cleanup work, and the majority of the organizational tasks. Although this labor was pivotal to the actual functioning of the political movement, it was seen as women's work and therefore devalued....

Las Chicanas de Aztlán at Cal State Long Beach began to develop a critique of the sexual politics of the movement.... While it was only some men who abused their status as leaders for sexual gain, the sexual objectification and harassment of women was fairly widespread and shaped movement political practice and culture.

Activist Chicanas critiqued the fact that women were sexualized within movement spaces, seen as sexual objects instead of political comrades.... [They] became critical of the ways young women faced a form of sexual initiation into the movement whereby men, under the guise of mentorship and political education, would initiate sexual relationships with incoming freshmen [women].... Chicanas broke the silence surrounding these practices and ... warned others of this practice, which they called having your pants "radicalized" off. Another form of sexual politics involved the notion of male prerogative whereby being "down for the revolution," Chicanas were expected to make themselves sexually available to movement men.... In *Hijas de Cuauhtémoc*, women called their male counterparts to task for what they saw as an informal political strategy to undermine the power of more experienced Chicanas by playing them off younger (or less politically seasoned) women through sexual relations with their male antagonists.... [W]omen who stepped outside of normative gender roles to provide leadership in the organization or challenged sexual politics in the movement were portrayed as sexually immoral or deviant and often labeled as dykes or lesbians....

According to [Sylvia] Castillo, the philosophy of hermanidad was the "result of a series of discussions that had been going on with the freshman class of Chicanas who were at Cal State Long Beach," and the more veteran organizers like "Anna NietoGomez who was present as the convener of [the meeting] through her role as an EOP adviser.... Our philosophy was la hermanidad, and even that term was very controversial because it wasn't really a word. We kind of made it up."

Much of the debate over hermanidad revolved around how to make the concept of *hermandad*, or brotherhood, relevant for women to create a specific form of solidarity and sisterhood....

[T]he group did create a new political philosophy of Chicana sisterhood and solidarity.... Hermanidad began to name gendered racism and the way patriarchal power divided women.... [T]he platform sought to establish a political program for Chicanas. It called for counseling and support in the areas of finance, education, sex, legal matters, and medical care. There was a call to action for Chicanas to work together to identify how perceived cultural values impeded social change.... The power of this call to hermanidad is that it saw women as vital and necessary agents of social change, and it named the specificity of oppression and the issues facing them.... The Basic Beliefs ... [asserted,] "... We recognize that we are oppressed as Raza and as women. We believe that the struggle is not with the male but the existing system of oppression. But the Chicano must also be educated to the problems and oppression of La Chicana so that he may not be used as a tool to divide by keeping man against women."...

The informal rap groups of 1968 and 1969 became a mobilized group in 1970. In addition to the group that formed at Long Beach State, las Chicanas de Aztlán at San Diego State University and Concilio Mujeres at San Francisco State University ... formed for similar reasons. Between 1970 and 1972 Chicana groups formed at Fresno State College, Cal State Los Angeles, and Stanford University. These young women organized themselves to address their common political needs ... [and] began a dialogue with other Chicanas that facilitated a shift in consciousness and the articulation of an explicitly Chicana gendered political identity....

★ ★ ★

Despite the critique of the day that asserted that feminism was part of the dominant culture's attempt to divide the movement, a specifically Chicana agenda and *ideologically* diverse forms of Chicana feminism were created from within the ranks of the Chicano movement. For example, the Cal State Los Angeles [Comisión Femenil Mexicana (CFM)] chapter's goals included visiting penal institutions, constructing a dormitory for Chicanas ..., and fomenting leadership of women in the student movement. Over forty women gathered to decide on four resolutions: a "woman's right to self-determination in order to be free to make decisions affecting her own body," the need to establish links with other women's organizations throughout the world, the need to ensure resources for Chicanas at the state and federal level, and that the group become a [CFM] chapter....

At Long Beach State the Chicana group was never really a "separate" organization from MEChA; the women worked in both groups, ... which was common among Chicana activists. Because their political needs were not being addressed in MEChA, they organized on their own behalf.... NietoGomez ... saw their work as part of the mission of MEChA, and the Chicana group often did fund-raising for *El Alacrán*, the MEChA newspaper....

Understanding that these Chicana groups were not separate or separatist is crucial ..., because the emergence of Chicana feminisms is often narrated as occurring outside of and after the Chicano Movement rather than within it....

Generational and Political Conflicts in Cuban American Communities

MARÍA DE LOS ANGELES TORRES

As hopes of returning to Cuba faded, Cuban exiles became more concerned with life in the United States.... [M]ore immediate immigrant issues emerged, such as the search for better jobs, education, and housing. Class divisions sharpened, and advocacy groups seeking improved social services emerged.... [T]he Cuban National Planning Council, a group of Miami social workers and businesspeople formed in the early 1970s. As an organization that provided services to needy exiles, this group defied the prevailing notion that all exiles had made it in the United States. Life in the United States created new needs and interests that could only be resolved, at least in part, by entering the domestic political arena.

Although there had always been ideological diversity within the Cuban émigré community, it was not until the 1970s that the political spectrum finally

María de los Angeles Torres, "The 1970s: Pluralization, Radicalization, and Homeland," in *In the Land of Mirrors: Cuban Exile Politics in the United States* (Ann Arbor: University of Michigan, 1999), pp. 84–105.

began to reflect this outwardly.... Those groups that were not preoccupied with the Cuban revolution met with hostility from those that were....

... Organizations such as the Spanish American League against Discrimination (SALAD) dedicated themselves to fighting discrimination, a taboo subject for Cubans. Although their advocacy was moderate compared to the efforts of other civil rights groups, it was controversial within the exile community. To admit that there was discrimination at all was somehow to give the communist Cuban regime ammunition against the United States....

Many of the organizations involved in armed action against the Cuban government had disintegrated by this time, but splinter groups remained. Some of these, such as Alpha 66, a group dedicated to the armed struggle against Castro, and Cuban Power, headed by Orlando Bosch, relied on terrorist actions. Bosch's group developed a strategy ... that internationalized terrorist actions. His aim was to prevent any country or corporation from conducting business with Cuba or from recognizing the Cuban government. Cuban Power bombed the offices of governments and corporations that maintained a relationship with the Cuban government, such as the Mexican Tourist office in Chicago, which was bombed in 1968. Bosch's organization reportedly was responsible for over 150 bombings before Bosch was jailed for firing a bazooka at a Polish freighter.... After leaving jail, Bosch took his fight to the Cuban community, vowing to kill anyone who supported detente with communist countries. Shortly thereafter José Elías de la Torriente, another anti-Castro leader, was assassinated. Among those targeted by extremist groups were people in the exile community who had abandoned the struggle to overthrow the Cuban government or who simply did not give it a high enough priority. In 1975 Luciano Nieves, an advocate of peaceful coexistence with the Cuban government, was assassinated. And Emiliano Milián, a Miami radio commentator who advocated dialogue with Cuba, lost both legs when he triggered a bomb that had been rigged to his car.

Yet in the 1970s the Cuban émigré community as a whole seemed less concerned with returning to Cuba than with making it in the United States.... The very existence of groups serving the needy—evidence that some Cubans faced problems in the United States—posed a challenge to the Cuban Right, which either ignored or denied the social and economic problems some within the community were encountering in the United States.

... [S]ome individuals involved in social service organizations also began to consider the possibility that the revolution in their homeland had resulted in gains for the poor. As a rule, the social service movement, including the Cuban émigré sector, was not generally concerned with foreign policy. But these sectors were allies in challenging the previously monolithic control over Cuban exile life held by Cuban conservatives. Those advocating normalization of relations disputed the then unquestioned aim of overthrowing the revolution, thereby creating the possibility of new discussion in regard to Cuba.

The challenge to the hegemony of the Cuban Right first became evident in academic circles.... El Instituto de Estudios Cubanos[,] ... which held its first meeting in Washington, DC, in the spring of 1969, brought together Cuban émigré scholars who studied Cuba.... The goal of this first meeting was to allow Cubans of divergent ideologies and generations to share their views of Cuba within a climate of respect and camaraderie. Unlike the prevalent Cuban exile scholarship of the late 1960s, the institute encouraged a less antagonistic approach to the Cuban government.

In the early 1970s debate began over whether Cubans should engage in dialogue with the government from which so many of them had fled.... Young people seeking some kind of relationship with their homeland entered this debate with a more positive, perhaps more romantic, appraisal of the revolution. Little by little they started to form political organizations of their own.

★ ★ ★

... Ironically, as the émigré community at large turned its attention toward the United States, many young Cubans in search of roots, identity, and political alternatives looked to Cuba and to their relationship with other minorities in the United States. Some of the first political groupings of young Cubans emerged in Washington and Chicago. These groups, composed of students and newly graduated young professionals, wanted to infuse the debate about Cuba with the voice of the younger generation....

... Confronted with the civil rights and antiwar movements, a significant number of Cuban students on North American campuses underwent a political conversion that was to have surprising long-term political implications. The first signs of this movement were in publications such as *Nueva Generación* and the more politically defined *Areíto* and *Joven Cuba*. *Joven Cuba*, a New York–based progressive magazine published by Cuban émigrés, called on Cubans to become part of the civil rights struggles of the black and Latino communities. It focused on the problematic position of Cubans as a national minority in the United States and stressed the importance of their relationship with other Latinos. *Areíto*, first published in Miami, was aimed instead at building bridges between Cubans in the United States and Cuba. The first few issues of *Areíto* addressed the identity of Cuban youth while focusing on the exile's relationship with their homeland [See Document 7]....

At the time there was no way for Cubans to return to the island, even as tourists. Travel to Cuba was prohibited by both the United States and Cuba. But young Cubans began to lobby Cuban government officials at the United Nations.... After intense lobbying efforts, the Cuban government granted a small number of visas to young Cuban émigrés who worked with *Areíto* and *Joven Cuba*. As a result, during the 1970s the Cuban government allowed a select number of Cuban exiles to visit the island.

The Cuban government first exempted from travel restrictions those who had emigrated prior to the 1959 revolution. These Cubans, many of whom were in fact sympathetic to the revolution, until then had been lumped together with the early 1960s émigrés. In the mid-1970s the Cuban government began to allow Cubans who were under eighteen years of age at the time of the revolution to visit the island. Entry permits were granted for a small number at a time.... [T]he visits influenced the attitude Cuban officials had of those who had left, and, finally, in 1977 the Cuban government shifted its policy and agreed to grant *Areíto* entry visas for a larger group visit.

The Areíto group was composed of middle-class Cubans who had come to the United States when they were young. They were raised in many different parts of the United States but shared a common longing to return to Cuba. Some worked with various publications, and others were scholars. Most faced stiff opposition from their parents for wanting to return to Cuba [See Document 8]....

By the mid-1970s tensions between the two countries had eased, and congressional representatives began to question the utility of the U.S. embargo against Cuba. Some even traveled to the island.... These legislators strongly felt that the time had come to normalize relations with Cuba. U.S. policy, they believed, was hurting the United States by making it appear isolated and unable to negotiate settlements. Cuban-American Democrats in cities such as New York, Chicago, and Boston were urging a new approach to U.S.-Cuban relations, while international pressure was mounting for warmer relations. In 1975 the Organization of American States (OAS) voted to lift its embargo of the island....

During the Carter presidency U.S. foreign policy again experienced a significant change in direction.... This new vision—recognition by a U.S. president of the need for reconciliation and dialogue—had marked effects on specific foreign policies, especially those aimed at Cuba and Latin America.

Early in his administration Carter became the first U.S. president since the revolution to make peace overtures to the Cuban government. After a series of talks both governments agreed to open "interests sections"—quasi-embassies hosted by third countries.... Travel to Cuba was permitted for the first time in almost twenty years, and some embargo restrictions against Cuba ... were relaxed....

Carter's domestic policies also contributed to strengthening the position of reformers within the Cuban community.... [T]he Carter administration developed relations with the Cuban National Planning Council, a group of moderate Cuban-Americans who advocated providing more social services for the exile community....

The flexibility of Carter's policies toward Latin America and Latinos in the United States spawned a climate in which the more reformist elements in the Cuban community, and the Latino community in general, could organize and exert influence on governmental policies. The Cuban government responded in kind: one of its conciliatory actions was to allow visits of exiles to their homeland.

First to be granted reentry was the Areíto group. Little by little its numbers expanded, and by 1977 the Cuban government gave the group fifty-five permits for a three-week tour of the island. Fear of reprisal from extremist exile groups required that the application and selection process be conducted in secret. Applicants had to be approved both by the group and by the Cuban Ministry of the Interior, which was charged with insuring that the returning exiles were not infiltrators. Once on the island the visit by these young Cubans had a tremendous impact on the government and the people of Cuba.... Prior to the visit Cubans on the island accepted the myth that everyone who left was an enemy of the revolution. Just as Cubans in the United States had broken with the island, Cubans on the island severed ties with those who had left....

But, when the youth who had left Cuba (or who had been taken out during the years of flight) returned, a sense of national recovery permeated their welcome. The group, traveling as the Antonio Maceo Brigade, was met with open arms and much emotion. Unlike earlier visits, this tour was covered extensively on Cuban television, which broadcast images of brigade members visiting relatives they hadn't seen in twenty years, working with construction crews building apartments, touring the island, dancing, and singing until dawn....

Upon returning to the United States, the initial group decided to expand the Antonio Maceo Brigade [See Document 7].... [T]he brigade defended the right of all Cubans to travel to the island in order to become reacquainted with the new Cuba and define their relationship to the homeland. The group was named after Antonio Maceo, the mulatto general of the Cuban War of Independence, because "of our desire to maintain a continuity with the history of our homeland ... our rebellion against the foreign decisions and against the historical circumstances which uprooted us from our homeland ... and our protests against the blockade which impedes our need to get to know the Cuban reality." Within a year of the first trip to Cuba more than three hundred young Cubans had signed up to join the brigade's second contingent, myself included.

Most were middle-class students united by their desire to return to their homeland. But this second group was not as politically homogeneous as the first group had been. I became a coordinator of the brigade and, along with the other coordinators, resisted demands by Cuban bureaucrats who wanted participants to pass an ideological litmus test. Because of the group's diversity, island organizers tightened the program in order to minimize contact between the brigade and the island's residents. Many brigade members had been part of the counterculture movement in the United States. We were advocates of gay rights and freedom of speech. Many of us were pacifists. Many still experimented with soft drugs. These beliefs and actions were punishable crimes in Cuba. Thus, contact between island youth and brigade members was discouraged.

Nonetheless, the brigade trips paved the way for future relations between the Cuban government and Cuban communities abroad. Both in Cuba and in the United States the myth of a monolithic Cuban community had been shattered, along with the myth of no return....

★ ★ ★

In September 1978 Castro announced that he would hold talks with representatives of the Cuban communities abroad. Numerous factors facilitated "the Dialogue," as these discussions were called. The Carter years marked a detente between the United States and Cuba.... Also, the Cuban revolutionary government had consolidated its power and was finally in a secure enough position to address those who had left the country. Furthermore, there were Cubans abroad who were ready to talk to the Castro government....

... The Dialogue, which was held over two sessions in November and December 1978, brought 140 Cubans from abroad to Havana.

This was my first return trip…. Its personal significance was tied to my return to Cuba, but it also had a broader meaning for the exile community as a whole. I met Cubans from throughout the United States who represented a broad range of political factions (even former Bay of Pigs prisoners joined in the Dialogue) and varying social backgrounds. Nuns, priests, and businesspeople all boarded the Cubana plane that took us to Cuba.

The formal agenda, consented to at the first meeting, included the release of political prisoners, permission for those prisoners and their families to leave Cuba, the reunification of divided families, and the right of Cubans living abroad to visit their relatives on the island. The Antonio Maceo Brigade presented the Cuban government with a more radical agenda than that agreed to by the overall group. This included the right of repatriation, the right to study in Cuba, the creation of an institute within the Cuban government to represent the interests of Cubans abroad, the opportunity to participate in social and professional organizations within Cuba, and the establishment of cultural and professional exchanges between Cubans on the island and abroad. We also supported the plea by a group of former political prisoners that the Cuban government release its female political prisoners….

The talks resulted in the following agreements: the release of three thousand political prisoners and permission for current and former prisoners and their families to emigrate; permission for those with family in the United States to leave; and permission for Cubans living abroad to visit the island…. [A]t the time such agreements were extraordinary. Prior to the Dialogue, not only were those who left considered traitors, but severe penalties were imposed against those leaving without government permission. Persons requesting such permission automatically lost jobs and other benefits. The stigma for family members remaining on the island was difficult to overcome. Yet in 1978 the Cuban government negotiated an opening with Cubans who had left, including many who had participated in military actions against Cuba….

Implementing the Dialogue agreements proved more difficult than reaching them. The release of political prisoners was to take place with the full cooperation of the United States. And, while the release proceeded as promised, the processing of visas for emigration to the United States was very slow….

Another agreement between the Cuban government and Cubans abroad resulted in more than 120,000 Cubans visiting the island in a year. At first traditional exile groups tried to convince people not to visit their relatives. Eventually, they gave in and instead encouraged exiles visiting relatives to help them gather intelligence information about life in Cuba, economic conditions, and military maneuvers. It became clear that, while Cubans abroad had broken with the revolution, they were still interested in visiting their families and homeland. Committees to defend and implement the accords of the Dialogue sprang up throughout the United States and in Puerto Rico, Venezuela, Mexico, and Spain….

The visitors also had an important effect on the Cuban population. Many island residents objected to the uneven distribution of consumer products between those who had relatives in other countries who could purchase these items on their behalf and those who did not. While there was discontent among Cubans before the 1979 visits, many blamed the exiles' visits for the increasing number of people wanting to leave the country, culminating in the dramatic exodus of more than 120,000 Cubans through the port of Mariel....

Still, the willingness of the U.S. and Cuban governments to negotiate during and after the Dialogue changed the political climate between the two countries and, consequently, opened a new political space within the Cuban exile community. U.S. Cuban organizations that called for normalizing relations between the two countries found that their demands were now more politically acceptable. As a result, organizations that aimed to reestablish relations with the island flourished.

The first organization that emerged from the Dialogue was the Miami-based Committee of 75. Headed by Albor Ruíz, a member of the *Areíto* editorial board, the committee was organized to monitor the implementation of the Dialogue accords in the United States and Cuba.... Other organizations, such as El Grupo de Reunificación Familiar, sought to bring together divided families.

The increased contact between Cuba and the United States gave rise to organizations that provided services to the Cuban community in relation to the island. The most notable of these were the travel agencies that chartered flights from the United States to Cuba.... [Different] services developed, including agencies that forwarded care packages to Cuba and pharmacies that sent medicine....

Other Cubans in the United States focused on advocating changes in U.S. policy toward Cuba, concentrating their efforts on organizing Washington-based groups that would lobby U.S. officials to lift the economic embargo on the island. One such group was the Cuban-American Committee (CAC).... In 1979 the committee presented the State Department with a petition signed by more than ten thousand Cubans requesting a speedy normalization of relations between the United States and Cuba....

Still other organizations concentrated on academic and cultural exchanges between Cubans in the United States and those on the island.... Many organizations promoting some form of exchange emerged within the U.S. Cuban exile community during this period. No doubt they surfaced, at least in part, because a new generation had come of age and felt strongly the need to maintain a link to the homeland....

★ ★ ★

... [G]roups that continued their quest to overthrow the revolution by violent means grew increasingly isolated. Their aim of invasion and return to the island—a promise extended relentlessly since the revolution's beginning and financed partially through community fund-raising efforts—became less realistic and more desperate and was recognized as such by most Cuban exiles. These groups reacted violently to the new developments. Their first attack was on Dialogue participants.

In 1979 Omega 7, one of the most active terrorist organizations, claimed credit for more than twenty bombings aimed at the homes and business of Dialogue members.... Communiqués were sent to the Miami offices of the Associated Press and United Press International vowing that any Cuban who traveled to Cuba would be killed. In April 1979 Omega 7 claimed credit for the assassination of Carlos Muñiz Varela, a twenty-six-year old member of the Antonio Maceo Brigade who coordinated the Puerto Rican offices of Viajes Varaderos, an agency that arranged travel to Cuba.

Members of the Antonio Maceo Brigade lived in constant fear. We were afraid that the events we sponsored would be bombed. Our names appeared in press communiqués under the headline "Castro's Agents," or we were called *dialogueros*, a term that came to have negative connotations.... The FBI's first response to a call to investigate Muñiz's murder was to assert that Puerto Rico was outside its jurisdiction.... In November 1979, in Union City, New Jersey, terrorists killed Eulalio Negrin, another Dialogue member. His killers were never found.

In response to terrorist acts, more open-minded Cuban exiles launched a national campaign against terrorism, demonstrating that they had learned how to use the U.S. political system.... [A] task force successfully lobbied several congressmen to establish special congressional hearings on Cuban exile right-wing terrorism, although ultimately these were more symbolic than effective in halting criminal acts or in pushing the FBI to investigate them....

... [T]he White House eventually established a special FBI task force and named Omega 7 the most dangerous terrorist group in the United States. But it was another two years before the FBI would make its first arrests of Omega 7 members....

The political legitimacy gained by those calling for a rapprochement with the revolution continued to shift the political middle ground in the Cuban community. Supporters of the Dialogue successfully organized a base of support among émigrés....

★ ★ ★

Within this expanded political spectrum new issues emerged. The Cuban émigré community became a vocal supporter of bilingual programs in Dade County, Florida.... This issue, along with Cuban support for bilingual voting materials, aligned Cubans with other Latinos throughout the United States. Furthermore, an unprecedented number of Cubans became naturalized U.S. citizens, a necessary requirement for voting. Thus, when the Democratic Party formed a caucus of Hispanic-American Democrats in 1979, with the goal of unifying Latinos of different national origin under a single banner, traditional Cuban-American Democrats and representatives from the Dialogue movement played a key role. By 1976 most Cuban voters in Dade County were registered Democrats. No longer did conservative Cubans monopolize connections with the formal political structures....

For Cuban émigrés Cuba—the homeland—continued to be at the center of political debate and life. Those promoting a better relationship found sympathetic ears in Washington.... But for the community new forms of political participation emerged that were related to the status of Cubans as U.S. citizens and residents.

FURTHER READING

Maylei Blackwell, *¡Chicana Power! Contested Histories of Feminism in the Chicano Movement* (2011).

Ernesto Chávez, *"¡Mi Raza Primero!" (My People First): Nationalism, Identity, and Insurgency in the Chicano Movement in Los Angeles* (2002).

José E. Cruz, *Identity and Power: Puerto Rican Politics and the Challenge of Ethnicity* (1998).

María de los Angeles Torres, *In the Land of Mirrors: Cuban Exile Politics in the United States* (1999).

Darrel Enck-Wanzer, ed., *The Young Lords: A Reader* (2010).

Johanna Fernández, "The Young Lords and the Postwar City: Notes on the Geographical and Structural Reconfigurations of Contemporary Urban Life," in Kenneth Kusmer and Joe William Trotter, Jr., eds., *African American Urban History since World War II* (2009).

Alma M. García, ed., *Chicana Feminist Thought* (1997).

Tato Laviera, *AmeRícan* (1985).

Sonia S. Lee and Ande Diaz, "'I Was the One Percenter': Manny Diaz and the Beginnings of a Black-Puerto Rican Coalition," *Journal of American Ethnic History* 26, no. 3 (2007), 52–80.

David Montejano, *Quixote's Soldiers: A Local History of the Chicano Movement, 1966–1981* (2010).

Carlos Muñoz, *Youth, Identity, Power: The Chicano Movement* (2007).

Achy Obejas, *We Came All the Way from Cuba So You Could Dress Like This?* (1994).

Lorena Oropeza, *¡Raza Si!, ¡Guerra No!: Chicano Protest and Patriotism during the Viet Nam War Era* (2005).

Pedro Pietri, *Puerto Rican Obituary* (1973).

Vicki L. Ruiz, "La Nueva Chicana: Women and the Movement" in *From Out of the Shadows: Mexican Women in Twentieth-Century America* (2008; originally published 1998).

Andrés Torres and José Velázquez. *The Puerto Rican Movement: Voices from the Diaspora* (1998).

Young Lords Party and Michael Abramson, eds., *Palante: The Young Lords Party* (1970).

CHAPTER 12

Dominican Migration and

Transnational Lives

In the 1960s, Dominican migration to the United States increased dramatically. Here, as elsewhere, U.S. intervention in the Dominican Republic fueled migration. In 1961, Rafael Leonidas Trujillo was assassinated, as the United States withdrew its long-term backing of this repressive dictator, who had ruled since 1930. In the aftermath, the United States sought to prevent communism or left-leaning politics from taking hold, by influencing Dominican politics and by sending U.S. marines in 1965. With Trujillo's prohibition of emigration lifted and with the United States expediting visas, migration rose sharply and then continued as a result of ongoing political and economic turmoil. Changes in U.S. immigration policy also shaped migration. In 1965, the United States ended its national origins quota system, based on immigrants' countries of origin and hence explicitly on immigrants' ethnicity and race. The Immigration Act of 1965 prioritized immigration based on family reunification, which some policymakers thought would sustain the predominance of European immigration. Instead, Dominicans, along with many Latin Americans and Asians, migrated through the family reunification provisions and through provisions for workers in certain occupations. Despite the Act's proclaimed emphasis on family reunification, the U.S. notion of the nuclear family and bureaucratic hurdles conflicted with Dominicans' notion of the extended family and their desires for more rapid family reunification. At times, the result could be migration without proper documentation.

Initially, most Dominicans settled in New York City, particularly in Washington Heights. Like migrants before them, Dominican sought to influence U.S. policies toward their home country and remained engaged in home-country politics. At the same time, they worked to build communities and improve conditions within their new U.S. home. Dominicans arrived as New York City was undergoing economic restructuring that entailed the decline of manufacturing jobs, wages, and working conditions, as well as the increasing polarization of very high- and very low-wage jobs, with the middle economic tier eroding. Sought as low-wage workers for the city's declining manufacturing sector and for service jobs, Dominicans became concentrated in particular sectors of the economy. Nevertheless, they managed to send remittances to their families in the Dominican Republic, sustaining their transnational households and bolstering the national economy. Arriving during an era of civil rights activism, Dominicans participated in and shaped the political and social movements of the era. Their sense of themselves in their new environment was shaped by differing notions of race in the Dominican Republic and the United States, by the U.S. lingering biracial system of classification that defined people as either white or black, by the emerging category of "Hispanic," and by their daily interactions with their diverse neighbors in Washington Heights and the broader U.S. society. Advances in transportation and communications facilitated ongoing connections with communities in both nations. This chapter examines Dominicans' transnational experiences through political involvement, economic linkages, and cultural interactions in the United States and the Dominican Republic.

 # DOCUMENTS

The U.S. role in the Dominican Republic shaped Dominican immigration. Document 1 is a declassified document in which the U.S. State Department reveals its program for influencing Dominican politics and expediting visas for travel to the United States in 1962. Continuing to leave their country for political and economic reasons, many Dominicans had settled in New York City by 1971, as the *New York Times* reports in Document 2. While some Dominicans migrated without proper documentation, others came through the provisions of the Immigration Act of 1965, which replaced national origin quotas with preference categories that emphasized family reunification. In Document 3, a government task force explores the 1965 Immigration Act's role in increasing migration to the United States. Arriving in large numbers during the late 1960s and early 1970s, Dominican youth, like writer Sherezada "Chiqui" Vicioso, were influenced by the political and social movements of the times, as Document 4 reveals. Even as Dominicans retained strong ties to their country of origin, they established firm roots and built communities in New York City through businesses and local politics, as a 1991 newspaper article depicts in Document 5. Document 6 is an excerpt from writer Junot Díaz's short story "Negocios," published in 1996. In portraying a father's migration story, he explores challenges, complex negotiations, inter-Latino dynamics, and more. Beyond New York City, Dominicans like Felicia Díaz settled in smaller cities such as Waterbury, Connecticut. In a 2003 interview, Document 7, Díaz stresses the role of social networks in facilitating migration and in building communities.

1. U.S. State Department Outlines Program in the Dominican Republic, 1962

PROGRAM OF ACTION FOR THE DOMINICAN REPUBLIC

A. General

1. Period Covered: The program outlined below is designed to cover the period from the present to February 1963, when a government chosen in elections scheduled for December 1962 will take office.

U.S. Department of State. "Program of Action for the Dominican Republic," April 30, 1962, Declassified Documents Retrieval System, United States; and "Dominican Republic: Status of Plan of Action Approved by the President as of July 17, 1962."

2. Basic Considerations:

(a) The United States has no other choice or interest than to support the Council of State until it is replaced by an elected government;

(b) The judgment of the Council and the parties on political and economic questions confronting them cannot be fully relied upon;

(c) Because of that fact and the continuing reliance of the Council and major party leaders on U.S. guidance—as well as our own determination to attain our objectives in the Dominican Republic—we should continue to take an active part in Dominican affairs and should not be unduly concerned about intervention.

3. U.S. Objectives for Period:

(a) The maintenance of the Council in effective power;

(b) Control of the threat from the far left (Castro/Communists) and the far right (Trujillistas);

(c) Resolution of the current Dominican economic and financial difficulties;

(d) Sound preparation of the Dominican people for participation in the electoral process.

B. Key Problems....

(a) "Purge" of the military: Partly to guard against a coup and partly to meet pressure from the National Civic Union (UCN), the Council plans to retire, assign abroad, exile or arrest and try a group of military officers. Although a selective weeding out of dangerous elements is desirable, the operation has to be executed carefully in order to avoid precipitating the violent action by disaffected military which the Council seeks to forestall. Two members of the Council have very recently approached Ambassador Martin for assurances of U.S. opposition to a military coup. Prior to these approaches, the Ambassador had made known to various Dominican leaders, civilian and military, the Department's position that "the United States Government would view with grave concern the replacement of the present Government by elements of, or allied with, the far left or the far right" and "in the event of the overthrow of the Council from any direction, the United States Government would be obliged to reexamine its entire policy toward the Dominican Republic"....

(h) Visa backlog: Because of the freer atmosphere following the end of the Trujillo regime and because of the desire of many Dominicans to insure a haven in the event of further upheavals, the Visa Section of the Embassy in Santo Domingo has been overwhelmed by a flood of visa applications. Although the Department has supplied the Embassy with extra visa personnel to meet the emergency, there are very substantial delays in processing applications (48 weeks for non–immigrant visas and 64 weeks for immigrant visas). The situation has taken on political importance, and the public image of the United States is being impaired. A visa expert from the Department of State is now in Santo Domingo to study the situation and make recommendations for immediate corrective measures....

C. Program of Action....

(d) ...

- Be prepared to consider very carefully a delay in the elections, if the OAS mission so recommends.

- Be prepared to seek a delay in the elections if it becomes apparent that the results would be contrary to our interests, and attempt to influence the OAS mission in that direction....

(f) Be prepared to provide very substantially increased economic assistance to the Dominican Government if, as a result of changes in U.S. sugar legislation, Dominican sugar ceases to earn the U.S. premium price....

(g) Define the U.S. economic and social objectives in the Dominican Republic as the basis for a finely coordinated approach by AID and international agencies under the Alliance for Progress....

(k) Continue, with all available means, to control and reduce Castro/ Communist influence in the student and labor movements.

DOMINICAN REPUBLIC: Status of Plan of Action Approved
by the President as of July 17, 1962

... (j) The Department has taken action to alleviate the problem of the large backlog of visa applications in Santo Domingo. A visa expert surveyed the situation, three officers have been assigned on temporary duty, and authorization has been given the Embassy to hire seven additional local employees. A contract has been signed to provide additional office space for an enlarged consular section, and it is expected that it will be occupied within a few days. The Department is prepared to send two additional visa officers as soon as space is available to accommodated them.

2. Dominicans Settle in New York City, 1971

... Dominicans have abandoned their island en masse in the years of economic and political instability following the 1962 assassination of Generalissimo Rafael Leónidas Trujillo Molina, and have settled in the eastern section of this country, particularly New York.

Many of them concede that a large proportion—perhaps a majority—are illegal residents. They entered the country on tourist or student visas and settled in New York State....

As a result, estimates of their numbers in the city—where they are concentrated in the Corona section of Queens, the Upper West Side of Manhattan, the East Bronx and South Brooklyn—vary widely. They range from a conservative 100,000 figure used by the Dominican Consulate at 1270 Avenue of the Americas to a probably inflated 200,000 cited by some community leaders. At any rate, many say that New York is the second largest Dominican city in the world, out-ranked only by Santo Domingo....

The illegal residency status of many Dominicans has in large measure shaped the character of their community....

But the possibility of more stringent enforcement of immigration laws in the near future—including fines against employers who hire illegal residents—has brought open expressions of concern from virtually the entire community.

"The Cubans are allowed in because of political reasons, and the Puerto Ricans are citizens: we should be given a chance also," said Francisco Leo, 35, a Dominican of Chinese descent, who runs a small Caribbean restaurant at 145th Street and Broadway.

A number of the Dominicans do not plan to stay here....

The influx of Dominicans has also shown up in the schools. George Washington High School at 549 Audubon Avenue on Manhattan's Upper West Side has the largest contingent of Dominican students in the city. Until two years ago, a majority of the pupils were black, but now, more than half the enrollment is Latin....

During the last five years, about 35,000 Dominicans have settled in the Corona section of Queens....

At 38-05 100th Street, in the basement of a stone townhouse, 77 residents have formed a neighborhood club—Dominicanos Unidos Social Club—"to improve the image of Dominicans," in the words of one member, Rafael Vasquez, 25, a red-haired bus driver who has lived in New York for nine years....

"Until recently, we had the best Latin community in New York," said Rafael Peralta, 45, a stern, straight-forward man wearing darkly tinted glasses, who works as a shipping clerk in a textile company.

"But the influx of poorer, rural Dominicans has lowered the level. It's not their fault. Many were brought here like cattle to work in the factories and res-taurants. They don't have any place to spend their free time but in the streets."

The year-old club, which meets every Sunday afternoon, sponsors dances, lectures on Dominican culture, and explanations of American laws and city reg-ulations, but pointedly remains aloof from politics, including the issue of illegal immigration.

"We feel sorry for our less fortunate companions, but if the immigration laws are enforced, we must obey them—all illegal Dominicans will have to leave," said Luis Medina, a dapper public accountant in his 40's, who is president of the club.

"Among members, there are perhaps five or six who are illegal immigrants," he continued....

In Corona, also, just two blocks away, in a white split-level storefront, which is the Queens headquarters of the Dominican Revolutionary party, or P.R.D., a group of Dominicans met on a recent Friday night.

Under the harsh glare of bare light bulbs, about 25 men, most in their early 30's and some wearing black berets, sat on wooden chairs, their arms folded, facing party officials who were seated behind a table.

Among them were shopkeepers, clerks, part-time students, factory laborers and waiters—some of them illegal immigrants who worked for "74 poisoned dollars a week," the New York State minimum wage.

The purpose of the P.R.D., according to the New York secretary-general, Pircilio Peña, is "to maintain alive the Dominican revolution until the individuals who have illegally taken power in Santo Domingo are over thrown or voted out of office."

Calling themselves non-Communists, P.R.D. members are followers of Dr. Juan Bosch, a deposed President of the Dominican Republic, and address each other as "compañero."

Party activity consists mainly of rallies, petitions to Representatives and Senators, and distribution of posters detailing alleged atrocities by the Dominican Government headed by President Joaquín Balaguer, against his opponents....

"The United States Government intervened in the Dominican Republic to destroy a democratic movement and left behind a repressive machine which has tried to exterminate Dominican youth," Mr. Peña asserted, tears welling in his eyes.

"Because of our economic misery, we have been forced to come to the United States and place ourselves in the grips of the monster that forced us to flee," said Winston Arnaud, 28, a student. "Fortunately, American public opinion would not permit the American Government to suppress us here the way it has in Santo Domingo."

Turning to the subject of illegal immigration, Nelson Beato, 31, a shipping clerk, said:

"The economic crisis in the United States has caused a nationalist cry against the immigrant, who is supposedly taking away jobs from Americans. We hold the jobs that are too dirty, too hard for Americans. But we are the weakest link in the Latin community, and we'll end up being the sacrificial guinea pigs."

3. U.S. Immigration Policy Shapes Dominican Immigration, 1979

The Immigration and Nationality Act of 1952 was substantially modified in 1965. The 1952 Act had promoted immigration from some nations while restricting it from others. The 1965 Amendments substituted a universalist approach, facilitated family reunification and deemphasized the immigration of "needed" workers....

... [T]he seeds of the demand for immigration in the 1980's were planted in the decade between 1967 and 1976, by the arrival of immigrants who may seek to bring their relatives to the United States in the future.

Worldwide immigration to the United States averaged 388 thousand annually over the past decade, with numbers ranging from 362 thousand in 1967 to over 454 thousand the next year. This level represents an increase of over one-third

U.S. Departments of Justice, Labor, and State, Interagency Task Force on Immigration Policy, Staff Report (March 1979), pp. 117–183.

from the level of immigration preceding the 1965 Amendments, when total immigration averaged 288 thousand a year. As well as increasing the number of immigrants, the 1965 Amendments also significantly changed the origin of the flow of immigration especially from the Eastern Hemisphere (Europe, Asia, Africa, and Oceania). Overall, immigration from Europe decreased. Southern and Eastern Europe replaced Northern and Western European nations as principal immigrant sources. On the other hand, immigration from Asia increased dramatically. Simultaneously, immigration from the Western Hemisphere (North and South America) increased moderately....

On July 1, 1968, an annual ceiling of 120,000 immigrant visas was imposed on Western Hemisphere (North and South American) immigration which previously had been unrestricted. The preference system was not extended to the "New World" because it was believed that the domestic labor market, through the labor certification process already in place, provided a more flexible tool to control Western Hemisphere immigration.... [N]umerically limited immigration from the Western Hemisphere was predicated on labor market conditions, while the preference system applicable in the Eastern Hemisphere favored family reunification....

In practice, however, the labor certification process did not regulate the composition of immigration from the Western Hemisphere effectively. Whereas in 1969 almost all Western Hemisphere entrants other than the statutorily exempted Cuban refugees were labor certified immigrants or accompanying family members, by 1976 that figure had plummeted to only 5 percent and at least 80 percent were exempt from labor certification by virtue of certain family ties in the United States. In 1976, Congress amended the law to impose more effective control, and beginning January 1, 1977, the preference system and per country limit were applied to Western Hemisphere immigration.

Over the 1967 to 1976 decade, Western Hemisphere immigration, which numbered 1,356,899, accounted for a little over one third of all immigration.... [A]bout half of the increase between the two decades is attributable to the newly gained independence of such former colonies as Barbados, Jamaica, and Trinidad and Tobago during the 1960's.... [T]he Act of November 2, 1966 authorized the adjustment of Cuban refugees after two years' presence in the United States. Over 166 thousand Cubans who had previously entered as paroled refugees adjusted their status during 1967 and 1968.... [P]olitical and economic difficulties in nearby countries, such as the Dominican Republic and Haiti, increased emigration from them. Finally, travel to the United States became easier and less expensive in the late 1960's, and as more information about the United States became widespread throughout the hemisphere, the lure of immigration became stronger....

About 81 percent of the immigration subject to the numerical limitations of the Western Hemisphere was of immigrants other than Cuban refugee adjustments of status.... Of the total admissions of Western Hemisphere natives, 84 percent were of immigrants from North America [Canada, Mexico, the Caribbean Islands, and Central America], with the largest number of these coming from Mexico

(42 percent), Jamaica (13 percent), the Dominican Republic (11 percent), and Canada (10 percent)....

... [C]ertain groups of immigrants have traditionally been exempt from numerical limitations. Immediate relatives of U.S. citizens have always been the major category....

The number of immigrants entering outside the numerical limitations increased considerably through the 1967 to 1976 period.... This upward trend can be expected to continue and probably accelerate as the larger numbers of immigrants admitted in the late 1960's and 1970's naturalize and petition for immediate relatives....

... [T]he spouses and minor children of U.S. citizens and the parents of adult U.S. citizens were admitted outside the numerical ceilings of the two hemispheres. Parents, admitted as second preference immigrants under the 1952 Act, were added to the numerically exempt immediate relative category in the 1965 Amendments....

Although generally increasing over the period since 1969, the immigration of immediate relatives from North and South America varied between 30 and 45 percent of the total during that time....

Spouses of U.S. citizens comprise the largest group (64 percent) of the immediate relative category and are the most likely to adjust their status in the United States....

Fifty-five percent of the 156,525 spouses from North America came from Mexico during the 1967 through 1976 period. Another 14 percent came from Canada, and 8 percent were from the Dominican Republic. The proximity of these nations, frequency of travel between them and the United States, and the large number of aliens, both legal and illegal, of these nationalities in the United States undoubtedly played an important role in the large numbers of spouses admitted as immigrants. Although much smaller in number, spouses of U.S. citizens comprised substantial portions of total immigration from such Central American nations as El Salvador, Honduras, Nicaragua, and Panama. Similarly, although relatively small in number, substantial proportions of the total immigration from the South American countries of Brazil, Chile, Peru and Venezuela were of spouses of U.S. citizens....

The number of admissions in all categories of immediate relatives increased between 1967 and 1976, but the rise in the number of minor children of U.S. citizens entering was the most dramatic. The 23,889 children admitted in 1976 was 179 percent higher than the 8,567 such entries at the beginning of the decade.

Not surprisingly, minor children of U.S. citizens, which includes both natural and adopted children under the age of 21, came from much the same countries as U.S. citizen spouses.... Of the 177,650 children of citizens immigrating to the United States over the 1967 through 1976 period, 19 percent (33,152) were from Europe.... Thirty-six percent (63,779) of all immediate relative children were from Asia.... Of the 41 percent (72,157) from North America, 65 percent were from Mexico; 10 percent were Canadian, and 7 percent were Dominican. Only 4 percent (6,249) of all children were from South America, with Colombia and Ecuador accounting for most of these.

4. Writer Sherezada "Chiqui" Vicioso Defines Herself during the 1970s

... I first came to the United States in April 1967. Initially, I had wanted to be a lay nun and work in the *barrios*. Marriage repelled me, especially when I looked at my aunts, practically all of whom were divorced. I couldn't stand the idiocy of the whole scene: the danger of getting mixed up with someone when you were thirteen or fourteen, worrying about not having a boyfriend when you were sixteen. To me, becoming a nun was my path to freedom. I also wanted to study medicine. The one year I planned to stay eventually became seventeen.

My mother, who had left a year earlier, said I should go to the States in order to improve my English and to get to know the world before embarking on becoming a nun. I was very angry with her at the time, but she was right.

I come from a very special family with an intellectual background. On my father's side, my grandfather was a journalist and a writer, and my father is a poet and a well-known composer. My mother is a better poet than I am, but has never dared to write. She is the daughter of a peasant woman who worked in a tobacco factory and a Dominican oligarch who owned the factory and literally bought her when she was sixteen. My mother is a hybrid of two very distinct classes. I felt this when I went to school in Santiago.

In spite of having studied English in school, I found out, on my arrival in New York, that I didn't know very much. Like most Dominicans who come to the United States, I went to work in a factory: first a hat, and then a button factory (the acetone in which we had to wash the buttons damaged my eyes so that I have had to wear glasses ever since). I went to night school for a while, and then was accepted into a city-sponsored intensive English program, where I was paid to study.

My next job was as a telephone operator, and I quickly acquired a reputation as being extremely courteous to the customers, as my English still wasn't all that good and I said "Thank you" to everyone, even if they insulted me. Then Brooklyn College opened its doors to minority students. They responded to a policy, initiated under the Johnson administration, whereby colleges were paid federal funds to admit minorities. I was one of eight Dominican students admitted to Brooklyn College.

Since there were only eight of us, and it was very tough to survive in such a racist atmosphere, we joined up with other minority students, principally Puerto Ricans, blacks, other people from the Caribbean—we formed a Third World Alliance.

This was a real threshold for me; I had never known the people from Barbados or Trinidad, etc. My concept of the Caribbean, up to that time, had been limited to the Spanish-speaking part, and I discovered my identity as a *caribeña* in New York.

"Sherezada 'Chiqui' Vicioso: An Oral History," in Denis Lynn Daly Heyck, ed., *Barrios and Borderlands: Cultures of Latinos and Latinas in the United States* (New York: Routledge, 1994), pp. 270–275.

I was also racially classified at Brooklyn College, which was an interesting experience for me. In Santo Domingo, the popular classes have a pretty clear grasp of racial divisions, but the middle and upper-middle classes are very deluded on this point. People straighten their hair and marry "in order to improve the race," etc., etc., and don't realize the racist connotations of their language or their attitude. In the United States, there is no space for fine distinctions of race, and one goes from being "*trigueño*" or "*indio*" to being "mulatto" or "black" or "Hispanic." This was an excellent experience for me. From that point on, I discovered myself as a Caribbean *mulata* and adopted the black identity as a gesture of solidarity. At that time, I deeply admired and identified with Angela Davis, and ever since then, I have kept on identifying myself as a black woman.

This opened another door; I learned about Frantz Fanon and other Caribbean theoreticians, and that finished Europe for me. I learned about the triangular trade and how we had financed Europe's development. I realized that capitalism was an impossible model to follow in our development. For me, this was discovering a universe. I only became a feminist much later.

When I first became more radical I was very much put off by feminism and people like Gloria Steinem and Betty Friedan—to me they were representatives of the white U.S. middle class who were busy telling us how *we* were being screwed up by *machismo*. In a first stage I rejected this and ... I also had a false sense of solidarity with our men, who were racially oppressed as well. I felt that if we women criticized our men, we were only providing the racists with ammunition. This created a conflict of loyalties for me.

Discovering myself as a woman came much later. First I had to discover that I was part of certain geographical area, and then, that I was Latin American. The great majority of the Latin American exiles converged on New York at that time—the Argentineans, the Uruguayans, the Chileans (Allende fell during those years)—so that, for me, New York became a kind of great doorway to this Latin American world.

Being in New York was very essential to my development. I would not be the woman I am today had I not gone to New York. I would have been the classic *fracasada* (failure) in my country because I know that I would not have found happiness in marriage and having children. I would have been frustrated, unhappy in a marriage, or divorced several times over because I would not have understood that within me was a woman who needed to express her own truths, articulate her own words. That, in Santo Domingo, would have been impossible.

Nevertheless, for the first ten years that I lived in New York, I was engulfed by a great silence; I could write nothing at all....

Still, all these experiences were being stored up inside of me. It's that kind of a process; things go in stages.

It was going to Africa that restored my essence as a *caribeña* for me. I went for three and a half months to work on coordinating the first meeting of ministers of education of the Portuguese-speaking African nations....

When I returned to the States, I was a different person; I suffered from severe depressions, which I now realize marked the death of one Chiqui and the birth of another....

I had to go back to Santo Domingo because, after a few years, living in the United States gave me a kind of physical malaise.... When you first get here from your country, full of strength and energy, you get involved in a first stage of learning, absorbing, discovering. Then comes a time when you have to go back in order to revitalize yourself. If you stay in New York too long, you begin to get worn down by it. Anyone who is in the least sensitive can't help but feel bruised by the destruction of our people. Really. I saw it all the time in the Dominican community....

The New York experience, which was so crucial to my discovery of my Caribbean and racial identity, has made me a very, very critical person with respect to my own society. Things I never noticed before, I now see. Like racism, for example. Class differences. Santo Domingo is a very societally structured city. The situation of women is atrocious. I get almost rude about this because I can't stand the kind of sexist behavior that exists in my country. And for that, you pay the price of ostracism. It's really hard. By dint of having lived in the United States, I am considered a "liberated woman," which means that the men feel they have a green light to harass me sexually while the women distrust me. That's the most painful part....

Because so many of my potential readers live in New York, I am definitely moving ... toward publishing in the United States. I think people on the island would be interested as well.... We cannot avoid the "invasion" of the Dominicans from the U.S. The whole country is changing: English is spoken all over—you feel the influence of the Dominicans who come back everywhere. I also think there will be interest in my writing in the States, first of all, because there are so many of us there, and second, because I will approach things with the particular viewpoint of a woman. I have a lot to tell about what New York did to my family.

5. Dominicans Build Transnational Lives, 1991

Martin Gomez starts all his mornings in America in the same place, at the foot of the George Washington Bridge, waiting for his ride and his future.

As the commuters from New Jersey begin to flow across the bridge to their jobs in midtown Manhattan, Mr. Gomez and hundreds of other Dominican immigrants are heading the other way, in an alternative rush hour imported from the streets of Santo Domingo.

In a caravan of livery cabs, broken-down cars, vans and school buses painted bright blue, they are going to sew dresses in factories, make beds in hotels and scrub office floors in central and northern New Jersey.

Those Dominicans, the largest group of recent immigrants, stand for a new wave of immigration that is transforming the New York metropolitan region.

Their economically ravaged homeland, where the average salary is $40 a month, sent more people to New York in the 1980's than any other country.

By an inexact official count, the Dominicans in the city are now 400,000 strong. Their entrepreneurial zeal has apparently bought them most of the city's bodegas and many of its livery cabs, and, to an exuberant merengue beat, they have revived a decaying Washington Heights.

The Dominicans have crowded into tenements that once were home to German Jews and the Irish. But while new arrivals are from somewhere else now, their story is in many ways the same. Their lives are still defined by money: earning it, saving it, and sending it back to their families.

Worker by worker by worker, they send so much home, an estimated $300 million to $600 million a year, that their remittances are the Dominican Republic's second-largest industry. Entire Dominican towns are dependent on money from New York.

All immigrants live suspended between two worlds, the old country and the new. The Dominicans just do so more than most. They may complain incessantly about how bad things are at home—the incompetent bureaucracy, the daily blackouts, the steep price of everything from plantains to sugar, but they talk just as much of returning. Home is a three-hour flight and a $489 round-trip ticket away.

"The Dominicans are like sojourners, or permanent immigrants," said Luis Guarnizo, a doctoral candidate in sociology at the Johns Hopkins University who has extensively studied and written about Dominican immigrants. "They have two lives, one back home and one here. It adds up to almost no life.

"They come here thinking, 'I'm going to save money, buy a house back home, and go back and start a business.' But life here is more difficult than they think. Time goes by, and their stay lengthens. Because of the bureaucracy and corruption in the Dominican Republic, going back is harder than they expected."

In the strict accounting of Mr. Gomez's existence, there are no meals out, no movies, not even television. Back in the Dominican Republic, he made about $10 a week as a cook. In America, depending on how much overtime he can find, he makes from $1,000 to $3,200 a month cleaning offices and factories....

By force of thought, if not fact, he said, "My wife and my children get me up every morning at 5." The pressure is enormous.

"Everyone is depending on me," he said. "Sometimes I don't want to work on weekends, but I have to do it. I have to feed my family, I have to feed myself. I have to pay the rent here—and there. I have to pay the light bill here—and there. I don't want to let anyone down."

He budgets $489 in air fare for his yearly trip home. When he has saved enough money, he says, he will build a house and stay in the land of beautiful beaches.

To judge from their rising economic profile, more and more Dominicans, like Mr. Gomez, are wistfully planting both feet on their new land, doing, in their own way, what generations of immigrants have done before them. The Dominicans, redefining the nature of "Hispanic" in a city where the word has long been synonymous with "Puerto Rican," have gone from driving livery cabs to operating fleets of them, from owning bodegas to buying supermarkets. Some have moved from the tenements of Washington Heights to houses in the suburbs.

And after cutting their political teeth on the local school board, the Dominicans last week all but won their own district on the City Council, which is about to expand, to 51 from 35 members, in an effort to give greater political power to the minority groups that now constitute a majority of the city's population....

"Now we are beginning to put down roots in this country," said Dr. Rafael Lantigua, an internist at the Columbia-Presbyterian Medical Center who was a leader in the drive for a Dominican Council district. "We know the only way to get services in a country like ours, and I say ours because this is our country, is through political empowerment."

6. Writer Junot Díaz Depicts a Father's Migration Experience, 1996

My father, Ramón de las Casas, left Santo Domingo just before my fourth birthday. Papi had been planning to leave for months, hustling and borrowing from his friends, from anyone he could put the bite on. In the end it was just plain luck that got his visa processed when it did. The last of his luck on the Island, considering that Mami had recently discovered he was keeping with an overweight puta he had met while breaking up a fight on her street in Los Millonitos. Mami learned this from a friend of hers, a nurse and a neighbor of the puta. The nurse couldn't understand what Papi was doing loafing around her street when he was supposed to be on patrol.

The initial fights, with Mami throwing our silverware into wild orbits, lasted a week. After a fork pierced him in the cheek, Papi decided to move out, just until things cooled down. He took a small bag of clothes and broke out early in the morning. On his second night away from the house, with the puta asleep at his side, Papi had a dream that the money Mami's father had promised him was spiraling away in the wind like bright bright birds. The dream blew him out of bed like a gunshot. Are you OK? the puta asked and he shook his head. I think I have to go somewhere, he said. He borrowed a clean mustard-colored guayabera from a friend, put himself in a concho and paid our abuelo a visit.

Abuelo had his rocking chair in his usual place, out on the sidewalk where he could see everyone and everything. He had fashioned that chair as a thirtieth-birthday present to himself and twice had to replace the wicker screens that his ass and shoulders had worn out. If you were to walk down to the Duarte you would see that type of chair for sale everywhere. It was November, the mangoes were thudding from the trees. Despite his dim eyesight, Abuelo saw Papi coming the moment he stepped onto Sumner Welles. Abuelo sighed, he'd had it up to his cojones with this spat. Papi hiked up his pants and squatted down next to the rocking chair.

I am here to talk to you about my life with your daughter, he said, removing his hat. I don't know what you've heard but I swear on my heart that none of it is true. All I want for your daughter and our children is to take them to the United States. I want a good life for them.

Abuelo searched his pockets for the cigarette he had just put away. The neighbors were gravitating towards the front of their houses to listen to the exchange. What about this other woman? Abuelo said finally, unable to find the cigarette tucked behind his ear.

It's true I went to her house, but that was a mistake. I did nothing to shame you, viejo. I know it wasn't a smart thing to do, but I didn't know the woman would lie like she did.

If you don't think I can do anything for your daughter then I won't ask to borrow that money.

Abuelo spit the taste of car exhaust and street dust from his mouth. He might have spit four or five times. The sun could have set twice on his deliberations but with his eyes quitting, his farm in Azua now dust and his familia in need, what could he really do?

Listen Ramón, he said, scratching his arm hairs. I believe you. But Virta, she hears the chisme on the street and you know how that is. Come home and be good to her. Don't yell. Don't hit the children. I'll tell her that you are leaving soon. That will help smooth things between the two of you.

Papi fetched his things from the puta's house and moved back in that night. Mami acted as if he were a troublesome visitor who had to be endured. She slept with the children and stayed out of the house as often as she could, visiting her relatives in other parts of the Capital. Many times Papi took hold of her arms and pushed her against the slumping walls of the house, thinking his touch would snap her from her brooding silence, but instead she slapped or kicked him. Why the hell do you do that? Don't you know how soon I'm leaving?

Then go, she said.

You'll regret that.

She shrugged and said nothing else.

In a house as loud as ours, one woman's silence was a serious thing. Papi slouched about for a month, taking us to kung fu movies we couldn't understand and drilling into us how much we'd miss him. He'd hover around Mami while she checked our hair for lice, wanting to be nearby the instant she cracked and begged him to stay.

One night Abuelo handed Papi a cigar box stuffed with cash. The bills were new and smelled of ginger. Here it is. Make your children proud.

You'll see. He kissed the viejo's cheek and the next day had himself a ticket for a flight leaving in three days. He held the ticket in front of Mami's eyes. Do you see this?

She nodded tiredly and took up his hands. In their room, she already had his clothes packed and mended.

She didn't kiss him when he left. Instead she sent each of the children over to him. Say good-bye to your father. Tell him that you want him back soon.

When he tried to embrace her she grabbed his upper arms, her fingers like pincers. You had best remember where this money came from, she said, the last words they exchanged face-to-face for five years.

★ ★ ★

He arrived in Miami at four in the morning in a roaring poorly booked plane. He passed easily through customs, having brought nothing but some clothes, a towel, a bar of soap, a razor, his money and a box of Chiclets in his pocket. The ticket to Miami had saved him money but he intended to continue on to Nueva York as soon as he could. Nueva York was the city of jobs, the city that had first called the Cubanos and their cigar industry, then the Bootstrap Puerto Ricans and now him.

He had trouble finding his way out of the terminal. Everyone was speaking English and the signs were no help. He smoked half a pack of cigarettes while wandering around. When he finally exited the terminal, he rested his bag on the sidewalk and threw away the rest of the cigarettes. In the darkness he could see little of Northamerica. A vast stretch of cars, distant palms and a highway that reminded him of the Máximo Gómez. The air was not as hot as home and the city was well lit but he didn't feel as if he had crossed an ocean and a world. A cabdriver in front of the terminal called to him in Spanish and threw his bag easily in the back seat of the cab. A new one, he said. The man was black, stooped and strong.

You got family here?

Not really.

How about an address?

Nope, Papi said. I'm here on my own. I got two hands and a heart as strong as a rock.

Right, the taxi driver said. He toured Papi through the city, around Calle Ocho. Although the streets were empty and accordion gates stretched in front of storefronts Papi recognized the prosperity in the buildings and in the tall operative lampposts. He indulged himself in the feeling that he was being shown his new digs to ensure that they met with his approval. Find a place to sleep here, the driver advised. And first thing tomorrow get yourself a job. Anything you can find.

I'm here to work.

Sure, said the driver. He dropped Papi off at a hotel and charged him five dollars for half an hour of service. Whatever you save on me will help you later. I hope you do well.

Papi offered the driver a tip but the driver was already pulling away, the dome atop his cab glowing, calling another fare. Shouldering his bag, Papi began to stroll, smelling the dust and the heat filtering up from the pressed rock of the streets. At first he considered saving money by sleeping outside on a bench but he was without guides and the inscrutability of the nearby signs unnerved him. What if there was a curfew? He knew that the slightest turn of fortune could dash him. How many before him had gotten this far only to get sent back for some stupid infraction? The sky was suddenly too high. He walked back the way he had come and went into the hotel, its spastic neon sign obtrusively jutting into the street. He had difficulty understanding the man at the desk, but finally the man wrote down the amount for a night's stay in block numbers. Room cuatro-cuatro, the man said. Papi had as much difficulty working the shower but finally was able to take a bath. It was the first bathroom he'd been in that hadn't curled the hair on his body. With the radio tuned in and incoherent, he trimmed his mustache. No photos exist of his mustache days but it is easily imagined. Within an hour he was asleep. He was twenty-four. He didn't dream about his familia and wouldn't for many years. He dreamed instead of gold coins, like the ones that had been salvaged from the many wrecks about our island, stacked high as sugar cane.

★ ★ ★

Even on his first disorienting morning, as an aged Latina snapped the sheets from the bed and emptied the one piece of scrap paper he'd thrown in the trash can, Papi pushed himself through the sit-ups and push-ups that kept him kicking ass until his forties.

You should try these, he told the Latina. They make work a lot easier.

If you had a job, she said, you wouldn't need exercise.

He stored the clothes he had worn the day before in his canvas shoulder bag and assembled a new outfit. He used his fingers and water to flatten out the worst of the wrinkles. During the years he'd lived with Mami, he'd washed and ironed his own clothes. These things were a man's job, he liked to say, proud of his own upkeep. Razor creases on his pants and resplendent white shirts were his trademarks. His generation had, after all, been weaned on the sartorial lunacy of the Jefe, who had owned just under ten thousand ties on the eve of his assassination. Dressed as he was, trim and serious, Papi looked foreign but not mojado.

That first day he chanced on a share in an apartment with three Guatemalans and his first job washing dishes at a Cuban sandwich shop. Once an old gringo diner of the hamburger-and-soda variety, the shop now filled with Óyeme's and the aroma of lechón. Sandwich pressers clamped down methodically behind the front counter. The man reading the newspaper in the back told Papi he could start right away and gave him two white ankle-length aprons. Wash these every day, he said. We stay clean around here.

Two of Papi's flatmates were brothers, Stefan and Tomás Hernández. Stefan was older than Tomás by twenty years. Both had families back home. Cataracts were slowly obscuring Stefan's eyes; the disease had cost him half a finger and his last job. He now swept floors and cleaned up vomit at the train station. This is a lot safer, he told my father. Working at a fábrica will kill you long before any tíguere will. Stefan had a passion for the track and would read the forms, despite his brother's warnings that he was ruining what was left of his eyes, by bringing his face down to the type. The tip of his nose was often capped in ink.

Eulalio was the third apartment-mate. He had the largest room to himself and owned the rusted-out Duster that brought them to work every morning. He'd been in the States close to two years and when he met Papi he spoke to him in English. When Papi didn't answer, Eulalio switched to Spanish. You're going to have to practice if you expect to get anywhere. How much English do you know?

None, Papi said after a moment.

Eulalio shook his head. Papi met Eulalio last and liked him least.

Papi slept in the living room, first on a carpet whose fraying threads kept sticking to his shaved head, and then on a mattress he salvaged from a neighbor. He worked two long shifts a day at the shop and had two four-hour breaks in between. On one of the breaks he slept at home and on the other he would handwash his aprons in the shop's sink and then nap in the storage room while the aprons dried, amidst the towers of El Pico coffee cans and sacks of bread. Sometimes he read the Western dreadfuls he was fond of—he could read one in about an hour. If it was too hot or he was bored by his book, he walked the neighborhoods, amazed at streets unblocked by sewage and the orderliness of the cars and houses....

At the apartment, he'd lie down on his mattress, stretching out his limbs to fill it as much as he could. He abstained from thoughts of home, from thoughts of his two bellicose sons and the wife he had nicknamed Melao. He told himself, Think only of today and tomorrow. Whenever he felt weak, he'd take from under the couch the road map he bought at a gas station and trace his fingers up the coast, enunciating the city names slowly, trying to copy the awful crunch of sounds that was English. The northern coast of our island was visible on the bottom right-hand corner of the map.

★ ★ ★

He left Miami in the winter. He'd lost his job and gained a new one but neither paid enough and the cost of the living room floor was too great. Besides, Papi had figured out from a few calculations and from talking to the gringa downstairs (who now understood him) that Eulalio wasn't paying culo for rent. Which explained why he had so many fine clothes and didn't work nearly as much as the rest. When Papi showed the figures to the Hernández brothers, written on the border of a newspaper, they were indifferent. He's the one with the car, they said, Stefan blinking at the numbers. Besides, who wants to start trouble here? We'll all be moving on anyway.

But this isn't right, Papi said. I'm living like a dog for this shit.

What can you do? Tomás said. Life smacks everybody around.

We'll see about that.

There are two stories about what happened next, one from Papi, one from Mami: either Papi left peacefully with a suitcase filled with Eulalio's best clothes or he beat the man first, and then took a bus and the suitcase to Virginia....

7. Felicia Díaz Recalls Networks and Community Formation in Waterbury, 2003

I was born in Santo Domingo ... in a small town ... in 1956.... I immigrated to the United States with two children, it was not easy for me. It was very hard....
[I was] 19 years old.... I came to the U.S. searching for a better opportunity for the family. I came here to Waterbury because ... my sister was already living

Felicia Díaz interviewed by Ruth Glasser, August 13, 2003; transcribed by Delmaliz Medina; translated by Taisha Rodríguez.

here.... My sister immigrated in 1973, she was the first to immigrate and, through immigration, she brought us here. My mother and seven siblings.... Her name is Josefina, one of the oldest, ... she used to work in a factory in New York, in the Bronx. And the factory moved her to Connecticut, and she had to travel every weekend, travel from New York to Connecticut. Then she decided to live here in Waterbury....

I arrived in 1978.... the community was also very united, there were few of us Dominicans and we were always looking for each other, helping one another. ... One would provide transportation or if they needed to go to the hospital, we would also get an interpreter. They would help one out. They would help find jobs and tell the person who came from Santo Domingo or New York where there were jobs, where they sold cheap clothes, where one could find Hispanic food....

In Santo Domingo, I worked over there also for the community.... When I arrived here, I learned about where I could continue to do the same things that I was doing over there....

There were always people that came and with no place to live. And if one was humanitarian, one would say 'Come stay with me until you find a job.' When they'd find a job then the person would leave but then when that person would leave another one would arrive ..., but it was hard to see people arrive here without having a place to live....

I think one should lend a hand even more to those. Because they don't have papers....

[When someone first arrived], ... we gave them good advice. Where to get vaccines for the children without having to pay. Where to find social services, where to take their children to school. I lasted a long time taking all the kids that arrived from Santo Domingo to take a test so that they could get into school.... I was interested in that children entered school as fast as possible. And that the kids were evaluated exactly and not lowered a grade.... I was always fighting for that in the bilingual program. At the time, I was the vice-president.... That was around 1990. I continued working in the immigration program and I was also vice-president of the immigration program and the bilingual program....

In the beginning I always looked for ways to have my own business.... And I would say to myself that I wanted to take care of children in their first few years. Because the first few years are always important for children, and one day I read in a newspaper that Luz Lebron was giving a class ... on opening a daycare.... I obtained my license, there were about seven or six of us that obtained the license. We were united, we were a support group. If something happened in my daycare, I would call the other ones, we would lend toys because there were only seven or six of us. I say seven because we counted Luz, she was the teacher.... And from then on, well, we started and founded the association [the *Organización de las Proveedoras,* or the Organization of Child-care Providers] and it's already been eight years.... But yes, the association has about 55 women consistently. From the ones that come and go there are about 100 something.... We only have about four men....

In the association, we meet once a month, we bring entertainment, we bring news about what has been happening in our community.... We also visit convalescent homes, we visit, we clean the streets, areas that are very filthy. All the providers, we take a day and do that, we are always doing different activities in the community, or for Christmas, or for Halloween. We are always celebrating all the traditions for the children, through our association....

But here, what we do is that there are always a few Dominicans involved in politics.... We are always trying to help, looking, through politics, to improve our community. Well, that is what I'm always trying to do. Always trying to see what party can help us.... Independently, we don't belong to any, we say to them, 'What are you going to offer us?' Are they going to improve education, health care, what can they offer us? We have a Dominican Club and the association, I tell them! The care of children and I don't tell them that we are about 57, I tell them we are about 150. Always give a higher number. Consider that most of us are married, most of us are citizens, and account for spouses and children over 18 years old can also vote....

 # ESSAYS

Although other Latinas and Latinos also built their lives via connections to their home countries and to their local communities in the United States, the scholarship on Dominican immigration has been particularly attentive to transnationalism. In the first essay, Jesse Hoffnung-Garskof, professor of history at the University of Michigan, explores how Dominicans in New York City in the late 1960s and early 1970s became both dominicanos ausentes (Dominicans living abroad) and New Yorkers. For Hoffnung-Garskof, these identities, as well as Dominicans' racial identities, took shape within the specific context of Washington Heights, where Dominicans interacted in their daily lives with African Americans, Puerto Ricans, and white ethnics, who remained in a neighborhood undergoing racial change. In the second essay, Carmen Teresa Whalen, professor of history and Latina/o Studies at Williams College, examines the impact of a globalizing garment industry on Puerto Rican and Dominican women, with special attention to parallels in the histories of these two groups. The garment industry relocated in search of low-wage workers first to Puerto Rico and then to the Dominican Republic. Puerto Rican and Dominican women found garment-industry jobs in their home countries, as well as deteriorating wages and working conditions in New York City's garment industry. Ruth Glasser, lecturer in urban and community studies at the University of Connecticut–Waterbury, turns our attention to Dominican migration to Waterbury, Connecticut, in the third essay. As Dominicans and other Latinas/os have increasingly settled beyond large cities, Waterbury provides an example of a smaller city, where Dominicans encountered an established Puerto Rican population and a city undergoing deindustrialization. Here, Dominicans relied on social networks to establish businesses and build a Dominican community.

Building Local and Transnational Lives in Washington Heights

JESSE HOFFNUNG-GARSKOF

During the first century of Dominican independence, businessmen, political representatives, soldiers, goods, and media images from the United States regularly crossed the border into the Dominican Republic. Then, in the political turmoil after the death of Trujillo, the border gates swung open in the other direction. Over the following decade, more than one hundred thousand Dominicans filed through the Visa Office, rode the escalators to baggage claim at John F. Kennedy Airport, and settled in a handful of neighborhoods in Manhattan and Queens. In so doing, they transplanted the long encounter between the two societies, in large part, from Dominican to U.S. soil. Dominican ideas of urban life and belonging in the modern world, ideas that had been fashioned in the shadow of the United States, would be transformed by a new experience of living inside the United States. But, most accounts agree, Dominicans first arrived in New York with little plan to refashion themselves into "American" ethnics. In 1969 an elderly journalist reporting on Dominican life in New York for a Santo Domingo magazine wrote that Dominican migrants dreamed of nothing but their homeland, "and long for the happy day of their return."

Dominican plans to return to their native land distinguished them little from earlier generations of immigrants to the United States. Despite the common presumption that immigrants have always sought to become Americans, a great many of the foreign workers who flooded into New York City in the early decades of the twentieth century saw the city as a temporary stopover before returning to the old country, whether it was Italy, Russia, Bulgaria, Turkey, or elsewhere. Dominican migrants in the 1960s expressed similar desires to work abroad only long enough to return to the Dominican Republic with the savings to invest in a small home, a colmado (corner store), a beauty shop, or some other business. They called their settlements the *colonia,* or colony, emphasizing the relationship between colonists and their home territory. Some saw themselves as political exiles, paying dues in the Dominican opposition parties in New York until the Balaguer regime could be overthrown. Some saw themselves as "economic exiles," who had escaped from the misery and unemployment created by their government. When the regime finally changed in the Dominican Republic and new economic policies were implemented, these economic exiles would return to the Dominican Republic triumphantly, and there enjoy the fruits of their hard sacrifice. Migrant *progreso* would eventually be measured in terms of the social and political geography of Santo Domingo, not New York.

Documents from the early Dominican experience in New York suggest that two ideas rarely occurred to migrant Dominicans: that they were a social group that would become a permanent fixture of Dominican social life, the "dominicanos ausentes," or that they were "domínicans" (with an accent on the second syllable, as it is pronounced in English), a new ethnic or racial minority with a permanent role in the economic, political, and social life of New York City. Yet in the years between the U.S. invasion in 1965 and the return to electoral democracy in Santo Domingo in 1978, Dominican identities and politics in New York evolved in both of these unexpected directions. Many Dominicans came to be, by the end of this period, simultaneously incorporated into both local and homeland politics. They reorganized their families, business, and culture, as well, to span the distance between New York and the Dominican Republic.... They began too to build institutions for participating in the politics and society of the Dominican Republic from abroad. Again, the simultaneous engagement with both homeland and neighborhood did not distinguish Dominicans dramatically from many earlier immigrant groups to the United States. But what was new about this process, and what has received very little study, is *how* these new migrants became New Yorkers and dominicanos ausentes in the specific contexts of the late 1960s and early 1970s.

Most dramatically, in adjusting their sense of self to this new neighborhood, Dominican migrants confronted an uncomfortable reality. Moving from the periphery of the imperial system to the center meant coming to occupy the position of a racial minority inside the United States, even for Dominicans who viewed themselves as white or mulatto, or simply Dominican. This meant confronting the differences between the racial identities they carried with them and the ones proposed to them by New York racial politics, in particular the politics that pitted black community activists against a white backlash in Washington Heights.... Indeed, while the new migrants took many paths to local racial identities, it is fair to say that Dominicans, as a group, became New Yorkers who, while held to be racially distinct from whites, were not simply collapsed into the existing categories of African American and Puerto Rican. Dominican became a kind of person one could be, in its own right. It also became a subset of both the broader category of Hispanic (or Latino) and of the even broader category of racial minority. Judging what it meant for Dominicans to be or not to be black, to be or not to be Hispanic, to be or not to be minorities requires turning to the particulars of the city and neighborhood they settled in the late 1960s.

★ ★ ★

The first decade of mass Dominican settlement in New York did not definitively settle the complex alliances and boundaries among white, black, Puerto Rican, and Dominican New Yorkers. It was merely an early act in the drama of Dominican ethnic and racial identity, with crucial scenes played against a backdrop provided by the turbulent racial politics of the city in the late 1960s. In particular, Dominicans worked out their new status as New Yorkers in the context of the northern Manhattan neighborhood called Washington Heights, which grew into the largest Dominican settlement outside the Republic. With the benefit of hindsight, it is clear that the Dominicans settling the neighborhood were an early wave of the new migration that would return New York to its age-old status as a city of racial and ethnic multitudes. But when they arrived, the neighborhood was fully engrossed in midcentury processes that were seemingly erasing the city's immigrant origins. The exclusion of new immigration from Europe in 1924 and the participation of the U.S.-born children of immigrants in the New Deal, World War II, and the postwar economic expansion had helped transform the many foreign races catalogued by Congress in 1911 into a new, white, ethnic American middle class. At the same time, the decline of ideas about Anglo-Saxon racial superiority after the fall of Hitler had repudiated the notion of inferior Hebrew, Celtic, and Italian races and confirmed the notion of a unified Caucasian race marked by relatively mild variations in ethnicity. But the very process that consolidated a supposed Caucasian race reinforced a notion that race relations in the city were defined by the "problem" of black and Puerto Rican New Yorkers. The transformation of off-white racial multitudes into ethnic Americans left the city increasingly divided between white and nonwhite.

This shift from a city of many races to a city with a white majority and two racial "minorities" reached a dramatic climax in neighborhoods like Washington Heights in the 1960s, just as Dominicans began arriving.... When the elevated train arrived in the early twentieth century and developers first built apartment buildings there, the neighborhood became a preferred residential area for second- and third-generation Jewish and Irish families eager to move out of the old working-class sectors of the Lower East Side and Harlem. During World War II, African Americans too began moving across the border of overcrowded Harlem into neighboring Washington Heights.... They generally saw the move north and west into middle-class Washington Heights as a move up in social status.

Similarly large numbers of Puerto Ricans began moving into eastern Washington Heights ... from other city neighborhoods in the decade after the war. This new influx joined the handful of Puerto Rican, Cuban, and Dominican settlers who had settled along upper Broadway in the 1930s. Scattered evidence suggests that Puerto Ricans also saw the neighborhood as a space for upward mobility.... Puerto Rican residents, like African Americans, told investigators that they saw a clear boundary line between Harlem and the higher-status Washington Heights. While white residents often saw the arrival of people of color as a shifting of neighborhood boundaries, Puerto Rican and black residents argued that the boundaries were the same and that they had crossed them.

... The Jews and Irish of Washington Heights interpreted the shifting color line as a shift northward in the boundary between Harlem and Washington Heights. They also responded to the arrival of African Americans and Puerto Ricans of various complexions with considerable anxiety and frequent hostility....

In 1963, just as the new consulate in Santo Domingo began issuing thousands of visas to new Dominican migrants, the break between black civil rights activism and Jewish community politics came to a head in Washington Heights. Hamilton Heights parents proposed desegregating neighborhood schools by busing students among the ethnic enclaves, north, south, east, and west. In 1964 Puerto Rican parents in Washington Heights joined with the African American school reformers in a one-day citywide school boycott. Black and Puerto Rican parents kept an estimated 360,000 students home from school to protest segregated and inferior schools in their neighborhoods. The boycott gave birth to an alliance between Puerto Rican and African American civil rights activists in Washington Heights. But the school system, under pressure from white constituents, responded with weak voluntary busing programs. The bulk of Jewish residents opposed the idea. Despite continued goodwill toward civil rights measures, protecting their own children from the inferior schools in black districts and from the violence they feared at the hands of black and Latino children was paramount. As Jewish leaders successfully flexed their muscles in local politics, these expressions of white privilege, no matter how anguished, became ways to resist neighborhood change....

Not all of the Jews in Washington Heights opposed busing. Ellen Lurie, a Jewish social worker, broke with her neighbors as they migrated toward the politics of white backlash, becoming a fiery leader in a continued alliance between radical whites and black liberation struggles....

The defeat of the desegregation movement in Washington Heights (as in the rest of New York) set the terms for conflicts that would even more violently divide the neighborhood and city along racial lines at the end of the decade. In 1966 and 1967, as the newly installed Balaguer government "cleaned up" the remnants of political opposition in Santo Domingo and many thousands made the decision to move to New York, civil rights leaders in New York gave up on desegregation (and more generally on the liberal allies who had proved so unreliable) and issued a new call for local control of neighborhood schools. This idea of community self-determination had strong roots in New York's black neighborhoods, stretching back especially to the movement led by Marcus Garvey in the 1920s. Among mainstream civil rights leaders the ideal of integration eclipsed the ideal of self-determination in the decades after World War II, but the two were always in tension. By 1966, as the desegregation movement floundered, the appeal of community control grew. If black students were going to be stuck in segregated districts, proponents reasoned, at least the educational and budgetary decisions should be made locally....

The Ford Foundation decided to fund an experiment in local control in the Ocean Hill–Brownsville section of Brooklyn in September 1967, granting a locally elected school board ... the same power to decide about curriculum and personnel that elected boards in comparably sized suburban districts already enjoyed....

New York's teachers, including many Jewish residents of Washington Heights, walked off the job in 1968 to protest the forced transfers [of teachers] in Ocean Hill–Brownsville....

Although participants in these conflicts did not anticipate the arrival of Dominicans ..., the racial conflicts bred during the teacher's strike helped define local politics in Washington Heights for nearly a decade....

By the end of the 1960s, when Dominican children arrived in neighborhood schools in Washington Heights, school politics were aligned along the same racial fault lines that had emerged in the city as a whole. Yet in Washington Heights, earlier than in other city neighborhoods, the enrollment of what were known in school board documents as "other Spanish" disrupted the three-way racial division of black, white, and Puerto Rican even as it took hold. First Cubans and then, much more profoundly, Dominicans reshaped the terrain of ethnicity and race in the neighborhood, and changed what it meant to be Latino in the city. Conversely, this moment in New York City history played a crucial role in shaping Dominicans' own experiments with their new role as ethnic New Yorkers. To the extent that other New Yorkers noticed newly arrived Dominicans in the early 1970s, they saw them in terms of the racial category "minorities," and the panethnic categories "Spanish" or "Hispanic," rather than viewing them in terms of what they shared with other immigrants, other Catholics, or other workers, or primarily in terms of the divides between modern and marginal, urban and rural, decent and indecent that were common in Santo Domingo. Being a racial minority meant something specific as the tide of antipoverty programs begun in the early 1960s began to recede and school elections became the central terrain for dividing up scarce resources. When New York politicians and activists first sought Dominicans out, it was to enlist them in school politics. And when Dominican activists and politicians began running for public office, it was in local school elections....

★ ★ ★

Some Dominicans entered the fray of school elections and sought to define community politics in what was becoming a majority Dominican neighborhood. But in the early years of the 1970s, ethnic and racial boundaries in Washington Heights, and the dangers associated with becoming a minority, provided dubious attractions to all but a few Dominicans. Dominicans' plans to return home and the symbolic opposition between Dominican nationalism and U.S. imperialism also helped to push the center of Dominican politics in Washington Heights away from questions of local schooling. Whatever was transpiring in the streets, schools, and community meetings of Washington Heights seemed a distant reality to many Dominicans, who, by contrast, felt deeply immersed in daily events in Santo Domingo. The Partido Revolucionario Dominicano (PRD) particularly infused the Dominican colonia with the sentiments of an opposition faction exiled by Balaguer's authoritarian regime. This pattern stretched back several decades. Many of the exiles who had escaped Santo Domingo in the final years of the Trujillo regime settled in New York. Then after the coup deposed PRD president Juan Bosch in 1963, and especially after the defeat of the Constitutionalists at the hands of the U.S. Marines in 1965, the opposition again set up shop in New York. Several thousand Constitutionalist combatants made their way to the city that was the historic home to their party. They found work in factories, taxicabs, and restaurants. Public employees and bureaucrats allied with the opposition, and therefore shut out of Balaguer's spoils system, also joined this exile community piecemeal as a means for economic survival.

The emergence of the opposition PRD as the most active political and social institution in the colonia shaped Dominican public life in Washington Heights around a particular symbolism of frustrated social revolution. The PRD, for instance, organized annual celebrations and demonstrations to commemorate the anniversary of the April 24 uprising in Santo Domingo. Each year, thousands marched up Broadway from 139th Street to the party headquarters at 159th Street, where they chanted, debated, listened to speeches by party leaders, and even tussled with onlookers suspected of being FBI agents. Dominicans in New York were not immigrants or minorities, ... they were an active resistance against Joaquín Balaguer and against Yankee imperialism, only temporarily displaced to the "belly of the beast.". ...

Side-by-side with the PRD, with its essentially transplanted leadership and institutional base, a scattering of left-wing Dominican parties and groups flourished in the colonia. Some of these were cells of island-based revolutionary movements reconstituted by students or labor leaders who had been deported or fled the repression of the regime since the early 1960s. But many of the most public left-wing activists were middle-class immigrants in their teens or early twenties, who were not political refugees. They were llevados, the young radicals taken along to New York when their families migrated for reasons unrelated to politics. Some were veterans of the growing revolutionary student movement in the Dominican Republic and some were not. In New York ..., these llevados became a vociferous intellectual and political elite in Washington Heights.

... The Frente Unido was then reborn in the early 1970s as the Comité de Defensa de los Derechos Humanos en la República Dominicana (Committee in Defense of Human Rights in the Dominican Republic), under the leadership of several Dominican high school students in Washington Heights, [Ramón] Bodden (still an uptown activist), a Brooklyn College student named Scherazada (Chiqui) Vicioso (now a prominent Dominican poet and intellectual), and a young middle-class woman named Dinorah Cordero (now a longtime community activist in Washington Heights) [See Document 4]. They set about organizing international public opinion against the assassinations, disappearances, and general brutality of the regime, and debating heartily the proper interpretations of Marx, Mao, Fanon, and Juan Bosch. But most notably, their constant vigils and protests in front of the Dominican Consulate and the United Nations became a familiar part of Dominican youth social life in Manhattan.

These marches, debates, and vigils took place only blocks from the heated school protests and contested elections that dominated Washington Heights politics in these years, and many of the young Dominican revolutionaries attended schools in the neighborhood. But these militant groups neither required nor desired that Dominicans become involved in U.S. politics, except as critics of foreign policy, and occasionally as aggrieved victims of police or INS abuses. Since they believed that the revolution back home, and the end of exile, was "just around the corner," the Frente Unido, the Comité de Defensa, and even the PRD put little or no energy into organizing around local issues in New York. In fact, in the words of one journalist, their politics called for "a patriotic attitude and conduct, the systematic rejection of that which is North American." This homeland-centered politics also required skepticism about what the left increasingly saw as the formality of elections. The dubious demonstration elections that the United States had sponsored in 1966 and the fraudulent Dominican elections that followed convinced Juan Bosch and many of his admirers that formal democracy was a sham designed to prevent real social change. In the years between 1966 and 1975, the suggestion that Dominicans should participate in the electoral process in Santo Domingo was enough to elicit cries that one was an "agent of yankee imperialism." The idea of participating in elections in New York was farther still from the ideals of revolutionary exiles. Calls for naturalization and forays into New York City electoral politics were met still more harshly with denunciations such as *vendepatrias* (sellout).

When it came to organizing apolitical Dominican migrants in New York, as one young revolutionary in New York wrote to the Dominican newspaper *El Nacional* in 1971, the role of the politically active left in New York was not to encourage migrants to take on local ethnic struggles. It was rather to "go about raising the consciousness of the hundreds of thousands of Dominican residents of New York ... so that they will return to their humiliated and exploited homeland." Left-wing parties and young llevados distributed leaflets at subway stations and tried to politicize the social clubs, like the Dominican Sporting Club on 173rd Street and Amsterdam Avenue, where migrants gathered to play dominoes, organize softball leagues, participate in beauty pageants, drink, listen to *son* or merengue, and catch up with the news from Santo Domingo. They did their best to give institutions the kind of political edge that Sporting and Cultural Clubs had in Santo Domingo....

The Dominican left in New York also forged an easy alliance with the growing local movement against U.S. foreign policy in Latin America and Vietnam. In fact, the Dominican left enjoyed a minor celebrity status in radical circles between 1968 and 1975. A range of political groupings in New York, from white antiwar radicals to proponents of Black Power, were entering a period of romance with anticolonial heroes like Che Guevara and Ho Chi Minh and were beginning to model their own politics on these exotic images of martial discipline and self-sacrifice. In the late 1960s and early 1970s these revolutionaries saw Dominicans as "third world brothers." The activists in the Comité de Defensa, for instance, mingled happily with the luminaries of the North American left: Norman Thomas, Stokely Carmichael, and the young intellectuals of Students for a Democratic Society and the North American Conference on Latin America (NACLA), all of whom recognized the young Dominican radicals as veterans of an actual popular revolution for national liberation. Dominican leftists joined demonstrations against the war in Vietnam. They used ties with the Socialist Workers Party to publish a newsletter called *La Trinitaria*. Their friendships with the organizers of NACLA pushed liberal North Americans into a much more critical stance on U.S. foreign policy and helped publicize the worst of Balaguer's human rights abuses.... As a result, a full spectrum of left-wing groups, from the Young Lords to antiwar organizations, began attending anti-Balaguer rallies and signing anti-Balaguer petitions.

In a sense, this was a form of political integration and acculturation. The Dominican immigrant left mingled with the native left in the student movements and antiwar rallies of the city. Eventually, this alliance would lead to deeper ties between veterans of the Dominican left and progressive student and community politics in New York, especially in the context of the student movement at City College and other City University of New York campuses.... [D]espite the strong thirst for social justice among these revolutionaries and a theoretical sympathy with any group that opposed the U.S. government, they had little interest in the kinds of neighborhood politics practiced by black and Puerto Rican neighbors.... [T]he Dominican left saw itself as a sympathetic ally to black and Puerto Rican militants in *their* local struggles for civil rights and social power. And it accepted the support of the U.S. left in its *own* international struggle. But the young revolutionaries did not imagine any unified local struggle about schooling and other resources in the neighborhood. To radical Dominican leaders, Dominicans were exiles with a properly international vision, not an ethnic constituency with a local one.

How much this small group of activists managed to instill their nationalist political vision within the much broader community of migrants is hard to judge. Yet, despite themselves, these young activists laid the foundations for the subsequent emergence of ethnic politics in New York. The PRD began providing basic legal services to migrants and economic assistance for needy party loyalists in New York and mobilizing public opinion about the injustices against Dominican New Yorkers committed by both the United States and the Balaguer regime. In particular, PRD leaders protested antiimmigrant abuses by the INS and police, and they pointed out the abuses of Dominican police and customs officials during the annual Christmas vacations many New Yorkers took on the island. From Santo Domingo, party leader José Francisco Peña Gómez argued that the rights of migrant workers should be part of the bilateral negotiations between the United States and the Dominican Republic. PRD leaders in Santo Domingo traveled to New York and Washington and met with Democratic members of Congress about the problem of INS abuses against Dominican New Yorkers. That is, despite the argument that the colonia was a space of temporary exile, the main institution of the Dominican opposition began to advocate for the rights of Dominicans as long-term members of both U.S. and Dominican polities. Activists on the far left also eventually turned to Dominican community politics, waging the first successful campaign to put a Dominican on the community school board, working to elect a Dominican to the city council, and creating some of the first neighborhood-based assistance organizations funded by the city government.

Confronting Garment Sweatshops at Home and in New York City

CARMEN TERESA WHALEN

... From the post-World War II era to the present, the US garment industry has turned to Latinas as a source of low-wage workers in their countries of origin and as migrants to the United States. The globalization of the garment industry has meant the proliferation of export processing zones overseas and of sweatshops in US cities. Sweatshops, here and there, have become a locus of Latinas's labor in the global economy. As a result, the globalization of labor intensive industries,

Carmen Teresa Whalen, "Sweatshops Here and There: The Garment Industry, Latinas, and Labor Migrations," *International Labor and Working-Class History*, 61 (Spring 2002): pp. 45–68. Reprinted with the permission of Cambridge University Press.

like the garment industry, has fostered the labor migrations of Latinas, both within their countries and to the United States.... As the garment industry relocated to Puerto Rico, Puerto Rican women migrated and found garment industry jobs, not only in New York City, but also in urban areas in Puerto Rico and elsewhere in the States. Yet the postwar economic boom in New York gave way to the industry's continued relocation to lower-wage areas, and Puerto Rican women confronted fewer jobs and deteriorating working conditions. Dominican women then encountered this changed labor market, as they became the next group of Latinas incorporated into New York's garment industry, while also experiencing the impact of export processing in the Dominican Republic.

Immigration is often portrayed as something that happens *to* the United States and that is problematic precisely because the United States does *not* control the process. This perspective ignores the impact of US political and economic interventions in shaping economic development and in causing out-migration, as well as the continuing reliance of US economic interests on low-wage immigrant labor in the United States. The globalization of the garment industry provides an example of the economic and political connections between the United States and countries of origin that shape migrations, particularly from the region that the United States has historically defined as its backyard. In addition, the experiences of Puerto Rican and Dominican women provide an important basis for exploring how the globalization of labor-intensive industries, like the garment industry, fostered the labor migrations of women and deteriorating economic conditions in the inner cities....

★ ★ ★

... [I]n the postwar era Puerto Rico became in essence the first export processing zone. The political ties between the United States and Puerto Rico facilitated the emergence of patterns of investment and migration that would be repeated in other countries. Puerto Rico's policymakers crafted an economic development strategy based on industrialization by invitation, and the US garment industry relocated to Puerto Rico to take advantage of low wages for women, as well as tax and other incentives. Puerto Rico became the model for a particular strategy of economic development that was based on foreign investment and export oriented industrialization, and that was accompanied by massive migration....

Puerto Rico illustrates key elements of the export-processing zones that then proliferated along the U.S.-Mexico border, in the Caribbean, Central America, and Asia. Because of the political ties between Puerto Rico and the United States, Puerto Rico provided a safe and profitable investment site for US capital.... Despite political ties, federal minimum wages were not applied in Puerto Rico until the late 1970s, so that wages were significantly lower than those in the States....

Promotional efforts touted Puerto Rico's advantages, including low wages [and tax exemptions]....

The garment industry came to Puerto Rico to reap the potential profits, establishing the dynamics of an export-processing zone in its wake....

The garment industry was central to Puerto Rico's industrialization, and women's labor was central to the garment industry.... By 1963, plants established by Puerto Rico's Economic Development Administration or Fomento, employed 70,000 workers, with sixty percent of the new jobs filled by women. In 1970, apparel was the largest industrial employer and eighty-seven percent of the workers were women.... Wage differentials, tax exemptions, and profits remained central to Fomento's efforts to recruit the US apparel industry....

Puerto Rico demonstrated that economic development based on export processing and labor intensive industries failed to generate sufficient employment. New manufacturing jobs in urban areas did not replace the jobs lost in rural areas, as Puerto Rico's agriculture and home needlework industry declined.... Total employment in Puerto Rico declined during the 1950s. As a result, Puerto Rico's industrialization coincided with massive migration.

As Puerto Rico's rural economies declined, Puerto Rican women became labor migrants, going to nearby towns, as well as to urban areas in Puerto Rico and the States in search of work. Doña Genara, who was born in 1926 in a rural area recalled ... moving to the nearby town to live with her sister in the early 1950s, [which] enabled her to attend a vocational training program that taught embroidering, knitting, and sewing by machine.... Her first job was in a knitting shop, where she earned $12.80 for the week.... After two years, the shop closed. Doña Genara turned to knitting homework, working longer hours and earning less money, "Three dozen, it was thirty-six hats to earn four dollars ... I didn't have time for anything. I worked about ten or twelve hours [a day]."...

Seeing few options in Puerto Rico's rural areas and towns, other women migrated to urban areas in Puerto Rico and the States....

Both government programs and informal networks facilitated women's labor migration to the States. In their efforts to reduce Puerto Rico's population, policymakers fostered migration, providing training programs and alerting potential migrants to the availability of jobs in the States.... A sister already living in Philadelphia eased [Doña Genara's] migration in 1954.... She found work easily.... The wage differentials that lured the US garment industry to Puerto Rico also made garment work in the States appealing to migrants. "I wanted to come for a better life ...," said Doña Genara, adding, "... in Puerto Rico I earned twelve dollars a week and here I earned forty, they took out two, I kept thirty-eight."...

At the end of World War II, Puerto Rican women in New York City were entering what was still the center of the US garment industry. The war had temporarily halted the industry's relocation and had pent-up consumer demand....

As a result of their labor migrations, Puerto Rican women became concentrated in New York City's garment industry, but only within certain trades.... Successful in finding jobs, Puerto Rican women were more likely than other women in the city to be in the labor market by 1950, forty compared to thirty-five percent. The overwhelming majority of Puerto Rican women, seventy-two percent, worked as operatives....

Even with the postwar boom in the garment industry, Puerto Rican women encountered a range of working conditions in union and non-union shops. For journalist Dan Wakefield, "The seventy-two hour week, at less than a dollar an hour, ... it was not a remote fact of history but a fact of life in Spanish Harlem in 1958." [A female garment worker] earned $.35 per garment, regardless of the difficulty of the piece, and the most she had ever earned was seventy dollars in a week, a feat she accomplished by working from 7:00 a.m. to 7:00 p.m. for six days. In union shops, piece rates were set based on the difficulty of the piece, with some set at $.70 to $.90.... Wakefield considered the "farmed-out needle-work of garment shops" and "the small often fly-by-night dress shops" as "the main chance of employment within the neighborhood," and concluded that "very few girls grow up in these streets without getting a touch of it."...

The availability of garment industry jobs gave women a certain leverage in the labor market, enabling them to switch jobs for better conditions or to strug-gle to improve conditions in their shops. Doña María, who had confronted her boss about piece-work rates, ... waited until her skills on the machine were needed and then quit, creating a predicament for her boss, "I worked Monday and Tuesday and on Wednesday I didn't report to work. I went next door and I find another job, this time in bathing suits.... They paid me about seventy-five cents a garment which at that time, this was in 1956, was good money."...

... Globalization brought the U.S. garment industry to Puerto Rico. Puerto Rican women became labor migrants as they were displaced from rural econo-mies and migrated in response to the availability of garment industry jobs. Dur-ing the postwar economic boom, Puerto Rican women found jobs easily, which increased their migration and concentration in the garment industry, and gave them a certain leverage in the industry. Puerto Rican women, however, had entered and become concentrated in an industry that was on the verge of funda-mental changes. After slowing during and immediately after the Second World War, the relocation of the garment industry was about to accelerate as the indus-try continued its search for lower-wage workers. Both working conditions and Puerto Rican women's position in the industry would change as a result.

★ ★ ★

Responding to increased competition from imports, the US garment industry relied increasingly on contractors, which fostered sweatshops in US cities and facilitated the industry's relocation to lower-wage areas at greater distances.... [C]ompetition and contracting exerted downward pressure on wages in the United States, as well as overseas. They hastened the continued relocation of the industry and the low-wage incorporation of Puerto Rican women in New York....

As Puerto Ricans entered the garment industry in large numbers, wages declined. The garment industry was shifting from a higher paying to a lower paying industry, and New York City itself was changing from a high to a low wage area.... The deskilling of the industry continued. As consumer demand shifted to casual wear, the more simple, standardized garments could be pro-duced by unskilled workers. Garment production was broken down into partic-ular tasks or section work, with each worker responsible for a single task. These tasks were increasingly parceled out to contracting shops, which relied heavily on the labor of Puerto Rican and African American women. Manufacturers and jobbers were larger employers responsible for several dimensions of garment production, while contractors were smaller employers that focused on a particular task, usually sewing. Between 1953 and 1961, … [t]he proportion of dress workers in contracting shops increased from sixty-nine to seventy-nine percent. This contributed to declining wages, as workers in shops operated by manufacturers and jobbers earned 1.6 times more than their counterparts in contracting shops.…

Also, deskilling, section work, and contracting lessened the industry's dependence on New York City, with its skilled labor force.… Improvements in transportation lowered the costs of conducting business beyond the city's limits, at the same time that high rents, limited manufacturing space, and traffic congestion increased the cost of doing business in the city.

Employment in New York's apparel industry plummeted, as did the quality of the remaining jobs. Between 1947 and 1982, New York City's share of production of women and children's apparel decreased from forty-two to sixteen percent. Employment in the apparel industry decreased by 54,000 jobs between 1947 and 1958, and the next decade witnessed the loss of another 72,000 jobs.… While manufacturing jobs that were secure, unionized and paid above the minimum wage declined during the 1970s, … a "downgraded manufacturing sector" expanded, relying on sweatshops and homework. Small garment shops provided flexibility and absorbed the risks and instability of the market. Wages in the apparel industry continued to decline relative to other manufacturing wages.…

The continued globalization of the garment industry meant that Puerto Rican women in New York City confronted fewer jobs, economic displacement, and deteriorating working conditions.…

As the garment industry continued its search for cheap labor via sweatshops in the States and continued relocation, Puerto Rican women became displaced labor migrants. Puerto Rican women's labor force participation decreased as the garment industry declined, [and] poverty among Puerto Ricans in the inner city increased.… In Philadelphia Doña Genara described the change, "All those lots that are vacant over there, those were factories." … Hence, the garment industry shaped not only Puerto Rican women's labor migration patterns, but also their economic wellbeing and that of their households and communities.… This was the labor market that Dominican women then confronted.

★ ★ ★

Like Puerto Rican women, Dominican women were affected by export processing in their home country, as well as by the continuing decline of New York's garment industry. The growth of export processing zones in the Dominican Republic echoed Puerto Rico's economic development. Policymakers in the Dominican Republic lured foreign investment through incentives that resembled those in Puerto Rico, while US policymakers instituted trade policies to promote the assembly of manufactured goods abroad. US investment and the garment industry dominated export-oriented manufacturing. Wage differentials and women's labor remained key ingredients in the economic development strategy and in the industry's relocation. Here too, economic development based on foreign investment and export processing failed to generate sufficient employment, and was accompanied by internal and international migration. Women figured prominently in both migration streams, finding garment work in export processing zones and in New York City. Although not a colony of the United States, export processing zones in the Dominican Republic highlight the impact of US political and economic interventions in shaping economic development and migration.

US policymakers facilitated overseas investment in ways that made the Dominican Republic and other Caribbean nations more like Puerto Rico. Trade policies reduced tariffs and hence the costs for US firms doing business beyond the boundaries of the United States.... In addition to favorable trade policies, the US government has provided financial assistance to firms that invest overseas, as well as to the governments of host countries that welcome them....

As in Puerto Rico, policymakers in the Dominican Republic shifted from import substitution to export-oriented industrialization with foreign investment. Establishing free trade zones in ... 1968, policymakers exempted industries from local taxes, from customs duties on imported capital and semi-finished goods, and from export duties on finished or semi-finished goods. Employment in manufacturing increased from 20,000 to 47,562 between 1968 and 1977.... The number of free trade zones, foreign investment, and imports to the United States all increased dramatically between the mid-1980s and the early 1990s. By 1988, garments accounted for seventy-eight percent of manufacturing exports. In that same year, sixty-three percent of export-processing firms were US owned, while only ten percent were Dominican owned....

The US garment industry relied on the low-wage labor of Dominican women in the export processing zones.... Wages in the Dominican Republic were significantly lower than in the United States, and they were declining. In 1984, US apparel workers earned an average of $7.00 an hour. Between 1984 and 1990, wages in the Dominican Republic plummeted from $1.33 to $.56 an hour.... By 1991, women held three-fourths of the 135,000 jobs in the free trade zones....

Economic development via export-oriented industrialization fostered internal and international migration, and the rural population decreased from sixty-five to forty-five percent between 1965 and 1984. The assassination of Trujillo in 1961 and changes in US immigration policies in 1965 increased Dominican immigration to the United States....

Dominican women became labor migrants.... Many headed to the export processing zone in Santiago, which employed 6,275 workers in 1980, almost all of whom were women. With the availability of jobs in New York City's secondary labor market a key reason for their migration, women were fifty-two percent of international migrants, as well.

Dominican women found garment industry jobs readily available in New York City....

As Dominican women continued to migrate to New York City, they became concentrated in the now downgraded garment industry....

... In search of work at the age of fifteen, Nerida left a rural area in the Dominican Republic and came to New York in 1993.... Nerida had left her child in the care of family and joined her parents in the city. After working in a couple of stores, she found work in the garment industry. Nerida was not alone. Women accounted for fifty-nine percent of all Dominican immigrants in the United States in 1996, and most immigrants were young, sixteen percent were between sixteen and twenty-four years of age, and forty-nine percent were between twenty-five and forty-four. Like Puerto Rican women, Dominican women who migrated in search of work, found themselves concentrated in low-wage jobs and then displaced.

★ ★ ★

Confronting the two-tiered garment industry, Nerida's work experiences in New York City suggest the conditions Dominicans confronted and the effects on their households and community.... [M]ost Dominican women, like Nerida, found low-paid, dead-end jobs, less demand for labor, and deteriorating working conditions. Their options and leverage in the garment industry were much more circumscribed than those initially encountered by Puerto Rican women in the post-war era.

In 1998, Nerida was working in New York's garment district in a nonunion packing shop that handled women's sportswear for several brand-name labels....

In describing their shop, workers emphasized the long hours, strict supervision, the tiring pace of the work, and the low wages. One worker summarized the conditions as, "a lot of work and a little money." Their regular work week was Monday through Fridays ... and Saturdays ... [for] a total of fifty-three and-a-half hours. During busy times, they were expected to work late and occasionally on Sundays and holidays.... While stating that overtime was optional, workers suggested that there were repercussions for those unwilling to work overtime and added that they needed the money.

The work pace is intense, Nerida explained.... The faster pace also increased the potential for injuries:

> The machine that is used for packing, if you put your hand in, it can cut it. If it doesn't completely catch your hand, it will burn it.... I have burned myself many times, many times.... Almost always it happens when you are more pressured because there is a lot of work....

Having worked in two other garment shops, Nerida considered this shop neither the best nor the worst. Her first garment industry job was in a union shop that sewed collars on t-shirts, paid above the minimum wage, and provided benefits.... Hers was the night shift, however, and because she had a child to care for, Nerida kept this job for just two to three weeks. When she was laid off from her current shop for three months, she went to work in a large shop in Brooklyn that occupied two floors and made sweaters. While most of the work was sewing, a small packing section employed about six workers, including Nerida. She traveled two hours to work and discovered that this shop paid the minimum wage but not overtime....

For Nerida, ... [h]ousehold finances were tight, "If the work is good, I work the whole week, ... I can pay my bills.... If this week I don't work much, I pay the babysitter, I can't pay any bills."...

... Long hours, low wages, and layoffs strained her household economy and her aspirations....

... Dominican women's concentration in the garment industry had consequences for their households and for the Dominican community. As manufacturing employment declined by almost 90,000 between 1989 and 1995, so did Dominican women's labor force participation. By 1997, forty-two percent of Dominican women were in the labor force compared to fifty-one percent of all women citywide. Like Puerto Rican women, Dominican women had gone from higher than average to lower than average labor-force participation. And Dominicans were still overrepresented as operators, laborers, and fabricators: thirty-six percent of all Dominicans in contrast to twelve percent of workers citywide.... As New York began to witness a growing disparity in incomes during the 1990s, Dominicans' earnings decreased.... While their low-wage labor may have kept some garment industry jobs in New York City, for Dominican women, working in the garment industry has increasingly meant a life of working poverty for individuals, as well as households and communities confronting poverty.

★ ★ ★

Parallels in the experiences of Puerto Rican and Dominican women suggest that the globalization of the garment industry is resulting in repeating patterns of economic displacement, labor migration, and sweatshop jobs in US cities. The garment industry continues to be marked by relocation and by the persistence of sweatshops.... The garment industry figures prominently in a particular model of economic development based on export-oriented industrialization and foreign, often US, investment. In both Puerto Rico and the Dominican Republic this model was accompanied by internal and international migration as insufficient employment and wages too low to sustain households sent people in search of work; Latinas became labor migrants. These economies remain dependent and mired in low-wage assembly jobs that are always poised to relocate to even lower-wage areas.... Indeed, ... export-processing zones and the garment industry have spread to Central American countries and elsewhere, bringing the same model of economic development to different countries at different times. Displaced, Latinas will likely continue their search for paid employment that will sustain their households.

Meanwhile, Latinas working in New York City's garment industry have become more diverse, with many coming from countries where the US garment industry and export processing zones have taken hold. Here too, competition and contracting exert a relentless downward pressure on wages, creating jobs that are notable for their low wages, long hours, pressured pace, [harsh] supervision, poor working conditions, and instability, as the possibility of shop relocation to lower-wage areas remains a constant and very real threat. For Puerto Rican and Dominican women, as well as for newcomer Latinas, the garment industry has been one of few avenues for employment. Yet garment industry jobs have translated into working poverty, offering few opportunities for improvements. For Puerto Rican and Dominican women, concentration in the garment industry was followed by economic displacement as employment continued to decline, at the same time that employers' search for the lowest-wage labor appears unrelenting.

Dominicans Reshape Formerly Puerto Rican Waterbury, Connecticut

RUTH GLASSER

Connecticut is experiencing a cultural reconfiguration, and Waterbury is literally and figuratively in its middle. The state with the highest proportion of Puerto Ricans among its Latinos, the highest per capita Puerto Rican city in the United States (Hartford), the first capital city with a Puerto Rican mayor (also Hartford) is becoming more nuanced, as newcomers from a variety of Spanish-speaking countries arrive daily to make their homes here.

Dominicans are the most prominent group of newcomers reshaping Waterbury's social, cultural, and economic landscape: Dominican-owned grocery stores abound. Dominican children form the core of a group dancing Colombian *cumbia* in Waterbury's schools. Local funeral homes now advertise that they can send bodies to Santo Domingo as well as San Juan.

Unlike most northeastern states, Connecticut's urban life takes place in small cities—its largest, Bridgeport, has only 139,529 people. These are cities with heavily industrial economies in steady decline since World War II, when their factories began to shut down. Waterbury was in the most industrialized corridor of the state, the center of the brass industry and related manufacturing, and was among the hardest hit.

This study is a preliminary investigation of two questions: (1) how has the arrival of a new group of Latino immigrants affected the nature of Latino Waterbury and Waterbury as a whole, and (2) what does the addition of new Latino groups have to tell us about interethnic interaction in general and the reshaping of U.S. Latino identities in particular? Since World War II, Puerto Ricans have been the dominant Latino group in Connecticut. However, in the last twenty years, Connecticut's Latino communities have become more multiethnic, as illustrated in the story of Waterbury. Waterbury is also emblematic of the kind of small city to which Puerto Ricans, Dominicans, and other Latino groups have increasingly migrated during the last several decades. This trend is a departure from the traditional pattern of migration to New York City, still the main focus of studies about Puerto Rican migrants and Dominican immigrants.

This chapter intends to bring such smaller but increasingly popular destinations into the historical literature on Latinos in the United States....

★ ★ ★

Ruth Glasser, "Mofongo Meets Mangú: Dominicans Reconfigure Latino Waterbury," in Andrés Torres, ed., *Latinos in New England* (Philadelphia, PA: Temple University Press, 2006), pp. 103–124.

In small cities, even a few hundred or thousand migrants or immigrants from one country have a significant impact. Waterbury's population has long hovered between 100,000 and 110,000.

Waterbury's Dominican arrivals came to a multiethnic city colonized over time by thousands from Europe, Lebanon, Cape Verde, and French Canada and by African American migrants from the U.S. South. The city was already "Latinized" by Puerto Ricans. From the 1940s onward Puerto Ricans arrived in significant numbers to work in area factories. Most came from small towns in the south-central mountains and southern coast of the island. Boricuas usually spent only a brief period in New York City—sometimes only long enough to board the railroad to Waterbury. Others came directly, through agricultural contracts arranged by the Puerto Rican Department of Labor. After working on vegetable farms, in orchards, and nurseries in nearby towns, they arrived in Waterbury, where factories offered better pay and more independent lifestyles.

... The community grew through chain migration, secondary migration from New York, and through generations born here.

With relatively well-paying factory jobs, many Puerto Rican *pioneros* were able to buy homes and educate their children. Scores of these children became professionals, many social service workers and teachers who ministered to the newer Puerto Rican migrants and the growing population of Spanish-speaking immigrants....

Like previous immigrant groups, Puerto Rican pioneros and their children achieved upward mobility with a base of good factory jobs and created small businesses, churches, and clubs. Such achievements were short-lived, for the physical havoc of highway building and urban renewal starting in the 1960s, along with the closing of the "Big Three" brass mills and other factories not only destroyed many of these institutions but also made it difficult for ensuing migrants to scale similar social and economic ladders.

... Both sending country conditions and those of New York City made smaller cities like Waterbury still an attractive choice for Latin American immigrants....

Dominican immigration differed from Puerto Rican migration in ways that fed into the economy. The industrial jobs that remained in Waterbury were mostly in smaller factories that paid relatively low wages and mostly employed women. And it was women who were coming in significant numbers from the Dominican Republic....

... Whereas many of the earlier Puerto Rican migrants had come from smaller towns, Dominicans came from larger cities such as Santo Domingo and Santiago. Many had been born and raised in smaller settlements but had migrated to ever-larger, urbanized areas in search of education and jobs. Moreover, many Dominican immigrants spent several years in New York City before coming to Waterbury.

Perhaps because immigration from the Dominican Republic was more difficult and expensive than migrating from Puerto Rico, many Quisqueyans came from higher economic positions than most Boricua migrants. Whereas the latter were often struggling small farmers, farm laborers, or fishermen, Dominican immigrants interviewed were more typically children of small business proprietors or farmers or ranchers with sizable landholdings or themselves had operated businesses thwarted by a teetering economy. Francisco Hernández, for example, was born in the town of Guaranico, where his family had a farm. He later moved to the capital to pursue his education. Hernández had trouble finding work in Santo Domingo, so he moved to Bonao, where he worked in a bank and then started a restaurant. Finally, economic difficulties forced him to close up shop and migrate to the United States.

According to interviewees, the first Dominicans came to Waterbury in the late 1960s. They had started off in New York City with no plans to move anywhere else. Apparently, close ties between New York City and Waterbury area manufacturers made the smaller city part of immigrants' mental geography. Gladys Maldonado explained:

> I came [to New York] in 1966. First my brother-in-law came looking
> to improve his life as a barber. A friend who had a barbershop helped
> him to come legally. Then after some time passed, he put in a request for
> my mother. My mother was a seamstress and seamstresses had a lot of
> work in New York in the 1960s.

Maldonado's cousin's tailor husband moved with his company from New York to Waterbury. Maldonado joined her relatives there after seven years in New York. Similarly, Judith Mariñez recounted how she, a talented designer working in a garment factory in New York, was asked by a Waterbury area couple to work in their factory.

Those immigrants established a beachhead in Waterbury and now "sold" it as a place with a better *ambiente* for the children. Maldonado recalled:

> In the year '73 my nieces and nephews were in the elementary
> grades. We were worried because [they] were very shy, and the public
> school in New York, well, it was a bit of a problem. So my cousin
> Carmen said, "Why don't you move to Waterbury?" Carmen told us
> it was a very peaceful city.

Others found the city through community connections. Adelaida Garcia, who had lived in Puerto Rico and then New York, discovered Waterbury through a friend in her Pentecostal church. She left her troubled marriage behind and came north with several children:

> I lived in the Bronx, a dangerous place where if a woman went out
> alone at such and such an hour something could happen to her. The
> "sisters" in New York visited the "sisters" in Waterbury. I began to
> explore the place, and then I decided to take the step to come and live
> here. There were about five Christian families who helped me to move.

Once single mothers such as Garcia had come to Waterbury, they urged others to migrate. Looking back, they believed that they had had a historical role in creating a community made up of their families and friends...

Within such a small city that they had helped shape, Dominican pioneras felt effective as recruiters and ultimately, as we shall see, as community leaders....

★ ★ ★

Perhaps because of the long, arduous process of acquiring visas, it has taken many years for this Dominican chain migration to yield a sizable community. Only in the 1980s and the 1990s has Dominican Waterbury become visible to outsiders....

While the large brass factories were declining into nonexistence, a cluster of small garment and metal-parts factories in Waterbury's North End provided jobs for Dominican newcomers. Leather jackets, pocketbooks, gloves, and cosmetics cases were manufactured in small workshops.... Immigrants particularly recall cutting, stitching, and packing for "La Correa" and "La Chalina," local belt and tie manufacturers. As more immigrants arrived and factories shut down, Dominicans could be found on construction sites, as certified nurses' aides, and in restaurants. In most cases, they worked alongside Puerto Ricans as well as members of other immigrant groups with a growing presence in Waterbury.

Puerto Ricans who came to Waterbury after World War II talk about a city without stores to service their needs. The closest they could come to their products was at Italian grocery stores, where they could get espresso coffee and short grain rice. Otherwise, Boricuas had to make special trips to New York. From the mid-1950s, however, a vibrant Puerto Rican business community began to form in Waterbury's South End neighborhood. People who worked in factories got loans from relatives and friends to start furniture stores, record and jewelry stores, and groceries with Caribbean products.

When Dominicans first arrived in Waterbury some ten or fifteen years later, they found a few bodegas run by Puerto Rican pioneros where they could get most of what they needed. However, they still longed for specific products from home, as Felicia Díaz recalled: "Upon arriving here one found nothing from Santo Domingo. All the seasonings from Santo Domingo people brought from over there, the mints, the candies, until a short time ago. It was difficult because [those things are] part of one's culture."

Dominicans were eventually served by compatriots looking for alternative livelihoods to the increasingly insecure factory jobs. As in New York, one of the most popular niches was the bodega. Juan Laras felt that the time was right to start his own business as the job market in the Waterbury area declined: "I lasted for eight or nine years working in several factories because before it was easy, people would move from one place to another for a dollar. Now the level of unemployment in Connecticut is too high."

Interviewees have described an explosion of Dominican-owned bodegas in Waterbury and throughout Connecticut during the last five to ten years. Some saw it as natural ethnic succession. Just as Puerto Ricans had previously taken over stores from Italian and Jewish merchants, now Dominicans were replacing Puerto Ricans. These Boricuas were aging. Their children had climbed the occupational ladder and had livelihoods that did not include grueling shop-keepers' hours. As Juan Laras put it:

> I have to be in here for fourteen hours, seven days a week. It looks easy. That man is a bodeguero and in five years he has X amount of money, yes, but in those five years he's there 150 hours a week, 362 days a year. On New Year's, when you're in your house unwrapping your gifts, I have to open up the bodega.
>
> The Puerto Ricans were the ones who began the bodega business. It's not easy. Probably that's why those who made their money got tired and they retired to enjoy what they earned. So they've passed the baton to the Dominicans. That's the future here.

As with the factories, New York City connections played a role in the development of Waterbury bodegas. Dominicans who had started in New York began to expand into Connecticut in order to find new markets and investment opportunities—bolstered by credit from New York bodegueros....

As in New York, a small percentage of Dominicans in Waterbury become bodegueros. But their number is belied by the visual strength of their presence—all over Waterbury are groceries that have been opened or bought out by Dominicans. Support by co-ethnics has helped. Juan Lara, for example, is buying his bodega gradually from his brother-in-law. Family support is often compounded by economic and social capital. Libio Rosado's mother owned a bodega in Santiago where he worked from a young age. Amado Vargas describes one family of bodegueros, close friends from his hometown of La Boca:

> They were like my family, well-known cattle people, upper middle class. When they came here, the first thing they did was open up a business.... [The] first little bodega was on Bank Street....

Even with little or no English, [they] had the material resources and the savvy to deal with the city bureaucracy. As Vargas observed: "It takes someone with skills to come here and open up a business.

★ ★ ★

After many years spent working in clothing and metal parts factories, Sonia Rosario decided she wanted her own business. Long-standing, close ties with Puerto Ricans enabled her to do so. She had met Joaquín and Hilda Batista in local factories. The couple had a daughter who owned a party shop, which Sonia admired:

> I decided it was nice work, entertaining, not too hard. We were all good friends and finally she said to me, "You've always wanted to work here. I'll sell it to you!"

Sonia wanted to give the shop a Dominican feel and so she renamed it Merengue Party Shop: "I was looking for a name that was more Dominican. Sonia, there are twenty thousand Sonias. So I said to myself, everyone knows 'merengue.' Now as I walk around that's how everyone knows me. 'Look, there's Sonia Merengue!'"

Through the accretion of such small actions, Dominican women have helped to alter Waterbury's Latino landscape, as they become bodegueras, clothing shop owners, and beauty salon operators. Some make "Dominican cakes," prepare and sell food from their homes, or clean houses. Single mothers like Felicia Díaz [See Document 7] have always cultivated more than one income stream, looking for jobs that allowed them the flexibility to be with their children:

> I always had a full-time and a part-time job. I did jobs at home, like
> those where you pack things and send them back by mail, manicures
> and pedicures on the weekends. People said, "I'm cleaning houses" and
> I said, "Do you need a helper?" There were days when [my children]
> went with me to work.

But the most unusual niche among Dominican women in Waterbury is the child care business, becoming as ubiquitous and organized as any bodegueros' association. As with bodegas, opportunity and changing economic circumstances combined to create this niche....

Adelaida Garcia, for example, had brought clothes and knickknacks up from New York City and sold them from her home, where she also worked as a beautician. But then came welfare reform: "The majority of my customers were people who lived on welfare. When they began to take away welfare, I began to prepare myself, because my customers were going! So I began to take day care classes."

It was that very welfare-to-work transition that inspired the formation of the Waterbury Hispanic Professionals Day Care Association, in which Adelaida Garcia, Felicia Díaz, and dozens of other Waterbury Dominicanas are active members. In 1996, Luz Lebrón, a Puerto Rican single mother, formed a group of women transitioning off welfare. They brainstormed about their skills and how they could deploy them to earn a living. The most important skill that emerged was child rearing. It seemed the perfect solution—form a group of women who could provide affordable, culturally appropriate day care in a city with few Spanish-speaking providers. Women with limited English and relatively low levels of formal education would train to have their own businesses, providing needed services to other mothers returning to the workforce.

The first ten women began classes to get their state-approved day care certifications. Felicia Díaz was one of them....

Although the association is multicultural, Dominicans such as Díaz and Garcia have been instrumental in making licensed, home-based day cares an attractive economic niche for their female compatriots. Felicia Díaz assiduously works her ethnic networks, making day care a counterpart to the chain-like opening of bodegas among men:

> I go to see my Dominican *compañeras* and I say to them, "Look, things
> are going well for me, why don't you come with me?" So I get them
> into the association. In fact today a Dominican called and asked me

about it. I told her, "This is a great business, what area do you live in? There? Magnificent, we don't have providers in that area." It's a way for them to be able to work while staying in their homes. The majority of Dominican women love children.

Membership in the association provides educational opportunities, licensing in different areas, leadership positions. Members believe they provide educational and cultural services to their young charges and beyond....

The variety of local Dominican business enterprises, be they bodegas or day care centers, become jumping-off points for larger activities along the continuum between community work and politics....

Increased organization and visibility among local Dominicans have drawn them into leadership roles, some of which reflect immigrants' homeland experiences....

Dominicans who have attained their citizenship and are deeply concerned about local affairs also work to make sure that people who represent community interests are elected....

Bodegas are important sites for political discussion. By the very nature of what they do, bodegueros, like the day care providers, must be intensely aware of politics as it plays out around them....

★ ★ ★

Dominicans are an increasingly integral part of Waterbury, and their presence is subtly altering the city's Latino community. As the children and grandchildren of Puerto Rican pioneros forsake shopkeeping careers and inner-city neighborhoods, Dominicans have filled the gaps. Their presence as the second major Spanish-speaking group has influenced their settlement strategies. Dominicans have integrated already-formed institutions, such as St. Cecilia's Church, injecting bits of their own culture through special celebrations such as the Fiesta de la Virgen de la Altagracia. When Dominicans found their own stores and social clubs, they are careful to balance Dominicanidad with a broader pan-Latino perspective, offering everything from grocery products to social activities to an increasingly multicultural Hispanic community. Thus, their presence enriches the Spanish-speaking community overall.

Dominicans have come to Waterbury during an era of shrinking economic opportunities, but the strength of the dollar in their homeland, their social capital, and their somewhat elevated class position have allowed many to make a better place for themselves....

Connections between New York City and Connecticut churches, bodegas, and factories have been an important catalyst for the growth of Waterbury's Dominican community. Waterbury is relatively far from New York and extremely different. However, Waterbury may be more typical of the small, deindustrialized cities of the Northeast where Dominicans and other Latino immigrants are settling in growing numbers. The physical configurations of such cities are more elusive than New York's, consisting of scattered pockets rather than dense districts.

Dominicans in Waterbury have established institutions such as the Dominican Club that allow them to provide social and political activities for members and link up with similar institutions in other cities. Thus, local Dominicans and those in Danbury, Hartford, Bridgeport, and other cities used preexisting connections to organize voters for the 2004 election. While Dominicans in Connecticut cities could not muster the political clout to obtain a local polling place, their growing level of political organization presages a future in which Dominican communities such as Waterbury's will be increasingly visible to politicos from home as well as to non-Latino locals accustomed to thinking of all Spanish-speakers as Puerto Ricans.

 # FURTHER READING

Ginetta E. B. Candelario, *Black behind the Ears: Dominican Racial Identity from Museums to Beauty Shops* (2007).

Junot Díaz, *The Brief and Wondrous Life of Oscar Wao* (2007).

Junot Díaz, *Drown* (1996).

Jorge Duany, *Blurred Borders: Transnational Migration between the Hispanic Caribbean and the United States* (2011).

Eugenia Georges, *The Making of a Transnational Community: Migration, Development, and Cultural Change in the Dominican Republic* (1990).

Vivian Garrison and Carol I. Weiss, "Dominican Family Networks and United States Immigration Policy," in Constance Sutton and Elsa Chaney, eds., *Caribbean Life in New York City: Sociocultural Dimensions* (1987).

Sherri Grasmuck and Patricia R. Pessar, *Between Two Islands: Dominican International Migration* (1991).

Luis E. Guarnizo, "Los Dominicanyorks: The Making of a Binational Society," in Mary Romero, Pierrette Hondagneu-Sotelo, and Vilma Ortiz, eds., *Challenging Fronteras: Structuring Latina and Latino Lives in the U.S.* (1997).

Jesse Hoffnung-Garskof, *A Tale of Two Cities: Santo Domingo and New York after 1950* (2008).

Jesse Hoffnung-Garskof, "'Yankee Go Home … and Take Me with You': Imperialism and Migration in the Dominican Republic, 1961–1966," *Canadian Journal of Latin American and Caribbean Studies* 28, nos. 57/58 (2004).

José Itzigsohn, "Immigrant Incorporation among Dominicans in Providence, Rhode Island: An Intergenerational Perspective," in Andrés Torres, ed., *Latinos in New England* (2006).

Peggy Levitt, "Transnational Ties and Incorporation: The Case of Dominicans in the United States," in David G. Gutiérrez, ed., *Columbia History of Latinos in the United States since 1960* (2004).

Peggy Levitt, *The Transnational Villagers* (2001).

Patricia R. Pessar, *A Visa for a Dream: Dominicans in the United States* (1995).

David Reimers, *Still the Golden Door: The Third World Comes to America* (1992).

Ernesto Sagás and Sintia E. Molina, eds., *Dominican Migration: Transnational Perspectives* (2004).

CHAPTER 13

The 1980s: U.S. Intervention and Central American Immigration

The 1980s witnessed a dramatic increase in immigration from El Salvador and Guatemala, as well as from other Central American countries. In the context of the Cold War, U.S. anti-communist perspectives and policies shaped the increased migration and the reception of those who came to the United States. While the wars began as struggles against extreme disparities in wealth and the repressive states that maintained them, U.S. intervention intensified the wars and the resultant refugee crisis. The U.S. government supported right-wing governments in El Salvador and Guatemala, despite widespread human rights abuses and the resultant international and domestic criticism of its policies. In Guatemala, the government attacked the Maya majority. Guatemalans were killed and "disappeared," and whole villages were decimated by the Guatemalan military's "scorched earth" policies. In Nicaragua, the U.S. government worked to topple the Sandinista government, which had overthrown a long-term, repressive dictatorship that the United States had supported. As the wars raged, people sought refuge in neighboring countries, and in the United States and Canada. By the mid-1980s, an estimated quarter million Guatemalans and more than 1 million Salvadorans had fled to other countries. Despite atrocities in their home countries, the U.S. government labeled Salvadorans and Guatemalans as economic immigrants and hence "illegal aliens," as they arrived without refugee status or proper authorization. Many argued, however, that they were "refugees," fleeing persecution.

During the 1960s and 1970s, smaller numbers of Central Americans came to the United States. Returning from Central America to Washington, D.C., U.S. government and international agencies' employees brought their domestic workers with them. This labor recruitment of women sparked social networks, as tens of thousands of immigrants then made their way to the city. Yet most who arrived during the 1980s did so without the benefit of earlier networks or communities. Instead, they turned to each other and to activism to meet their immediate needs, to challenge U.S. policies in their home countries and the U.S. denial of refugee status, and to improve conditions in their new communities. In Los Angeles, they formed community-based organizations, joined unionization and other workplace struggles, and engaged in a wide variety of political activities.

By the late 1980s, multinational efforts sought to restore peace in Central America. During the 1990s, peace accords were negotiated in El Salvador and Guatemala. Still violence continued. The countries' economies remained in shambles following more than a decade of wars, which had not fully resolved the underlying causes of those wars. While some refugees returned home, migration continued. By the 2000 census, more than 655,000 Salvadorans, 372,000 Guatemalans, and 177,000 Nicaraguans had made the United States their home. This chapter explores U.S. policies in Central America, the debate over Central Americans' status in the United States, and the struggles of Central Americans to gain recognition and rights.

DOCUMENTS

As Salvadorans and Guatemalans arrived in the United States, U.S. policy defined them as "illegal aliens," while others defined them as "refugees." Document 1, a 1981 *Hartford Courant* newspaper article, illustrates the debate over the U.S. policy of deporting Salvadorans. Those who defined Salvadorans and Guatemalans as refugees included several U.S. religious denominations, and churches initiated a sanctuary movement to protect them from deportation, as Document 2 reveals. In Document 3, a nursing student describes the conditions in El Salvador that made her the target of government repression and that fostered both her migration and her self-definition as a "refugee." While the U.S. government continued to deport Salvadorans, Document 4, a letter from the U.S. Government Accounting Office to U.S. Representative Hamilton Fish, Jr., suggests tensions over how to classify and interpret the risks to Salvadoran returnees. Document 5 is an excerpt of a woman's journey from Nicaragua to Los Angeles, revealing both the risks of the journey and erroneous expectations about life in the United States. Salvadoran activists and the sanctuary movement sought to redefine Salvadorans and Guatemalans as refugees, to halt deportations, and to stop U.S. funding of the governments of El Salvador and Guatemala. In 1991, a U.S. district court's ruling in *American Baptist Churches v. Thornburgh* was a victory for activists, calling for asylum to be based on individual fears of persecution, not U.S. foreign policy considerations, as Document 6 reveals. In Document 7, Victor Montejo describes growing up as a Maya in Guatemala, the impact of the violence of the 1980s, and his experiences as a refugee in camps and in coming to the United States. Having become an anthropologist, he addresses the dynamics between scholars and the study of indigenous peoples.

1. Associated Press Reveals Debate over Salvadorans' Status, 1981

U.S. immigration officials are still sending hundreds of Salvadoran refugees back to their war-torn country despite possible dangers that await them there and a freeze on pending asylum requests.

Critics of U.S. immigration policy claim many refugees are pressured into signing statements in which they waive their right to seek political asylum and agree to return voluntarily to El Salvador.

"If not certain death, they face persecution of one form or another" upon their return, said Polly Pittman of the Council on Hemispheric Relations.

However, immigration officials deny that pressure is applied, saying Salvadorans caught entering the United States illegally are advised of their right to request asylum if they feel they would be endangered by returning.

Administration officials also contend that many of the Salvadoran immigrants are entering the United States for economic, not political reasons.

Verne Jervis, spokesman for the Justice Department's Immigration and Naturalization Service, said about 1,000 Salvadorans are being allowed to remain in the United States while their asylum requests are pending.

In the final days of the Carter administration, the State Department imposed a 90-day freeze on processing Salvadoran asylum requests. That move allowed Salvadorans seeking asylum to remain in the United States for at least that period.

The freeze is scheduled to expire in mid-April and Reagan administration officials say no decision has been made on whether to begin granting asylum to Salvadorans fleeing their country's bloody civil war.

Officials say the administration fears that by granting asylum, the United States could undercut the U.S.-backed Salvadoran government by implying that it cannot protect its own people or that its security forces might actually be carrying out the political repression.

About 9,000 Salvadorans were expelled from the United States last year, Jervis said. And despite the freeze, nearly 100 a week are currently being deported from the Los Angeles area alone, the California immigration office said.

A State Department official, who requested anonymity, said the United States was investigating the fate of Salvadorans who had been shipped back and had thus far found no evidence that those returned were persecuted.

But refugees and their U.S. supporters contend that Salvadorans who are sent back face real danger.

2. Churches Launch Sanctuary Movement for Central American Refugees, 1982

Identifying immigration as the "civil rights issue of the 1980s," representatives of the nation's major churches announced in Hollywood Monday that they are escalating their support of Central American refugees to new levels of organized political activism.

The church leaders said they will offer their churches as sanctuaries to illegal immigrants, stage protests at stockholders meetings, set up a national bail-bond

"Laurie Becklund, "Church Leaders Pledge Crusade for Refugees," *Los Angeles Times,* February 16, 1982, p. OC-A1. Copyright © 1982. Los Angeles Times. Reprinted with Permission.

fund to free refugees from detention, and step up lobbying efforts in Washington, D.C., to try to halt the deportation of Salvadoran immigrants.

The religious leaders, representing about 100 million church members including Catholics, Lutherans, Baptists, Episcopalians and others, announced their plans at a press conference at St. Thomas Episcopal Church after their first national conference this weekend of the "Central American Refugee Defense Network."

"I think you will begin seeing heavier pressure on government because there is now really a national consensus of church bodies to try to stop the deportation of Salvadoran refugees," said Bishop Anthony J. Bevilacqua of Brooklyn, N.Y., head of migration of the U.S. Catholic Conference of Bishops.

"We represent about half the U.S. population," he said. "I know not all that population agrees with our position on undocumented aliens because this is a period of antagonism to outsiders. But we are taking a leadership position on this issue. It will become an integral part of churches, of their budgets, of their commitments,"

Mary Solberg, of the New York-based Lutheran Immigration and Refugee Service, said she considered the conference a critical transition for church groups with mainstream congregations.

"The voluntary (church-affiliated) agencies are involved in a key issue," she said. "We have always been helping bonafide, approved refugees. Now we are moving into helping those refugees who have not been approved—the Guatemalans, the Salvadorans. Our hearts breaks for Poland. But it makes no sense to recognize Poles as refugees and not Salvadorans."

The fact that churches oppose U.S. policy in some foreign nations, for example, El Salvador, is not new. Many church organizations have come out against U.S. military aid to El Salvador and have lobbied for the granting of temporary asylum to Salvadoran refugees while their country is at war.

Both the Reagan and Carter administrations have refused to grant temporary asylum to Salvadorans that the United States has granted in the past to Nicaraguans, Cambodians and other immigrants whose countries are at war.

What is new, the church officials said Monday, is a coordinated program nationwide that will have a political edge that many American churchgoers are unaccustomed to.

Although not every church group will participate in every activity, the conference endorsed the following measures:

—The naming of individual churches as sanctuaries that will welcome undocumented aliens who come to their doors and assist them in avoiding deportation.

—The establishment of a nationwide bail bond fund in which congregations will put up their own church properties as collateral to help free Salvadorans from detention as they seek political asylum here.

—The funding of a new council made up of church leaders and Salvadoran refugees that will operate a toll-free telephone number to help illegal immigrants.

—The purchase of Western Airlines stock by church leaders who plan to challenge the airline's contract with the U.S. Immigration and Naturalization Service to fly Salvadorans back toward their embattled homelands.

—The sponsoring of a nationwide speaking tour in which Salvadoran refugees will address congregation members in an informal setting and introduce them to Salvadoran cooking.

3. Nursing Student Describes Persecution in El Salvador, 1985

My name is Adriana Rodriguez. I am twenty-seven years old. I was a nursing student, but could not finish my training because of the problems in my country, El Salvador. I was forced to leave the country in 1982.

In 1981 I was studying to be a nurse in San Salvador, and had the opportunity to help people who had fled from the war zones in the countryside. They were refugees inside El Salvador. These refugees were mainly elderly people, women and children who had left their homes in the countryside and towns around the capital, San Salvador. They were forced to come to the city for refuge because their home towns had been destroyed by army bombings.

I started working with three other nursing students at the San José de la Montaña Refuge. It was the refugee camp that Monsignor Oscar Romero had been planning to open, before his murder in 1980. The refugee camp was in a seminary, twenty minutes south of the capital. We used to take medicine from the hospital and our school to the camp. It offered food, clothing and moral support to the refugees because the government was refusing to provide any aid. They were happy to see us because it meant that someone cared about them....

Each person there had lived a tragedy. They had all gone through traumatic experiences, such as the murder of a husband, child or parent. They had seen their relatives die after being tortured and burned. Some were the only survivors in their families. They suffered psychologically as well as physically. Seeing this suffering made the four of us realize that it was our duty as human beings, as Christians and as nurses, to help the refugees as much as we could, even though we were only students.

The director of our school, a conservative, bitter woman, called us into her office. She said that the work we were doing was subversive. She threatened to suspend us if we did not stop working at the camp. I answered, "In school we are told that it is a nurse's duty to tend to those who need help. I feel that to be a dedicated nurse I must use what I am learning to help those whose rights have been taken away."

We continued our work at the refugee camp, thinking that she wouldn't carry out her threat. But she did. She expelled us when we had only one year left of nursing school. Since I had learned the basics during the first two years of school, and my friends and I had plenty of practical experience from our work with the refugees, we went on working at the refugee camp.

Adriana Rodriguez, "'I Had Never Thought of Leaving My Country,'" in *A Dream Compels Us: Voices of Salvadoran Women* (Cambridge, MA: South End Press, 1989), pp. 211–215.

It was at this time that one of three other students I worked with was captured. She was carried off in a truck by heavily armed men. We never heard from her again. Her mother went crazy looking for her, hoping at least to find her remains. The rest of us were frightened. We realized that the army wasn't kidding, and that our fate could be the same.

... I continued to work with the nuns and other religious people who ran the small clinic at the camp. We had medicine, first aid equipment and fluids to treat diarrhea. Mostly we educated people about how to prevent diarrhea.

One afternoon a boy came to us asking for medical help. He said that someone was needed in Aguilares, a little town about thirty minutes outside San Salvador that had been bombed. So a nun and I went by car. We sent medicines with the boy, who traveled on foot through the hills, because we were afraid of being stopped and searched on the highway. If the army found medicines in our possession, they would have accused us of being rebels.

When we arrived, we found a lot of wounded.... The army claimed that it had been conducting a "cleanup operation" to rid the town of guerrillas. But in reality the army bombs towns where the people are unarmed. There were many such bombings in 1981....

At that time I was living in San Salvador, where I rented a room from a woman. One night some men came looking for me. I wasn't there because sometimes I spent the night at the refugee camp. Angry at not finding me, they took the woman's seventeen-year-old son. The people I lived with weren't related to me, and had nothing to do with my work, although we had become close friends. The boy resisted, and they shot him until his intestines fell out. He died right there, outside his house. His mother came looking for me, to warn me because she knew they wanted to kill me.

Then they captured my fiancé. We had planned to get married in 1981. He was twenty years old. They grabbed him as he was walking down the street. It was a death squad, heavily armed plainclothesmen. They killed him, stabbing him repeatedly, in front of people walking by on the street. Neither I nor his family claimed his body. We were afraid. We didn't understand why they had to kill him. He was only a student. He wasn't involved in anything. We don't even know where he is buried—perhaps in a common grave with twenty others.

My family, too, was persecuted. My father, who was fifty-two years old, was killed in 1981 in Morazán, where my family came from. It was another "cleanup operation." They bombed the town of Morazán—they obliterated it. After they bombed it with napalm and 200- and 500-pound bombs, the troops arrived. They took my father and some other elderly people away. They burned my father alive, along with eleven others.

I became very frightened after all these deaths. I knew they were looking for me. I had done nothing except help those who needed medical attention, but I had to leave the country to survive. I had no idea of where to go. I had never thought of leaving my country.... I went to Mexico with a dozen other Salvadorans who were in the same situation....

I had a distant cousin living in Texas. I called him to ask him for help, for money. He said the only thing I could do was to come to the United States.

He sent me money for a "coyote"—that's a guide across the border.... It took ten days. We had to walk for five nights. It was raining and our feet were covered with sores....

After a year in this country, I began to work with the Committee of Central American Refugees (CRECEN). I still wanted to be a nurse, and they told me there was a health project, a clinic, where I could work. I worked there for a year, and then moved on to Long Island, New York, to work on a similar project—establishing a clinic there for refugees....

I have to clean houses to earn money. I'd like to resume nursing studies, but I'm undocumented and don't speak much English. The Sanctuary Movement can help me find work and help with other problems, like getting medicine, but they can't get me a visa....

CRECEN is working to get political refugee status for us. After all, we are political refugees. We left our country because of the war, because it's dangerous to live in the middle of a war, even if one is not actively participating in it. Providing health care to people who need it the most is a crime in El Salvador. It is because of the war that we had to leave.

That makes us political refugees.

4. U.S. Government Labels Salvadorans as "Illegal Aliens," 1987

This report is in response to your request that we investigate certain issues concerning Salvadoran nationals. As agreed with your office, our review covered those Salvadorans who, whether through deportation, voluntary departure proceeding, or otherwise, have been required to return to El Salvador. Specifically, you asked us to comment on (1) whether they have been targeted for violence or persecution upon their return and (2) the reliability and use made of reports by the Intergovernmental Committee for Migration (ICM) on its reception program for returning Salvadorans....

First, to what extent have Salvadoran returnees experienced violence or persecution? The State Department has stated that ICM has not reported a single case of political persecution involving returnees to El Salvador. Our review of ICM's reports showed that, while the reports do not specifically state that individuals have experienced political persecution, they do state that some returnees have reported personal security problems. ICM's records showed that, as of February 1987, 70 returnees have reported personal security problems. ICM, based on personal interviews or correspondence with returnees, classifies reports of threats of violence or persecution as "personal security problems." ICM has decided that such cases warrant its assistance to individuals to apply for emigration to other countries that have humanitarian resettlement programs. Australia, Canada, and Sweden have accepted 5 returnees determined to be in

U.S. General Accounting Office, Briefing Report to the Honorable Hamilton Fish, Jr., House of Representatives, "Illegal Aliens: Extent of Problems Experienced by Returned Salvadorans Not Determinable" (May 1987), pp. 1–3.

life-threatening situations from either government security or guerrilla forces and were considering the applications of 32 others. We did not attempt to verify the validity of ICM's determinations or whether, in fact, the reported violence or persecution had occurred.

The ICM program covered only about two-thirds of returnees from the United States during the period December 1, 1984 to December 31, 1986. The reliability of information developed by ICM, human rights organizations, and the U.S. embassy in San Salvador is limited, and therefore the frequency or extent of political violence or persecution experienced by returnees cannot be determined.

Second, what is the extent of violence or persecution experienced by the general population of El Salvador? Evidence obtained from the U.S. embassy and human rights monitoring organizations in San Salvador indicates that human rights abuses in El Salvador are still occurring but with distinctly less intensity and frequency than previously. However, the limitations on data collection that exist for all organizations monitoring human rights violations in San Salvador weaken the validity of information on the extent of such occurrences. U.S. and Salvadoran officials we contacted in San Salvador believe that Salvadorans continue to have a pervasive fear of random violence. They told us that Salvadorans are concerned about the consequences of being viewed as sympathetic to either government security or guerrilla forces. Some officials reported a widespread Salvadoran mistrust of government judicial institutions and processes.

Third, have Salvadoran returnees experienced more violence or persecution than the general population? It cannot be determined whether Salvadoran returnees, as a group, have experienced more violence or persecution than the general population. This is because (1) organizations that gather data on returnees do not have adequate information about returnees' experiences after they return to El Salvador and (2) organizations that gather data on human rights violations do not identify returnees as a separate group. Officials we interviewed said that, while some returnees may have greater personal fear of violence and persecution, than does the general population, the likelihood that they would actually experience such violence or persecution depends more on the reasons individuals left El Salvador in the first place than it does on the status of being a returnee....

In its comments on the report, the Department of State said that there was no evidence that returnees have suffered political persecution. While we agree that ICM reports do not specifically refer to returnees experiencing political persecution, they do report on returnees having personal security problems. ICM's basis for such a determination includes evidence that returnees have reported life-threatening situations and, as a result, other nations have accepted some returnees for humanitarian resettlement.

Although the Department stated it agreed with the observation that returnees encounter the same problems as do similarly situated persons in the general Salvadoran population, it was not our intention to infer that we had reached that conclusion. We believe that due to the data limitations described in this report, a comparison cannot be made of the problems encountered by returnees versus the general population in El Salvador.

The Department stated that civil strife and other violence in El Salvador have created circumstances that cause people to experience personal security problems. Also, the Department noted that, while human rights abuses are not authorized or condoned by the highest level of the Salvadoran government, lower-level government security forces and guerrillas are responsible for some human rights abuses from time to time....

5. Nicaraguan Woman Recounts Her Undocumented Journey, 1988

"I talked with Miguel, who said he wanted to go because he believed, from what Leticia and other people had told him, that it'd be like going to another world, to a paradise where everything would be within our reach....

"I called Leticia right back and said yes....

"I didn't sleep much. I talked with my brother Omar. He said, 'I'm not telling you to go or stay. You're responsible for your own actions and you know what you want.... Personally, I wouldn't like to go because people tell me it's a lie that you can have anything you want. Anywhere in the world, you have to work hard to have something.... It's true I don't live well, but we're more or less all right. If I get sick here, I get paid. If you get sick there, they aren't going to pay you.' ...

"We spent a long time at the Honduran border....

"We traveled all day through Honduras.... The place seems sad. No country is nice when you have to stay there a long time, only your own country....

"Since we got to the Honduran-Guatemalan border early, we had to wait until it opened, which was some time after seven in the morning. There was no problem, really, because we were on the shopping excursion bus. The tour leader charges a lot in order to pay off officials, both in Honduras and in Guatemala. The visa allows you to stay only a week or so, but the bribe is for Immigration. They know that some people aren't there just to shop, that some of them, like us, won't return. But they don't know which ones....

"We left Guatemala City with Uncle Mundo. I carried a bag containing one change of clothes for each of us: a blouse, pants, and underwear. 'We have to get moving. Walk fast. Let's go!' he yelled at us. We hurried to a bus stop.... Mundo warned us not to talk with anyone on the trip. Nothing, we should say nothing.

"We reached Tecún Umán on the Guatemalan-Mexican border around two or three o'clock that afternoon. It's a nice town, simple and pretty. People use bicycles for taxis....

"At the river, Mundo told us to act as if we were looking around and to pretend he wasn't with us. Since we rarely said anything out loud and instead communicated by small gestures and glances, he motioned for us to go to the group of people washing clothes on the river's edge and blend in with them.

Dianne Walta Hart, *Undocumented in L.A.: An Immigrant's Story* (New York: Scholarly Resources Books, 1997), pp. 9–29.

"When we got there, a woman approached us, asking, 'Are you crossing to the other side?' ...

"I said yes to the woman, but added that we were with a relative. She whispered, 'Then watch out because *la migra*'s close by. They [Immigration officials] can catch you and take you up there, up to the prison. Be careful.' ...

"The Immigration officer, dressed in his uniform, stopped us. 'What are you doing here?'

"Marisa answered. 'We're just looking around,' she said. 'We like it here, and my little sister is swimming.' ...

"The Immigration officer... took our passports, and told us that we had to go with him.... I told the officer that ... I first had to dry off and dress Nora. I was trying to stall him, trying to give Mundo time to cross the river.

"Mundo arrived while I was still dressing Nora. 'What happened?' he asked me.

"'This man from Immigration said we had to show him our papers, our passports.'

"'Don't move,' he mumbled. 'I'll take care of it. All he wants is money.'

"Mundo was right. He went to talk with the officer, gave him some money, and returned with our passports. We waited for a half hour, got on the raft, and crossed to the other side, to Mexico.

"The crossing itself was scary. The river is narrow but deep. Since we had to sit close to the edge of the raft, we all thought we'd fall in. Some people swam with the raft, pulling and pushing it. When we reached Mexico, we got off quickly, ran past the Immigration office, and once more got on bicycles that were taxis....

"By the time we arrived in Mexico City, we had spent so much time in buses that we didn't know what day it was. I just remember it was dark, although it was morning. At first, I thought it was going to storm or rain, but it was just dark, cloudy, and polluted....

"The six of us and Mundo traveled by bus for probably the next two or three days. We went through many towns, but I don't remember the names....

"We got off somewhere near Tijuana.... We took another bus to Tijuana, and then another one to a place near the border crossing. We arrived at a hotel around four o'clock in the afternoon, and Mundo got Cokes and bread for us....

"We left somewhere between six and half past.... Mundo warned us and said, 'As soon as the taxi stops, get out quickly, and follow me.' The taxi stopped, and Mundo got out and went through an opening in the chain-link fence that divides Mexico from the United States. Beyond the fence is a river-bed, and beyond that, up a little higher, is a road where the Immigration vehicles go back and forth, making sure that no one gets across. We were tired of the cold. The entire trip had been horribly cold....

"There must have been twenty to twenty-five people just where we were, and even more farther on. In the riverbed we saw, near a stream of dirty water, lots of empty cartons and bags. But we also saw a dead man, or it could have been a woman. No one paid any attention to the body. It seemed to be a common occurrence....

"Uncle Mundo called a taxi from a woman's house, and an hour later we were in a San Diego park. It must have been around noon because people were having lunch.... It was January 1, 1989, but none of us knew that. Maybe Mundo knew, but the rest of us were confused about the time, day, everything....

"Sergio arrived.... It had been nearly two years since Sergio had seen his daughters. He had forgotten their ages and didn't know the dates of their birthdays, so he said to each one, 'How old are you? Oh, so grown up!' He didn't keep up with their ages, their birthdays, that sort of thing, as other fathers do....

"He drove us to Los Angeles. I didn't expect the city to look like that. I had seen postcards that people sent to Nicaragua. Some of them had tall buildings with beautiful lights and the card said 'New York,' so I thought all cities, no matter what they were called, looked like that. But Los Angeles wasn't like that at all....

"Sergio's whole family—mother, brothers, sisters—and Leticia were waiting for us in an apartment. We were relieved and happy to finally be there. Leticia was emotional, crying and hugging us. She'd been afraid that something would happen to us in the crossing, as has happened to many people. But there we were. We all made it....

"I didn't understand the situation.... The problem was that I didn't know if Sergio and Leticia had their own apartment or not. I knew Leticia didn't like to live with Sergio's family since they've never gotten along well, so it seemed strange to me from the very moment I saw all of them in that one-room apartment. Maybe they had just gotten together for our arrival. I simply didn't know. It hadn't occurred to me that they all, including Sergio's two brothers, two sisters, and mother, lived in one room....

"The apartment was ... just a tiny box of a room that had a bathroom, a closet, and a kitchen along the wall. There was no furniture, no bed, nothing.... It was so small and cost four hundred fifty dollars a month. Just looking at it, as we say in Nicaragua, I felt my batteries go low. I was demoralized, without the strength to go on, and with the urge to cry.

"Leticia couldn't explain it. She tried, but for me it was too much of a surprise. Miguel gestured, showing that he was as astounded as I was. The apartment didn't matter to the girls, and really not to me, either, but the lie mattered. What we had been told, the lie, was the biggest surprise.

"I didn't tell Miguel, but I thought about how I had my bed in Nicaragua, I had my room, my house where Miguel could shout and play with the boys in the little yard. There we could talk with our neighbors, but here, no, there was nothing. Miguel couldn't play because Sergio wouldn't let him go outside and didn't want him to disturb the neighbors. You always had to be quiet.... It was like when you want to sing a happy song and you can't because it bothers the people next door."...

6. Activists' Lawsuit Wins New Asylum Hearings for Salvadorans and Guatemalans, 1991

WHEREAS, the system of asylum processing has been significantly changed by regulations effective October 1, 1990; and

---

American Baptist Churches v. Thornburgh, 760 F.Supp. 796, N.D. Cal. 1991.

WHEREAS, under the new asylum regulations as well as the old:

foreign policy and border enforcement considerations are not relevant to the determination of whether an applicant for asylum has a well-founded fear of persecution;

the fact that an individual is from a country whose government the United States supports or with which it has favorable relations is not relevant to the determination of whether an applicant for asylum has a well-founded fear of persecution;

whether or not the United States Government agrees with the political or ideological beliefs of the individual is not relevant to the determination of whether an applicant for asylum has a well-founded fear of persecution;

the same standard for determining whether or not an applicant has a well-founded fear of persecution applies to Salvadorans and Guatemalans as applies to all other nationalities....

THEREFORE, Plaintiffs and Defendants enter into and stipulate that this agreement imposes binding obligations on the parties and their successors and that this agreement constitutes a full and complete resolution of the issues raised in this action.

7. Victor Montejo Describes His Life as a Maya, a Refugee, and an Anthropologist, 1999

I ARRIVED IN the world on Lahunh Tox, October 9, 1951, the firstborn child of Eusebio Montejo and Juana Esteban Méndez, both originally from Jacaltenango in the department of Huehuetenango in Guatemala. When he was young my father could not attend school because there were no schools at that time and because he had to work on the land with his father.... When he was twelve years old he began attending a school in Yinhch'ewex that was run voluntarily by a local man.... In return the villagers gave the teacher corn, beans, and firewood to help sustain his family.... My father had to walk three kilometers each morning to get to the school.... This is how my father learned to read, write, and speak Spanish.

My mother had no opportunity to attend school, even though there was a public school in Jacaltenango run by ladino schoolteachers. Education for Maya women was not considered necessary, and her parents did not encourage her. Because her father was often sick, she had to help her mother take care of the other children and travel to nearby towns to sell her weavings. My mother speaks only Popb'al Ti', the Jakaltek Maya language. After my parents married in Jacaltenango, they moved to the Jakaltek village of La Laguna, within the

Republished with permission of University of Oklahoma Press, from "The Anthropologist and the Other," by Victor Montejo in *Voices from Exile: Violence and Survival in Modern Maya History* (1999), pp. 3–14; permission conveyed through Copyright Clearance Center, Inc.

municipio (municipality) of Jacaltenango, to cultivate corn, sugarcane, *achiote*, peppers, and beans. It is in this village that I grew up.

There were two more sons and three daughters born into our family.... My brothers and I studied to become primary school teachers. My sisters completed their studies up to the sixth-grade level. All of my family were severely affected by the violence in the Kuchumatan highlands in the 1980s. My brother Pedro Antonio, with whom I had the closest emotional ties, was killed by soldiers during the town's patronal festival on February 1, 1981. My brother José and his family are now living in Ottawa, where he moved as a landed immigrant in 1986 after living in a refugee camp in Chiapas. He is studying at a college in Ottawa. My sisters also moved to Canada in 1986 and live there with their families....

I grew up speaking Popb'al Ti', and I went with my mother to various Maya ceremonies and festivities. She would tell me stories about my grandfather, who was an Alkal Txah, a Prayer Maker.... I learned the names of the sacred places and the stories of our culture heroes.... We learned all these stories from the elders, who passed on to us through the oral tradition the knowledge of the world around us and the greatness of our people.

My upbringing also included attendance at Catholic church ceremonies, many of which coincided with or were superimposed on traditional Maya ones.... More direct contact with the Catholic church came when a group of Maryknoll nuns arrived in La Laguna to recruit Maya children for a boarding school in Jacaltenango. I was one of the children who decided to attend the Fray Bartolomé de Las Casas school, and at the age of seven, I left my parents and home community for Jacaltenango. I began to attend mass regularly and even became an altar boy, learning Latin so as to make the proper responses during the mass. At this point in my life I became a Catholic because I received my education from Catholic missionaries. I also started to learn Spanish.

... My good grades in the last years of primary school called me to the attention of the parish priest, Fr. Bill Mullan, who obtained a scholarship so that I could attend the Seminary of San José in Sololá. And so I moved again, this time very far away from my family and home village.

I received my *educación básica* (basic education) at the seminary, which was run by Benedictine priests. I learned a great deal there, but the distance from my family and the culture shock of being in a different town where the spoken Maya was different from my language gave rise to some adjustment problems.... It was at this school that I discovered world literature and found in ethnohistorical books such as the *Popol Vuh* and the *Annals of the Kaqchikels* that these ancient stories bore great similarity to those in the oral tradition in my small village. We had not considered those stories very important, nor had we paid much attention to them. This was the beginning of my interest in writing....

After three years at the seminary, I received a scholarship to study at the Instituto Indígena para Varones Santiago in Antigua, Guatemala. This school was run by the Brothers of LaSalle, who were very strict but who also inculcated in us great respect for ourselves, our people, and our culture. I had, by now, decided to become a schoolteacher and work among my own people.... I became a primary school teacher in the village of Yinhch'ewex in January 1973....

I taught with another teacher who disappeared in the violence of 1982.... I worked for a decade in Maya communities in Jacaltenango, until the violence became unbearable and the massacres forced me into exile.

In early November 1982 I left Jacaltenango and went to Guatemala City to apply for a visa to come to the United States. Wallace Kaufman, a friend of my recently deceased brother, Pedro Antonio, invited me to come to the United States to lecture on Maya culture.... I could only get a tourist visa that permitted me to stay for six weeks.... As I was preparing to leave the United States, my wife sent someone to call me with the news that I should not come back to Guatemala because my name was on a death list. The army and the civil patrols were looking for me. They did not believe that I was in the United States but thought that I had gone to the mountains to join the guerrillas. So I did not return to my wife and children and resume my work as a teacher. With great sadness, in mid-December I decided to go to Mexico to search for my parents, brother, and sisters who were living in a refugee camp in Chiapas and to join them in exile.

In the refugee camp in Guadalupe Victoria, I found a typewriter and started to write about the events that had forced me and thousands of others into exile and had caused the massacre of thousands more innocent people in Guatemala. In the tenuous safety of the refugee camp, I decided to speak for those whom the army wished to silence through death, disappearance, or exile....

I applied for an H-1 visa, for writers and people with special skills, and came to the United States.... In February 1984 ... I found some part-time work, but my main concern was to get my family to safety.... Because I did not return to Jacaltenango, the civil patrols began to retaliate against my family. My wife and children were under virtual house arrest and were warned that they would be killed if I did not return. Again my resourceful wife sent someone to call to let me know that she could not leave town because of the civil patrols. With the help of friends in the United States and members of the Friends Meeting House in Washington, D.C., we devised a plan to rescue my family. Congressmen and senators wrote letters to the U.S. Embassy for the appropriate visas, and Sister Tina, a nun from Philadelphia long past the age when such service should be required of her, courageously went to Jacaltenango and helped Mercedes and the children leave the town and the country. It had been two years since I had seen them, and I was overjoyed to greet them at Washington's National Airport on March 4, 1984.

At that time of joyous reunion, we met Gloria Halbritter, an Oneida Indian clan mother from Oneida, New York. She was drawn to us because our children looked like her grandchildren. She welcomed us into her life, her home, and her family, giving us deep and abiding ties to a Native American community here.

The challenge now was to find ways to survive with my family in the United States. Dr. Poteet arranged for me to be a consultant in Latin American Studies at Bucknell University, and I began to study English.... I spent a great deal of time in the Bucknell library reading books on Maya culture. I knew I could write about my culture, but I needed the tools and the academic training to do it well. I decided that I wanted that training to be in anthropology, and

I began to search for universities where there was both a Maya Studies program and the possibility of scholarships.... SUNY–Albany gave me the opportunity to fulfill my dreams.... Mercedes took all kinds of jobs to help support us....

I graduated from SUNY in the spring of 1989 and moved to the University of Connecticut to work on my doctorate....

Recently the field of anthropology has seen much discussion on the relationship between the anthropologist and the people studied, the "other." Usually the anthropologist is from a dominant Western culture or a former colonial power while those studied are less powerful, less literate, and less sophisticated in the ways of the "first" world. This dichotomy is not as relevant in my case. I am a Maya, I was a refugee, I lived in exile, and as an anthropologist I returned to the refugee camps to investigate the situation of those remaining there. I have the advantage of a Western education *and* a Maya upbringing. I speak two Maya languages, Popb'al Ti' and Q'anjob'al, in addition to Spanish and English. However, I have lived outside my culture for the past ten years and have acquired some Western and academic ethnocentrisms from that experience. Because of my double identity, this work is directed to two audiences: the Maya themselves, so that they have this document as a commemoration of their struggles; and the general Western community, academic and nonacademic, so that our work becomes relevant to and respectful of indigenous cultures.

 # ESSAYS

Wars in Central America were ignited by extremely uneven distributions of wealth and by the political repression used to maintain that status quo. These wars were fanned by U.S. intervention to protect what it saw as its own interests during the Cold War, as well as U.S. economic investments in those countries. As María Cristina García, professor of history at Cornell University, details in the first essay, the United States supported repressive, right-wing governments in El Salvador and Guatemala, despite flagrant human rights abuses. In contrast, in Nicaragua the United States sought to undermine the government that had unseated a long-standing repressive dictatorship. The result was a refugee crisis that had its greatest impact on neighboring countries, but also sent people fleeing to the United States.

Geopolitics also shaped how the United States defined those seeking refuge in the United States. Those fleeing from El Salvador and Guatemala, governments that the United States supported, were deemed economic immigrants and hence "illegal aliens," rather than refugees. In the second essay, Susan Bibler Coutin, associate dean and professor of Criminology, Law, and Society at the University of California, Irvine, describes how Salvadoran activists in the United States sought to define Salvadorans as refugees, in order to prevent deportations back to El Salvador and to challenge the U.S. government's financial support of a government that was brutally repressing opposition. With time, however, as peace accords were signed and Salvadorans remained in the United States, activists worked to redefine Salvadorans as immigrants, deserving of the legal rights of citizens and permanent residents.

Central American Wars, U.S. Interventions, and a Refugee Crisis

MARÍA CRISTINA GARCÍA

The revolutions in Nicaragua, El Salvador, and Guatemala were each the product of decades of struggles over land, resources, and power. However, what began as localized conflicts became international crises that affected dozens of nations, including neighboring Costa Rica, Honduras, and Mexico; hemispheric allies such as the United States and Canada; and even Cuba, the Soviet Union, and the European Community. Thousands of Central Americans died, and millions were uprooted as a consequence of the domestic and foreign policy decisions of these various actors. But just as local political conflicts became internationalized, so, too, did their eventual resolution. The negotiated peace settlements and the reintegration of the displaced involved some of these very same actors, who through diplomacy, investment, and aid tried to establish peace, social and political stability, and economic opportunity in the region.

★ ★ ★

In 1979, the Sandinista rebels overthrew the US-supported government of Anastacio Somoza Debayle. The Somoza family ... had controlled Nicaraguan politics since 1934.... From the Truman to the Ford administrations, the Somozas were regarded by the United States government as reliable allies in the Cold War and were rewarded with millions of dollars in economic and military aid, much of which found its way to private coffers.... US corporations also controlled thousands of acres of Nicaragua's most fertile land and owned or managed the leading mines, the railroads, and the lumber and banking industries.

The extensive US presence in Nicaragua's national life never guaranteed the people peace or socioeconomic mobility. The majority of the three million Nicaraguans lived in extreme poverty, and high infant mortality, illiteracy, and unemployment were common features of day-to-day life. Two percent of the farms controlled nearly half of the tillable land, and over two hundred thousand peasants were landless. In turn, the Somoza family's wealth was estimated at more than a billion dollars.... American investors made handsome profits from their ventures in Nicaragua: US investments yielded hundreds of millions of dollars in yearly income that was exported back to the United States.

The extreme disparities in wealth and the corruption in the highest echelons of the government raised the consciousness of the citizenry, especially labor organizers, university students, journalists, and public intellectuals. Prior to 1972, the US-trained Nicaragua National Guard helped to keep the opposition weak and disorganized by assassinating over thirty thousand of the dictator's opponents and driving thousands more into exile.... [A]fter an earthquake devastated the capital city of Managua in December 1972, ... [s]trikes and demonstrations

Seeking Refuge: Central American Migration to Mexico, the United States, and Canada, by María Cristina García. © 2006 by the Regents of the University of California. Published by the University of California Press.

increased ... as Nicaraguans protested the blatant theft of international aid and the shameless corruption of government officials who financially profited from the devastation. Inspiring the protests was the politically moderate editor Pedro Joaquin Chamorro, who used his small opposition newspaper, *La Prensa,* to meticulously document the corruption and abuse of authority.

The Sandinista National Liberation Front (FSLN) ... favored a revolutionary political and socioeconomic agenda.... [T]he Sandinistas, as members the FSLN were popularly called, waged war against the dictatorship.... Determined to eliminate the FSLN, the Nicaragua National Guard increased its surveillance of the population as well as its campaign of imprisonment, torture, and assassination.... Even the political moderates came under attack: Chamorro was jailed and finally assassinated in 1978. This action, more than any other, turned the political tide. A two-week general strike calling for Somoza's unconditional resignation evolved into a full-scale, nationwide insurrection. By May 1979 the Sandinistas controlled the nation's major towns and cities, including parts of Managua.

On July 17, 1979, Somoza fled to Miami with some of the senior commanders of the National Guard.... On July 19, a coalition of moderates and leftists took control of Nicaragua's government....

While all were committed to agrarian reform and basic social welfare programs such as universal health care, literacy, and free public education, they disagreed on the roles that the private sector and the multiparty political system would play in the new Nicaragua—if any. The more radical members of the FSLN saw no role for such institutions in their socialist state. As this segment assumed control of the national directorate and the armed forces, moderates in the coalition ... felt increasingly silenced and shut out of the decision making.... By 1982 several moderates had resigned from the coalition or gone into exile....

Most nations in the hemisphere, with the notable exception of Central American neighbors Costa Rica, El Salvador, Guatemala, and Honduras, cautiously welcomed the change in Nicaragua's government. Despite its thirty-plus years of assistance to the Somoza government, in the final year of the revolution Mexico offered the Sandinistas tactical support and then recognized the new government almost immediately....

Canada ... officially welcomed the end of the Somoza era and even prohibited Somoza's entry into the country when he asked to relocate there, but postponed recognition of the Sandinista government. Throughout the 1980s Canadian policymakers opposed US policy in Nicaragua and criticized the militarization of the region, but avoided any official condemnation of the United States that might strain US-Canadian relations, especially in trade and commerce....

As the most powerful nation in the hemisphere, the United States shaped the tone and content of the political debate over Nicaragua throughout the next decade.... [T]he United States had a geopolitical interest in containing revolution in the Americas. However, US policy shifted dramatically in a relatively short period of time. Immediately following his inauguration in January 1977, President Jimmy Carter declared US aid to individual Latin American countries contingent upon their human rights policies, and thus withdrew economic and military aid from the Somoza dictatorship.... Carter officially recognized the

Sandinista government and hoped that it would offer its country peace, security, and basic civil liberties. The United States granted Nicaragua close to a hundred million dollars in emergency aid during 1979–1980 … with the goal of maintaining positive relations and avoiding the mistakes the United States had made with Cuba twenty years earlier.…

US-Nicaraguan relations collapsed after Ronald Reagan moved into the White House in January 1981.… [T]he Cold War framed the gathering of intelligence, the interpretation of the data, and ultimately the policymaking in this administration. They were determined not to let post-Vietnam guilt interfere with the containment of what they saw as a growing Cuban–Soviet–East European presence in the region. Congress … supported the economic embargo on Nicaragua and redirected aid to the "Contras": *contra-revolucionarios* on the Honduras–Nicaragua border, whom the Reagan administration directed to stop the flow of arms from the Sandinista government to the leftist guerrillas … in El Salvador.

By the end of Reagan's first term it was clear that the administration … was using the Contras to destabilize—and overthrow—the Nicaraguan government.… [T]he Contras' military maneuvers were designed to force the Sandinistas to commit the Nicaraguan armed forces to domestic defense and to create a climate of political instability that would erode popular support and encourage revolt.… By 1983, the CIA itself was directly engaged in sabotage—bombing Nicaraguan oil reserves and mining harbors …—in clear violation of international law and the United States' own Boland Amendment, which prohibited assisting or using the Contras to overthrow the Nicaraguan government or to provoke conflict between Nicaragua and Honduras. Congress responded with the second Boland Amendment in 1984, which severed lethal aid to the Contras once and for all. Nicaragua filed a complaint against the United States in the World Court for the mining of its harbors, and two years later the court officially condemned the United States. However, neither domestic pressure nor international sanction deterred the Reagan administration from its foreign policy objectives: the administration turned to the illegal sale of arms to Iran in order to redirect the profits to its Contra protégés.

… Critics argued that US policy only served to increase poverty and homelessness in Nicaragua, destabilize neighboring countries and [produce] a large-scale regional migration. NGOs … documented the human toll produced by the militarization of Central America.… [A] vocal and influential minority [of Americans] protested US policy and ultimately forced Congress to monitor the administration's support of the Contras.… Such popular pressure undoubtedly influenced the congressional and judicial scrutiny that followed the discovery of the illegal sale of arms to Iran.

… [T]he Bush administration continued to undermine the Sandinistas, albeit through more traditional pressure—the economic embargo, diplomatic isolation, and financial support of opposition groups. In 1989, when the Sandinista government finally agreed to elections … the United States funneled millions of dollars to the opposition parties to ensure the Sandinistas' defeat. In February 1990, Violeta Barrios de Chamorro … was elected president of Nicaragua by over half of the war-weary electorate.... The United States finally lifted its economic embargo and provided millions of dollars to help rebuild the society that, only months before, it had tried to destroy.

The opposition's victory came at a high price for the Nicaraguan people: thirty thousand dead; fifty thousand wounded; and three hundred thousand left homeless. And over half a million Nicaraguans remained outside their country, the majority of them in the United States, waiting to see what type of society would evolve in their homeland.

★ ★ ★

As in Nicaragua, the civil war in El Salvador was rooted in the unequal distribution of power. An oligarchy of landed elites known as the Fourteen Families controlled 60 percent of the farmland, the entire banking system, and most of the nation's industry. Eight percent of the nation's five million people controlled half of the nation's income, while over one-quarter of the rural population was poor and had been pushed off their land to make room for agricultural estates dedicated to the production of coffee, the country's principal export. Since 1932, the country was ruled by a series of generals with close ties to the oligarchy, whose interests they protected, and they were equally zealous in weeding out any challenges to their authority. A peasant uprising in 1932 ... led to *la matanza:* the murder of over thirty thousand Salvadorans by the army and vigilante groups.

... After the fraudulent elections of 1972, more and more Salvadorans engaged in strikes, demonstrations, and other acts of civil disobedience against the government.... As one of the principal institutions in El Salvador (and Latin America), the Catholic Church had historically helped to maintain the unequal power relationships by encouraging the poor and the oppressed to passively accept their fate on earth in hopes of greater glories in heaven. However, by the 1960s, a more radical wing of the Catholic Church preached what it called a "theology of liberation": the fundamental idea that poverty and oppression were not God's will, and that God's children had the right to challenge oppressive institutions, structures, and conditions in every sector of society. Moreover, according to liberation theology, the Catholic Church was obligated to condemn these unjust institutions and assist the faithful in their struggle for liberation.... To those who held power in Salvadoran society, this theology ... was certainly radical enough to threaten their positions of privilege. Particularly worrisome was the fact that this theology was preached by even the highest-ranking clergyman of their society, the archbishop of San Salvador, Oscar Arnulfo Romero, who used his weekly radio sermons to condemn the abuses in Salvadoran society and to urge President Carter to withdraw military aid.

Whether influenced by liberation theology or the Sandinista and Cuban revolutions, a number of groups emerged in El Salvador to demand social justice.... Each drew its rapidly growing membership from different segments of Salvadoran society—university students, teachers, trade unionists, as well as the urban and rural poor—and used a variety of tactics to challenge the authority of the elites, from traditional forms of civil disobedience to guerrilla warfare....

The principal agencies of Salvadoran national security tried to eliminate the rebels and dissenters.... Protesters were arrested and beaten, expelled from the country, or murdered. The armed forces were assisted in these efforts by privately funded paramilitary groups.... [T]he paramilitary groups received their funding from members of the oligarchy.... These groups, appropriately nicknamed ... "death squads," employed particularly gruesome tactics. Those believed to have ties to insurgent groups or who challenged the established order in any way—through labor organizing, sermons and public speaking, classroom instruction, publications and journalism—were tortured, raped, and killed. Thousands of mutilated corpses appeared in town sewers, garbage dumps, street gutters, and shallow graves, left by their torturers as a warning to others.... A favorite target of these death squads were nuns and priests, especially those affiliated with the more liberal Maryknoll and Jesuit orders that preached liberation theology....

Nineteen eighty was a particularly violent year: over eight thousand civilians were killed, and yet no one was arrested for the murders.... In March, Archbishop Oscar Romero was shot and killed while saying mass at the cathedral. At his funeral procession, the military fired into the crowd of thirty thousand mourners, killing thirty and wounding hundreds. , , ,

As in Nicaragua, the assassination of prominent leaders ... served to unite reformers and revolutionaries.... [T]he various political parties, religious organizations, trade unions, and peasant groups joined forces to create the Revolutionary Democratic Front (FDR).... Five guerrilla groups also joined forces under the FMLN. The FDR and FMLN eventually ... united under the banner FDR-FMLN....

... Assassinations decreased by the end of 1984, as a result of US pressure, but the Salvadoran military increased its bombing of villages on which the guerrillas depended for shelter and food. Over seventy thousand were left homeless as a result of this campaign.

US military aid to El Salvador continued despite the blatant human rights violations and intense international opposition, and despite the December 1980 United Nations resolution calling for an end to military support of the Salvadoran government. As in Nicaragua, the hard-liners in the Reagan administration portrayed the Salvadoran civil war as part of the East–West struggle, in which the United States had a moral duty to contain Cuban/Soviet expansionism.... As early as February 1980, Canadian and Mexican representatives met to discuss their mutual opposition to US intervention in Central American affairs. Canada cut off aid to El Salvador in November 1980, and along with Mexico and most nations in the hemisphere supported the UN resolution....

In order to continue providing aid, the US Congress required evidence that El Salvador was making significant improvements in human rights. Members of the Reagan administration either denied or downplayed news reports of civilian casualties, claiming that only leftist guerrillas were caught in the crossfire....

Congress found the administration's arguments and evidence compelling enough to continue sending aid. Throughout the 1980s, El Salvador remained on the list of the top five nations to receive aid from the United States. All in all, the United States provided six billion dollars in economic and military aid to El Salvador during its twelve-year civil war....

While the different parties struggled for control of the Salvadoran government, thousands of people were uprooted from their homes or murdered. By 1986, over half a million Salvadorans were internally displaced, dependent on the government for their survival, and over one million had fled to other countries.

★ ★ ★

In Guatemala, a state of war began in 1954, when a CIA-sponsored military coup overthrew the democratically elected government of Jacobo Arbenz Guzman and thwarted the country's decade-long campaign for agrarian reform. For the next forty years, a series of military officers ruled the country. As in Nicaragua and El Salvador, opposition groups in Guatemala during this time frame challenged the institutions that concentrated wealth and power in the hands of a small percentage of the population. Two percent of the population controlled 72 percent of all private land, while 60 percent of Guatemalans earned roughly two dollars a day harvesting export crops such as coffee, sugar, and cotton. Workers and their families endured inhumane conditions at home and at work: inferior housing with no running water, sewers, or electrification; and access to health care and education was limited. Workers were offered few legal protections, and attempts at unionization were violently discouraged.

The Maya of the highlands of Guatemala, who comprised half of Guatemala's population of eight million and were the backbone of the agricultural economy, were especially poor and victimized. Multinational corporations, with the encouragement and support of various dictatorships, confiscated Indian land for oil production, mining, and cattle raising.... They were a voiceless and heavily exploited majority, whose intense poverty made them, the government feared, prone to insurgency. As early as the 1960s, the army moved into the highlands and kidnapped and killed those suspected of trying to form agricultural cooperatives, unions, or political groups. Between 1966 and 1976, fifty thousand people were murdered....

In 1982, the four principal guerrilla armies joined to form the Guatemalan National Revolutionary Unity (URNG). Their platform included agrarian reform and price controls; equality between Indians and *ladinos;* democratic representation; and civil liberties such as freedom of expression and religion. The government tried to control the population and erode the guerrillas' popular base through special programs ..., which provided food and other aid in exchange for service in the ... civilian defense patrols.... The army burned fields and killed livestock to destroy the guerrillas' food supplies. Individuals remotely suspected of assisting the guerrillas, no matter how young, were viciously tortured and killed.

The Mayas were especially targeted. Accused of harboring or supporting the rebels, entire villages were burned to the ground by the *kaibiles,* the government's elite counterinsurgency units, many of whom were young Indians forced to wage war against their own people. Entire communities were slaughtered. Soldiers used guns, knives, and machetes, or doused their victims with gasoline and burned them alive. Bodies were mutilated before and after death....

Survivors and nearby villagers ... who appealed for amnesty or who were caught by the Guatemalan military and allowed to live were "reoriented": interrogated for information on the guerrillas and then subjected to "reeducation" classes for twelve to fifteen hours every day for several months, where they were lectured on the "falsehoods" of the guerrillas' political campaign. Finally, in strategic areas, ... inhabitants of towns and villages were relocated to heavily patrolled "model villages," where their actions were strictly regulated.

The government's policy of indoctrination and cultural annihilation continued in the model villages. Residents were allowed to speak only Spanish, and Catholicism and indigenous rituals were strongly discouraged in favor of some form of evangelical Protestantism ... that taught subservience to authority. The traditional Maya government was replaced with army-appointed commissioners and the civilian defense patrols that spied on camp residents and controlled the movement of the villagers. As part of the government's rural pacification policy, the Maya populations were forced to engage in public works projects, including rebuilding the structures and communities that the army had so assiduously burned down.

From 1978 to 1984, approximately 100,000 Guatemalans were killed and 40,000 "disappeared" (their whereabouts unknown and presumed dead); 440 villages were destroyed, and 750,000 people internally displaced. Over a quarter-million people fled the country. The Catholic Church was one of the few institutions to denounce the human rights violations.... As in El Salvador, clergy, nuns, and missionaries became popular targets for the counterinsurgency units, forcing many to flee the country and form the Guatemalan Church in Exile.

US aid to Guatemala shifted according to human rights reports and the domestic pressure that these elicited. Military aid was temporarily suspended in 1977, but the United States continued to train officers in the Guatemalan armed forces, facilitate corporate investments, and provide ... development assistance to those in power. After a meeting with General Ríos Montt in Honduras in 1982, President Reagan remarked that Ríos Montt was a man of "great integrity" whom human rights monitors had given a "bum rap." Military aid was reinstated a few years later. But in March 1990, under domestic and international pressure, the Bush administration recalled its ambassador in protest over the Guatemalan government's failure to investigate and punish human rights abuses; and military aid once again ceased in 1992.

As with the rest of the United States' Central America policy, its actions in Guatemala drew international criticism, particularly from its neighbors. This time, Canada served as cosponsor of the 1982 UN resolution condemning Guatemala.... Mexico ... was surprisingly less critical of Guatemala's human rights violations than it was of El Salvador's rightist regime.... The silence was inconsistent but pragmatic: the Guatemalan conflict was closer to home and threatened to spill over into Mexico's southern states. Thousands of Maya refugees crossed Mexico's southern border and sought safety in the state of Chiapas, also home to a large Maya population.... Domestic concerns far outweighed ideological commitments.

★ ★ ★

Before 1970, migration within Central America was common. People migrated within and across borders for temporary work in farming, construction, and domestic service. Salvadorans had the longest tradition of cross-border migration, particularly to Honduras, where 350,000 had settled by the end of the 1960s, lured by the higher wages offered by the banana companies....

Guatemalans, particularly Maya Indians, also had a migratory tradition, especially to Mexico's Soconusco region and Chiapas in general.... There they found a Maya and mestizo population that shared cultural similarities. As Mexican workers sought employment in higher-paying industries, the Guatemalans provided the labor critical to the region's agricultural industry: an estimated twenty thousand to one hundred thousand seasonal workers in Mexico each year. Until the 1990s, ... [t]he border was fluid, and trade, commerce, and family ties extended across national boundaries....

Migration to more distant countries such as the United States and Canada was less common, although a few thousand Central Americans lived in cities such as Washington, San Francisco, New York, and Miami by end of the 1970s. As the wars escalated, these smaller northern populations served as magnets, encouraging further migration. The 1980 census in the United States ... counted 94,447 Salvadorans and 63,073 Guatemalans, and close to half had arrived in the previous five years. The detention of undocumented Central Americans on the United States–Mexico border also increased. In 1977, the first year for which such statistics are available, more than seven thousand Salvadorans and over five thousand Guatemalans were apprehended.

Despite a migratory tradition within the region, the Central American nations were ill prepared to deal with the refugee crisis of 1974–1996. The wars in Central America displaced millions of people and forced them to migrate internally and across borders. As with most migrations, people traveled wherever they had networks of family, friends, or countrymen that could take them in and assist them in finding jobs [See Document 7]. They followed established patterns of migration: Salvadorans traveled to Honduras and Guatemala because they had done so for decades; and Guatemalans crossed the border into Chiapas. But with each passing year, populations emerged in less traditional areas of settlement: Salvadorans settled in Mexico, Guatemalans in Belize, and Nicaraguans in Costa Rica....

The international press commonly referred to these migrants as refugees because political upheaval played a role in their migration, but their legal status was far from clear and varied from country to country [See Document 1]....

Complicating matters, most Central American migrants did not meet the strict UN definition of refugee status, having fled their countries because of the generalized climate of violence rather than a "well-founded" fear of persecution for the listed categories. By 1980, the United Nations High Commissioner for Refugees (UNHCR) readily admitted that the Convention and Protocol were too restrictive, and advocated a more lenient response to the so-called *nonconvention refugees:* those who did not meet the strict definition of the term but who had fled their homes, crossed an international border, and were living in refugee-like conditions....

Each country conducted its own domestic debate on what constituted a refugee, and what types of programs should be made available to those so designated (i.e., asylum or temporary safe haven; resettlement; work authorization;

social services, repatriation, etc.). Most governments preferred to view the Nicaraguans, Salvadorans, and Guatemalans living among their populations as economic migrants because it freed them from any responsibility [See Document 4]....

The lack of protection offered by states, then, became one more means by which migrants became the victims and pawns of foreign policy decisions. Human rights organizations and other NGOs were at times the migrants' only advocates, urging a broader definition of their status that would facilitate their accommodation, and assisting in their temporary or long-term integration into host societies.

In Nicaragua, the first large-scale migration out of the country began during the mid- to late 1970s, when the fighting between Sandinista rebels and the Somoza dictatorship was most intense. An estimated two hundred thousand Nicaraguans fled to other countries during this period, although the majority are believed to have returned after the Sandinista victory in 1979. A second wave of emigrants left after 1979 because of the Sandinistas' policies and/or the upheaval caused by the Contra war. For those who chose to leave the country, wealth, language, availability of transportation, and historical patterns of migration all played a role in determining the country of first asylum. The majority of middle- to upper-class exiles ... traveled to cities like Miami, Los Angeles, and Houston, where they found employment in the large Latino enclaves. Those interested in supporting the counterrevolution were particularly drawn to Miami, where exile groups such as the Nicaraguan Democratic Front were working with the US government to oust the Sandinistas. Other exiles/refugees migrated to neighboring and more familiar Spanish-speaking countries such as Costa Rica, Honduras, and Panama.

... Salvadoran migration increased after October 1979, when the death squads intensified the campaign against the opposition. According to the UNHCR, half a million Salvadorans fled their homeland during the period 1979–1982. By the end of the 1980s, one million people were estimated to have migrated, and over half a million were internally displaced. In turn, Guatemalan migration increased during 1982–1984, when the governments of Ríos Montt and Mejía Víctores escalated their counterinsurgency campaigns. According to UNHCR estimates, over one million people became internal migrants or refugees in Guatemala during the 1980s....

The countries that bordered Nicaragua, El Salvador, and Guatemala suddenly found themselves reluctant hosts to thousands of refugees. Humanitarian concern for the refugees was tempered by political and economic considerations: politicians feared that comprehensive assistance would encourage the refugees to stay permanently within their borders and increase resentment among nationals, who would have to compete with the refugees for jobs, housing, and social services. The presence of thousands of dissidents and rebels could also potentially destabilize their own countries. Central American governments therefore tried to discourage large-scale migration.... [P]aramilitary groups often equated assistance to refugees and displaced persons with support for guerrilla insurgents, and interfered with the delivery of humanitarian assistance and harassed, arrested, and even murdered aid workers [See Document 3].

The UNHCR advocated resettlement in neighboring countries because such an arrangement would facilitate eventual repatriation. The UNHCR provided millions of dollars in funding to local government agencies to establish camps and to provide emergency food and medical care.... Camps that were designed as a temporary measure became permanent housing; some residents remained in their camps for as long as ten years with limited opportunities for education and recreation. In many cases, camps housed thousands more than they were designed to hold.... Others decided to try their luck further north, seeking employment in the more developed economies of Mexico, the United States, and Canada.

By 1989, six nations—Costa Rica, Honduras, Nicaragua, El Salvador, Guatemala, and Belize—reported an aggregate eight hundred thousand immigrants, of which 10 percent were officially documented as refugees and received assistance from local governments and international agencies....

Salvadorans Challenge the U.S. Label of "Illegal Aliens"

SUSAN BIBLER COUTIN

Irrespective of its other goals, U.S. immigration law establishes the terms through which immigrants who are in the United States without authorization negotiate their legal statuses. Although it is primarily designed to regulate legal immigration and to prevent unauthorized entry or sojourn, U.S. immigration law also identifies various criteria, such as political necessity, labor skills, and family ties, that are used to decide which of the individuals who are illegally present in the United States can regularize their stay. Immigration law simultaneously establishes various proceedings, such as asylum hearings, labor certification, and family petitions, through which these criteria are applied. These criteria and proceedings enable unauthorized immigrants and their advocates to devise legalization strategies. These strategies in turn shape immigration policy in that efforts to legalize sometimes redefine not only individual immigrants but also the criteria and proceedings that determine legalization. Moreover, policymakers sometimes change policies to counter particular legalization strategies. Attending to the relationship between immigration law and legalization strategies therefore helps to account for the formulation, impact, and ongoing redefinition of immigration policies....

★ ★ ★

Salvadorans' initial legalization strategies were formulated in the early 1980s, when the outbreak of civil war in El Salvador led unprecedented numbers of Salvadorans to enter the United States. By the mid-1980s, there were 500,000 to 800,000 Salvadorans in the United States, and by the early 1990s, community activists estimated that this number had grown to approximately 1 million individuals. While the laws barring unauthorized entry did not prevent these individuals – most of whom entered the country without authorization – from coming to the United States, immigration law did make their stay in this country precarious. If apprehended, Salvadorans, like other undocumented persons, faced detention and possible deportation. Given the pervasiveness of civil war and human rights violations in El Salvador, many were willing to accept lengthy detention in the United States rather than agreeing to depart voluntarily. Even if they avoided apprehension, Salvadorans, again like other unauthorized immigrants, found their ability to live and work hampered by their lack of documents.... The passage of the 1986 Immigration Reform and Control Act [IRCA], which imposed sanctions on employers who hired unauthorized workers, made life even more difficult for the undocumented.

The only way for most Salvadorans to be in the United States legally in the early and mid-1980s was to apply for political asylum. Other means of legalization, such as family petitions, suspension of deportation, and labor certification, required having close family members with legal status, seven years of continuous residence in the United States, or specialized job skills, all of which were in short supply within this newly immigrated community. Political asylum, in contrast, was available to migrants who could demonstrate a well-founded fear of persecution in their homelands, a characteristic that, unfortunately, was all too common among these early Salvadoran migrants. Prior to the passage of IRCA, Salvadorans' primary legal need was to avoid deportation, not to legalize their stay, therefore few Salvadorans applied for asylum unless they were first apprehended by the INS [Immigration and Naturalization Service]. If they were apprehended, applying for asylum could delay or prevent deportation. Although only 2.6 percent of the asylum applications filed by Salvadorans were being approved during this period, filing an application would allow applicants to remain in the United States while their original case and any appeals were pending, a process that could last several years.

For Salvadoran activists, defining Salvadorans as "refugees" was part of a political strategy that sought not only to save lives and prevent deportations, but also to affect the course of the Salvadoran civil war. Among the Salvadorans who came to the United States in the early 1980s were members of the political groups that made up the FMLN (Farabundo Marti National Liberation Front), the force opposing the Salvadoran government. These activists formed political committees in the United States that corresponded to their organizations in El Salvador.... In addition to helping detained Salvadorans apply for political asylum, refugee committees lobbied for federal legislation that would grant extended voluntary departure (EVD) status to Salvadorans on the grounds that they were refugees. Activists hoped that if the U.S. government formally recognized Salvadorans as refugees, the U.S. government would be unable to continue sending military aid to the Salvadoran government, which would in turn promote either a guerrilla victory or a negotiated settlement.

... [T]he Reagan administration, which by 1987 was supplying over $1 million a day in military and other aid to the Salvadoran government, adopted the stance that the human rights situation in El Salvador was improving and that the vast majority of Salvadorans in the United States were economic immigrants who did not deserve asylum [See Document 4]. State Department officials favored resettlement in the region instead of asylum in the United States for those Salvadorans who did face danger in their homelands....

★ ★ ★

During the 1980s, the large numbers of Salvadoran immigrants, the high profile of U.S. Central American policy, and the organizing efforts of Salvadoran activists gave rise to political movements that sought to define Salvadorans as refugees who deserved political asylum. One of the strongest components of this activism was the sanctuary movement, a network of congregations that declared themselves "sanctuaries" for Salvadoran and Guatemalan refugees. The sanctuary movement began in 1982, when U.S. religious activists who had helped detained Salvadoran and Guatemalan immigrants file for political asylum decided to also help unapprehended Central Americans avoid being detected by U.S. immigration authorities [See Document 2]. Activists took this step because the routine denial of Salvadorans' and Guatemalans' asylum petitions led them to conclude that the U.S. government was discriminating against asylum seekers from noncommunist countries.... By 1986, there were approximately 400 congregations participating in the sanctuary movement.

The methods through which sanctuary activists sought to change U.S. refugee and Central American policy derived from U.S. immigration law itself. In seeking to define Salvadorans and Guatemalans as "refugees," sanctuary activists were taking advantage of the fact that, according to U.S. law, being a victim of political persecution is one of the grounds on which a person who has entered the United States illicitly can change his or her status from that of an illegal alien to an authorized resident.... [W]hen a Central American requested the movement's assistance in entering the United States, movement members "screened" the individual to determine whether he or she was a "refugee." ... Individuals who were deemed to be political refugees were brought into the United States, whereas those who were considered economic immigrants were either left to cross the border on their own or given some other sort of assistance.

... [W]hen they housed undocumented Central Americans, religious activists took advantage of the fact that U.S. immigration law increasingly holds private citizens accountable for the legal status of those around them. By publicly sheltering Central Americans, activists asserted that if they were required to assess the legal status of other individuals, then they also were entitled to act on their own understandings of immigration law.... Such actions not only defined Salvadorans and Guatemalans as "refugees" but also reinterpreted this category, suggesting that refugee status is conferred by the experience of fleeing persecution, not by the decision of a judge or asylum official, and that private citizens as well as government authorities have the ability to recognize refugees....

Movement members' efforts to define Salvadorans and Guatemalans as refugees defined movement members as criminals in the eyes of U.S. authorities. In 1984 and 1985, sanctuary activists were convicted in Texas on charges of transporting illegal aliens, and in 1986, eight movement members were convicted of conspiracy and alien smuggling in Tucson, Arizona.... [I]n response to the indictment of sanctuary activists in 1985, sanctuary congregations and Central American service organizations sued the U.S. Attorney General and the INS Commissioner, charging that the prosecution of sanctuary activists violated activists' rights to freedom of religious practice and that the INS had discriminated against Salvadoran and Guatemalan asylum applicants in violation of U.S. and international refugee law. The lawsuit, advocates' legislative work, and religious activists' attempts to define Central Americans as refugees eventually produced policy changes permitting Salvadorans and Guatemalans to apply for temporary legal status in the United States.

★ ★ ★

In 1990, hard work, strategic alliances, and changed circumstances resulted in legislation granting Salvadorans the right to apply for Temporary Protected Status (TPS) and an out-of-court settlement of the lawsuit filed by sanctuary congregations and Central American service organizations in 1985.... A provision allowing Salvadorans who had been in the United States since September 19, 1990, to apply for eighteen months of TPS was incorporated into the [1990 immigration] act. Blanket protection for most Salvadorans who were in the United States had become possible.

The TPS provision of the 1990 Immigration Act was a factor in advocates' second policy success – a negotiated settlement in what came to be known as the *ABC* lawsuit, after the American Baptist Churches, the lead plaintiff in the suit.... Congress had granted Salvadorans the right to apply for TPS, and, in response to heavy criticism by human rights activists, the INS had already revised its asylum procedures. For these reasons, the defense agreed to grant Salvadorans who had been in the United States since September 19, 1990, and Guatemalans who had been present since October 1, 1990, the right to *de novo* asylum interviews. To eliminate bias against applicants, asylum officers were to receive special training regarding conditions in El Salvador and Guatemala, previous denials were not to be held against applicants, and officers were to base their initial decisions solely on the most recently submitted asylum petition. To obtain these benefits, *ABC* class members had to either register directly with the INS or, in the case of Salvadorans, apply for TPS and then submit an asylum application before a deadline to be imposed by the INS. Plaintiffs in the *ABC* case hailed this agreement as a victory [See Document 6]....

Though the purpose of the agreement was to ensure that Salvadoran and Guatemalan asylum applicants had fair hearings, some applicants used the *ABC* asylum process to preserve their rights to remain in the country.... While waiting for their cases to be decided, applicants would receive work permits, gain time in the country, and perhaps become eligible for other forms of legalization, such as being petitioned for by a family member. Moreover, the special rules governing *ABC* class members' asylum interviews with INS officials improved applicants' chances of obtaining asylum....

As they filled out asylum applications under the terms of the *ABC* agreement, community organizations not only negotiated the legal status of individual applicants but also the boundaries of the *ABC* agreement's target population and thus the meaning of the "political asylee" category. Each of the organizations whose legal services programs I observed developed broad notions of eligibility, reflecting staffmembers' understanding of the arbitrary and pervasive nature of civil war and human rights abuses in El Salvador. Legal workers at each of these organizations told me that, because persecution was so widespread in El Salvador, many Salvadorans took experiences like being forced off a bus by soldiers or being forced to give food to the guerrillas for granted and did not see themselves as victims of persecution.... By submitting asylum applications that reflected their staffs' understanding of the pervasiveness of persecution in El Salvador, community organizations were asserting that Salvadorans had been driven to the United States by the war and were also promoting a broader definition of the "refugee" category than that which INS officials seem to be using. If their clients ultimately obtain either asylum or another status, then community organizations will have succeeded in legalizing a group of people whom they consider deserving....

★ ★ ★

... During the 1980s, Salvadoran activists had found it both empowering and politically necessary to define themselves and their community as refugees, given the Reagan Administration's contention that Salvadorans were economic immigrants. By the 1990s, when many Salvadorans had decided to remain in the United States instead of returning to El Salvador, activists redefined this term, associating refugees with helplessness, dependency, and lack of control.... As they rejected the term refugee as disempowering, activists claimed the notion of immigrant that is part of the American immigrant story, according to which self-reliant individuals who are interested in bettering themselves set down permanent roots in the United States.... [A]ctivists contend that Salvadorans are entitled to legal status in the United States, given their now lengthy period of residence, the ties they have created, the work they have performed, the taxes they have paid, and the role that the United States played in the conflict that caused them to emigrate. This argument manipulates the potentially stigmatizing category "immigrant" by suggesting that immigrants benefit rather than harm U.S. society.

As they redefined their community, Salvadoran activists and legal advocates devised new legalization strategies. In contrast to the early 1980s, when Salvadorans saw legalization as a means of preventing untimely and perhaps life-threatening deportations, by the 1990s the goal of legalization had become securing the legal rights enjoyed by citizens and legal permanent residents for Salvadorans who had made their lives in the United States. The TPS program and the *ABC* agreement advanced this goal in that they permitted formerly undocumented Salvadorans to obtain work authorization and other identity documents. Moreover, by the 1990s, the 1986 amnesty program, Salvadorans' marriages to U.S. citizens or legal permanent residents, and the amount of time that Salvadorans had been in the United States expanded the avenues of legalization available to Salvadorans. With U.S. citizen and legal permanent resident siblings, spouses, parents, and children, Salvadorans could qualify for family visa petitions. Those Salvadorans who had immigrated more than seven years ago were eligible to apply for suspension of deportation, which requires demonstrating seven years of continuous residence in the United States, good moral character, and that deportation would be an extreme hardship. Ties with employers made work-related visas and labor certification an option for some. Accordingly, community organizations whose legal programs had focused exclusively on political asylum added suspension of deportation, adjustment of status, family petitions, and naturalization to services they offered clients....

The legalization strategies pursued by Salvadoran immigrants and advocates demonstrate that immigrants have some ability to shape not only their own legal situation but also conditions in their homelands. Just as foreign policies have domestic implications, domestic policies can affect foreign relations and political realities. During the 1980s, activists' efforts to obtain refugee status for Salvadorans addressed not only the domestic problem posed by the sudden influx of Central Americans, but also foreign policy issues regarding human rights violations in El Salvador and the United States' stance regarding the civil war.... [I]n the 1990s, activists argue that enabling Salvadorans in the United States to become legal immigrants would promote democratization in El Salvador by maintaining remittances, forestalling potentially destabilizing deportations, and increasing Salvadorans' political clout in the United States. In short, in defining themselves first as refugees and then as immigrants, activists and advocates have pursued policies that have transnational political and economic implications. Salvadoran immigrants' legalization strategies therefore have the potential to affect the conditions that caused Salvadorans to emigrate in the first place....

FURTHER READING

Arturo Arias, "Central American-Americans: Invisibility, Power and Representation in the US Latino World," *Latino Studies* 1, no. 1 (2003), 168–187.

Arturo Arias, ed., *The Rigoberta Menchú Controversy* (2001).

Arturo Arias, *Taking Their Word: Literature and the Signs of Central America* (2007).

Brenda Carter, Kevan Insko, David Loeb, and Marlene Tobias, eds., *A Dream Compels Us: Voices of Salvadoran Women* (1989).

Norma Stoltz Chinchilla and Nora Hamilton, "Central American Immigrants: Diverse Populations, Changing Communities," in David G. Gutiérrez, ed., *Columbia History of Latinos in the United States since 1960* (2004).

Susan Bibler Coutin, *Legalizing Moves: Salvadoran Immigrants' Struggle for US Residency* (2003).

José Luis Falconi and José Antonio Mazzotti, eds., *The Other Latinos: Central and South Americans in the United States* (2007).

Leon Fink, *The Maya of Morganton: Work and Community in the Nuevo New South* (2003).

María Cristina García, "'Dangerous Times Call for Risky Responses': Latino Immigration and Sanctuary, 1981–2001," in Gastón Espinosa, Virgilio Elizondo, and Jesse Miranda, eds., *Latino Religions and Civic Activism in the United States* (2004).

María Cristina García, *Seeking Refuge: Central American Migration to Mexico, The United States, and Canada* (2006).

Nora Hamilton and Norma Stoltz Chinchilla, *Seeking Community in a Global City: Guatemalans and Salvadorans in Los Angeles* (2001).

Dianne Walta Hart, *Undocumented in L.A.: An Immigrant's Story* (1997).

James Loucky and Marilyn M. Moors, eds., *The Maya Diaspora: Guatemalan Roots, New American Lives* (2000).

Sarah J. Mahler, *American Dreaming: Immigrant Life on the Margins* (1995).

Rigoberta Menchú, *I Rigoberta Menchú: An Indian Woman in Guatemala* (1984).

Cecilia Menjívar, *Fragmented Ties: Salvadoran Immigrant Networks in America* (2000).

Cecilia Menjívar, "Global Processes and Local Lives: Guatemalan Women's Work at Home and Abroad," *International Labor and Working Class History* 70, no. 1 (2006), 86–105.

Victor Montejo, *Voices from Exile: Violence and Survival in Modern Maya History* (1999).

Terry Repak, *Waiting on Washington: Central American Workers in the Nation's Capital* (1995).

CHAPTER 14

Continuing Immigration Debates

Latinas and Latinos have long been recruited as a source of low-wage labor for U.S. indus-
tries, but they have not always been welcomed as permanent residents. This contradiction
continues to shape U.S. immigration policies and the treatment of Latinas/os, regardless of
their legal status and whether they are recent arrivals or members of families that have been
in the United States for many generations. Additional contradictions stem from the inter-
sections of U.S. foreign policy considerations and immigration. Rather than exploring the
complex interactions in the political and economic causes of migration or making decisions
based on individual circumstances, the U.S. government continues to treat most Latina/o
immigrants as economic migrants but characterizes arrivals from Cuba as political migrants
fleeing a repressive government. As a result, debates rage over who should be admitted to
the United States, how undocumented immigrants should be treated, and even who can be
considered an "American" or part of U.S. society.

As employers and the U.S. government have continued to recruit Latinas and Latinos
as low-wage laborers, undocumented immigrants have become vital workers in the agricul-
ture, construction, and service industries. Yet the enforcement of immigration laws in work-
places has been uneven. U.S. officials have generally been more aggressive in punishing
unauthorized immigrants apprehended at workplaces or during routine traffic stops than
they have been in enforcing sanctions on employers for hiring them. Various states and
municipalities have passed anti-immigrant laws. In 1994, California's Proposition 187
sought to eliminate public services for undocumented immigrants, shifting attention away
from Latinas/os' productive labor and their contributions to society, and arguing that
undocumented immigrants were a drain on social services and hence on taxpayers. While
this and other laws have targeted unauthorized immigrants, they have had broader effects.
Legal immigrants and native-born Latinas/os have felt unwelcomed and stigmatized by
this legislation because the general U.S. population often fails to make distinctions among
Latinas/os.

The U.S. government's struggle to reform immigration policies or to pass the DREAM
Act suggests the intensity of these contradictions and debates. Brought to the United
States as minor children by their parents, undocumented children feel the long-term

consequences of the nation's broken immigration system. They face attending college with little financial support due to their lack of legal status, or entering the workforce as undocumented workers. The DREAM Act would provide U.S. citizenship for undocumented students who graduate from college or enlist in the military. This legislation, opponents argue, rewards lawbreakers and encourages others to enter the country illegally. Proponents counter that legalizing the status of exemplary immigrant youth would help the nation make use of their valuable skills and knowledge, and that it is needed on humanitarian grounds since the United States is the only home many of these youth have known. This chapter explores the ongoing contradictions and debates over U.S. immigration policy, as well as the consequences for Latinas/os.

DOCUMENTS

California's Proposition 187 gained national notoriety in 1994, by attempting to deny education and nonemergency health care to undocumented immigrants, as Document 1 reveals. In 1999, an international custody battle was ignited when a Cuban mother perished at sea and her five-year-old child, Elián González, made it to Florida. In Document 2, a journalist describes the struggle that pitted the child's relatives in Florida against his father and paternal grandparents in Cuba. An undocumented student from Costa Rica testifies, in Document 3, before Congress in support of the DREAM Act, which would provide a path to citizenship for youth brought to the United States as children, and who pursue higher education or military service. In 2008, Immigration and Customs Enforcement conducted the largest workplace raid in the nation's history at a meat-processing plant in Postville, Iowa. In Document 4, a court interpreter shares his misgivings about the federal government's unusual legal procedures, which led to the deportation of some 300 unauthorized workers. The United States has long granted asylum to refugees facing persecution in their home countries based on race, religion, nationality, political opinion, or social group. In 2009, a Guatemalan woman obtained political asylum based on domestic abuse. Her case, described in Document 5, was the first in which domestic abuse was accepted as a form of persecution in U.S. asylum petitions. The congressional debate over the DREAM Act, excerpted in Document 6, pitted those opposed to the legislation as a form of amnesty against those who supported it for exemplary youth. Passed in 2010, Arizona's SB 1070 became the nation's most restrictive anti-immigrant law, expanding the immigration enforcement duties of law officers and placing restrictions on undocumented immigrants, as Document 7 depicts. Others states, including Georgia, passed similar anti-immigrant legislation. These laws, however, curtailed the low-wage labor force that domestic agricultural employers relied on, as described in Document 8.

1. California's Proposition 187 Seeks to Deny Education and Non-Emergency Health Care to Undocumented Migrants, 1994

Proposition 187: Text of Proposed Law

SECTION 1. Findings and Declaration.

The People of California find and declare as follows:

That they have suffered and are suffering economic hardship caused by the presence of illegal aliens in this state.

That they have suffered and are suffering personal injury and damage caused by the criminal conduct of illegal aliens in this state.

That they have a right to the protection of their government from any person or persons entering this country unlawfully.

Therefore, the People of California declare their intention to provide for cooperation between their agencies of state and local government with the federal government, and to establish a system of required notification by and between such agencies to prevent illegal aliens in the United States from receiving benefits or public services in the State of California.

SECTION 2. Manufacture, Distribution or Sale of False Citizenship or Resident Alien Documents: Crime and Punishment....

113. Any person who manufactures, distributes or sells false documents to conceal the true citizenship or resident alien status of another person is guilty of a felony, and shall be punished by imprisonment in the state prison for five years or by a fine of seventy-five thousand dollars ($75,000).

SECTION 3. Use of False Citizenship or Resident Alien Documents: Crime and Punishment....

114. Any person who uses false documents to conceal his or her true citizenship or resident alien status is guilty of a felony, and shall be punished by imprisonment in the state prison for five years or by a fine of twenty-five thousand dollars ($25,000).

SECTION 4. Law Enforcement Cooperation with INS....

834b. (a) Every law enforcement agency in California shall fully cooperate with the United States Immigration and Naturalization Service regarding any person who is arrested if he or she is suspected of being present in the United States in violation of federal immigration laws....

SECTION 5. Exclusion of Illegal Aliens from Public Social Services....

(b) A person shall not receive any public social services to which he or she may be otherwise entitled until the legal status of that person has been verified as one of the following:

(1) A citizen of the United States.

(2) An alien lawfully admitted as a permanent resident.

(3) An alien lawfully admitted for a temporary period of time....

Selections from Proposition 187, California Secretary of State, California Ballot Pamphlet, General Election, November 8, 1994.

SECTION 6. Exclusion of Illegal Aliens from Publicly Funded Health Care....

(b) A person shall not receive any health care services from a publicly-funded health care facility, to which he or she is otherwise entitled until the legal status of that person has been verified....

SECTION 7. Exclusion of Illegal Aliens from Public Elementary and Secondary Schools....

48215. (a) No public elementary or secondary school shall admit, or permit the attendance of, any child who is not a citizen of the United States, an alien lawfully admitted as a permanent resident, or a person who is otherwise authorized under federal law to be present in the United States....

(e) Each school district shall provide information to the State Superintendent of Public instruction, the Attorney General of California, and the United States Immigration and Naturalization Service regarding any enrollee or pupil, or parent or guardian, attending a public elementary or secondary school in the school district determined or reasonably suspected to be in violation of federal immigration laws within forty-five days after becoming aware of an apparent violation. The notice shall also be provided to the parent or legal guardian of the enrollee or pupil, and shall state that an existing pupil may not continue to attend the school after ninety calendar days from the date of the notice, unless legal status is established.

(f) For each child who cannot establish legal status in the United States, each school district shall continue to provide education for a period of ninety days from the date of the notice. Such ninety day period shall be utilized to accomplish an orderly transition to a school in the child's country of origin. Each school district shall fully cooperate in this transition effort to ensure that the educational needs of the child are best served for that period of time.

SECTION 8. Exclusion of Illegal Aliens from Public Postsecondary Educational Institutions....

66010.8. (a) No public institution of postsecondary education shall admit, enroll, or permit the attendance of any person who is not a citizen of the United States, an alien lawfully admitted as a permanent resident in the United States, or a person who is otherwise authorized under federal law to be present in the United States....

(c) No later than 45 days after the admissions officer of a public postsecondary educational institution becomes aware of the application, enrollment, or attendance of a person determined to be, or who is under reasonable suspicion of being, in the United States in violation of federal immigration laws, that officer shall provide that information to the State Superintendent of Public Instruction, the Attorney General of California, and the United States Immigration and Naturalization Service. The information shall also be provided to the applicant, enrollee, or person admitted.

SECTION 9. Attorney General Cooperation with the INS....

53069.65. Whenever the state or a city, or a county, or any other legally authorized local governmental entity with jurisdictional boundaries reports the presence of a person who is suspected of being present in the United States in violation of federal immigration laws to the Attorney General of California, that report shall be transmitted to the United States Immigration and Naturalization Service. The Attorney General shall be responsible for maintaining on-going and accurate records of such reports, and shall provide any additional information that may be requested by any other government entity.

2. Cuba Longs for a Little Boy; Family Battles U.S. Relatives for Return of Rescued 6-year-old, 1999

CARDENAS, Cuba, Dec. 9—The door is open to the small house on Cosio Street, a narrow, potholed avenue of crumbling wood and plaster dwellings near the center of this dilapidated town 90 miles east of Havana. Just inside, neighbors are quietly chatting, and a woman is weeping softly into the telephone. Atop a television is a school photo of a smiling, 5-year-old boy dressed in red shorts and a crisp white shirt, knee socks and new sneakers.

The boy is Elian Gonzalez, who on Monday celebrated his sixth birthday away from home....

Elian's fate seems unlikely to be resolved soon, however. In the two weeks since the boy was found floating in an inner tube off the Miami coast and then released by U.S. authorities into the custody of relatives in Miami, he has become a symbol of everything that divides the two countries and Cubans themselves both here and in southern Florida.

The Cuban government has fully mobilized, organizing daily demonstrations, including one that drew hundreds of thousands to Havana's costal highway today. At the rallies, community leaders shout that the child was kidnapped by his mother, who drowned when their small craft capsized during a clandestine voyage to Florida, and is now being held hostage by the United States, despite demands by his father here to send him home.

Washington seems unsure how to proceed. The U.S. government still has legal control of Elian until an immigration hearing, currently scheduled for Dec. 23. American officials here have asked to meet with his father, ... Juan Gonzalez, so that he can document his paternity and demonstrate his active participation in the boy's upbringing. The Cuban government is not yet sure it wants the father to cooperate. It asked Washington today to clarify whether the Immigration and Naturalization Service (INS) or the Florida courts ultimately have jurisdiction over the case.

But the Miami relatives, and the politically powerful Cuban exiles who have embraced Elian in the United States, may have the biggest influence over the long term. They say they won't give the boy back, no matter what.

And therein lies the roots of a family tragedy that, at least in this sad household, dwarfs all the government pronouncements and political arguments in both capitals. Grandfather Gonzalez says he hasn't spoken to his five siblings in Miami since they called with the fantastic news that Elian was with them, and he doesn't want to.

He also said his son, Elian's father, was appalled when relatives in Miami offered to give the boy $2 million as an example of how much better his life would be if he stays in the United States. And he said the boy himself has been tugged in different directions....

"They were divorced about 3 1/2 years ago," [Grandfather Gonzalez, 53,] said of his 31-year-old elder son and Elian's mother, Elizabet, but that didn't prevent them from sharing Elian.

Elian was here most weekends, since his mother usually worked then.... On Monday, when Elian's godmother went to pick him up from school, ... the school said he hadn't been there all day.

The godmother went by the mother's house "and there was nobody there," Gonzalez said. "She met a friend of Elizabet in the street, who said, 'She's gone, they're all gone,'" referring to Elizabet, her live-in boyfriend and Elian.

Later, he said, they learned that the three, and 10 others, had left Sunday morning for good. For Florida.

"I can't imagine that she would do something that would give us such pain," he said.

"I called my brother in Miami that Monday. I spoke to my sister, Caridad," Gonzalez said. "We all had good relations with each other—they've been back here to visit" since the siblings fled in the massive Cuban emigration of the early 1960s. "I said, 'I think they left in a small boat. You have to find out if they got there.' She called back and said they had had no news. They were not in Krome," the INS detention camp in Miami.

On Thursday, Thanksgiving Day in the United States, he said the family here heard on a Miami radio station that a boat had sunk, that people were dead and "that one boy had been found" by local fishermen and been taken to a hospital. Again, they called Miami. "I said, 'Take his photo to the hospital and see if it is him.'"

"Imagine how overjoyed we were when we found out it was Elian," Gonzalez said. "He was two days in the water."

Elian's great aunts and uncles picked him up at the hospital on Friday. "When they got home they called us, and put Elian on the phone" with his father. "He didn't talk much. He said 'Poppy, I saw my mother' go into the water and die." ...

His son started to gather birth and marriage certificates, and had a friend in Havana contact authorities, Gonzalez said. The Cuban government sent diplomatic notes to Washington asking for Elian's return....

... Pointing to a rusted 1956 Rambler, Gonzalez said his son has put the car up for sale to pay for the long distance telephone calls and other expenses....

At Elian's school, ... a sort of shrine has been created. The small, blue table and chair where he sat in his first grade class is there, with his workbooks and a pencil holder on which a photograph of his father, and one of the family together, are pasted. On one table is an array of children's letters and drawings about the missing boy....

As ... [Grandfather] Gonzalez says goodbye to his guest, he hesitates and then reaches into his pocket for his wallet. He opens a wrinkled sheet of yellow paper on which two names and Florida telephone numbers are written—the fishermen who rescued Elian. "I'd like you to do something for me," he says. "Tell them we appreciate with all our hearts what they did for him. We are so grateful.

"Tell them that here in Cuba, they have a family."

3. Costa Rican Student Marie Nazareth Gonzalez Testifies in Congress in Support of DREAM Act, 2007

... [M]y name is Marie Nazareth Gonzalez. I am 21 years old, and I am a junior from Jefferson City, MO, currently attending Westminster College in Fulton, MO.... My family is originally from Costa Rica. I was born in Alajuela, Costa Rica, but have been living in the U.S. since the age of 5. My parents, Marvin and Marina, brought me to the United States in November 1991. Having come over legally, their plan was to become U.S. citizens so we could one day all benefit from living in the land of the free. We sought to live the American dream— the promise of a better education, a better life and, altogether, a better future, what any parent would want for their child....

In April of 2002, after an anonymous person called the Governor's office, where my father was working, our immigration status came into question. Later on, it was confirmed that we were undocumented. From that day forward, my life became a haze of meetings with attorneys, hearings, and rallies. When they heard what we were facing, deportation, the community that knew us in Jefferson City rallied behind my family and me to an overwhelming degree. They knew that we were hardworking, honorable, taxpaying people, and they fought to allow us to stay in the United States.

Members of our Catholic parish, where my mom worked as a volunteer Spanish teacher and after-school care director, joined with other community members to form the Gonzalez Group to rally support by collecting signatures, petitions and organizing phone calls. My classmates, teachers and others also got involved because they considered me to be an important part of their community.

I became involved in advocacy for the DREAM Act right after my senior year of high school.... I had little to fear from speaking out since I was already facing deportation. When I was asked to give the valedictorian speech at the mock graduation in front of the Capitol, I became a national symbol for the DREAM Act.

Eventually, all of the work of so many people on my behalf began to pay off....

On July the 1st of 2005, I got word that the Department of Homeland Security would allow me to stay and defer my departure for 1 year.

My life since April of 2002 can be easily compared to a roller coaster. There have been times when I have felt like I was on top of the world, living out my and my parents' dream of being a successful young woman in college, only to be brought down by the realization that it can be taken away at any moment. The deferral of my deportation has been renewed twice, each time for a year. Last month, when they gave me until June of 2008, they told me it would be my last renewal. If the DREAM Act does not pass by then, I will have to leave, and I will not be able to graduate from college.

U.S. Congress, House Judiciary Committee Hearing on "Comprehensive Immigration Reform: The Future of Undocumented Immigrant Students," 110th Congress, 1st Session, May 18, 2007.

I am only one student and one story. In the course of fighting to remain here, I have been lucky to meet many other students who would also benefit from the DREAM Act. Unlike them, I can speak about this issue in public without risking deportation. I share with them in their fear and their pain and uncertainty. I can personally attest to how life in limbo is no way to live. I have been torn apart from my parents for almost 2 years and have been struggling to make it on my own. I know what it is like to face difficulty and how hard it is to fight for your dreams. No matter what, I will always consider the United States of America my home. I love this country. Only in America would a person like me have the opportunity to be standing in front of you. Many may argue that, because I have a Costa Rica birth certificate, I am Costa Rican and should be sent back, but I tell you I do not feel that way. I hope one day not only to be a U.S. citizen, but to go to law school and to live in D.C. and to continue advocating for others who cannot speak for themselves. Whether that will happen, though, is up to you, our Nation's leaders, and to God.

Thank you....

4. A Court Interpreter Reflects on the Arrests of Undocumented Guatemalan Workers in Iowa, 2008

On Monday, 12 May 2008, at 10:00 a.m. in an operation involving some 900 agents, Immigration and Customs Enforcement (ICE) executed a raid of Agriprocessors Inc, the nation's largest kosher slaughterhouse and meat-packing plant, located in the town of Postville, Iowa. The raid—officials boasted—was "the largest single-site operation of its kind in American history". At that same hour, 26 federally certified interpreters from all over the country were en route to the small neighboring city of Waterloo, Iowa, having no idea what their mission was about. The investigation had started more than a year earlier. Raid preparations had begun in December. The Clerk's Office of the US District Court had contracted the interpreters a month ahead, but was not at liberty to tell us the whole truth, lest the impending raid be compromised....

... I was instructed over phone to meet at 7:00 a.m.... We arrived at the heavily guarded compound, went through security and gathered inside the retro "Electric Park Ballroom", where a makeshift court had been set up.... The [National Cattle Congress] is a 60-acre cattle fairground that had been transformed into a sort of concentration camp or detention center. Fenced in behind the ballroom/courtroom were 23 trailers from federal authorities, including two set up as sentencing courts; ... scores of ICE agents and US Marshals; and ... a gymnasium filled with tight rows of cots where some 300 male detainees were kept, the women being housed in county jails....

... Then began the saddest procession I have ever witnessed, one the public would never see because cameras were not allowed past the perimeter of the

Erik Camayd-Frexias, "Interpreting after the largest ice raid in US history: A personal account," *Latino Studies* 7 (2009), pp. 123–139. Reproduced with permission of Palgrave Macmillan.

compound.... Driven single-file in groups of 10, shackled at the wrists, waist and ankles, chains dragging as they shuffled through, the slaughterhouse workers were brought in for arraignment, and sat and listened through headsets to the interpreted initial appearance, before marching out again to be bused to different county jails, only to make room for the next row of 10. They appeared to be uniformly no more than 5-ft tall, mostly illiterate Guatemalan peasants with Mayan last names, some being relatives ..., some in tears, others with faces of worry, fear and embarrassment. They all spoke Spanish, a few rather laboriously. It dawned on me that aside from their nationality, which was imposed on their people in the 19th century, they too were Native Americans, in shackles. They stood out in stark racial contrast to the rest of us.... They had all waived their right to be indicted by a grand jury, and had accepted instead an *information* or simple charging document by the US Attorney, hoping to be quickly deported, as they had families to support back home. But it was not to be. They were criminally charged with "aggravated identity theft" and "Social Security fraud"—charges they did not understand ... and, frankly, neither could I....

... Of Agriprocessors' 968 current employees, approximately 75 per cent were illegal immigrants. There were 697 arrest warrants, but late-shift workers had not arrived, so "only" 390 were arrested: 314 men and 76 women, 290 Guatemalans, 93 Mexicans, four Ukrainians and three Israelis who were not seen in court. Some were released on humanitarian grounds: 56 mostly mothers with unattended children, a few with medical reasons and 12 juveniles were temporarily released with ankle monitors or directly turned over for deportation. In all, 306 were held for prosecution. Only five of the 390 originally arrested had any kind of prior criminal record. There remained 307 outstanding warrants.

This was the immediate collateral damage. Postville, Iowa (pop. 2273), where nearly half the people worked at Agriprocessors, had lost one-third of its population by Tuesday morning. Businesses were empty, amid looming concerns that if the plant closed it would become a ghost town. In addition to those arrested, many people had fled the town in fear. Several families had taken refuge at St. Bridget's Catholic Church, terrified, sleeping on pews and refusing to leave for days. Volunteers from the community served food and organized activities for the children.... [A]t the elementary and middle school, 120 of the 363 children were absent. In the following days, the principal went around town on the school bus and gathered 70 students after convincing the parents to let them come back to school; 50 remained unaccounted for. Some American parents complained that their children were traumatized.... The principal reported the same reaction in the classrooms, saying that for the children it was as if 10 of their classmates had suddenly died. Counselors were brought in. American children were having nightmares that their parents too were being taken away.... In some cases, both parents were picked up and small children were left behind for up to 72 hours. Typically, the mother would be released "on humanitarian grounds" with an ankle GPS monitor, pending prosecution and deportation.... [T]he mother would have no income and could not work to provide for her children. Some of the children were born in the United States and are American citizens. Sometimes one parent was a deportable alien, whereas the other was not. "Hundreds of families were torn apart by this raid", said a Catholic nun. "The humanitarian impact of this raid is obvious to anyone in Postville. The economic impact will soon be evident"....

... So I faced a frustrating dilemma. I seriously considered withdrawing from an assignment, for the first time in my 23 years as a federally certified interpreter, citing conflict of interest. In fact, I have both an ethical and contractual obligation to withdraw if a conflict of interest exists that compromises my neutrality.... In all my years as a court interpreter, I have taken a front-row seat in countless criminal cases ranging from rape, capital murder and mayhem to terrorism, narcotics and human trafficking. I am not the impressionable kind. Moreover, as a professor of interpreting, I have confronted my students with every possible conflict scenario, or so I thought. The truth is that nothing could have prepared me for the prospect of helping our government put hundreds of innocent people in jail. In my ignorance and disbelief, I reluctantly decided to stay the course and see what happened next.

Wednesday, 14 May, our second day in court, was to be a long one.... Through the day, the procession continued, 10 × 10, hour after hour, the same charges, the same recitation from the magistrates, the same faces, chains and shackles, on the defendants. There was little to remind us that they were actually 306 individuals, except that occasionally, as though to break the monotony, one would dare to speak for the others and beg to be deported quickly so that they could feed their families back home.... Later in the day, three groups of women were brought, shackled in the same manner....

The ... attorney [explained] the uniform Plea Agreement that the government was offering.... "There are three possibilities. If you plead guilty to the charge of 'knowingly using a false Social Security number', the government will withdraw the heavier charge of 'aggravated identity theft', and you will serve 5 months in jail, be deported without a hearing, and be placed on supervised release for 3 years. If you plead not guilty, you could wait in jail for 6–8 months for a trial (without right of bail, as you are on an immigration detainer). Even if you win at trial, you will still be deported, and could end up waiting longer in jail than if you had just pled guilty. You would also risk losing at trial and receiving a 2-year minimum sentence, before being deported"....

That first interview, though, took 3 hours. The client, a Guatemalan peasant afraid for his family, spent most of that time weeping at our table, in a corner of the crowded jailhouse visiting room.... His case and that of a million others could simply be solved by a temporary work permit as part of our much-overdue immigration reform. "The Good Lord knows I was just working and not doing anyone any harm." This man, like many others, was in fact *not* guilty. "Knowingly" and "intent" are necessary elements of the charges, but most of the clients we interviewed did not even know what a Social Security number (SSN) was or what purpose it served. This worker simply had the papers filled out for him at the plant, as he could not read or write Spanish, let alone English.... To him we were part of the system keeping him from being deported back to his country, where his children, wife, mother and sister depended on him. He was their sole support, and he did not know how they were going to make it with him in jail for

5 months. None of the "options" really mattered to him.... He had failed his family, and was devastated.... He stared for a while at the signature page.... Before he signed with a scribble, he said, "God knows you are just doing your job to support your families, and that job is to keep me from supporting mine." There was my conflict of interest, well put by a weeping, illiterate man....

Created by Congress in an Act of 1998, the new federal offense of identity theft ... bears no relation to the Postville cases. It specifically states, "knowingly uses a means of identification of another person with the *intent to commit any unlawful activity or felony*". The offense clearly refers to harmful, felonious acts, such as obtaining credit under another person's identity. Obtaining *work,* however, is not an "unlawful activity." There is no way that a grand jury would find probable cause of identity theft here. But with the promise of faster deportation, their ignorance of the legal system, and the limited opportunity to consult with counsel before arraignment, all the workers, without exception, were led to waive their 5th Amendment right to grand jury indictment on felony charges....

... [T]he Postville charges—document fraud and identity theft—treat every illegal alien as a potential terrorist, and with the same rigor. At sentencing, as I interpreted, there was one condition of probation that was entirely new to me: "You shall not be in possession of an explosive artifact". The Guatemalan peasants in shackles looked at each other, perplexed.

When the executive responded to post-9/11 criticism by integrating law enforcement operations and security intelligence, ICE was created as "the largest investigative arm of the Department of Homeland Security (DHS)" with "broad law enforcement powers and authorities for enforcing more than 400 federal statutes". A foreseeable effect of such broadness and integration was the concentration of authority in the executive branch, to the detriment of the constitutional separation of powers. Nowhere is this more evident than in Postville, where the expansive agency's authority can be seen to impinge on the judicial and legislative powers.... Opportunistically raised by DHS, the sad specter of 9/11 has come back to haunt illegal workers and their local communities across the USA....

5. Guatemalan Woman Obtains Asylum for Spousal Abuse, 2009

In an unusually protracted and closely watched case, the Obama administration has recommended political asylum for a Guatemalan woman fleeing horrific abuse by her husband, the strongest signal yet that the administration is open to a variety of asylum claims from foreign women facing domestic abuse.

The government's assent, lawyers said, virtually ensures that the woman, Rody Alvarado Peña, will be allowed to remain in the United States after battling in *immigration* court since 1995.

Immigration lawyers said the administration had taken a major step toward clarifying a murky area of asylum law and defining the legal grounds on which battered and sexually abused women in foreign countries could seek protection here.

After 14 years of legal indecision, during which several immigration courts and three attorneys general considered Ms. Alvarado's case, the *Department of Homeland Security* cleared the way for her in a *one-paragraph document* filed late Wednesday in immigration court in San Francisco. Ms. Alvarado, the department found, "is eligible for asylum and merits a grant of asylum as a matter of discretion." ...

[Karen] Musalo, director of the *Center for Gender and Refugee Studies* at Hastings College of the Law at the *University of California,* said Ms. Alvarado's "has been the iconic case of domestic abuse as a basis for asylum." ...

In a phone interview Thursday, Ms. Alvarado, who has not been detained and lives in California, where she is a housekeeper at a home for elderly nuns, said she was pleased but also a little dazed and disbelieving....

She said she hoped the outcome in her case would mean that other abused women would receive quicker decisions from the courts.

Homeland Security Department officials were cautious in assessing the implications of the administration's recommendation. The department "continues to view domestic violence as a possible basis for asylum," a department spokesman, Matthew Chandler, said. But such cases ... continue to depend on the specific abuse....

After enduring a decade of violence by her husband, Francisco Osorio, a former soldier in Guatemala, Ms. Alvarado came to the United States in 1995. Over the years, immigration judges have not questioned the credibility of her story. According to court documents, she married when she was 16, and became pregnant soon afterward. In a beating that he apparently hoped would induce an abortion, Mr. Osorio dislocated her jaw and kicked her repeatedly. He also "pistol-whipped Ms. Alvarado, broke windows and mirrors with her head, punched and slapped her, threatened her with his machete and dragged her down the street by her hair," a court filing states....

The large legal question in the case is whether women who suffer domestic abuse are part of a *"particular social group"* that has faced persecution, one criteria for asylum claims....

In a declaration filed recently to bolster Ms. Alvarado's argument that she was part of a persecuted group in Guatemala, an expert witness, [Guatemalan lawyer] Claudia Paz y Paz Bailey, reported that more than 4,000 women had been killed violently there in the last decade. These killings, only 2 percent of which have been solved, were so frequent that they earned their own legal term, *"femicide."* ... In 2008 Guatemala enacted a law establishing special sanctions for the crime....

The resolution of her case is coming too late for Ms. Alvarado to be able to raise her two children, whom she has not seen since she left them in Guatemala. The children, now 22 and 17, were raised by their paternal grandparents, whom they call Mama and Papa.

"It has been tremendously painful for me to know that they do not see me as their mother," Ms. Alvarado said in court papers.

6. Congress Debates the DREAM Act, 2010

Mr. KING of Iowa....

... I would like to be able to say that you are dreaming if you think you can impose amnesty on 2 or more million people that came here illegally and set it up as a reward just because the compassion of your heart says that is what you should do. The people that support the DREAM Act are the people that are looking at this thing in the same way they are supporting the broader overall amnesty policy.... [W]e have seen the immigration law in America has simply been pushed off the edge and hijacked towards the line of opening up our border for the cynical political purposes of wanting to provide for people to come here and vote that will vote for a certain party....

The foundation of [the DREAM Act] ... remains—in-State tuition discounts for kids who are in the United States illegally and then suspends the enforcement of the law against them so that they can't be deported as long as they are going to college—or now we expand it to the military....

... [W]e have someone who is in the country illegally.... So we'll say to them, ... we're going to give you this in-State tuition discount to go to the University of Iowa, and it's going to save you $10,000 a year. That's the equivalent of a $10,000-a-year scholarship fund for someone who is not in the United States legally....

We should also understand that one of the essential pillars of American exceptionalism is the rule of law. And if we have contempt for the rule of law, if we have some of the highest profile people in America openly speak about hiring illegals to take care of their home and at the same time advocate for the DREAM Act, which is amnesty for a specific class of people, reward for illegal behavior, a magnet for bringing more children into the United States that would be here illegally, and getting them to qualify under the DREAM Act so they can go off and be funded partly by the taxpayers and go off to college, or the argument that comes from the Department of Defense, which is that it's good for our military readiness to have the DREAM Act.... Now, how can it be that a Nation of 306 million people can't field an army without granting citizenship to people that are here illegally? ...

It's inconsistent with the rule of law to propose the idea that for national security purposes, we should pass the DREAM Act and put these people that came here illegally into the military and give them citizenship along the way. That undermines the American dream....

★ ★ ★

Mr. CARDIN. Mr. President, I rise today to express my support for the DREAM Act amendment to the 2010 National Defense Administration Act. This is bipartisan legislation that provides sound economic and national security benefits to our Nation.

Congressman Steve King (R-IA), *Congressional Record,* 111th Congress, 2nd Session, September 22, 2010; and Senator Benjamin L. Cardin (D-MD), *Congressional Record,* 111th Congress, 2nd Session, September 23, 2010.

I have long supported the DREAM Act primarily because it provides a pathway forward for young men and women who have played by the rules all of their lives, graduated high school and now want to give back to this country. These are young people who had no say in how or when they came to our country, but somehow, their parents or other relatives brought them here to live a better life.

... We are talking about the innocent children, who, for the most part, have known no other home than America and deserve a way forward now that they are reaching adulthood.

Every year, thousands of undocumented students who live in the United States graduate from high school. Among these students you will find valedictorians, honor roll students, and community leaders who are committed to the United States and their local communities. It is estimated that there are 65,000 such young people who graduate from high school in the United States and find themselves unable to work, go to college, or serve this country in the military.

The young people who would be DREAM Act eligible would have graduated high school, passed a background check and be of good moral character.... DREAM Act-eligible young people are exactly the type of individuals we want to be part of our great society.

The DREAM Act is a smart, targeted piece of legislation that will only benefit children who were brought to this country before the age of 16 and have been living here for at least 5 years....

... the DREAM Act provides clear fiscal benefits to our local communities and our Nation. State and local taxpayers have invested time and money in these young people through elementary and secondary education expecting that eventually they will become contributing, tax-paying members of our society.... [W]hy would any community throw away such an investment?

... Additionally, our own Department of Defense recommended in their 2010–2012 strategic plan the passage of the DREAM Act to help the military "share and maintain a mission-ready All Volunteer Force." The former Secretary of the Army, Louis Caldera, stated "the DREAM Act will materially expand the pool of individuals qualified, ready and willing to serve their country in uniform." The DREAM Act provides a smart and narrow pathway for eligible young people to go on to college or enter our military....

No child should be held accountable for the sins of their parents. This targeted, bipartisan legislation recognizes this fact and shows compassion to the innocent.... These are young people who truly deserve a second chance....

7. Arizona Enacts Immigration Restriction Legislation, 2010

Section. 1. *Intent*

The legislature finds that there is a compelling interest in the cooperative enforcement of federal immigration laws throughout all of Arizona. The legislature declares that the intent of this act is to make attrition through enforcement

---

Selections from State of Arizona's (SB 1070), "Support Our Law Enforcement and Safe Neighborhoods Act," 2010. http://www.azleg.gov/legtext/49leg/2r/bills/sbl070s.pdf.

the public policy of all state and local government agencies in Arizona. The provisions of this act are intended to work together to discourage and deter the unlawful entry and presence of aliens and economic activity by persons unlawfully present in the United States.

Sec. 2. Title 11, chapter 7, Arizona Revised Statutes, is amended by adding article 8, to read:

ARTICLE 8: ENFORCEMENT OF IMMIGRATION LAWS

11-1051. *Cooperation and assistance in enforcement of immigration laws; indemnification*

A. NO OFFICIAL OR AGENCY OF THIS STATE OR A COUNTY, CITY, TOWN OR OTHER POLITICAL SUBDIVISION OF THIS STATE MAY ADOPT A POLICY THAT LIMITS OR RESTRICTS THE ENFORCEMENT OF FEDERAL IMMIGRATION LAWS TO LESS THAN THE FULL EXTENT PERMITTED BY FEDERAL LAW.

B. FOR ANY LAWFUL CONTACT MADE BY A LAW ENFORCEMENT OFFICIAL OR AGENCY OF THIS STATE OR A COUNTY, CITY, TOWN OR OTHER POLITICAL SUBDIVISION OF THIS STATE WHERE REASONABLE SUSPICION EXISTS THAT THE PERSON IS AN ALIEN WHO IS UNLAWFULLY PRESENT IN THE UNITED STATES, A REASONABLE ATTEMPT SHALL BE MADE, WHEN PRACTICABLE, TO DETERMINE THE IMMIGRATION STATUS OF THE PERSON....

C. IF AN ALIEN WHO IS UNLAWFULLY PRESENT IN THE UNITED STATES IS CONVICTED OF A VIOLATION OF STATE OR LOCAL LAW, ON DISCHARGE FROM IMPRISONMENT OR ASSESSMENT OF ANY FINE THAT IS IMPOSED, THE ALIEN SHALL BE TRANSFERRED IMMEDIATELY TO THE CUSTODY OF THE UNITED STATES IMMIGRATION AND CUSTOMS ENFORCEMENT OR THE UNITED STATES CUSTOMS AND BORDER PROTECTION....

E. A LAW ENFORCEMENT OFFICER, WITHOUT A WARRANT, MAY ARREST A PERSON IF THE OFFICER HAS PROBABLE CAUSE TO BELIEVE THAT THE PERSON HAS COMMITTED ANY PUBLIC OFFENSE THAT MAKES THE PERSON REMOVABLE FROM THE UNITED STATES.

F. EXCEPT AS PROVIDED IN FEDERAL LAW, OFFICIALS OR AGENCIES OF THIS STATE AND COUNTIES, CITIES, TOWNS AND OTHER POLITICAL SUBDIVISIONS OF THIS STATE MAY NOT BE PROHIBITED OR IN ANY WAY BE RESTRICTED FROM SENDING, RECEIVING OR MAINTAINING INFORMATION RELATING TO THE IMMIGRATION STATUS OF ANY INDIVIDUAL OR EXCHANGING THAT INFORMATION WITH ANY OTHER FEDERAL, STATE OR LOCAL GOVERNMENTAL ENTITY....

13-2319. *Smuggling; classification: definitions*

A. It is unlawful for a person to intentionally engage in the smuggling of human beings for profit or commercial purpose....

E. NOTWITHSTANDING ANY OTHER LAW, A PEACE OFFICER MAY LAWFULLY STOP ANY PERSON WHO IS OPERATING A MOTOR VEHICLE IF THE OFFICER HAS REASONABLE SUSPICION TO BELIEVE THE PERSON IS IN VIOLATION OF ANY CIVIL TRAFFIC LAW AND THIS SECTION....

13-2928. *Unlawful stopping to hire and pick up passengers for work: unlawful application, solicitation or employment; classification; definitions*

A. IT IS UNLAWFUL FOR AN OCCUPANT OF A MOTOR VEHICLE THAT IS STOPPED ON A STREET, ROADWAY OR HIGHWAY TO ATTEMPT TO HIRE OR HIRE AND PICK UP PASSENGERS FOR WORK AT A DIFFERENT LOCATION IF THE MOTOR VEHICLE BLOCKS OR IMPEDES THE NORMAL MOVEMENT OF TRAFFIC.

B. IT IS UNLAWFUL FOR A PERSON TO ENTER A MOTOR VEHICLE THAT IS STOPPED ON A STREET, ROADWAY OR HIGHWAY IN ORDER TO BE HIRED BY AN OCCUPANT OF THE MOTOR VEHICLE AND TO BE TRANSPORTED TO WORK AT A DIFFERENT LOCATION IF THE MOTOR VEHICLE BLOCKS OR IMPEDES THE NORMAL MOVEMENT OF TRAFFIC.

C. IT IS UNLAWFUL FOR A PERSON WHO IS UNLAWFULLY PRESENT IN THE UNITED STATES AND WHO IS AN UNAUTHORIZED ALIEN TO KNOWINGLY APPLY FOR WORK, SOLICIT WORK IN A PUBLIC PLACE OR PERFORM WORK AS AN EMPLOYEE OR INDEPENDENT CONTRACTOR IN THIS STATE....

13-2929. *Unlawful transporting, moving, concealing, harboring or shielding of unlawful aliens; vehicle impoundment; classification*

A. IT IS UNLAWFUL FOR A PERSON WHO IS IN VIOLATION OF A CRIMINAL OFFENSE TO:

... 2. CONCEAL, HARBOR OR SHIELD OR ATTEMPT TO CONCEAL, HARBOR OR SHIELD AN ALIEN FROM DETECTION IN ANY PLACE IN THIS STATE, INCLUDING ANY BUILDING OR ANY MEANS OF TRANSPORTATION, IF THE PERSON KNOWS OR RECKLESSLY DISREGARDS THE FACT THAT THE ALIEN HAS COME TO, HAS ENTERED OR REMAINS IN THE UNITED STATES IN VIOLATION OF LAW.

3. ENCOURAGE OR INDUCE AN ALIEN TO COME TO OR RESIDE IN THIS STATE IF THE PERSON KNOWS OR RECKLESSLY DISREGARDS THE FACT THAT SUCH COMING TO, ENTERING

OR RESIDING IN THIS STATE IS OR WILL BE IN VIOLATION
OF LAW....

*23-212. Knowingly employing unauthorized aliens; prohibition; false
and frivolous complaints; violation; classification; license suspension
and revocation; affirmative defense*

A. An employer shall not knowingly employ an unauthorized alien. If, in
the case when an employer uses a contract, subcontract or other independent
contractor agreement to obtain the labor of an alien in this state, the employer
knowingly contracts with an unauthorized alien or with a person who employs
or contracts with an unauthorized alien to perform the labor, the employer
violates this subsection....

8. Arizona-Type Legislation Creates Labor Shortages in Georgia, 2011

Reporting from Wray, Ga.—It was a Tuesday afternoon at the height of
blackberry season, and the Paulk family farm was short 100 pickers. It was Don
Pedro's job to find them.

Pedro Guerrero, 54, the smiling, soft-spoken man in black cowboy boots
whom everyone calls Don Pedro, was barreling down two-lane roads in a compact Chevy on a hunt for his own people. He was searching amid the trailers and
tumbledown rental houses and mercados that have sprung up since the 1990s,
when waves of Latinos began arriving in Georgia to harvest food, serve it in restaurants and scrape it from soiled plates.

... On a flip phone, he punched in numbers for guys named Felipe and
Miguel and Sixto, surfing an analog network of cousins and friends of friends
and old sources who might know where the hard workers were....

Don Pedro—like farmers across Georgia—is worried that the state's tough
new immigration law, set to take effect July 1, is scaring away an illegal immigrant labor force.

The Georgia Department of Agriculture this month released a survey of
farmers who said they needed to fill more than 11,000 positions lasting from
one day to a year. Critics of U.S. farming practices have long said Americans
would take such jobs if they paid better.

Don Pedro said his job has never been so tough, nor workers so scarce. His
boss had told the state Labor Department he needed pickers, but he had
received no responses. He wasn't surprised, even though the jobless rate in
Irwin County was 13%. Few here believe that native Southerners, white or
black, wish to return to the land their ancestors once sharecropped or tended in
bondage.

The Paulks, like many of the large landowners in these parts, are white, and
have been working their fields since the late 1800s. For years, they grew row

crops tended by African American sharecroppers using mule power: cotton, then tobacco, then peanuts.

As that farm work became mechanized, many sharecroppers moved away. But in the 1970s, the Paulks switched to delicate fruits—mostly muscadine grapes, and later blackberries—and needed field hands once again. Latinos like Don Pedro were eager to help.

He arrived in 1988, an illegal immigrant from the Mexican countryside who had spent some time in California. He knew his way around a farm, he spoke some English, and he worked hard. Soon he was working for the Paulks as a crew leader and state-licensed labor contractor.

It was a pinnacle of sorts, and a position of stature. Nearly every Latino around here has been hired by Don Pedro or has a relative who has. He is the godfather to many of their children.

He earned his citizenship and eventually saved enough, with the help of a Wal-Mart job on the side, to buy a little 9-acre ranchito....

The five children Don Pedro and his wife raised in Georgia, ages 14 to 30, all work at the farm, full or part time. Son Jesus has an associate's degree; son Eric, 19, is in college. Daughter Nancy, 18, plans to attend in the fall. The five are as much Georgian as Mexican, gliding between Spanish and a Southern-inflected English....

They are some of the most rooted members of an otherwise rootless population. But they too are worried about what the new law might mean for them. With no laborers, what use is a labor contractor? ...

They stood straddling the bushes, working fast and quietly to harvest berries that will be shipped to Sam's Clubs, Costcos and other stores on the East Coast. They were young and old, men and women. Some had pulled tube socks over their arms to protect against the sun. Some wrapped their faces in bandanas. They were almost all Mexican or Guatemalan....

... The picking itself is not strenuous. But the 10-hour shifts in the powerful Georgia sun can be grueling, and dangerous....

The pickers, under federal law, must present identifying documents to work. Farmers acknowledge that some IDs must be phony, but as the Paulks' office manager said, "I don't know what a fake one looks like."

Many other farmers have turned to Don Pedro this year. He found workers to pick Lynn McKinnon's blueberries, but had to lure them over to the Paulks' farm before the job was done, forcing her to finish the job by machine. Blueberries, unlike blackberries, can be machine-picked, but it is not as efficient as hand-picking.

"That made me lose 30% of my fruit," she reminded Don Pedro, who had stopped by to pick up some checks she owed his workers.

McKinnon had been passing out fliers in Florida, promising workers free transportation to Georgia, and free motel stays. She had no takers....

The law, like others around the country, will force many employers to check potential employees' legal status using the federal E-Verify database. It will also give police the power to check the immigration status of criminal suspects. On Monday, a federal judge in Atlanta will consider the argument of immigrant rights activists that the law is unconstitutional and should be blocked.

The activist said farm owners had signed on in solidarity against the law. Tonight, J.W. Paulk was the only farmer in attendance.

The Paulks have been talking about moving to less labor-intensive crops, or using a federal guest-worker program, a move they say will cut into their profits. For now, they need pickers....

About 30 Latinos had come to the meeting. Police had already become more aggressive, they said, with more traffic stops and more arrests. We are not rateros, a man said, not criminals. If we go back to Mexico, said a woman who has lived in Georgia for nine years, what will we go back to? We are from here, she said....

 # ESSAYS

Reflecting the tension between wanting immigrants as a source of low-wage labor but not welcoming them as full members of society, nativist discourse has often grown during periods when economic downturns follow rising immigration. In the first essay, Leo Chavez, professor of anthropology at the University of California, Irvine, traces the emergence of the "new" nativist discourse from the 1994 passage of California's Proposition 187. This law sought to eliminate public services for undocumented immigrants in California, shifting attention from Latinas/os' productive labor to the reproductive sphere of social services. Its passage encouraged national proposals for broader restrictions that would also affect documented immigrants and Latina/o citizens. For Chavez, the new nativist discourse characterizes immigrants as illegitimate residents and highlights the contradictions of recent immigration history, as some claim that nonwhite immigrants threaten U.S. culture, while others insist that the U.S. economy is dependent on immigrant labor.

Continuing to reflect the foreign policy imperatives of U.S. immigration policies, Cubans have enjoyed special treatment among Latina/o immigrants since 1959, because the U.S. government treats them as refugees from a communist country. As Ted Henken, professor of sociology and anthropology at Baruch College, explains in the second essay, U.S. policy toward Cuban immigrants changed in the mid-1990s, when the numbers of Cuban rafters attempting to reach U.S. soil increased dramatically. Yet the new U.S. policy continued to give Cuban immigrants special status by guaranteeing a high number of visas, and by allowing rafters who reach U.S. soil to remain, returning only those rafters apprehended at sea. In contrast, U.S. officials deport rafters from the Dominican Republic and Haiti even if they reach land. According to Henken, more Cuban immigrants arrive with visas than as unauthorized rafters as a result.

Immigration Reform and Nativism

LEO R. CHAVEZ

On November 8, 1994, the voters of California overwhelmingly passed Proposition 187, which was, in the words of its supporters, to "Save Our State" by preventing "illegal aliens in the United States from receiving benefits or public services in the State of California." As with many trends that begin in California, the anti-immigrant sentiment expressed in Proposition 187 rolled across the nation, as other states, some congressional representatives, and presidential candidates expressed the need to deny health care, education, and other publicly funded benefits to immigrants.

... [T]he discourse of immigration reform is situated in a space that crosses over the borders of micropolitics and macropolitics. Local immigration reform discourse can become the national discourse, but in becoming national the local can become transformed.

As California's anti-immigrant discourse flowed across the nation, the anti-"illegal alien" focus of Proposition 187 broadened considerably. Discourse about immigration reform became a way of expressing anger about demographic changes brought on by immigration, targeting anyone who might be suspected of being "immigrant," "foreign looking," "un-American," or different. By eliminating or reducing these stigmatized groups, immigration reform would, in theory, "do something" about the source of the "problems" facing U.S. citizens, problems in the economy, education system, health care, and even the relations of local governments with the federal government. To the proponents of immigration reform, illegal immigrants are not the only problem; immigration in general is a threat to the "nation" that is conceived of as a singular, predominantly Euro-American, English-speaking culture. The "new" immigrants are *transnationalists*, or people who maintain social linkages back in the home country; they are not bound by national borders and their multiple identities are situated in communities in different nations and in communities that cross nations. Transnational migrants threaten a singular vision of the "nation" because they allegedly bring "multiculturalism" and not assimilation....

Proponents of immigration reform, therefore, often cast their net on issues much wider than just illegal immigration. For example, flush with victory after passage of Proposition 187, the proposition's backers announced that their agenda was actually much broader and included affirmative action, bilingual education, and the promotion of English as the official language. Their concerns led U.S. Representative Toby Roth (a Republican from Wisconsin) to introduce a bill that would effectively halt funding for bilingual education, abolish bilingual

Leo R. Chavez, "Immigration Reform and Nativism: The Nationalist Response to the Transnational Challenge," in Juan F. Perea, ed., *Immigrants Out! The New Nativism and the Anti-Immigrant Impulse in the United States* (New York: New York University Press, 1997), pp. 61–78.

electoral ballots, and allow individuals to bring civil suits against institutions that violate English-only federal statutes....

The question of who is an "American" and anti-immigrant discourse become entangled in revealing ways. For instance, on October 18, 1994, California State Senator Craven, a Republican from Oceanside, was quoted as saying "that the [California] state legislature should explore requiring all people of Hispanic descent to carry an identification card that would be used to verify legal residence." By targeting "all Hispanics," citizens, legal residents, and undocumented immigrants, California Senator Craven defines all Hispanics as belonging to a suspect class. Why Senator Craven focuses only on Hispanics is not clear. After all, California's ethnic diversity includes many other ethnic groups, including undocumented Canadians and Europeans who overstay their visas. Perhaps the answer has to do with the assumptions about social evolution and progress implicit in immigration discourse. Discredited nineteenth-century scientific notions about social evolution continue to underlie present-day discourse on national encounters. This discourse positions Euro-Americans and Europeans at the top of a hierarchical ordering of civilized ("developed" and "technologically advanced" being common metaphors for this hierarchy) societies in contrast to less civilized ("less developed" and "technologically backward") societies. Senator Craven expressed these assumptions when addressing a senate hearing on migrant workers held in San Diego in February 1993; he said that "migrant workers were on a lower scale of humanity."

... Pat Buchanan, a presidential candidate during the 1992 and 1996 elections ... said: "A non-white majority is envisioned if today's immigration continues." ... Buchanan would like a moratorium on all immigration to the United States, not merely closing the borders to undocumented immigrants.

The extent to which the anti-immigrant debate is racially polarized is suggested by voting patterns in California. Proposition 187 passed with 59 percent of the votes cast. But white Californians, in particular, appeared to be expressing sentiments of unease over immigration. Two out of three voting whites in California (about 67 percent) voted for the proposition, a significantly larger proportion than the vote among African Americans and Asian Americans (about half of each group voted for it) and Latinos (only 23 percent voted for it). The voting block provided by white voters ensured passage of Proposition 187. Importantly, even though whites account for about 57 percent of California's population, they account for about 80 percent of the voters, thus their views take on tremendous power. In contrast, while Latinos account for 25 percent of the state's population, they accounted for only 8 percent of those voting. White voters in California appear to be sending a symbolic statement about their concern over immigration and the "new" immigrants.

Since passage of Proposition 187 by the voters of California, a number of U.S. Representatives and Senators have submitted bills dealing with the "immigration problem." Following the assumption put forward by proponents of Proposition 187, that social services, not jobs, are the magnet drawing undocumented immigrants to the United States, national immigration reform proposals target aid to immigrants.... In June 1995, a House task force chaired by

Representative Elton Gallegly (Republican from Simi Valley) submitted its report urging an approach similar to Proposition 187 at the national level. The task force recommended denying all public services, except emergency health care, to undocumented immigrants. In order for hospitals to receive reimbursement for treating undocumented immigrants, however, they would have to notify the Immigration and Naturalization Service of the patients before they are discharged. The task force also recommended allowing states to cut off public education to undocumented students. One of the task force's most contentious recommendations is to amend the U.S. Constitution to end automatic citizenship for U.S.-born children whose parents are undocumented immigrants.

Representative Gallegly was an early proponent of this policy. In October 1991, he introduced legislation into Congress to amend the U.S. Constitution to deny citizenship to a child born in the United States if neither of the parents are citizens and if the child's mother is not at least a legal resident. His argument is that even though this is a nation of immigrants, we must reduce immigration—both legal and undocumented:

> ... Today, in many parts of this country our cities and towns are being overrun with immigrants, both legal and undocumented, who pose major economic and law enforcement problems for local governments and place an added burden on their already strained budgets.

Although Gallegly's legislation focuses on the children of undocumented immigrants, his statement clearly makes little differentiation between legal and illegal immigrants. He views immigrants generally as a "problem," as outsiders, regardless of immigration status. Thus, his attempts to stop conferring citizenship on the children of undocumented immigrants appears as but one part of a broader agenda to rid the country of all "outsiders," that is, immigrants and their U.S.-born children....

These emerging views on legal immigration set the context for national immigration reform proposals that target all immigrants, including those legally in the country. For example, Representative E. Clay Shaw, Jr. (a Republican from Florida), proposed that only citizens be provided benefits such as Aid to Families with Dependent Children, food stamps, and Medicaid. Denying these benefits to legal residents, would, according to Representative Shaw, take away the attraction of people to come to this country, that is, welfare and the social safety net. In all, the Republican legislative program for immigration reform that was brought to the U.S. House of Representatives in Proposition 187's wake would deny sixty kinds of federal assistance to millions of legal immigrants, including health programs, Social Security, Supplementary Security Income, disability payments, housing assistance, childhood immunizations, subsidized school lunches, job training, and aid to the homeless. On March 24, 1995, the House of Representatives passed the Personal Responsibility Act, which included many of these proposals to limit social services to legal immigrants.

The U.S. Senate followed the House's example when it passed its own bill on welfare policy on September 19, 1995. The Senate's bill cuts fewer benefits for legal immigrants than the House's but also restricts benefits for naturalized citizens who immigrate after the bill's enactment. If enacted, this would be the first time in U.S. history that government benefits were denied naturalized citizens because they were not born in the United States, thus establishing a two-tiered or segmented structure for citizenship. But even if these parts of the bill are ultimately dropped, they indicate the willingness of policy-makers to treat naturalized citizens differently from U.S.-born citizens. This is a sign of a major reconceptualization of the relationship of immigrants to the nation.

Finally, the U.S. Congress is considering legislation that would reduce the number of legal immigrants from 800,000 to about 535,000 per year. This reduction would be accomplished by eliminating several preference categories for family reunification ... to stop the network migration of extended family members, while allowing nuclear families to continue to reunite in the United States. Eliminating these preferences would shut the door on an estimated 2.4 million foreigners—mostly Mexicans and Filipinos—waiting in queues to enter the United States on the basis of family ties.

In sum, the nativist revolt against undocumented immigrants that began in California quickly reached national proportions, targeting all immigrants. The policy recommendations emanating from state and federal legislators and the discourse spewing forth from presidential candidates are of the sort not heard with such force since the nativist movements of the late 1800s and the early twentieth century.... Traditional definitions of who deserves to be an American and receive the benefits of the social contract are being challenged and redefined in unprecedented ways....

★ ★ ★

Why is anti-immigrant rhetoric so prominent in the contemporary discourse on the state of the nation? To answer this question, we must remember that Americans have always had a love-hate relationship with immigration, despite a congratulatory self-image as a "nation of immigrants." ... [N]ativism and xenophobia have been constant themes in American history, although they become prominent during specific historical moments. Contemporary anti-immigrant posturing can be traced to changes in immigration law, continued undocumented immigration, an economy undergoing repeated cycles of recession, and the end of the Cold War.

In many ways, the "new" nativism sounds strikingly similar to the "old" nativism. In their book *The Immigration Time Bomb,* Richard Lamm, the ex-Governor of Colorado, and Gary Imhoff, an ex-official of the Immigration and Naturalization Service, warn about the perils of immigration in a way that is reminiscent of older laments:

> At today's massive levels, immigration has major negative consequences—
> economic, social, and demographic—that overwhelm its advantages....
> To solve the immigration crisis, we Americans ... have to face the
> necessity of passing laws to restrict immigration and the necessity of
> enforcing those laws. If we fail to do so, we shall leave a legacy of strife,
> violence, and joblessness to our children.

More recently, Peter Brimelow, himself an immigrant from ... Great Britain, has vociferously echoed Lamm and Imhoff's dark scenario for a future of continued immigration. America's problems, according to Brimelow, are due to immigrants who lack the cultural background of earlier European, especially British, immigrants.... Failure to restrict immigration, Brimelow warns, will lead America on the road to becoming an "alien nation."

... In arguing for the urgency of their cause, the proponents of immigration reform often characterize the immigrant as the "enemy" in metaphors of war. Immigrants become the new threat to national security and identity, filling the void left by the loss of the old enemies after the collapse of the Soviet Union and the end of the Cold War....

Immigrants as foreigners who threatened the American way of life was a central part of the Proposition 187 campaign in California. Proponents of Proposition 187 banked on the widely held perception that an "invasion" of undocumented immigrants was the cause of California's economic problems and eroding the lifestyles of U.S. citizens to the point of reducing the nation to a "Third World" country. The reference to "Third World" is a strategic marker that metaphorically alludes to social evolution and the threat of immigration leading to a de-evolution of "American civilization."

... [A] proponent of Proposition 187, Ruth Coffey, the director of Stop Immigration Now, frequently raised the specter of "multiculturalism," commenting that "I have no intention of being the object of 'conquest,' peaceful or otherwise, by Latinos, Asians, blacks, Arabs or any other groups of individuals who have claimed my country." Of course, the irony of Ms. Coffey's statement appears to go unnoticed; as a result of the Mexican American War in the mid 1800s, the United States "conquered" California. An appeal to historical memory, however, can be subtle yet telling. Ronald Prince, one of the cofounders of the Save Our State (SOS) initiative, speaking to a gathering in Orange County, explaining how Proposition 187 would stop undocumented immigration, used a metaphor that harkened back to images of frontier justice, when Mexicans were routinely hanged by vigilante mobs: "You are the posse and SOS is the rope."

Glenn Spencer, founder of the Voice of Citizens Together, ... argued for passage of Proposition 187 because illegal immigration is "part of a reconquest of the American Southwest by foreign Hispanics...." After the passage of Proposition 187, at a rally to deny public education to illegal immigrants and to denounce the Clinton Administration's proposed $40-billion aid package to Mexico, Spencer said, "It boils down to this: Do we want to retain control of the Southwest more than the Mexicans want to take it from us?" ... Spencer's comment was that "What we have in Southern California is not assimilation—It's annexation by Mexico."

Immigrants as a threat to national security, sovereignty, and control of territory is central to the war metaphors as used in debates about immigration....

According to Linda B. Hayes, the Proposition 187 media director for southern California, the loss of U.S. territory can occur as a result of the rapid demographic shifts caused by Mexican immigration. As she wrote in a letter to the *New York Times,*

... If these trends continued, a Mexico-controlled California could vote to establish Spanish as the sole language of California, 10 million more English-speaking Californians could flee, and there could be a statewide vote to leave the Union and annex California to Mexico.

Why people who left a country in search of economic opportunity and a better life would vote to return the state to that country is not explained. Nor is it clear why, in the year 2004, the children and grandchildren of immigrants—all U.S. citizens who did not grow up in Mexico and who will not have the same nostalgia for Mexico as their parents or grandparents—would vote to annex California to Mexico. Of course, such questions may be beside the point since nativist arguments rely more on emotional resonance than the marshaling of empirical evidence and support found in academic treatises.

Proposition 187 and the proposals for immigration reform that followed, then, can be traced to xenophobia related to the changing complexion of immigrants, frustration with the ineffectiveness of the 1986 immigration law to control undocumented immigration, economic recessions, and a new nationalism. As anti-immigrant as the discourse appears, immigration reform targets predominantly women and children, that is, the reproduction of the immigrant labor force....

* * *

... Proposition 187 and most of the immigration reform proposals that followed it target social services, especially health care and education, as the principal attraction to immigrants, both legal and undocumented. The logic is that denial of social services to immigrants reduces the incentives for immigration and thus fewer immigrants will decide to come to the United States. This logic, however, targets reproduction—women and children—and does very little to stop the production-work of immigrant labor.

This is not to suggest that some proposals do not advocate increased funding for the Border Patrol and that the Justice Department does not occasionally "get tough" on employers, because both of these are true. Rather, the point here is that most of the proposals for immigration reform focus on social services, targeting reproduction of the immigrant family and thereby reducing the costs associated with immigrant labor while maintaining, or even increasing, the profits of that labor. It is certainly true that immigrant families have reproductive costs, some of which are subsidized by society, such as education. Immigrant workers, on the other hand, have many benefits for production, since they cost society little to produce (the costs of raising and educating them were borne by their families and home societies), are often willing to perform low-wage work, are typically young and relatively healthy, and are often afraid to pursue, or are unaware of, their rights as workers. By targeting reproduction, immigration reform does very little to undermine the lucrative and highly profitable relationship between employers and workers.

Proposition 187 and most of the immigration reform proposals discussed above do not target production. They leave immigrant workers and their employers curiously out of the picture. For example, Proposition 187 did not advocate more funds for ensuring fair labor standards and practices, thus reducing the incentive for hiring immigrant, especially undocumented, labor. As Labor Secretary Robert B. Reich noted: "One reason that employers in the United States are willing to risk employer sanctions right now and hire illegal immigrants is because they can get those illegal immigrants at less than the minimum wage, put them in squalid working conditions, and they know that those illegal immigrants are unlikely to complain." Nor did the proposition propose increased enforcement of employer sanctions. The implicit message is that we are going after the reproduction of the undocumented labor force not the laborer nor the employer.

The debate surrounding Proposition 187 provides further insight into this point. The proposition's proponents targeted those who are "breaking the law" and don't deserve social service benefits.... Proposition 187, however, targeted only undocumented immigrants' use of social services, not employers who might be breaking the law by hiring undocumented workers. Indeed, in correspondence between Pete Wilson and immigration authorities, Wilson often encouraged the immigration commissioner to stop raids on California companies, arguing that sweeping up undocumented workers caused unnecessary disruptions to business. Such actions stand in marked contrast to anti-immigrant discourse, suggesting that production must be safeguarded but reproduction of the worker's family must be stopped.

Getting rid (the euphemism is "voluntary return migration") of spouses and children would reduce the costs associated with immigrant labor by removing those most likely to use social services. Parenthetically, a more cynical argument is that the objective in denying education and health care to undocumented immigrants is not to pressure them to return to their country of origin but to create a permanent underclass of low-educated, available low-wage workers.... Research has shown, however, that undocumented immigrants come to the United States to work and rarely come to get an education.... Despite the medical and financial implications, the first action Governor Wilson took after passage of Proposition 187 was to move to cut off prenatal care to undocumented women. However, there is absolutely no evidence that if you deny health care for women and children, or deny education or school lunches for children for that matter, that it will do anything to reduce the economic magnet—jobs—that draws immigrant labor to the United States. This is true for both undocumented and legal immigration.

... At the same time that proponents of immigration reform appear to be clamoring for an end or reduction in immigration, there are serious proposals to bring foreign workers to the United States on a temporary basis to work in agriculture and highly competitive high-technology companies. Shortly after the November 1994 elections were over in California, Governor Wilson was in Washington promoting just such a new *bracero* or guest-worker program. An advocate of providing California agribusiness low-cost seasonal labor (guest-workers) when he was a U.S. senator, Wilson again made his plea for a guest-worker program.... Wilson clearly stated his vision of a return to a use of primarily Mexican male labor that would exclude the workers' families: "It makes sense … to have some sort of guest-worker program. But not the kind of thing we have been seeing where there has been massive illegal immigration, where whole families have come and where they are … requiring services that are paid for by state taxpayers." …

This is the logical next step since a guest-worker program institutionalizes the perfect cost-benefit ratio for immigrant labor: bringing foreign workers produced with no costs and who are not allowed to bring their families, thus not incurring reproductive costs (health care, education) here. In essence, production without reproduction, workers without families, sojourners not settlers.…

Even undocumented workers, our unofficial guest-workers, and their families have a remarkable capacity to develop a sense of community in the United States. Although they may have come originally as temporary migrants, over time they marry or bring their spouse and children to join them in the United States, have children born here who therefore become citizens (what I have termed "binational families"), have other relatives and friends living nearby, and have important networks in the labor market. These social and familial developments increase the likelihood of settlement in the United States.

★ ★ ★

What is new in the "new" nativism, perhaps, is the extent to which immigrants, even those who are legal residents and citizens, are being reimagined as less deserving members of the community.… The benefits immigrants have historically brought to this "nation of immigrants" have become overshadowed by the cost of immigration. To be [an] "immigrant" today is tantamount to being a "cost" to society, a cost that must be reduced if the nation is to get its house in order and balance its budget. In the discourse of contemporary social sciences, immigrants have become the less moral, undeserving, and threatening Other in society.

In the current discourse on immigration, race matters but in a less than obvious way.… [T]he category of immigration has replaced the notion of race. In other words, rather than speaking in terms of biological differentiation, genetic inferiority, or social evolution, proponents of immigration reform cloak a "neo-racism" in a language that talks about "scales of humanity," "us and them," "conquest and sovereignty" and "a nonwhite majority." Such phrasing alerts us to the fact that the "new" immigration from Latin America, particularly Mexico, and Asia is qualitatively different from the "old" immigration from Europe.

The new immigrants pose a transnationalist challenge to a narrow nationalist construction of the nation. In this sense, the current wave of immigration reform proposals reflect a nationalist response to this transnational challenge. Immigrants, it is said, are harbingers of a "nonwhite majority," multiculturalism, and an end of English dominance. As a consequence, they are depicted as posing a threat to the fiction of the "national culture" and the nationalist order of society. They undermine the notion of a singular American identity.…

Thus enters the recurrent contradiction in America's immigration history. On the one hand, there are those who have desired immigrant labor because it provides a valuable asset to the economy. On the other hand are those Americans who believe immigrants threaten that which is "American." The specific nature of that threat may find different emphasis during any particular historical moment. In the current epoch, the threat is both cultural and fiscal. The families of immigrant workers have costs to society. Reducing society's obligations and responsibilities to immigrant families is [a] way of balancing the budget but not necessarily a way to produce healthy and educated members of society. Nor are such policies sure to reduce the flow of immigrants, legal or otherwise.... Rather than giving us an accurate portrayal of immigrant motives and behavior, the discourse of immigration reform tells us more about the fears and character of a nation under stress. In this sense, the new nativism is a lot like the old nativism.

Cuban Immigration and the Persistence of Special Treatment

TED HENKEN

Special treatment of Cuban immigrants to the United States since 1959 seemed to end abruptly in May 1995 as a result of migration accords between the US and Cuba following the rafter crisis of 1994. Cubans picked up at sea would now be sent home like other "illegal" immigrants. While the Clinton Administration allowed rafters still in detention at Guantánamo Bay to be paroled into the US, it also sent a message to Castro, the Cuban people, and the increasingly restrictionist US public: the US had control of its borders and would not allow illegal immigration, even from enemy states like communist Cuba.

Notwithstanding Washington's effort to construct a consistent policy toward illegal immigration, this [essay] argues that changes in US policy toward Cuban refugees were neither sudden nor complete. First, resistance to the free entry of Cubans had been mounting for years prior to the 1995 changes, especially during the 1980 Mariel boatlift which brought 125,000 Cubans. Secondly, the Clinton Administration's supposed 180-degree policy shift turned out to be only partial. Rafters *intercepted at sea* are routinely *repatriated* to Cuba, but are rarely *deported* to Cuba after *reaching US soil*. Special treatment of Cuban immigrants continues despite the fact that both the original intent and immediate consequences of the May 1995 accords were to halt unsafe, disorderly, and unauthorized immigration from Cuba to the US....

★ ★ ★

... During the first three-and-a-half years of the [Cuban] revolution (1959–1962), Cubans already in the US were joined by an explosion of 215,000 more. The 1959–1962 period has been characterized as the "golden age" of the Cuban

Ted Henken, "Balseros, Boteros, and El Bombo: Post-1994 Cuban Immigration to the United States and the Persistence of Special Treatment," *Latino Studies* v. 3 (2005): pp. 393–416. Reproduced with permission of Palgrave Macmillan.

exodus. No other US refugee resettlement program has been more generous and accommodating than the Cuban Refugee Program (CRP) set up for the "Golden exiles" and later applied to continuing waves of Cubans.

Four different resettlement agencies were active in assisting the first group to find housing and jobs in Miami or elsewhere. The US government also funded an extensive bilingual education program. Job retraining services were created, a college loan program organized, and unprecedented exceptions made to residency and citizenship laws to enable Cuban success and integration ... American generosity to Cubans went beyond simple humanitarianism. The US had underlying ideological motivations and foreign policy goals during the Cold War. First was the strategic goal of overthrowing the new, Communist government. At the time, Kennedy could easily justify special treatment, claiming that it would end when the Cuban government was overthrown and Cuban exiles went home.

The 1961 Bay of Pigs fiasco made it evident that the exiles would not return soon. Thereupon, a second goal emerged. The US would continue to readily accept Cubans as political refugees because their exit was symbolic proof both of the repressive nature of Cuban Communism and the attractiveness of US democracy. Maintenance of this ideological goal required the practical step of expediting legal regularization and integration of a group initially admitted as temporary exiles. Effectively, all Cuban arrivals were considered to be "refugees from Communism," providing them with virtually unrestrained access to legal immigration.

All told, more than 260,000 additional Cubans immigrated to the US via the 1965–1973 air-lift....

Gradually, members of Congress and officials in the State and Justice departments began to point out the contradiction of an open-door policy, reasoning that open immigration, while good for individual immigrants and as a democratic symbol, actually strengthened the Cuban government by allowing Castro to export dissent to the US. Such concerns intensified over time as Congress was faced with rising costs associated with the air-lift and the various assistance measures of the CRP....

Superficially, the Mariel exodus looks like more of the same special treatment. Indeed, Cubans arriving between May and September of 1980 equaled 250% of the annual world-wide refugee quota of 50,000 set just 3 weeks prior to the Mariel exodus by the Refugee Act of 1980. Furthermore, President Carter's initial welcome seemed to revert to the Cold War definition of a refugee which the new Refugee Act had just changed. Instead of individual asylum determinations based on "persecution or a well-founded fear of persecution," as the new law required the Cubans were again accepted *en masse*.

However, the appearance that *Marielitos* were receiving traditional Cuban advantages belies a more complex reality. "... Reports that the Cuban government was placing convicted criminals and inmates from mental institutions on boats headed for the US fueled calls for halting the exodus." In fact, the US refused them status as "refugees." Instead, the ambivalent term "entrant (status pending)," was used....

The new status reflected intense debate over continued special treatment and some argued that the change was proof that the 1980 Refugee Act had effectively denied Cubans preferential treatment.... The new "entrant" status signaled the first time since the revolution that US immigration policy had turned restrictionist toward Cubans.

When the media emphasized the criminality and low job skills among a fraction of the entrants, President Reagan decided to deny them refugee status, reasoning that they fled poverty, not political repression, and were therefore economic migrants. Additionally, the Congressional Black Caucus pressured the Reagan administration to be consistent in its immigration policy, citing a history of blatant discrimination against Haitian boat-people. This led to the creation of the Justice Department's Cuban-Haitian entrant program which temporarily improved terms for Haitians and began to spread advantages more evenly. By continuing Carter's designation for *Marielitos,* Reagan was able to satisfy those who saw the political refugee designation for Cubans as inaccurate or unfair. However, he succeeded in retaining special programming for entrants, which appeased the Cuban-American community....

... US immigration policy toward Cuban arrivals prior to 1994 was clearly exceptional. The vast majority was welcomed as refugees and received substantial material support after arrival. Even the *Marielitos,* who were not officially labeled refugees, managed to receive many of the same benefits as their predecessors. At the same time, ... the arrivals from Mariel in 1980 were met with even greater ambivalence and concerted official action to deny them special status....

★ ★ ★

By 1994, after five successive years of growth in the number of Cuban rafters rescued by the USCG, unconventional escapes from Cuba reached crisis proportions....

Rafters were still being pulled by the certainty of refugee status upon arrival in the US. Between 1987 and 1994, the US Interest Section in Havana issued visas to only 11,222 (7.1 percent) of the 160,000 maximum allowable number of visas over that period (20,000 per year). "During the same period," however, "the US admitted 13,275 Cubans [mostly rafters] who had arrived in Florida illegally." Moreover, as the number of Cubans granted legal immigrant visas gradually dropped, the numbers of rafters interdicted rapidly increased. From the mid-1980s with an average of 40 annual interceptions of Cuban rafters, numbers shot up to 391 in 1989 and 467 in 1990. Then, in the early 1990s, as economic impact from lost Soviet aid combined with the already acute lack of political and civil liberties on the island, the rafter exodus exploded....

From January to July, 1994, the USCG rescued 4,731 rafters. The US willingness to accept all comers and the increasingly explosive atmosphere in Havana led a frustrated Castro to call Washington's bluff by opening Cuba's harbors in early August allowing thousands more rafters to flee to Florida. As a result, the number of rafters surged to 21,300 rescued in the month of August alone.

The Clinton administration made three tactical responses. First, on August 19, 1994, Clinton reversed policy, announcing that any Cuban rafter picked up in the future would *not* be allowed to enter the US and would be indefinitely detained at a "safe-haven" on the US Naval Base at Guantánamo Bay, Cuba.

Second, those who had successfully made it to Miami before the announcement would be allowed to stay in the country and receive asylum under the 1966 Cuban Adjustment Act. Third, the terms of the US embargo would be strengthened to punish the Cuban government for allowing mass emigration. Despite the denial of refugee status in the past to *Marielitos,* Clinton's first decision was criticized by many observers at the time as complete betrayal of a thirty-five-year-old immigration policy designed to welcome any Cuban as a political refugee....

The Clinton administration opened negotiations with the Cuban government early in September with Cuba agreeing to encourage Cubans to stay "using mainly persuasive means" and promising not to punish returnees. The US agreed to persuade detainees at Guantánamo to return to Cuba and apply to immigrate through official channels. As a result of these measures, by mid-September the exodus had come to a close.

The most important change in US immigration policy toward Cuba stipulated in the accords was a US promise to treat the 20,000 legal immigrant limit as a quota to be filled each year.... [W]hile 20,000 was now the minimum, the inclusion of special refugee admittances and direct relatives of US citizens made 27,845 the new maximum. Furthermore, ... the thousands of Cubans already on the immigration waiting list would be issued visas immediately.... [M]any other immigrant groups such as Haitians and Chinese complained at continuance of special treatment for Cubans....

Following a series of secret negotiations in New York between Cuba's National Assembly chairman, Ricardo Alarcón, and US State Department representative Peter Tarnoff, Clinton reversed his August 1994 policy. On May 2, 1995, he announced that all Cuban rafters still held in the camps at Guantánamo would gradually be paroled into the US over the next nine months but "Cuban emigrants intercepted on the high seas by the US attempting to enter the US will be returned to Cuba" if they could not show proof of having suffered persecution in Cuba.

Although most leaders in the Cuban-American community had acquiesced to both the August 19 safe-haven policy and to the September 9 migration accords, this new move to repatriate Cubans for the first time caused a strong backlash. Rep. Ileana Ros-Lehtinen (R-FL) saw the May 2 agreement as an insidious deal that allowed the Guantánamo rafters into the US, "at the price of 11 million enslaved people in Cuba." ... The Clinton administration openly rejected such an interpretation. "We're not repatriating anyone," explained a senior White House official. "We're rescuing people at sea and doing what we do with anyone – return them to their country when they are trying to immigrate illegally." Finally, the official pointed to the growing desire among the US public to see illegal immigrants deported: "We think there is a general consensus in the US that we can't allow people to arrive on our shores in a disorderly, illegal manner". However, the new *de facto* Cuban immigration policy, often called "wet-foot, dry-foot," allows and even encourages the practice.

★ ★ ★

Legal Cuban immigrants can be divided into three groups. The first and smallest group is the 2,000–3,000 yearly beneficiaries of the US Interest Section's special in-country refugee program and their family members. Special in-country US refugee programs have periodically been set up, as in the case of Cuba, after the President, in conjunction with the US Congress, declares a group of potential refugees "of special humanitarian concern to the US." The limit on refugee admissions for the entire Western Hemisphere is set at 3,000 and most of these go to Cubans who apply for protection at the US Interest Section in Havana. This in-country refugee program currently exists in only a few other countries, including Croatia, Kenya, and Vietnam.

The second group is the direct relatives of US citizens or legal residents who are issued visas each year based on the family reunification criteria of US immigration law. These immigrants must be sponsored by a close relative who is either a US citizen or resident, and while not subject to an absolute numerical limit, often must wait a number of years to immigrate based on yearly global immigration totals and the degree of family priority.

The third, and by far largest group, is the winners of the Cuban visa lottery and their family members. Officially called the Special Cuban Migration Program (SCMP), this lottery ... was set up as a result of the September, 1994 US–Cuba migration talks. Intended to promote safe, legal, and orderly immigration, the SCMP is held biannually and open only to applicants between 18 and 55 years old who must satisfy two of the following three conditions: (1) have a high-school diploma or the equivalent, (2) have three years job experience, or (3) have relatives in the US. Lottery winners are interviewed by the US Interest Section and have a background check. The SCMP was initiated explicitly to bring the total annual number of Cuban immigrants up to the 20,000 minimum commitment made by the US government in the 1994 migration accords. Thus, when lottery winners and their family members are counted, lottery immigrants consistently number around 15,000 each year making them the single largest portion of the Cuban flow since 1994. This special immigration path is open exclusively to Cubans. The 20,000 annual visas guaranteed to Cubans equal the maximum possible number of visas allowed to other countries.

... [A]lthough the persistence of Cuban sea exits has attracted sustained media attention in the 10 years since the 1994 crisis, an arguably much more significant result of the 1995 migration accords is the fact that the number of *legal* Cuban immigrants admitted to the US (more than 200,000) has dwarfed the 10,000 who have managed to arrive by sea. Moreover, Cuba has sent roughly 20 times more legal immigrants between 1995 and 2004 than it did in the preceding decade. In fact, Cuba's yearly total of legal immigrants in each of the past 10 years has placed it among the top 10 sending nations each year.

Therefore, when discussing *unauthorized* Cuban immigration, we would do well to keep in mind that Cuba currently enjoys an extremely generous policy of *legal* immigration and that the major Cuban immigration flow since 1995 has been an orderly, safe, and legal one....

Even with access to such a high number or immigrant visas over the past decade, in each of the three visa lotteries taking place every two years from 1994 to 1998 the number of visa applications has far exceeded the supply.

★ ★ ★

The best-known case of Cuban migrants attempting to make it to the US by means of a hired speedboat is that of Elizabeth Brotóns and her son, Elián González. [See Document 2.] While the tragic deaths of Brotóns and 10 of her fellow passengers and the hotly contested fate of the rescued boy has been the subject of intense media coverage, relatively little attention or analysis has been given to the important shifts in underlying Cuban migration trends of which this episode is a part. In fact, well before the Elián saga, Cuban migration strategies had already begun undergoing an important change by the summer of 1998 from a rafter (*balsero*) to a boater (*botero*) phenomenon.

... [B]etween 1998 and 1999 Cubans stopped trying to evade capture by the Border Patrol once on shore....

... [O]ver the past decade, US officials have detained 9,848 Cubans after making landfall, while just 466 have thought it necessary to run away.... [T]his discrepancy arises from the fact that Cubans know that they need not fear capture once on US soil, rather they must avoid it at sea....

The trend toward utilizing smugglers is more pronounced when we compare the proportion of Cuban "arrivals" (land apprehensions plus estimated escapes) to USCG interdictions during these same years. For example, in 1997 the ratio was roughly 2:5 arrivals to interdictions (171 Cubans arrived on American shores, while 421 were intercepted at sea).... By 1999, however, so many Cubans successfully made landfall that the ratio was reversed, with 2,424 land arrivals and 1,619 interdictions....

... [M]ost Cubans had clearly abandoned non-motorized rafts for more reliable speedboats and successful landing in the US is likely due to increased use of migrant smugglers in the Caribbean.

★ ★ ★

Cuba is not the only nation sending rafters to the US, nor does it send the greatest number. The total flow from the three leading Caribbean countries over the past 10 years shows that Cuba's overall flow during this period is the smallest of the three (19,845), making up less than two-thirds of the Haitian flow (31,058) and less than half of the Dominican flow (44,545)....

... [T]he desperation and hopelessness that lead many Cubans to embark on dangerous sea voyages, while originating from a unique combination of political and economic factors specific to Cuba, are not found only in Cuba. Haitians, Dominicans, Chinese, Ecuadorians, Mexicans, and many others share this desperation and hopelessness. My point is to question Cuban "exceptionalism" by comparing the well-publicized Cuban migration flow in a regional perspective, where other, larger flows are rarely reported on or discussed.

The high numbers of Haitian and Dominican rafters is especially surprising given the fact that neither nationality stands to benefit from the special status granted Cubans under the Cuban Adjustment Act if they succeed in making it to the US. Moreover, Cuba's population of 11.2 million is larger than that of either the Dominican Republic (8.7 million) or Haiti (7.5 million).... As officials from the USIS openly admit, the 20,000 immigrant visas it issues each year in

Havana act as a kind of safety valve allowing Cubans to immigrate safely and legally who may otherwise choose to risk their lives coming by sea without authorization....

... The total number of Coast Guard interdictions for each of the three countries over the past decade shows clearly that Cuban interdictions, though substantial (8,675), have been significantly less common than those of Haitians (14,956) and especially those of Dominicans (19,953).

... Cuban migrants have become adept at successfully evading capture at sea over the past decade and have taken advantage of their special status once ashore.... [W]hen compared with Dominicans and especially Haitians, Cubans have enjoyed a very high probability of making landfall. Thus, the major trend evidenced in these USCG migrant flow statistics is the fact that what has been interpreted largely as a Cuban crisis, is in fact a global phenomenon, including other sending nations in the Caribbean Basin, as well as other farther flung locations such as the People's Republic of China and Ecuador (both of which have been sending large numbers of migrants by sea over the past five to 10 fiscal years).

... [W]hile the initial open-armed welcome given to the "golden exiles" of 1960 has eroded significantly, special treatment has indeed survived efforts at evenhandedness.

The US-Cuba migration accords of 1994 and 1995 achieved short-term success in reducing dangerous maritime migration and encouraging safe, legal, and orderly migration through a generous policy of granting 20,000 immigrant visas annually. However, a policy shift that seemed at the time to be "a complete reversal," has turned out to be much more complex and nuanced in practice. After May 2, 1995, all Cubans picked up at sea were to be returned to Cuba. This important policy change has been consistently enforced.

The great majority of the 8,678 Cubans interdicted at sea between 1995 and 2004 have been repatriated either directly to Cuba, the Bahamas (when interdicted in Bahamian waters), or to a third country (a total of 7,472 out of 8,678 or roughly 86%).... Only 5 percent of the more than 8,600 Cuban migrants intercepted by the Coast Guard have been allowed into the US to pursue claims for political asylum or due to involvement in a crime or for medical emergency....

Despite the fact that the US has complied with the 1994 and 1995 accords by repatriating the vast majority of Cubans interdicted at sea, at the time few observers realized that neither migration accord addressed the continued applicability of the 1966 Cuban Adjustment Act.... In practice, this has meant that virtually all Cubans who make it to US territory, by whatever means, are permitted to stay.

... [B]oth bureaucratic and interest group politics can explain the continuance of Cuban exceptionalism. First of all, the many different local, state, and federal agencies involved in border enforcement often work at cross-purposes and heed different sets of laws leading to what I call "policy by default." For example, the US Coast Guard sees it as its mission to both ensure safety at sea and protect US borders. Thus, it is empowered to halt unauthorized maritime migrants and enforce the US–Cuba migration accords, which require it to intercept and repatriate Cubans (wet-foot), as it does with unauthorized maritime migrants from all sending countries. However, when the Coast Guard must evacuate Cuban migrants to the US in the case of medical emergencies (as in the case of Elián González) or when Cubans successfully make landfall, the USCG loses jurisdiction over them and ... laws such as the Cuban Adjustment Act come into play (dry-foot).

... Although originally passed during the Cold War, the Act was not initially intended as an ideological beacon giving welcome and granting protection to refugees from communism. Instead, it was a practical solution to the fact that most Cuban immigrants to the US after 1959 had entered without a fixed legal status, as they had not expected to stay for very long. However, by 1965 it was apparent that the revolution had been consolidated and Cubans in the US who had expected to return home would need to legalize their immigration status. Thus, the original intent and function of the passage of the Act in 1966 was simply to allow Cubans already physically present in the US to adjust their immigration status from a situation of limbo to that of permanent residency.

... [T]he granting of parole to all Cuban arrivals is *not a mandate* of the Cuban Adjustment Act. Instead, the Act "simply gives the attorney general the authority to parole them." ...

★ ★ ★

The first lesson is that ..., despite all the media attention Cuban rafters have received, little attention has been focused on an arguably much more significant phenomenon of Cuba sending a constant, orderly, and substantial flow of *legal* immigrants to the US over the decade since the 1994–1995 migration accords. Second, the Dominican Republic and Haiti have each had more of their citizens intercepted at sea over the past 10 years than has the more populous island of Cuba.... [T]he Cuban case gets a highly disproportionate amount of attention relative to other rafter-sending countries in the Caribbean.

A second lesson concerns the amount of unauthorized Cuban immigration over the past decade. Directly contradicting common assumptions that unauthorized Cuban immigration is "out of control," what is most surprising about the Cuban flow over the past 10 years is that more Cubans have *not* come to the US as *balseros* or *boteros* given the fact they still suffer from an economic crisis and the lack of many basic political freedoms at home and continue to benefit from exceptional policies upon arrival in the US.... It is clear that the generous allowance of a minimum of 20,000 immigrant visas each year stipulated in the migration accords has had the desired effect of channeling these potent push and pull forces into a safe, legal flow....

A third lesson addresses the admittedly anachronistic Cuban Adjustment Act.... [T]he current interpretation of the Act is a direct violation of the September 1994 migration agreement.... [T]he existence of the Act allows each government to attempt to blame the other for contradictory and often inhumane migration policies. Both governments are right.

On the US side, the USIS in Havana has repeatedly sought to discourage potential Cuban rafters from departing, yet the same government rewards those who make it across successfully by allowing them to stay. The US also seeks to prosecute migrant smugglers for the crime of transporting illegal immigrants to the US, yet allows those who pay them to obtain parole and eventual legal residency if they reach land. Finally, the US government places an increasingly harsh economic embargo on Cuba, yet ignores the fact that the embargo itself contributes to conditions whereby more people will seek to emigrate by any means available, contradicting our efforts to achieve a safe, legal, and orderly migration policy.

There is a strange illogic to having an overall US policy, ... aimed at toppling the Cuban government by cutting off revenue to the island and exacerbating the economic crisis, yet at the same time allowing entry to all Cuban arrivals under the pretext that they are fleeing political persecution and not economic hardship. Furthermore, if the US allows Cubans access to the Cuban Adjustment Act based on their fear of persecution in Cuba, how is it that the Cuban government welcomes the vast majority of these same migrants back within a few years as family visitors? Finally, providing Cubans with exceptional access to the US continues to have the ironic, if unintended, consequence of aiding in the survival of Cuba's current regime by providing an effective safety valve in a time of economic crisis.

On the Cuban side, Cuba's justified criticisms of the Act for encouraging perilous sea crossings ring hollow given its own restrictive and manipulative policies on the free emigration and return of its own citizens.... [T]he Castro government has little credibility in complaining about US immigration policy, which already provides Cuba with access to an extremely generous level of legal immigration.

... [T]he statistics and trends described above give the lie to the Cuban government's claim that it is merely the Cuban Adjustment Act ... that pulls Cubans to the US and causes them to unnecessarily risk their lives at sea. Dominicans, Haitians, Ecuadorians, Chinese, Mexicans, and persons of many other nationalities continue to set out for the US in great numbers, knowing that upon arrival they will not be able to take advantage of such a generous exception to US immigration law, as can Cubans.

... While the end of the Cold War was used for a time as an explanation of the reduced numbers of refugees around the world, such logic only reinforces problematic ideological refugee criteria based on the dubious assumption that only communist regimes practice repression. While the Cuban government likes to claim that all Cuban émigrés are economic immigrants and the US has its own tradition of labeling all Cuban arrivals political refugees, the determination of a migrant's actual mix of motivations is rarely so simple. There continues to be a need to treat all Cuban (and Haitian and Dominican) migrants with the dignity that any human being deserves, without blindly labeling them all illegal immigrants on the one hand or political refugees on the other.

FURTHER READING

Linda Allegro, "Welfare Use and Political Response: Urban Narratives from First and Second-Generation Puerto Ricans and Dominicans in New York City," *Centro Journal* 17, no. 1 (2005), 220–241.

Sarah Banet-Wiser, "Elián González and 'The Purpose of America': Nation, Family and the Child-Citizen," *American Quarterly* 55, no. 2 (2003), 149–178.

Héctor R. Cordero-Guzmán, Robert C. Smith, and Ramón Grosfoguel, eds., *Migration, Transnationalization, and Race in a Changing New York* (2001).

Nicholas De Genova and Ana Y. Ramos-Zayas, *Latino Crossings: Mexicans, Puerto Ricans, and the Politics of Race and Citizenship* (2003).

William V. Flores and Rina Benmayor, eds., *Latino Cultural Citizenship: Claiming Identity, Space, and Rights* (1997).

María Cristina García, "'Dangerous Times Call for Risky Responses': Latino Immigration and the Sanctuary, 1981–2001," in Gastón Espinosa, Virgilio Elizondo, and Jesse Miranda, eds., *Latino Religions and Civic Activism in the United States* (2005).

Greta Gilbertson and Audrey Singer, "The Emergence of Protective Citizenship in the USA: Naturalization among Dominican Immigrants in the Post-1996 Welfare Reform Era," *Ethnic and Racial Studies* 26, no. 1 (2003), 25–51.

Juan Gonzalez, *Harvest of Empire: A History of Latinos in America* (2000, 2011).

Cecilia Menjívar, "Educational Hopes, Documented Dreams: Guatemalans and Salvadoran Immigrants' Legality and Educational Prospects," *The ANNALS of the American Academy of Political and Social Science* 620 (2008), 177–193.

Cecilia Menjívar, "Family Reorganization in a Context of Legal Uncertainty: Guatemalan and Salvadoran Immigrants in the United States," *American Journal of Sociology* 32, no. 2 (2006), 223–245.

Suzanne Oboler, ed., *Latinos and Citizenship: The Dilemma of Belonging* (2006).

Juan F. Perea, ed., *Immigrants Out!: The New Nativism and the Anti-Immigrant Impulse in the United States* (1997).

Alejandro Portes, "The New Latin Nation: Immigration and the Hispanic Population of the United States," in Juan Flores and Renato Rosaldo, eds., *A Companion to Latina/o Studies* (2007).

Alejandro Portes and Rubén G. Rumbaut, *Immigrant America: A Portrait* (2006).

Clara E. Rodríguez, *Changing Race: Latinos, the Census, and the History of Ethnicity in the United States* (2000).

Nestor P. Rodriguez and Cecilia Menjívar, "Central American Immigrants and Racialization in a Post-Civil Rights Era," in José A. Cobas, Jorge Duany, and Joe R. Feagin, eds., *How the United States Racializes Latinos: White Hegemony and its Consequences* (2009).

Victor Rodríguez, *Latino Politics in the United States: Race, Ethnicity, Class, and Gender in the Mexican Americans and Puerto Rican Experience* (2005).

Francisco H. Vázquez, ed., *Latino/a Thought: Culture, Politics, and Society* (2003, 2009).

Carlos G. Vélez-Ibáñez and Anna Sampaio, *Transnational Latina/o Communities: Politics, Processes, and Cultures* (2000).

CHAPTER 15

Pan–Latino Identities

Throughout most of the twentieth century, pan-Latino alliances and identities were difficult to create and sustain. Regional concentrations of Mexican Americans in the Southwest, Puerto Ricans in the Northeast, and Cuban Americans in the Southeast fostered few opportunities for collaboration. Alliances were most frequent in a few specific cities that attracted various Latino populations. The diversity of Latinas and Latinos also complicated efforts to create pan-Latino alliances. Along with distinct national origins and varied migrant/immigrant experiences, citizenship status, socioeconomic class, race, religion, gender, sexuality, and political affiliations were additional factors that influenced alliances. Toward the end of the twentieth century, however, the rapid demographic growth of Latinas/os and their dispersal throughout the nation created more opportunities for inter-Latino interactions. Dominicans, Central Americans, and South Americans joined long-established communities of Mexican Americans, Puerto Ricans, and Cuban Americans. Moreover, as migration from Mexico, Puerto Rico, and Cuba continued, many new arrivals avoided the traditional regions of settlement, finding jobs and social opportunities elsewhere. Mexican immigrants began settling in the Northeast and South, while Puerto Ricans journeyed to the Southeast and Southwest. Others fanned out across rural areas, attracted by a slower pace of life, affordability, and less crime, or recruited there as low-wage agricultural and food-processing workers. These dispersed settlement patterns broke down previous regionalisms, and also created daily opportunities for interactions among Latinas/os of different backgrounds, as they went to school, worked, shared neighborhoods, and sometimes started families together.

By the 1970s, government agencies began using the term "Hispanic" as an umbrella label for all groups whose ancestry linked them to Spanish-speaking countries. Critics charged that this label obliterated the distinct histories, national origins, and cultures of widely divergent populations, and facilitated the negative stereotyping of the entire group. Challenging the term's homogenizing and stigmatizing propensities, "Latino" emerged as a more grassroots term that sought to embrace diversity while building bridges. Many Latinas/os recognized parallels in their histories and experiences, often beginning with the role of U.S. imperialism in their countries of origin and continuing with the ways in which they were racialized in the United States.

Although national identities remained significant, several community efforts forged pan-Latino alliances through political activism, sports, music, and other forms of popular culture. Beginning in the 1980s, movements to restrict bilingual education and to pass English-only laws spurred coalitions among Latinas/os who viewed these nativist efforts as attacks against their communities. Moreover, the daily intermingling of Latinas/os of different backgrounds fostered pan-Latino cultural events such as music and film festivals, as well as sports competitions. While some cultural events originated from community organizations, others were shaped by business concerns. Advertisers and businesses sought to create a broad market for products by promoting the idea of a generic Hispanic audience and clientele. Despite some corporate influence, musical concerts, dance clubs, and sporting events helped bring together distinct Latino populations and fostered pan-Latino identities. This chapter examines various constructions of Latino identities through activism, popular culture, and sports.

DOCUMENTS

College campuses have been one of the arenas where pan–Latino identities have been developed. In 1991, Latino undergraduates launched a hunger strike to pressure Williams College to create courses in Latina/o Studies. Their letter of demands, Document 1, included hiring Latina/o faculty and administrators. The passage of anti-immigrant laws also helped unite Latinas/os in opposition. Document 2 describes a march in Washington, D.C., in which Latinas/os of various national backgrounds protested anti-immigrant legislation and celebrated their commonalities. Like others before them, Latinas/os of Generation X, born roughly between the early 1960s and early 1980s, have created their own cultural mix, incorporating their families' immigrant traditions with U.S. popular culture. The linguistic practices, popular culture contributions, and changing gender roles of Latinas/os in Generation X are the focus of Document 3. Two issues that drew widespread support among Latinos were the campaign to stop the navy's bombardment of the Puerto Rican island of Vieques and the efforts to pass comprehensive immigration reform. In a 2001 speech, in Document 4, Illinois Congressman Luis Gutiérrez ties the movement for peace in Vieques to the struggle to stop the deportation of undocumented workers and provide a path to legalization. Dance clubs, music, and sports are three areas where pan–Latino identities have also been forged. Document 5 describes the pan-Latino nightclub atmosphere of Pan Dulce, a gay nightclub in San Francisco. The musical contributions of various Latina/o artists are the focus of Document 6, which describes the winners of the 2006 Latin Grammys. In Document 7, a journalist depicts the international nature of a St. Louis, Missouri, soccer league, in which many Latino immigrants participate. The diversity of the Latino population found in the 2010 U.S. Census is described in Document 8.

1. Latina/o Students at Williams College Go on Hunger Strike, Calling for Latina/o Studies, 1991

Strikers want respect and official action

To the editor:

We write to you concerning a situation that for Lationo/a, Mexican, and Puerto Rican students here at Williams has become unbearable: the negation of our existence as students with a culture and reality of our own.

When Latino/a, Mexican and Puerto Rican students first come to this college to obtain an education, we come with high hopes for our futures, those of our families, and those of the communities from which we are displaced. Within ourselves, because of our quasi-privileged position, we carry the responsibility to show those brothers and sisters in our race and culture the advantages of rising from the abject socio-economic situation our people have been relegated to since colonization. However, after a few weeks on campus we realize that we have been deceived by the literature of the Admissions Office claiming a utopian multicultural diversity—many of us here, and some who are no longer here, realize that in reality this campus is more oppressive than the societies from which we come.

For the last three years we have talked with as many people as we could in the administration, faculty, and Williams community at large, trying to express what we felt was needed in terms of accepting the dignity of our culture, needs and goals. Yet, we were always told that "in time, this will happen," or that "we must start slow." We are told that we are not sub-citizens culturally, intellectually, or any other form in this community. Yet when a petition is put forth for something as simple as spending a few dollars to bring a salsa band to this college, we have to profusely justify the importance and universality of such an event.

We cannot be part of this community any longer. This college denies the existence of a society that is multicultural, multiracial and multiclass. The bigotry of academia and of this campus can perhaps be ignored by you, but not by us who must deal with it every day (while trying to be normal students).

Today, we start a hunger strike because suddenly we are faced with the reality that offers nothing either for us who are almost graduating nor for those who we leave behind. While our hope would be to change the injustices suffered by us and our families, our petition is much simpler: we want to have at least two classes offered for next fall, one on the Chicano Experience and one on the Puerto Rican Experience in the United States. These classes must be taught by Chicano and Puerto Rican professors.

After wasting three or four education years here at Williams we find ourselves at a crossroads. Nothing but your positive answer on our petition will change our minds. We believe that this is not a fight against what is called do facto racism but rather against institutional racism since it is Williams and its

Benjamin Soriano, Vicente Medrano, Manuel Alfaro, Letter to Williams College administration, April 18, 1991 [copy held by Carmen Whalen].

community that have, by bureaucratic policy, delayed the small petitions put forth by us years ago. Consequently, we have been driven to the point where we will lose even our self-respect if we remain inactive.

We urge you to act, inaction only confirms our accusations.

Manuel Alfaro '91, Vicente Medrano '92, and
Benjamin Soriano '91

A copy of this letter was sent to the college administration and faculty.

2. March on Washington for Immigrant Rights Draws Diverse Latina/o Supporters, 1996

Waving flags of Mexico, El Salvador, Cuba and the United States, tens of thousands of Hispanic people marched here today, mixing ethnic pride with political protest against what they see as growing anti-immigrant and anti-Hispanic sentiment.

"Gone are the days when people could talk about Latinos as a mob without ideas and without a political program," said Juan Jose Gutierrez, director of Coordinadora 96, the coalition that organized the march.

The event, called the Latino and Immigrants' Rights March, was billed as the first mass protest by Hispanic people in the nation's capital. Its organizers, a coalition of labor and liberal advocacy groups, had predicted that 100,000 people would participate. It was difficult to determine whether the event met that goal, since under a new policy mandated by Congress, the United States Park Service is banned from providing crowd estimates.

The major point of the march, the organizers said, was to protest new laws that cut off benefits to legal immigrants who are not citizens, make it more difficult to prove discrimination against companies that fail to hire people they believe to be illegal immigrants and making political asylum harder to get. The Republicans who control Congress were held to blame for the laws, which President Clinton signed....

Organizers presented seven demands, including an end to cutbacks in affirmative-action programs; an increase in the minimum wage, to $7 an hour from $4.75, and the establishment of an amnesty program for illegal immigrants who came to this country before Jan. 1, 1992.

"We're using what we learned in the civil rights movement," said Representative Jose E. Serrano, a Bronx Democrat. "It's like the 60's all over again, which is good and bad. It's good because of the level of activism, but bad because the issues are the same."

But as much as the march and rally reflected Hispanic anger, it was also an attempt by many participants to display pride in their heritage. As if to underscore their double heritage, the rally, held on the Ellipse, south of the White House, began with a choir singing the national anthem in Spanish and English.

"For me, this is a way to validate our presence in the United States in a very friendly way," said Dr. Regina Reanteria Weitzman, a doctor from Washington who immigrated from Mexico City 10 years ago. She added that she hoped "to send a message to Congress and to the President of the United States that we are a people who came here to work, who came here to do good, and we just want to be part of mainstream America."

Javier Salas, a 25-year-old from Germantown, Md., held a hand-lettered sign that said in Spanish, "Soy de la tierra y me llaman extra-terrestre." On the other side was the translation: "I am from Earth and they call me an alien."

The march, which had been planned for three years, took place at a time when a number of Federal reports show that Hispanic people, about 10 percent of the United States population, are not sharing in the nation's general prosperity. While incomes for blacks and whites rose last year, the earnings of Hispanics, who may be of any race, dropped.

A major theme of the event was the need for Hispanic people to unite and not be divided by national origins....

The march began in a park about a mile from the White House and snaked through the streets; sometimes it seemed as much a festival as a protest. The crowd danced to salsa music from compact disc players. The Danza Azteca group, from Washington and Boston, in feathers and costumes worn by Americans before the arrival of Europeans, danced to drums.

But along with an air of gaiety, the talk kept returning to what marchers said was a growing hostility toward Hispanic people, as evidenced by proposals to ban the use of any language except English in government documents and proceedings.

"People are really concerned," said Juan Marinez from East Lansing, Mich., as he walked alongside his father, Efrain, who came from Mexico 73 years ago and whose great-grandfather was born in San Antonio when it was still part of Mexico. "They hear Spanish spoken at the grocery store or at the Kmart, and they say, 'My God, we're being invaded.' But if you really look at it, what was the first European language that was spoken in this hemisphere? It wasn't English."

3. Journalists Describe Generation X Latinos, 1999

... Unlike their Anglo peers, they do not live in the shadow of a more populous baby boom. The Latino population is young and getting younger. "This generation is going to permanently change things," says Rudy Acuña, founding chair of Chicano Studies at Cal State Northridge. "Past generations have always assimilated. This time around, there are enough of them to say, 'We aren't going to make it *your* society. We want to make it on our own terms'."

Bill Teck, 31, set out to name this new power generation. Growing up in Miami, the son of Cuban and American parents, he felt left out of the Generation X rubric, especially the slacker part. "If you're the first generation born and educated in the U.S., you really can't have a slacker mentality." Nothing if not entrepreneurial, he coined the term Generation Ñ—it's pronounced EN-yay, the extra flavor unit in the Spanish alphabet—and copyrighted it in 1995 as a full-service brand. The following year, in the first issue of Generation Ñ magazine, he published a letter that was part come-on, part manifesto. "If you know all the words to [the merengue hit] 'Abusadora' and 'Stairway to Heaven',", it ran, "If you grew up on cafe, black beans and 'Three's Company'... If you're thinking of borrowing one of your father's guayaberas ... You're Generation Ñ." As peers in California toyed with their own rubric, Generation Mex, a cohort—or at least a marketing target—was born.

Better versed in American pop culture than their parents, Ñ's can also be more assertively Latin. In a special NEWSWEEK Poll, Latinos over 35 were most likely to identify themselves as American; those under 35 were more likely to identify as Hispanic or Latino. Often generations removed from the immigrant experience, many Ñ's are now rediscovering—and flaunting—their roots. The son of migrant farm workers, Jaime Cortez, 33, has an Ivy League education—and a San Francisco apartment full of traditional guayabera shirts.... "More and more, you see literary, educated guys doing things that immigrants wanted to get away from.... America has this weird optimism that dictates that we have to leave the past behind. My generation of Latinos doesn't feel that way at all. We know we come from a rich history and culture, and we want to celebrate that. I think that's our defining trait."

The cultural mix, though, is not all salutary. Like other immigrant groups, Latinos in the second and third generations begin to absorb the worst of America: poorer health and diet, higher delinquency and dropout rates, more divorce and domestic abuse. Latino girls recently passed blacks with the highest rates of teen pregnancy, more than double that for whites. "The longer [families] have been in the United States, the better the kids speak English and the higher their self-esteem," says Michigan State sociologist Rubén Rumbaut. "But they also do less homework, have lower GPAs and lower aspirations." The reasons for this pattern are complicated and little-studied, says Rumbaut. Children's superior English skills may upset the family order. Also, second- and third-generation Latinos, who grow up with higher expectations than their immigrant parents, may be less resilient when they encounter discrimination....

At its best, the new wave of Latin-based music now riding the charts reflects the generation's bicultural lives. Though Latin audiences are in large part regionally divided—tropical grooves in the East, Mexican sounds in the South and West—young stars like Ricky Martin and the Colombian rocker Shakira break down the divisions by mixing a variety of pop styles, Latin and Anglo. "We are made of fusion," says Shakira, 22. "It's what determines our identity: the way in one mouthful we take rice, plátanos, meat." Her own music combines Alanis Morissette, reggae and Mexican mariachi sounds.... The musicians' breakthrough, for many Latinos, has become a measure of collective success in

North America. "When I was growing up, it really wasn't cool to be Hispanic," says Adan Quiñones, 22, a real-estate broker in La Puente, a suburb of L.A. "There was pressure to act white. Now, everyone wants to be Latino. If Ricky Martin has helped bring that about, then I certainly admire him."

The attention from Anglo audiences is not always gratifying. [Marc] Anthony, 30, bristles over a recent magazine article that featured jalapeño peppers beside his picture. "Jalapeños are Mexican. I've never eaten one in my life.... This whole 'crossover wave' thing really displaces me," [the singer] says. "Like I'm coming in and invading America with my music. I was born and raised in New York, man."...

Many young Latinas are rejecting the traditional roles that their mothers embraced. "The main difference between our generations is that women are less tolerant," says Ana Escribano, 30, a student at Florida International University who works part-time at Generation Ñ. "Less tolerant of the machismo. Less tolerant of the cheating and doing everything for men." The result is often a culture clash between mother and daughter. The poet and writer Michele Serros, 33, a fourth-generation Mexican-American, calls herself a Chicana Falsa because she felt she didn't live up to ethnic expectations. The women in her family, she says, lived at home until they were married, and wouldn't dream of being on their own. "I grew up on TV, idolized Mary Tyler Moore and 'That Girl'." Her mother and aunts especially "would have never considered dating outside the race." Though her family accepts her Anglo husband, they don't understand why she kept her maiden name. "They think it is disrespectful [toward] my husband."...

Many Ñ's are also wrestling with an even more deeply entrenched tradition: religion. Like their parents, young Hispanics are overwhelmingly Roman Catholic. But their faith is more fluid. In their home in San Francisco, Rod Hernández and Olivia Armas have a traditional big red felt Virgin of Guadalupe over the bed, and they were married in the church. Their future children, they say, will be baptized. Yet they call themselves cultural Catholics. "We respect and honor Catholic traditions, but don't practice it," says Olivia. Enrique Aguilar, 25, says most of his friends feel the same ambivalence. Born in El Salvador, Aguilar came to the United States in 1981, during the revolution, and now manages and co-owns a wireless-accessories company in San Antonio. Although he is a practicing Catholic, he feels less devout than his parents. "In El Salvador there is so much hardship that you have to lean on religion or you will go crazy," he says. "But here we have so much opportunity. We believe in the religion, but we also question it much more."

As some take advantage of these opportunities, though, many are left behind. To get to her classes at Michigan State University, Rosa Salas, 21, drives first past the Mexican-American community in North Lansing, where children walk to a school that is falling apart. A few minutes later, she passes the brand-new high school in neighboring Okemos, where white Anglo kids surf the Internet. "I've got my sociology books in the car so I can discuss race and ethnicity with all the other white kids in my class who never had to deal with race," she says. The trip is a daily reminder that Latinos still trail the rest of the country economically and still have to deal with Anglo prejudice. "I'm tired of people thinking that I just came over the border," says Salas. "I'm tired of people asking me if I got my green card or if I eat tacos every night."

Many face prejudice from other Hispanics as well. With their jumble of races and national origins, Latinos can be as color-conscious as anyone else, says the Dominican-born author Junot Díaz. "Dominicans are anti-Haitian because of anti-African feelings; Puerto Ricans treat Dominicans like Americans treat Puerto Ricans." At the very hip Miami nightclub La Covacha recently, the crowd is energetic, well dressed and universally fair-skinned. Though Miami has a growing Central American community, it is not represented here, either in the clientele or staff. This is no accident, admits promoter Aurelio Rodriguez, a former Armani model. "I'm catering to an upscale South American crowd," he says. "There's big discrimination against Nicaraguans. [They're] considered lower-class."

In Generation Ñ this tension is showing signs of easing. Among other reasons, the threat of recent movements to end affirmative action and restrict immigrants' access to some social benefits has fostered a broader solidarity. At a June press conference by the boxers Oscar De La Hoya and Félix Trinidad to promote their Sept. 18 title fight, most fans hold the national line. Puerto Ricans scream for Trinidad, Mexicans for De La Hoya. But a number switch camps. Amid the cheering, Omar Ortiz, 36, explains, "I'm Puerto Rican, but I'm for De La Hoya. He's proud of his culture, and that gives all Latinos pride."

These are the borders that Generation Ñ is crossing. Their elders may not always understand the new territory, but they are welcome there. In a quiet moment, Rod Hernández's mother, María, takes stock of her son's generation. Maria Hernández, 53, is a supervisor at the U.S. Bankruptcy Court in Riverside, Calif. Rod, she says, is better educated than she or her husband, and has also taught them things about Mexican history and art. For all Olivia's teasing, his Spanish is better than his parents'. And if his life is more chaotically American than theirs, it is in some ways even more respectful of its Latin roots. "My husband and I have always been comfortable with our heritage," María says. "But we were never as demonstrative about it as Rod and Olivia. They've taken it to a higher plane." In these and other ways, Generation Ñ is creating a new Latino America.

4. Congressman Luis Gutierrez Links Amnesty for Undocumented Migrants and Peace in Viequez in a Chicago Speech, 2001

… And what happens in Vieques happens here to us. We want the people of Vieques to be able to do what?—to live in peace and in harmony with the natural resources of that island. And so yesterday I was happy, delighted to be in jail

---

Congressman Luis Gutiérrez, speech at Human Chain demonstration in Chicago, May 1, 2001 (transcription by Mérida Rúa).

with, with the Catholic priest who is in charge of Vieques, with the mayor of Vieques, with Danny Rivera, with Robert Kennedy, with, James Olmos was there with us. I was happy and delighted to be there with them. I was delighted and happy to be there to do what?—to raise the level of awareness about the abuses that the US Navy. The United States cannot continue to be a symbol of freedom, democracy, and the defender of human rights when it abuses the human right of the people of Vieques with the continuing contamination....

... And we're gonna create a movement for the undocumented worker.

They don't need amnesty because they've done nothing wrong. They don't need amnesty cause they've done nothing wrong. They work hard. Sweat and toil everyday and make this nation a better more prosperous place for all.

What we have to do is have a legalization process. A legalization process that allows them to get their documents so that they can *continue* to pay their taxes. So they can continue to contribute. We wanna make sure however that after a long day at work they can get to go home to their families, to their wives, to their children, to their community.

We are tired—of families coming together for dinner and missing a father. Of families coming—together for mass on Sunday and missing a member of their community because the INS has deported them. We're tired of people living in fear and exploitation in a subclass.... Thousands of Americans [hand] their ... most cherished possession[,] hand their children to undocumented workers so they can bathe them and feed them and raise them. If they're good enough to raise the children of future Americans then [they're] good enough to have their documents.

It's unfair for them to raise the children of American citizens and not be able to come home to their children. Everybody in this room knows that you've eaten on a plate that's been cleaned by an undocumented worker. Everybody in this room stayed in a hotel room with toilets been cleaned. Everybody's gone to the supermarket and eaten fruits and vegetables that have been picked with pesticides in terrible conditions by undocumented, 11 million. Does anybody have a plan to deport 11 million—NO. They want to continue to benefit from their work and not give them the respect and the dignity that comes with permanent residency. That's a situation that we won't tolerate anymore.

... If you really love your neighbor as you love yourself and are going to live by that Christian credo.... Their children play with your children. We go to Church with them. We build communities together. What would Chicago be without the Asian [community] along Lawrence and the rest of the city of Chicago? What would Chicago be without the contributions of the Polish community...? What would Chicago be without the Irish and the Italian community? What would Chicago be without immigrants from Africa and from Mexico and Central and South America that built this city?...

We're gonna continue to fight together as members of congress. I am real proud of bring people together around Vieques.... [D]on't you think that it's just wrong that high school students, some of our finest minds in this city and in this nation graduate from high school? From our public school system with high honors and cannot go on to college because they are undocumented[?] They are American as Thomas Jefferson. They came here at an early age and they can't go to college.... They can't get a social security. They speak English. This is their country. And they wanna contribute.

ENGLISH TRANSLATION OF CONGRESSMEN GUTIÉRREZ'S REMARKS IN SPANISH (MAY 1, 2001)

... Here we have to stop the abuse that exists in this country. And let me tell you, I have my daughter Jessica, my daughter Omaira, and my wife.... I will go tonight, I have the honor, the privilege, and the joy to know that my daughters, my family will be together. Shouldn't we want the same for all families? That the father, the mother, the children, and the grandparents—that everyone can be together every night with the security that comes from what?—from legalization.... And my family and I, we don't live in fear of bombardment from the navy. We live here where there is order. We want the same for those who live in Vieques. Therefore, as a Puerto Rican, I ask all of you, Puerto Ricans, Mexicans, Central and South Americans, and of every nationality—Let's remain united because there will be those who want to divide us. Please—let's applaud all the participants of civil disobedience on Vieques.

5. Rafa Negrón and Patrick Herbert Describe a Pan-Latino Nightclub Atmosphere, 2001–2002

Rafa Negrón (2001): "Tim Martinez–a straight boy–and I created Pan Dulce [Sweat Bread]. We created the name [for a nightclub] together. Tim knew. I can't express or emphasize enough how important it was to have someone who knew, that I didn't have to explain – like we were tasting the same thing. And it's important that I say 'tasting.' That's why we really liked the name 'Pan Dulce.' '[C]ause it was always on the tip of our tongue. It was something that was so Latino; it was about food. It is a f-l-a-v-a! that you had to know, that you couldn't tell people. You can *tell* someone about tamarindo, but you can't *explain tamarindo.*"

Patrick Herbert (2002): "I was always clear that Pan Dulce was a pan-Latino, highly caribeño space. One, because of the music – 'cause it was salsa. Two, because I always experienced house as being at the very least African diasporic, and only a certain kind of fluid mexicano, centroamericano appreciated house in my experience in the Bay Area. So, the best house D.J.s I knew were Salvadoran. I mean, it was truly very different than [the club] Futura, and the house music that was spun in Pan Dulce was not the electronica stuff you would hear at Esta Noche or wherever. So, caribeño to me basically means— one of the key components to me is connection to Africa, and so house and salsa both felt caribeño. And because of Rafa, and Adela in particular, who

Interview of Rafa Negrón by Horacio Roque Ramírez, Los Angeles, California, December 26, 2001; interview of Patrick "Pato" Herbert by Horacio Roque Ramírez, Los Angeles, California, September 2, 2002.

were sort of the aesthetic makers, it felt like it was sort of the first Latino social space in San Francisco that felt caribeño. The Mission Cultural Center has felt Latin American, which was one of the first times I've felt the sense of a Latin intelligentsia, and it was what one of the first pan-Latino spaces. But Pan Dulce felt caribeño."

6. Colombian Performer Shakira, the Latin Grammys, and Latina/o Popular Culture, 2006

Shakira, the Colombian singer and songwriter who is both an ambitious artist and a hip-swiveling sex symbol, reigned over Latin music at the Latin Grammy Awards, which were held for the first time in New York City last night at Madison Square Garden. The show began and ended with New York City's durable Latin style, salsa.

Shakira's 2005 Spanish-language album, "Fijación Oral Vol. 1," won awards for album of the year and best female pop vocal album, and her single "La Tortura" won song of the year and record of the year.

She dedicated one of her awards to hard-working Latin immigrants in search of a dream, and another to the city where she grew up, Barranquilla, Colombia....

Last night's show was the seventh Latin Grammy Awards. For its first five years, the show was conducted in English (though it was often bilingual) and was broadcast on the CBS network. Last year, it moved to the Spanish-language network Univision and switched to Spanish throughout.

Even New York City's mayor, Michael R. Bloomberg, spoke Spanish when he arrived onstage behind a chorus line of women in red, though he seemed unaware that "Hasta la vista" is a goodbye, not a greeting.

With awards in 47 categories, from pop to samba to norteño to merengue to Colombian vallenato, the show has from the start juggled many Latin constituencies. This year it emphasized both New York's largest Latin community, Puerto Ricans, and the largest Hispanic group in the United States, Mexican-Americans.

The show's finale was a tribute to New York City as a stronghold of the salsa style developed by Puerto Ricans. It included performances by the Fania All-Stars with two Puerto Rican award winners, the singers Gilberto Santa Rosa (best salsa album) and Andy Montañez (best traditional tropical album).

The program also included a tribute to the Puerto Rican pop star Ricky Martin, named Person of the Year by the Latin Academy of Recording Arts and Sciences, which presents the Latin Grammys. In his speech, after the thank yous, he condemned human trafficking.

An elaborate production number, complete with fireworks, celebrated the Puerto Rican reggaetón beat that has won young audiences across Latin America. Calle 13, a reggaetón group, was named best new artist, and its self-titled debut also won the award for best urban music album....

It was a good night for Gustavo Cerati, who helped invent Latin alternative rock in the 1980s as the leader of Soda Stereo. He was one of the producers on Shakira's album; he also won awards for best rock song and best rock solo album with his own album "Ahí Vamos."...

A collaboration between the Cuban songwriter Pablo Milanés and Mr. Montañez, the Puerto Rican salsa singer, was named best traditional tropical album, while the Puerto Rican singer Olga Tañon won the best contemporary tropical album award. Mr. Milanés also won the award for best singer-songwriter album for his "Como un Campo de Maíz."

The award for Brazilian contemporary pop album went to Sergio Mendes's hip-hop-flavored album "Timeless." Other Brazilian winners included the singers Marisa Monte and Maria Rita and the rock band Os Paralamas do Suceso.

Mexican songwriters won for best rock album, "Casa" by Natalia y la Forquetina, and for best alternative music album, Julieta Venegas's "Limón y Sal."...

Gustavo Santaolalla, the Argentine composer and producer who won an Academy Award for the score for "Brokeback Mountain," shared a Latin Grammy for best tango album for "Café de Los Maestros." The album brought together the elder generation of Argentine tango performers, including some of the final performances by musicians in their 90s who have since died.

Backstage, Mr. Santaolalla said, "It's never too late."

7. Immigrants Create "International" Soccer League in St. Louis, 2008

On a recent Sunday in north St. Louis' DeSoto Park, several hundred onlookers are gathered around two rocky soccer fields. On this sun-kissed afternoon they've come to see a group of weekend warriors do battle in the city's most hardcore amateur soccer league: La Liga Latino Americana de Fútbol.

Brian Bourgschulte, a forward for Real Mardel, a squad mostly composed of Saint Louis University alumni and native St. Louisans, has just scored to put his team up 2-0 over Dinamo, a predominantly Hispanic team....

A graduate of Parkway West High School and a full-time soccer bum, Bourgschulte plays in two other weekly leagues, but says La Liga is "by far the best in terms of competitiveness."

Nearly two decades old, the league has grown from a weekend assemblage of 4 teams—all hailing from the same small town in southwestern Mexico—to 28 teams, with more than 1,000 players representing nearly every corner of the map: Nigeria, Kenya, Iraq, Brazil and Hungary among them. Virtually every country in Latin America fields at least one player, while two, El Salvador and Honduras, have their own teams.

"The more competitive the soccer game is, the more heated it gets. Plus people from Europe and Mexico, or South America, they take the soccer so serious," says the league's president, Alberto Gutiérrez. "Generally speaking, they want to win no matter what."

The smell of Mexican food wafts across DeSoto Park, emanating from food vendors who, on soccer Sundays, throw up tents around the fields to cater to hungry players and their families.

With a propane-powered griddle for warming tortillas and a barbecue to grill large cuts of flank steak, one family cooks authentic asada tacos: They chop the meat into small pieces on a wooden block and sprinkle it with onions and cilantro. Others sell traditional Mexican street fare including bags of fresh fruit and chicharrones—crisp-fried pork skins....

Depending on the popularity of the teams playing, crowds of several hundred people might encircle the fields, from the season's beginning in April to its October finale. Grizzled old Mexican men pace the sidelines, drinking cans of Busch beer and heckling the referees in Spanish. Money slyly changes hands in friendly wagers. Women line up in chairs to gossip and watch their children and husbands play....

The style of play within the ranks of La Liga Latino Americana de Fútbol alternates between fluid, efficient performances and clunky, lumbering ones. For every man who's in peak shape, there's the guy with an ample beer belly. Many players boast college or semiprofessional soccer experience, while many others have never advanced beyond pickup games.

Still, Tom Lutkar, a referee for many of the league's matches and the district administrator for the U.S. Soccer Federation, says the quality of soccer in La Liga is at times topnotch.

"They have an amazing first touch. It's a quick tap-tap-tap. You very seldom see a wild kick," recounts Lutkar. "They have phenomenal ball control and a passion for the game. The level of play depends on which team, but sometimes their skill level is as good as any area college."...

There is no shortage of colorful clubs and players in La Liga. Cobras, currently second in league standings, wears the same uniforms as the elite Champions League team FC Barcelona. Their starting lineup features Hispanic and African players from six different countries. One team member, like their squad's European counterpart, is a Brazilian with a curly ponytail. Naturally, his teammates call him "Dinho," after Barcelona's Brazilian star Ronaldinho.

With players from so many different countries on the field, communication would seem to pose a problem. But the players say it works—as long as they're wearing the same colors.

"It's not hard; it's just the language of soccer," says Barry Meneh, a Nigerian who is one of five African-born players on the club Olimpico. "We don't have to be able to talk to each other for them to give me the ball."

"It does cause problems sometimes," counters Rafael Lopez, a former player for team Alianza who now maintains the league's website, www.futbolstl.com. "If you say a word in a match, the other team's player thinks it's against them."

What is now La Liga Latino was founded in the early 1990s when a small group of friends and family, almost all from the small town of El Llano in the southwestern Mexican state of Michoacán, would gather to play soccer in Tower Grove Park.

The dramatic changes in the area's Hispanic population over the years help explain the expansion. Census statistics show that from 1990 to 2006, St. Louis' Latin-American population doubled from 15,000 to 28,000.

With the city's immigration boom, places like DeSoto Park have become the de facto cultural hubs, settings where many go to speak their native tongue, eat familiar foods and engage in their national pastime.

"We have a great time. We're usually hanging out and barbecuing after the game," says Mario Madera, a seventeen-year veteran of the league and a player and coach of the club Necaxa, which borrows its name from a team in the Mexican professional league.

Moreover, for many players, the soccer matches are as integral a part of their lives in America as the jobs they work during the week.

"Most of the guys on my old team worked with me at a landscaping company," says Jesse Lippert, a former player. "They come in and work in the spring and summer for eight months and play soccer. When the grass stops growing, they go home."

The phenomenon of Hispanic immigrants organizing soccer teams is nothing new. La Liga, in fact, isn't the only Hispanic soccer association in the St. Louis area; both Granite City and St. Charles have their own leagues. Still, everyone knows that La Liga is the premier league....

With a full head of salt-and-pepper hair and cinnamon-colored skin, Alberto Gutierrez, La Liga's president, rarely misses a Sunday match at DeSoto....

Now 49, Gutiérrez immigrated to Southern California from El Llano when he was 13. He moved to St. Louis in 1980 to work at Norfolk Southern Railway, and he's stayed with the company ever since, raising a family in South St. Louis County.

As the volunteer president of La Liga for the past seven years, he has watched the league grow from a small, almost exclusively Hispanic affair into the vast, multicultural network it is today. In addition to implementing fines and suspensions for fighting and leaving trash after games, he handles all the scheduling and player registration and obtains permits from the City of St. Louis to use the fields....

Jack Lyons, codirector of the St. Louis Soccer Hall of Fame and its small museum located just off of South Kingshighway, says that immigrants have long been an integral part of St. Louis' rich soccer tradition.

"One of the first teams was from an area around Carondelet Park that was predominantly Spanish. They had the Spanish Society, which fielded some pretty good teams," Lyons says. "The church is where soccer started. Most of the parishes were made up of immigrants: Irish, German, Italian, English. They gathered socially to play soccer."

Lyons explains that the early amateur leagues set the foundation for St. Louis' place in soccer history. The American team that upset England in the 1950 World Cup consisted largely of Italians from the Hill neighborhood. The Cinderella story, widely regarded as the greatest upset in soccer history— England was a 3-1 favorite to win the Cup; the United States, a 500-1 underdog—was the subject of the Hollywood film The Miracle Match. The movie was filmed partially in Marquette Park, one of the secondary fields where La Liga plays each week....

"The thing I've learned from working these games is that Mexico is not homogenous," adds Roger Morley, a referee in the league. "There tends to be regional affiliations and teams don't always like each other because of that."...

Even with ... confrontations Lutkar, a referee himself, says he admires the players' competitive zeal and La Liga's generally family-friendly environment. "During the playoffs you get people lined up, cheering. You can't even get up next to the field; it's almost a festival atmosphere," he says. "You can see how much passion they have when they get a chance to play organized."...

8. U.S. Census Depicts Latino Diversity, 2010

Hispanics of Mexican, Puerto Rican, and Cuban origin or descent remain the nation's three largest Hispanic country-of-origin groups, according to the 2010 U.S. Census. However, while the relative position of these three groups has remained unchanged since 2000, the next four Hispanic sub-groups grew faster during the decade.

Hispanics of Salvadoran origin, the fourth largest Hispanic country-of-origin group grew by 152% since 2000. The Dominican population grew by 85%, the Guatemalan population by 180% and the Colombian population by 93%. Meanwhile, the Cuban and Puerto Rican populations grow more slowly—44% and 36% respectively.

Country of origin is based on self-described family ancestry or place of birth in response to questions in the Census Bureau's American Community Survey and on the 2010 Census form. It is not necessarily the same as place of birth, nor is it indicative of immigrant or citizenship status. For example, a U.S. citizen born in Los Angeles of Mexican immigrant parents or grandparents may (or may not) identify his or her country of origin as Mexico. Likewise, some immigrants born in Mexico may identify another country as their origin depending on the place of birth of their ancestors.

The 2010 Decennial Census counted 50.5 million Hispanics. Among them, there were 31.8 million Mexican-origin Hispanics—the largest Hispanic country-of-origin group. They are followed by Puerto Rican origin Hispanics, who number 4.6 million in the U.S. and make up 9.2% of all Hispanics. Next are Cubans at 1.8 million or 3.5%, Salvadorans at 1.6 million or 3.3% and Dominicans at 1.4 million or 2.8%.

Census 2010 also revealed that there are now more than one million Guatemalan-origin Hispanics in the U.S. Together, Hispanic-origin populations with more than one million people comprise nine-in-ten (90.7%) of the nation's Hispanics.

T A B L E 15.1   U.S. Hispanic Population, by Country of Origin, 2010

Origin Group	Population (thousands)	Share (%)
Mexican	31,798	63.0
Puerto Rican	4,624	9.2
All other Hispanic	3,452	6.8
Cuban	1,786	3.5
Salvadoran	1,649	3.3
Dominican	1,415	2.8
Guatemalan	1,044	2.1
Colombian	909	1.8
Spaniard	635	1.3
Honduran	633	1.3
Ecuadorian	565	1.1
Peruvian	531	1.1
Nicaraguan	348	0.7
Argentinean	225	0.4
Venezuelan	215	0.4
Panamanian	165	0.3
Chilean	127	0.3
Costa Rican	126	0.3
Bolivian	99	0.2
Uruguayan	57	0.1
Other Central American	32	0.1
Other South American	22	<0.1
Paraguayan	20	<0.1

SOURCE: 2010 U.S. Census (Ennis, Rios-Vargas and Albert, 2011).

ESSAYS

Music, performance, and dance are some of the cultural manifestations in which pan-Latino identities emerge. In the first essay, Horacio N. Roque Ramírez, professor of Chicana/o Studies at the University of California, Santa Barbara, describes a queer Latino nightclub in San Francisco that became an avenue for *latinaje,* the hybrid process of creating pan-Latino spaces from below. Established by a gay Puerto Rican who grew up in California, Pan Dulce was a nightclub where gay Latinas/os could feel at home enjoying Caribbean-inflected music. Pan Dulce had strong community roots because its promoter was involved in

T A B L E 15.2 U.S Hispanic Population Growth, by Country of Origin, 2000–2010

	Population		Growth	
	2010	*2000*	*Number*	*(%)*
All Hispanics	**50,478**	**35,306**	**15,172**	**43.0**
Guatemalan	1,044	372	672	180.3
Salvadoran	1,649	655	994	151.7
Colombian	909	471	438	93.1
Dominican	1,415	765	650	84.9
Mexican	31,798	20,641	11,158	54.1
Cuban	1,786	1,242	544	43.8
Puerto Rican	4,624	3,406	1,218	35.7

NOTE: Hispanic population growth among country of origin groups with a population of 900,000 or more in 2010. Growth rates are computed from unrounded data.

SOURCE: 2010 Census and 2000 Census (Ennis, Rios-Varoas and Albert, 2011).

HIV prevention projects and queer Latino organizations, to which the nightclub's audience was also connected.

Soccer is one of the sports popular among several, though not all, Latino populations. In the second essay, Christopher A. Shinn, lecturer in English at Georgetown University, describes the ways that soccer unites Latinas/os as spectators, consumers, and participants. Television broadcasts of Latin American soccer league games keep recent immigrants connected to their homelands, while the Major League Soccer league in the United States has cultivated fans among immigrant and U.S.-born Latinas/os. While corporate sponsorship injects consumerism into international and national soccer leagues, soccer fans and participants share transnational ties. Local soccer leagues have become arenas where recent immigrants and U.S.-born Latinas/os participate in cross-cultural and community-building processes. Shinn argues that soccer can both promote and undermine nationality, as well as foster new U.S.-based Latina/o identities.

Pan Dulce: A Queer Pan-Latino Space

HORACIO N. ROQUE RAMÍREZ

You have just entered a queer space of Latino desires in San Francisco. It is the summer of 1996, and you are in Pan Dulce on a Sunday night, *boricua* Rafael "Rafa" Negrón's cultural mix and multigendered dance experiment. Here are the bodies and motions of transgender, bisexual, lesbian, and gay women and men (and a few heterosexuals as well) sweating out and drinking away another

Horacio N. Roque Ramirez "'Mira, Yo Soy Boricua y Estoy Aquí': Rafa Negrón's Pan Dulce and the Queer Sonic Latinaje of San Francisco," *Centro: Journal of the Center for Puerto Rican Studies* 19, no. 1 (Spring 2007), pp. 274–313.

weekend in the foggy City by the Bay. The queer complexity of the bodies, genders, and desires present at Pan Dulce fit well into the city's larger history of "alternative" sexualities and cultures, including the generally freer way in which queer and non-queer Latinas and Latinos share social and cultural spaces. Geographically, you are in the South of Market District (SOMA), walking distance from the historically Latino barrio; the Mission District. SOMA is an area of the city historically identified since the early 1960s most easily in relation to leather communities (especially before AIDS), not the place generally for (queer) Latinas and Latinos. Still, we Latinas and Latinos, excited with this new non-white queer space, got on the bus, walked, drove, rode our bike, or went on a quick taxi ride to the corner of 11th and Folsom streets for the promise of pleasures Pan Dulce signified. When you know you don't have a permanent social space, when you realize that you don't have musical and dancing choices every night of the week, or even once a week, as queer *Latinas* have experienced as far back as queer Latino anything in San Francisco goes, being in the house of dance matters. Dancing and music are hardly frivolous, escapist moments from the everyday politics of survival. Dancing and performance can be and have been moments for survival in the racialized late-capitalist queer geography of San Francisco. Pan Dulce was precisely an opportunity to build a momentary queer Latino home.

... I write with a strong historical sense of the relationship among cultures, identities, and survival for queer Latinos and Latinas, centering the life of the short-lived Pan Dulce and what it meant in 1990s Bay Area queer Latino history. I also write with appreciation of the tensions among notions of *latinidad,* specifically Puerto Rican and Caribbean cultures as manifested through Pan Dulce's music and performances on the dance floor and on stage. In particular, the essay illustrates the centrality of Calirican Rafa Negrón's shaping Pan Dulce and, as such, of those spaces queer Latinas and Latinos have sought to build and sustain. Indeed, this is a generation-, West Coast-, and San Francisco-specific pan-Latino configuration of queer latinidad, illustrating the centrality of some Latino cultures at the relative exclusion of others.

... I discuss pieces of the music and dance club scene in relation to the idea of cultural citizenship for queer Latinos in San Francisco. I foreground queer Latino-*caribeño* musical citizenship because it is intimately connected to history, identity making, and community survival. If we agree that music and dance are forms of identity, history, and politics, then explicit attempts to create space and community around these forms are struggles for history and survival.... In the local context of queer and Latino urban realities, Pan Dulce achieved what Ricardo A. Bracho and José Mineros refer to as *latinaje:* the always already plural process of making Latino worlds from below....

★ ★ ★

Anthropologist Renato Rosaldo first proposed the idea of cultural citizenship as a way to describe Latinsos' claims for space, visibility, identity, and rights. These claims, he and others have argued, emerge from people's struggles for inclusion in a society that actively marginalizes them. Whether through voters' initiatives, such as California's Propositions 187 and 209 in the 1990s, respectively targeting undocumented Latino immigrants and affirmative action, or the dismantling of bilingual HIV prevention programming, Latinos remain embattled members of the body politic. As blue-collar workers (nannies, maids, gardeners, day laborers, cooks, janitors), Latinas and Latinos fit well in the national body: they work hard while serving others, generally middle-class whites. But when they claim rights and visibility as Latinas and Latinos with a history and a sense of entitlement— through language rights, for curricular democratization, for effective, non-homophobic HIV services—their "differences" become problematic, even "subversive" for the status quo. When they step off the commodified, exoticised "Latin" space—where and when Latino and Latina identities and subjectivities are meant to add "flavor" and "spice" to otherwise bland consumer cultures— and create their own cultures for inclusion and belonging, Latina and Latino bodies achieve cultural citizenship. The making of the musical space of Pan Dulce was such a space for queer Latino presence in San Francisco in the mid-1990s.

Despite its conceptual breadth, the notion of cultural citizenship has yet to respond to sexual differences, to non-heterosexual Latino communities. All of us do not have access to the same spaces based on our genders and sexualities, real or perceived. While presumably sexually "unmarked" Latinos (but read straight) can lay claim to urban cultural space through festivals and dances, often by invoking strong heteronormative notions of *familia,* queer Latinas and Latinos outside specifically prescribed spaces and events (gay pride, for example) have other issues with which to contend. Safety from sexual violence in the streets, access to clubs or bars catering to queers of color, or the ability to remain "invisible" as a paying customer in a queer space where racial fetishization is common-place—there are relative risks in the search for space where racialized queer genders and sexualities are involved. The question of space and safety for queer Latinas and Latinos cannot be taken for granted.

However useful the notion of cultural citizenship may ultimately be to understand queer sexual community formations, its emphasis on identity and visibility is fitting for conceptualizing a larger queer historical frame. In my research on San Francisco queer Latino/a history, identity and visibility have been central notions in narrators' memories of how they have created cultural and political space. In their narratives, music emerges as a critical tool for community building. The nighttime world of music and dance has afforded opportunities for suspending at least momentarily rigid gender and sexual codes. In the late 1960s and early 1970s, for example, also on Folsom Street but more in the heart of the Mission District, the late Ruben Salazar's nightclub El Intimo housed the performances of the gay Mexican woman-impersonator and dancer Manuel Castillo....

The yet unwritten queer sonic Latino histories of El Intimo more than three decades ago and that of Pan Dulce in the 1990s speak to what Frances R. Aparicio and Susana Chávez-Silverman call *tropicalizations....* "A different, more radical sort of *tropicalization* emerges from the cultural productions, political struggles, and oppositional strategies deployed by some U.S. Latinos/as." It is this ... form of tropicalization that interests me for analyzing the story of Pan Dulce, for the queer Latino club represented a multilayered process for simultaneously creating queerness and Caribbean-inflected latinidades in San Francisco. In doing so, it created a new geography on the border of two predominant ones, what could be differentiated between the gay and predominantly white leather South of Market district and the more straight Latino-dominant Mission. Pan Dulce tropicalized this border zone with multiple bodies and ingredients that offered new possibilities for multigendered queer Latino urban life, and certainly for disrupting this differentiation between bordering communities in this city of neighborhoods. In this momentary, weekly tropicalization from below of the Mission and the city, it was to be a Calirican-inflected version of latinidad in a culturally Mexican-dominant pan-Latino barrio.

... While queer Latinizations can publicly disrupt heteronormativity and whiteness (often simultaneously), the tools, discourses, and symbols for both queerness and latinidad lend themselves easily for consumer capitalism and its profitable projects through commodification. Far from occupying antagonistic positions, projects on behalf of Latino/queer cultural resistance or affirmation in white/straight-majority conditions, and consumer capitalism based precisely on these collective goals for visibility can coexist well. A most (dis)pleasurable example is beer companies' sponsorship of queer, Latino, and queer Latino celebrations. In these effervescent partnerships between capitalist consumption and cultures of marginalized identity and visibility, the most easily recognizable and reductive icons take center stage. Two discourses predominate: that of "*la familia*" (via a Latino picture of brown/dark *mamá, papa, hija e hijo* huddled in happiness, or a "queer family" version of young queers together with smiles, often holding filled beer cups), or that of "*culturas*" invoked again through predictable iconography (for "Latinos," perhaps the sun over a colorful rural vista, or nationally specific icons such as flags, clothing, or musical instruments, and for "queers," the ever popular rainbow flag or pink triangle). In these visual and narrative discourses, Latinizations and tropicalizations can come and go, for they are multidimensional processes that can simultaneously function as exercises in cultural affirmation (in making the space and financial resources available for a festival or a dance) and the means for corporate profits (for the companies successfully selling their goods)....

[Agustín] Laó-Montes's "Latinization from below" comes close to what gay Chicano playwright Ricardo A. Bracho and gay Los Angeles native and San Francisco-based Honduran club promoter José Mineros refer to as latinaje. In large urban centers with significant Latin American and Caribbean populations, they argue, latinaje speaks to that which we Latinos make and create, not quite that which we "are" in a culturally predestined, formulaic way. What is useful about latinaje as well, Bracho explains further, is the term's distancing from the dangerously essentializing and rigidly identitarian notion of latinidad, one primarily functioning on literary, often elite realms. What is particularly useful about latinaje in understanding the lives and meanings in Pan Dulce is its collectivist character in the creation of public cultures, as opposed to a more individual and exclusive latinidad. In the context of the queer Latino club Pan Dulce, latinaje was very much that taking place in the collective experience of the dance floor, the refashioning of queer and Latino space through performance, the (re) interpretation of sound and movement, and the fluidity of genders, sexualities, and identities. Pan Dulce as a structured venue/space allowed for latinaje to create multiple queer latinidades....

★ ★ ★

Rafael "Rafa" Negrón is at the center of the history of Pan Dulce. Born in Germany to his *nuyorican* mother while his Puerto Rican-born father was in military service, Rafa became a traveler and cultural border crosser from a young age, learning the intricacies of identity (re)formation, of intersecting sexual and racial memberships, and of cultural crossings. Settling in New York when Rafa was still a baby, the Negróns made their way to California when young Rafa was seven years old, in part because, as he remembers, his parents wanted a backyard; he was the second oldest and first son, with his three sisters and one brother completing their family unit. Once in California, Rafa learned that while clearly he was not white, neither was he *mexicano* or Chicano, the dominant Latino minority group he saw facing daily discrimination. The most prominent markers of *mexicanidad* he recalls from his youth in the Los Angeles region were poverty and youth violence, along with those of the United Farm Workers (UFW) and its popular grape boycotts, part of the burgeoning Chicano Movement. His politically active mother, engaged in struggles for welfare, educational, and workers' rights, brought the activist energy home and, with it, Chicanos and mexicanos from the community with whom Rafa negotiated learning Spanish. Feeling "special" as a Puerto Rican in California, somewhere between white and Chicano cultures, Rafa recalls strong codes of respect, sacrifice, and honesty from his mother. She herself came out as a lesbian to her children when he was a young teen, which Rafa interpreted as a sign of her honesty with them, opening yet another window for him and his siblings into the possibilities of political and sexual expression. As a gifted student, Rafa functioned in this context of family life around politics, social protest, and sexual difference, combined with his own early covert explorations of gay public sex as a junior high school student in Long Beach. This multicultured, multiracial, and multigendered/sexual background shaped Rafa's persona. Troubling the categories of Whiteness and Latino/Chicano/mexicano in California, but also heterosexuality in both constructs, Rafa straddled these aspects of his experience and identity precisely because of his diasporic Puerto Rican roots. While his Puerto Rican family history was central in shaping his consciousness, so was the racial, cultural, and sexual maneuvering he did as a young gay Calirican.

Music played a central role in the Negrón family household, and it was a space Rafa, as the oldest son, shared closely with his mother. As he explains, Disco was the first sonic medium through which family and neighborhood came together, with home performances becoming a bridge between the two and making economic challenges in the family more bearable.... The experience of blood *and* gay/queer kinship within the Negrón household, then, revolved around a great deal of the experiences shaping the Puerto Rican diaspora: racialized and gendered poverty, resulting economic family dislocation and instability, and a hybrid cultural blending of mainstream forms (Disco) with Latin American, Caribbean diasporic forms, like the boleros which Rafa recalls also being part of the repertoire at the Negrón's. He distinctly remembers Noel Estrada's "En mi Viejo San Juan" as one of the classics heard at home. There and in his surrounding community, musical cultures, languages, sexualities, and racial ethnic political struggles shaped the multifaceted L. A. world through which Rafa made his way as a young gay Calirican....

Finding himself again with other queer Latinos in the San Francisco Bay Area, Rafa navigated a rich geography of social, cultural, and sexual opportunities, often criss-crossing cities, racial groups, nationalities, and genders. It was not unusual for him to seek several spots for nighttime fun and pleasure the same evening.... Still, Rafa and his friends complained to each other that they could not go to a single place to get what they felt they needed as young gay urban Latinos in San Francisco: a racially and nationally mixed Latino cultural style, with the energy of the mostly-white house music scene they could experience in clubs like Universe, and the Black urban male-female energy feel of the Hip-Hop at The Box. These literal sonic movements across the city brought together the categories of Latino, Puerto Rican, Black, and "of color" for Rafa and his friends, and supported what he himself was about to bring together in a single space. The idea was not to collapse these markers, so that they became interchangeable, but to appreciate how opening questions of latinidad and queerness allowed for these borrowings while recognizing the specific contributions from each category.

Several key experiences in Rafa's life coalesced just before giving birth to Pan Dulce. As Rafa ventured musically and sexually in multiple geographies in the early 1990s, he was also becoming a well-known maître d' in the city's restaurant industry. He had also become part of the HIV agency El Ambiente, an English-dominant HIV prevention and education project targeting gay and bisexual Latinos in the city. Rafa had additionally found his way into the Círculo Familiar, a Bay Area group of queer women and men with varying degrees of Puerto Rican identities. Throughout all these associations, Rafa remained a consistent consumer of queer Latino nightlife, a regular "club child" at clubs like the End Up, where he had met promoter and D.J. Joseph Solis. These four corners—El Ambiente, his well-profiled job as Maître D' of the popular restaurant LuLu, the Círculo Familiar, and the city's gay club world—brought Rafa closer to many queer and Latino communities that were becoming more and more visible, and that were recreating the terms for simultaneous racial and sexual identification in the region. At this intersection, placed between communities of color and white communities, between straight and queer, and between several cultural and political settings, Rafa was not then a banner-carrying activist, but a Puerto Rican member at large of the city's queer Latino community who, through sociocultural organizing, was contributing back to his community.

Pan Dulce took form out of these interconnecting queer communities. When the new owners of a club at the corner of 11th Street and Folsom called the respected club promoter and D.J. Joseph Solis to have a Latino night, Solis referred them to Rafa. Hearing the message in his answering machine after returning from a trip to Los Angeles, where he had just met someone who would eventually become a role model and boyfriend, Rafa knew he would need a partner to get a club night going. Thinking of what he and his club friends had wanted for years, he considered seriously the proposition for a club. But Rafa had his own conditions for taking on the challenge…. The D.J. Rafa would meet was to help create a queer version of the multisexual and multinational Latino tropics the Mission District had already experienced in a more straight-dominant form. Unbeknown to Rafa, this simultaneity between pan-national and multisexual Latina and Latino nightlife had a tradition in the Bay Area in clubs like El Intimo in the late 1960s and 1970s, the dances and other social gatherings of organizations like the Gay Latino Alliance in the 1970s, the women's monthly club COLORS since the mid-1980s, and the multigendered but woman-dominant El Río since the 1980s.

Though invested in creating a multiracial, Puerto Rican-inflected Latino queer spot in the city, Rafa recognizes the foundational role the "straight boy" Tim Martinez had for creating Pan Dulce…. Queer and straight club social networks intersected in the creation of Pan Dulce through Rafa's and Tim's collaboration, but so did the pan-Latino histories of migration into the region: Central Americans (Nicaraguans and Salvadorans) and Caribbean peoples (Cubans and Puerto Ricans) were moving into a city where Chicano/mexicano culture was still dominant. As Rafa explains further, the queer Latino club sensation that Pan Dulce became in 1996 and its queer and straight roots had a mix that had everything to do with the feel and flavor for a cultural space that could not be "explained" but experienced [See Document 5]…. Rafa uses the popular Mexican fruit flavor tamarindo to suggest the experiential quality of what he describes Tim and he—as diasporic *caribeños*—just "knew" again suggests the mixing of latinidades in the Mission. His use of "flava" additionally suggests his Puerto Rican-Black intersection through this Hip-hop term, itself a product of diasporic cultures between Jamaica and New York City. Despite this tamarindo reference, the recipe for the *musical* taste for Pan Dulce was jointly created between Rafa and Tim to reflect a *Caribbean* and house music intersection. In the words of Rafa, it was to be "30 to 45 minutes of salsa and merengue, and … a *little* cumbia—if we have to—and then 30 to 45 minutes of good house."…

Invoking the consumption of food, culture, and homoeroticism at the same time, Rafa connects again a distinctly diasporic Puerto Rican tradition with his queer Calirican project of Pan Dulce. In part a response to the relative absence of queer Caribbean Latino cultures in San Francisco, Pan Dulce was not outside circuits of capital accumulation; the club's success, like any other, depended largely on alcohol sales and an overall profit margin for the building owners. Rafa, however, not dependent on the club for personal economic subsistence, followed a more artisan-entrepreneurship model, not focusing on profits but on a creative queer-Latino-centered space for consuming *and* producing queer Caribbean cultures, that is, a queer Latino production from below, a queer latinaje.

From the beginning Pan Dulce was a relatively young crowd of mostly 20-something queer and Latino, but actually multiracial, folk. The crowd included professionals and non-professionals, women and men, students, artists and health workers, (im)migrant and native, white and blue collar, and the working poor. A great many there were connected to the work of the sex-positive HIV agency Proyecto. This link between the HIV agency and the club was no coincidence. Although by the mid-1990s the crisis of AIDS in (gay) Latino communities that began in the mid-1980s had become less extreme than in previous years, HIV and AIDS were still present, for some literally in their bodies as they danced. The few Latino HIV agencies like Proyecto and clubs like Pan Dulce came at a historical juncture in the city: not only was HIV still present, but the gentrification of many of the neighborhoods in the Mission District was a reminder of the precariousness of life for these residents in the city. AIDS and gentrification, in the larger context of poverty, political, and educational disempowerment, literally have been removing Latino bodies from the city for decades. Like the collective experiences of Black queer men in the city, queer Latinos have been overrepresented in the HIV-infection and AIDS-related body count in San Francisco. In addition, the overwhelming context and reminder of the city's cultural and political queer whiteness set yet more markers for our disappearance and marginality.

To speak of Pan Dulce's queer Latina and Latino bodies in motion involves the literal and the figurative. Again, accounting for who was there literally entails the two interrelated histories of AIDS and gentrification in San Francisco. Rafa had been a long-term volunteer with El Ambiente. Well known in the gay Latino community through that work, Rafa was also a friend of poet and activist Ricardo A. Bracho, former underground house club promoter himself and then-coordinator of Proyecto's Colegio ContraSIDA. Many of the bodies that eventually made their way to Pan Dulce were staff, clients, volunteers, or friends and supporters of these agencies, especially of Proyecto. The social networks facilitated through these two well-known gay Latinos and these two queer HIV agencies, in addition to the cadre of club promoters both Rafa and Ricardo knew, made Pan Dulce possible.

The connection to Proyecto in particular made the club's multi-gender character more apparent. Because Proyecto emphasized cogender (women and men) and generally multigender educational programming (an even wider opening for gender expressions that included transgenders), the networks that were facilitated through the agency and that led individuals to Pan Dulce were also more than just gay and male, an audience which would be expected from an HIV agency, and which was true for El Ambiente. Like the space that Proyecto had made in its offices and through its workshops, Pan Dulce had queer women and men: transgender, bisexual, gay, and lesbian, including some in transition from one sex or gender to another. Thus, while gentrification continued in high gear in 1995 in the Mission District, with the rise of the dot-coms in the city, and a young, white professional class displacing many Latino families, and as agencies like El Ambiente and Proyecto continued to carry out preventive AIDS education especially with younger, 20-something queer populations, Pan Dulce became a queer Latino space for respite....

Inside the club on the first floor, several rooms, two bars, and the center dancing floor in front of the performing stage gave ample opportunities for flirting, catching up with friends, and gossiping. Upstairs, on the outside patio, we could smoke, drink, and continue the dialogue and the bodily play with a sense of freedom under the night sky, the fog rolling by above our heads. On the dance floor, with house music and salsa marking the steps, and a few contra-band cumbias occasionally snuck in by long-standing, butch Chicana DJ "Chili D" (Diane Felix), and which, ironically, typically drew the largest crowds to the dance floor, the musical space was one for exciting possibilities. As performance scholar Fiona Buckland explains, "queer world-making" takes specific dimensions in dance clubs. In her case, New York's queer clubs in the 1990s were sites for understanding the relationship between physical space and sexual meanings....

... For the mixed-race, bisexually identified *panameño* and photographer-in-residence Patrick "Pato" Hebert, who was part of Proyecto's network and cadre of cultural workers and art instructors, Pan Dulce represented a new Latino formation straddling musical, geographic, and national boundaries [See Document 5].... In the mixed sonic geography of Pan Dulce that Pato recalls, several identity vectors and national aesthetics take central place: the popular *cubana* transgender health worker and performer Adela Vázquez; Salvadoran D.J.s and their talents spinning house music; and, most centrally in the sonic space, salsa. Through all of these musical forms, (im)migrant bodies, and gendered styles, a local queer Caribe took form through diasporic black and brown cultures.... Given that it was a nightclub, it was through the medium of the music that this particular Caribbean Latino feel emerged....

... To understand contemporary queer Latina and Latino history specifically in the ongoing public health, capitalist, sexual, and gendered and racialized crises that AIDS, gentrification, and incarceration represent in most urban centers, we need to remember that the steps to our resistance are multiple.... The queer sonic *latinaje* that the Calirican Rafa Negrón's Pan Dulce became was precisely one form of such resistance to these forms of domination. A tropicalizing Latinization from below, Pan Dulce produced cultural affirmations and resistance to both heteronormative and whitening practices in the City by the Bay....

U.S. Latinos and Fútbol Nation

CHRISTOPHER A. SHINN

U.S. LATINOS COMING from diverse homelands throughout the Americas nonetheless speak a distinct and widely popular Latin idiom: "fútbol." As the world's most popular sport, the game of fútbol enables Latinos to maintain strong social and cultural ties to Latin America, building upon a long-standing sports history that recalls the beginnings of the World Cup in Uruguay in 1930 and counts a remarkable half of the World Cup titles won by South American countries (Brazil, Uruguay, Argentina). The sport itself necessitates a paradigm shift

Christopher A. Shinn, "Fútbol Nation: U.S. Latinos and the Goal of a Homeland," in Michell Habell-Pallan and Mary Romero, eds., *Latina/o Popular Culture* (New York: NYU Press, 2002), pp. 240–251.

because, historically speaking, the United States never became a fútbol nation as did many of its neighbors in the South. Indeed, the game has often instilled particularly fierce loyalties and deep divisions throughout Latin America in its celebrated and checkered sports past. Close to four thousand casualties resulted in the summer of 1969, for example, when El Salvador mobilized armed forces and invaded Honduras in the so-called Central American Soccer War following the outcome of a qualifying round of the World Cup championship, a clear indication of just how serious this type of play can be.

The wide popularity of fútbol among Latinos, then, might be best understood within the larger cultural and historical framework of the game's privileged position among the various and dispersed peoples of Latin America. For Latino communities, given the history of fútbol in Latin America and their ties to this history, the game clearly constitutes a source of Latino/a pride, cultural tradition, popular folklore, and psychic and social connection to distant homelands [See Document 7]. Thanks to media and closed-circuit television, Guatemalans in the United States can continue to follow the Central American games (CONCACAF), while Mexican Americans can watch Mexican fútbol matches on Univisión, Fox Sports, World Español, or Galavisión. At the same time, as a spectator sport, the game provides intimate occasions for Latino/a fans to congregate in clearly defined U.S. Latino/a social spaces such as the home, the taqueria, the cantina, or the local community center in order to follow their favorite national teams and players in Latin America. The sport thus actively engages what is culturally specific among Latinos and leads us to ask how fútbol contributes to the shared and discrepant meanings of the terms "Latinoamericano" and "U.S. Latino." Their entanglement becomes a matter of deep play, for the game captures the sense of movement and flow appropriate to the dynamic exchange of diverse Latin American and U.S. Latino/a identities. The prominence of fútbol among a growing immigrant and native Latino/a population ... coincides with a deep and abiding transnational connection with Latin America and symbolizes the cultural future for Latinos, forging new gendered, pan-ethnic, and corporate structures that seek to create and capitalize on an emerging sense of homeland in the United States.... [T]he establishment of Major League Soccer and the growth of Latino fútbol leagues in Washington state ... indicate[s] how Latinos themselves participate in a complex process of intercultural and transnational exchange with multiple homelands.

★ ★ ★

Rather than debate the degree of actual connectedness to distant homelands that the game may or may not allow, one might note simply how, by definition, the game creates a space of exaggerated meanings through the element of play and always exceeds the boundaries of what it is. The game thus imagines popular Latino/a alliances that reflect the experiences of migrating peoples and the cultural traditions that come to define them. The sense of pan-Latino-ness, Latin male sentimentality, and the comradery of aficionados globally, for instance, are based in part on the game's romance as it comes to represent the "passion of the people," the "beautiful game," or, in the Uruguayan Eduardo Galeano's poetic words, "soccer in sun and shadow." Within this romance, fútbol allows for an imaginary sense of peoplehood among Latinos that frequently becomes a lasting expression of the sport's popular nostalgia.

To love fútbol, then, is essentially to take part in what it means to be, or not be, culturally "Latino" in the Americas and ask how U.S. Latino communities define or reinvent themselves in relation to the game. The issue of gender clearly remains a critical factor in this equation. The love of the game coincides with the practice of established male rituals that are part of Latino socialization. Traditionally, the game follows conventional male codes of homosocial bonding and behavior, including such popular subcultural trends as wearing solid colored jerseys and shiny shorts along with black hip hop styles. U.S. Latinas and women in Latin America in turn participate in the sport primarily as fans and supporters, spectators and on-site vendors, and occasionally as referees. Latin American women are largely discouraged from playing fútbol (except in locations such as Brazil, where the women's national team has achieved some prominence internationally), while soccer in the United States has become the leading sport among women. Latina contributions to the game demonstrate how women can uniquely participate in and observe the game, testing the boundaries of place and purpose against a traditional Latin male sports world. This participation usually means, however, that Latinas must challenge conventional norms of femininity and sexuality in order to revise what Barbara Cox and Shona Thompson have referred to as the standard male "soccer body."

While soccer is the largest growing sport among women in the world, the World Cup champion U.S. women's soccer team did not include a single Latina player. Ironically, Mexico, by contrast, chose to recruit ten Mexican American women, that is, U.S. citizens of Mexican descent, to play fútbol for the national team under the direction of former California State Los Angeles coach Leonardo Cuellar, filling a vacuum created by the absence of women players in their own country. Although local fútbol leagues in U.S. Latino communities include a very small percentage of women (less than 10 percent in the Los Angeles area, for example, compared to Latino soccer programs among men), recent trends suggest that the presence of U.S. Latinas in the sport is increasing—in part as a result of the visibility of women's World Cup soccer. The same slow but incremental gains for women can also be seen in Latin America as national pride becomes a factor in reclaiming territory associated with the game as it is played among Latin American men. As Patrick Escobar, vice president of the Amateur Athletic Foundation in the United States, predicts, "You're going to see national pride take over [in women's World Cup soccer]. Mexico and Brazil are not going to want to be relegated to fifth or sixth place." The game of fútbol is indeed a major battleground for international competition in the form of women's and men's amateur and professional sports. Such international appeal, as we shall see, represents the guiding force behind the development of Major League Soccer (the official governing body of professional soccer in the United States) as well as the growth of local fútbol leagues among U.S. Latinos. While these organizations retain their local character, they promote and market national and transnational networks and alliances, part of the way that Latinos create and contest the imaginary spaces of homeland both on and off the field.

★ ★ ★

As the official soccer league of the United States, Major League Soccer (MLS) welcomes a fan base of an estimated 40 percent Latinos, imprinting a unique Latino presence on the game. MLS openly courts Latino/a populations in the United States as fans and players according to their multiple national allegiances, capitalizing on the game's popularity among diverse Latino communities across the Americas and promoting the growth of soccer in the United States. Indeed, the MLS organization strategically markets the game according to the national backgrounds of U.S. Latino/a fans. As former MLS commissioner Doug Logan explained in 1997 to *Hispanic* magazine,

> Mexican goalkeeper Jorge Campos and Salvadoran Muricio Cienfuegos
> [play] for the Los Angeles Galaxy (since the metropolis has huge
> Mexican and Salvadoran communities), while Bolivian midfield star
> Marco Etcheverry is with the D.C. United (since Washington, D.C.
> is a city with a vibrant Bolivian community), and Colombian player
> Antony de Avila is with the MetroStars in New York (since there's
> a sizeable Colombian and South American community in Queens).

Hence, MLS seeks to build upon the popularity of fútbol among U.S. Latinos in a larger effort toward making the magical crossover into the American main-stream, transforming the United States into a competitive fútbol nation.

Most U.S. soccer clubs notably reside in metropolitan areas in which Latinos constitute a significant proportion of the population: the Los Angeles Galaxy, the New York/New Jersey MetroStars, the Miami Fusion, the San Jose Clash, the Chicago Fire, the Dallas Burn, and the D.C. United, among others. This fact has been a logical part of the marketing of MLS from the beginning in hopes that the popularity of the sport itself, building upon its traditional Latino/a fan base, would expand and become self-generating in the United States as a whole. The fact that the United States hosted the World Cup in 1994 has bolstered MLS's vision and has helped gain a small but increasing level of interest among Anglo audiences. Among Latino/a fans, the presence of Latino players on the United States national team gave further reason to follow the United States' performance in the 1994 and 1998 World Cup....

As the marketing strategy of MLS indicates, the construction of a fútbol nation depends on an imaginary projection of a nation itself—otherwise known as the "national league." Ironically, because of the ownership of players and the benefits of free agency, the players are not necessarily from the countries they come to represent. MLS has lost its better young players to European clubs (a condition quite familiar to Argentina and Brazil), while European players ... have been courted to play for the United States teams. Martin Vasquez ... once played for the Mexican national team in the World Cup until he was granted citizenship in the United States to play for the Tampa Bay Mutiny, then later became part of the U.S. national team.... In short, the game retains its sense of peoplehood according to a nationally defined, though internally differentiated, sports organization where the players do not always hold to the nationality they come to defend. This condition reflects the wider multinational corporate structure of the game, in which the level playing field is broadly organized by the free market. While the United States might not be victorious on the field, it can nonetheless market the Latino athlete's iconic status and control the game according to the $135 million it contributes to MLS....

Despite the corporate influences and controlling mechanisms surrounding the sport, fútbol alliances bring together nations and peoples that also cut across more restrictive definitions of "Latin Americans" and "Latinos." Who can forget the 1970 World Cup finals in Mexico City, for instance, in which the Brazilian player Pelé was hoisted on the shoulders of Mexicans who carried him off the field wearing a Mexican sombrero? Pelé was essentially deemed an honorary Mexican citizen, participating in a larger Latin American collectivity.... In a general sense the game of fútbol has already created popular alliances under a larger *regional* configuration that speaks to other possible transnational and cross-cultural linkages.

... [W]e might ask why "U.S. Latino" excludes U.S. Brazilians and whether this distinction is in fact necessary. To address this question, we might examine a second related example: when Mexico lost to Germany in the sixteenth round of the 1998 World Cup, U.S. Latino communities, which had been supporting the Mexican national team, subsequently realigned their popular allegiance to Brazil in the finals against France. Why did Latino/a fans overwhelmingly root for Brazil and why not France? The nationalist rivalries among countries in the Americas yield to a larger regional imaginary within a global context as the circle of play expands to include countries from around the world. The game reinforces alliances in the Americas created by hemispheric models of play and brings together various American countries according to the long-standing cultural affinities shared among diverse Latino/a peoples. By contrast, the Old World comes to represent the *other* continent, if not more pointedly, the empire of the colonial past. As C. L. R. James reminds us, the playing field enacts social and political dramas in which present and former colonized countries often take revenge on their historic oppressors. Indeed, Iran's defeat of the United States in the 1998 World Cup symbolized a conquest of the "Great Satan" himself.

★ ★ ★

In spite of soccer's indelible association to professional players and organizations in the United States and Latin America, the game has also cut across the Americas and the globe and has made its way into one's very own home and neighborhood, public parks and fields, schools and locally sponsored soccer leagues. Here the people represent not the all-star players who remain larger than life, but the game's romance for everyday folks who constitute members of the local community. In a more localized world, Latinos participate in spontaneous "pick-up" games known as *cascaritas,* though much focus tends to be placed on the emergence of soccer leagues throughout the country. La Liga Hispana, based in Seattle, Washington, for instance, has expanded into thirty-six teams and over six hundred members as part of a larger statewide Latino membership that includes close to two hundred teams and more than three thousand players. Latino communities, hence, create subcultures and enlarge other sporting alliances to engage diverse Latino/a populations into a new—or renewed—sense of homeland.

The growth of soccer leagues in the state of Washington attests to the arrival and settlement of diverse native and immigrant Latino/a populations that increasingly need and value leisure in the form of Latino/a communal life. Mexican service workers—approximately 125,000—travel the migrant circuit to Washington each year in order to labor for long hours in the fields, supporting the state's $5.23 billion agricultural economy. Undocumented Mexican workers constitute 70 percent of all seasonal pickers, arriving in eastern Washington (i.e., Yakima Valley) from such rural villages as Pajacuarán, in the state of Michoacán, which sends a third of its residents to work in the United States. These workers often spend Sundays, their only day of rest, on the fútbol field, participating, for example, in Yakima's Liga Mexicana and Sunnyside's League of the Lower Valley. Many foreign- and native-born Latinos have also moved to western Washington—to places like King County and Seattle and its suburbs. Washington's overall Latino population has experienced an unprecedented boom as a result of two key historical events. In 1986 Congress made legal residents out of about 2.3 million Mexican migrant workers nationwide, allowing for Mexican immigrants to bring their families to the United States. Then, in an immigration backlash in the early 1990s, California passed Proposition 187 in the wake of economic recession, prompting Latino immigrants to move north to Washington. According to Marc Ramirez, staff writer for the *Seattle Times,* "From 1990 to 1997, Washington's Latino population grew by nearly 50 people a day, almost four times the rate of the overall population. In that seven-year period, the number of Latinos statewide rose 58 percent, from 214,568 to 339,618."

The growth of fútbol leagues has come to represent the cultural future for many Latino immigrants as the game fosters gradual but steady movement toward local, community-based activity, leading to national affiliation and the establishment of homes in the United States.... Local sponsors, who are themselves part of the Latino community, promote an already traditional sport among Latino/a fans. Members of the Hispanic Business Chamber and restaurant owners support La Liga Hispana and participate in developing Latino/a communities and their independently owned businesses. Team jerseys advertise Latino nightclubs, car dealers, La Española market, or the Azteca and Jalisco restaurants. On the other hand, as the popularity of fútbol continues, the leagues increasingly demand larger corporate sponsors in order to survive. The Liga de Fútbol de Pasco in Washington state, for example, consists of teams whose names are called "Albertsons," "Budweiser," or "Best Foods" instead of "Morelos," "El Aguíla," and "Hidalgo."

Despite the U.S.-based corporate sponsorship of these teams, the relationship between the local community and the wider affiliations of homeland created by fútbol indeed remains integral to the game. Local teams in the United States often take the name of fútbol clubs in distant homelands: teams in the Liga de Fútbol de Pasco, for example, assume names such as "San José," "Guadalajara," and "Mexico," to reinforce important symbolic equivalences. The Guadalajara Chivas are so named after the Mexican First Division team, and the Pasco jerseys bear the likeness of the Mexican team. This close association is not simply an expression of popular nationalist nostalgia, but is a further attempt to re-create Mexico in the United States. Indeed, many local players emigrated from the cities of Guadalajara and San José and have subsequently made Pasco, Washington, their home. The Mexican government itself frequently sponsors fútbol tournaments through the Programa para las Communidades Mexicanas en el Extranjero and the Mexican consulate. The annual tournament "Copa México," held in Washington and throughout the United States, ... brings together local teams under a wide array of jurisdictions, corporate and national sponsorships, and mass media. The players and audiences generally belong to local communities throughout the Washington area but have migrated from multiple homelands. The radio station La Deportiva (KXPA—1540 AM) provides Raúl Sandoval's distinct play-by-play commentary, while local vendors sell products and programs to U.S. Latino/a fans. The fútbol leagues are supported by businesses such as Rosella's Produce and *La Voz* or *Siete Días,* popular Latino newspapers in the Pacific Northwest. At the same time, the games are sponsored by larger multinational corporations such as BuenaVista Travel and TELMEX, among others. The regional winner of "Copa México" eventually moves on to compete on a national stage, bringing together Mexican American communities throughout the United States.

As with other forms of Latino/a cultural life from food to popular folklore, athletic competition reflects deep nationalist feelings even at this local level. In La Liga Hispana, national and ethnic pride often turns violent when teams collide on the field over loyalties to homeland. As the *Seattle Times,* for instance, notes, "La Española's players [of La Liga Hispana] have seen civil wars erupt on opposing squads between teammates claiming superiority for the mother countries. Some say La Española itself is targeted for having so many non-Latinos on its roster." Among these "non-Latinos" are often second-generation Mexican Americans, whose Latino ties to the homeland are challenged by recent Mexican immigrants.

The weekend soccer league, moreover, can facilitate a process of Latino/a cross-cultural fertilization. Just as the consumer can purchase his or her mole, plantains, and guaraná all in the same ethnic grocery store, the game can also form multiethnic and transnational communities that emerge among those living in the same neighborhoods and playing the same game. La Liga Hispana includes players with roots in Mexico, Brazil, Chile, Nicaragua, and Ecuador as well as foreign and native-born Latinos and non-Latino players. Though predominantly Mexican American, La Liga Hispana nonetheless includes a range of Latinos from Latin America and a few Anglos from the United States. This cross-section of Latinos not only reveals a shared history of migration and settlement in the United States but also creates local leagues with a distinct international flavor united by a common love of the game. In this instance, the game of fútbol serves as a popular site of U.S. and Latin American transcultural formation that links the United States and Mexico, parts of the Caribbean, and Central and South America.

The game of fútbol thus remains entangled in the popular projections of multiple Latino/a identities, national affiliations, and sporting alliances. The interrelatedness of the controversial terms "Latino/a," "American," and "Latin American," among others, applies to the game and its players in relation to the popularity of the sport throughout the United States and Latin America. This wider context of the Americas informs the introduction of Latino stars in MLS and explains the strong interest and consumptive patterns of U.S. Latino/a fans and players. The growth of Latino soccer leagues attests to the continuation and alteration of long-standing cultural traditions in Latin America and contributes to the formation of distinct U.S. Latino/a identities. Fútbol promotes as well as undermines the popular construction of nationality as U.S. Latino/a fans' allegiances are subsequently redrawn according to a wider, regionally based Latino/a configuration. Throughout the United States, the growth of fútbol coincides with an evolving sense of Latino/a identity that has indeed traveled down field as it continues to pursue the far-reaching goal of a homeland.

 # FURTHER READING

Frances R. Aparicio and Susana Chávez, eds., *Tropicalizations: Transcultural Representations of Latinidad* (1997).

Charles Ramírez Berg, *Latino Images in Film: Stereotypes, Subversion, and Resistance* (2002).

Adrian Burgos, *Playing America's Game: Baseball, Latinos, and the Color Line* (2007).

María Elena Cepeda, *Musical ImagiNation: U.S.-Colombian Identity and the Latin Music Boom* (2010).

José A. Cobas, Jorge Duany, and Joe R. Feagin, eds., *How the United States Racializes Latinos: White Hegemony and Its Consequences* (2009).

Celeste Fraser Delgado and José Esteban Muñoz, eds., *Everynight Life: Culture and Dance in Latin/o America* (1997).

Michelle Habell-Pallán and Mary Romero, eds., *Latina/o Popular Culture* (2002).

Denis Lynn Daly Heyck, ed., *Barrios and Borderlands: Cultures of Latinos and Latinas in the United States* (1994).

Agustin Lao-Montes and Arlene Davila, eds., *Mambo Montage: The Latinization of New York* (2001).

Anthony F. Macias, "Bringing Music to the People: Race, Urban Culture, and Municipal Politics in Postwar Los Angeles," *American Quarterly* 56, no. 3 (September 2004), 693–717.

Isabel Molina-Guzmán, *Dangerous Curves: Latina Bodies in the Media* (2010).

Chon A. Noriega and Ana M. López, eds., *The Ethnic Eye: Latino Media Arts* (1996).

Suzanne Oboler, *Ethnic Labels, Latino Lives: Identity and the Politics of (Re)Presentation in the United States* (1995).

Enrique C. Ochoa and Gilda L. Ochoa, eds., *Latino LA: Transformations, Communities, and Activism* (2005).

Felix M. Padilla, *Latino Ethnic Consciousness: The Case of Mexican Americans and Puerto Ricans in Chicago* (1985).

Juan Javier Pescador, "¡Vamos Taximaroa! Mexcian/Chicano Soccer Associations and Translational/Translocal Communities, 1967–2002," *Latino Studies* 2, no. 3 (2004), 352–376.

Milagros Ricourt and Ruby Danta, *Hispanas de Queens: Latino Panethnicity in a New York City Neighborhood* (2003).

Clara E. Rodríguez, *Heroes, Lovers, and Others: The Story of Latinos in Hollywood* (2004).

Clara E. Rodríguez, ed., *Latin Looks: Images of Latinas and Latinos in the U.S. Media* (1997).

Horacio N. Roque Ramírez, "'That's My Place!': Negotiating Racial, Sexual, and Gender Politics in San Francisco's Gay Latino Alliance, 1975–1983," *Journal of the History of Sexuality* 12, no. 2 (2003), 224–258.

Mérida Rúa, "Colao Subjectivities: PortoMex and MexiRican Perspectives on Language and Identity," *Centro: Journal of the Center for Puerto Rican Studies* 8, no. 2 (2001), 117–133.

Marcelo M. Suárez-Orozco and Mariela M. Páez, eds., *Latinos: Remaking America* (2002).

Angharad N. Valdivia, *A Latina in the Land of Hollywood and Other Essays on Media Culture* (2000).